THE ORGANIZATION AND ORDER OF BATTLE OF MILITARIES IN WORLD WAR II

VOLUME VI
ITALY and FRANCE

Including the Neutral Countries of
SAN MARINO, VATICAN CITY (HOLY SEE), ANDORRA, and MONACO

By the same author in this series

The Organization and Order of Battle of Militaries in World War II

Volume I: Germany	2005	ISBN: 1-4120-7498-3
Volume II: The British Commonwealth	2006	ISBN: 1-4120-8565-5
Volume III: The United States	2006	ISBN: 1-4251-0659-5
Volume IV: Japan	2007	ISBN: 1-4251-2422-4
Volume V - Book A: Union of Soviet Socialist Republics	2009	ISBN: 1-4269-0281-9
Volume V - Book B: Union of Soviet Socialist Republics	2009	ISBN: 1-4269-2251-0

Next Book in the Series

Volume VII: Germany's Allies & the Neutral Nations of Europe   To Be Published Summer 2010

THE ORGANIZATION AND ORDER OF BATTLE OF MILITARIES IN WORLD WAR II

VOLUME VI
ITALY and FRANCE

Including the Neutral Countries of
SAN MARINO, VATICAN CITY (HOLY SEE), ANDORRA, and MONACO

CHARLES D. PETTIBONE

Order this book online at www.trafford.com
or email orders@trafford.com

Most Trafford titles are also available at major online book retailers.

© Copyright 2010 Charles D. Pettibone.

All rights reserved. No part of this publication may be reproduced, stored in a retrieval system, or transmitted, in any form or by any means, electronic, mechanical, photocopying, recording, or otherwise, without the written prior permission of the author.

The views expressed in this work are solely those of the author and do not necessarily reflect the views of the publisher, and the publisher hereby disclaims any responsibility for them.

Printed in the United States of America.

ISBN: 978-1-4269-4633-2 (sc)

Our mission is to efficiently provide the world's finest, most comprehensive book publishing service, enabling every author to experience success. To find out how to publish your book, your way, and have it available worldwide, visit us online at www.trafford.com

Trafford rev. 10/12/2010

 www.trafford.com

North America & international
toll-free: 1 888 232 4444 (USA & Canada)
phone: 250 383 6864 ♦ fax: 812 355 4082

To the men and women who served in the armed forces
throughout the world from 1985 to 2010.

To Austin Rasbach, Ryan Boline, & Jonathan Zodarecky
two of my former Eagle Scouts, and one of my friend's sons,
who are still serving their country at this time.

Contents

	Page
Introduction	vii
How To Use This Book	viii

SECTION A - ITALY, SAN MARINO & VATICAN CITY STATE (THE HOLY SEE)
Part 1 - THE ITALIAN GOVERNMENT AND THE ORGANIZATION AND STRUCTURE OF ITALY'S MILITARY HIGH COMMAND

Italian Government	5
Armed Forces High Command	18
Army High Command	21
Territorial Defense Commands	29
Royal Navy High Command	40
Royal Air Force High Command	42
Italian Socialist Republic	43
The Military of the Italian Social Republic - 1944	45
German Command of Northern Italy	49
Partisan Resistance	51
Italian Partisan Republics of 1944	52
Allied Military Government of Italy	53

Part 2 - ITALY'S ORDER OF BATTLE 1937 - 1945

Army Groups Italy	57
Army Groups	58
Italian Royal Fleet Afloat	62
Armies	63
General Headquarter Units That Approach Army Status	74
Fascists Militia (Army Status)	76
Corps, Air Forces, and Fleets	78
Army Corps	78
Royal Navy Fleets	97
Royal Navy Sea Departments	98
Royal Air Force Corps Commands	99
Fascist Militia (Corps Status)	102
Battle Groups	103
Divisions	104
Infantry Divisions	104
Garrison Divisions	125
Coastal Defense Divisions	128
Motorized and Semi-Motorized Divisions	133
Motorized Divisions	133
Semi-Motorized Divisions	135

Armored	139
Mountain and Alpine Divisions	142
Mountain Divisions	142
Alpine Divisions	144
Celeri (Fast) Divisions	147
Parachute Divisions	149
Assault and Landing Divisions	151
Colonial Divisions	153
Territorial Zones	156
Royal Navy Squadrons (Division Status)	159
Royal Air Force Commands	163
Fascist Militia (Division Status)	166
Blackshirt (CCNN) Divisions	166
Other Blackshirt Units with Division Status	169
Royal Carabinieri (CCRR) Units	174
Brigades	175
Infantry Brigades	175
Division Depots	186
Territorial Districts	189
Border Guard Sectors	191
Miscellaneous Units (Brigade Status)	192
Foreign Volunteers in the Italian Military	192
Colonial Brigades	193
Royal Navy Squadrons (Brigade Status)	196
Fascist Militia (Brigade Status)	199
Royal Air Force Brigades	207
The Military of the Italian Social Republic	208
National Republican Army	208
Army	208
Divisions	209
Brigades	210
National Republican Air Force	211
National Republican Navy	212
The Military of the Royal Italian Government - 09/08/43	213
Italian Co-Belligerent Army (Army of the South)	213
Corps (Italian Co-Belligerent Army)	214
Division (Italian Co-Belligerent Army)	215
Brigades (Italian Co-Belligerent Army)	220
Italian Co-Belligerent Air Force	221
Italian Co-Belligerent Navy	222

Part 3 - SAN MARINO

San Marino Government	225
German Occupation of San Marino	227
Allied Occupation of San Marino	227
Military of San Marino	228

Part 4 - VATICAN CITY STATE (THE HOLY SEE)

Government of Vatican City State	231
The Holy See	233
Military of Vatican City State	234

APPENDIX FOR SECTION A - ITALY

Appendix A Table of Equivalent Ranks	237
Appendix B Senior Commanders	239
Appendix C Military Units in Selected Campaigns	241
Appendix D The Fleet of the Royal Italian Navy	261
Aircraft Carriers	261
Seaplane Carriers/Tenders	261
Battleships	262
Heavy Cruisers	263
Light Cruisers	265
Destroyer Divisions	269
Submarine Divisions	270
Fast Torpedo Boat [MAS] Divisions	272
Torpedo Boat Divisions	273

SECTION B - FRANCE, MONACO & THE VALLEYS OF ANDORRA
Part 1 - THE FRENCH GOVERNMENT AND THE ORGANIZATION AND STRUCTURE OF FRANCE'S MILITARY HIGH COMMAND

Government of France	279
Minister of National Defense and War	283
The Army Council	286
The Supreme Council of National Defense	288
Armed Forces High Command	290
General Headquarters [Army High Command]	291
Colonial Forces	298
Air Force Headquarters	299
Navy High Command	300
Naval General Staff	301
Military Districts	302
Overseas Colonies & Protectorates (under Minister of War)	318
Overseas Colonies & Protectorates (under Minister of Colonies)	321
Japanese Military Commanders in Indochina	327
German Occupied France (Frankreich)	328
Pas-de-Calais and Nord 1940-1944	331
German Territory of Southern Vichy France	332
Italian Occupied French Zone	332
Government of Vichy France	333
Vichy Armed Forces High Command	338
Vichy France in North Africa	343

National Committee of the Free French	344
Free French Armed Forces	347
Free French in North Africa	348
Resistance Organizations	350
French Committee of National Liberation	353
Provisional Government of France	354
Provisional Government Armed Forces	355

Part 2 - FRANCE'S ORDER OF BATTLE 1939 - 1945

Theater	361
Army Groups	363
Armies	365
Army Detachments	371
Air Forces	372
Major Naval Commands and Fleets	374
Army Corps (pre-July 1940)	379
Cavalry Corps and Armored Groups	392
Miscellaneous Units: Fronts, Groups	393
Naval Commands (Corps equivalent)	394
Divisions	399
Motorized Infantry Divisions	399
Infantry Divisions	403
Mountain Divisions	422
Light Mountain Divisions	425
North African Infantry Divisions	427
Colonial Infantry Divisions	430
Overseas Infantry Divisions	435
Light Infantry Divisions	441
Foreign Infantry Divisions	444
Cavalry Divisions	445
Light Cavalry Divisions	446
Light Mechanized Divisions	448
Armored Divisions	450
Fortress Infantry Divisions	452
Commands Equivalent to Divisions	454
Commands of the Maginot Line (Division Status)	456
Divisions in Overseas Colonies and Protectorates	462
Air Divisions	468
Naval Commands (Division Equivalent)	470
Brigades	473
Commands of the Maginot Line (Brigade Status)	473
Infantry Brigades	476
Armored and Mechanized Brigades	480
Cavalry Brigades	483
Miscellaneous Brigades	485
Air Force Wings	485

Naval Commands (Brigade Equivalent)	486
Vichy French Army	490
Corps	490
Divisions	492
Free French Forces (1941 - 1944)	500
Corps	500
Divisions	500
Brigades	501
Free French Naval Forces	501
Rebuilt French Army of 1943 - 1945	502
Armies	502
Corps	503
Infantry Divisions	505
Armored Divisions	509

Part 3 - MONACO

Government of Monaco	513
Monaco Government under Italian Control	514
Monaco Government under German Control	514
Military of Monaco	515

Part 4 - ANDORRA

Government of Valleys of Andorra	519
Military of Andorra	521

APPENDIX FOR PART B - FRANCE

Appendix A Table of Equivalent Ranks	525
Appendix B Military Units in Selected Campaigns	527
Appendix C The Fleet of the Royal Italian Navy	532
Light Aircraft Carriers	532
Escort Aircraft Carriers	532
Seaplane Carriers	533
Battle Cruisers	533
Battleships	534
Heavy Cruisers	536
Light Cruisers	537
Minelayers	539
Submarine Tenders	539
Destroyer Divisions	540
Light Destroyer Divisions	541
Submarine Divisions	543

Bibliography

Books Used in this Series	545
Internet Sites	559
Index	560

INTRODUCTION

What started out as five books, is now nine. Book five being split into three books. This book represents the seventh of nine I plan to write. The series will contain: Volume I - Germany; Volume II - The British Commonwealth; Volume III - The United States; Volume IV - Japan; Volume V, Book A - Union of Soviet Socialist Republics; Volume V, Book B - Union of Soviet Socialist Republics; Volume VI - Italy and France; Volume VII - Germany's Allies (Bulgaria, Croatia, Finland, Hungary, Romania, Serbia, Slovakia) and the Neutral Nations (Portugal, Spain, Sweden, and Switzerland); and Volume VIII - Other Nations at War (Albania, Belgium, Brazil, China, Czechoslovakia, Denmark, Estonia, Greece, Latvia, Lithuania, Luxembourg, Netherlands, Norway, Poland, Yugoslavia).

After being discharged from the service in January 1970, I developed an interest in World War II. I wanted to know everything I could about the war. As I read, I started to collect names of different military unit leaders. While other people were collecting stamps or baseball cards, I collected names. The careers of Marshals Pietro Badoglia, Rodolfo Graziani and Giovanni Messe of Italy; and Marshal Henri-Phillippi-Benoni-Omar-Joseph Pétain, Generals Maurice Gamelin and Brigadier General Charles-André-Joseph-Marie de Gaulle of France, can easily be traced. But, I wanted to know about the generals who commanded the Army Groups and Armies of 1944 and 1945. Who were these men like Italy's Lieutenant Generals Paolo Berardi, Guiseppe de Stefanis, and Raffele Cadorna? What about French Lieutenant Generals Jean-Joseph-Marie-Gabriel de Lattre de Tassigny, Marie-Joseph-Pierre-François Kœnig, and Alphonse-Pierre Juin? What were their careers like? So as I read, I wrote down names and the commands of units.

This series of books is a composite of more than forty years of collecting names. Military leaders of General or Admiral ranks are listed. In a few cases there are leaders listed below the rank of a general officer, such as staff positions within an Army or the Commander of a naval ship. The majority are military commanders from division level on up.

This book is broken down into two sections of four parts each. Section A contains Italy and the two smaller neutral countries of San Marino and the Vatican City State which falls within Italian Territory. Section B contains France and the two smaller neutral countries of Monaco and the Valleys of Andorra which falls within French Territory. Each section is broken down as follows: Part one contains the organization of Military Structure and Commands of the different branches of service, army, air force, navy, and marine corps of the major nation. The second part is an Order of Battle of the major nation, either Italy or France, covering 1941 to 1945. Parts three and four contain the governments and information of the two neutral nations in the major country's territory. This is followed by an Appendix for each section. The major difference between this Order of Battle from others that have been written is, one can trace the career of individual commanders as they advanced through the ranks and the commands they held. This will be described in the next few pages.

Over the years, this book has been rewritten numerous times. As new information became available, the book has been updated. I do not claim this to be the book's final form and to be 100% accurate. This author would be grateful to anyone who has any information pertaining to any of the United States leaders listed; such as their given name, date of birth, date of death, dates leader commanded unit, etc. If anyone can assist me with any additions or corrections, please write me in care of the publisher.

Charles D. Pettibone
Rochester, New York
June 19, 2010

HOW TO USE THIS BOOK

This book and the others in the series are an excellent resource tool. Each book in the series actually started out as an addendum to another book that I was going to write, "A Directory of Military Leaders". But, each addendum when finally written ended up being between three and five (300-500) hundred pages in length, making each of them no addendum, but a book in their own right. So I decided to put my original idea aside and just concentrate on then five (5), now seven (7) books in this series. I plan on writing and publishing a book a year for the next three (3) years.

There are numerous Order of Battle books on the market. So what makes this series so special? Why should one decide on this particular book?

First, the first part of each book contains the overall command structure of the country's armed forces. Then it gives command structure for the army, navy, and air force, in the case of Germany, the command structure of the Schutzstaffel (SS) is included. For the British Commonwealth, the armed force's command structure of Great Britain, including India, Australia, Canada, New Zealand and South Africa are included. For the United States, the Marine Corps, although part of the Navy, is listed separately. For Japan, only the Army and Navy are listed, with the Air Forces divided between them. And for the Soviet Union, the Soviet Army makes up the majority of the Armed Forces, with the Soviet Navy and Soviet Air Force just beginning to become separate entities from the Army.

Second, a complete Order of Battle is given. Most Order of Battle usually deal with only the armies of the country/countries involved, and then only at the division and sometimes at the corps level. Higher echelons of commands are usually not covered. In this series of books, all of the commanders known are spelled out, and not just for the army, but all the branches of the armed forces; giving a breakdown of all the major echelons of command, from theater level down to division. Under each major component, in the book (Army Group, Armies, Corps, and Divisions), the equivalent commands of the other military branches (navy, air force, marine, etc.) of the country's armed forces are included.

For the Volumes on the British Commonwealth and the United States, there is a third part in the book that contains the overall command structure of each Anglo-American Theater of Operation.

Third, most Order of Battles list the commanders and their dates of tenure. This one includes those, but also lists of their next duty assignment, where the officer went after leaving this post. One can literally trace a general or flag officer's career through the upper echelons of command with these books. Making this series of books completely different from all the others on the market.

Fourth, military unit and/or ship insignia, crest, emblem, or patch is pictured next to the unit/ship, whenever it was found.

Fifth, the Appendix is broken down into several parts. There is an appendix that has the usual table of Equivalent Ranks. An appendix that lists senior officers, Field Marshal,

Admiral of the Fleet, Colonel General, full Generals and Admirals. Another appendix lists some Military Units used in different campaigns.

Sixth, there is a unique appendix that lists the Major Naval Warships and their commanders. I know of no other book on the market that offers this. This appendix shows: 1) the silhouette of the major warship whenever found. A major ship is classified as aa aircraft carrier (to include fleet, light, and escort), battleship, battlecruiser, heavy and light cruiser. Two, an Order of Battle for the ship's commanders; and third, in some cases, the ship's crest and emblem when found is also given.

So how does one use this book? Let's look at the entry for the Italian 3rd "Ravenna" (Mountain) Infantry Division.

3rd "Ravenna" (Mountain) Infantry Division (reduced) (pre-war as **3rd "Manferrato" Infantry Division**; /39, redesignated **3rd "Ravenna" (Mountain) Infantry Division**; 06/40, on French border; has mountain equipment in it's TO&E; 04/05/41?, part of XI Army Corps, Second Army; Greece and Yugoslavia; 05/41, transferred back to Italy; 07/42, Soviet Union, part of Eighth Army; 01/43, severely damaged on the Don; 05/43, Italy for reforming in Tuscany; 09/08/43, surrendered and disbanded): /39 MG Matteo Roux (Commanding General, XI Army Corps) 06/10/40? MG Edoardo Nebbia [+ /40, acting Commanding General, II Army Corps] (Commanding General, X Army Corps) 10/03/42 MG Francesco Du Pont (?) 09/08/43 surrendered and disbanded.

Following the unit's name, it states that the 3rd "Ravenna" (Mountain) Infantry Division was as pre-war division known as the 3rd "Manferrato" Infantry Division. In 1939, it was redesignated the 3rd "Ravenna" (Mountain) Infantry Division, and in June 1940 it was stationed on the French border, and has mountain equipment in it's Table of Organization and Equipment. Around April 5, 1941, it was part of the XI Army Corps, Second Army, and transferred to Greece and Yugoslavia. In May 1941, it was transferred back to Italy. In July 1942, the 3rd became part of the Eighth Army in the Soviet Union. In January 1943, it was severely damaged on the Don River. In May 1943, it was reforming in Italy, and on September 8, 1943, it surrendered and was disbanded.

In 1939, MG Matteo Roux took command of the division. After his name appears (Commanding General, XI Army Corps) 06/12/40?. This stands for: around June 12, 1940, MG Roux gave up command of the 3rd "Ravenna" (mountain) Infantry Division and his next duty assignment was Commanding General of the XI Army Corps. Also on that date, the 3rd (Mountain) Infantry Division was taken over by MG Edoardo Nebbia.

There will be four different endings following a General officer's name:
    1. Officer's name followed by a date.
    2. Officer's name followed by (new assignment) then a date.
    3. Officer's name followed by [concurrent assignment] then a date.
    4. Officer's name followed by [concurrent assignment] (new assignment) then a date.

Ending one (1) will occur if a General officer took a leave of absence but returned to take command of that unit again (see example A below) or if the officer involved has the rank of Colonel (Captain in the Navy) or lower. In the majority of these cases, these officers next assignments have not been tracked (see example B below).

Example A: from **Italian Eleventh Army**:
... Gen. Carlo Geloso /41 LG Sebastiano Visconti Prasca (acting; /43 to /45, German prisoner-of-war) 04/41 Gen. Carlo Geloso ...

Explanation of Example A:
Gen. Carlo Geloso, for whatever reason, medical, leave, rest, etc, left being the Commander-in-Chief of the Eleventh Army in 1941 and returned to command that unit later in April 1941.

Example B: from **Italian "Legnano" Artillery Regiment**:
... /35 Col. Antonio Formisano /37 Col. Giuseppe ...

Explanation of Example B:
Colonel Antonio Formisano assignment ended in 1937. Since his rank was Colonel (Captain in the Navy) or lower, and his name does not appear on any list as a Major General/Rear Admiral or higher, his next assignment or duty is not tracked.

Ending two (2) will occur in the majority of the General/Flag officers listed. This will be their new duty assignment followed by the date their present assignment ended (see Example C).

Example C: from **Italian 7th "Lupi di Toscana" Infantry Division (reduced)**:
... / 41 MG Angelico Carta (Commanding General, 51st "Sienna" Infantry Division) /41 MG Ernesto Cappa ...

Explanation of Example C:
MG Angelico Carta held command of the 7th "Lupi di Toscana" Infantry Division (reduced) from sometime in 1941. In 1941, he was given his new assignment, Commanding General of the 51st "Sienna" Infantry Division.

Ending two (2), may have three (3) different conclusions. The first one, as stated above, the new duty assignment, and shown in Example C. Second, it may contain a question mark (see Example D); or, third, it may state a date, assignment, (see Example E).

Example D: from **Italian 15th "Bergamo" Infantry Division**:
... /39 MG Ugo Gigliarelli Fiumi (?   ) 06/10/40? ...

Explanation of Example D:
MG Ugo Gigliarelli Fiumi left command of the 15th "Bergamo" Infantry Division around June 10, 1940, but his next duty and/or future duty assignment are unknown.

Example E: from **Italian 18th "Messina" Infantry Division**:
... /39 Col. Attilio Amato (acting; /43, Commanding General, 14th Coastal Division) /39 MG

Francesco Zani ...

Explanation of Example E:
Col. Attilio Amato was acting commander and gave up command of the 18th "messina" Infantry Division in 1939. What duty he assumed next is unknown, but in 1943, he became the Commanding General, 14th Coastal Division. Since there was a difference of one year between assignments, the date of the next assignment and the future duty will be listed. Anytime a future duty assignment can be listed; it will be used instead of the question mark in example D.

Another ending that does not show a person's new assignment may be:

Example F: also from **18th "Messina" Infantry Division**.
... /39 MG Francesco Zani (attached to General Headquarters, Albania) 06/41? MG Guglielmo ...

Explanation of Example F:
MG Francesco Zani gave up the command of the 18th "Messina" Infantry Division around June 1941. At that time he was attached to the General Headquarters, Albania, with no particular assignment.

Ending three (3) will occur if a General officer is holding a concurrent command. At the date next to the bracket occurs, that officer gave up this command and went back to his other concurrent command (see Example G).

Example G: from **Army Group South [Gruppo Armate Sud]**:
... Mar. [Retired '20] Emilio De Bono [+ Member, Fascists Grand Council] /41 Mar. His Royal ...

Explanation of Example G:
Mar. [Retire '20] Emilio De Bono who was Commander-in-Chief, Army Group South, was concurrently a Member of the Fascists Grand Council.. In 1941 when Army Group South was turned over to Mar. His Royal Highness Crown Prince Umberto Piemonte [di Savoia], Mar. Emilio De Bono did not get a new assignment but continued as a Member of the Fascists Grand Council.

Ending four (4), the General/Flag officer gave up both this command and his concurrent command and was given a new duty assignment; with the old assignment ending on that date (see Example G).

Example H: from **Army Group East (#1)**.
... 12/39 LG Carlo Geloso [+ Commanding General, XXVI Army Corps] (Commander-in-Chief, Third Army) 06/10/40 Gen Camillo Grossi

Explanation of Example H:
LG Carlo Geloso was made Commander-in-Chief of Army Group East (#1), while concurrently serving as Commanding General, XXVI Army Corps. On June 10, 1940, he became Commander-in-Chief of the Third Army, giving up both assignments.

Dates before and/or after an officers name and assignment.

A date may appear in several forms. They are:

Date	Explanation
09/01/39	This is the true date the assignment began and/or ended.
09/01/39?	When it appears before the name, the officer had his present assignment on this actual date, but it might be earlier. When it appears after the assignment, the officer in question had a new assignment on this actual date, but the assignment might be earlier
09/39	This is the true month and year the assignment began and/or ended. The actual date is unknown.
09/39?	When it appears before the name, the officer had his present assignment n this month and year, but it might be earlier. When it appears after the assignment, the officer in question had a new assignment in this month and year, but the assignment might be earlier
/39	This is the year the assignment began and/or ended. The actual month and date are unknown.
/39?	When it appears before the name, the officer had his present assignment n this year, but it might be earlier. When it appears after the assignment, the officer in question had a new assignment in this year, but the assignment might be earlier
/4?	No date was found to suggest when assignment was made. In this case, /4?, the assignment started/ended in the 40's. Sometimes only a (/) may be found.

Other assistance that will help you with this book are:
There may be a time when two officers appear to hold the same post. When this happens, the officers will be listed one under the other with the date of their assignment before their name and what their next duty assignment is and the date they left their assignment. See example I.

Example I: from **206th Regional Military Tribunal (Judical) Torino [Turin]**:
206th Regional Military Tribunal (Judical) Torino [Turin] (10/43): MG America Cappi or BG Cino Gaggiotti

Explanation of Example I: It appears that in October 1943, two commanders, MG America Cappi and BG Cino Gaggiotti, were both found to be Chief, 206th Regional Military Tribunal (Judical) in Torino [Turin]. But, the problem lies that both have been listed with a starting date of 1941, so they are listed either side by side with an "or" between them or, under one another by order in they left for their next duty assignment. It is possible In some circumstances that there could be more than one officer in a position at the same time.

Sometimes you will come across another strange entry as in Example J.

Example J: from **Army Group South [Gruppo Armate Sud]**:
... (0610/40): Mar. [Retired '20] Emilio De Bono [+ Member, Fascists Grand Council] /41 Mar. His Royal ...

Explanation of Example J: When Army Group South was formed on June 10, 1940, Mar. [Retired '20] Emilio De Bono was brought out of retirement, placed on active duty, and assigned as Commander-in-Chief, Army Group South. He was retired in 1920, since the subscript [Retired '20] appears after his rank. In a lot of cases, a General or Admiral would retire and then be recalled back to active duty, sometimes the same year they retired, to fill a position permanently or until some other officer could be appointed, and then they would be retired again. Whenever I found a General/Flag Officer who retired and was recalled to active duty, the subscript "[Retired and either the month and year of retirement, if known, will be listed; or, the year of retirement]" as in this case, [Retired '20]. If I could not find a year only Retired appears, [Retired].

SECTION A

ITALY

SAN MARINO

&

VATICAN CITY STATE
(THE HOLY SEE)

Part 1

THE ITALIAN GOVERNMENT AND THE ORGANIZATION AND STRUCTURE OF ITALY'S MILITARY HIGH COMMAND

Part 1

THE ITALIAN GOVERNMENT AND THE ORGANIZATION AND STRUCTURE OF THE HIGH COMMAND

Italian Government

King of Italy: His Royal Highness King VICTOR EMMANUEL III [Victor Emmanuel di Savoia, Royal House of Savoy] [+ Supreme Commander of all Armed Forces; + 05/36 to 11/43, Emperor of Ethiopia; + 05/39 to 09/08/43, King of Albania [see Volume VII]] 05/45

A. **Chief Aide-de-Camp to the King**: /31 LG Duke Giuseppe Marion Asinari Rossillon (Member, Commission Supervising the Supreme Court, Senate & Member, Commission for the Armed Forces) /40 LG Ilio Iorio (?) /41 LG Mario Vercellino (Commander-in-Chief, Fourth Army) /41 MG Adolfo Infante (Commanding General, 132nd "Ariete" Armored Division) /42 BG Antonio Cavallo

B. **First Aide-de-Camp to the King**: /40 BG Paolo Puntoni (?) /43

C. **Aide-de-Camp to the King**: /41? Col. Tancredi Bianchi (Military Attaché Switzerland) /42

D. **Honorary Aide-de-Camp to the King**: /41 [Retired] LG Giullo Marinetti

E. **Chief Administration Officer, Royal Household in Tuscany**: /39 Count MG Giovanni Amico di Meane (in reserve) 07/41

Head of Government:
Primer: 10/31/22 Il Duce 1st Mar. of Italy BENITO AMILCARE ANDREA MUSSOLINI 07/25/43 vacant 07/27/43 1st Mar. of Italy [Retired 12/40] Pietro Badoglio, Duke of Addis Abeba, Marquess of el Sabotino [+ 02/11/44, Foreign Minister & acting Minister of Italian Africa] (resigned & replaced) 06/09/44 IVANOE BONOMI [+ 06/18/44 to 12/10/44, Foreign Minister; + 06/18/44, Interior Minister].

A. **Supreme Commander of all Armed Forces (Comandante Supremo delle Forze Armate dello Stato)**: His Royal Highness King VICTOR EMMANUEL III, King of Italy [+ 05/36 to 11/43, Emperor of Ethiopia; + 05/39 to 09/08/43, King of Albania [see Volume VII]]

  1. **War Minister**: Il Duce 1st Mar. of Italy BENITO AMILCARE ANDREA MUSSOLINI 07/43
  2. **Air Minster**: Il Duce 1st Mar. of Italy BENITO AMILCARE ANDREA MUSSOLINI 07/43
  3. **Navy Minister**: Il Duce 1st Mar. of Italy BENITO AMILCARE ANDREA MUSSOLINI 07/43

B. **Supreme Commission of Defense:**
  1. **Chairman:** Il Duce BENITO AMILCARE ANDREA MUSSOLINI 07/43

C. *Ministers*
  1. **Foreign Minister**: /32 Il Duce BENITO AMILCARE ANDREA MUSSOLINI /36 GIAN GALEAZZO CIANO, 2nd Count of Cortellazzo and Buccari (Ambassador to the Holy See) 07/20/40 BG Vincenzo Mezzacapo (acting) /40 GIAN GALEAZZO CIANO, 2nd Count of Cortellazzo and Buccari (Ambassador to the Holy See) 02/43 Il Duce 1st Mar. of Italy BENITO AMILCARE ANDREA MUSSOLINI 07/25/43 RAFFAELE GUARIGLIA 02/11/44 1st Mar. of Italy [Retired 12/40] Pietro Badoglio, Duke of Addis Abeda, Marquess of el Sabotino [+ acting Minister of Italian Africa] 06/08/44 vacant 06/18/44 IVANOE BONOMI [+ Primer & Interior Minister] 12/10/44 vacant 12/12/44 ALCIDE de GASPERI.

a. ***Ambassadors***
   i. **Ambassador to the Holy See (Vatican)**: /39 BG Dino Alfieri [MVSN] (Ambassador to Germany) /39 unknown? 02/43 GIAN GALEAZZO CIANO, 2nd Count of Cortellazzo and Buccari [+ Member, Grand Council of Fascism]
   ii. **Ambassador to Germany**: /39 BG Dino Alfieri [MVSN] (?) /43 Gen. [Rtetired '39] Alberto Pariani (arrested by the German and placed in prison; /45, arrested by the Italian government as a pro-fascist but acquitted) 09/08/43 dissolved.
   iii. **Ambassador to Spain**: /38 MG Gastone Gambara [+ to /39, Commanding General, Volunteer Corps of Troops to Spain] (Commanding General, XV Army Corps) 06/10/40

b. ***Governors***
   i. **Governor-General of Dodecanese Islands**: /36 BG Count Cesare Maria de Vecchi di Val Cismon (Commanding General, Dodecanese Islands) /40 Gen. Ettore Bastico [+ to /41 Member, Commission for the Armed Forces, Senate] (Governor-General, Libya & Commander-in-Chief, North Africa) /42 unknown? 01/01/43 VA Inigo Campioni [+ Commander-in-Chief, Headquarters, Aegean Sea] (shot to death) 05/24/44
   ii. **Governor-General of Libya**: /40 Mar. Rodolfo Graziani [+ Chief of the Army General Staff & Commander-in-Chief, North Africa] 03/25/41 LG Italo Gariboldi [+ Commander-in-Chief, General Headquarters North Africa] (in reserve) 07/41 unknown? /42 Mar. Ettore Bastico [+ Commander-in-Chief, North Africa] /43 dissolved.
   iii. **Governor of Montenegro** (10/41; HQ: Cetinje, Montenegro; part of Ninth Army): Gen. Alessandro Pirzio-Biroli [+ Governor of Montenegro] (?) 09/08/43 disbanded.
      A. **Chief of the Cabinet of the Military Government of Montenegro**: unknown? /43 BG Giovanni Stirati (to /45, German prisoner-of-war) 09/43 dissolved.
      B. **President, Border Commission for Montenegro**: /43 BG Fausto Ghemi (to /45, German prisoner-of-war) 09/08/43 dissolved.
   iv. **Governor of Italian Somaliland**: /36 LG Ruggero Santini [+ Commanding General, Somaliland] /37 unknown? /40 LG Gustavo Pesenti (retired; 06/42?, 14th Territorial Zone) 11/40 MG Carlo de Simone [+ Commanding General, Italian Somaliland Corps; + to 03/10/41, Commanding General, 102nd Colonial Infantry Division; + 03/10/41 to 04/24/41, Italian Governor of Harar] 05/17/41 ceased to exist.

c. ***High Commissioners***
   i. **High Commissioner Lubiana, Yugoslavia**: /41 Gen. [Retired '23?] Francesco Grazioli [+ Vice President, Commission for the Affairs of Italian Africa, Senate] /42

d. ***Consuls***

i. **Italian Consul, Marseilles (France)**: 07/41 BG (Res.) Egido Liberati
2. **War Minister**: Il Duce 1st Mar. of Italy BENITO AMILCARE ANDREA MUSSOLINI 07/43 LG Antonio Sorice (?) /44 LG Taddeo Orlando (Commander-in-Chief, Royal Carabinieri) /44
    a. **Undersecretary of War**: /36 Gen. Alberto Pariani [+Chief of the Army General Staff] (retired; /43, recalled & Commander-in-Chief, General Headquarters, Albania) /39 LG Ubaldo Soddu (Deputy Chief of the Supreme General Staff & Commander-in-Chief, Army Group East) 11/29/40 Gen. Alfredo Guzzoni [+ Deputy Chief of the Supreme General Staff] (/43, Commander-in-Chief, Sixth Army) 05/41 LG Antonio Scuero (Commanding General, V Army Corps) 02/43 LG Antonio Sorice (War Minister) 07/43 LG Giovanni Battista Oxilia [+ Deputy Chief of the General Staff].
        i. **Territorial Army**:
    b. **Chief of the General Staff (Army High Command)**: /36 Gen. [Rtetired '39] Alberto Pariani [+ Undersecretary of War] (retired; /43, recalled & Commander-in-Chief, General Headquarters, Albania) /39 Mar. Rodolfo Graziani, Marquis [Marchese] of Neghelli [+ /40, Governor-General, Libya & Commander-in-Chief, North Africa] (resigned; 09/08/43, joins Social Republic of Italy; 09/08/43, Minister of War & Commander-in-Chief, Armed Forces, Social Republic of Italy) 05/41 LG Mario Roatta (Commander-in-Chief, Second Army) 01/42 Gen. Vittorio Ambrosio [+ Commander-in-Chief, Royal Army] (Commander-in-Chief of the Armed Forces or Chief of the Supreme General Staff) 02/43 Gen. Ezlo Rosi (Commander-in-Chief, Army Group East) 05/43 LG Mario Roatta [+ 07/43, Commanding General, General Headquarters Rome] (dismissed) 09/43 Mar. Giovanni Messe (Chief of the Supreme General Staff) 11/12/43 LG Paolo Berardi (Commanding General, XI Territorial Defense Command) /45.
        i. **Field Army**:
    c. **Undersecretary of State for War Manufacture**:
        i. **War Manufacture Committee**:
            07/41 BG Giovanni Marciani
3. **Air Minster**: Il Duce 1st Mar. of Italy BENITO AMILCARE ANDREA MUSSOLINI 07/27/43 MG Renato Sandali [RIAF] [+ Undersecretary of Air & Chief of Staff, Air Force] (Governor-General of Libya) 06/18/44
    a. **Undersecretary of Air & Chief of Staff (Air Force High Command)**: 03/22/34 MG Giuseppe Valle [RIAF] (?) 11/10/39 MG Francesno Pricolo [RIAF] (?) 11/15/41 LG Rino Corso Fougier [RIAF] (?) 07/27/43 MG Renato Sandali [RIAF] [+ Air Minister & Chief of Staff, Air Force] (Governor-General of Libya) 06/18/44 MG Pietro Piacentini [RIAF] (?) 12/13/44 MG Mario Ajmone-Cat [RIAF].
4. **Navy Minister**: Il Duce 1st Mar. of Italy BENITO AMILCARE ANDREA MUSSOLINI 07/25/43 VA Raffaele de Courten [RIN] [+ Chief of Staff, Italian Royal Navy]
    a. **Undersecretary of Navy & Chief of Staff (Navy High Command)**:

/35? Adm. Domenico Cavagnari [RIN] (retired; President of Admiraldy Committee) 12/10/40 VA Arturo Riccardi [RIN] (President of Admiralty Committee) 07/25/43 VA Raffaele de Courten [RIN] [+ Naval Minister]

5. **Interior Minister**: 11/06/26 Il Duce BENITO AMILCARE ANDREA MUSSOLINI 07/26/43 BRUNO FORNACIARI 08/09/43 BG (Res.) Umberto Ricci [+ attached to VI Territorial Defense Command & Administrator, 8th Territorial Zone] 02/11/44 VITO REALE 04/17/44 vacant 04/22/44 SALVATORE ALDISIO 06/08/44 vacant 06/18/44 IVANOE BONOMI [+ Primer; + to 12/10/44, Foreign Minister].

    a. **Undersecretary**: GUIDO BUFFARINI-GUIDI 02/43 BG Umberto Albini [MVSN] [+ Member, Fascist Grand Council]

    b. **Commandant of Police**: ARTURO BOCCHINI (died of cerebral ictus) 11/20/40 CARMINE SENISE (replaced) 04/43 MG Renzo Chierici [MVSN] (?) 07/25/43 CARMINE SENISE (arrested by the Germans, deported to a concentration camp) 09/08/43 dissolved.

    c. **Organization for Vigilance and Repression of Anti-Fascism [Organizzazione per la Vigilanza e la Repressione (OVRA)]**: FRANCESCO NUDI /?? GUIDO LETO

    d. **Royal Carabinieri (CCRR)**: /35 MG Riccardo Moizo (retired, relinquished command on reaching age limit; Member, Commission of the Armed Forces, Senate) 08/26/40 LG Remo Gambelli (retired for age and given a post in War Ministry) 02/28/43 LG Azzolino Hazon (killed in an air raid on Rome) /43 LG Angelo Cerica (/45, Commanding General, VI Terrtiorial Defense Command) /43 MG Giuseppe Pieche (?) /44 LG Taddeo Orlando.

        i. **Deputy Commander-in-Chief, Royal Carabinieri**: /37 MG Carlo Contestabile (retired?) /40 MG Cesare Cantù (retired?) /40 MG Crispino Agostinucci [+ to /41, Commanding General, Royal Carabinieri Albania] (09/08/43, German prisoner-of-war; /47, President, National Association of Carabinieri) /42 MG Azzolono Hazon (Commander-in-Chief, Royal Carabinieri) 02/28/43 MG Giuseppe Pieche (Commander-in-Chief, Royal Carabinieri) /43

        ii. **King's Bodyguard (Carabinieri Guardia del Re, popularly known as Cuirassiers (Corazzieri))**:

        iii. **Administration Divisions**:
            A. **1st Pastrengo Carabinieri Division** (Milan):
            B. **2nd Podaga Carabinieri Division** (Rome):
                1. **Autonomous Group of Carabinieri. Aegean Islands**:
            C. **3rd Ogaden Carabinieri Division** (Naples):
            D. **High Command of Carabinieri, Albania**:
            E. **Royal Carabinieri, North Africa**:

        iv. **Administration Divisions**:
            A. **Royal Carabinieri Central Italy**: /44 MG Filippo

Caruso.
- v. **President National Association of Carabinieri**: /34 Col. Amedeo Ademollo.
- e. **Special Division of Public Security (Division Speciale Pubblica Sicurezza)**:
  - i. **Public Security Police**

6. **Minister of Justice**:
   a. **President for Special Tribunal for the State Defense**: 11/32 MG Casanuova Antonino Tringali [MVSN] [+ Member, Fascist Grand Council] (09/43, joins Social Republic of Italy; 09/23/43, Italian Social Republic Minister of Justice) 07/43
   b. **Supreme Tribunal, Rome**: /41 BG (Res.) Luigi Lenti
      i. **Attached to Supreme Tribunal, Rome**:
         /41 BG (Res.) Giovanni Losurdo
   c. **Special Tribunal for Defense of State, Rome**:
      /40 BG Fernando Cianci [MVSN]
      /41 BG (Res.) Pietro Lanari
      /41 BG (Res.) Gioacchino Milazzo

7. **Finance Minister**: 07/41 BG Salvatore Gangi (?) /41 REVAL 02/43 GIACOMO ACERBO
   a. **Royal Customs Guard (Regia Guardio di Finanza, commonly known as Finance Guards)** (General Headquarters: Rome): /34 MG Riccardo Calcagno (Member, Commission of the Affairs of Italian Africa, Senate) 12/38 LG Ugo Pignetti (retired?) /41 LG Aldo Aymonino
      i. **Deputy Commander, Royal Customs Guards**: /33 Col. Antonio Papaleo (retired?) /40 BG Paolo Gamondi (?) /42 BG Francesco Poli (/48, Deputy Commander, Customs Guard) 09/08/43 dissolved.
      ii. **Firenze [Florence] Royal Customs Guard Zone Inspectorate**: Col. Riccardo Conti (/45, Deputy Commander, Royal Customs Guard) /44
      iii. **Genova [Genoa] Royal Customs Guard Zone Inspectorate**: /37 Col. Francesco Poli (Inspector of the Royal Customs Guard, Albania, Yugoslavia & Greece) /40
      iv. **Napoli [Naples] Royal Customs Guard Zone Inspectorate**: /37 Col. Paolo Gamondi (Deputy Commander, Royal Customs Guards) /40 Col. Filippo Crimi (joins Social Republic of Italy; /43 Commanding General, National Republican Customs Guards) /43
      v. **Rome Special Customs Guard Zone Inspectorate**: /44 BG Filippo Crimi.
      vi. **Rome Royal Customs Guard Legion**: /39? Col. Filippo Crimi (Commanding Officer, Naples Royal Customs Guard Zone Inspectorate) /40
      vii. **Inspector of the Royal Customs Guard Albania, Yugoslavia & Greece**: /40 BG Francesco Poli (Deputy Commander, Royal

Customs Guard) /42
8. **Corporation Minister**: /39 MG Renato Ricci [MVSN] [+ /40, Member, Directorate of the National Fascist Party] (Commanding General, Voluntary Militia for National Security) 02/43 TIENGO 04/43 TULLIO CIANETTI
   a. **Commerce**:
   b. **Industry**:
      i. **President, Commission Requesting Wool**: 07/41 MG Antonio Barbato
9. **Minister of Public Works**: /39 BG Adelschi Serena [MVSN] [+ Secretary of the National Fascist Party] (Member, Fascist Grand Party) /40
   a. **Council of Public Works**:
      i. **Member, Council of Public Works**:
         /38 MG (Res.) Pietro De Lauso
10. **Minister of Communication**:
    a. **Assistant Minister of Communication**: /41 MG Giovanni Calini
    b. **Chief, War Correspondents, North Africa**: /41 MG Carlo Fettarappa Sandri
11. **Minister of Labor**:
12. **Minister of War Production**: unknown? 04/43? Gen. (Res.) Giuseppe Gatti (?) /43 LG Carlo Favagrossa
    a. **Undersecretary of State for War Production**:
       i. **At Disposal of, Attached to, or on Special Duties, Undersecretary of State for War Production**:
          02/42 (attached to) BG (Res.) Erico Zannini
    b. **Chief General Commissariat for War Production**: /39 MG Carlo Favagrossa (Minister of War Production) /43
13. **Minister of Education**: /35 BG Count Cesare Maria de Vecchi di Val Cismon (Governor of Italian Aegean Islands) /36 unknown? 02/05/43 CARLO ALBERTO BIGGINI (09/23/43, Italian Social Republic Minister of National Education) 07/43
14. **Minister of Popular Culture**: /37 BG Dino Alfieri [MVSN] (Ambassador to the Vatican) /39 MG Alessandro Pavolini (joins the Social Republic of Italy; 09/23/43, Leader of the Republican Fascist Party & Commanding General, National Republican Guard Brigade "Nere", Social Republic of Italy) 09/08/43 dissolved.
15. **Minister of Agriculture and Forestry**
16. **Presidency of Grand Council of Fascism [Gran Consiglio del Fascism]** (1923, the main body of the Fascist government in Italy; the body held and applied great power to control the institutions of government and became a state body on 12/09/28). Il Duce BENITO AMILCARE ANDREA MUSSOLINI 07/25/43 1st Mar. of Italy [Retired 12/40] Pietro Badoglio, Duke of Addis Abeda, Marquess of el Sabotino.
    a. *Members*
       i. **The Quadrumvirs** (the people who lead the March on Rome). 12/09/29 MICHELE BIANCHI (died a natural death) 02/03/30 /40 Mar. [Retired '20] Emilio De Bono [+ to /41, Commander-in-Chief, Army Group South] (arrested by Mussolini, after

Mussolini was set freed by the Germans, tried, convicted, and executed by firing squad) 01/11/44 /41 BG Count Cesare Maria de Vecchi di Val Cismon Mar. of the AF Italo Balbo

ii. **The President of the Senate** (the Senate is the upper house of the Parliament of Italy):

iii. **The President of the Italian Chamber of Deputies [Camera dei Deputati]** (1939, **Chamber of Fasci and Corporation**; the Chamber of Deputies is the lower house of the Parliament of Italy):

iv. **Minister of Justice**:

v. **Minister of Foreign Affairs**: 32 Il Duce BENITO AMILCARE ANDREA MUSSOLINI /36 GIAN GALEAZZO CIANO, 2nd Count of Cortellazzo and Buccari (Ambassador to the Holy See) 07/20/40 BG Vincenzo Mezzacapo (acting) /40 GIAN GALEAZZO CIANO, 2nd Count of Cortellazzo and Buccari (Ambassador to the Holy See) 02/43 Il Duce 1st Mar. of Italy BENITO AMILCARE ANDREA MUSSOLINI 07/25/43 RAFFAELE GUARIGLIA 02/11/44 1st Mar. of Italy $_{[Retired\ 12/40]}$ Pietro Badoglio, Duke of Addis Abeda, Marquess of el Sabotino [+ acting Minister of Italian Africa] 06/08/44 vacant 06/18/44 IVANOE BONOMI [+ Primer & Interior Minister] 12/10/44 vacant 12/12/44 ALCIDE de GASPERI.

    A. **Military-Governor, Rhodes**: 01/01/43? ? Adm. Inigo Campioni [+ Commanding Officer, General Headquarters, Aegean] /43 MG Raffaello Calzini (to /45, German prisoner-of-war) 09/08/43

vi. **Minister of Agriculture and Forestry**:

vii. **Minister of Education**: /36 unknown? 02/05/43 CARLO ALBERTO BIGGINI (09/23/43, Italian Social Republic Minister of National Education) 07/43

viii. **Minister of Corporations**:

ix. **Minister of Popular Culture**:

x. **President of the Royal Academy of Italy**: The Marquis [Marchese] GUGLIELMO MARCONI

xi. **The Secretary of the National Fascist Party** (also **Secretary of the Grand Council**): BG Achille Starace $_{[MVSN]}$ [+ /35 to /37?, Commanding General, Celere Column A. O.] (Chief of Staff, Voluntary Militia for National Security) /39 BG Adelschi Serena $_{[MVSN]}$ (Member, Fascist Grand Party) /40 unknown? /43 MG Carlo Scorza $_{[MVSN]}$

    A. **Vice-Secretary of the National Fascist Party**: /33 Col. Adelschi Serena $_{[MVSN]}$ [+ /34 to /37, Member Fascist Grand Council] (Minister of Public Works & Secretary of the National Fascist Party) /39 unknown? /42 BG Carlo Scorza [MVSN] (Secretary of the National Fascist Party) /43

      xii. **various people chosen by Mussolini himself, who held a 3-year position**
GIAN GALEAZZO CIANO, 2nd Count of Cortellazzo and Buccari [+ Ambassador to the Holy See]
/34 Col. Adelschi Serena [MVSN] [+ Vice-Secretary of the National Fascist Party] /37
/40 Mar. [Retired '20] Emilio De Bono
/40 BG Adelschi Serena [MVSN] (?) /41
/40 MG Casanuova Antonino Tringali [MVSN] [+ President, Tribunal for the State Defense] (09/43, joins Social Republic of Italy; 09/23/43, Minister of Justice, Social Republic of Italy) 07/43
05/14/40 LG Ottavio Zoppi [MVSN] [+ Member, Commission for the Armed Forces, Senate; + President, National Adriti (Shock-Troop) Federation] 09/08/43 dissolved.
/41 BG Unberto Albini [MVSN] [+ Undersecretary of Interior]
02/05/43 CARLO ALBERTO BIGGINI
02/43 BG Umberto Albini [MVSN] [+ Undersecretary of Interior]

  b. **National Security Volunteer Militia [Milizia Voluntaria per la Sicurezza Nazionale (MVSN) {Fascist Militia}]** (or commonly known as the **Black Shirts (Camicie Nere (CCNN))**: 02/43 MG Renato Ricci [MVSN] (joins Social Republic of Italy; /43 Commanding General, National Republican Guard, Social Republic of Italy) 09/08/43
Director, National Security Volunteer Militia (MVSN): 04/43? MG Allessandro Melchiori [MVSN]
Chief of Staff, National Security Volunteer Militia (MVSN) (Commander, National Security Volunteer Militia): /35 MG Luigi Russo [MVSN] (Undersecretary to President, Council of Ministers) /39 MG Achille Starace [MVSN] (/45, executed by Partisans) /41 MG Sergio Biraghi [MVSN] (?) /41 MG Enzo Emilio Galbiati [MVSN] (arrested) /43 MG Giuseppe Conticelli [MVSN]

17. **Minister of Italian Africa**: /39 MG Attillo Teruzzi [MVSN] (?) /43 MG (Res.) Cesare Cesari (acting; retired?) /43 Gen. [Retired '36] Melchiade Gabba (acting; retired) /44
  a. **Undersecretary of Ministry of Italian Africa**: /37 MG Attillo Teruzzi [MVSN] (Minister of Italian Africa) /39
  b. **Commissioner for Italian East Africa**: /35 Gen. [Retired '20] Emilio De Bono [+ Member, Grand Council of Fascist; + to 11/35, Commander-in-Chief, Italian East Africa] 11/35 Gen. Pietro Badoglio, Duke of Addis Ababa, Marquess of el Sabotino (Viceroy and Governor-General, Italian East Africa) 05/09/36 disbanded.

c. **Viceroy and Governor-General, Italian East Africa** (05/09/36, Ethiopia) Gen. Pietro Badoglio, Duke of Addis Ababa, Marquess of el Sabotino [+ Commander-in-Chief, General Headquarters East Africa] (Chief of the Supreme General Staff) 06/11/36 Mar. Rodolfo Graziani [+ Commanding General, XI Army Corps] /37 vacant12/21/37 Mar. Rodolfo Graziani (/39, Chief of the Army General Staff) /38 Gen. His Royal Highness Prince Amadeo Umberto Isabella Luigi Filippo Maria Giuseppe Giovanni di Savoia [Savoy-Aosta], 3rd Duke of Aosta [+ Commander-in-Chief, General Headquarters East Africa] (British prisoner-of war; 03/03/42, died in a British Prison of War Camp in Kenya from tuberculosis and maleria) 05/19/41 vacant 05/23/41 Gen. Pietro Gazzera [acting; + Commander-in-Chief, General Headquarters East Africa; Italian Governor of Galla-Sidama; Commanding General, 24th Colonial Infantry Division] (to /43, British prisoner-of-war; /43 to /45, German prisoner-of-war) 07/06/41 LG Guglielmo Ciro Nasi [+ Member, Commission of the Affairs of Italian Africa, Senate; & Italian Governor of Amhara; & Commanding General, Western Ethiopia] (British prisoner-of-war) 11/27/41 surrendered; reinstated 02/11/44 1st Mar. of Italy [Retired 12/40] Pietro Badoglio, Duke of Addis Abeba, Marquess of el Sabotino [+ Foreign Minister]

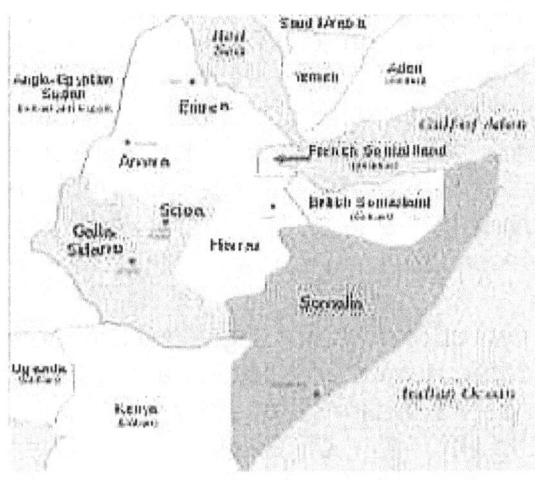

i. **Italian Governor of Addis Ababa** (05/05/36): GIUSEPPE BOTTAI 05/27/36 vacant 06/01/36 ALFREDO SINISCALCHI 09/23/38 FRANCESCO CAMERO MEDICI 01/01/39 ENRICO CERULLI [+ Italian Governor of Showa] (Italian Governor of Harar) 05/05/39 LG Guglielmo Ciro Nasi [+ Member, Commission for the Armed Forces, Senate; & Italian Governor of Showa] (Italian Governor of Harrar) 06/02/40 GIUSEPPE DAODICE [+ Italian Governor of Showa] 04/03/41 AGENORE FRANGIPANI [+ Italian Governor of Showa] 04/06/41 surrendered.

ii. **Italian Governor of Amhara** (06/01/36): LG Alessandro Pirzio-Biroli (/41, Commander-in-Chief, Ninth Army) 12/15/37 LG Ottorino Mezzetti (Member, Commission for the Affairs of Italian Africa, Senate) 01/01/39 LG Luigi Frusci [+ /40 to 05/17/41, Governor of Eritrea & Commanding General, Eritrea Corps; + 06/40, Commanding General, 4th (Eritrean) Colonial Infantry Division] (British prisoner-of-war) 05/19/41 LG Guglielmo Ciro Nasi [+ to 07/41, Member, Commission for the Armed Forces, Senate; + 07/06/41, Viceroy and Governor-General, Italian East Africa & Member, Commission of the Affairs of Italian Africa, Senate; + Commanding General, Western Ethiopia] 11/27/41 surrendered.

A. **Commanding Officer, Amhara, Ethiopia**: /36 BG

      Quirino Armellini (Commanding General, "Piave" Infantry Brigade) /39
   iii. **Italian Governor of Galla-Sidama** (06/01/36): MG Carlo Geloso (Commanding General, V Army Corps) 07/10/38 ARMANDO FELSANI 08/12/38 Gen. Pietro Gazzera [+ /39 to /40, Member, Commission for the Affairs of Italian Africa, Senate; /40, Commanding General, 24th Colonial Infantry Division; + /41, acting Governor-General, Italian East Africa (to /43, British prisoner-of-war; /43 to /45, German prisoner-of-war) 07/06/41 surrendered.
   iv. **Italian Governor of Harrar**: 06/01/36 LG Guglielmo Ciro Nasi (Member, Commission for the Armed Forces, Senate; & Italian Governor of Addis Ababa; & Italian Governor of Showa) 05/05/39 ENRICO CERULLI 06/11/40 LG Guglielmo Cero Nasi [+ Member, Commission for the Armed Forces, Senate] (05/19/41, Italian Governor of Amhara) 02/04/41 POMPEO GORINI (acting) 03/10/41 MG Carlo de Simone [+ Governor of Italian Somaliland & Commanding General, Juba Sector, Italian Somaliland Corps] 04/24/41 surrendered.
   v. **Italian Governor of Showa** (01/01/39): ENRICO CERULLI [+ Italian Governor of Addis Ababa] (Italian Governor of Harar) 05/05/39 LG Guglielmo Ciro Nasi [+ Member, Commission for the Armed Forces, Senate; & Italian Governor of Addis Ababa] (Italian Governor of Harrar) 06/02/40 GIUSEPPE DAODICE [+ Italian Governor of Addis Ababa] 04/03/41 AGENORE FRANGIPANI [+ Italian Governor of Addis Ababa] 04/06/41 surrendered.
   vi. **Italian Governor of Eritrea**: /36 LG Alfredo Guzzoni (Commanding General, XI Army Corps) /37 unknown? /40 LG Luigi Frusci [+ Italian Governor of Amhara, Ethiopia & Commanding General, Eritrea Corps; + 06/40, Commanding General, 4th (Eritrean) Colonial Infantry Division] (British prisoner-of-war) 05/17/41 ceased to exist.
   vii. **Italian Africa Police [Polizia del'Africa Italiana (PAI)]**: BG Ubaldo Presti $_{[MVSN]}$ (?) /41 BG Riccardo Maraffa (German prisoner-of-war; sent to Dachau Concentrate Camp where he died) 09/08/43
  d. **Head of the Cabinet, Government of East Africa**: /37 MG Giovan Battista Volpini (killed by Abyssinian partisans) /41
 18. **Minister of Occupied Italy** (1944, responsible for the reconstruction of liberated northern Italy and for the relations with the different resistance movements): MAURO SCOCCIMARRO.

Italian Senate
 A. **The President of the Senate** (the Senate is the upper house of the Parliament of Italy):

B. **Vice-President of the Senate**: 12/42? LG [Retired '31] Count Giovanni Romei Longhena

C. **Senators; Members (ex-Servicemen) of the Senator**
    03/25/39 Gen. [Retired '39] Ruggero Santini [+ to /41, Vice President of the Affairs of Italian Africa, Senate; + /41, Member, Commission for the Armed Forces, Senate] /43
    07/41? Gen. [Retired] Ettore Mambretti

D. **Commission for the Armed Forces, Senate**:
    1. **Members**:
        /39 Gen. [Retired] Pietro Ago
        /39 Gen. Valentino Bobbio (?) /40
        /39 Mar. [Retired '20] Emilio De Bono [+ Member, Commission of Affairs of Italian Africa, Senate & Inspector of Overseas Troops] (Commander-in-Chief, Army Group South & Member, Fascist Grand Council) /40
        /39 Gen. Ettore Bastico [+ to 40, Commanding General, Army of Po; + /40, Governor-General, Dodecanese Islands] /41
        /39 Gen. Camillo Grossi [+ to -6/10/40, Commander-in-Chief, Fourth Army; + 06/10/40 Commander-in-Chief, Army Group East; + 06/40, Head, Italian Armistice Commission to France] (died) /41
        /39 Gen. [Retired] Arturo Vacca-Maggiolini (Head, Italian Armistice Commission to France) /41
        /39 LG Adriano Marinetti [+ to /40, Commander-in-Chief, First Army] /43 dissolved.
        /39 Gen. [Retired '20] Count Federico Baistrocchi (?) 09/08/43 dissolved.
        /39 LG (Res.) Eugenio Graziosi (?) 09/08/43 dissolved.
        /39 Gen. Angelo Tua [04/20/40, retired] (?) 09/08/43 dissolved.
        /39 LG Ottavio Zoppi [MVSN] [+ 05/14/40, Member, National Directorate of Fascist Party; + President, National Adriti (Shock-Troop) Federation] 09/08/43 dissolved.
        05/05/39 LG Guglielmo Ciro Nasi [+ to 06/02/40 Italian Governor of Addis Ababa & Italian Governor of Showa; + 06/01/40 to 02/04/41, Italian Governor of Harrar; + 06/10/40 to 05/07/41, Commanding General, Eastern Sector, Italian East Africa] (Viceroy and Governor-General Italian East Africa & Member, Commission of the Affairs of Italian Africa, Senate) 07/06/41
        /40 LG Fidenzio Dall'Ora (?) /41
        /40 LG Duke Giuseppe Marion Asinari Rossillon [+ Member, Commission Supervising the Supreme Court, Senate] 09/08/43 dissolved.
        /40 Mar. [Retired '20] Emilio De Bono (Inspector of Overseas Troops) 09/08/43 dissolved.
        /40 LG Count Ambrogio Clerici (?) 09/08/43 dissolved.
        /40 Gen. Francesco Guidi (?) 09/08/43 dissolved.
        08/26/40 LG [Retired '40] LG Riccardo Moizo (?) 09/08/43 dissolved.
        /41 Gen. [Retired '39] Ruggero Santini [+ Senator] (?) 09/08/43 dissolved.
        /43 Gen. [Retired] Arturo Vacca-Maggiolini (?) 09/08/43 dissolved.

E. **Commission of Affairs of Italian Africa, Senate:**
1. **President, Commission of Affairs of State for Africa, Senate:**
/43 Gen. [Retired '23?] Francesco Grazioli (Head, unknown? Mission to Rumania) 09/08/43 dissolved.
2. **Vice President, Commission of Affairs of Italian Africa, Senate:**
/39 Gen. [Retired '23?] Francesco Grazioli (High Commissioner Lubiana, Yugoslavia) /41
/39 Gen. [Retired '39] Ruggero Santini [+ Senator] (Member, Commission for the Armed Forces, Senate) /41
/41 Gen. [Retired '36] Melchiade Gabba (Minister of Italian Africa) 09/08/43 dissolved.
/41 Gen. [Retired '23?] Francesco Grazioli [+ to /42, High Commissioner Lubiana, Yugoslavia] (President, Commission of Affairs of State for Africa, Senate) /43
3. **Secretary, Commission of Affairs of Italian Africa, Senate:**
/41 LG Umberto Somma (?) /43
4. **Members, Commission of Affairs of Italian Africa, Senate:**
01/01/39 LG Ottorino Mezzetti (?) 09/08/43 dissolved.
/39 Mar. [Retired '20] Emilio De Bono [+ Member, Commission for Armed Forces, Senate & Inspector of Overseas Troops] (Commander-in-Chief, Army Group South & Member, Fascist Grand Council) /40
/39 Gen. Pietro Gazzera [+ Italian Governor of Galla-Sidama] (Commanding General, 24th Colonial Infantry Division) /40
/39 LG [Retired '39] Glacomo Appiotti (President, Council of the Military Union) 09/08/43 dissolved.
/39 LG Riccardo Calcagno (?) 09/08/43 dissolved.
/39 Gen. [Retired '36] Melchiade Gabba (Vice President, Commission of Affairs of Italian Africa) /41
/40 LG Ambrogio Bollati (?) 09/08/43 dissolved.
/40 LG Umberto Somma (Secretary, Commissiion of the Affairs of Italian Africa, Senate) /41
07/06/41 Gen. Guglielmo Ciro Nasi [+ Viceroy and Governor-General, Italian East Africa; & Commanding General, Western Ethiopia] (British prisoner-of-war) 11/27/41

F. **Commission Supervising the Supreme Court, Senate:**
1. **Members:**
/40 LG Duke Giuseppe Marion Asinari Rossillon [+ Member, Commission for the Armed Forces] 09/08/43 dissolved.

Italian Chamber of Deputies [Camera dei Deputati] (1939, **Chamber of Fasci and Corporation**; the Chamber of Deputies is the lower house of the Parliament of Italy):
A. **The President of the Italian Chamber of Deputies [Camera dei Deputati]** (1939, **Chamber of Fasci and Corporation**; the Chamber of Deputies is the lower house

of the Parliament of Italy):

Armed Forces High Command

Supreme Commander of all Armed Forces (Comandante Supremo delle Forze Armate dello Stato): His Royal Highness King VICTOR EMMANUEL III, King of Italy [+ 05/36 to 11/43, Emperor of Ethiopia; + 05/39 to 09/08/43, King of Albania [see Volume VII]]

Supreme Commission of Defense:
A. **Chairman:** Il Duce 1st Mar. of Italy BENITO AMILCARE ANDREA MUSSOLINI 07/43
B. **Commander-in-Chief of the Armed Forces**: 12/40 Mar. Ugo Cavallero 01/43 Gen. Vittorio Ambrosio (Inspector-General of the Army) 09/08/43
C. **Undersecretary of War**: /36 Gen. [Rtetired '39] Alberto Pariani [+Chief of the Army General Staff] (retired; /43, recalled & Commander-in-Chief, General Headquarters, Albania) /39 LG Ubaldo Soddu (Deputy Chief of the Supreme General Staff & Commander-in-Chief, Army Group East) 11/29/40 Gen. Alfredo Guzzoni [+ Deputy Chief of the Supreme General Staff] (/43, Commander-in-Chief, Sixth Army) 05/41 LG Antonio Scuero (Commanding General, V Army Corps) 02/43 BG Antonio Sorice (?) /44 LG Giovanni Battista Oxilia [+ Deputy Chief of the General Staff].
D. **Chief of the General Staff (Army High Command)**: /36 Gen. [Rtetired '39] Alberto Pariani [+Undersecretary of War] (retired; /43, recalled & Commander-in-Chief, General Headquarters, Albania) /39 Mar. Rodolfo Graziani, Marquis [Marchese] of Neghelli [+ /40, Governor-General, Libya & Commander-in-Chief, North Africa] (resigned; 09/08/43, joins Social Republic of Italy; 09/08/43, Minister of War & Commander-in-Chief, Armed Forces, Social Republic of Italy) 05/41 LG Mario Roatta (Commander-in-Chief, Second Army) 01/42 Gen. Vittorio Ambrosio [+ Commander-in-Chief, Royal Army] (Commander-in-Chief of the Armed Forces or Chief of the Supreme General Staff) 02/43 Gen. Ezlo Rosi (Commander-in-Chief, Army Group East) 05/43 LG Mario Roatta [+ 07/43, Commanding General, General Headquarters Rome] (dismissed) 09/43 Mar. Giovanni Messe (Chief of the Supreme General Staff) 11/12/43 LG Paolo Berardi (Commanding General, XI Territorial Defense Command) /45.
E. **Undersecretary of Air & Chief of Staff (Air Force High Command)**: 03/22/34 MG Giuseppe Valle [RIAF] (?) 11/10/39 MG Francesno Pricolo [RIAF] (?) 11/15/41 LG Rino Corso Fougier [RIAF] (?) 07/27/43 MG Renato Sandali [RIAF] [+ Air Minister & Chief of Staff, Air Force] (Governor-General of Libra) 06/18/44 MG Pietro Piacentini [RIAF] (?) 12/13/44 MG Mario Ajmone-Cat [RIAF].
F. **Undersecretary of Navy & Chief of Staff (Navy High Command)**: /35? Adm. Domenico Cavagnari (retired; President of Admiraldy Committee) 12/10/40 VA Arturo Riccardi [RIN] (President of Admiralty Committee) 07/25/43 VA Raffaele de Courten

Chief of the Supreme General Staff (Capo di Stato Maggiore Generale; also known as **Supreme Commander** or **Commander-in-Chief of the Armed Forces (Comandante Supremo delle Forze Armate dello Stato)** (in times of war, appointed by Royal Decree and approved by Council of Ministers): 06/11/36 Mar. Pietro Badoglio Duke of Addis

Ababa, Marquess of el Sabotino (resigned and retired) 12/40 Gen. Count [Retired '19 & '27] Ugo Cavallero [+ 12/40, Commander-in-Chief, General Headquarters Albania; + to 05/41, Commander-in-Chief, Army Group East (#1)] (committed suicide) 01/43 Gen. Vittorio Ambrosio (Inspector-General of the Army) 09/08/43 vacant 11/12/43 Mar. Giovanni Messe.

- A. **Deputy Chief of the Supreme General Staff**: 11/29/40 Gen. Ubaldo Soddu [+ Commander-in-Chief, Army Group East] (retired?) 12/40 LG Alfredo Guzzoni [+ Undersecretary of War] (07/43, Commander-in-Chief, Sixth Army) /41 unknown? 03/11/43 LG Francesco Rossi
- B. **Vice Chief of the Supreme General Staff**: /40 MG Quirino Armellini (Commanding General, 80th "La Spezia" Air Landing Division) /40 MG Giovanni Magli [+ /42, Commanding General, I Army Corps] (Commanding General, VII Army Corps) 01/01/43?
- C. **Chief of Staff to Chief of the Supreme General Staff**: /40 MG Francesco Rossi (Deputy Chief of the Supreme General Staff) 03/11/43
- D. **War Minister**: Il Duce 1st Mar. of Italy BENITO AMILCARE ANDREA MUSSOLINI 07/43 LG Antonio Sorice (?) /44 LG Taddeo Orlando (Commander-in-Chief, Royal Carabinieri) /44
- E. **Air Minster**: Il Duce 1st Mar. of Italy BENITO AMILCARE ANDREA MUSSOLINI
- F. **Navy Minister**: Il Duce 1st Mar. of Italy BENITO AMILCARE ANDREA MUSSOLINI
- G. **Military Intelligence Service [Servizio Informazioni Militari]**: /39 BG Giacomo Carboni (Commandant, Modena Military Acadmey) /40 BG Cesare Amé (?) /43 MG Giacomo Carboni (Commanding General, XX Army Corps) 07/43
- H. **Chief of the Operations Branch, Supreme General Staff**: MG Silvio Rossi (?) /43 MG Umberto Utili (Commanding General, I Motorized Group) /44
- I. *Commissions:*
  1. **Italian Armistice Commission to France (CIAF)** (06/40): Gen. Ben Pietro Pintor (killed in an air crash) /40 Gen. Camillo Grossi [+ Member, Commission for the Armed Forces, Senate] (died) /41 Gen. [Retired] Arturo Vacca-Maggiolini (Member, Commission for the Armed Forces, Senate) /43
     - a. **Deputy Head, Italian Armistice Commission to France** (06/40): unknown? /42 LG Carlo Vecchiarelli (Commander-in-Chief, Eleven Army) /43
     - b. **Chief of Staff, Italian Armistice Commission to France** (06/40): BG Cesare Gandini (Infantry Commander, 9th "Pasubio" Semi-Motorized Infantry Division) /40 MG Ferruccio Bignamini (Commanding General, Vicenza Military Province) /43
     - c. **Members**:
       /40 BG Giuseppe Mancinelli (Italian Liaison Officer to German Armistice Commission to France) /40
       /40 BG Guglielmo Bazzarello (/42, Commanding General, Ajaccio Fortified Area) /41
       /41 BG Felice Gonnella (Commanding General, 211th Coastal Division) 12/41
       /41 BG Quinto Mazzolini
     - d. **Army Sub-Delegation, Italian Armistice Commission to France:**
       /42 BG Leone Santini (at disposal of, VI Territorial Defense Command) /43

03/42 (in Tunisia) BG Giacomo Silimbani [MVSN]
J. *Liaison Officers*:
1. **Liaison Officer to the Supreme Commander**: BG E. Mattioli
2. **Liaison Officer to German Armistice Commission to France**: /40 BG Giuseppe Mancinelli (/43, Chief of Staff, First Army) /42
K. **President, Military Tribunal**: /43 LG [Retired?] Nino Salvatore Villa Santa (retired?) /43 BG Alessandro Aporti (British-American prisoner-of-war, Tunisia) 05/15/43
1. **Judge Advocate-General, Supreme Military Tribunal**: /41 MG Ovidio Ciancarini
    a. **Judge**:
       10/01/41 MG Nicola Spinelli
       04/42? MG Achille Rosmini
2. **Advocate-General, Supreme Military Tribunal**: /39? BG Ovidio Ciancarini (Judge Advocate-General, Supreme Military Tribunal) /41
    a. **Assistant Advocate General, Supreme Military Tribunal**: /39 MG (Res.) Arrigo Mirabelli
    b. **Attached to Advocate-General Office**:
       /41 BG Leone Zingales (assigned to Italian Expeditionary Corps, Russia) /42
3. **Military Advocate [Judicial Branch], Reserve**: BG Enrico Capra
4. **Advocate Supply, Military Tribunal**: /41 BG (Res.) Vittorio Pasini
L. **President, Administration Council of the Military Union**: /43 LG [Retired '39] Giacomo Appiotti
M. *Armed Forces Schools*
1. **Commandant, Supreme Institute of War**: /38 MG Count Curio Barbasetti di Prun (Commanding General, 1st "Superga" Infantry Division) /39 MG Luigi Mentasti (Commanding General, XIV Army Corps) /41 unknown? 08/08/42 MG Alberto Ferrero (Commanding General, XXIII Army Corps) /42 MG Giovanni Angelo Pivano (to /45, German prisoner-of-war) 09/08/43 disbanded.
N. *Military Missions, Delegations*
1. **Military Mission to German High Command**: /40 MG Efisio Marras [+ Military Attaché, Germany] (fled to Switzerland) 09/08/43 dissolved.
2. **Military Mission to Vichy**: /43 MG Duke Carlo Avarna di Gualtieri
3. **Military Mission to Croatia**: /08/05/41 BG Giovanni Carlo Re [+ Military Attaché, Croatia] (/45, Commanding General, Legnano Division) 09/08/43 dissolved.
4. **Head, Delegation for Control of War Industry, France**: /42 MG Giuseppe Comerci
O. **For Special Employment for the Chief of the Supreme General Staff**:
/43 BG Giuseppe Castellano (Commander Security, Aosta Division) /44
P. **Attached to Supreme Headquarters**:
01/41 BG Augusto Muzzioli

Army High Command
(Royal Army [Regio Esercito])

War Minister: Il Duce 1st Mar. of Italy BENITO AMILCARE ANDREA MUSSOLINI 07/43 LG Antonio Sorice (?) /44 LG Taddeo Orlando (Commander-in-Chief, Royal Carabinieri) /44

A. **Undersecretary of War**: /36 Gen. [Rtetired '39] Alberto Pariani [+ Chief of the Gneral Staff] (retired; /43, recalled & Commander-in-Chief, General Headquarters, Albania) /39 LG Ubaldo Soddu (Deputy Chief of the Supreme General Staff & Commander-in-Chief, Army Group East) 11/29/40 Gen. Alfredo Guzzoni [+ Deputy Chief of the Supreme General Staff] (/43, Commander-in-Chief, Sixth Army) 05/41 LG Antonio Scuero (Commanding General, V Army Corps) 02/43 LG Antonio Sorice (War Minister) 07/43 LG Giovanni Battista Oxilia [+ Deputy Chief of the General Staff].
   1. **Central Administration of the Army (Rear Echelon)**:
      a. **Cabinet and Secretariat**: /36 BG Antonio Sorice [+ Quartermaster-General] (02/43, Undersecretary of War, War Ministry) /41
         i. **Office of Generals**:
         ii. **Office of Military Publications**:
         iii. **Foreign Liaison Section**:
         iv. **Autonomous Company of Carabinieri Reali (CCRR)**:
      b. **General Directorates**:
         i. **Officer Personnel**: /42 BG Roberto Grimaldi
         ii. **Civilian Personnel and General Affairs**:
         iii. **Artillery**: /41? BG (Res.) Marrigo Falasca (?) /42 BG Cicito Frongia (?) /43 LG Ubaldo Fautilli
            A. **Artillery Technical Service, Ministry of War**: /39? BG Umberto Ruggeri (07/41, Head, Experimental & Research Section, Inspectorate of Mechanized Forces) 06/40? MG Vittorio Pallieri (?) /41? MG Luigi Sarracino
            B. **Attached to General Headquarters, Artillery, War Ministry**:
            01/40 MG (Res.) Enrico Monti
         iv. **Engineers**: /33 MG Giuseppe Dall'Ora (retired?) /39
            A. **Deputy Director-General of Engineers, Ministry of War**: unknown? /41 BG Armando Mazzetti
            B. **Service of Technical Studies & Engineering Experience, Ministry of War**: /40 BG (Res.) Curgio Giamberini (?) /42 BG Tito Ricci.
               1. **Head, Unknown? Department, Service of Technical Studies & Engineering Experience, Ministry of War**: 12/01/41 Col. Carlo Micheletta

2. **Attached to Engineers Directorate**: 06/42? BG Giuseppe Perotti
v. **Logistic Services [Quartermaster-General]**: /36 BG Antonio Sorice [+ Chief of Cabinet, Ministry of War] (02/43, Undersecretary of War, War Ministry) /41 unknown? 08/42? LG Matteo Roux
    A. **Chief, Motorizarion Service, Ministry of War**: /42? MG Alfio Marziani (Commanding General, Italian Forces on Samos) /43
    B. **Chief Motorized Technical Services, Ministry of War**: 01/40 BG Mario Manera
    C. **Attached to Logistic Services, War Ministry**: 09/41 BG (Res.) Gino Stefanini
vi. **Medical Services**:
    A. **Directorate-General Military Health**: 04/41 MG Paolo Modestini
vii. **Chemical Services**: /38 BG Achille Rosmini (/42?, Judge, Supreme Military Tribunal) /40 MG Guido Coiro (?) /43
viii. **Administrative Services**:
c. **Superior Directorate for Studying & Testing Engineer Equipment**:
d. **General Accounting Office**:
e. **Inspectorate General of Recruiting**:
    i. **Assistant Inspector-General, Recruiting**: /41 BG Carlo Ferrero
2. **Territorial Army**:

B   **Chief of the General Staff (Army High Command)**: /36 Gen. Alberto Pariani [+ Undersecretary of War] (retired; /43, recalled & Commander-in-Chief, General Headquarters, Albania) /39 Mar. Rodolfo Graziani, Marquis [Marchese] of Neghelli [+ /40, Governor-General, Libya & Commander-in-Chief, North Africa] (resigned; 09/08/43, joins Social Republic of Italy; 09/08/43, Minister of War & Commander-in-Chief, Armed Forces, Social Republic of Italy) 05/41 LG Mario Roatta (Commander-in-Chief, Second Army) 01/42 Gen. Vittorio Ambrosio [+ Commander-in-Chief, Royal Army] (Commander-in-Chief of the Armed Forces or Chief of the Supreme General Staff) 02/43 Gen. Ezlo Rosi (Commander-in-Chief, Army Group East) 05/43 LG Mario Roatta [+ 07/43, Commanding General, General Headquarters Rome] (dismissed) 09/43 Mar. Giovanni Messe (Chief of the Supreme General Staff) 11/12/43 LG Paolo Berardi (Commanding General, XI Territorial Defense Command) /45.
[NOTE: acting Chief of the General Staff 11/42 LG Giuseppe de Stefanis (09/43, Commanding General, LI Army Corps) /42**]**
    1. **Field Army**:

C   **Undersecretary of State for War Manufacture**:
    1. **Staff, Undersecretary of State for War Manufacture**: BG (Res.) Camillo Calamani
D. **Mobilization Branch, Ministry of War**: unknown? 09/42 LG [Retired '39?] Angelo Stirpe
E. **Recruiting Office, Ministry of War**: /41 BG Giulio Cappa
F. **Overseas Section, Ministry of War**: /41 BG Ernesto Cappa (Commanding

General, 7th "Lupi di Toscana" Infantry Division) /41?
G. **War Ministry Supply Services**: /41? MG (Res.) Michele d'Admo
H. **Director of Heath, Ministry of War**: /40 BG Ignazio Fiorenza (?) /41 MG Dante Casella
I. **Central Commission on War Contracts, War Ministry**:
   1. **Members**: BG Savario Costa [MVSN]
J. **Commissariat Service, Ministry of War**: /39? MG Arturo Quarto (?) 07/41? MG Giuseppe Pipito
K. **Special Duties, War Ministry**
   01/40 LG [Retired?] Pietro Maravigna
   12/40 MG Marquis [Marquise] Orazio Toraldo di Francia
   07/41 LG Giovanni Majoli
   07/41 LG Umberto Testa
   11/10/41 BG Enrico Rovebe
   02/18/42 LG Riccardo Balocco
L. **"Attached to" or "At Dispoal of" War Ministry**
   06/40 LG Luigi Perego
   07/41 MG (Res.) Vincenzo Iacoe
   07/41 LG [Retired] Leonida Pacini (to /45, German prisoner-of-war) 09/08/43
   /43 LG Francesco Paolo Loasses (to /45, German prisoner-of-war) 09/08/43

Chief of Staff of the Army [Superesercito] (also **Commander-in-Chief, Royal Army**): /36 Gen. Alberto Pariani [+ Undersecretary of War] (retired; /43, recalled & Commander-in-Chief, General Headquarters, Albania) /39 Mar. Rodolfo Graziani, Marquis [Marchese] of Neghelli [+ 06/40, Governor-General of Libya & Commander-in-Chief, Armed Forces Libya] (resigned; 09/08/43, joins Social Republic of Italy; 09/08/43, Minister of War & Commander-in-Chief, Armed Forces, Social Republic of Italy) 03/41 LG Mario Roatta (Commander-in-Chief, Second Army) 01/42 Gen. Vittorio Ambrosio [+ Commander-in-Chief, Royal Army] (Commander-in-Chief of the Armed Forces or Chief of the Supreme General Staff) 02/43 Gen. Ezlo Rosi (Commander-in-Chief, Army Group East) 05/43 LG Mario Roatta + 07/43, Commanding General, General Headquarters Rome] (dismissed) 09/43 Mar. Giovanni Messe (Chief of the Supreme General Staff) 11/12/43 LG Paolo Berardi (/45, Commanding General, XI Territorial Defense Command)
A. **Deputy Chief of the Army General Staff (Sottocapo di Stato Maggiore)**: /39 MG Mario Roatta (Chief of the Army General Staff) 03/41 unknown? /43 MG Giacomo Zanussi (/45, Commanding General, Cremona Division) /43 MG Antonio Gandin (executed by the Germans) 09/43 unknown? /44 LG Giovanni Battista Oxilia [+ Undersecretary of War].
B **Assistant Chief of Staff, Operations (Sottocapo di Stato Maggiore per le Operazioni)** (supervised territorial and colonial operations, training, records, and intelligence): /37? MG Ubaldo Soddu (Undersecretary of War, Ministry of War) /39 unknown? /42 MG Antonio Gandin (Commanding General, 33rd "Acqui" Infantry Division) /43
   1. **Intelligence**:
   2. **Discipline**:
   3. **Clerical Personnel**:
   4. **Training**: 04/05/41? BG Emilio Faldella (Chief of Staff, Sixth Army) 01/43

C. **Assistant Chief of Staff, Intendance [Administration] (Sottocapo di Stato Maggiore Intendente)** (supervised organization, mobilization, transportation, and services):
1. **Army Optical Section, Army General Staff**: /41 MG Vito Artale [MVSN] (arrested by the fascists; /44, executed by the fascists) /43
2. **Chief Motorized Technical Services**: /41 BG Giovanni Astuti (?) /4? BG Mario Carrera
3. **President, Civilian Mobilization**: /39 BG Carlo Favagrossa (Commanding General, 16th "Fossalta" Infantry Division) /39

D. **Assistant Chief of Staff, Territorial Defense (Sottocapo di Stato Maggiore per la Difensa Territoriale)** (responsible for all defense, including Coast defense, but excluding frontier defense): /42 BG Angelo Odone
1. **Attached to Assistant Chief of Staff, Territorial Defense**: LG [Retired] Emilio Bucci

E. *Assistant Chief of Staff, Unknown?*: /42? BG Aldo Rossi

F. **Army Artillery Directorate**:
1. **Anti-Aircraft Artillery Command**: unknown? /43 MG Guiseppe Romano
2. **Head, Artillery Experimental Center**: unknown? /43 BG Guido De Corné (to /45, German prisoner-of-war) 10/43

G. **Army Engineer Directorate**:
1. **Directorate Service Studies & Practical Engineering**:
   a. **Special Duties, Directorate Service Studies & Practical Engineering**: /41? BG Augusto d'Alfonso
2. **Research and Experimental Directorate, Engineering**: 07/41? BG Domenico Leone

H. *Intendance*:
1. **Intendance's Department**:
2. **Army Medical Directorate**: /39? MG Loreto Mazzetti (?) 04/40? MG Alfredo Ingravalle
3. **Army Veterinary Directorate**:
4. **Army Commissariat Directorate**:
5. **Army Rail Transport Directorate**:
6. **Army Transport Directorate**:
7. **Army Postal Directorate**:
8. **Army Timber Directorate**

I. **Headquarters Personnel (Quartiere Generale)**:

J. **Army Aircraft Headquarters**:

K. *Army Schools*
1. **Commandant, Modena Military Academy**: /40 BG Giacomo Carboni (Commanding General, 20th "Friuli" Division) /41 unknown? 09/08/43 disbanded.
2. **Commandant, Rome Military School**: /41 BG Marquis Alberto Trionfi (Infantry Officer, 59th "Cagliari" Infantry Division) /42
3. **Commandant, Royal Academy of Infantry & Cavalry**: /39? Col. Giuseppe Romano (/41, Commanding General, 207th Coastal Division) /40? Col. Gaetano Cantaluppi (Commanding General, "Ariete" Combat Group; /42?,

Commanding General, 185th "Folgore" Airborne Division) /41? BG Matteo Negro (to /45, German prisoner-of-war) 09/08/43 disbanded.

4. **Commandant, Central School of Infantry**: /39? BG Benvenuto Gioda (Commanding General, 4th "Livorno" Infantry Division) /40 Col. Mario Bignami (/41, British prisoner-of-war) /40? Col. Carlo Biglioni (Intendant-General, Italian Expeditionary Force) /42 BG Ugo Abbondanza (Infantry Commander, 11th "Brennero" Infantry Division) /43 BG Francesco Montagna [MVSN] (joins Social Republic of Italy; 10/43, Commanding General, 2nd Group Italian Youth "Sassello") 09/08/43 disbanded.

5. **Commandant, Central Military School of Mountaineering [Alpinism]**: /40? Col. Giacomo Lombardi (Commanding General, 27th "Brescia" Infantry Division) /41 unknown? 09/08/43 disbanded.

6. **Commandant, School of Application of Cavalry** (/43, disbanded by the Germans): /36 BG Umberto Berardi (/41, British prisoner-of-war) /38 unknown? /40 BG Raffele Cadorna (Commanding General, 132nd "Ariete" Armored Division) 02/43 BG Count Guglielmo Barbò di Caselmorano (German prisoner-of-war; died of illness in Flossenburg Concentration Camp) 09/08/43 disbanded.

7. **Commandant, Central School for Cavalry Troops**: /39? BG Emanuelle Beraudo di Pralorme (Commanding General, Unknown? Colonial Division) /40? BG Ugo De Carolis (Infantry Commander, 52nd "Torino" Infantry Division) 08/05/41 unknown? 09/08/43 disbanded.

8. **Commandant, Royal Academy & Artillery School in Torino**: /43 MG Carlo Pellegrini (to /45, German prisoner-of-war) 09/08/43 disbanded.

9. **Commandant, Central School of Artillery**: /37? Col. Umberto Utili (Artillery Commander, Unknown? Army Corps; /41, Chief of Staff, Italian Expeditionary Corps) /39? BG Pietro Belletti (Commanding General, 15th "Bergamo" Infantry Division) /40 Col. Auturo Fortunato (Commandant, Royal Military Academy of Artillery & Engineering) /40 BG Mario Balotta (acting Commanding General, 132nd "Ariete" Armored Division) /41 BG Brunetto Brunetti (Commanding General, 27th "Brescia" Infantry Division) /42 Col. Giuseppe Carnellutti (Commandant of Royal Military Academy of Artillery & Engineering) /42? BG Stefano Degiani (Inspector of Engineers) 09/08/43? disbanded.

10. **Commandant, School of Artillery Shooting**: /38? Col. Augusto de Pignier (Inspector of Artillery) /39? Col. Lorenzo Caratti /41? Col. Bartolomeo Pedrotti (Artillery Commander, IV Army Corps) /42 unknown? 09/08/43 disbanded.

11. **Commandant, Royal Military Academy of Artillery & Engineering**: /36 BG Antonio Basso (/40, Commanding General, XIII Army Corps) /37 BG Arnaldo Forgiero (/39, Commanding General, 11th "Brennero" Infantry Division) /38 BG Luigi Manzi (Commanding General, 1st "Cosseria" Infantry Brigade) /40 BG Auturo Fortunato (/42, Engineer-in-Chief, Eleventh Army) /41 BG Adolfo Sardi (?) /42 BG Giuseppe Carnellutti (?) /43 BG Balilla Rima (?) /43 BG Emilio Sacchi (German prisoner-of-war; /43, joins Social Republic of Italy) 09/08/43 disbanded.

12. **Commandant, Non-Commissioned Officers of Artillery**: /38? BG Luigi

                Mazzini (Commanding General, 33rd "Acqui" Infantry Division) /39? unknown? /40? BG Gastano Alagia (Artillery Commander, Fourth Army) /42 unknown? 09/08/43 disbanded.
        13.   **Commandant, Central School of Engineering**: MG Armando Bianchi (Engineer in Chief, Sixth Army) /40 unknown? 09/08/43 disbanded.
        14.   **Commandant, Officer's School of Complementary Engineering**: /4? BG Enrico Frattini (/42, Commanding General, 1st "Folgore" Airborne Division) /4? BG Oreste Crivaro (Engineer-in-Chief, XVII Army Corps) /42 unknown? 09/08/43 disbanded.
        15.   **Commandant, 4th Regimental School of Engineering**: BG Aldo Beghi (prisoner-of-war) /41 unknown? 09/08/43 disbanded.
        16.   **Commandant, School of Application (Law) of Military Medicine**: 07/01/37 MG Alfredo Bucciante (?) /38? BG Loreto Mazzetti (Director-General of Military Medical Services) /39? unknown? 09/08/43 disbanded.
        17.   **Commandant, Medical Tactical School**: /40 BG Alfredo Germino
        18.   **Commandant, Milan Military School**: 08/08/42? BG Epifanio Chiaramonti
        19.   *Commandant, Central Military Schools*: /42 MG Luigi Chiolini

L.   *Military Attaché*
        1.   **Military Attaché, Croatia (Zagreb)**: /08/05/41 BG Giovanni Carlo Re [+ Head, Italian Military Mission to Croatia] (/45, Commanding General, Legnano Division) /09/08/43 dissolved.
        2.   **Military Attaché, Denmark (Copenhagen)**: /36 BG Efisio Marras [+ Military Attaché, Germany] (Commanding General, VIII Army Corps) /39
        3.   **Military Attaché, France (Paris)**: /38 MG Sebastiano Visconti Prasca (Military Attaché, Germany) /39
        4.   **Military Attaché, Germany (Berlin)**: /36 BG Efisio Marras [+ Military Attaché, Denmark] (Commanding General, VIII Army Corps) /39 MG Mario Roatta (Deputy Chief of the Army General Staff) /39 MG Sebastiano Visconti Prasca (Commanding General, 2nd "Emanuele Filiberto Testa di Ferro" Cavalry [Celere] Division) /39 MG Efisio Marras [+ Head, Italian Military Mission to German High Command] (fled to Switzerland) 09/08/43 dissolved.
        5.   **Military Attaché, Hungary (Budapest)**: /43 BG Emilio Voli
        6.   **Military Attaché, Switzerland (Berne)**: /42 BG Tancredi Bianchi
        7.   **Military Attaché, United States (Washington, D. C.)**: /40 MG Adolfo Infante (Chief Aide-de-Camp to the King) /41

M.   **Italian Liaison Officer to German Field Marshal Erwin Rommel**: /41 MG Count Giorgio Calvi di Bergolo (Commanding General, 131st "Centauro" Armored Division) 01/01/43

N.   **On General Staff, Unknown Position**:
04/42 BG Mario Grosso (II)

O.   **At Disposal of or Special Employment of the Chief of the General Staff**:
/40? BG Pietro Carlino
/40 BG Achille D'Havet (Commanding General, 47th "Bari" Infantry Division) /40
07/41 MG (Res.) Noe Grassi
/42 BG Giuseppe Castellano (for special employment for the Chief of the Supreme
    General Staff) /43

P.   **Field Army**

1. **Army Group West**
2. **Army Group East**
3. **Army Group South**
4. **Army Group North Africa**

Inspectorate of the Royal Army
A. *Inspectorates of Arms*:
   1. **Inspectorate of Infantry**: /35 MG Valentino Bobbio (/39, Member, Commission for the Armed Forces, Senate) /37 MG Luigi Frusci (Commanding General, Llamas Negras - XIII de Marzo Division) /37 MG Adriano Marinetti (Commanding General, VII Army Corps) /38 MG His Royal Highness Umberto Piemonte, the Crown Prince of Italy (Piedmont) and Viceroy (Commander-in-Chief, Army Group West) /39
      a. **Inspector of Camps of Mobile Troops**: /42 Gen. His Royal Highness Prince Filiberto Lodovico Massimiliano Emanuele Maria di Savoia [Savoy-Genoa], Duke of Pistoia
      b. **At Disposal of, Attached to, or on Special Duties, Inspectorate of Infantry**:
      07/42? (special duties) MG (Res.) Bortolo Zambon
   2. **Inspectorate of Mechanized Forces (STAM)**: /41 BG Enrico Guido Girola
      a. **Experimental & Research Section, Inspectorate of Mechanized Forces**: 07/41 MG Umberto Ruggeri
      b. **At Disposal of, Attached to, or on Special Duties, Inspectorate of Mechanized Forces**:
      07/41? (attached to) BG Alberto Pescatore
      07/41? (attached to) BG Ugo Russo
      12/20/42 (attached to) BG Giovanni Maria Scalabrino
   3. **Inspectorate of Artillery**: /39 MG Marquis Ettore Manca di Mores (retired) /40 MG Augusto de Pignier (Commanding General, XIII Army Corps) 06/10/40? MG Raffaelo D'Antonio
      a. **At Disposal of, Attached to, or on Special Duties, Inspectorate of Artillery**:
      01/42 (special duties) BG Luigi Podio
      b. **At Disposal of, Attached to, or on Special Duties, Inspectorate of Technical Services, Artillery**:
      07/41? (attached to) BG (Res.) Achille Rosica
   4. **Inspectorate of Engineers**: /42 MG Oreste Crivaro (Commanding General, II Terrtiorial Defense Command) /42 MG Frederico Amoroso (?) /43 LG Arnaldo Forgiero (Commandant of Rhodes) /43 MG Stefano Degiani (Director, Historical & Culture Institute of Engineers) 10/43? LG Oreste Crivaro.
      a. **Director, Historical & Culture Institute of Engineers**: 10/43? MG Stefano Degiani
      b. **At Disposal of, Attached to, or on Special Duties, Inspectorate of Engineers**:
      05/40? (attached to) BG Francesco Paladino
      07/40? (special duties) MG (Res.) Augusto Lussiana

            07/41 (attached to) BG Luigi Lastrico
            01/42? (special duties) MG (Res.) Agostino Papone
   5. **Inspectorate of Alpine (Mountain) Troops**: /43 LG Gabrielle Nasci (?   ) /43 MG Giovanni Esposito (joins Social Republic of Italy; 10/43, Commanding General, 204th Regional Military Command Trieste) 09/08/43
      a. **At Disposal of, Attached to, or on Special Duties, Alpine Troops**: 05/04/43 (at disposal) BG Carlo Filippi ((to /45, German prisoner-of-war) 09/08/43
   6. **Inspectorate of Cavalry (Celere) Troops**: /36 MG Giovanni Messe (/39, Commanding General, 3rd "Principe Amedeo Duca d'Aosta" Cavalry (Celere) Division) /38 MG Count Sebastiano Murari della Corte Brà (Commanding General, XIV Army Corps) /39 MG Lorenzo Dalmazzo (Commanding General, XI Army Corps) /39 unknown? /41 MG Mario Marazzani /42 LG Federico Ferrari Orsi (Commanding General, XXII Army Corps) /42 LG Mario Marazzani (/47, Commanding General, III Territorial Defense Command) 01/01/43 MG Count Carlo Ceriana-Mayneri (?   ) /43 MG Mario Badino-Rossi (Commanding General, 224th Coastal Division) /43
   7. **Inspectorate of Overseas Troops:** /39 Mar. [Retired '20] Emilio De Bono [+ Member, Commission for the Armed Forces, Senate & Member, Commission for the Affairs of Italian Africa] (Commander-in-Chief, Army Group South & Member, Fascist Grand Council) /40 unknown? /43 Mar. [Retired '20] Emilio De Bono (condemned to death and executed as a traitor) /44
B. *Inspectorates of Services*
   1. **Inspectorate of Motorizarion**:
   2. **Inspectorate of Armaments** (Rome):
      a. **At Disposal of, Attached to, or on Special Duties, Inspectorate of Armaments**:
         07/41 (special duties) BG Arturo Barbacini
   3. **Inspectorate of Animal & Veterinary Services**:
   4. **Inspectorate of Commissary Services**:
   5. **Inspectorate of MT Technical Services**: /39 LG Mario Caracciolo di Feroleto (Commander-in-Chief, Fourth Army) /40 MG Giovanni Battista Bachelet

Territorial Defense Commands

I Territorial Defense Command (HQ: Torino [Turin], Italy): /41 LG Attilio Grattarola (Commanding General, II Territorial Defense Command) /43
- A. *Components - I Territorial Defense Command*
    1. **1ˢᵗ Territorial Zone** (HQ: Torino [Turin], Italy; division status)
        - a. **1ˢᵗ "Superga" Infantry Division Depot** (brigade status)
        - b. **36ᵗʰ "Forlì" Infantry Division Depot** (brigade status)
        - c. **37ᵗʰ "Modena" Infantry Division Depot** (brigade status)
        - d. **1ˢᵗ "Taurineense" Mountain Division Depot** (brigade status)
        - e. **40ᵗʰ Territorial District** (HQ: Cuneo, Italy; brigade status)
    2. **4ᵗʰ Territorial Zone** (HQ Novara, Italy; division status)
        - a. **2ⁿᵈ "Sforzesca" Division Depot** (brigade status)
        - b. **24ᵗʰ Territorial District** (HQ: Novara, Italy; brigade status)
    3. **1ˢᵗ DICAT Blackshirt (CCNN) Legion** (HQ: Torino [Turin], Italy; also under 1ˢᵗ DICAT Blackshirt (CCNN) Legion Group)
- B. **Inspector, Technical Services, Torino [Turin]**: 07/41? BG (Res.) Giuseppe Licari
- C. **Torino [Turin] Royal Carabinieri Brigade**: /40 BG Count Eduardo Odetti
- D. *Prefects and Commandants, I Territorial Defense Command*
    1. **Prefect of Torino [Turin]**: /43 BG Dino Borri ₍MVSN₎ (joins Social Republic of Italy) /43
- E. **At Disposal of, Attached to, or on Special Duties with I Territorial Defense Command**
    10/41 (attached to) MG (Res.) Enrico Signorelli
    11/01/41 (special duties) BG Alfredo Obici
    12/42? (special duties) BG Oscar Ulrich Bansa
    /43 (at disposal) BG Luigi Ninci (to /45, German prisoner-of-war) 09/08/43

II Territorial Defense Command (HQ: Alessandria, Italy): unknown? /42 LG Oreste Crivaro (Inspector of Engineers) /43 LG Attilio Grattarola (to /45, German prisoner-of-war) 09/43 LG Arnaldo Forgiero (Inspector of Engineers) /44 MG Emilio Magliano (?) /44 LG Carlo Gotti.
- A. *Components - II Territorial Defense Command*
    1. **2ⁿᵈ Territorial Zone** (HQ: Alessandria, Italy; division status)
        - a. **3ʳᵈ "Ravenna" Infantry Division Depot** (brigade status)
        - b. **26ᵗʰ "Assietta" Infantry Division Depot** (brigade status)
        - c. **4ᵗʰ "Cuneense" Mountain Division Depot** (brigade status)
        - d. **1ˢᵗ Territorial District** (HQ: Alessandria, Italy; brigade status)
        - e. **86ᵗʰ Territorial District** (HQ: Casale Monferrato, Italy; brigade status)
    2. **4ᵗʰ DICAT Blackshirt (CCNN) Legion** (HQ: Alessandria, Italy; also under 1ˢᵗ DICAT Blackshirt (CCNN) Legion Group)
- B. **Engineer-in-Chief, II Territorial Defense Command**: unknown? /43 BG Rodolfo Stivala (to /45, German prisoner-of-war) 09/43 dissolved.
- B. *Provincial Inspector Anti-Aircraft, II Territorial Defense Command*:
    1. **Provincial Inspector Anti-Aircraft, Alessandria**: /41? MG (Res) Giuseppe Ceccarini

      2. **Provincial Inspector Anti-Aircraft, Turin**: /41? BG (Res) Carlo Fenoglietto
C. *Prefects and Commandants, II Territorial Defense Command*
   1. **Commandant, Alessandria**: /42 BG Giuseppe Bellocchi
   2. **Commandant, Turin**: /43 LG [Retired] Enrico Adami-Rossi (joins Italian Social Republic; Commanding General, 201st Regional Military Command Firenze [Florence]) 09/08/43

III Territorial Defense Command (HQ: Milano [Milan], Italy): /41 LG Antero Canale (at disposal of the Minister of War; 09/08/43 to /45, German prisoner-of-war) /43 MG Bernado Cetroni (to /45, German prisoner-of-war) /43 MG Vittorio Ruggero (to /45, German prisoner-of-war) 09/08/43
A. *Components - III Territorial Defense Command*
   1. **3rd Territorial Zone** (HQ: Milano [Milan], Italy; division status)
      a. **6th "Cuneo" Infantry Division Depot** (brigade status)
      b. **7th "Lupi di Toscana" Infantry Division Depot** (brigade status)
      c. **58th "Legnano" Infantry Division Depot** (brigade status)
      d. **59th "Cagliari" Infantry Division Depot** (brigade status)
      e. **23rd Territorial District** (HQ: Milano [Milan], Italy; brigade status)
      f. **42nd Territorial District** (HQ: Bergamo, Italy; brigade status)
      g. **44th Territorial District** (HQ: Cremona, Italy; brigade status)
      h. **54th Territorial District** (HQ: Pavia, Italy; brigade status)
      i. **65th Territorial District** (HQ: Lodi, Italy; brigade status)
      j. **67th Territorial District** (HQ: Ivrea, Italy; brigade status)
      k. **68th Territorial District** (HQ: Lecco, Italy; brigade status)
      l. **73rd Territorial District** (HQ: Varese, Italy; brigade status)
      m. **75th Territorial District** (HQ: Vercelli, Italy; brigade status)
      n. **76th Territorial District** (HQ: Monza, Italy; brigade status)
   2. **XI Border Guard Sector** (HQ: Varese, Italy; brigade status)
   3. **XII Border Guard Sector** (HQ: Sondrie, Italy; brigade status)
   4. **5th DICAT Blackshirt (CCNN) Legion** (HQ: Milano [Milan], Italy; also under 2nd DICAT Blackshirt (CCNN) Legion Group)
   5. **7th DICAT Blackshirt (CCNN) Legion** (HQ: Brescia, Italy; also under 2nd DICAT Blackshirt (CCNN) Legion Group)
B. *Components - III Territorial Defense Command* (09/43)
   1. **Como Province** (09/43): MG Gastano Binacchi (to /45, German prisoner-of-war) /43
C. **Engineer-in-Chief III Territorial Defense Command**: /41 BG (Res.) Michale Gerboni
D. **Director, Metals Distribution Organization, Milano [Milan]**: /42? BG (Res.) Mario Grosso (I) (?) /43
E. **Medical Division, III Territorial Defense Command**: 03/42 BG (Res.) Celestino Gozzi
F. *Military Tribunal Milano [Milan]*
   1. **President, Military Tribunal Milano [Milan]**: /41 BG Gino Gagliotti
   2. **Advocate, Military Tribunal Milano [Milan]**: unknown? /43 BG Gaetano Tei
G. *Provincial Inspector Anti-Aircraft, III Territorial Defense Command*:

1. **Provincial Inspector Anti-Aircraft, Milano [Milan]**: 05/43 BG (Res) Renzo Giovannelli
H. *Prefects and Commandants, III Territorial Defense Command*
   1. **Commandant, Casalmaggiore**: /43 BG Vitaliano Visconti di Oleggio (to /45, German prisoner-of-war) 09/08/43 dissolved.
   2. **Prefect of Milano [Milan]**: /43 BG Giovanni D'Antoni (to /45, German prisoner-of-war) 09/08/43 dissolved.
   3. **Prefect of Vercelli**: /38 MG Carlo Baratelli [MVSN] (in reserve) /42 unknown? 09/08/43 dissolved.
   4. **Commandant, Vercelli**: /43 BG Alessandro Blanchi (to /45, German prisoner-of-war) 09/08/43 dissolved.
I. **At Disposal of, Attached to, or on Special Duties with III Territorial Defense Command**:
   07/41 (special duties) MG Count Girolamo Masnoni D'Intignano [MVSN]
   03/43 (attached to) BG Mario Zanotti
   05/43 (special duties) MG [Retired?] Pier Domenico Mazzari
   /43 (at disposal) BG Alfredo Tortella (to /45, German prisoner-of-war; /43, joins Social Republic of Italy) 09/08/43

IV Territorial Defense Command (HQ: Bolzano, Italy): /38 MG Giovanni Corte (?) /43 MG Attilio Fantoni (to /45, German prisoner-of-war) /43 LG Arturo Taranto (to /45, German prisoner-of-war) 10/43 dissolved; reformed 06/45 MG Giacomo Negroni.
[NOTE: also listed around /39? BG Adolfo Zauli (acting; /41, British prisoner-of-war) /39?]
A. *Components - IV Territorial Defense Command* (1940)
   1. **5th Territorial Zone** (HQ: Verona, Italy; division status)
      a. **9th "Pasubio" Infantry Division Depot** (brigade status)
      b. **10th "Piave" Infantry Division Depot** (brigade status)
      c. **132nd "Ariete" Armor Division Depot** (brigade status)
      d. **3rd Celere [Fast] Division Depot** (brigade status)
      e. **7th Territorial District** (HQ: Parma, Italy; brigade status)
      f. **45th Territorial District** (HQ: Verona, Italy; brigade status)
      g. **61st Territorial District** (HQ: Mantova, Italy; brigade status)
      h. **62nd Territorial District** (HQ: Vicenza, Italy; brigade status)
      i. **63rd Territorial District** (HQ: Rovigo, Italy; brigade status)
   2. **7th Territorial Zone** (HQ: Trento, Italy; division status)
      a. **11th "Brennero" Infantry Division Depot** (brigade status)
      b. **33rd "Acqui" Infantry Division Depot** (brigade status)
      c. **102nd "Trento" Infantry Division Depot** (brigade status)
      d. **2nd "Tridentina" Mountain Division Depot** (brigade status)
      e. **9th "Pusteria" Mountain Division Depot** (brigade status)
      f. **77th Territorial District** (HQ: Belluno, Italy; brigade status)
      g. **88th Territorial District** (HQ: Sulmona, Italy; brigade status)
      h. **89th Territorial District** (HQ: Sondrio, Italy; brigade status)
      i. **90th Territorial District** (HQ: Treviglio, Italy; brigade status)
      j. **91st Territorial District** (HQ: Bassano, Italy; brigade status)
      k. **92nd Territorial District** (HQ: Trento, Italy; brigade status)

        l.   **93rd Territorial District** (HQ: Bolzano, Italy; brigade status)
     3.   **Bolzano Border Guards**: /43 BG Lorenzo Brovarone Carnaro (German prisoner-of-war) /43
        a.   **XIII Border Guard Sector** (HQ: Merano, Italy; brigade status)
        b.   **XIV Border Guard Sector** (HQ: Bressanone, Italy; brigade status)
        c.   **XV Border Guard Sector** (HQ: Brunico, Italy; brigade status)
     4.   **8th DICAT Blackshirt (CCNN) Legion** (HQ: Verona, Italy; also under 2nd DICAT Blackshirt (CCNN) Legion Group)

B.   *Components - IV Territorial Defense Command* (09/43)
     1.   **Vicenza Military Province** (09/43): LG Ferruccio Bignamini (to /45, German prisoner-of-war) 09/08/43 dissolved.

C.   **Engineer-in-Chief, IV Territorial Defense Command**: unknown? /43 MG Donato Vox (German prisoner-of-war) 09/08/43 dissolved.

D.   **Medical Director, IV Territorial Defense Command**: 07/40? BG Francesco Pellegrini

E.   *Prefects and Commandants, IV Territorial Defense Command*
     1.   **Prefect of Belluno**: /39 BG Francesco Bellini $_{[MVSN]}$ (in reserve; Prefect of Gorizia, V Territorial Defense Command) /43
     2.   **Prefect of Treviso (ENR)**: /44 BG Francesco Bellini $_{[MVSN]}$.
     3.   **Commandant, Parma**: /43 BG Giovanni Moramarco (to /45, German prisoner-of-war) 09/08/43 dissolved.
     4.   **Commandant, Trento**: /43 BG Carlo Canegallo (to /45, German prisoner-of-war) 09/08/43

V Territorial Defense Command (HQ: Trieste, Italy): /43 LG Ernesto Cappa (?) 09/44 LG Gino Granata.

A.   *Components - V Territorial Defense Command*
     1.   **10th Territorial Zone** (HQ: Trieste, Italy; division status)
        a.   **12th "Sassari" Infantry Division Depot** (brigade status)
        b.   **94th Territorial District** (HQ: Trieste, Italy; brigade status)
     2.   **11th Territorial Zone** (HQ: Pola, Italy; division status)
        a.   **15th "Bergamo" Infantry Division Depot** (brigade status)
        b.   **57th "Lombardia"" Infantry Division Depot** (brigade status)
        c.   **97th Territorial District** (HQ: Pola, Italy; brigade status)
     3.   **11th DICAT Blackshirt (CCNN) Legion** (HQ: Trieste, Italy; also under 3rd DICAT Blackshirt (CCNN) Legion Group)

B.   **Engineer-in-Chief, V Territorial Defense Command**:
     1.   **Assistant Engineer-in-Chief, V Territorial Defense Command**: /40 MG (Res.) MG Ginesio Mercadante

C.   **Fiume Military Tribunal, V Territorial Defense Command**: /42 MG Umberto Vaccari

D.   *Prefects and Commandants, V Territorial Defense Command*
     1.   **Prefect of Gorizia**: BG Francesco Bellini $_{[MVSN]}$ (joins the Social Republic of Italy, Prefect of Imperia, XV Territorial Defense Command) 09/08/43
     2.   **Prefect of Trieste**: /39 BG Dino Borri $_{[MVSN]}$ (Prefect of Genova [Genoa], XV Territorial Defense Command) /41

VI Territorial Defense Command (HQ: Bologna, Italy): /41 LG (Res.) Alberto Terziani (?) /45 LG Angelo Cerica
- A. *Components - VI Territorial Defense Command*
    1. **8th Territorial Zone** (HQ: Bologna, Italy; division status)
        - a. **16th "Pistoia" Infantry Division Depot** (brigade status)
        - b. **6th Territorial District** (HQ: Bologna, Italy; brigade status)
        - b. **47th Territorial District** (HQ: Modena, Italy; brigade status)
    2. **9th Territorial Zone** (HQ: Ravenna, Italy; division status)
        - a. **17th "Pavia" Infantry Division Depot** (brigade status)
        - b. **56th "Casale" Infantry Division Depot** (brigade status)
        - c. **2nd Celere [Fast] Division Depot** (brigade status)
        - d. **8th Territorial District** (HQ: Ravenna, Italy; brigade status)
        - e. **55th Territorial District** (HQ: Ferrara, Italy; brigade status)
        - f. **56th Territorial District** (HQ: Forli, Italy; brigade status)
    3. **15th Territorial Zone** (HQ: Piacenza, Italy; division status)
        - a. **101st "Trieste" Infantry Division Depot** (brigade status)
        - b. **133rd "Littorio" Armor Division Depot** (brigade status)
        - c. **2nd Territorial District** (HQ: Piacenza, Italy; brigade status)
        - d. **57th Territorial District** (HQ: Reggio Emilia, Italy; brigade status)
    4. **6th DICAT Blackshirt (CCNN) Legion** (HQ: Piacenza, Italy; also under 2nd DICAT Blackshirt (CCNN) Legion Group)
    5. **12th DICAT Blackshirt (CCNN) Legion** (HQ: Bologna, Italy; also under 3rd DICAT Blackshirt (CCNN) Legion Group)
- B. **Assistant Director, Health, VI Territorial Defense Command**: /41? BG Nicola Bruni
- C. *Provincial Inspector Anti-Aircraft, VI Territorial Defense Command*:
    1. **Provincial Inspector Anti-Aircraft, Bologna**: 07/41? MG (Res.) Angelo Soati
    2. **Provincial Inspector Anti-Aircraft, Ravenna**: 07/41? BG (Res.) Luigi Peluso
- D. *Prefects and Commandants, VI Territorial Defense Command*
    1. **Prefect of La Spezia**: /39 BG Giuseppe Aventi $_{[MVSN]}$ (in reserve; /43, killed in action) /41
    2. **Commandant, Pistoia**: /43 BG Giuseppe Volpi (to /45, German prisoner-of-war) 09/08/43 dissolved.
- E. **At Disposal of, Attached to, or on Special Duties with VI Territorial Defense Command**:
    01/18/42 (special duties) BG Antonio Mori
    /43 (at disposal) BG Alpinoio Paoletti (to /45, German prisoner-of-war) 09/08/43
    /43 (at disposal) BG Leone Santini (to /45, German prisoner-of-war) 09/08/43
    09/43 BG (Res.) Umberto Ricci [+ to 02/11/44, Interior Minister; + Commanding General, 8th Territorial Zone, VI Territorial Defense Command]

VII Territorial Defense Command (HQ: Firenze [Florence], Italy):
- A. *Components - VII Territorial Defense Command*

1. **13th Territorial Zone** (HQ: Firenze [Florence], Italy; division status)
   a. **19th Division Depot**
   b. **41st Division Depot**
   c. **131st Division Depot**
2. **17th Territorial Zone** (HQ: Livorno, Italy; division status)
   a. **20th Division Depot**
   b. **44th Division Depot**
3. **13th DICAT Blackshirt (CCNN) Legion** (HQ: Livorno, Italy; also under 4th DICAT Blackshirt (CCNN) Legion Group)
4. **14th DICAT Blackshirt (CCNN) Legion** (HQ: Firenze [Florence], Italy; also under 4th DICAT Blackshirt (CCNN) Legion Group)

B. *Provincial Inspector Anti-Aircraft, VII Territorial Defense Command*:
   1. **Provincial Inspector Anti-Aircraft, Grossetto**: /41? BG (Res) Arturo Concialini
   2. **Provincial Inspector Anti-Aircraft, Firenze [Florence]**: 06/39? BG Leonido Matarelli

C. **President, Military Tribunal Firenze [Florence]**: /43 BG Samuele Balbo-Bertone (German prisoner-of-war; /45, executed by the Germans) 09/08/43 dissolved.

D. **At Disposal of, Attached to, or on Special Duties with VII Territorial Defense Command**:
/43 (at disposal) BG Mario Fattori (to /45, German prisoner-of-war) 09/08/43

VIII Territorial Defense Command (HQ: Rome, Italy): unknown? /42 MG Umberto di Giorgio (Commanding General, Rome Corps) /43

A. **Chief of Staff, VIII Territorial Defense Command**: unknown? /41 BG Marquis Alberto Trionfi (Commandant, Rome Military School) /41

B. *Components - VIII Territorial Defense Command*
   1. **16th Territorial Zone** (HQ: Rome, Italy; division status)
      a. **2nd Division Depot**
      b. **4th Division Depot**
      c. **52nd Division Depot**
   2. **16th DICAT Blackshirt (CCNN) Legion** (HQ: Terni, Italy; also under 4th DICAT Blackshirt (CCNN) Legion Group)
   3. **18th DICAT Blackshirt (CCNN) Legion** (HQ: Rome, Italy; also under 4th DICAT Blackshirt (CCNN) Legion Group)

C. *Provincial Inspector Anti-Aircraft, VIII Territorial Defense Command*:
   1. **Provincial Inspector Anti-Aircraft, Rome**: 03/07/42? LG (Res) Oscar Fiorentino
   2. **Inspector Anti-Aircraft Defenses, Viterbo**: 11/41 BG Carlo Montuorisanseverino

D. **Military Tribunal, Rome**: /41? BG Francesco Traina

E. **Assistant Director, Health, VIII Territorial Defense Command**: 07/41? BG Verecondo Paoletti

F. *Prefects and Commandants, VIII Territorial Defense Command*
   1. **Commandant of Rome**: /44 MG Roberto Bencivenga (Governor of Salerno) /44

G. **At Disposal of, Attached to, or on Special Duties with VIII Territorial Defense Command**:
09/42? BG (Res.) Luigi Zo

IX Territorial Defense Command (HQ: Bari, Italy): /42? MG Alberto Aliberti (?) /43 MG Carlo Gotti (Commanding General, II Territorial Defense Command) /44 MG Ismaele Di Nisio.
- A. *Components - IX Territorial Defense Command*
    1. **18th Territorial Zone** (HQ: Perugia, Italy; division status)
        - a. **22nd Division Depot**
        - b. **48th Division Depot**
        - c. **61st Division Depot**
        - d. **64th Division Depot**
    2. **22nd Territorial Zone** (HQ: Bari, Italy; division status)
        - a. **23rd Division Depot**
        - b. **47th Division Depot**
        - c. **43rd Division Depot**
    3. **23rd Territorial Zone** (HQ: Chieti, Italy; division status)
        - a. **24th Division Depot**
        - b. **62nd Division Depot**
    4. **24th Territorial Zone** (HQ: Ancona, Italy; division status)
        - a. **18th Division Depot**
        - b. **49th Division Depot**
    5. **15th DICAT Blackshirt (CCNN) Legion** (HQ: Ancona, Italy; also under 3rd DICAT Blackshirt (CCNN) Legion Group)
    6. **20th DICAT Blackshirt (CCNN) Legion** (HQ: Bari, Italy; also under 5th DICAT Blackshirt (CCNN) Legion Group)
- B. *Prefects and Commandants, IX Territorial Defense Command*
    1. **Prefect of Bari**: /35 Col. Dino Borri [MVSN] (Prefect of Trieste, V Territorial Defense Command) /39
    2. **Prefect of Foggia**: /37 BG Giuseppe Aventi [MVSN] (Prefect of La Spezia, VI Territorial Defense Command) /39

X Territorial Defense Command (HQ: Napoli [Naples], Italy): /39? LG Silvio Rossi (?) /41? MG Nicolangelo Carnimeo (?) /43 MG Giuseppe Romano (Commanding General, Anti-Aircraft Artillery Command) /43 MG Gastano Frichione
- A. *Components - X Territorial Defense Command*
    1. **19th Territorial Zone** (HQ: Napoli [Naples], Italy; division status)
        - a. **25th Division Depot**
        - b. **51st Division Depot**
        - c. **60th Division Depot**
    2. **20th Territorial Zone** (HQ: Salerno, Italy; division status)
        - a. **55th Division Depot**
    3. **19th DICAT Blackshirt (CCNN) Legion** (HQ: Napoli [Naples], Italy; also under 5th DICAT Blackshirt (CCNN) Legion Group)
- B. **Artillery, X Territorial Defense Command**: 11/11/41 BG (Res.) Pasquale

Salvatores (?) /42
- B. **Rear Inspector, Commissariat, X Territorial Defense Command**: /41? BG Armando Alleva (retired) 08/09/41
- C. *Provincial Inspector Anti-Aircraft, X Territorial Defense Command*:
    1. **Provincial Inspector Anti-Aircraft, Benovento**: 07/41? MG (Res) Gaetano Napoletano
    2. **Provincial Inspector Anti-Aircraft, Napoli [Naples]**: /41? MG (Res) Alfredo de Rosa
    3. **Provincial Inspector Anti-Aircraft, Reggio Calabria**: 07/41? BG (Res) Fortunato Sandicchi
- D. **Medical Inspector, X Territorial Defense Command**: unknown? 01/43? BG Antonio Rombola
- E. *Governors, Prefects, Commandants, & Inspectors, X Territorial Defense Command*
    1. **Governor of Salerno**: /44 MG Roberto Bencivenga
    2. **Prefect of Napoli [Naples]**: /41 BG Unberto Albini $_{[MVSN]}$ (Undersecretary of Interior & Member, Fascist Grand Council) 02/43
    3. **Inspector of Naples Port**: /41? MG Giovanni Caruso
    4. **Naples Defenses**: 07/41? BG Ettore Marino
- F. **At Disposal of, Attached to, or on Special Duties with X Territorial Defense Command**:
08/20/41 (attached to) MG Emilio Radice

XI Territorial Defense Command (HQ: Udine, Italy): 01/01/43? MG Guilio Perugi (to /45, German prisoner-of-war) /43 MG Cesare Del Ponte (German prisoner-of-war; /43, joins Social Republic of Italy) /43 unknown? /45 MG Lazzaro Maurizio de Castiglione.
- A. *Components - XI Territorial Defense Command*
    1. **12th Territorial Zone** (HQ: Gorizia, Italy; division status)
        a. **13th Division Depot**
        b. **14th Division Depot**
        c. **38th Division Depot**
        d. **1st Celere [Fast] Division Depot**
        e. **3rd Mountain Division Depot**
    2. **10th DICAT Blackshirt (CCNN) Legion** (HQ: Udine, Italy; also under 3rd DICAT Blackshirt (CCNN) Legion Group)
- B. **Artillery, XI Territorial Defense Command**: /43 BG Antonio Carusi
- C. **Engineer-in-Chief, XI Territorial Defense Command**:
    1. **Assistant Engineer, XI Territorial Defense Command**: 07/41? MG (Res.) Ferruccio Zicavo
- D. **Military Health, XI Territorial Defense Command**:
    1. **Assistant Director, Military Health, XI Territorial Defense Command**: 01/38? Col. (Res.) Giuseppe Matucci
- E. **At Disposal of, Attached to, or on Special Duties with XI Territorial Defense Command**:
/43 (at disposal) BG Peitro Sisinni (German prisoner-of-war; 10/43, joins Social Republic of Italy) 09/43

XII Territorial Defense Command (HQ: Palermo, Sicily; also known as **Sicily Territorial Defense Command**): unknown? /44 LG Adamo Mariotti.
A. *Components - XII Territorial Defense Command*
   1. **21st Territorial Zone** (HQ: Catanzaro, Italy; division status)
      a. **27th Division Depot**
      b. **48th Division Depot**
      c. **61st Division Depot**
      d. **64th Division Depot**
   2. **25th Territorial Zone** (HQ: Palermo, Sicily; division status)
      a. **28th Division Depot**
      b. **54th Division Depot**
   3. **26th Territorial Zone** (HQ: Messina, Sicily; division status)
      a. **29th Division Depot**
   4. **21st DICAT Blackshirt (CCNN) Legion** (HQ: Catanzaro, Italy; also under 5th DICAT Blackshirt (CCNN) Legion Group)
   5. **22nd DICAT Blackshirt (CCNN) Legion** (HQ: Palermo, Sicily; also under 5th DICAT Blackshirt (CCNN) Legion Group)
B. **Artillery, XII Territorial Defense Command**: unknown? /42 BG Federigo Vannetti
C. *Provincial Inspector Anti-Aircraft, XII Territorial Defense Command*:
   1. **Provincial Inspector Anti-Aircraft, Catanzaro**: /41? MG (Res) Basilio Fiore
   2. **Provincial Inspector Anti-Aircraft, Messina**: 08/41? BG (Res) Guiseppe Paleologo
D. **Advocate, Military Tribunal (Judical), Palermo**: /41? BG Domenico Chinnici
E. *Prefects and Commandants, XII Territorial Defense Command*
   1. **Commandant, Messina**: /43 MG Aurelio Bozzoni [MVSN] (to /45, German prisoner-of-war) 08/43 disbanded.
   2. **Commandant, Palermo**: /42 MG Giuseppe Molinero (Allied prisoner-of-war) 08/43
   3. **Commandant, Rugusa**: /43 BG Davide Dusmet (German prisoner-of-war) 10/43
F. **At Disposal of, Attached to, or on Special Duties with XII Territorial Defense Command**:
   11/03/41 (special duties) BG Ettore Cimino
   01/14/42 (special duties) MG Pasquale Marotta

XIII Territorial Defense Command (HQ: Cagliari, Sardina)
A. *Components - XIII Territorial Defense Command*
   1. **27th Territorial Zone** (HQ: Cagliari, Sardina; division status)
      a. **30th Division Depot**
      b. **31st Division Depot**
   2. **13th DICAT Blackshirt (CCNN) Legion** (HQ: Cagliari, Sardinia; also under 4th DICAT Blackshirt (CCNN) Legion Group)

XIV Territorial Defense Command (HQ: Treviso, Italy): /41 LG Francesco Loasses (at disposal of the Ministry of War) /43

A. ***Components - XIV Territorial Defense Command***
   1. **6th Territorial Zone** (HQ: Trieste, Italy; division status)
      a. **32nd Division Depot**
   2. **XVI Border Guard Sector** (under control of the Italian Army; brigade status)
   3. **XVII Border Guard Sector** (HQ: Vinadio, Italy; brigade status)
   4. **9th DICAT Blackshirt (CCNN) Legion** (HQ: Padova, Italy; also under 3rd DICAT Blackshirt (CCNN) Legion Group)
B. ***Components - XIV Territorial Defense Command*** (09/43)
   1. **Padova Military Zone** (09/43): BG Alfonso Binelli (to /45, German prisoner-of-war) 09/08/43
C. **Artillery, XIV Territorial Defense Command**: /43 BG (Res.) Pietro Fietta d'Asolo
D. **Engineer-in-Chief, XIV Army Corps**: /42 BG Luigi Petromilli
E. **Frontier Guards, XIV Army Corps**: /40 Col. Marcello Piccone (Commanding General, 104th "Mantova" Semi-Motorized Infantry Division) /42
F. **Attached to XIV Territorial Defense Command**:
   /42 BG Luigi Gherzi (Infantry Commander, 154th "Murge" Garrison Division) /42
   /43 BG Alessandro Croce (German prisoner-of-war; /43, joins Social Republic of Italy) /43

XV Territorial Defense Command (HQ: Genova [Genoa], Italy): unknown? /42 MG Americo Coppi
A. ***Components - XV Territorial Defense Command***
   1. **14th Territorial Zone** (HQ: Genova [Genoa], Italy; division status)
      a. **5th Division Depot**
      b. **63rd Division Depot**
   2. **2nd DICAT Blackshirt (CCNN) Legion** (HQ: Savona, Italy; also under 1st DICAT Blackshirt (CCNN) Legion Group)
   3. **3rd DICAT Blackshirt (CCNN) Legion** (HQ: Genova [Genoa], Italy; also under 1st DICAT Blackshirt (CCNN) Legion Group)
B. ***Provincial Inspector Anti-Aircraft, XV Territorial Defense Command***:
   1. **Provincial Inspector Anti-Aircraft, Genova [Genoa]**: /41? MG (Res) Ettore Crepas
   2. **Provincial Inspector Anti-Aircraft, Savona**: 07/41? MG (Res) Pietro Garasano
C. ***Prefects and Commandants, XV Territorial Defense Command***
   1. **Prefect of Genova [Genoa]**: /33 Col. Unberto Albini [MVSN] (Prefect of Napoli [Naples], X Territorial Defense Command) /41 BG Dino Borri [MVSN] (Prefect of Turin) /43
   2. **Prefect of Imperia (ENR)**: 09/43 BG Francesco Bellini [MVSN] (in reserve, Prefect of Treviso, IV Territorial Defense Command) /44
   3. **Liguria Military Area**: /43 BG Cesare Rossi (Gernan prisoner-of-war; /45, killed in an Allied air attack) 09/08/43 dissolved.
D. **At Disposal of, Attached to, or on Special Duties with XV Territorial Defense Command**:
   /41? (special duties) BG Francesco Beggiato
   11/42? (special duties) MG Pietro Zaglio

Tirana Territorial Defense Command: /42 MG Egidio Levis
A. **President, Military Tribunal, Tirana**: /42 BG Umberto Maranghini (?) /43 BG Giacomo Anderson (German prisoner-of-war) 09/08/43 dissolved.
B. **General Military Procurator, Tirana**: /42 BG Umberto Meranghini
C. **At Disposal of, Attached to, or on Special Duties with Tirana Territorial Defense Command**:
12/40? (attached to) BG Half Ismali Permeti
12/20/42 (attached to) BG Perrizi Prenk

Naval Ensign

Royal Navy High Command (Royal Navy [Regia Marina])

Undersecretary and Chief of Staff of the Navy [Capo di Stato Maggiore]: /35? Adm. Domenico Cavagnari [RIN] (retired; President of Admiraldy Committee) 12/10/40 VA Arturo Riccardi [RIN] (President of Admiralty Committee) 07/25/43 VA Raffaele de Courten [RIN]

A. **Deputy Chief of Staff of the Navy [Sottocapo di Stato Maggiore]:** RA Inigo Campioni [RIN] (Commander-in-Chief, Royal Italian Navy Afloat & Commander-in-Chief, 1st Fleet) 08/15/39 RA Enrico Accoretti [RIN] (04/07/43, Commanding Officer, 9th Battleship Squadron) /41? RA Franco Rogadeo [RIN]

B. **Director General of Personnel:** /35 RA Arturo Riccardi [RIN] (06/41, Undersecretary and Chief of Staff of the Navy) 12/11/40 RA Ferdinando Casardi [RIN] (Vice President of Naval Council) /40 RA Angelo Parona [RIN] (Commanding Officer, 3rd Heavy Cruiser Squadron) 11/13/41 RA Antonino Toscano [RIN] (Commanding Officer, 4th Light Crusier Squadron) 01/12/42

C. **Director General of Naval Intelligence:** /41 RA Franco Maugeri [RIN]

D. **Vice Chief (Director General) of Naval Operations:** 04/24/41 VA Luigi Sansonnetti [RIN] (Commanding Officer, 3rd Heavy Cruiser Squadron) 07/25/43

E. **Director General, Naval Armament [Direttore Generale Armamenti Navali]:** RA Carlo Bergamini [RIN] (Commanding Officer, 5th Battleship Squadron) 08/01/39? RA Antonio Pasetti [RIN] (Commander-in-Chief, Ionian & Lower Adriatic Sea Department) 04/25/40

F. **Naval Academy Command [Comando Accademia Navale]:** RA Riccardo Paladini (Commanding Officer, Ionian and Lower Adriatic Sea Department) /37? RA Guido Bacci [RIN] (Commander-in-Chief, Upper Tyrrenhian Sea Department) /38? RA Carlo De Angelis [RIN] (?) /39? RA Bruno Brivonesi [RIN] (Commanding Officer, 3rd Heavy Cruiser Squadron) 04/24/40

G. **President of Naval Council [Presidente del Consiglio Navale]:** /?? VA Romeo Bernotti [RIN] (President of Admiralty Committee) /?? VA Giotto Maraghini (?) /43? VA Ildebrando Goiran [RIN]

    1. **Vice President of Naval Council [Vice Presidente del Consiglio Navale]:** /37 RA Luigi Sansonetti [RIN] (Commanding Officer, 7th Light Cruiser Squadron) 08/03/39 RA Ferdinando Casardi [RIN] (Commanding Officer, 2nd Light Cruiser Suuadron) 05/24/40

H. **President of Admiralty Committee [Presidente del Comitato Ammiragli]:** VA Angelo Jachino [RIN] (Commanding Officer, 2nd Light Cruiser Squadron) 07/25/40 VA Salvatore Denti Amari [RIN] (?) 12/11/40 Adm. [Retired 12/11/40] Domenico Cavagnari [RIN] (?) /4? VA Romeo Bernotti [RIN] (?) 07/25/43 Adm. Arturo Riccardi [RIN]

I. **Anti-Submarine Inspectorate:** 08/41 RA Alberto Da Zara [RIN] (Commanding Officer, 7th Light Cruiser Squadron) 03/07/42

J. **Commander-in-Chief, Italian Royal Fleet Afloat [Comando in Capo Forze Navali da Battaglia]:** VA Inigo Campioni [RIN] [+ Commander-in-Chief, 1st Fleet] (01/01/43,

Commander-in-Chief, Aegean Sea & Governor of Italian Dodecanese Islands) 12/09/40 Adm. Angelo Jachino [RIN] [+ to 01/07/43, Commanding Officer, 2nd Light Cruiser Squadron; + 01/12/42 to 01/07/43, Commanding Officer, 1st Heavy Cruiser Squadron] (?) 04/01/43 Adm. Carlo Bergamini [RIN] [Flag: RIN battleship *Roma*] [+ Commander-in-Chief, 1st Fleet] (killed in action; died when his flagship was sunk) 09/08/43

Royal Air Force High Command (Royal Air Force [Regio Aeronautica])

Undersecretary of Air & Chief of Staff of the Italian Air Force: Gen. Italo Balbo (Governor-General of Libya) 03/22/34 MG Giuseppe Valle [RIAF] (?) 11/10/39 MG Francesno Pricolo [RIAF] (?) 11/15/41 LG Rino Corso Fougier [RIAF] (?) 07/27/43 MG Renato Sandali [RIAF] [+ Air Minister] (Governor-General of Libya) 06/18/44 MG Pietro Piacentini [RIAF] (?) 12/13/44 MG Mario Ajmone-Cat [RIAF].

A. **Aeronautical Arm:**
    1. **Navigation:**
    2. **Ground Service:**
B. **Specialist Branch:**
C. **Air Force Branch:**
    1. **Aerial Army:**
    2. **Air Forces for the Army:**
    3. **Air Forces for the Navy:**
    4. **Air Forces for Colonial Garrisons:**
D. **Military School Command:**
E. **Commissariat Corps:**
F. **Medical Corps:**
G. **Aeronautical Engineering Corps:**
H. **Parachute Brigade:**

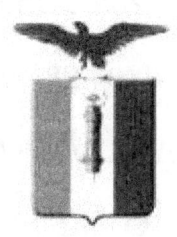

Coat of Arms

Social Republic of Italy
[Italian Social Republic]
[Repubblica Sociale Italiana (RSI)]
(September 23, 1943 to April 28, 1945)

[The Italian Social Republic [Repubblica Sociale Italiana (RSI)] also known as the Salò Republic [Repubblicia di Salò] was a puppet government formed in northern Italy after the Germans released Mussolini from his imprisonment]

Head of Government (09/23/43, northern Italy): Il Duce BENITO AMILCARE ANDREA MUSSOLINI (assassinated) 04/25/45

A. **Ministers**
1. **Minister of Foreign Affairs** (09/23/43): Il Duce BENITO AMILCARE ANDREA MUSSOLINI (assassinated) 04/25/45 dissolved.
2. **Minister of Defense** (09/23/43): Mar. Rodolfo Graziani, Marquis [Marchese] of Neghelli [+ Commander-in-Chief, Armed Forces, Social Republic of Italy] (arrested; /50, sentenced to 19 years imprisonment for collaboration with the Nazis; released after a few months; /55, died in Rome) 04/25/45 dissolved.
    a. **Secretary-General of the Army** (09/23/43): MG Unberto Giglio (Commanding General, 202nd Regional Military Command Bologna) /45?
        i. **Undersecretary of the Army** (09/23/43): MG Umberto Giglio (Secretary-General of the Army, Ministry of National Defense, Social Republic of Italy) /43 CARLO EMANUELE BASILE 04/25/45 dissolved.
    b. **Undersecretary of the Navy** (09/23/43): VA Antonio Legnani $_{[RIN]}$ (?) /43 FERRUCCIO FERRINI /44 GIUSEPPE SPARZANI /45 BRUNO GEMELLI 04/25/45 dissolved.
    a. **Undersecretary of the Air Force** (09/23/43): ERNESTO BOTTO /44 ARRIGO TESSARI /44 MANILO MOLFESE /44 MG Ruggero Bonomi 04/25/45 dissolved.
3. **Minister of the Interior** (09/23/43): GUIDO BUFFARINI GUIDI (07/10/45, shot by partisans) /45 PAOLO ZERBINO (04/28/45, shot by partisans) 04/25/45 dissolved.
    a. **Undersecretary of Interior** (09/23/43): BG Umberto Albini [+ Member, Fascist Grand Council]
4. **Minister of Justice** (09/23/43): MG Casanuova Antonino Tringali $_{[MVSN]}$ (died of natural causes, angina pectoris) 10/30/43 PIETRO PISENTI 04/25/45 dissolved.
5. **Minister of Finance** (09/23/43): DOMENICO GIAMPIETRO PELLEGRINI 04/25/45 dissolved.
6. **Minister of Industrial Production** (09/23/43): SILVIO GAI /43 ANGELO TARCHI 04/25/45 dissolved.

7. **Minister of Public Works** (09/23/43): RUGGERO ROMANO (04/28/45, shot by partisans) 04/25/45 dissolved.
8. **Minister of Communications** (09/23/43): AUGUSTO LIVERANI (04/28/45, shot by partisans) 04/25/45 dissolved.
9. **Minister of Labor** (09/23/43): unknown? /45 GIUSEPPE SPINELLI 04/25/45 dissolved.
10. **Minister of National Education** (09/23/43): CARLO ALBERTO BIGGINI (11/19/45, died of natural causes) 04/25/45 dissolved.
11. **Minister of Popular Culture** (09/23/43): FERNANDO MEZZASOMA (04/28/45, shot by partisans) 04/25/45 dissolved.
12. **Minister of Agriculture** (09/23/43): EDOARDO MORONI 04/25/45 dissolved.
13. **Leader of the Republican Fascist Party** (09/23/43): MG Alessandro Pavolini [+ Commanding General, National Republican Guard Brigade "Nere"] (/45, executed by Partisans) 04/25/45 dissolved.
    a. **2nd Group Italian Youth "Sassello"** (09/23/43): BG Francesco Montagna [MVSN]

The Military of the Italian Social Republic
(October 28, 1943)

National Republican Army
[Esercito Nazionale Repubblicano (ENR)]

Minister of Defense (09/23/43): Mar. Rodolfo Graziani, Marquis [Marchese] of Neghelli [+ Commander-in-Chief, Armed Forces, Social Republic of Italy] (arrested; /50, sentenced to 19 years imprisonment for collaboration with the Nazis; released after a few months; /55, died in Rome) 04/25/45 dissolved.
- A. **Undersecretarey of State for the Army, Ministry of National Defense, Social Republic of Italy** (09/23/43): LG Alfonso Ollearo
- B. **Military Secretary, Ministry of National Defense, Social Republic of Italy**: BG Rosario Sorrentino
- C. **Directorate-General of Motorization, Ministry of National Defense, Social Republic of Italy** (09/23/43): BG Biagio Carrara
- D. **Directorate-General of Engineers, Ministry of National Defense** (09/23/43): BG Gualtiero Frattali (Directorate-General of Technical Services, Ministry of National Defense) /44
- E. **Directorate-General of Technical Services, Ministry of National Defense** (09/23/43): unknown? /44 BG Gualtiero Frattali
- F. **Directorate-General of Logistics Services, Ministry of National Defense** (09/23/43): BG Francesco Marrajeni
- G. **Directorate-General of General Affairs, Civilian, Personnel, Administration Service; Ministry of National Defense** (09/23/40): BG Francesco Medoni

Commander-in-Chief, Armed Forces, Social Republic of Italy (09/23/43): Mar. Rodolfo Graziani, Marquis [Marchese] of Neghelli [+ Minister of Defense, Social Republic of Italy] (arrested; /50, sentenced to 19 years imprisonment for collaboration with the Nazis; released after a few months; /55, died in Rome) 04/25/45 dissolved.

Chief of the General Staff, Social Republic of Italy (10/28/43): Gen. Gastone Gambara (?) /45 LG Archimede Mischi [MVSN].
- A. **Deputy Chief of the General Staff, Social Republic of Italy** (10/28/43): LG Alessandro Scala
- B. **Secretary-General of the Army, Social Republic of Italy** (10/28/43): BG Emilio Canevari (Head, Military Mission to Germany) /44
- C. *Directorate-Generals*
  1. **Directorate-General of Artillery** (09/23/43): BG Marcello Gignolini
  2. **Directorate-General of Security** (09/23/43): unknown? /44 MG Renzo Montagna [MVSN] (Commanding General, 205th Regional Military Command Milano [Milan]) /45
- D. **National Security Volunteer Militia [Milizia Voluntaria per la Sicurezza Nazionale (MVSN) {Fascist Militia}]** (or commonly known as the **Black Shirts**

(Camicie Nere (CCNN)) (HQ Rome, Italy): 10/28/43 LG Quirino Armellini (Commanding General, V Territorial Defense Command) /45

    1. **Chief of Staff, National Security Volunteer Militia (MVSN)** (Commander, National Security Volunteer Militia): /35 MG Luigi Russo [MVSN] (Undersecretary to President, Council of Ministers) /39 MG Achille Starace [MVSN] (/45, executed by Partisans) /41 MG Sergio Biraghi [MVSN] (?) /41 MG Enzo Emilio Galbiati [MVSN] (arrested) /43 MG Giuseppe Conticelli [MVSN]

    2. **Military Advocate (Judical Branch), Rome HQ National Security Volunteer Militia**: BG (Res.) Sebastiano Cascella

E. **National Republican Guard, Social Republic of Italy** (10/43): MG Renato Ricci [MVSN] (/45, arrested; /50, released) /43 MG Italo Romegialli [MVSN] (?) /44 MG Renzo Montagna [MVSN]

    1. **Deputy Commander, National Republican Guard, Social Republic of Italy** (10/43): MG Italo Romegialli [MVSN] (Commanding General, National Republican Guard, Social Republic of Italy) /43

    2. **Chief of Staff, National Republican Guard, Social Republic of Italy** (10/43): MG Niccolò Nicchiarelli [MVSN] (condemned to 12-1/2 years imprisonment) 05/45.

F. **Publications & Propaganda Office, Social Republic of Italy** (10/43): MG Fattarappa-Sandri

G. *Regional Military Commands*

    1. **1st Provincial Military Command Torino [Turin]** (10/43): BG Massimo De Castiglione [MVSN] (Commanding General, 206th Regional Military Command Torino) /44?

    2. **200th Regional Military Command Rome [Roma]** (10/43): BG Federico Magri (?) /43 BG Gherardo Magaldi (Commanding General, 202nd Regional Military Command Bologna) /44? MG Giunio Ruggiero

        a. **200th Regional Military Tribunal (Judical) Rome** (10/43): BG Alfredo Arnera

    3. **201st Regional Military Command Firenze [Florence]** (10/43): LG Enrico Adami-Rossi (Commanding General 206th Regional Military Command Torino [Turin]) /45

        a. **201st Regional Military Tribunal (Judical) Firenze [Florence]** (10/43): BG Raffaele Berti.

    4. **202nd Regional Military Command Bologna** (10/43): BG Guglielmo Bocassi (?) /44? BG Gherardo Magaldi (?) /45? MG Unberto Giglio

        a. **202nd Regional Military Tribunal (Judical) Bologna** (10/43): MG Cesare Corvino

    5. **203rd Regional Military Command Padova-Verona** (10/43): BG Ottavio Peano [MVSN] (?) /43 MG Umberto Piatti del Pozzo (Commandant, Center for Training of Special Units, Social Republic of Italy) /44 MG Nino Sozzani (?) /44 MG Attilo Pognisi

    6. **204th Regional Military Command Trieste** (10/43): MG Giovanni Esposito

        a. **204th Regional Military Tribunal (Judical) Trieste** (10/43): BG Augusto Moretto

7. **205th Regional Military Command Milano [Milan]** (10/43): MG Giaocchino Solinas (Commandant, Center of Mobilization of Major Units, Social Republic of Italy) /45? MG Filippo Diamanti [MVSN]
8. **206th Regional Military Command Torino [Turin]** (10/43): LG Enrico Broglia (?) /44 BG Massimo De Castiglione [MVSN] (?) /45 LG Enrico Adami-Rossi (?) /45 MG Renzo Montagna [MVSN].
    a. **206th Regional Military Tribunal (Judical) Torino [Turin]** (10/43): MG America Cappi or BG Cino Gaggiotti
9. **206th Regional Military Command Allessandria** (10/43): BG Felice Valletti Borgnini (acting) /44 MG Renzo Montagna [MVSN] (Director-General, Republican Security, Social Republic of Italy) /44
10. **207th Regional Military Command Perugia** (10/43): BG Goffredo Ricci (Commanding General, 4th "Monte [Mount] Rosa" Alpine Division, Social Republic of Italy) /44 BG Michele Lotti
    a. **207th Regional Military Tribunal (Judical) Perugia** (10/43): BG Florenzo Chirubini
11. **208th Regional Military Command Macerata** (10/43): unknown? /43 MG Renzo Montagna [MVSN] (Commanding General, 206th Regional Military Command Allessandria) /44
12. **209th Regional Military Command Chieti** (10/43): BG Ilo Giacomo Perugini (Commanding General, 209th Regional Military Command Aquila) /44
13. **209th Regional Military Command Aquilla** (/44): BG Ilo Giacomo Perugini
14. **210th Regional Military Command Genova [Genoa]** (10/43): MG Marlo Guassardo (?) /43 MG Filippo Diamanti [MVSN] (Commandant, Center of Mobilization of Major Units, Social Republic of Italy) /44 BG Luigi Jalla (?) /44 MG Amedeo De Cia

H. *Regional Inspectors*
1. **Regional Inspector, National Republican Guard Emilia, Social Republic of Italy)** (10/28/43): MG Giovanni D'Oro [MVSN]
2. **Regional Inspector, National Republican Guard Lazio, Social Republic of Italy)** (10/28/43): BG Aristide Chiappe [MVSN].
3. **Regional Inspector, National Republican Guard Liguria, Social Republic of Italy)** (10/28/43): BG Mario Bertoni [MVSN].
4. **Regional Inspector, National Republican Guard Lombardia, Social Republic of Italy)** (10/28/43): BG Amedeo Mosca [MVSN].
5. **Regional Inspector, National Republican Guard Marche, Social Republic of Italy)** (10/28/43): BG Eichi Di Rodeano [MVSN] (?) /44 MG Guido Felici [MVSN].
6. **Regional Inspector of National Republican Guard Piemonte, Social Republic of Italy** (10/28/43): BG Domenico Mittica [MVSN] (?) /44 BG Raffaele Castriotta [MVSN].
7. **Regional Inspector of National Republican Guard Toscany, Social Republic of Italy** (10/28/43): unknown? /44 MG Mario Marino [MVSN].
8. **Regional Inspector of National Republican Guard Venetian Gulf, Social Republic of Italy** (10/28/43): BG Italo De Pasquale [MVSN] (?) /44 BG Angelo Sommavilla.

I. ***Centers & Schools***
   1. **Commandant, Center for Training of Special Units** (10/43): MG Amilcare Farina (Commanding General, 3rd "San Marco" Marine Division, Social Republic of Italy) /44 BG Giovanni Del Giudice (?) /44 LG Enea Navarini (?) /44 MG Umberto Piatti del Pozzo
   2. **Commandant, Center of Mobilization of Major Units**: /44 MG Goffredo Ricci (?) /44 MG Filippo Diamanti [MVSN] (Commanding General, 205th Military Regional Command Milano [Milan]) /45? MG Giaocchino Solinas
   3. **Commandant, National Republican Guard Non-Commissioned Officers School** (10/43): BG Giuseppe Volante [MVSN] (Commanding General, National Republican Guard Division Etna) /43 MG Mario Marino [MVSN] (Regional Inspector of National Republican Guard Toscany, Social Republic of Italy) /44

J. **Military Mission to Germany** (10/43): BG Emilio Canevari (?) /43 MG Umberto Morera

German Command of Northern Italy

German Plenipotentiary and Ambassador in Italy (de facto Ruler): 09/23/43 RUDOLF RAHN [German] 04/28/45

Highest SS and Policeleader, Gestapo Italy [HoeSSPf [HöSSPf] South (Italy)] (HQ: Rome): 09/23/43 SS-Gen. Karl Wolff [German].
A.   **SSPf Bozen**: 09/15/43 SS-MG Karl Brunner [German].
B.   **SSPf Middle Italy-Verona**: 12/01/43 SS-Col. Karl-Heinz Buerger [Bürger] [German].
C.   **SSPf Upper Italy-Center**: 04/44 SS-BG Ernst Hildebrandt [German] (?) 10/44
D.   **SSPf Upper Italy-West**: 01/23/44 SS-MG Willi Tensfeld [German].

Head of the Military Administration: /44 LG Friedrich-Karl Otto Gustav von Waechter [Wächter] [German] /45

[NOTE: In charge of German troops in Italy prior to the 09/08/43 German takeover of Northern Italy, Military Mission prior to 1943; Commander-in-Chief [Oberbefehlshaber (OB)] South after 09/2343]

Head of Military Mission and **Military Attaché**: GdFl Enno von Rintelen [German-Luft] (Regional Commander, Corsica) 09/10/43 position eliminated.

Commander-in-Chief [Oberbefehlshaber (OB)] South (09/08/43): FM Albert Kesselring [German-Luft] (Commander-in-Chief [Oberbefehlshaber (OB)] Southwest) 11/16/43 dissolved, new command **Commander-in-Chief [Oberbefehlshaber (OB)] Southwest** 11/16/43 FM Albert Kesselring [German-Luft] (leave) 10/44 CG Heinrich Gottfried von Vietinghoff genannt Scheel [German] [temporary; + Commander-in-Chief, Army Group "C"] (Commander-in-Chief, Army Group North (Russia #1)) 01/17/45 FM Albert Kesselring [German-Luft] (Commander-in-Chief [Oberbefehlshaber (OB)] West) 03/10/45 CG Heinrich Gottfried von Vietinghoff genannt Scheel [German] [+ Commander-in-Chief, Army Group "C"] 04/30/45 LG Hans Roettiger [Röttiger] [German] (acting) 04/30/45 GdI Friedrich Wilhelm "Fritz" Schulz [German] (deposed by SS-Gen. Karl Wolff [German] after his refusal of surrender to the Allies) 05/02/45.
A.   **Chief of Staff, Commander-in-Chief [Oberbefehlshaber (OB)] South**: 08/42 LG Paul Deichmann [German-Luft] (Commanding General, Luftgau [Air District] IV) 06/25/43

jointly with

ARMY GROUP "B" (Italy-France #2) (09/08/43): FM Erwin Johannes Eugen Rommel [German] 11/20/43 Army Group "B" moved to France.
A.   **Regional Commander, Corsica** (09/10/43): MG Enno von Rintelen [German-Luft] (?) 10/43
B.   **Regional Commander, Adriatic Coast** (07/22/43): LG Wather Lucht [German] (Commanding General, LXVI Reserve Army [Infantry] Corps) 11/01/43 GdGebTr Ludwig Kuebler [Kübler] [German] (Commanding General, XCVII Army [Infantry] Corps) 09/28/44 redesignated <u>XCVII Army [Infantry] Corps</u> - see **XCVII Army [Infantry]**

        Corps.
C.   **Regional Commander, Venetian Coast** (08/44): GdI Joachim Witthoeft [Witthöft] [German] (?) 09/01/44 GdI Anton Dostler [German] (Commanding General, LXXIII Army [Infantry] Corps) 11/25/44 redesignated **LXXIII Army [Infantry] Corps** - see **LXXIII Army [Infantry] Corps**.

Commanding Officer of the Waffen-SS Italy (08/01/44): SS-Gen. Lothar Debes [German]
A.   **Chief of Staff, Commanding Officer of the Waffen-SS Italy**: 08/01/44 SS-Col. Eugen von Elfenau [German]

Partisan Resistance
(1943)

Even before the fall of Benito Mussolini on September 25, 1943, delegates of non Fascist parties met in Rome and founded the **Anti-Fascist United Freedom Front**. After the German occupation of Italy, it was renamed the **Committee of National Liberation [Comitato di Liberazione Nationale (CLN)]**. Other cities in Italy also set up liberation committees. In the course of a few months these committees were regrouped into three regional committees, acting independently of the Italian Government.

President, Central Committee of National Liberation [Comitato Centrale di Liberazione Nationale (CCLN)]. (1943, Rome): IVANOE BONOMI [FORMERLY President, Anti-Fascist United Freedom Front] (Primer) 06/09/44 disbanded after the recapturing of Rome by the Allies and restoring the authority of the Italian government.

President, Committee of National Liberation of Toscania [Comitato Toscano di Liberazione Nationale (CTLN)]. (1943, Firenze [Florence]): GAETANO PIERACCINI /43 CARLO RAGGHIANTI 08/44 disbanded after the recapturing of Rome by the Allies and restoring the authority of the Italian government.

President, Committee of National Liberation of Upper Italy [Comitato di Liberazione Nationale per Alta Italia (CLNAI)]. (1943, Milano [Milan]) ALFREDO PIZZONI "LONGHI" 04/45 RODOLFO MORANDI.

Italian Partisan Republics of 1944

In 1944, the **Committee of National Liberation of Upper Italy** staged a general revolt which resulted in the establishment of a number of free zone (also called **Partisan Republics**), which were destroyed by the Germans before the year was over. They were:

Alto Monferrato (09/44 to 12/02/44)
Alto Tortonese (09/44 to 12/44)
Bobbio e Torriglia (07/07/44 to 08/27/44)
Cansiglio (07/44 to 09/44)
Carnia (07/44 to 10/44)
Friuli Orientale (06/30/44 to 09/44)
Imperia (08/44 to 10/44)
Langhe (09/44 to 11/44)
Montefiorino (06/17/44 to 08/01/44)
Ossola (09/10/44 to 10/23/44
Val Ceno (06/10/44 to 07/11/44)
Val d'Enza e Val Parma (06/44-07/44)
Val Maira e Val Varaita (06/44 to 08/21/44)
Val Taro (06/15/44 to 07/24/44)
Valli di Lanzo (06/25/44 to 09/44)
Valsesia (06/11/44 to 07/10/44)
Varzi (09/44 to 11/29/44)

Ossola or **Domodossola** was the only republic which received some recognition by both Swiss officials and by local Allied representatives. Italian partisans established the **Free Republic of Ossola** on the shore of Lake Maggiore including Cannoba, Intra, Verbania, Omegna, and Domodossola. It comprised 35 municipalities situated along the Swiss frontier. The partisan republics of **Alto Tortonese**, **Bobbio e Torriglia**, and **Varzi** were adjacent to **Ossola**, forming one vast liberated territory. By the end of 1944, the Germans reoccupied these areas.

President, Provisional Junta of Government of Ossola (09/10/44): ETTORE TIBALDI 10/23/44 reoccupied by the Germans.

A new revolt in 1945 was more successful as it resulted in the destruction of the **Italian Social Republic** and the end of German authority in most of northern Italy.

After the liberation, the **Committee of National Liberation of Upper Italy (CLNAI)** acted as a de facto government for North Italy until an agreement was reached with the centarl government. The liberated territories being handed over to the **Allied Military Administration for Italy**.

Allied Military Government of Italy
(June 11, 1943)

Head of the Allied Military Government [AMGOT]: 06/11/43 Gen. Dwight David Eisenhower [American] (Supreme Commander-in-Chief, Supreme Headquarters, Allied Expeditionary Force) 01/08/44 FM Sir Henry Maitland Wilson [British] [+ Supreme Commander-in-Chief, Allied Mediterranean Theater of Operations] (Head of British Joint Staff Mission, Washington, D. C.) 12/16/44 FM Sir Harold Rupert Leofric Geogre Alexander [British] [+ Supreme Commander-in-Chief, Allied Mediterranean Theater of Operations].

Chief Commissioner of the Allied Control Commission for Italy: 11/10/43 MG Kenyon Ashe Joyce [American] (retired) 01/16/44 LG Sir (Frank) Noel Mason-MacFarlane [British] (acting Head of the Allied Military Government of Italy) 06/44 ELLERY W. STONE [American] 01/31/47.
[NOTE: From 10/27/44 to 01/31/47, acting for ELLERY W. STONE [aMERICAN] was MAURICE HAROLD McMILLAN [British].**]**

Military Governors of the Occupied Territories (07/10/43): FM Sir Harold Rupert Leofric Geogre Alexander [British] [+ Deputy Supreme Commander-in-Chief, Allied Mediterranean Theater of Operations] 12/11/44 Gen. Mark Wayne Clark [American].

Part 2

ITALY'S ORDER OF BATTLE 1937 - 1945

Part 2

ITALY'S
ORDER OF BATTLE
1937 - 1945

Army Groups Italy

Army Groups Italy (the armies of Italy remained under the nominal control of the crown prince [Titular Commander of Army Groups]): /40 Gen. His Royal Highness Crown Prince Umberto Piemonte [di Savoia], the Crown Prince of Italy (Piedmont) and Viceroy [+ /42 to /43, Commander-in-Chief, Army Group South] (05/09/46, King of Italy for 35 days) 09/08/43 disbanded.

    1. **First Aide-de-Camp to the Crown Prince**: /41? LG (Res.) Emilio Gamerra

A. **Army Group West** (06/40): /39 LG His Royal Highness Crown Prince Umberto Piemonte [di Savoia], the Crown Prince of Italy (Piedmont) and Viceroy (Commander-in-Chief, Army Groups Italy) /40 unknown? 09/08/43 disbanded.
    1. *Components* (06/10/40):
        a. **First Army**
        b. **Fourth Army**

B. **Army Group Central** (1940):
    1. *Components* (1942):
        a. **Third Army**
        b. **Sixth Army**
        c. **Seventh Army**

C. **Army Group South** (06/10/40): Mar. [Retired '20] Emilio De Bono [+ Member, Fascists Grand Council] /41 Mar. Of Italy His Royal Highness Crown Prince Umberto Piemonte [di Savoia], the Crown Prince of Italy (Piedmont) and Viceroy [+ Commander-in-Chief, Army Groups Italy] (05/09/46, King of Italy for 35 days) 09/08/43 disbanded.
    1. *Components* (09/43):
        a. **General Headquarters Sardinia**
        b. **General Headquarters Corsica,**
        c. **Fifth Army**
        d. **Seventh Army**

D. **Reserves** (06/10/40)
        a. **Third Army**
        b. **Seventh Army**
        c. **General Headquarters East Africa** (Army Status)
        d. **General Headquarters Albania** (Sub-Army Status)
        e. **General Headquarters Aegean** (Corps Status)
        f. **Zara** (Division Status)

Army Groups

General Headquarters East Africa [Africa Orientale Italiana (AOI)] (1934, Abyssinia [Ethiopia], Eritrea, and Somaliland): /35 Gen. [Retired '20] Emilio De Bono [+ Member, Grand Council of Fascist; + to 11/35, Commissioner for Italian East Africa] (/39, Inspector of Overseas Troops; /39, Member, Commission of Armed Forces, Senate; /39, Member, Commissioner for the Affairs Italian Africa) 11/35 Gen. Pietro Badoglio, Duke of Addis Ababa, Marquess of el Sabotino [+ Viceroy and Governor-General, Italian East Africa] 06/11/36 Gen. His Royal Highness Prince Amadeo Umberto Isabella Luigi Filippo Maria Giuseppe Giovanni di Savoia [Savoy-Aosta], 3rd Duke of Aosta [+ Viceroy and Governor-General, Italian East Africa] (British prisoner-of war; 03/03/42, died in a British Prison of War Camp in Kenya from tuberculosis and maleria) 05/19/41 vacant 05/23/41 Gen. Pietro Gazzera [+ acting Viceroy and Governor-General, Italian East Africa] (British prisoner-of-war) 05/19/41 disbanded

A. **Chief of Staff, General Headquarters East Africa**: /36 MG Italo Gariboldi (/38, Commanding General, V Army Corps) /37 MG Felice Valetti Borgnini (?) /38 MG Claudio Trezzani (to /44, British prisoner-of-war) 11/27/41 dissolved.
B. *Components - General Headquarters East Africa* (06/10/40):
  1. **Northern Sector** (corps status):
  2. **Eastern Sector** (corps status):
  3. **Southern Sector** (corps status):
  4. **Giuba Sector** (corps status):
C. *Components - General Headquarters East Africa* (04/41):
  1. **Jimma Area** (04/41): Gen. Pietro Gazzera (British prisoner-of-war) 05/19/41 surrendered.
  2. **Western Ethiopia** (04/41): Gen. Guglielmo Ciro Nasi [+ to 07/06/41, Member, Commission for the Armed Forces, Senate; + 05/27/41, Italian Governor of Amhara; 07/06/41, Viceroy and Governor-General, Italian East Africa & Member, Commission of the Affair of Italian Africa, Senate] (British prisoner-of-War)11/27/41 surrendered.
D. *Components - General Headquarters East Africa* (1942):
  1. **Eritrean Corps**
  2. **Italian Somaliland Corps**
  3. **4 divisions**
  4. **Central Reserve in Ethiopia**
E. **Deputy Chief of Staff, General Headquarters East Africa**: /39 BG Odoardo Majnardi (British prisoner-of-war; /41, died in a British hospital in Berbera) 05/19/41 dissolved.

Army Group East (04/07/39, Albania; 05/41, disbanded when Albania was incorporated into Italy; 09/08/43, reformed for possible Allied invasion of Albania and Yugoslavia; 05/41 incorporated into Italy and General Headquarters Albania took over control; reformed 09/08/43): **Army Group East (#1)** 1939 LG Alfredo Guzzoni (Commander-in-Chief, Fourth Army) 12/39 LG Carlo Geloso [+ Commanding General, XXVI Army Corps] (Commander-in-Chief, Third Army) 06/10/40 Gen Camillo Grossi [+ Member, Commission for the Armed Forces, Senate] (Head, Italian Armistice Commission to France) 06/40 LG Sebastiano

Visconti Prasca [+ Commander-in-Chief, General Headquarters Albania] (Commanding General, XXVI Army Corps) 11/29/40 Gen. Ubaldo Soddu [+ Deputy Chief of the Supreme General Staff] (retired?) 12/40 Gen. Count [Retired '19 & '27] Ugo Cavallero [+ Chief of the Supreme General Staff; + to 12/40, Commander-in-Chief, General Headquarters Albania] (Commander-in-Chief, Army Group Albania) 04/05/41 redesignated **Army Group Albania** 04/05/41 Gen. Count [Retired '19 & '27] Ugo Cavallero [+ Chief of the Supreme General Staff] 05/41 reformed **Army Group East (#2)** 05/43 Gen. Ezio Rosi (to /45, German prisoner-of-war) 09/05/43 disbanded.

- A. **Chief of Staff, Army Group East**: /40 BG Gugleilmo Negro (Commanding General, 16th "Pistola" Motorized Infantry Division) /41 unknown? /43 MG Emilio Giglioli (?) 09/05/43 dissolved.
- B. *Components - Army Group East* (04/07/39):
    1. **Ninth Army** (also known as **General Headquarters Albania and East**)
- C. *Components - Army Group East* (06/10/40):
    1. **Second Army**
    2. **Sixth Army**
    3. **Eighth Army**
    4. **Eleventh Army** (added 11/40; also known as **General Headquarters Greece**)
- D. *Components - Army Group Albania* (04/07/41):
    1. **Ninth Army** (also known as **General Headquarters Albania and East**)
- E. *Components - Army Group East* (09/43):
    1. **Ninth Army**
    2. **Eleventh Army**
    3. **General Headquarters Aegean**

Army Group West [Gruppo Armate Ovest] (/39; France): Gen. His Royal Highness Crown Prince Umberto Piemonte [di Savoia], the Crown Prince of Italy (Piedmont) and Viceroy (Commander-in-Chief, Army Groups Italy) /40
- A. **Chief of Staff, Army Group West** (06/10/40): BG Emillio Battisti (Commanding General, 49th "Parma" Alpini Division) /41?
- B. *Components - Army Group West* (06/10/40):
    1. **First Army**
    2. **Fourth Army**
- C. **Chief Operations, Army Group West** (06/10/40): Col. Clemente Primieri (Chief of Staff, 3rd "Ravenna" Infantry Division) /40

Army Group South [Gruppo Armate Sud] (06/10/40): Mar. [Retired '20] Emilio De Bono [+ Member, Fascists Grand Council] /41 Mar. His Royal Highness Crown Prince Umberto Piemonte [di Savoia], the Crown Prince of Italy (Piedmont) and Viceroy [+ Commander-in-Chief, Army Group Italy] (05/09/46, King of Italy for 35 days) 09/08/43 disbanded.
- A. **Chief of Staff, Army Group South** (06/10/40): BG Vittorio Ruggero (Commanding General, 58th "Legnano" Infantry Division) /41 unknown? 09/08/43 dissolved.
- B. *Components - Army Group South* (06/10/40):
    1. **XII Army Corps**
    2. **XIII Army Corps**

C. ***Components*** - **Army Group South** (09/43):
 1. **General Headquarters Sardinia**
 2. **General Headquarters Corsica**
 3. **Fifth Army**
 4. **Seventh Army**

General Headquarters North Africa (Supreme Commander's Headquarters in Libya; responsible for all Italian troops in North Africa): /37 LG Mario Caracciolo di Feroleto [+ Commanding General, XXI Army Corps] /38 Mar. of AF Italo Balbo (died) 06/40 Mar. Rodolfo Graziani, Marquis [Marchese] of Neghelli [+ Chief of The Army General Staff & Governor-General, Libya] (resigned; 09/08/43, joins Social Republic of Italy; 09/08/43, Minister of War & Chief of the Armed Forces General Staff, Social Republic of Italy) 03/25/41 LG Italo Gariboldi [+ Governor-General of Libya] (in reserve; 07/42, Commander-in-Chief, Eighth Army) 07/12/41 FM Ettore Bastico (Commander-in-Chief, Italian Armed Forces Supreme Command of Libya) /42 redesignated **Italian Armed Forces Supreme Command of Libya** 10/23/42? Mar. Ettore Bastico (returned to Italy) 02/43 unknown? 05/43 disbanded.
 A. **Deputy Commander, General Headquarters North Africa** (06/10/40): LG Italo Gariboldi [+ Commander-in-Chief, Fifth Army; + 11/40, acting Commander-in-Chief, Tenth Army] (Commander-in-Chief, General Headquarters North Africa & Governor-General of Libya] /40 BG Oliviero Miele (?) 02/41 unknown? 05/43 dissolved.
 B. **Chief of Staff, General Headquarters North Africa**: /39 LG Guiseppe Tellera (Commander-in-Chief, Tenth Army) 12/40 LG Gastone Gambara [+ Commanding General, XX Army Corps] 12/41 MG Count Curio Barbasetti di Prun (Logistic Commander, General Headquarters, North Africa) /42 MG Ottorino Giannantoni [MVSN] (?) /42 MG Emilio Giglioli (Chief of Staff, Army Group East) 05/43 dissolved
 C. ***Components*** - **General Headquarters North Africa** (06/10/40):
  1. **Fifth Army**
  2. **Tenth Army**
  3. **Reserves**
 D. ***Components*** - **General Headquarters North Africa** (10/42):
  1. **X Army Corps**
  2. **XX Army Corps**
  3. **XXI Army Corps**
  4. ***German Africa Corps*** (usually operated independently under FM Erwin Johannes Eugen Rommel [German])
 E. **Italian Armed Forces Supreme Command of Libya** (10/23/42)
  1. **Tripolitania Defense Command** (army status)
  2. **Cyrenaica Defense Command** (army status)
  3. **5th Air Force [Squadra 5]** (corps status)
  4. **Libya Naval Command [Comando Marilibia]** (status)
 F. **Engineer-in-Chief, North Africa**: /42? MG Luigi Grosso (?) 05/43 dissolved.
  1. **Chief Executive, Engineers, North Africa**: /42 BG (Res.) Giuseppe Rossi
  2. **Chief Engineer, Delease, North Africa**: /42 BG Guido Saltini (died of an illness onboard a hospital ship being evacuated from North Africa to Italy) /42 unknown? 05/43 dissolved.

G. **Logistic Commander, General Headquarters, North Africa** (06/10/40): unknown? /42 MG Count Curio Barbasetti di Prun (Commanding General, XIV Army Corps) 05/43 dissolved.
H. **Inspector-General, Italian African Police**: /41 BG Raffaele Catardi $_{[MVSN]}$ (?) 05/43 dissolved.
I. **Advocate, Military War Tribunal, North Africa**: /42 MG (Res.) Bernardo Olivieri
J. **Royal Caribinieri, North Africa**: /42 BG Umberto Giani (possible Commanding General, 1st Pastrengo Carabinieri Division) 03/43 vacant 05/43 dissolved.
    1. **3rd Bureau, Royal Carabinieri, North Africa**: /42 BG Raul Masi (?) 05/43 dissolved.
K. **At Disposal of, Attached to, or on Special Duties with General Headquarters, North Africa**
/41 (attached to) Col. Alessandro Albert

Italian Royal Fleet Afloat [army group status]

Commander-in-Chief, Italian Royal Fleet Alfoat [Comando in Capo Forze Navali da Battaglia]: VA Inigo Campioni [RIN] [+ Commander-in-Chief, 1st Fleet] (01/01/43?, Commander-in-Chief, Headquarters, Aegean Sea & Governor of Italian Dodecanes Islands) 12/09/40 Adm. Angelo Jachino [RIN] [+ to 01/07/43, Commanding Officer, 2nd Light Cruiser Squadron; + 01/12/42 to 01/07/43, Commanding Officer, 1st Heavy Cruiser Squadron] (?) 04/01/43 Adm. Carlo Bergamini [RIN] [Flag: RIN battleship *Roma*] [+ Commander-in-Chief, 1st Fleet] (killed in action; died when his flagship was sunk) 09/08/43 disbanded.

- A. **Deputy Commander, Italian Royal Fleet Alfoat [Comando in Seconda Forze Navali]**:
- B. *Components* - **Royal Navy Afloat** (06/10/40)
    1. **1st Fleet** (corps status)
    2. **2nd Fleet** (corps status)
    3. **Submarine Fleet** (corps status)
    4. **Upper Tyrrenhian Sea Department** (Italy; corps status)
    5. **Lower Tyrrenhian Sea Department** (Italy; corps status)
    6. **Upper Adriatic Sea Department** (Italy; corps status)
    7. **Ionian and Lower Adriatic Sea Department** (Italy; corps status)
    8. **Aegean Sea Naval Command** (division status)
    9. **Albania Naval Command** (division status)
    10. **Libya Naval Command** (division status)
    11. **Italian East Africa Naval Command** (division status)
    12. **Far East Naval Command** (brigade status)
    13. **Naval Fleet Train** (division status)
    14. **Anti-Submarine Division** (division status)

Armies

Army of Padova: /38 LG Ettore Bastico (Commanding General, Army of the Po) /38 LG Vittorio Ambrosio (Commander-in-Chief, Second Army) /39 redesignated **Second Army** - see **Second Army**.

Army of the Po: /38 Gen. Ettore Bastico [+ /39, Member, Commission for the Armed Forces, Senate] /40 (Governor-General, Dodecanese Islands) /40 unknown? /41 disbanded.
A. **Chief of Staff, Army of the Po**: /39 BG Luigi Reverberi (/41, Commanding General, 2nd "Tridentina" Alpine Division) /39 BG Guglielmo Spicacci (Chief of Staff, Ninth Army) /41 dissolved.

Army of Torino (/39, disbanded): /38 LG Adriano Marinetti (Commander-in-Chief, First Army) /39 Gen. Angelo Tua (Member, Commission for the Armed Forces, Senate) disbanded.

Army of Verona: /38 LG Adriano Marinetti (designated Commander-in-Chief, Army of Torino) /38? Gen. Camillo Grossi (designated Commander-in-Chief, Fourth Army) /38 redesignated **Fourth Army** - see **Fourth Army**.

Army S (/40, disbanded): /39 LG Edoardo Monti (retired) /40 disbanded.

First Army (/39; 06/10/40, part of Army Group West; France; Libya; Tunisia; 05/43, destroyed in Tunisia): <u>**First Army (#1)**</u> /39 Gen. Adriano Marinetti [+ Member, Commission for the Armed Forces, Senate] (retired?) 06/10/40? Gen. Ben Pietro Pintor Head, Italian Armistice Commission to France) /40 LG Remo Gambelli (acting; Commander-in-Chief, Royal Carabinieri) /40 disbanded; reformed <u>**First Army (#2)**</u> /42 Mar. Giovanni Messe (Commander-in-Chief, First Italo-German Army) 02/43 redesignated **First Italo-German Army** 02/43 Mar. Giovanni Messe (Allied prisoner-of-war; 09/43, Chief of Army General Staff) 05/43 destroyed.
A. **Chief of Staff, First Army**: /39 BG Giuseppe Mancinelli (Member, Italian Armistice Commission to France) /40 MG Adolfo Infante (Military Attaché, Washington, D. C.) /40 unknown? /43 MG Giuseppe Mancinelli (to /44, Allied prisoner-of-war; /45, Commanding General, Custom Guards) 05/43 dissolved.
B. *Components - First Army* (06/10/40):
   1. **II Army Corps**
   2. **III Army Corps**
   3. **XV Army Corps**
   4. **7th "Lupi di Toscana" Infantry Division**
   5. **16th "Pistoia" Infantry Division**
   6. **22nd "Cacciatori della Alpi" Infantry Division**
   7. **5th "Pusteria" Mountain Infantry Division**
   8. **7th "Lupi di Toscana" Infantry Division**
   9. *Support Units* **(regiment sized listed only)**
      a. **205th Artillery Regiment**

C. ***Components - First Italo-German Army*** (02/43):
1. ***German Africa Corps***
2. **XX Army Corps**
3. **XXI Army Corps**
D. **Artillery Commander, First Army** (1939): unknown? /40 disbanded; reformed **Artillery Commander, First Italo-German Army** 02/43 MG Pietro Belletti (Allied prisoner-of-war; after released, Inspector of Artillery) 05/43 dissolved.
E. **Royal Carabinieri, First Army**: Col. Raffaele Castriotta [MVSN] (/44, Regional Inspector, National Republican "Piemonte" Guard, Special Republic of Italy) 05/43 dissolved.

Second Army (/39, from **Army of Padova**; part of Army Group East; also known as **General Headquarters Solvenia-Dalmatia**; Yugoslavia; 04/41 invaded and occupied western Slovenia and garrison unit for Dalmatia; occupied northern Yugoslavia and defended the coast; /43, extended into northeast Italy): **Second Army (#1)** /39 Gen. Vittorio Ambrosio (Chief of the Army General Staff) /42 LG Mario Roatta (Commander-in-Chief, General Headquarters Slovenia-Dalmatia) 01/42 redesignated **General Headquarters Slovenia-Dalmatia** /42 LG Mario Roatta (Commander-in-Chief, Sixth Army) /43 LG Mario Robotti (Commander-in-Chief, Second Army (#2)) /43 redesignated **Second Army (#2)** /43 LG Mario Robotti (?) 09/08/43 disbanded.
A. **Chief of Staff, Second Army** (06/10/40): unknown? /43 BG Clemente Primieri (/46, Commanding General, Cremona Division) 09/08/43 dissolved.
B. ***Components - Second Army*** (06/10/40):
1. **V Army Corps**
2. **XI Army Corps**
3. **"Alto Isonzo" Mountain Infantry Brigade**
C. ***Components - Second Army*** (04/42):
1. 4 divisions
D. ***Components - Second Army*** (03/43):
1. **V Army Corps**
2. **XI Army Corps**
3. **XVIII Army Corps**
4. **158th Division**
E. ***Components - Second Army*** (09/43):
1. **V Army Corps**
2. **XI Army Corps**
3. **XVII Army Corps**
4. **1st Cavalry Division**
F. **Deputy Chief of Staff, Second Army** (06/10/40): unknown? /41? Col. Giacomo Zanussi (Chief of Staff, Sixth Army) /43
G. **Artillery, Second Army**: /41 MG Giuseppe Gianni (to /43, German prisoner-of-war) 09/08/43 dissolved.
H. **Engineer-in-Chief, Second Army**: unknown? /43 MG Luigi Fogliani (to /45, German prisoner-of-war) 09/08/43 dissolved.
I. **Intendant-General (Quartermaster), Second Army**: /40 BG Raffaele Pelligra (Commanding General, 13th "Re" Infantry Division) /42 BG Umberto Giglio (joins the

Social Republic of Italy; /43, Undersecretary of State for the Army, Ministry of National Defense, Social Republic of Italy) 09/08/43 dissolved.
I. **Solvenia-Dalmatia Area**; /43 MG Alfonso Cigala-Fulgosi [+ Commanding General, 15th "Bergano" Infantry Division] (executed by the Germans) /43 BG Salavtore Pelligra (executed by the Germans) 09/08/43 dissolved.
J. **At Disposal of, Attached to, or on Special Duties with Second Army**:
/41 (attached to) MG Vittorio Emanuele La Rocca
01/42? (attached to) BG (Res.) Luigi Sabatini

Third Army (06/10/40, in Lazio Abruzzi area of Central Italy;06/40, part of Army Group Central; moved to Albania; became basis of Eleventh Army): 06/10/40 LG Carlo Geloso (Commander-in-Chief, Eleventh Army) 10/40 redesignated **Eleventh Army** - see **Eleventh Army**.
A. *Components - Third Army* (06/10/40):
   1. **IX Army Corps**

Fourth Army (1938, from **Army of Verona**; 06/10/40, part of Army Group West; France; Italy; occupied southeast France; moved into Italy (Piedmont and Liguria) to defend against Allied attack): Gen. Camillo Grossi [+ /39, Member, Commission for the Armed Forces, Senate] (Commander-in-Chief, Army Group East 12/39 Gen Alfredo Guzzoni (Undersecretary of War & Deputy Chief of the Supreme General Staff) /40 LG Mario Vercellino (Commander-in-Chief, Ninth Army) 11/29/40 Gen. Mario Caracciolo di Feroleto (Commander-in-Chief, Fifth Army) /41 LG Mario Vercellino (?) 09/08/43 disbanded.
A. **Chief of Staff, Fourth Army** (1939): MG Giuseppe Amico (Chief of Staff, Seventh Army) 06/10/40 unknown? /42 BG Alessandro Trabucchi (Commanding General, Division "Cremona") 09/08/43 dissolved.
B. *Components - Fourth Army* (06/10/40):
   1. **I Army Corps**
   2. **IV Army Corps**
   3. **Alpini Corps**
   4. **11th "Brenniero" Infantry Division**
   5. **58th "Legnano" Infantry Division**
   6. **2nd "Tridentina"Alpini Division**
   7. **4th "Celere di Armata" Cavalry Brigade**
   8. **VI Border Guard Sector** (HQ: Pinerolo, Italy; brigade status)
   9. *Support Units* **(regiment sized listed only)**
      a. **7th Corps Artillery Regiment**
      b. **22nd Corps Artillery Regiment**
C. *Components - Fourth Army* (09/43):
   1. **I Army Corps**
   2. **XV Army Corps**
   3. **XXII Army Corps**
   4. **2nd Cavalry Division**
D. **Artillery Commander, Fourth Army**: unknown? /42 BG Giovanni Battista Oxilia (Commanding Geeral, 27th "Brescia" Semi-Motorized Infantry Division) 08/42 MG Gastano Alagia (?) 09/08/43 dissolved.

E. **Intendence Commissariat, Fourth Army**: unknown? /43 BG Tito Fuselli (to /45, German prisoner-of-war; /45, died in a hospital) 09/08/43 dissolved.
F. **Military Tribunal, Fourth Army**: unknown? /43 BG Giuseppe Capelli (to /45, German prisoner-of-war) 09/08/43 dissolved.
G. **At Disposal of, Attached to, or on Special Duties with Fourth Army**:
/43 BG Eligio Rosso (to /45, German prisoner-of-war) 09/08/43

Fifth Army (06/10/40, part of General Headquarters North Africa; western Libya; 02/41, badly damaged; /42, reformed in Italy; 09/43, part of Army Groups Italy): /39 LG Italo Gariboldi [+ 06/40, Deputy Commander, North Africa] (acting Commander-in-Chief, Tenth Army) 11/40 Gen. Mario Caracciolo di Feroleto (?) /41 unknown? 01/01/43? Gen. Mario Caracciolo di Feroleto (?) 09/08/43 disbanded.

A. **Chief of Staff, Fifth Army**: /39 MG Efisio Marras (Military Attaché, Germany) /40 unknown? 09/08/43 dissolved.
B. *Components* - **Fifth Army** (06/10/40):
   1. **X Army Corps**
   2. **XX Army Corps**
   3. **XXIII Army Corps**
   4. **Tripoli Fortress** (corps status)
   5. **XXVIII Border Guard Sector** (HQ: Zuara; brigade status)
   6. **XXIX Border Guard Sector** (HQ: Nalut; brigade status)
C. *Components* - **Fifth Army** (1942):
   1. **VII Army Corps**
   2. **XIII Army Corps**
   3. **184th Nembo Division**
D. *Components* - **Fifth Army** (09/43):
   1. **General Headquarters Corsica**
   2. **II Army Corps**
   3. **XVI Army Corps**

Sixth Army (from **Army of the Po**; 06/10/40, part of Army Group East; Italy; /42, part of Army Groups Italy; Sicily; 08/43, badly damaged): **Army of the Po** 06/10/40 LG Mario Vercellino (Commander-in-Chief, Fourth Army) /40 Gen. Ezio Rosi (Commander-in-Chief, Sixth Army) /41 redesignated **Sixth Army** /41 Gen. Ezio Rosi (Chief of the Army General Staff) 02/43 LG Mario Roatta (Chief of the Army General Staff) 05/43? Gen. Alfredo Guzzoni (joins Social Republic of Italy; 07/03/44, Commander-in-Chief, Italo-German Army Group Liguria [XLVII "Liguria" Army]) 08/43 disbanded.

A. **Deputy Commander, Sixth Army** (06/10/40): unknown? /42 MG Adamo Mariotti (Commanding General, Sicily Military Command) 08/43 dissolved.
B. **Chief of Staff, Sixth Army**: /41 MG Adamo Mariotti (Deputy Commander, Sixth Army) /42 BG Carlo or Mario Vanden Heufel (?) 01/43 BG Giacomo Zanussi (Infantry Commander, 44th "Cremona" Infantry Division) /43 MG Emilio Faldella (Member of the Resistance in Northern Italy; /44, arrested by the Germans; /45, released) 08/43 dissolved.
C. *Components* - **Sixth Army** (06/10/40):
   1. **Celere [Fast] Corps**

       2.   **Truck Borne Corps**
       3.   **Armored Corps**
       4.   *Support Units* (regiment sized listed only)
           a.   **10th Army Artillery Regiment**
           b.   **19th Coastal Defense Artillery Regiment**
           a.   **26th Army Artillery Regiment**

D.   *Components* - Sixth Army (09/43):
       1.   **XII Army Corps**
       2.   **XVI Army Corps**

E.   **Engineer-in-Chief, Sixth Army** (06/10/40): MG Armando Bianchi (?) 08/43 dissolved.

F.   **Intendant-General (Administration), Sixth Army**: /42 BG Alberto Aliberti (Commanding General, Folgore Division) /43 unknown? 08/43 dissolved.

Seventh Army (06/10/40, in Italy; France; /42, part of Army Groups Italy; southern Italy; 09/08/43, disbanded): 06/10/40 Gen. Designate His Royal Highness Prince Filiberto Lodovico Massimiliano Emanuele Maria di Savoia [Savoy-Genoa], Duke of Pistoia (Inspector of Camps of Mobile Troops) /42 Gen. Designate His Royal Highness Prince Adalberto di Savoia [Savoy-Genoa], Duke of Bergamo (?) 09/02/43 LG Mario Arisio (?) 09/08/43 disbanded.

[NOTE: also listed /41 LG Francesco Zingales (acting; Commanding General, XX Army Corps) /42]

A.   **Chief of Staff, Seventh Army** (06/10/40): MG Giuseppe Amico (Commanding General, 64th "Catanzaro" Infantry Division) /41? unknown? /43 MG Paolo Berardi (Commanding General, XXI Army Corps) /43 MG Raffaele Relligra (/45, Director-General of Administration, Ministry of Defense) 09/08/43 dissolved.

B.   *Components* - **Seventh Army** (06/10/40):
       1.   **VII Army Corps**
       2.   **VIII Army Corps**

C.   *Components* - **Seventh Army** (09/43):
       1.   **IX Army Corps** (Italy heel)
       2.   **XIX Army Corps** (Salerno area)
       3.   **XXXI Army Corps** (Italy's toe)
       4.   **II General Headquarters**

D.   **Artillery, Seventh Army** (06/10/40): unknown? /43 MG Giovanni Battista Guiccione (10/43, acting Commanding General, LI Army Corps) 09/08/43 dissolved.

Eighth Army (06/10/40, part of Italian Army Group East; 07/42, from **Expeditionary Force**, Soviet Union; 12/10/42, part of German Army Group "B"; 03/43, virtually destroyed in Soviet Union; rebuilding in northern Italy (South Tyrol and Venezia [Venice])): **Eighth Army (#1)** 06/10/40? LG His Royal Highness Prince Adalberto di Savoia [Savoy-Genoa], Duke of Bergamo (Commander-in-Chief, Italian Expeditionary Force) **Italian Expeditionary Force** Gen. Designate His Royal Highness Prince Adalberto di Savoia [Savoy-Genoa], Duke of Bergamo (01/01/43, Commander-in-Chief, Seventh Army) 07/42 redesignated **Eighth Army (#2)** 07/42 Gen. Italo Gariboldi (German prisoner-of-war; /44, condemned to death as a traitor by Social Republic of Italy; /44, liberated by the Allies)

09/08/43 disbanded.
- A. **Chief of Staff, Eighth Army**: /40 BG Giovanni Battista Oxilia (Artillery Commander, Fourth Army) /42 MG Bruno Malaguti (Commanding General, 52nd "Torino [Turin]" Semi-Motorized Infantry Division) /42 BG Lorenzo Richieri (to /45, German prisoner-of-war) 09/08/43 dissolved.
- B. *Components - Eighth Army* (06/10/40):
    1. **VI Army Corps**
    2. **XIV Army Corps**
    3. *Support Units* **(regiment sized listed only)**
        - a. **9th Army Artillery Regiment**: /34 Col. Guido Cipriani
        - b. **30th Corps Artillery Regiment**
        - c. **201st Motorized Artillery Regiment**
- C. *Components - Eighth Army* (08/08/42):
    1. **II Army Corps**
    2. **XXXV Alpini Corps**
    3. **Alpini [Alpine] Corps**
    4. **156th "Vicenza" (Security) Infantry Division**
    5. **"Barbo" Cavalry Brigade:**
    6. **Air Force Command, Eighth Army** (brigade status)
    7. **Croatian Blackshirt (CCNN) Legion** (regiment status)
- D. *Components - Eighth Army* (11/42):
    1. *German XXIX Army Corps*
    2. *German XXIV Panzer Corps*
    3. **II Army Corps**
    4. **XXXV Alpini Corps**
- E. *Components - Eighth Army* (09/43):
    1. **XIII Army Corps**
    2. **XXIV Army Corps**
    3. **XXXV Alpini Corps**
- F. **Artillery Commander, Eighth Army**: 08/08/42? MG Mario Balotta (?) 09/08/43 dissolved.
    1. **9th Army Artillery Regiment**
    2. **201st Motorized Artillery Regiment**: 08/08/42? Col. Enrice Altavilla 09/08/43 dissolved.
    3. **4th Artillery Group** (becomes **4th Anti-Aircraft Artillery Regiment**): /40? Col. Gastano Alagia (Commandant, School for Non-Commissioned Officers of Artillery) /41? Col. Paolo Fantazzini 08/08/42? Col. Giuseppe di Marino 09/08/43 dissolved.
    4. **Cavalry Artillery Regiment**: 08/08/42? Col. D. Montella 09/08/43 dissolved.
- G. **Engineer Commander, Eighth Army**: 08/08/42? MG Arnaldo Foriero 09/08/43 dissolved.
- H. **Chemical Troops, Eighth Army**: LCol. Cesiro Mischi 09/08/43 dissolved.
- I. **Aviation Commander, Eighth Army**: 08/01/42? BG Enrico Pezzi $_{[RIAF]}$ (missing in action, Russia) /42 unknown? 09/08/43 dissolved.
- J. **Intendant General (Quartermaster), Italian Expeditionary Force** (07/42): BG Carlo Biglioni (Commanding General, 9th "Pasubio" Semi-Motorized Infantry

Division) /42 unknown? 09/08/43 dissolved.
1. **Transport Command, Quartermaster, Eighth Army**: 08/08/42? LCol. A. Gualano 09/08/43 dissolved.
2. **Medical Command, Quartermaster, Eighth Army**: 08/08/42? Col. Dr. N. Maugeri /42 Col. Prof. Federico Bocchetti (killed in an air crash) 12/29/42 unknown? 09/08/43 dissolved.
3. **Commissariat Command (Rations Administration), Quartermaster, Eighth Army**: 08/08/42? Col. F. Pirro 09/08/43 dissolved.
4. **Line of Communication Command, Quartermaster, Eighth Army**: 08/08/42? BG G. Musinu (?) 09/08/43 dissolved.
5. **Veterinary Command, Quartermaster, Eighth Army**: 08/08/42? unknown? 09/08/43 dissolved.
6. **Motor Vehicle Command, Quartermaster, Eighth Army**: 08/08/42? unknown? 09/08/43 dissolved.
7. **Artillery Support Service, Quartermaster, Eighth Army**: 08/08/42? Col. G. Bottari 09/08/43 dissolved.
8. **Engineer Support Service, Quartermaster, Eighth Army**: 08/08/42? Col. V. Caniglia 09/08/43 dissolved.
9. **Chemical Support Service, Quartermaster, Eighth Army**: 08/08/42? Maj. G. Rosa 09/08/43 dissolved.
10. **Recovery Maintenance Support Service, Quartermaster, Eighth Army**: 08/08/42? Col. F. Graziani 09/08/43 dissolved.
11. **Field Postal Support Service, Quartermaster, Eighth Army**: 08/08/42? Maj. A. Zocchi 09/08/43 dissolved.
12. **Requisitioning Support Service, Quartermaster, Eighth Army**: 08/08/42? unknown? 09/08/43 dissolved.
13. **Roads Support Service, Quartermaster, Eighth Army**: 08/08/42? Maj. A. Perdomo 09/08/43 dissolved.

K. **German General with the Italian Eighth Army**: 08/27/42 Gdl Kurt von Tippelskirch [German] (Commanding General, German, XII Army Corps) 02/01/43 dissolved.
1. **Chief of Staff, German General with the Italian Eighth Army**: 09/18/42 Col. Walter Nagel [German] 01/05/43 MG Dr. phil. Hans Speidel [German] (Chief of Staff, German Army Group South) 02/05/43 dissolved.

Ninth Army (04/07/39, part of Army Group East; 04/05/41?, part of Army Group Albania; 05/41, also known as **General Headquarters Albania and East**; occupied Montenegro and Albania; /42, designated **General Headquarters Albania**; /43, redesignated **General Headquarters East**): /40 LG Mario Vercellino (Aide-de-Camp to the King) 02/41 Gen. Alessandro Pirzio-Biroli (Commanding General, Headquarters Albania) 10/41/42 redesignated **General Headquarters Albania** [see entry]; reformed **Ninth Army (#2)** 07/43 LG Lorenzo Dalmazzo (German prisoner-of-war) 10/43 disbanded.
A. **Chief of Staff, Ninth Army**: /40 BG Guglielmo Spicacci (Commanding General, 18th "Messina" Infantry Division) /42
B. *Components - Ninth Army* (04/07/41):
1. **III Army Corps**
2. **XIV Army Corps**
3. **XVII Army Corps**

        4.   **XXVI Army Corps**
        5.   **Librazhd Sector** (corps status)
C.   ***Components - Ninth Army*** (09/43):
        1.   **General Headquarters Albania**
        2.   **General Headquarters Montenegro**
D.   **Engineer-in-Chief, Ninth Army** (04/7/39): unknown? /43 MG Giuseppe Piacentini (to /45, German prisoner-of-war) /43 MG Ugo Buoncompagni (to /45, German prisoner-of-war; /48, Commanding General, IV Territorial Defense Command) 09/08/43 dissolved.
E.   **Royal Carabinieri, Ninth Army**: unknown? /43 BG Silvio Robino (to /45, German prisoner-of-war) 09/08/43 dissolved.

Tenth Army (06/10/40, part of General Headquarters North Africa; Libya; Egypt; 02/41, destroyed in Egypt and Libya; 02/41, destroyed): /39 Gen. Francesco Guidi (Member, Commission for the Armed Forces, Senate) /40 LG Mario Berti (sick leave) 11/40 LG Italo Gariboldi (acting) [+ Deputy Commander, General Headquarters North Africa] 12/40 LG Giuseppe Tellera (killed in action) 02/41 destroyed.
A.   ***Components - Tenth Army*** (06/10/40):
        1.   **XXI Army Corps**
        2.   **XXII Army Corps**
        3.   **Tobruk Fortress** (Corps Status)
        4.   **1st Libyan Infantry Division**
        5.   **XXX Border Guard Sector** (HQ: Berdia; brigade status)
        6.   **Banghazi Fortress** (brigade status)
B.   ***Components - Tenth Army*** (09/43):
        1.   **Berdia Corps**
        2.   **XXII Army Corps**
        3.   **1st CCNN Division**
        4.   **2nd CCNN Division**
        5.   **3rd CCNN Division**
        6.   **4th CCNN Division**
        7.   **62nd Colonial Division**
        8.   **63rd Colonial Division**
        9.   **64th Colonial Division**
        10.   **Maletti Armor Group**
        11.   **Babini Armor Group**
C.   **Engineer-in-Chief, Tenth Army**: /40 BG Romolo La Strucci (British priosner-of-war) /40 unknown? 02/41 dissolved.

Eleventh Army (11/40, from **Third Army**; part of Army Group East; also known as **General Headquarters Greece**; Greece; also designated **General Headquarters Greece**, under Gen. Geloso): Gen. Carlo Geloso /41 LG Sebastiano Visconti Prasca (acting; /43 to /45, German prisoner-of-war) 04/41 Gen. Carlo Geloso [+ /42, Military-Governor, Greece; to /45, German prisoner-of-war; /45, interned by the Soviets) 06/43 Gen. Carlo Vecchiarelli (to /45, German prisoner-of-war) 09/08/43 disbanded.
A.   **Chief of Staff, Eleventh Army** (11/40): unknown? /43 MG Cesare Gandini (to /45,

German prisoner-of-war; /49 Commanding General, "Cremona" Infantry Division) 09/08/43 dissolved.
- B. ***Components - Eleventh Army*** (11/40):
  1. 8 divisions
  2. ***Support Units*** (regiment sized listed only)
     a. 7th "Milano [Milan]" Cavalry Regiment
- C. ***Components - Eleventh Army*** (07/43):
  1. **III Army Corps**
  2. **VIII Army Corps**
  3. **XXIV Army Corps**
  4. **11th Division**
- D. ***Components - Eleventh Army*** (09/43):
  1. **III Army Corps**
  2. **VIII Army Corps**
  3. ***German LXVIII Army Corps***
- E. **Artillery, Eleventh Army** (11/40): unknown? /42 MG Giovanni Fontana (?) /43 MG Camillo Zarri (to /45, German prisoner-of-war) 09/08/43 dissolved.
- F. **Engineer-in-Chief, Eleventh Army** (11/40): unknown? /42 BG Auturo Fortunato (?) 09/08/43 dissolved.
  1. **Engineer Commander & Military Governor, Volo, Greece**: 10/42 BG Giovanni Nicotra (?) 09/08/43 dissolved.
- G. **Intendent-General [Quartermaster], Eleven Army** (11/40): unknown? /43 BG Attilio Calendi (to 45, German prisoner-of-war) 09/08/43 dissolved.
- H. **Inspector of Intendance, Eleven Army** (11/40): unknown? /43 BG Guiseppe Cerrutti (to /45, German prisoner-of-war) 09/08/43 dissolved.
- I. **Transport Service, Eleven Army** (11/40): unknown? /43 BG Alessandro Vaccaneo (to /45, German prisoner-of-war; /45, executed by the Germans) 09/08/43 dissolved.
- J. **Military Advocate [Judicial Branch], Greece** (11/40): unknown? /42 BG Numzio Caldone (?) 09/08/43 dissolved.
  1. **Military Police, Athens**: /41 MG (Res.) Luigi Ganini (?) 09/08/43 dissolved.
- K. **President, Military Tribunal, Eleventh Army** (11/40): unknown? /43 BG Mario Ferrannini (to /45, German prisoner-of-war) 09/08/43 dissolved.
- L. **Royal Carabinieri, Eleventh Army** (11/40): unknown? /43 BG Francesco Mazzerelli (to /45, German prisoner-of-war) 09/08/43 dissolved.
- M. **Commanding Black Shirt Units, Eleven Army** (11/40): MG Enzo Emilio Galbiati (Commanding Black Shirt Group, Greece) /41 redesignated **Commanding Black Shirt Group, Greece** /41 MG Enzo Emilio Galbiati (Chief of Staff, Voluntary Militia for National Security) /41 unknown? 09/08/43 dissolved.
- N. ***Area and Sector Commanders***
  1. **Commanding General, Atene [Athens] Area** (11/40): unknown? /43 BG Umberto Broccoli (to /45, German prisoner-of-war) 09/08/43 dissolved.
  2. **Commanding General, Argolide Sector, Greece** (11/40): unknown? /43 MG Italo Caracciolo (to /45, German prisoner-of-war) 09/08/43 dissolved.
  3. **Commanding General, Argolide-Kossovo Sector, Greece-Serbia** (11/40): unknown? 04/43 Federico d'Arle (?) 09/08/43 dissolved.

4. **Commanding General, Northern Attica, Greece** (11/40): unknown? /43 BG Augusto Moretto (German prisoner-of-war; 09/43, joins Social Republic of Italy; 10/43, Commanding General, 204th Regional Militray Tribunal Trisete) 09/08/43 dissolved.

O. **At Disposal of, Attached to, or on Special Duties with General Headquarters Greece**:
/42 (attached to) BG Giovanni Fava

Army of the Alps (Italy): /38? LG His Royal Highness Crown Prince Umberto Piemonte [di Savoia], the Crown Prince of Italy (Piedmont) and Viceroy (Commander-in-Chief, Army Group West) /39

Tripolitania Defense Command (/40; 10/23/42, part of Italian Armed Forces Supreme Command of Libya; 05/43, dissolved): /41 LG Carlo Vecchiarelli (Commanding General, XX Army Corps) /41 MG Mario Soldarelli [acting; + Commanding General, 60th "Sabratha" Infantry Division] /42 LG Enrico Armando 05/43 disbanded.
  A. *Components* - **Tripolitania Defense Command** (10/23/42)
    1. **Tripoli Fortress** (corps status)
    2. **80th "La Spezia" Airlanding Division**
    3. **Sirte Sector, Tripolitania Defense Command** (division status)
    4. **Homs Sector, Tripolitania Defense Command** (division status)
    5. **Garian Sector, Tripolitania Defense Command** (division status)
    6. **Zuara Sector, Tripolitania Defense Command** (division status)

Cyrenaica Defense Command (/40; 10/23/42, part of Italian Armed Forces Supreme Command of Libya): /42 LG Giuseppe Cesare Ivaldi (?) 05/42 disbanded.
  A. *Components* - **Cyrenaica Defense Command** (10/23/42)
    1. **Benghazi Fortress** (division status)
    2. **16th "Pistoia" Motorized Infantry Division**
    3. **Agedabia-Jalo Sector, Cyrenaica Defense Command** (division status)
    4. **Barce Sector, Cyrenaica Defense Command** (division status)
    5. **Jarabub-Siwa Sector, Cyrenaica Defense Command** (division status)
    6. **Derna Fortress** (division status)
    7. **Tobruk Fortress** (division status)

Italian Armed Forces Logistics Command of Libya [Delegazione Africa Settentrionale]: 10/23/42? MG Count Curio Barbasetti di Prun (Commanding General, XIV Army Corps) 05/43 dissolved.
  A. *Components* - **Italian Armed Forces Logistics Command of Libya** (10/23/42)
    1. **1st Delease Support Corps** (Tripoli, Libya; responsible for logistics Tripolitania Defense Command):
    2. **2nd Delease Support Corps** (Benghasi, Libya; responsible for logistics Cyrenaica Defense Command):
    3. **3rd Delease Support Corps** (Mersa Matruh, Libya; responsible for logistics the three combat corps):
    4. **Intendant-General, North Africa [Intendenza Africa Settentrionale**

Corps]: 10/23/42? BG Vittorio Palma (?   ) 09/08/43 dissolved.
a. **Transport Department**
b. **Supply Department**
c. **Medical Department**
d. **Motor Vehicle Department**
e. **Rear Area Security (Lines of Communication) Department**

General Headquarters Units That Approached Army Status

General Headquarters Corsica (unknown?; 09/43, part of Fifth Army, Army Groups Italy): unknown?
- A. *Components - General Headquarters Corsica* (09/43):
  1. VII Army Corps
- B. **Commandant, Bastia, Corsica**: unknown? /42 BG Rodolfo Stivala (Engineer-in-Chief, II Territorial Defense Command) /43 unknown?

General Headquarters Albania (04/39; HQ: Tirana, Albania; part of Ninth Army; 05/41, incorporated into Italy; 09/08/43, disarmed by Germans): LG Alfredo Guzzoni (Commander-in-Chief, Army Group East) /39 MG Matteo Roux (acting; Commanding General, 3rd "Ravenna" Infantry Division) /40 LG Sebastiano Visconti Prasca [+ acting Commander-in-Chief, Army Group East (#1)] (Commanding General, XXVI Army Corps) 12/40 Mar. of Italy Ugo Cavallero [+ Chief of the Supreme General Staff & Commander-in-Chief, Army Group East (#1)] 12/40 BG Viceroy Francesco Jacomoni (?) 10/41 Gen. Alessandro Pirzio-Biroli (Commanding General, General Headquarters, Montenegro & Governor of Montenegro) 10/41 LG Camillo Mercalli (/43, Commanding General, XXXI Army Corps) /42 LG Lorenzo Dalmazzo /43 Gen. [Rtetired '39] Alberto Pariani (Ambassador to Germany) /43 LG Lorenzo Dalmazzo (Commander General, Ninth Army) 07/43 disbanded.
- A. **Deputy Commander, General Headquarters Albania** (04/39): MG Giovanni Messe (Commanding General, Celere (Cavalry {Fast}) Army Corps) /40 unknown? 09/08/43 dissolved.
- B. **Chief of Staff, General Headquarters Albania**: unknown? /40 BG Salvatore Bartiromo (?) /41 MG Alberto Ferrero (Commanding General, 4th "Cuneense" Alpine Division) /41 BG Umberto Ricagno (Commanding General, 3rd "Julia" Alpine Division) 11/41 MG Carlo Tucci (German prisoner-of-war) 09/08/43 dissolved
- C. *Components - General Headquarters Albania* (06/10/40):
  1. XXV Army Corps
- D. *Components - General Headquarters Albania* (09/43):
  1. IV Army Corps
  2. XXV Army Corps
  3. Fieri Sub-Sector: /43 BG Salvatore D'Agostino (to /45, German prisoner-of-war) 09/08/43 dissolved.
- E. **Artillery, General Headquarters Albania** (04/39): unknown? /43 BG Alberto De Agazio (German prisoner-of-war; .43, died in prison) 09/08/43 dissolved.
- F. **Cavalry (Celere) Units, Albania** (04/39): unknown? /43 Col. Francesco Mayer (to /45, German prisoner-of-war) 09/08/43 dissolved.
- G. **Technical Troops, Albania** (04/39): unknown? /43 MG Giambattista Zanuccoli (?) 09/08/43 dissolved.
- H. **Royal Carabinieri Albania** (04/39): MG Crispino Agostinucci [+ Deputy Commander-in-Chief, Royal Carabinieri] /41 BG Silvio Robino (Commanding General, Royal Carabinieri, Ninth Army) /43 BG Giovanni Scopelliti (to /45, German prisoner-of-war) 09/08/43 dissolved.

I. **President, War Tribunal, Albania** (04/39): unknown? 05/42? BG Feruccio Paganuzzi 09/08/43 dissolved.
J. **Military Advocate, Albania** (04/39): unknown? /41 BG Salvatore Scordato (?) 09/08/43 dissolved.
K. **President, Regional Commission Albanian Frontier** (04/39): unknown? 03/42 BG Giovanni Grassi (?) 09/08/43 dissolved.
L. **Albanian Fascist Militia** (04/39): /41 BG G. Ballabio [MVSN] (?) 12/42 BG Giuseppe Volante [MVSN] (joins Social Republic of Italy; Commandant, National Republican Guard Non-Commissioned Officers School, Social Republic of Italy) 09/08/43 dissolved.
M. **Commandant, Durazzo** (04/39): unknown? 09/42 BG Ottavio Peano [MVSN] (joins the Social Republis of Italy; 10/43, Commanding General, 203rd Regional Military Command Padova) /43 BG Emilio Peano (to /45, German prisoner-of-war) 09/08/43 dissolved.
N. **At Disposal of, Attached to, or on Special Duties with General Headquarters Albania**:
06/41? MG Francesco Zani (Commanding General, 23rd "Ferrara" Infantry Division) /42

General Headquarters Montenegro (10/41; HQ: Cetinje, Montenegro; part of Ninth Army): Gen. Alessandro Pirzio-Biroli [+ Governor of Montenegro] (?) 09/08/43 disbanded.
A. *Components - General Headquarters Montenegro* (09/43):
1. **VI Army Corps**
2. **XIV Army Corps**

General Headquarters Rome (07/43, for defense of Rome): LG Mario Roatta [+ Army Chief of Staff] (dismissed) 09/09/43 Mar. [Retired] Enrico Caviglia.
A. *Components - General Headquarters Rome* (09/43):
1. **XVII Army Corps**
2. **XX Motorized Corps**
3. **Rome Corps**

General Headquarters Sardinia (1943; 09/43, part of Army Groups Italy): LG Antonio Basso (Commanding General, IX Army Corps) /43 MG Guido Boselli (Commanding General, IX Territorial Defense Command) or MG Giovanni Magli (?) /44 MG Carlo Petra di Caccuri (?) /45 MG Brunetto Brunetti (acting) /45.
A. *Components - General Headquarters Sardinia* (09/43):
1. **XIII Army Corps**
2. **XXX Army Corps**
3. 7 divisions
4. *German 90th Motorized Division*
B. **Group South [Sud], Sardinia**: /43 BG Carlo Ticchioni (Commanding General, "Granatieri" Division) /44

Fascist Militia (army status)

National Security Volunteer Militia [Milizia Voluntaria per la Sicurezza Nazionale (MVSN) {Fascist Militia}] (or commonly known as the **Black Shirts (Camicie Nere (CCNN))** (HQ Rome, Italy)
Director, National Security Volunteer Militia (MVSN): 04/43? MG Allessandro Melchiori [MVSN]
Chief of Staff, National Security Volunteer Militia (MVSN) (Commander, National Security Volunteer Militia): /35 MG Luigi Russo [MVSN] (Undersecretary to President, Council of Ministers) /39 MG Achille Starace [MVSN] (/45, executed by Partisans) /41 MG Sergio Biraghi [MVSN] (?) /41 MG Enzo Emilio Galbiati [MVSN] (arrested) /43 MG Giuseppe Conticelli [MVSN] 43 vacant 10/28/43 LG Quirino Armellini (Commanding General, V Territorial Defense Command) /45

- A. **Operations Section, National Security Volunteer Militia**: /39 MG Lorenzo Allegretti [MVSN]
- B. **Inspector-General of National Security Volunteer Militia [MVSN]**: /41? MG Benesperando Luraschi [MVSN]
    1. **Fascist Party Inspectors**:
       /41? BG Ennio Barberini [MVSN],
       /41? BG Sandro Bonamici [MVSN],
- C. **Training, National Security Volunteer Militia [MVSN]**:
    1. **Training Staff, Headquarters National Security Volunteer Militia [MVSN]**: 01/42 BG Count Diego Salazar y Munatores
- D. **Anti-Aircraft & Coast Defense Command [Comando Milizia Contaerei e Artiglieria Marittima]** (HQ: Rome; corps status): /43 MG (Res.) Count Alberto Galamini [MVSN]
- E. **Forest Militia [Milizia Forestale]** (HQ: Rome, Italy; division status): /35 Col. Augusto Agostini [MVSN] (joins Italian Social Republic; Commanding General National Republican Mountain & Forest Guard) /43 MG Guido Felici [MVSN] (Regional Inspector of National Republican Guard Marche, Social Republic of Italy) /44
- F. **Railway Militia [Milizia Ferroviaria]** (HQ: Rome, Italy; division status): /32 Col. Vittorio Raffaldi [MVSN] (joins Social Republic of Italy; 09/43, Head, Inspectorate of National Republican Railway Guard, Social Republic of Italy) 09/08/43 disbanded.
- G. **Harbor Militia [Milizia Portuaria]** (HQ: Rome, Italy, division status): 06/10/40? unknown? 03/43 BG Giuseppe Visconti [MVSN]
- H. **University Militia [Milizia Universitaria]** (HQ: Rome, Italy; division status): unknown?
- I. **Frontier Militia [Milizia Confinaria]** (HQ: Rome, Italy; division status): 06/10/40? unknown? /43 BG Antonio Cobianchi
- J. **Post and Telegraph Militia [Milizia Postelegrafica]** (HQ: Rome, Italy; division status): 06/10/40? unknown? /43 MG Rodolfo Tanese [MSVN] (joins Social Republic of Italy; 10/43, Commanding General, Republican Harbor Gurad, Social Republic of Italy) 09/08/43 disbanded.
- K. **Roads Militia [Milizia Stradadle]** (HQ: Rome, Italy; division status): /39 MG Ugo Leonardi [MVSN] (Commanding General, National Republican Roads Guard, Social Republic of Italy) 09/08/43

L.	**Construction General, National Security Volunteer Militia (MVSN) & Military Judge**: /41? BG Torello Dagnino
M.	**Military Advocate (Judical Branch), Rome HQ National Security Volunteer Militia**: BG (Res.) Sebastiano Cascella (?) /41? BG Giuseppe Ciardi
N.	**Procurator General of Special State Defense, National Security Volunteer Militia (MVSN)**: /41 MG Nicholas De Nobili [MVSN] /41 MG Francesco Dessy [MVSN]
O.	**Head, Supply Service, National Security Volunteer Militia (MVSN)**: /40 MG Count Giandavide Elti di Rodeano [MVSN]
P.	**President, Disabled Ex-Serviceman's Institute**: BG Giovanni Baccarini [MVSN]
Q.	**Association of Alpine [Alpini] Veterans**: 04/43 MG Alessandro Tarabin [MSVN]
R.	**National Councillor, National Security Volunteer Militia (MVSN)**: 07/41 MG Francesco Sacco [MVSN] 12/42 MG Nicola Sansanelli [MVSN]
S.	**At Disposal of, Attached to, or on Special Duties with National Security Volunteer Militia (MVSN)**: /41? (attached to) MG Roberto Farinacci [MVSN] /41? (At disposal) MG Georgio Vaccaro [MVSN]
T.	***Blackshirt [CCNN (Camicie Nere)] Zones*** (division status)

1. **1st CCNN (Camicie Nere) Zone**:
2. **2nd CCNN (Camicie Nere) Zone**:
3. **3rd CCNN (Camicie Nere) Zone**:
4. **4th CCNN (Camicie Nere) Zone**:
5. **5th CCNN (Camicie Nere) Zone**:
6. **6th CCNN (Camicie Nere) Zone**:
7. **7th CCNN (Camicie Nere) Zone**:
8. **8th CCNN (Camicie Nere) Zone**:
9. **9th CCNN (Camicie Nere) Zone**:
10. **10th CCNN (Camicie Nere) Zone**:
11. **11th CCNN (Camicie Nere) Zone**:
12. **12th CCNN (Camicie Nere) Zone**:
13. **13th CCNN (Camicie Nere) Zone**:
14. **14th CCNN (Camicie Nere) Zone**:
15. **Albanian Fascist Militia**:

Army Corps, Air Forces, and Fleets

Army Corps

I Army Corps (pre-war; 06/10/40, part of the Fourth Army, Army Group West; occupation duty; HQ: Sospel, France; Avignon, France; Grasse, France): /35 MG Ruggero Santini (Governor of Somaliland) /36 unknown? 06/10/40? LG Carlo Vecchiarelli (/41, Commanding General, Tripolitania Command) /40 MG Count Curio Barbasetti di Prun (Chief of Staff, Headquarters, North Africa) /42 MG Giovanni Magli [+ Vice Chief of the Supreme General Staff] (Commanding General, VII Army Corps) 01/01/43? LG Federico Romero (?) 09/08/43 disbanded.

A. **Components - I Army Corps** (06/10/40)
   1. **1st "Superga" Infantry Division**
   2. **24th "Pinerolo" Infantry Division**
   3. **59h "Cagliari" Infantry Division**
   4. **VIII Border Guard Sector** (HQ: Bardonecchia, Italy; brigade status)
   5. **IX Border Guard Sector** (HQ: Susa, Italy; brigade status)
   6. *Support Units* **(regiment sized listed only)**
      a. **1st Corps Artillery Regiment**
B. **Artillery Commander, I Army Corps**: /37 BG Paolo Berardi (Commanding General, 2nd "Varaita-Po" Alpine Brigade) 06/10/40 unknown? 09/08/43 disolved.
C. **Eingineer-in-Chief, I Army Corps**: unknown? 05/42? BG Francesco Ravera
D. **Military Judge, I Army Corps**: 04/11/42? BG (Res.) Camillo Franzini
E. **At Disposal of, Attached to, or on Special Duties with I Army Corps**:
   07/41 (special duties) BG Vittorio Grosso
   07/41 (attached to) MG Mario Zaccone

II Army Corps (pre-war; 06/10/40, part of the First Army; 08/08/42?, Eighth Army, Soviet Union; 12/42, largely destroyed; remnants withdrawn to Italy; 09/08/43, still rebuilding at Armistice; part of Fifth Army): /35 LG Pietro Maravigna (Commanding General, IX Army Corps) /36 LG Ettore Bastico (Commanding General, Volunteer Corps of Troops to Spain) /37 unknown? /40 LG Francesco Rossi (Chief of Staff, Chief of the Supreme General Staff) /40 LG Francesco Bertini /40 MG Edoardo Nebbia [+ Commanding General, 3rd "Ravenna" Infantry Division] (acting) /40 LG Francesco Bertini (retired?) /40 LG Giovanni Zanghieri (Commanding General, XVII Army Corps) 08/08/42? LG Gabrielle Nasci (Commanding General, Alpine [Alpini] Corps) /42 LG Gervasio Bitossi (acting Commanding General, XX Army Corps) 01/01/43 LG Arnaldo Forgiero (Commanding General, II Territorial Defense Command) /43 LG Vittorio Sogno (Allied prisoner-of-war, captured un Tunisia) 09/08/43 disbanded.

A. **Chief of Staff, II Army Corps**: Col. Ugo Almici 09/08/43 dissolved.
B. **Components - II Army Corps** (06/10/40)
   1. **4th "Livorno" Infantry Division**
   2. **33rd "Acqui" Infantry Division**
   3. **36th "Forlì" Infantry Division**
   4. **4th "Cuneense" Mountain Infantry Division**

5. **2nd Alpini Brigade**
6. **III Border Guard Sector** (HQ: Vinadio, Italy; brigade status)
7. **IV Border Guard Sector** (HQ: Saluzzo, Italy; brigade status)
8. *Support Units* **(regiment sized listed only)**
   a. **2nd Corps Artillery Regiment**: 08/08/42? Col. E. Grimaldi 09/08/43 dissolved.
C. **Artillery Commander, II Army Corps**: 08/08/42? BG Mario Martorrelli (?) 12/10/42? BG Italo Giglio (to /45, German prisoner-of-war) 09/08/43 dissolved.
D. **Engineer Commander, II Army Corps**: 08/08/42? BG Balilla Rima (Commandant, Royal Academy of Artillery & Engineering) /43 unknown? 09/08/43 dissolved.
E. **At Disposal of, Attached to, or on Special Duties with II Army Corps**: 12/01/41 (special duties) Col. (Res.) Renzo Vaccari (at disposal, 40th Territroial District) /43

III Army Corps (pre-war; 06/10/40, part of the First Army; occupation duty in Albania; 04/05/41?, part of Ninth Army; HQ: Thebes, Greece; Volos, Greece; 07/43, part of Eleventh Army): /35 MG Ettore Bastico (Commanding General, II Army Corps) /36 LG Augusto Grassi (to reserve) /38 LG Ruggero Santini (Senator & Vice President, Commission of the Affairs of Italian Africa, Senate) 03/25/39 LG Antero Canale (Commanding General, XVI Army Corps) /40 LG Sebastiano Visconti Prasca (Commander-in-Chief, General Headquarters Albania & acting Commander-in-Chief, Army Group East (#1)) 06/40 LG His Royal Highness Prince Adalberto di Savoia [Savoy-Genoa], Duke of Bergamo (Commander-in-Chief, Eighth Army) 06/10/40? MG Mario Arisio (Commanding General, XII Army Corps) /41 MG Vittorio Asinari di Bernezzo (/43, Commanding General, I Territorial Defense Command) /41 LG Angelo Rossi (to /45, German prisoner-of-war) 06/43 LG [Retired /40?] Camillo Rossi (retired?) /43 LG Luigi Manzi (?) 09/08/43 disbanded.
A. *Components* - **III Army Corps** (06/10/40)
   1. **3rd "Ravenna" Infantry Division**
   2. **6th "Cuneo" Infantry Division**
   3. **1st Alpini Brigade**
   4. **II Border Guard Sector** (HQ: Cuneo, Italy; brigade status)
   5. *Support Units* **(regiment sized listed only)**
      a. **3rd Corps Artillery Regiment**: /41? Col. Attilo Lazzarini (Commanding General, 226th Coastal Division) /42 unknown? 09/08/43 dissolved.
B. **Artillery, III Army Corps** (06/10/40): unknown? /43 BG Luigi Jalla (German prisoner-of-war; /43, joins Social Republic of Italy; Commanding General, 210th Regional Military Command Genova [Genoa]) 09/08/43 dissolved.

IV Army Corps (/36, Ethiopia, East Africa; 06/10/40, part of the Fourth Army; occupation duty; HQ: Berat, Albania; Durazzo, Albania): **IV (East African) Army Corps (#1)**: /36 LG Ezio Babbini (?) /37 disbanded; reformed as **Bolzano Corps** /35 LG Francesco Guidi (Commander-in-Chief, Tenth Army) /38 LG His Royal Highness Prince Filiberto Lodovico Massimiliano Emanuele Maria di Savoia [Savoy-Genoa], Duke of Pistoia (06/10/40, Commander-in-Chief, Seventh Army) /39 LG Mario Gamaleri (/40, Commanding General, XVIII Army Corps) /39 redesignated **IV Army Corps (#2)** /39 MG Camillo Mercalli (Commanding General, HQ Albania) /41 LG Carlo Spatocco /42 MG Pietro Maggiani (acting; Commanding General, 6th "Cuneo" Infantry Division) /42 LG Carlo Spatocco (to /45,

German prisoner-of-war; /45, executed by the Germans) /43 MG Carlo Rivolta (acting) 09/08/43 disbanded.
- A. **Chief of Staff, IV Army Corps** (06/10/40): Col. Guilio Martinat (Chief of Staff, Alpine Army Corps) /40 unknown? 09/08/43 dissolved.
- B. *Components - IV Army Corps* (06/10/40)
    1. **2nd "Sforzesca" Infantry Division**
    2. **26th "Assietta" Infantry Division**
    3. **VII Border Guard Sector** (HQ: Cesana, Italy; brigade status)
    4. *Support Units* **(regiment sized listed only)**
        a. **4th Corps Artillery Regiment**
- C. **Artillery, IV Army Corps** (06/10/40): unknown? /42 Col. Bartolomeo Pedrotti (Commanding General, 225th Coastal Division) /42 unknown? 09/08/43 dissolved.
- D. **Engineer-in-Chief, IV Army Corps** (06/10/40): unknown? /42 MG Carlo Tessiore (to /45, German prisoner-of-war; /45, died in Russian hospital following liberation) /43 BG Mario Granozio (to /45, German prisoner-of-war) 09/08/43 dissolved.

V Army Corps (06/10/40, part of Second Army; occupation duty; HQ: Susak, Slovenia; Crikvenica, Croatia; Cirquenizza, Croatia; 03/43, part of Second Army): /38 MG Carlo Geloso (Commanding General, IX Army Corps) /38 MG Italo Gariboldi (Commander-in-Chief, Fifth Army) /39 MG Riccardo Balocco (/42, special duties, War Minister) /39 LG Carlo Vecchiarelli (Commanding General, I Army Corps) /40 LG Benedetto Fiorenzuoli (?) /41 LG Renato Coturri (?) 01/01/43? LG Alessandro Gloria (Commanding General, XXXV Army Corps) /43 LG Antonio Scuero (retired for age) 02/12/43 unknown? 09/08/43 disbanded.
- A. **Chief of Staff, V Army Corps**: /37 Col. Guglielmo Spicacci (Artillery Commander, VI Army Corps) /39 unknown? /41 BG Clemente Primieri (Chief of Staff, Second Army) /43 unknown? 09/08/43 dissolved.
- B. *Components - V Army Corps* (06/10/40)
    1. **12th "Sassari" Infantry Division**
    2. **15th "Bergamo" Infantry Division**
    3. **XXV Border Guard Sector** (HQ: S. Pietro del Caorso; brigade status)
    4. **XXVI Border Guard Sector** (HQ: Villa del Nevoso; brigade status)
    5. **XXVII Border Guard Sector** (HQ: Fiume; brigade status)
    6. *Support Units* **(regiment sized listed only)**
        a. **5th Corps Artillery Regiment**
        b. **1st Army Artillery Regiment** (added by 04/05/41)
        c. **10th Army Artillery Regiment** (added by 04/05/41)
- C. **Artillery, V Army Corps** (06/10/43): unknown? /43 BG Guido Masserano (German prisoner-of-war) 09/08/43 dissolved.
- D. **Engineer-in-Chief, 5th Army Corps** (06/10/40): BG Luigi Fogliani (Engineer-in-Chief, Second Army) /43 BG Agostino Garavano (to /45, German Prisoner-of-war) 09/08/43 dissolved.

VI Army Corps (06/10/40, part of Eighth Army; occupation duty; HQ: Dubrovnik, Yugoslavia; Ragusa, Croatia): /39 LG Ezlo Rosi (/41, Commander-in-Chief, Army of the Po) /40 LG Lorenzo Dalmazzo (Commanding General, Headquarters Albania) /42 LG Ugo

Santovito (?) /43 MG Paride Negri (acting) /43 LG Alessandro Piazzoni (to /45, German prisoner-of-war) 09/08/43 disbanded.

- A. **Components - VI Army Corps (06/10/40)**
    1. **18th "Messina" Infantry Division**
    2. **49th "Parma" Infantry Division**
    3. **56th "Casale" Infantry Division**
    4. **Support Units (regiment sized listed only)**
        - a. **6th Corps Artillery Regiment**: /40 Col. Tancredi Bianchi (Aide-de-Camp to the King) /41? unknown? 09/08/43 dissolved.
        - b. **2nd Army Artillery Regiment** (added by 04/05/41)
        - c. **7th Army Artillery Regiment** (added by 04/05/41)
        - d. **9th Army Artillery Regiment** (added by 04/05/41)
- B. **Artillery, VI Army Corps**: /39 Col. Guglielmo Spicacci (Chief of Staff, Army of Po) /40 unknown? /43 Col. Vincenzo Catalano (to /45, German prisoner-of-war) 09/08/43 dissolved.
- C. **MVSN Troops, VI Army Corps**: unknown? /43 BG Michele Pallotta [MVSN] (to /44, German prisoner-of-war; /44, joined Social Republic of Italy) 09/08/43 dissolved.
- D. **At Disposal of, Attached to, or on Special Duties with VI Army Corps**:
01/40 (special duties) BG Vittorio Marangio
01/40 (special duties) BG Umberto Oddo

VII Army Corps (pre-war, part of Seventh Army; garrison duty; HQ: Corte, Corsica; Bastia, Corsica; /42, part of Fifth Army): /38 MG Adriano Marinetti (designated Commander-in-Chief, Army of Verona) /38 LG Aldo Aymonino (/41, Commanding General, Royal Customs Guards) /40 LG Vittorio Sogno (Commanding General, XVII Army Corps) /41 LG Mario Priore (Commanding General, XXXI Army Corps) 11/15/41 LG Mario Nicolosi (/42, Commanding General, X Army Corps) /41 LG Giuseppe Pafundi /42 LG Umberto Mondino (/43, Commanding General, XXV Army Corps) /42 LG Giuseppe Pafundi (?) /42 LG Giacomo Carboni (Chief, Military Intelligence Service) /43 MG Giovanni Magli (Commanding General, Sardinia Military Command) 09/08/43 disbanded.

- A. **Components - VII Army Corps (06/10/40)**
    1. **20th "Fruili" Infantry Division**
    2. **41st "Firenze [Florence]" Infantry Division**
    4. **Support Units (regiment sized listed only)**
        - a. **52nd Coastal Defense Artillery Regiment**
- B. **Artillery, VII Army Corps** (06/10/40): unknown? /42 Col. Guido Lama 09/08/43 dissolved.
- C. **Engineer-in-Chief, VII Army Corps** (06/10/40): unknown? /42 BG Gino Granata (Commanding General, "Legnano" Division) /43 unknown? 09/08/43 dissolved.
- D. **Medical Services, VII Army Corps** (06/10/40): Col. Enrico Bertelli 09/08/43 dissolved.
- E. **Rear Headquarters, VII Army Corps** (06/10/40): BG Corti 09/08/43 dissolved.
- F. **At Disposal of, Attached to, or on Special Duties with VII Army Corps**:
07/41? LG [Retired '40] Edmondo Rossi

VIII Army Corps (06/10/40, part of Seventh Army; occupation duty; HQ: Xylocastron,

Peloponnesus, Greece; 07/43, part of Eleventh Army): /39 MG Efisio Marras (Chief of Staff, Fifth Army) /39 LG Remo Gambelli (acting Commander-in-Chief, First Army) /40 MG Emilio Bancale (Commanding General, XV Army Corps) /41 LG Gastone Gambara (Chief of Staff, Commander-in-Chief North Africa) /41 MG Rodolfo Naldi (acting) [+ Commanding General, 29th "Piemonte" Infantry Division] /41 BG Matteo Negro (acting; Commandant, Royal Academy of Infantry & Cavalry) /42 LG Mario Marghinotti (to /45, German prisoner-of-war) 09/08/43 disbanded.

- A. **Deputy Commander, VIII Army Corps** (06/10/40): MG Mario Marghinotti (Commanding General, 11th "Brennero" Infantry Division) /41 unknown 09/08/43 dissolved.
- B. *Components* - VIII Army Corps (06/10/40)
    1. **21st "Granatieri di Sardegna" Infantry Division**
    2. **51st "Siena" Infantry Division**
    3. *Support Units* (regiment sized listed only)
        - a. **8th Corps Artillery Regiment**: /39? Col. Adolfo Sardi (/40, Commandant, Royal Artillery & Engineer Military Academy) /40? Col. Guido Lama (Artillery Commander, VIII Army Corps) /41 unknown 09/08/43 dissolved.
        - b. **169th Coastal Defense Artillery Regiment**
- C. **Artillery, VIII Army Corps** (06/10/40): unknown? /41 Col. Guido Lama (Artillery Commander, VII Army Corps) /42 Col. Aldo Menghini (to /45, German prisoner-of-war) 09/08/43 dissolved.
- D. **Engineer Commander, VIII Army Corps** (06/10/40): unknown? /41 Col. Pietro Andrea Baratelli 09/08/43 dissolved.
- E. **Advocate, Blackshirt (CCNN), VIII Army Corps** (06/10/40): unknown? /41? MG Cesare Federico Bevilacqua [MVSN] (?) 09/08/43 dissolved.
- F. **At Disposal of, Attached to, or on Special Duties with VIII Army Corps**:
    /40? (special duties) MG Natale Pentimalli
    07/41? (attached to) MG (Res.) Biagio Russo
    07/41? (special duties) BG (Res.) Ugo Sprega
    07/20/42 (special duties) MG Guglielmo Negro

IX Army Corps (HQ: Bari, later Putignano, Italy; part of Seventh Army in southern Italy; 10/43, disbanded by the Germans): /36 LG Pietro Maravigna (retired?; 01/40, Special Duties, War Ministry) /38 LG Carlo Geloso (Commander-in-Chief, Army Group East) /39 LG Count Ambrogio Clerici (Member, Commission for the Armed Forces, Senate) 06/10/40? LG Camillo Rossi (retired?; 06/43, Commanding General, III Army Corps) /40 MG Federico Romero (acting; /42, Commanding General, I Army Corps) /40 LG Luigi De Biase (?) /42 LG Umberto Spigo (Commanding General, XVIII Army Corps) /42 LG Quirino Armellini (Commanding General, National Security Volunteer Militia [MVSN]) /43 LG Antonio Basso (Commanding General, Army Forces in Campania) /43 LG Roberto Lerici (?) /43 MG Ismaele Di Nisio (Commanding General, IX Territorial Defense Command) 10/43 disbanded.

- A. *Components* - IX Army Corps (06/10/40)
    1. **29th "Piemonte" Infantry Division**
    2. **47th "Bari" Infantry Division**
    3. **48th "Taro" Infantry Division**

4. *Support Units* (regiment sized listed only)
   a. **9th Corps Artillery Regiment**: Col. Michelangelo Nicolini 09/08/43 dissolved.
   b. **13th Replacement Artillery Regiment**
   c. **110th Replacement Artillery Regiment**
   d. **111th Replacement Artillery Regiment**
   e. **113th Replacement Artillery Regiment**

B. **At Disposal of, Attached to, or on Special Duties with Headquarters, IX Army Corps**:
07/41 (attached to) BG (Res.) Luigi Ienco

X Army Corps (pre-war, part of Fifth Army; 12/42, destroyed in Egypt): 06/10/40? MG Alberto Barbieri (Commanding General, XVII Army Corps) /41 MG Mario Balotta (Artillery Commander, Eighth Army) /41 MG Luigi Nuvoloni (?   ) /41 MG Benvenuto Gioda (Commanding General, XIX Army Corps) /42? LG Marlo Nicolosi (?   ) /42 LG Federico Ferrari Orsi (killed by a mine in North Africa) /42 MG Edoardo Nebbia (Allied prisoner-of-war) 12/42 destroyed.

A. *Components* - **X Army Corps** (06/10/40)
   1. **25th "Bologna" Infantry Division**
   2. **55th "Savona" Infantry Division**
   3. **60th "Sabratha" Infantry Division**
   4. *Support Units* (regiment sized listed only)
      a. **10th Corps Artillery Regiment**
B. **Artillery, X Army Corps** (06/10/40): unknown? /42 Col. Arrigo Grillo (Allied prisoner-of-war) 11/07/42 dissolved.
C. **Engineer-in-Chief, X Army Corps** (06/10/40): unknown? /42 BG Lorenzo Converso (Allied prisoner-of-war) 11/07/42 dissolved.
D. **Rear Troops, X Army Corps** (06/10/40): unknown? /42 BG Dino Parri (Allied prisoner-of-war) 11/07/42 dissolved.

XI Army Corps (06/10/40. Part of Second army; occupation duty; HQ: Ljubljana, Slovenia; 03/43, part of Second Army): /35 LG Rodolfo Graziani [+ /36, Viceroy of Ethiopia] /37 LG Alfredo Guzzoni (Commanding General, Expeditionary Force to Albania; Commanding General, Albanian Army Corps) /39 LG Lorenzo Dalmazzo (Commanding General, XXI Army Corps) /39 LG Antero Canale (Commanding General, III Army Corps) /39 LG Ben Pietro Pintor (Commander-in-Chief, First Army) 06/10/40? MG Matteo Roux (/42, Logistic Services Directorate, War Ministry) /40 MG Mario Robotti (/43, Commander-in-Chief, General Headquarters Slovenia-Dalmatia) /42 LG Gastone Gambara (joins the Social Republic of Italy; /43, Chief of Staff, Social Republic of Italy) /43 BG Armando Lubrano (acting; to /45, German prisoner-of-war) 09/08/43 disbanded.

A. *Components* - **XI Army Corps** (06/10/40)
   1. **13th "Re" Infantry Division**
   2. **14th "Isonzo" Infantry Division**
   3. **XXI Border Guard Sector** (HQ: Tolmino; brigade status)
   4. **XXII Border Guard Sector** (HQ: Taggia; brigade status)
   5. **XXIII Border Guard Sector** (HQ: Postumia; brigade status)

B. **Engineer-in-Chief, XI Army Corps** (06/10/40): unknown? 07/01/42 BG Alberto Notari (?) 09/08/43 dissolved.
C. **At Disposal of, Attached to, or on Special Duties with XI Army Corps**:
12/42 (special duties) BG Annibale Gallo

XII Army Corps (06/10/40, part of Army Group South; HQ: Enna, Corleone, Sicily; 07/43, largely destroyed; 09/43, part of Sixth Army; 09/08/43, surrendered to Allies): /35 LG Vittorio Ambrosio (Commanding General, Army of Padova) /38 LG Angelo Rossi (Commanding General, III Army Corps) /41 LG Mario Arisio (Commander-in-Chief, Seventh Army) 07/43 LG Francesco Zingales [+ XVI Army Corps] 09/02/43 vacant 09/08/43 surrendered to Allies.
A. *Components - XII Army Corps* (06/10/40)
1. **28th "Aosta" Infantry Division**
2. **54th "Napoli [Naples]" Infantry Division**
3. *Support Units* (regiment sized listed only)
   a. **12th Corps Artillery Regiment**
B. **Artillery, XII Army Corps** (06/10/40): unknown? /43 Col. Ettore Monacci (10/43, Deputy Commander, Mantova Division) 09/08/43 dissolved.
C. **At Disposal of, Attached to, or on Special Duties with XII Army Corps**:
/41? (attached to) BG Domenico Angelica
/41? (at disposal) BG (Res.) Corrado De Franchis

XIII Army Corps (06/10/40, part of Army Group South; garrison duty; HQ: Florence; Cagliari, Sardinia; /42, part of Fifth Army; 09/43, part of Eighth Army): /38? LG Edoardo Monti (Commander-in-Chief, Army S) /40 LG Augusto De Pignier (?) /40 MG Antonio Basso (Commanding General, General Headquarters Sardinia) /43 LG Gustano Reisoli-Matthieu (?) /43 MG Giovanni Battista Zenati (acting) /43 LG Angelico Carta (?) 09/08/43 disbanded.
A. *Components - XIII Army Corps* (06/10/40)
1. **30th "Sabauda" Infantry Division**
2. **31st "Calabria" Infantry Division**
3. *Support Units* (regiment sized listed only)
   a. **46th Coastal DefenseArtillery Regiment**
B. **Artillery, XIII Army Corps** (06/10/40): Col. Ferrante Gonzga del Vodice (Artillery Commander, XXV Army Corps) /42 unknown? 09/08/43 dissolved.
C. **Engineer-in-Chief, XIII Army Corps** (0610/40): unknown? 02/42? MG Ugo Pession (?) /42 BG Agostino Garavano (Engineer-in-Chief, V Army Corps) /43 unknown? 09/08/43 dissolved.
D. **At Disposal of, Attached to, or on Special Duties with XIII Army Corps**:
10/40? (special duties) BG Arturo Vallesi

XIV Army Corps (06/10/40, part of Eighth Army; occupation duty in Albania; HQ: Citnje, Montenegro; 04/05/41?, part of Ninth Army; Greece and Yugoslavia; 09/08/43, disbanded by the Germans): /39 LG Count Sebastiano Murari della Corte Brà (?) 06/10/40? MG Giovanni Vecchi (/42, Commanding General, XXV Army Corps) /41 LG Luigi Mentasti (?) /43 LG Ercolo Roncaglia (to /45, German prisoner-of-war) /43 LG Count Curio Barbasetti di Prun (German prisoner-of-war) 09/08/43 disbanded.

A. ***Components* - XIV Army Corps** (06/10/40)
1. **32nd "Marche" Infantry Division**
2. **38th "Puglie" Infantry Division**
3. **XVI Border** ; brigade status **or** (HQ: Tolmezzo)
4. ***Support Units* (regiment sized listed only)**
   a. **14th Corps Artillery Regiment**

XV Army Corps (06/10/40, part of First Army; garrison duty northern Italy; HQ: Genoa; Carcare; 09/43, part of Fourth Army; 09/08/43, disbanded by the German): /39 LG Mario Berti (Commander-in-Chief, Tenth Army) /40 LG Fernandino Cona (Commanding General, XX Army Corps) 06/10/40 LG Gastone Gambara (Comnanding General, VIII Army Corps) /41 LG Emilio Bancale (?) 09/08/43 disbanded.
A. ***Components* - XV Army Corps** (06/10/40)
1. **5th "Cosseria" Infantry Division**
2. **37th "Modena" Infantry Division**
3. **44th "Cremona" Infantry Division**
4. **I Border Guard Sector** (HQ: Bordighera, Italy; brigade status)
5. **V Border Guard Sector** (HQ: Taggia, Italy; brigade status)
B. **Artillery, XV Army Corps** (06/10/40): unknown? /43 BG Vittorio de Bernadis (?) /43 BG Francesco Sclavo (to /45, German prisoner-of-war) 09/08/43 dissolved.
C. **At Disposal of, Attached to, or on Special Duties with XV Army Corps**:
/41? (attached to) BG Attilio Sannia

XVI Army Corps (HQ: Catania, Piazza Armerina, Sicily; disbanded at La Spezia; aided the escape of Italian Fleet from this port; 09/43, part of Sixth Army, later Fifth Army): /40 LG Carlo Rossi (I) (Commanding General, Ciamuria Corps) /40 LG Antero Canale (Commanding General, III Territorial Defense Command) /41 LG Carlo Rossi (I) (to /45, German prisoner-of-war) /43 LG Agostino Cinti (acting) 07/43 LG Francesco Zingales [+ XII Army Corps] (?) 09/08/43 disbanded.
A. **Chief of Staff, XVI Army Corps**: /39? Col. Guilio Martinat (Chief of Staff, IV Army Corps) /40 unknown? 09/08/43 dissolved.
B. ***Components* - XVI Army Corps** (06/10/40)
1. ***Support Units* (regiment sized listed only)**
   a. **40th Corps Artillery Regiment**
   a. **44th Coastal Defense Artillery Regiment**
C. **Artillery, XVI Army Corps**: /41 Col. Paolo Ottone /43 BG Giuseppe Cinti (to /45, German prisoner-of-war) 09/08/43 dissolved.
D. **At Disposal of, Attached to, or on Special Duties with XVI Army Corps**:
/43 (at disposal) BG Mario Marchi (to /45, German prisoner-of-war) 09/08/43 dissolved.
/43 (at disposal) BG Orazio Marescalco (to /45, German prisoner-of-war) 09/08/43 dissolved.

XVII Army Corps (1941; garrison duty in Italy; HQ: Rome; 04/05/41; part of Ninth Army; Greece and Yugoslavia; 09/43, part of Second Army): /40 LG Giuseppe Pafundi (Commanding General, Armored Corps) /40 LG Alberto Barbieri (/43, Commanding

General, Rome Corps) /41 LG Vittorio Sogno (Commanding General, XXX Army Corps) /42 LG Giovanni Zanghieri (?) 09/08/43 disbanded.
- A. **Components - XVII Army Corps** (04/05/41)
    1. **18th "Messina" Infantry Division**
    2. **32nd "Marche" Infantry Division**
    3. **131st "Centauro" Armor Division**
    4. **"Diamanti" Blackshirt (CCNN) Group** (brigade status)
    5. **"Skanderberg Albanian Blackshirt (CCNN) Legion** (regiment status)
    6. **19th "Cavalleggeri Guide" Cavalry Regiment**: /39 Col. Ugo De Carolis (Commandant, Central School for Cavalry (Celere) Troops) /40
    7. **21st Artillery Regiment**
- B. **Engineer-in-Chief, XVII Army Corps** (04/05/41): unknown? /42 BG Oreste Crivaro (Inspector of Engineers) 10/43 dissolved.
- C. **At Disposal of, Attached to, or on Special Duties with XVI Army Corps**:
01/42 (attached to) BG Ugo Ojetti
01/42? (special duties) BG (Res.) Filippo Tagliavacche
09/42? (special duties) BG Mario Varese

XVIII Army Corps (1940; occupation duty; HQ: Split, Yugoslavia; Spalato, Dalmatial; 03/43, part of Second Army): LG Mario Gamaleri (/43, President, Army Sub-Committee Commission for the Italian Armed Forces, Senate) /41 LG Gabriele Nasci (Commanding General, II Army Corps) 08/08/42 LG Quirino Armellini (Commanding General, IX Army Corps) /42 LG Umberto Spigo (?) 09/08/43 disbanded.
- A. **Artillery, XVIII Army Corps** (/40): unknown? /43 BG Salavtore Pelligra (Commanding General, Spalato Area) 09/08/43 dissolved.
- B. **Engineer-in-Chief, XVIII Army Corps** (/40): unknown? /43 BG Angelo Policardi (executed by the Germans) 09/08/43? dissolved.

XIX Army Corps (04/42; garrison duty; HQ: Naples; Bozen; Bolzano; 09/43, part of Seventh Army in southern Italy): LG Gastone Gambara (in reserve; /42, Commanding General, XI Army Corps) /42 LG Ugo Santovito (Commanding General, VI Army Corps) /42 LG Arturo Taranto (acting) /42 LG Benvenuto Gioda (?) 01/01/43? LG Enea Navarini (10/43, Commandant, Center for Training of Special Units, Social Republic of Italy) /43 LG Arturo Taranto (Commanding General, XXXV Army Corps) /43 LG Riccardo Pentimalli (retired; /44, condemned to 20 years imprisonment for misconduct of the defense of Naples) 09/08/43 disbanded.

XX Army Corps (1939; 06/10/40, part of Fifth Army; 02/43, part of First Italo-German Army; 05/43, destroyed in Tunisia; 07/43, recreated as **XX Motorized Army Corps**): /37 LG Ben Pietro Pintor (/39, Commanding General, XI Army Corps) /38 MG Luigi Frusci (Governor of Amhara, Ethiopia) 01/01/39 MG Alberto Barbieri (Commanding General, X Army Corps) 06/10/40? MG Ferdinando Cona (British prisoner-of-war; captured at Agedabia) 02/07/41 LG Enrico Armando (Commanding General, Tripolitania Defense Command) /41 LG Carlo Vecchiarelli (/42, Deputy Commander, Italian Armistice Commission to France) /41 MG Mario Soldarelli [acting; + Commanding General, 60th "Sabratha" Infantry Division] 12/11/41 MG Alessandro Piazzoni (acting; /42, Commanding General, 15th "Bergamo" Infantry Division) 12/41 LG Gastone Gambara [+ Chief of Staff,

Commander-in-Chief, North Africa] (Commanding General, XIX Army Corps) 04/42 LG Francesco Zingales (Commanding General, XXXI Army Corps) /42 LG Ettore Baldassare (killed in action) 10/23/42 MG Giuseppe de Stefanis (acting; Chief of the General Staff)11/42 MG Taddeo Orlando (Allied prisoner-of-war, captured in Tunisia; /44, Minister of War) 05/43 LG Gervasio Bitossi (Commanding General, XX Motorized Army Corps) 07/43 see **XX Motorized Army Corps**.
- A. *Components - XX Army Corps* (06/10/40)
  1. **17th "Pavia" Infantry Division**
  2. **27th "Brescia" Infantry Division**
  3. **61st "Sirte" Infantry Division**
  4. *Support Units* **(regiment sized listed only)**
     a. **20th Corps Artillery Regiment**
- B. **Artillery, XX Army Corps** (06/10/40): unknown? /42 BG Guido Piacenza (killed in action) /42 BG Alberto Roda (Allied prisoner-of-war, captured on Sicily) 07/43 dissolved.

XX Motorized Army Corps (07/43): LG Gervasio Bitossi (to /45, German prisoner-of-war) 10/43 LG Giacomo Carboni (?) 09/08/43 disbanded.
- A. **Chief of Staff, XX Motorized Army Corps** (07/43): Col. Salvi (?) 09/08/43 disbanded.

XXI Army Corps (06/10/40. Part of Tenth Army; HQ: Tirana; 02/43, part of First Italo-German Army;05/43, destroyed in Tunisia): /37 LG Mario Caracciolo di Feroleto [+ to /38, Commanding General, Libya] (Inspector-General of Technical Services) /39 LG Lorenzo Dalmazzo (Commanding General, VI Army Corps) /41 LG Enea Navarini /42 MG Alessandro Gloria (acting; Commanding General, V Army Corps) /42 LG Enea Navarini (?) /43 LG Paolo Berardi (Allied prisoner-of-war; 09/43, after released, Chief of the General Staff) 05/43 destroyed.
- A. *Components - XXI Army Corps* (06/10/40)
  1. **62nd "Marmarica" Infantry Division**
  2. **63rd "Cirene" Infantry Division**

XXII Army Corps (06/10/40, part of Tenth Army; 01/21/41, destroyed in North Africa; reformed and used for occupation duty; HQ: Brignoles, France; Hyeres, France; 09/43, part of Tenth Army, then Fourth Army): **XXII Army Corps (1)** /39 LG Umberto Somma (Member, Commission of the Affairs of Italian Africa, Senate) 06/10/40? LG Errico Pitassi-Manella (British prisoner-of-war; captured at Tobruk) 01/21/41 destroyed; reformed **XXII Army Corps (#2)** /42 LG Federico Ferrari Orsi (Commanding General, X Army Corps) 12/42 LG Alfonso Ollearo (joins Social Republic of Italy; 10/43, Undersecretary of State for the Army, Ministry of National Defense, Social Republic of Italy) 09/08/43 disbanded.
- A. **Chief of Staff, XXII Army Corps** (06/10/40): unknown? /41 Col. Adolfo De Leone (British prisoner-of-war) /41 unknown? 09/08/43 dissolved.
- B. *Components - XXII Army Corps* (06/10/40)
  1. **64th "Catanzaro" Infantry Division**
  2. **4th "3 Gennaio" Blackshirt (CCNN) Division**
  3. *Support Units* **(regiment sized listed only)**

        a.   **42ⁿᵈ Coastal Defense Artillery Regiment**
C.   **Engineer-in-Chief, XXII Army Corps** (06/10/40): unknown? /43 BG Romolo Borelli (to /45, German prisoner-of-war) 09/08/43 dissolved.

XXIII Army Corps (06/10/40, part of Fifth Army; occupation duty; HQ: Trieste, Italy): /38 MG Annibale Bergonzoli (to /45, British prisoner-of-war) /41 LG Alberto Ferrero (?) 09/08/43 disbanded.
- A.   *Components* - **XXIII Army Corps** (06/10/40)
    1. **1ˢᵗ "23 Marzo" Blackshirt (CCNN) Division**
    2. **2ⁿᵈ "28 Ottobre" Blackshirt (CCNN) Division**
- B.   **Artillery, XXIII Army Corps** (06/10/40): unknown? /43 BG Ralmondo Sesini (?) 09/08/43 dissolved.
    1. **At Disposal of Artillery Commander, XVI Army Corps**:
        /43 Col. Giovan Battista Salomon (to /44, German prisoner-of-war; /44, joins Social Republic of Italy) 09/08/43

XXIV Army Corps (HQ: Udine, Italy; 05/43, from Alpini Corps; 07/43, part of Eleventh Army; 09/43, Eighth Army): LG Licurgo Zannini (to /45, German prisoner-of-war) 09/08/43 dissolved.

XXV Army Corps (started out as **Ciamuria Corps**; /40, redesignated **XXV Army Corps**; occupation duty; HQ: Valona, Albania): **Ciamuria Corps** /40 LG Carlo Rossi (I) (Commanding General, XXV Army Corps) /40 redesignated **XXV Army Corps** /40 LG Carlo Rossi (I) (Commanding General, XVI Army Corps) /41 LG Giovanni Vecchi (?) /43 LG Umberto Mondino (to /45, German prisoner-of-war) 09/08/43 disbanded.
- A.   *Components* - **XXV Army Corps** (06/10/40)
    1. **19ᵗʰ "Venetia" Infantry Division**
    2. **23ʳᵈ "Ferrara" Infantry Division**
    3. **53ʳᵈ "Arezzo" Infantry Division**
    4. **3ʳᵈ "Julia" Alpini Division**
    5. **131ˢᵗ "Centauro" Armor Division**
    6. **13ᵗʰ Border Artillery Brigade** (brigade status)
    7. **I Albania Border Guard Sector** (brigade status)
    8. **II Albania Border Guard Sector** (brigade status)
    9. **III Albania Border Guard Sector** (brigade status)
    10. **Albania Coastal Border Guard Sector** (brigade status)
- B.   **Artillery, XXV Army Corps** (06/10/40): unknown? /42 BG Paolo Perrod (killed in Russia) /42 BG Conradino Tricoli (?) /42 BG Ferrante Gonzga del Vodice (Commanding General, 222ⁿᵈ Coastal Division) /43 unknown? 09/08/43 dissolved.

XXVI Army Corps (occupation duty in Albania; 04/05/41?, part of Ninth Army; HQ: Yannina, Greece; 09/08/43, disbanded by the Germans): /39 LG Carlo Geloso [+ Commander-in-Chief, Army Group East] /39 unknown? 06/10/40? LG Sebastiano Visconti Prasca (/41, acting Commander-in-Chief, Eleventh Army) /40 LG Gabrielle Nasci (Commanding General, Librazhd Sector) 04/05/41 MG Alessandro Gloria (acting; Commanding General, 25ᵗʰ "Bologna" Semi-Motorized Infantry Division) /41 LG Ugo

Santovito (/42, Commanding General, XIX Army Corps) /41 LG Guido Della Bona (?) 09/08/43 disbanded.
  A. **Artillery, XXVI Army Corps**: unknown? /42 BG Vincenzo Saporetti (to /45, German prisoner-of-war) 09/08/43 dissolved.
  B. **Engineer-in-Chief, XXVI Army Corps**: /41 BG Mario Perrelli (?) 09/08/43 dissolved.
  C. **At Disposal of, Attached to, or on Special Duties with XXVI Army Corps**: 07/41? (special duties) BG Ugo Marfuggi

XXX Army Corps (12/42; garrison duty; HQ: Sardinia; 09/08/43, surrendered to Allies): /41 LG Francesco Zingales (acting Commander-in-Chief, Seventh Army) /41 MG Dante Lorenzelli (?) /42 MG Enrico Frattini (British prisoner-of-war) /42 LG Umberto Mondino (Commanding General, VII Army Corps) /42 LG Renato Coturri (Commanding General, V Army Corps) /42 LG Vittorio Sogno (Commanding General, II Army Corps) /43 MG Giacomo Castagna [+ Commanding General, 31st "Calabria" Infantry Division] 09/08/43 surrendered to Allies.
  A. **Engineer-in-Chief, XXX Army Corps** (12/42): BG Flavio Gioia (Allied prisoner-of-war) 09/08/43 dissolved

XXXI Army Corps (11/15/41; HQ: Catanzaro, near Soveria Mamnelli; 09/43, part of Seventh Army in southern Italy): /40 LG Carlo Spatocco (Commanding General, Tripoli Fortress) /41 LG Mario Priore (?) /42 MG Felice Gonnella [+ Commanding General, 211th Coastal Division] (acting) /42 LG Taddeo Orlando (Commanding General, XX Army Corps) /42 LG Francesco Zingales (Commanding General, XXXV Army Corps) 11/42 MG Emilio Coronati (acting) 12/42 LG Camillo Mercalli (?) 09/08/43 disbanded.
  A. **Engineer-in-Chief, XXXI Army Corps** (12/42): BG Angelo Policardi (Engineer-in-Chief, XVIII Army Corps) /43 Col. Luigi Laccetti 09/08/43 dissolved.
  B. **At Disposal of, Attached to, or on Special Duties with XXXI Army Corps**: 12/15/41 (special duties) BG Amedeo Sorrentino (Commanding General, 4th Territorial Zone) /43

XXXV Army Corps (08/08/42?, part of Eighth Army; 12/42, largely destroyed in Soviet Union): 08/08/42? LG Giovanni Messe (Commander-in-Chief, First Army (#2)) 12/10/42? LG Francesco Zingales (XII Army Corps & XIV Army Corps) 07/43 LG Alessandro Gloria (Commanding General, Bolzano Army Corps) /43 LG Arturo Taranto (Commanding General, IV Territorial Defense Command) /43 unknown? 09/08/43 disbanded.
  A. **Chief of Staff, XXXV Army Corps** (08/08/42): BG Umberto Utili (Chief Operations, Supreme General Staff) /43 Col. Gaetano Vargas 09/08/43 dissolved.
  B. *Components* - **XXXV Army Corps** (08/08/42)
      1. **9th "Pasubio" Semi-Motorized Infantry Division**
      2. **52nd "Torino [Turin]" Semi-Motorized Infantry Division**
      3. **3rd "Principe Amedeo Duca d'Aosta" Cavalry (Celere) Division**
      4. **"3rd Gennaio" Blackshirt (CCNN) Brigade**
  C. **Artillery, XXXV Army Corps**: 08/08/42? BG Francesco Du Pont (Commanding General, 3rd "Ravenna" (Mountain) Infantry Division) 10/03/42 BG Adriano Perrod (?) 09/08/43 dissolved.
  D. **Engineer-in-Chief, XXXV Army Corps**: 08/08/42? BG Mario Tirelli (/46?,

Commanding General, "Avellino" Division) /43 MG Francesco Tessore (to /45, German prisoner-of-war) 09/08/43 dissolved.

Celere [Cavalry] {Fast} Corps (06/10/40, part of the Sixth Army; 04/05/41?, part of Second Army; Greece and Yugoslavia): /38 MG Claudio Trezzani (Chief of Staff, Italian East Africa) /38 unknown? 06/10/40? LG Giovanni Messe (Commanding General, Special Army Corps) /40 LG Federico Ferrari Orsi (Inspector of Cavalry [Celere] Troops) /42 09/08/43 dissolved.
- A. **Components - Cavalry [Celere] {Fast} Corps** (06/10/40)
    1. **1st "Eugenio di Savoia" Cavalry (Celere) Division**
    2. **2nd "Emanuele Filiberto Testa di Ferro" Cavalry (Celere) Division**
    3. **3rd "Principe Amedeo Duca d'Aosta" Cavalry (Celere) Division**

Armored Corps (06/10/40, part of the Sixth Army): /38 LG Fidenzio Dall'Ora (Member, Commission for the Armed Forces, Senate) /40 MG Ettore Baldassare (Commanding General, 132nd "Ariete" Armored Division) 06/10/40? LG Giuseppe Pafundi (Commanding General, VIII Army Corps) /41
- A. **Components - Armored Corps** (06/10/40)
    1. **101st "Trieste" Motorized Infantry Division**
    2. **102nd "Trento" Motorized Infantry Division**
    3. **132nd "Ariete" Armored Division**
    4. **133rd "Littorio" Armored Division**
- B. **Artillery, Armored Corps**: /38? BG Giuseppe de Stefanis (Commanding General, 24th "Pinerolo" Infantry Division) 06/10/40?

Truck Borne Corps (06/10/40, part of the Sixth Army; 04/05/41?, part of Second Army; Greece and Yugoslavia): 06/10/40? LG Francesco Zingales (Commanding General, Italian Expeditionary Corps) /41
- A. **Components - Truck Borne Corps** (06/10/40)
    1. **9th "Pasubio" Semi-Motorized Infantry Division**
    2. **10th "Piave" Motorized Infantry Division**
    3. **52nd "Torino [Turin]" Semi-Motorized Infantry Division**

Alpine [Alpini] Corps (06/10/40, part of the Fourth Army; 03/42, Eighth Army; Soviet Union; 01/43, destroyed in Soviet Union; 07/43, reforming): <u>**Commanding General, Alpine Troops**</u> /39 LG Gabrielle Nasci (Commanding General, XXVI Army Corps) /40 redesignated <u>**Alpine [Alpini] Corps**</u> /39 LG Luigi Negri Cesi (?) /40 LG Umberto Testa (Special duties, War Ministry) 07/41 unknown? 12/10/42? LG Gabriele Nasci (Inspector-General of Alpine Troops) 05/04/43 unknown? 09/08/43 disbanded.
- A. **Chief of Staff, Alpini [Alpine] Corps]** (06/10/40): Col. Giuilo Martinat (killed in action) /43
- B. **Components - Alpini Corps** (06/10/40)
    1. **1st "Taurino" Alpini Division**
    2. **"Levanna" Mountain Brigade**
    3. **X Border Guard Sector** (HQ: Vinadio, Italy; brigade status)
    4. *Support Units* (regiment sized listed only)

        a.   **11th Corps Artillery Regiment**: 08/08/42? Col. G. Maj
C. **Artillery Commander, Alpini [Alpine] Corps**: 08/08/42? BG Carlo Filippi (at disposal of Inspector of Alpine Troops) 05/04/43
D. **Engineer Commander, Alpini [Alpine] Corps** (06/10/40): unknown? 08/08/42? BG Cesare Tamassia (?) 05/04/43 unknown? 09/08/43 dissolved.

Volunteer Corps of Troops to Spain [Corpo di Truppe Volontarie] (1937, Spanish Civil War): LG Ettore Bastico (Commanding General, Army of Padova) /37 MG Mario Berti (Commanding General, XV Army Corps) /38 MG Gastone Gambara [+ Ambassador to Spain] /39
A. **Deputy Commander, Volunteer Corps of Troops to Spain**: /37 MG Mario Berti (Commanding General, Volunteer Corps of Troops to Spain) /37 MG Luigi Frusci (Commanding General, 20th "Friuli" Infantry Division) /37
B. **Chief of Staff, Volunteer Corps of Troops to Spain**: /37 BG Gastone Gambara (Commanding General, Volunteer Corps of Troops to Spain & Ambassador to Spain) /38

General Headquarters Aegean (composed of Dodecanese and Aegean Islands; 09/43, part of Army Group East): 06/10/40? BG Cesare Mario De Vecchi di Val Cisomon (retired?; 07/42, Commanding General, 215th Coastal Division) /40 unknown? 01/01/43? Adm. Inigo Campioni [+ Governor of Rhodes] (shot to death) 05/24/44
A. **Chief of Staff, General Headquarters Aegean** (06/10/40): unknown? /43 BG Roberto Sequi (?) 09/08/43 dissoloved.
A. *Components - General Headquarters Aegean* (06/10/40)
    1.   **50th "Regina" Infantry Division**
    2.   **Commandant, Rhodes**: /43 LG Arnaldo Forgiero (to /45, German prisoner-of-war) 10/43 disbanded.
        a.   **Chief of Staff, Rhodes**: /42 Col. Ercole Ronco (Commanding General, 30th "Sabauda" Infantry Division) /43 unknown? 09/08/43 dissolved.
    3.   **Commandant, Samos**: /43 MG Alfio Marziani (?) 10/43 disbanded.
        a.   **At Disposal of, Attached to, or on Special Duties with Samos Island**:
            06/42 (attached to) BG Bianco Zanotti [MVSN]
    4.   **Commandant, Zante Island**: /43 BG Luigi Paderini (to /45, German prisoner-of-war) 09/08/43 disbanded.
B. **Artillery, Aegean Islands**: unknown? /42 BG Silvio Tosatto (?) /43 BG Giuseppe Consoli (to /45, German prisoner-of-war) 10/43 dissolved.
C. **President, Military Tribunal (Judical) Aegean Islands**: unknown? /43 BG Carlo or Errico Chitti (to /45, German prisoner-of-war) 10/43 dissolved.

Tobruk Fortress (06/10/40, part of Tenth Army; corps status; /42, lowered to division status):
A. *Components - Tobruk Fortress* (06/10/40)
    1.   **XXXI Border Guard Sector** (HQ: Tobruk (Ras el Meduar); brigade status)
    2.   **XXXII Border Guard Sector** (HQ: Tobruk (Sidi Daud); brigade status)

Tripoli Fortress (06/10/40, part of Fifth Army; corps status; 10/23/42?, part of Tripolitania Defense Command): unknown? /41 LG Carlo Spatocco (Commanding General, IV Army Corps) /41 unknown? 10/23/42? LG Alberto Mannerini (Allied prisoner-of-war; /50, Commander-in-Chief, Royal Carabinieri) 05/43 BG Alessandro Santin (?) 05/43 disbanded.
A. **Components - Tripoli Fortress** (06/10/40)
   1. **XXXIII Border Guard Sector** (HQ: Tripoli; brigade status)
   2. **XXXIV Border Guard Sector** (HQ: Tripoli; brigade status)
   3. **XXXV Border Guard Sector** (HQ: Tripoli; brigade status)
   4. **South East Border Guard Sector** (HQ: Tripoli; brigade status)
B. **Components - Tripoli Fortress** (10/23/42)
   1. **30th Coastal and Anti-Aircraft Artillery Regiment**
   2. **31st Anti-Aircraft Artillery Regiment**
   3. **34th Coastal and Anti-Aircraft Artillery Regiment**
C. **Commandant, Tripoli Fortress**: /39 Col. Dino Parri (Deputy Commander, 10th "Pavia" Motorized Infantry Division) /41

Bardia Army Corps (Libya; 01/41, destroyed; 09/43, part of Tenth Army): MG Annibale Bergonzolli

Rome Army Corps (08/43, to reinforce XX Motorized Army Corps, and to provide for internal defense of Rome): /38 LG Domenico Siciliani (retired) /38 disbanded; reformed 08/43 LG Alberto Barbieri (?) /43 MG Umberto di Giorgio

Bolzano Army Corps (/43): LG Alessandro Gloria (to /45, German prisoner-of-war) 09/08/43

Florence Army Corps:
A. **Artillery, Florence Army Corps**: /38 Col. Odoardo Majnardi (Deputy Chief of Staff, Italian East Africa) /39

Royal Custom Guards: /34 MG Riccardo Calcagno (Member, Commission of the Affairs of Italian Africa, Senate) /39 unknown? /41 LG Aldo Aymonino.
A. **Components - Royal Custom Guards**
   1. **Custom Guards Albania**: /43 BG Michele Di Gaetano (to /45, German prisoner-of-war) 09/08/43 dissolved.
   2. **Royal Customs Guard Porto Empedoelo**: /41? BG Felice Piccolo
   3. **11th Custom Guards Group**: /43 BG Carlo Ghe (to /45, German prisoner-of-war) 09/08/43 dissolved.

Bersaglieri Corps (07/18/37, as a light infantry force for the Sardinian Army):
A. **Components - Bersaglieri Corps** (07/18/37)
   1. **1st Bersaglieri Regiment**: /39? Col. Giuseppe Molinero (Commanding General, 23rd Territorial District) /41? Col. Count Giullo Cesare Gotti-Porcinari (/43, Commanding General, 54th "Napoli [Naples]" Infantry Division) /42?
   2. **2nd Bersaglieri Regiment**

3. **3ʳᵈ Bersaglieri Regiment**: /37? Col. Attilio Amato (acting Commanding General, 2ⁿᵈ Infantry Brigade) /39? Col. Luigi Peluso (Provincial Inspector Anti-Aircraft, Ravenna) 07/41?
4. **4ᵗʰ Bersaglieri Regiment**
5. **5ᵗʰ Bersaglieri Regiment**
6. **6ᵗʰ Bersaglieri Regiment**:
7. **7ᵗʰ Bersaglieri Regiment**
8. **8ᵗʰ Bersaglieri Regiment**
9. **9ᵗʰ Bersaglieri Regiment**: /37 Col. Arturo Scattini (/42, Deputy Commander, 80ᵗʰ "La Spezia" Airlanding Division) /39?
10. **10ᵗʰ Bersaglieri Regiment**
11. **11ᵗʰ Bersaglieri Regiment**
12. **12ᵗʰ Bersaglieri Regiment**

Librazhd Sector (04/05/41?, part of Ninth Army; Greece and Yugoslavia): 04/05/41? LG Gabrielle Nasci (Commanding General, XVIII Army Corps) /41

A. *Components* - **Librazhd Sector** (07/18/37)
1. **24ᵗʰ "Pinerolo" Infantry Division**
2. **41ˢᵗ "Firenze [Florence]" Infantry Division**
3. **53ʳᵈ "Arezzo" Infantry Division**
4. **"Biscaccianti" Blackshirt (CCNN) Brigade**: 07/18/37 Col. Alessandro Biscaccianti [MVSN] (/43, Commanding General, 8ᵗʰ Blackshirt (CCNN) Zone) /3?
5. **4ᵗʰ Bersaglieri Regiment**: 04/05/41? Col. G. Scognamillo
6. **"Brisotto" Infantry Regiment** (temporary unit): 04/05/41? Col. Silvio Brisotto (Internal Security Commander, Aosta Infantry Division) /42
7. **7ᵗʰ "Lancieri di Milano [Milan]" Cavalry Regiment**: /38 Col. Cesara Lomaglio [acting; + Commanding Officer, 5ᵗʰ "Lancieri di Novara" Cavalry Regiment] /38 Col. Ugo De Carolis (Commanding Officer, 19ᵗʰ "Cavalleggeri Guide" Cavalry Regiment) /39 Col. Mario Badino-Rossi (Commanding General, 202ⁿᵈ Coastal Division) /40 unknown? 04/05/41? Col. Giorgi Morigi (Commanding General, Nembo Division) 09/08/43 dissolved.
8. **"Agostini" Forest Militia Regiment** (temporary unit): 04/05/41? MG Augusto Agostini [MVSN]
9. **8ᵗʰ Corps Artillery Regiment**: 04/05/41? Col. V. Petillo

Northern Sector, Italian East Africa (**Eritrean Corps**; 06/10/41, Eritrea; corps status; 05/17/41, ceased to exist): /35 Alessandro Pirzio-Biroli (Italian Governor of Amhara) 06/01/36 unknown? /40 LG Luigi Frusci [+ Italian Governor of Amhara, Ethiopia & Italian Governor of Eritrea; + 06/40, Commanding General, 4ᵗʰ (Eritrean) Colonial Infantry Division] (British prisoner-of-war) /41 MG Vincenzo Tessitore (acting; British prisoner-of-war, captured at Massawa) 04/08/41 unknown? 05/17/41 ceased to exist.

A. *Components* - **Eritrean Corps** (1940):
1. 3 divisions
B. *Components* - **Southern Sector** (06/10/41)
1. **3ʳᵈ Colonial Infantry Brigade**
2. **4ᵗʰ Colonial Infantry Brigade**

3. 5th Colonial Infantry Brigade
4. 6th Colonial Infantry Brigade
5. 8th Colonial Infantry Brigade
6. 12th Colonial Infantry Brigade
7. 16th Colonial Infantry Brigade
8. 19th Colonial Infantry Brigade
9. 21st Colonial Infantry Brigade
10. 22nd Colonial Infantry Brigade
11. 41st Colonial Infantry Brigade
12. 42nd Colonial Infantry Brigade
13. 43rd Colonial Infantry Brigade

Eastern Sector, Italian East Africa (06/10/40, Gondar District, Ethiopia; corps status; 05/17/41, ceased to exist): LG Guglielmo Ciro Nasi [+ Member, Commission for the Armed Forces, Senate; + to 02/04/41, Italian Governor of Harrar] (Italian Governor of Amhara) 05/17/41 ceased to exist.

A. *Components* - Eastern Sector (06/10/41)
1. 40th "African" Infantry Division
2. 65th "Granatieri di Savia" Infantry Division
3. 2nd Colonial Infantry Brigade
4. 7th Colonial Infantry Brigade
5. 11th Colonial Infantry Brigade
6. 13th Colonial Infantry Brigade
7. 14th Colonial Infantry Brigade
8. 15th Colonial Infantry Brigade
9. 17th Colonial Infantry Brigade
10. 70th Colonial Infantry Brigade

Southern Sector, Italian East Africa (06/10/41, Galla-Sidamo; corps status; 07/06/41, ceased to exist): Gen. Pietro Gazzera (British prisoner-of-war; captured at Dembedollo) 07/06/41 ceased to exist.

A. *Components* - Southern Sector (06/10/41)
1. 1st Colonial Infantry Brigade
2. 9th Colonial Infantry Brigade
3. 10th Colonial Infantry Brigade
4. 18th Colonial Infantry Brigade
5. 23rd Colonial Infantry Brigade
6. 25th Colonial Infantry Brigade
7. 85th Colonial Infantry Brigade
8. 86th Colonial Infantry Brigade

Juba [Giuba] Sector (Italian Somaliland Corps; 06/10/41, part of Italian East African Armed Forces; corps status): **Italian Somaliland Corps** /36 LG Ruggero Santini [+ to /37, Italian Governor of Somaliland] (Commanding General III Army Corps) /38 unknown? 11/40 redesignated **Juba [Giuba] Sector** 11/40 MG Carlo de Simone [+ Governor of Italian Somaliland; + to 03/10/41, Commanding General, 102nd Colonial Infantry Division;

+ 03/10/41 to 04/24/41, Italian Governor of Harar] (to /44, British prisoner-of-war; /45, Commanding General, VII Territorial Defense Command) 07/06/41 disbanded.
- A. **Chief of Staff, Italian Somaliland Corps**: /38 BG Marquis Luigi Trionfi (acting Commanding General, 37th "Modena" Infantry Division) /40
- B. *Components* - **Italian Somaliland Corps** (1940):
    1. **Harar Division**
    2. **5 brigades**
- C. *Components* - **Giuba Sector** (06/10/41)
    1. **20th Colonial Infantry Brigade**
    2. **91st Colonial Infantry Brigade**
    3. **92nd Colonial Infantry Brigade**
- D. **Intendant-General (Quartermaster), Italian Somaliland Corps**: /36 BG Eduardo Giordano

Special Army Corps (/40; disbanded /41): LG Giovanni Messe (Commanding General, Italian Expeditionary Corps) 08/05/41 LG Francesco Zingales (Commanding General, XXX Army Corps) /41 MG Ercole Roncaglia (/43, Commanding General, XIV Army Corps) /41 disbanded.

Italian Expeditionary Corps [Corpo di Spedizione Italiano (CSIR)] (07/10/41, in charge of all Italian units in Soviet Union until Eighth Army arrived in 07/42; 07/41, assigned to German Eleventh Army; 08/14/41, assigned to German Panzer Group 1; 06/03/42, assigned to German Seventeenth Army; 07/10/42, dissolved and used to form **XXXV Army Corps**): 07/41 LG Francesco Zingales (ill; Commanding General, Special Army Corps) 08/05/41 LG Giovanni Messe (Commanding General, XXXV Army Corps) 07/10/42 dissolved and used to form **XXXV Army Corps** - see **XXV Army Corps**.
- A. **Chief of Staff, Italian Expeditionary Corps** (07/10/41): Col. Guido Piacenza (acting Commanding General, 26th "Assietta" Mountain Infantry Division) 11/01/41 Col. Umberto Utili (Chief of Staff, XXXV Army Corps) /42
- B. *Components* - **Italian Expeditionary Corps** (08/05/41)
    1. **9th "Pasubio" Semi-Motorized Infantry Division**
    2. **52nd "Torino [Turin]" Semi-Motorized Infantry Division**
    3. **3rd "Principe Amedeo Duca d'Aosta" Cavalry (Celere) Division**
    4. **Air Assets, Italian Expeditionary Corps** (brigade status)
    5. **63rd "Tagliamento" Blackshirt (CCNN) Legion** (regiment status): 08/05/41 Col. Niccolò Nicchiarelli [MVSN] (Commanding General, 1st Blackshirt Zone) /43
    6. *Support Units* - **Italian Expeditionary Corps** (08/05/41)
        - a. **21st Transport Command, Italian Expeditionary Corps**: 08/05/41? Col. Ninchi
        - b. **14th Medical Command, Italian Expeditionary Corps**: 08/05/41? unknown?
        - c. **XXX Corps Artillery Regiment**: 08/05/41? Col. Lorenzo Matiotti
- C. **Artillery, Italian Expeditionary Corps** (07/10/41): BG Francesco Du Pont (Commanding General, 52nd "Torino [Turin]" Semi-Motorized Infantry Division) /41 unknown? 08/08/42 BG Luigi Jalla (Artillery Commander, III Army Corps) /43
- D. **Engineer-in-Chief, Italian Expeditionary Corps** (07/10/41): Col. Mario Tirelli

(Engineer-in-Chief, XXXV Army Corps) 08/08/42
- E. **Intendent General (Quartermaster), Italian Expeditionary Corps** (07/10/41): Col. Eugenio Gatti (Infantry Commander, 56th "Casale" Infantry Division) /42 BG Carlo Biglioni (Intendant-General, Eighth Army) 07/42
- F. **Aviation Command** (07/10/41): Col. Carlo Drago [RIAF] 02/25/42 BG Enrico Pezzi [RIAF]
- G. **German Liaison Officer** (07/10/41): Maj. Hans-Wessel von Gyldenfeldt [German] 10/41 Maj. I. G. Reinhold Fellmer [German] 11/20/42

Libyan Sahara Defense Command: /40? MG Alberto Mannerini (Commanding General, Tripoli Fortress) 10/23/42? Col. Umberto Piatti del Pozzo (09/43, joins Social Republic of Italy; 10/43, Commanding General, 203rd Regional Military Command Padova) 05/43 disbanded.
- A. *Components* - Libyan Sahara Defense Command (10/23/42)
    1. **Hon Sector, Sebha Sector, Libyan Sahara Defense Command** (division status)
    2. **Ghat Sector, Sebha Sector, Libyan Sahara Defense Command** (division status)
    3. **Sebha Sector, Sebha Sector, Libyan Sahara Defense Command** (division status)

Royal Navy Fleets

1st Fleet [Commando in Capo 1a Squadra] (HQ: Taranto, Italy; Flagship: RIN battleship *Giulio Cesare*): 06/10/40? VA Inigo Campioni [RIN] [+ Commander-in-Chief, Royal Italian Navy Afloat] (01/01/43, Commander-in-Chief, Headquarters, Aegean Sea & Governor of Italian Dodecanese Islands) 12/09/40 unknown? 01/01/43 VA Carlo Bergamini [RIN] [Flag: RIN battleship *Roma*] [+ to 01/07/43, Commanding Officer, 5th Battleship Squadron; + 03/05/43, Commander-in-Chief, Italian Fleet Afloat] (killed in action; died when his flagship was sunk) 09/08/43

A. **Deputy Commander, 1st Fleet**: 12/01/42 VA Carlo Bergamini [RIN] [+ Commanding Officer, 2nd Fleet; Commanding Officer, 5th Battleship Squadron] (Commander-in-Chief, 1st Fleet) 01/01/43

B. *Components - 1st Fleet* (06/10/40)
   1. **1st Heavy Cruiser Squadron**
   2. **4th Light Cruiser Squadron**
   3. **5th Battleship Squadron**
   4. **8th Light Cruiser Squadron**
   5. **9th Battleship Squadron**

2nd Fleet (HQ: La Spezia, Italy; Flagship: RIN heavy cruiser *Pola*): 08/16/39 VA Riccardo Paladini [RIN] (?) 07/24/41 unknown? 01/12/42 VA Carlo Bergamini [RIN] [+ Commanding Officer, 5th Battleship Squadron; + Deputy Commander, 1st Fleet] (Commander-in-Chief, 1st Fleet) 01/01/43

A. *Components - 2nd Fleet* (06/10/40)
   1. **2nd Light Cruiser Squadron**
   2. **3rd Heavy Cruiser Squadron**
   3. **6th Battleship Squadron**
   4. **7th Light Cruiser Squadron**

Submarine Fleet (HQ: unknown?, Italy; Flagship: unknown?): /38? RA Antonio Legnani [RIN] (Commanding Officer, 8th Squadron) 07/20/39 VA Mario Falangola [RIN] (?) 12/10/41 VA Antonio Legnani [RIN] (joins the Social Republic of Italy; 09/23/43, Undersecretary of the Navy, Social Republic of Italy) 09/08/43

A. *Components - Submarine Fleet* (06/10/40)
   1. **1st Submarine Squadron**
   2. **2nd Submarine Squadron**
   3. **3rd Submarine Squadron**
   4. **4th Submarine Squadron**
   5. **7th Submarine Squadron**

Royal Navy Sea Departments (Italy)

Upper Tyrrhenian Sea Department [Comando Circoscrizione Alto Tirreno] (HQ: La Spenza, Italy): VA Giotto Maraghini (President of Navy Council) 06/10/40? VA Guido Bacci [RIN] (?) /4? VA Ildebrando Goiran [RIN] (President, Naval Council) /43 VA His Royal Highness Prince Aimone Roberto Margherita Marie Giuseppe Torino di Savoia [Savoy-Aosta], Duke of Spoleto, from 05/18/41 to 10/12/43 King Designate of Croatia [see Volume VII], and from 03/03/42, 4th Duke of Aosta] [RIN]
    A.   ***Components*** - **Upper Tyrrhenian Sea Department** (06/10/40)
        1.   **1st Fast Torpedo Boat [MAS] Squadron**
        2.   **Torpedo Boat Division 10**
        3.   **Torpedo Boat Division 16**

Lower Tyrrhenian Sea Department [Comando Circoscrizione Basso Tirreno] (HQ: Napoli [Naples], Italy): 06/10/40? VA Vladimiro Pini [RIN]
    A.   ***Components*** - **Lower Tyrrhenian Sea Department** (06/10/40)
        1.   **Sicily Naval Command** (division status)
        2.   **Sardinia Naval Command** (division status)
        3.   **Torpedo Boat Division 3**
        4.   **Torpedo Boat Division 4**

Upper Adriatic Sea Department [Comando Circoscrizione Alto Adriatico] (HQ: Venice, Italy): 06/10/40? VA His Royal Highness Prince Ferdinando Umberto Filippo Adalberto di Savoia [Savoy-Genoa], 3rd Duke of Genova [Genoa] [RIN]
    A.   ***Components*** - **Upper Adriatic Sea Department** (06/10/40)
        1.   **Pola Naval Command** (division status)
        2.   **Torpedo Boat Division 15**
        3.   **Fast Torpedo Boat [MAS] Division 6**

Ionian and Lower Adriatic Sea Department [Comando Circoscrizione dello Ionio e Basso Adriatico] (HQ: Taranto, Italy): 35? VA Vladimiro Pini [RIN] (?) /37? VA Riccardo Paladini [RIN] (Commander-in-Chief, 2nd Fleet) 08/16/39 RA Bruto Brivonesi [RIN] (Commanding Officer, 5th Battleship Squadron) 04/25/40? VA Antonio Pasetti [RIN] (?) /42? VA Peitro Lodolo [RIN]
    A.   ***Components*** - **Ionian and Lower Adriatic Sea Department** (06/10/40)
        1.   **Brindisi Naval Command** (division status)
        2.   **RIN light cruiser *Bari***
        2.   **RIN light cruiser *Taranto***
        3.   **Destroyer Division 2**
        4.   **Destroyer Division 6**

Royal Air Force Corps Commands

1st Air Force [Squadra 1] (/35, Northwestern Italy; HQ: Milano [Milan]; northern Italy and southern French coastline): 06/10/40? LG Rino Corso Fougier [RIAF] (?) /40 MG Alberto Briganti [RIAF] (?) 08/42? LG Gennaro Tedeschini-Lalli [RIAF] (?) 09/08/43 disbanded.
A.   *Components - 1st Air Force [Squadra 1]* (06/10/40):
   1.   **2nd "Borea" Fighter Command** (division status)
   2.   **4th "Drago" Bomber Command** (division status)
   3.   **6th "Falco" Bomber Command** (division status)
   4.   **1st Air Force Support Command** (division status)

2nd Air Force [Squadra 2] (/35, Northeastern Italy; HQ: Palermo, then Padova; Sicily until 12/40, /41, for duty in the central Mediterranean; north-east Italy; HQ: Padua, Italy): 06/10/40? LG Gennaro Tedeschini-Lalli [RIAF] (08/42?, Commanding General, 1st Air Force) /40 MG Ettore Faccenda [RIAF] (?) 04/05/41? LG Tullio Toccolini [RIAF] (?) 08/42? LG Felice Porro [RIAF] (?) 09/08/43 disbanded.
A.   *Components - 2nd Air Force [Squadra 2]* (06/10/40):
   1.   **1st "Aquila" Fighter Command** (division status)
   2.   **3rd "Centauro" Bomber Command** (division status)
   3.   **11th "Nibbio" Bomber Wing** (brigade status)
   4.   **2nd Air Force Support Command** (division status)

3rd Air Force [Squadra 3] (/35, Central Italy; HQ: Rome; Rome and duty in the Western Mediterranean, defense of Sicily): 06/10/40? LG Aldo Pellegrini [RIAF] (?) /40 Col. Ribella [RIAF] (acting) /40 MG Mario Infante [RIAF] (?) 11/41 LG Mario Ajmone-Cat [RIAF] (?) 08/42? LG Eraldo Ilari [RIAF] (?) 09/08/43 disbanded.
A.   *Components - 3rd Air Force [Squadra 3]* (06/10/40):
   1.   **5th "Eolo" Fighter Command** (division status)
   2.   **8th "Astore" Bomber Wing** (brigade status)
   3.   **3rd Air Force Support Command** (division status)

4th Air Force [Squadra 4] (/35, Southern Italy; HQ: Bari; Bari and duty in central and eastern Mediterranean, Yugoslavia, Greek Islands, Adriatic Sea): 06/10/40? LG Eraldo Ilari [RIAF] (08/42?, Commanding General, 3rd Air Force) 10/28/40? MG A. Bonola [RIAF] (?) 08/42? LG Ferruccio Ranza [RIAF] (?) 09/08/43 disbanded.
A.   *Components - 4th Air Force [Squadra 4]* (04/07/39):
   1.   **35th Bombardment Group** (Base: Brindisi, Italy; regiment status): 10/28/40? Col. E. Grande Brindisi [RIAF]
   2.   **36th Bombardment Group** (Base: Foggia, Italy; regiment status; removed by 10/28/40)
   3.   **37th Bombardment Group** (Base: Lecce-Galatina, Italy; regiment status): 10/28/40? LCol. A. Bancheri Lecce [RIAF]
   4.   **6th "Caccia" Fighter Group** (Base: Grottaglie, Italy; regiment status; removed by 10/28/40)
   5.   **4th Air Force Support Command** (added 06/10/40; division status):
   6.   **42nd BT Bombardment Group** (added 10/28/40; Base: Italy; regiment

status): 10/28/40? Col. S. Tade Grottaglie [RIAF]

5th Air Force [Squadra 5] (07/25/40, from **Aeronautica Della Libya (ALIB)**; HQ: Tripoli, Libya; North Africa and Tunisia): LG Mario Ajmone-Cat [RIAF] (Commanding General, 3rd Air Force) 11/41 LG Vittorio Marchesi [RIAF] (?) 10/42 LG M. Bernasconi [RIAF] (?) 09/08/43 disbanded.
- A. *Components* - **5th Air Force [Squadra 5]** (10/23/42):
    1. **Tripolitania Air Command** (Base: Tripoli, Libya; division status)
    2. **Central Sector** (Base: Cyrenaica; division status)
    3. **Eastern Sector** (Base: Fulka, Egypt; division status)

Albania Air Command [Aeronautica Dell'Albania (AALB)] (06/10/40; HQ: Tirana, Albania; Balkans, Adriatic Sea, Greece, Yugoslavia): 10/28/40? LG Ferruccio Ranza [RIAF] (Commanding General, 4th Air Force) 08/42? MG Gino Sozzani [RIAF] (?) 09/08/43 disbanded.
- A. *Components* - **Albania Air Command** (06/10/40):
    1. **Albania Air Support Command** (division status)**Albania Air Support Command** (division status)
    2. **38th BT Bombardment Group** (Base: Tirana, Albania; regiment status): 10/28/40? Col. D. Ludovico Valona

Aegean Air Command [Aeronautica Dell'Egeo (AEGE)] (06/10/40; HQ: Rhodes, Dodecanese; Aegean Islands, escort duty from Greece to Libya): Col. Ezio Padovani [RIAF] /40 BG Umberto Cappa [RIAF] (?) /40 MG Ulisse Longo [RIAF] (?) /42? MG Alberto Briganti [RIAF] (?) 09/08/43 disbanded.
- A. *Components* - **Aegean Air Command** (06/10/40):
    1. **39th Bombardier Wing** (Base: Gadurra [Rhodes], Dodecanese)
- B. **At Disposal of, Attached to, or on Special Duties with Aegean Air Command**: 09/42 (attached to) BG Ettore Muti [MVSN]

Italian East Africa Air Command [Aeronautica Africa Orientale Italiana (AAOI)] (06/10/40; HQ: Addis Ababa, Abyssinia [Ethiopia]): LG Pietro Pinna [RIAF] (?) /41 disbanded.
- A. *Components* - **Italian East Africa Air Command** (06/10/40):
    1. **Italian East Africa Air Support Command** (division status)
    2. **Northern Sector Italian East Africa Air Command** (Base: Asmiara, Eritrea)
    3. **Western Sector Italian East Africa Air Command** (Base: Addis Ababa, Abyssinia [Ethiopia])
    4. **Southern Sector Italian East Africa Air Command** (Base: Mogadiscio, Italian Somaliland)

Libya Air Command [Aeronautica Della Libyan (ALIB)] (06/10/40; HQ: Tripoli, Libya): 06/10/40? LG Felice Porro [RIAF] (?) 07/25/40 redesignated **5th Air Force** 07/25/40 07/40 redesignated **5th Air Force** - see **5th Air Force**.
- A. *Components* - **Libyan Air Command** (06/10/40):
    1. **Libyan Eastern Sector** (division status)

2. **Libyan Western Sector** (division status)

Sardinia Air Command [Aeronautica Della Sardegna (ASAR)] (06/10/40; HQ: Cagliari; Sardinia, central Mediterranean, Vichy North Africa, Sicily): MG Ottorino Vespignani [RIAF] (?) /40 MG Aldo Urbani [RIAF] (?) 09/08/43 disbanded.
A. *Components* - **Sardinia Air Command** (06/10/40):
    1. **Sardinia Air Support Command** (division status)
    2. **10th Bombardier Wing** (brigade wing)

Sicily Air Command [Aeronautica Della Sicilia (ASIC)] (12/40, HQ: Palermo; Sicily, central Mediterranean, Tunisia): MG Renato Mazzucco [RIAF] (?) 12/40 MG Monti [RIAF] (?) 08/42? BG Silvio Scaroni [RIAF] (?) 07/43 disbanded.
A. *Components* - **Sicily Air Command** (11/08/42):
    1. **51st CT Fighter Group** (Base: Gela, Sicily; regiment status)
    2. **53rd CT Fighter Group** (Base: Chinisia, Sicily; regiment wing)

Special Air Transportation Service [Commando Servizi Aeri Speciali (CSAS)] (06/10/40; HQ: Rome-Littorio; responsible for air supply to Italian contingents abroad):

Air Force Command for the Army [Comando Aviazione Alto Comando del Regio Esercito]:

Air Force Command for the Navy [Aviazione Ausiliaria per la Regia Marina (RM)] (equivalent to the Royal Air Force Coastal Command):

Italian Air Corps [Corpo Aero Italiano (CAI)] (Brussels, for raids against Britain, 09/40 to 04/41):

[Aviazione per Il Regia Esercito (AVRE)] (units working with the Army; second half of 1942, found only in the Balkans):

Fascist Militia (corps status)

Anti-Aircraft & Coast Defense Command [Comando Milizia Contaerei e Artiglieria Marittima] (HQ: Rome): 06/10/40? unknown? 09/08/43 disbanded.
- A. *Components* - Anti-Aircraft & Coast Defense Command (06/10/40)
  1. **Anti-Aircraft Artillery Militia [Milizia Artiglieria Controaerei (MAC)]** (06/10/40)
     1. **1st DICAT Legion Group** (HQ: Torino [Turin], Italy)
     2. **2nd DICAT Legion Group** (HQ: Milano [Milan], Italy): 06/42? BG Ferruccio Quarra [MVSN]
     3. **3rd DICAT Legion Group** (HQ: Bologna, Italy)
     4. **4th DICAT Legion Group** (HQ: Rome, Italy)
     5. **5th DICAT Legion Group** (HQ: Napoli [Naples], Italy)
  2. **Coast Defense Militia [Milizia Artiglieria Marittima [MAM]** formerly **[MILMART]**
     1. **1st MILMART Legion Group** (HQ: Messina, Italy)
     2. **2nd MILMART Legion Group** (HQ: La Spezia, Italy)

[NOTE: The DICAT [Territorial Anti-Aircraft Defense (Difesa contraerea Territoriale)] operated under control of the Territorial Army. The MILMART (Milizia Marittima) was for coastal defense. The difference between the two was that the MILMART was directly subordinate to the Royal Navy (Regia Marina) for active service as opposed to the DICAT, which was directly subordinate to the Territorial Army.**]**

Battle Groups (Sub-Corps Status)

58th "Abruzzi" Infantry Battle Group: /37 MG Ferruccio Bignamini (/40, Chief of Staff, Italian Armistice Commission to France) /39

Divisions

Infantry Divisions
[Usually named after towns unless otherwise noted]

Littorio Division (/37, Italian Volunteer Division C. T. V.; Spanish Civil War): MG Annibale Bergonzoli (06/10/41, Commanding General, XXIII Army Corps) /38

Llamas Negras - XIII de Marzo Division (/37, Italian Volunteer Division C. T. V.; Spanish Civil War): /37 MG Luigi Frusci (Deputy Commander, Volunteer Corps of Troops to Spain) /37

Flechas (Arrow) Division (/37, Italian Volunteer Division C. T. V.; Spanish Civil War): MG Mario Roatta (Military Attache' Germany) /39
- A. **Flechas Negras (Black Arrows)**: /37 Col. Alessandro Piazzoni (Commanding Officer, 53rd "Umbria" Infantry Regiment) /40
- B. **Flechas Azules (Blue Arrows)**: Col. Gusberti

2nd "Sfòrzesca" (Mountain) Infantry Division (reduced) (pre-war; name meaning "of the Sforza family", the ancient warlords of Milano [Milan]; has mountain equipment in it's TO&E; 06/40, invasion of France; 01/41, Albania, Greece; 07/41, returned to Italy; 06/42, Soviet Union, part of II Army Corps ,Eighth Army; severely damaged on the Don; 03/43, Italy for reforming; 05/43, merged with **157th "Novara" Infantry Division**; 09/08/43, surrendered and disbanded by the Germans): /37 MG Luigi Mentasti (Commandant, Supreme Institute of War) /39? MG Alfonso Ollearo (12/42, Commanding General, XXII Army Corps) /41 MG Carlo Pellegrini (Commandant, Royal Academy & Artillery School in Torino) /43 BG Nicole Ruffo (acting) /43 MG Michele Vaccaro (German prisoner-of-war; /43, joins Social Republic of Italy) 09/08/43 disbanded.
- A. **Infantry Commander**: /41 BG Michele Vaccaro (Commanding General, 2nd "Sfòzesca" (Mountain) Infantry Division) 05/43 merged with **157th "Novara" Infantry Division**; 09/08/43 surrendered and disbanded.
- B. *Components* - **2nd "Sfòrzesca" Infantry Division** (06/10/40)
    1. **53rd "Umbria" Infantry Regiment** (named for in region in Italy): /38? Col. Pietro Maggiani (Commanding General, 2nd Infantry Brigade) /39? unknown? /40 Col. Alessandro Piazzoni (Commanding General, 50th "Regina" Infantry Division) /40 unknown? 08/08/42? Col. Massimo Contini
    2. **54th "Umbria" Infantry Regiment** (named for in region in Italy): unknown? 08/08/42? Col. Mario Viale
    3. **17th "Sfòrzesca" Motorized Artillery Regiment**: /37? Col. Alessandro Gloria (Commanding General, "Manferrato" Infantry Brigade) /38? unknown? 08/08/42? Col. Achille Tirindelli

3rd "Manferrato" Infantry Division (pre-war; /39, redesignated **3rd "Ravenna" (Mountain) Infantry Division** and disbanded): /37 MG Alberto Terziani (retired?; 12/10/41,

Commanding General, VI Territorial Defense Command) /39 MG Matteo Roux (acting Commanding General, General Headquarters Albania) /39 vacant /39 redesignated **3rd "Ravenna" (Mountain) Infantry Division** - see **3rd "Ravenna" (Mountain) Infantry Division**.

3rd "Ravenna" (Mountain) Infantry Division (reduced) (pre-war as **3rd "Manferrato" Infantry Division**; /39, redesignated **3rd "Ravenna" (Mountain) Infantry Division**; 06/40, on French border; has mountain equipment in it's TO&E; 04/05/41?, part of XI Army Corps, Second Army; Greece and Yugoslavia; 05/41, transferred back to Italy; 07/42, Soviet Union, part of Eighth Army; 01/43, severely damaged on the Don; 05/43, Italy for reforming in Tuscany; 09/08/43, surrendered and disbanded): /39 MG Matteo Roux (Commanding General, XI Army Corps) 06/10/40? MG Edoardo Nebbia [+ /40, acting Commanding General, II Army Corps] (Commanding General, X Army Corps) 10/03/42 MG Francesco Du Pont (?) 09/08/43 surrendered and disbanded.
- A. **Chief of Staff, 3rd "Ravenna" Infantry Division** (06/10/40): Col. Clemente Primieri (Chief of Staff, V Army Corps) /41 unknown? 09/08/43 dissolved.
- B. *Components* - **3rd "Ravenna" Infantry Division** (06/10/40)
    1. **37th "Ravenna" Infantry Regiment**: unknown? 08/08/42? Col. Giovanni Naldoni 09/08/43 dissolved.
    2. **38th "Ravenna" Infantry Regiment**: unknown? 08/08/42? Col. Mario Bianchi
    3. **121st Motorized Artillery Regiment**: unknown? 08/08/42? Col. Giacomo Manfredi 09/08/43 dissolved.
- C. **Infantry Commander**: 08/08/42? BG Manilo Capizzi (Commanding General, 104th "Mantova" Infantry Division) /43 unknown? 09/08/43 dissolved.

4th "Monviso" Infantry Division (pre-war; /39, redesignated **4th "Liverno" Assault and Landing (Mountain) Infantry Division**): MG Antero Canale (Commanding General, 4th "Liverno" Assault and Landing (Mountain) Infantry Division) /39 redesignated **4th "Liverno" Assault and Landing (Mountain) Infantry Division** - see **4th "Liverno" Assault and Landing (Mountain) Infantry Division**.

5th "Cosseria" Infantry Division (reduced) (pre-war; 06/40, French Alps; 07/42, Soviet Union; 01/43, virtually destroyed; 03/43, Italy for reforming near Milan; 09/08/43, surrendered and disbanded): /35 unknown? /38? MG Carlo Bracco (?) 06/10/40? MG Alberto Vasarri (/43, Commanding General, 40th Territorial District) /40 MG Umberto Mondadori (?) 08/08/42? MG Enrico Gazzale (?) /43 MG Vincenzo Robertiello (?) 09/08/43 surrendered and disbanded.
- A. *Components* - **5th "Cosseria" Infantry Division** (06/10/40)
    1. **89th "Saberno" Infantry Regiment**: /37? Col. Giuseppe Stefanelli (Commanding General, Armored Infantry Brigade) /38? Col. Ettore Cotronei (Commanding General, 20th "Friuli" Assault & Landing Infantry Division) /40 unknown? 08/08/42? Col. Paolino Maggio 09/08/43 dissolved.
    2. **90th "Saberno" Infantry Regiment**: unknown? 08/08/42? Col. A. Guasconi 12/10/42? LCol. Giacomo Lapenna 09/08/43 dissolved.
    3. **37th Artillery Regiment** (to 103rd "Piacenza" Infantry Division):

4. **108th Artillery Division** (/41): 08/08/42? Col. Ernesto Drommi 09/08/43 dissolved.

B. **Infantry Commander**: 08/08/42? BG Vincenzo Robertiello (Infantry Commander, 12th "Sassari" Infantry Division) /43 unknown 09/08/43 dissolved.

6th "Cuneo" Infantry Division (reduced) (pre-war; 06/40, invasion of France; 01/41, Albania, then Greece; after fall of Greece, garrison duty on the Islands of Nasso, Nicaria, Sira. Andro, Santorino, and Samos until armistice; 09/08/43, surrendered and disbanded by the Germans): /39 MG Carlo Melotti (?) /41 MG Pietro Maggiani (Commanding General, 56th "Casale" Infantry Division) /41 unknown? 11/42 MG Mario Soldarelli (/44, Commanding General, Territorial Defense Command) /43 MG Pietro Maggiani (to /45, German prisoner-of-war) 09/08/43 disbanded.

A. ***Components* - 6th "Cuneo" Infantry Division (reduced)** (06/10/40)
1. **7th " Cuneo" Infantry Regiment**:
2. **8th " Cuneo" Infantry Regiment**:
3. **27th "Legnano" Artillery Regiment**: /35 Col. Antonio Formisano /37 Col. Giuseppe Mancinelli (Chief of Staff, First Army) /39 unknown? 09/08/43 dissolved.
4. **24th "Carracio" Blackshirt (CCNN) Legion**:

B. **Infantry, 6th "Cuneo" Infantry Division** (06/10/40): unknown? /43 BG Eugenio Peirolo (to /45, German prisoner-of-war) 09/08/43 dissolved.

7th "Leonessa" Infantry Division (pre-war as **"Leonessa" Brigade**; /39 redesignated **7th "Leonessa" Infantry Division** /39, redesignated **7th "Lupi di Toscana" Infantry Division (reduced)**): <u>**leonessa" Brigade**</u> /37? BG Francesco Sartoris (Commanding General, 33rd "Acqui" Infantry Division) /39 redesignated **7th "Leonessa" Infantry Division** /39 MG Fernandino Cona (/40, Commanding General, XV Army Corps) /39 redesignated **7th "Lupi di Toscana" Infantry Division (reduced)** - see redesignated **7th "Lupi di Toscana" Infantry Division**.

7th "Lupi di Toscana" Infantry Division (reduced) (/39, from **7th "Leonessa" Infantry Division**; named for the Tuscany Wolves, the Tuscan volunteers of the Italian Independence Wars; 06/40, French Alps; 01/41, Albania; 11/42, invasion of Vichy France and occupied Toulon; 08/24/43, Italy; 09/08/43, dissolved): /37? MG Pier Domenico Mazzari (retired?; 05/43?, Special Duties, III Territorial Defense Command) /39 MG Edmondo Rossi (retired?; /41, attached to VII Army Corps) 06/10/40? MG Ottavio Bollea (?) /41 MG Angelico Carta (Commanding General, 51st "Sienna" Infantry Division) /41 MG Ernesto Cappa (Commanding General, V Territorial Defense Command) /42 MG Gustano Reisoli-Matthieu (Commanding General, XIII Army Corps) /43 BG Lauro Riviera (?) 09/08/43 disbanded.

A. **Chief of Staff, 7th "Lupi di Toscana" Infantry Division**: /40 Col. Alberto Roda (Artillery Commander, XX Army Corps) /42 unknown? 09/08/43 dissolved.
B. ***Components* - 7th "Lupi di Toscana" Infantry Division (reduced)** (06/10/40)
1. **77th "Toscana"Infantry Regiment** (named for in region in Italy):
2. **78th "Toscana" Infantry Regiment** (named for in region in Italy): /38? Col. Paolo Puntoni (First Aide-de-Camp to the King) /40? Col. Umberto Bonagura 09/08/43 dissolved.

3. **30th "Leonessa" Artillery Regiment** ("the Lioness", nickname of the town of Brescia, earned during the 1848 independence revolt):
C. **Infantry, 7th "Lupi di Toscana" Infantry Division** (/39): unknown? /43 Col. Claudio Gregori (to /45, German prisoner-of-war) 09/08/43 dissolved.

8th "di Marcia" (Training) Infantry Division (07/42, for replacements for Eighth Army in Soviet Union; 03/43? disbanded): MG Egisto Conti (Commanding General, 230th Coastal Division) 03/43? disbanded.
A. *Components - 8th "di Marcia" (Training) Infantry Division* (07/42)
 1. **1st Brigade** (03/43, redesignated **28th Coastal Brigade**):
 2. **2nd Brigade** (03/43, redesignated **29th Coastal Brigade**):
 3. **3rd Brigade** (03/43, assigned anti-partisan duty in Yugoslavia; 04/43, headquarters used to form **230th Coastal Division**):

11th "Brennero" Infantry Division (reduced) (pre-war; named after northernmost Alpine pass toward Austria; 06/40, France; 12/40, Albania; 09/08/43, the division chose to remain with the Axis and continued to fight against the allies; 10/43, because of German doubts, the division was disbanded): /39 MG Arnaldo Forgiero (/42, in Russia; /43, Commanding General, II Army Corps) /41 MG Mario Marghinotti (Commanding General, 25th "Bologna" Semi-Motorized Infantry Division) /41 MG Paolo Berardi (Commanding General, 12th "Sassari" Infantry Division) /42 MG Licurgo Zannini (Commanding General, XXIV Army Corps) /42 MG Aldo Princivalle (09/43, joins Social Republic of Italy; 10/43, Commanding General, 3rd "San Marco" Marine Division) 10/43 disbanded.
A. **Deputy Commander, 11th "Brennero" Infantry Division**: /42 BG Salavatore d'Arminio Monforte (Commanding General, 53rd "Arezzo" Infantry Division) 01/01/43
B. *Components - 11th "Brennero" Infantry Division (reduced)* (06/10/40)
 1. **231st "Avellino" Infantry Regiment**: /37 Col. Marquis Luigi Trionfi (Chief of Staff, Somalia) /38 unknown? /41? Col. Rodolfo Torresan (Chief, Recovery Section, General Staff; /43, Commanding General, 29th "Piemonte" Infantry Division) /42 Col. Antonio Cesaretti (Commanding General, 153rd "Macerata" Garrison Division) /43 unknown? 09/08/43 dissolved.
 2. **232nd "Avellino" Infantry Regiment**:
 3. **331st Infantry Regiment** (assigned to **50th "Regina" Infantry Division**):
 4. **9th "Brennero" Artillery Regiment**:
 5. **35th "Indomita" Blackshirt (CCNN) Legion**:
C. **Infantry Commander, 11th "Brennero" Infantry Division**: /43 BG Ugo Abbondanza (?) /43 BG Caretta (to /45, German prisoner-of-war) 10/43 dissolved.

12th "Del Timavo" Infantry Division (pre-war; /39, redesignated **12th "Sassari" Infantry Division (reinforced)**): /38? MG Lorenzo Dalmazzo (Inspector of Cavalry (Celere) Troops) /39 MG Riccardo Balocco (Commanding General, 12th "Sassari" Infantry Division) /39 redesignated **12th "Sassari" Infantry Division (reinforced)** - see **12th "Sassari" Infantry Division**.

12th "Sassari" Infantry Division (reinforced) (/39, from **12th "Del Timavo" Infantry Division**; 04/05/41?, part of VI Army Corps, Second Army; Greece and Yugoslavia;

09/08/43, disbanded by the Germans): MG Riccardo Balocco (/41, Commanding General, V Army Corps) 06/10/40? MG Giacomo Castagna (01/01/43?, Commanding General, 31st "Calabria" Infantry Division) /40 MG Michele Giacomo Scaroina (Commanding General, 50th "Regina" Infantry Division) 01/41 MG Furio Monticelli (?) /42 MG Paola Berardi (Chief of Staff, Seventh Army) /43 BG Ettore Giannuzzi (?) /43 MG Francesco Zani (?) 09/08/43 disbanded.

- A. **Components - 12th "Sassari" Infantry Division (reinforced)** (06/10/40)
    1. **151st "Sassari" Infantry Regiment**: /38 Col. Antonio Rizzo (Commanding Officer, 8th Colonial Brigade) /40? Col. Felice Gonnella (Member, Italian Armistice Commission to France) /41 Col. Mario Maggiani (Commanding General, 56th "Casale" Infantry Division) 01/01/43? unknown 09/08/43 dissolved.
    2. **152nd "Sassari" Infantry Regiment**: /39 Col. Aldo Princivalle (Infantry Commander, 9th "Pasubio" Infantry Division) 08/05/41 Col. Ugo Medori (Commanding General, 212th Coastal Division) /43 unknown? 09/08/43 dissolved.
    3. **34th Artillery Regiment**:
    4. **73rd "Boiardi" Blackshirt (CCNN) Legion**:
- B. **Infantry Commander, 12th "Sassari" Infantry Division** (06/10/40): unknown? /43 BG Vincenzo Robertiello (Commanding General, 5th "Cosseria" Infantry Division) /43 unknown? 09/08/43 dissolved.

13th "Rè" Infantry Division (reinforced) (pre-war; named for the word "King"; 04/05/41?, part of XI Army Corps, Second Army; Greece and Yugoslavia; Coratia; 01/43, Italy): /39 MG Benedetto Fiorenzuoli (Commanding General, 14th "Isonzo" Infantry Division) 08/05/41? BG Ottorino Battista Dabbeni (Commanding General, 105th "Rovigo" Semi-Motorized Infantry Division) /42 MG Raffaele Pelligra (Chief of Staff, Seventh Army) /43 BG Giovanni De Bonis (?) /43 BG Ottaviomo Traniello (?) 09/08/43 disbanded.

- A. **Components - 13th "Rè" Infantry Division (reinforced)** (06/10/40)
    1. **1st "Rè" Infantry Regiment**:
    2. **2nd "Rè" Infantry Regiment**:
    3. **23rd "Timavo" Artillery Regiment** (named for a river):
    4. **75th "Italo Balbo" or "20 Dicembre" Blackshirt (CCNN) Legion**:

14th "Isonzo" Infantry Division (reinforced) (pre-war, as **Isonzo Brigade**; named after a World War I battlefield; 04/05/41?, part of XI Army Corps, Second Army; Greece and Yugoslavia; 09/08/43, surrendered and disbanded by the Germans): **Isonzo Brigade** /37? BG Francesco Roluti (Commanding General, 14th "Isonzo" Infantry Division) /39 redesignated **14th "Isonzo" Infantry Division** /39 MG Francesco Roluti (retired?) /39 MG Giovanni Cocconi (?) 06/10/40? MG Federico Romero (acting Commanding General, XI Army Corps) /40 MG Benedetto Fiorenzuoli (Commanding General, V Army Corps) /40 MG Alessandro Maccario /42 MG Emilio Coronati (Commanding General, 152nd " Piceno" Garrison Division) /42 MG Alessandro Maccario (/44?, Commanding General, Internal Security Division "Calabria" /43 MG Guido Cerruti (German prisoner-of-war) 09/08/43 disbanded.

- A. **Components - 14th "Isonzo" Infantry Division (reinforced)** (06/10/40)
    1. **23rd "Como" Infantry Regiment**:

2. **24th "Como" Infantry Regiment**:
3. **6th "Isonzo" Artillery Regiment**:
4. **98th "Maremana" Blackshirt (CCNN) Legion**:

15th "Carnaro" Infantry Division (prewar; /39, redesignated **15th "Bergamo" Infantry Division (reinforced)**): /34 MG Achille Vaccarisi (retired?) /35 unknown? /37? MG Giovanni Majoli (07/41, Special duties with War Ministry) /38? MG Francesco Lavinao (Commanding General, 15th "Bergamo" Infantry Division) /39 redesignated **15th "Bergamo" Infantry Division (reinforced)** - see **15th "Bergamo" Infantry Division (reinforced)**.

15th "Bergamo" Infantry Division (reinforced) (/39, from **15th "Carnaro" Infantry Division**; 04/05/41?, part of V Army Corps, Second Army; Greece and Yugoslavia): MG Francesco Lavinao (Commanding General, 62nd "Marmarica" Infantry Division) /39 MG Ugo Gigliarelli Fiumi (?) 06/10/40? Pietro Belletti (Commanding General, 105th "Rovigo" Semi-Motorized Infantry Division; 10/43, destroyed and disbanded by the Germans) /42 BG Emilio Becuzzi (Commanding General, Dalmatia Coastal Defense) /42 MG Alessandro Piazzoni (Commanding General, 53rd "Arezzo" Infantry Division) /43 MG Alfonso Cigala-Fulgosi [+ Commanding General, Spalato Area, Dalmatia] (Executed by the Germans) 10/43 disbanded.

A. ***Components*** - **15th "Bergamo" Infantry Division (reinforced)** (06/10/40)
1. **25th "Bergamo" Infantry Regiment**:
2. **26th "Bergamo" Infantry Regiment**:
3. **4th "Carnaro" Artillery Regiment**:
4. **89th "Etrusca" Blackshirt (CCNN) Legion**:

B. **Infantry, 15th "Bergamo" Infantry Division** (06/10/40): unknown? /43 Col. Paolo Grimaldi (to /45, German prisoner-of-war) 09/08/43 dissolved.

16th "Fossalta" Infantry Division (pre-war as **"Fossalta" Brigade**; /39 redesignated **16th "Fossalta" Infantry Division**; /39, redesignated **16th "Pistola" Motorized Infantry Division**): <u>**"Fossalta" Brigade**</u> /38? BG Guido Perugi (Commanding General, 36th "Forli" Infantry Division) /39 redesignated <u>**16th "Fossalta" Infantry Division**</u> /39 MG Carlo Favagrossa (Chief, General Commissariat for War Production) /39 redesignated **16th "Pistola" Motorized Infantry Division** - see **16th "Pistola" Motorized Infantry Division**.

17th "Rubicone" Infantry Division (pre-war; /39, redesignated **17th "Pavia" Semi-Motorized Infantry Division**): /34 MG Ugo Pignetti (Commanding General, Royal Customs Guard) /38 MG Luigi Cubeddu (?) /39 redesignated **17th "Pavia" Semi-Motorized Infantry Division** - see redesignated **17th "Pavia" Semi-Motorized Infantry Division**.

18th "Messina" Infantry Division (reduced) (pre-war, as **"Metauro" Infantry Division**; /39, redesignated **18th "Messina" Infantry Division**; 04/05/41?, part of the XVII Army Corps, Ninth Army; Greece and Yugoslavia; 09/08/43, disbanded by the Germans): <u>**"Metauro" Infantry Division**</u> /38? MG Angelo Stirpe (Commanding General, 24th "Gran Sasso" Infantry Division) /39 redesignated <u>**"Messina" Infantry Division**</u> /39 MG Remo Gambelli (Commanding General, 18th "Messina" Infantry Division) /39 redesignated <u>**18th "Messina" Infantry Division**</u> /39 MG Remo Gambelli (Commanding General, VIII Army

Corps) /39 Col. Attilio Amato (acting; /43 Commanding General, 14th Coastal Brigade) /39 MG Francesco Zani (attached to, General Headquarters Albania) 06/41? MG Carlo Tucci (Chief of Staff, General Headquarters, Albania) /42 MG Guglielmo Spicacci (to /45, German prisoner-of-war; /45, lost without a trace) /43 BG Attilio Amato (German prisoner-of-war) 09/08/43 disbanded.

A. **Components - 18th "Messina" Infantry Division (reduced)** (06/10/40)
1. **93rd "Messina" Infantry Regiment**:
2. **94th "Messina" Infantry Regiment**:
3. **2nd "Metauro" Artillery Regiment** (named for a river):
4. **108th "Stamura" Blackshirt (CCNN) Legion**:

19th "Gavninana" Infantry Division (/38, disbanded): /35 MG Nino Salvatore Villa Santa (/43, President, Supreme Military Tribunal) /39 BG Mario Arisio (acting; Commanding General, 28th "Vespri" Infantry Brigade) /39 disbanded.

19th "Venezia [Venice]" Infantry Division (pre-war; Albania; Greece; 10/40, Balkans; 09/08/43, changed sides and fought against the Germans and Croatian forces; portions of the division were reorganized into the **Garibaldi Division** fighting along side of General Tito's Yugoslavian Partisans): /39 MG Errico Pitassi-Manella (Commanding General, XXII Army Corps) 06/10/40? BG Silvio Bonini (01/01/43?, Commanding General, 19th "Venezia [Venice]" Infantry Division) 09/10/40 MG Vito Ferroni (?) 01/01/43? MG Silvio Bonini (?) /43 MG Giovanni Battista Oxilia (joined the Yugoslav Partisans, Commanding General, Garibaldi" Division) 09/43 joined the Yugoslav Partisans as the **Garibaldi Division** - see **Garibaldi Division**.

A. **Components - 19th "Venezia [Venice]" Infantry Division** (06/10/40)
1. **83rd "Venezia [Venice]" Infantry Regiment**:
2. **84th "Venezia [Venice]" Infantry Regiment**: /39? Col. Giuseppe Falugi (/42, Commanding General, 16th "Pistola" Motorized Infantry Division) /40? Col. Carlo Ferrero (Assistant Inspector-General, Recruiting) /41? Col. Giorgio Masina (/42, Commanding Genera;, 102nd "Trento" Motorized Infantry Division) /41 Col. Rosario Assanti (Commanding General, 15th Territorial Zone) /42 Col. Ettore Giannuzzi (Commanding General, 12th "Sassari" Infantry Division) /43 unknown? 09/08/43 dissolved.
3. **383rd Infantry Regiment**:
4. **19th "Gavinana" Artillery Regiment** (named for a town and a location of a battle):
5. **72nd "Farini" Blackshirt (CCNN) Legion**:
B. **Infantry, 19th "Venezia [Venice]" Infantry Division**: 06/10/40): unknown? /43 BG Carlo Isasca (joins the Yugoslav Chetnics; /45, captured and executed by Yugoslav communists) 09/08/43 dissolved.

21st "Granatieri di Sardegna" Infantry Division (reduced) (pre-war; named after the Sardinia Grenadiers, the Royal Guards; 06/40, France; 07/41, Balkans; 12/42, Italy; 09/08/43, crushed and disbanded by the Germans): /37 MG Giovanni Vecchi (Commanding General, 31st "Caprera" Infantry Division) /39 BG Giunio Ruggiero (Commanding General, 36th "Forli" Mountain Infantry Division) 06/10/40? MG Taddeo Orlando (Commanding General, XXXI Army Corps) /42 MG Umberto Spigo (acting;

Commanding General, IX Army Corps) /42 MG Giunio Ruggiero (09/43, joins the Social Republic of Italy; /44?, Commanding General, 200th Regional Military Command Rome) /43 BG Alfredo de Rienzi (?) /43 MG Giaocchino Solinas (joins Social Republic of Italy; /44, Commanding General, 205th Military Regional Command Milano) 09/08/43 disbanded.

- A. **Components - 21st "Granatieri di Sardegna" Infantry Division (reduced)** (06/10/40)
    1. **1st "Granatieri di Sardegna" Infantry Regiment**: /39 Col. Ugo Fongoli (Commanding General, 41st Colonial Infantry Brigade) /40 Col. Alfredo de Rienzi (Commanding General, 21st "Granatieri di Sardegna" Infantry Division) /43 unknown? 09/08/43 dissolved.
    2. **2nd "Granatieri di Sardegna" Infantry Regiment**:
    3. **3rd "Granatieri di Sardegna" Infantry Regiment**: /37 Col. Marquis Alberto Trionfi (Chief of Staff, 51st "Siena" Infantry Division) /40 unknown? 09/08/43 dissolved.
    4. **13th "Granatieri di Sardegna" Artillery Regiment**: /37? Col. Gabriele Boglione /39? Col. Emilio Coronati (/42, Commanding General, 14th "Isonzo" Infantry Division) /40? Col. Alberto Aliberti (Intendant-General, Sixth Army) /42 unknown? 09/08/43 dissolved.
    5. **55th "Alpina Friuliana" Blackshirt (CCNN) Legion**:

22nd "Cacciatori della Alpi" Infantry Division [Alps' Light Infantry Division] (reduced) (pre-war; named for Garibaldi's Volunteers during the Italian Independence Wars; 06/40, France; 01/41, Balkans; 09/08/43, surrendered and disbanded by the Germans): /39 BG Emilio Giglioli (acting; Deputy Commander, 41st "Firenze" Infantry Division) 06/10/40? MG Dante Lorenzelli (Commanding General, 1st "Superga" Assault & Landing (Mountain) Infantry Division) /40 BG Guido Pialorsi (British prisoner-of-war; /44, Commanding General, Folgore Combat Group) 06/41 MG Giovanni Angelo Pivano (Commandant, Salsomagglore Garrison; /43, Commandant, Supreme Institute of War) 12/31/41 MG Vittorio Ruggero (Commanding General, Milano Territorial Defense Command) /43 BG Luigi Maggiore-Perni (German prisoner-of-war) 09/08/43 disbanded.

- A. **Components - 22nd "Cacciatori della Alpi" Infantry Division [Alps' Light Infantry Division] (reduced)** (06/10/40)
    1. **51st "Alpi" Infantry Regiment** (name for the Alps mountains):
    2. **52nd "Alpi" Infantry Regiment** (name for the Alps mountains): /39? Col. Nicola Spinelli (/40, Commanding General, 64th "Catanzaro" Infantry Division) /39 Col. Emilio Giglioli (acting Commanding Officer, "Cacciatori delle Alpi" Infantry Division) /40? Col. Paolo Angioj (Commanding Officer, 157th "Liguria" Infantry Regiment) /40? unknown? 09/08/43 dissolved.
    3. **1st "Cacciatori d'Alpi" Artillery Regiment** (name for the Alps mountains):
    4. **105th "Benito Moggioni" Blackshirt (CCNN) Legion**:

23rd "Murge" Infantry Division (pre-war; /39, redesignated **23rd "Ferrara" Infantry Division**): /37? MG Carlo Vecchiarelli (Commanding General, 132nd "Ariete" Armored Division) /39 MG Licurgo Zannini (Commanding General, 23rd "Ferrara" Infantry Division) /39 redesignated **23rd "Ferrara" Infantry Division** - see **23rd "Ferrara" Infantry Division**.

23rd "Ferrara" Infantry Division (pre-war, from **23rd "Ferrara" Infantry Division**; 10/40,

Balkans; 09/08/43, disbanded by the Germans): /39 Licurgo Zannini (Commanding General, 24th "Pinerolo" Infantry Division) /40 MG Francesco Zani (Commanding General, 12th "Sassari" Infantry Division) /43 MG Antonio Franceschini (German prisoner-of-war) 09/08/43 idsbanded.
- A. **Components 23rd "Ferrara" Infantry Division** (06/10/40)
    1. **47th "Ferrara" Infantry Regiment**:
    2. **48th "Ferrara" Infantry Regiment**: /39? Col. Francesco Sapienza (acting Commanding General, 185th "Folgore" Airborne Division) /41 unknown? 09/08/43 dissolved.
    3. **14th "Murge" Artillery Regiment**: /35 Col. Giacomo Castagna (Commanding General, 12th "Sassari" Infantry Division) /39? Col. Guido Boselli (Commanding General, 41st "Firenze [Florence]" Infantry Division) /40? unknown? 09/08/43 dissolved.
    4. **82nd "Benito Mussolini" Blackshirt (CCNN) Legion**:
- B. **Infantry, 23rd "Ferrara" Infantry Division**: unknown? /43 BG Giacomo Tonareli (to /45, German prisoner-of-war) 09/08/45 dissolved.

24th "Gran Sasso" Infantry Division (pre-war; /39, redesignated **24th "Pinerolo" Infantry Division**): /35 MG Enrico Maltese (retired?; 07/41, with National Council of Research, Rome) /36 MG His Royal Highness Prince Adalberto di Savoia, Duke of Bergamo (/41, Commanding General, III Army Corps) /39 MG Angelo Stirpe (Commanding General, 24th "Pinerolo" Infantry Division) /39 redesignated **24th "Pinerolo" Infantry Division** - see **24th "Pinerolo" Infantry Division**.

24th "Pinerolo" Infantry Division (reinforced) (pre-war, as **24th "Gran Sasso" Infantry Division**; France; 01/41, Balkans; 04/05/41?, part of Librazhd Sector, Ninth Army; 09/08/43, defected to the Greek ELAS Partisans and fought against the Germans): /39 MG Angelo Stirpe (retired?; 09/42, Mobilization Branch, War Ministry) /39 MG Giuseppe de Stefanis (Commanding General, 102nd "Trento" Motorized Infantry Division) /41 MG Licurgo Zannini (Commanding General, 11th "Brennero" Infantry Division) /41 MG Guglielmo Scalise (?) /42 MG Cesare Benelli (?) /42 BG Guglielmo Morgari (Infantry Commander, 36th "Forti" Mountain Infantry Division) 11/42 MG Adolfo Infante (/44, Aide-de-Camp to the Crown Prince) 09/08/43 remains of unit defected to the Greek ELAS Partisans.
- A. **Components - 24th "Pinerolo" Infantry Division (reinforced)** (06/10/40)
    1. **13th "Pinerolo" Infantry Regiment**: /41? Col. Giovanni Del Giudice (joins Social Republic of Italy; 10/43, Commandant, Center for Training of Special Units) /43) unknown? 09/08/43 dissolved.
    2. **14th "Pinerolo" Infantry Regiment**
    3. **313th Infantry Regiment**:
    4. **18th "Gran Sasso" Artillery Regiment** (named for a mountain): Col. Francesco De Rose (/41, British prisoner-of-war) /39? Col. Nicola Ciampa /41? Col. Armando Lubrano (Commanding Officer, 2nd "Tridentina" Alpine Artillery Regiment) /42? unknown? 09/08/43 dissolved.
    5. **136th "Tre Monti" Blackshirt (CCNN) Legion**:

25th "Volturno" Infantry Division (pre-war; /39, redesignated **25th "Bologna" Semi-**

Motorized Infantry Division): /38? MG Giuseppe Pafundi (Commanding General, 25th "Bologna" Semi-Motorized Infantry Division) /39 redesignated **25th "Bologna" Semi-Motorized Infantry Division** - see **25th "Bologna" Semi-Motorized Infantry Division**.

27th "Sila" Infantry Division (to /39, when it was disbanded and redesignated **27th "Brescia" Semi-Motorized Infantry Division**): /34 BG Francesco Bertini (/40, Commanding General, II Army Corps) /36? BG Attilio de Michelis (/42, Commanding General, 21st Territorial Zone) /39 disbanded and redesignated **27th "Brescia" Semi-Motorized Infantry Division** - see **27th "Brescia" Semi-Motorized Infantry Division**.

28th "Aosta" Infantry Division (reinforced) (pre-war; 06/40, Sicily; 08/43, destroyed by the Allies): /39 MG Mario Arisio ("Torino [Turin]" Semi-Motorized Infantry Division) /39 MG Pietro Maletti (Commanding General, 3rd Libyan Infantry Division) /40 MG Federico d'Arle (Commanding General, 38th "Puglie" Infantry Division) /41 MG Valentino Babini (British prisoner-of-war, captured at Agedabia ; released, /44, Commanding General, "Aosta" Infantry Division [see Italian Co-Belligerent Army]) 02/07/41 04/05/41? MG Emanuele Girlando (?) /42 MG Luigi Manzi (Commanding General, III Army Corps) /43 MG Giuseppe Romano (Commanding General, X Territorial Defense Command) 08/43 destroyed.
- A. ***Components - 28th "Aosta" Infantry Division (reinforced)*** (06/10/40)
    1. **5th "Aosta" Infantry Regiment**: /40? Col. Ugo Sprega (Special duties, VIII Army Corps) 07/41? unknown? 09/08/43 dissolved.
    2. **6th "Aosta" Infantry Regiment**:
    3. **22nd "Vespri" Artillery Regiment** (is a reference to the 1282 Vespri Siciliani revolt against the French Anjou royal house): /37 Col. Brunetto Brunetti (/41, Commandant, Artillery School) /3? Col. Giuseppe Castellano (Commanding Officer, 22nd "Aosta" Artillery Regiment; /42, Special employment for the Chief of the General Staff) /39 unknown? 09/08/43 dissolved.
    4. **171st "Vespri" Blackshirt (CCNN) Legion**:
- B. **Infantry, 28th "Aosta" Infantry Division** (06/10/40): unknown? /42 Col. Umberto Marchesi (acting Commanding General, 207th Coastal Division) /42? unknown? 09/08/43 dissolved.
- C. **Internal Security, 28th "Aosta" Infantry Division**: /42 Col. Silvio Brisotto (Commanding General, 58th "Legnano" Infantry Division) /43 unknown? 09/08/43 dissolved.

29th "Peloritana" Infantry Division (1935; 1939, disbanded): MG Enrico Adami-Rossi (/43, Commandant, Turin, II Territorial Defense Command) /39 disbanded.

29th "Piemonte" Infantry Division (pre-war; named for in region in Italy; 01/41, Balkans, Aegean; 09/08/43, disbanded by the Germans): 06/10/40? MG Giovanni Cerio (British prisoner-of-war) /40 MG Armellini Chiappi (09/08/43 to /44, German prisoner-of-war; /44, died in hospital) /41 MG Rodolfo Naldi [+ /41, acting Commanding General, VIII Army Corps; /42, acting Commanding General, VIII Army Corps] (died during the war) /43 MG Rodolfo Torresan (to/ 44, German prisoner-of-war; /44 died in hospital end of /44 or beginning of /45) 09/08/43 disbanded.
- A. ***Components - 29th "Piemonte" Infantry Division*** (06/10/40)

1. **3rd "Piemonte" Infantry Regiment**:
2. **4th "Piemonte" Infantry Regiment**:
3. **303rd Infantry Regiment**:
4. **24th "Peloritana" Artillery Regiment** (named for a mountain): /38? LCol. Vincenzo Saporetti (Artillery Officer, 21st "Piemonte" Artillery Regiment; /42, Artillery Officer, XXVI Army Corps) /39 unknown? 09/08/43 dissolved.
5. **166th Artillery Regiment**:

B. **Infantry, 29th "Piemonte" Infantry Division** (06/10/40): unknown? /43 BG Riccardo di Belfiore Mattioli (to /45, German prisoner-of-war) 09/08/43 dissolved.

30th "Sabauda" Infantry Division (reinforced) (pre-war; named for "of the House of Savoy"; 06/40, Sardinia; 09/08/43, surrendered to Allies): /35 MG Italo Gariboldi (Chief of Staff, Italian East Africa) /36 MG Luigi De Biase (Commanding General, IX Army Corps) 06/10/40? MG Ubaldo Scanagatta (?) 01/01/43? MG Giovanni Battista Zenati (acting; acting Commanding General, XIII Army Corps) /43 BG Gino Piccini (acting) /43 MG Nino Sozzani (09/43, joins Social Republic of Italy; Commanding General, 203rd Regional Military Command Padova) /43 BG Erole Ronco (12/43, Commanding General, Sabauda Internal Security Division) 09/08/43 surrendered.

A. *Components - 30th "Sabauda" Infantry Division (reinforced)* (06/10/40)
1. **45th "Reggio" Infantry Regiment**: /38 LCol. Gino Piccini (Commanding Officer, 60th "Calabria" Infantry Regiment) /40? unknown? 09/08/43 dissolved.
2. **46th "Reggio" Infantry Regiment**: Col. Arnaldo Azzi (Commanding General, 101st "Trieste" Motorized Infantry Division) /40 Col. Antonio Callierno (acting Commanding Officer, 65th "Granatieri di Savoia" Infantry Division) /40 unknown? 09/08/43 dissolved.
3. **16th "Sabauda" Artillery Regiment**:
4. **176th "San Elisio" Blackshirt (CCNN) Legion**:

B. **Infantry, 30th "Sabauda" Infantry Division** (06/10/40): unknown? /43 BG Giuseppe Vallerini (?) 09/08/43 dissolved.

31st " Caprera" Infantry Division (pre-war; /39, redesignated **31st "Calabria" Infantry Division (reinforced)**): /39 MG Giovanni Vecchi (Commanding General, "31st "Calabria" Infantry Division) /39, redesignated **31st "Calabria" Infantry Division** - see **31st "Calabria" Infantry Division (reinforced)**.

31st "Calabria" Infantry Division (reinforced) (pre-war; named for in region in Italy; 06/40, Sardinia; 09/08/43, surrendered to Allies): /39 MG Giovanni Vecchi (Commanding General, XIV Army Corps) /40 MG Giovanni Antonio De Benedetti (?) 06/10/40? MG Carlo Petra di Caccuri (acting Commanding General, 47th "Bari" Infantry Division) /42? BG Mario Nannei (acting) 01/01/43? MG Giacomo Castagna [+ /43, Commanding General, XXX Army Corps] /43 BG Antonio Garelli (Commanding General, "Calabria" Division) 09/08/43 surrendered.

A. *Components - 31st "Calabria" Infantry Division (reinforced)* (06/10/40)
1. **59th "Calabria" Infantry Regiment**:
2. **60th "Calabria" Infantry Regiment**: /39? Col. Enrico Broglia (Commanding General, "Pasubio" Infantry Brigade) /40? Col. Gino Piccini (Infantry

Commander, 41ˢᵗ "Firenzi [Florence]" Infantry Division) /42? unknown? 09/08/43 dissolved.
   3. **40ᵗʰ "Caprera" Artillery Regiment** (named after an island, the retirement home of the famous patriot Giuseppe Baribaldi):
   4. **177ᵗʰ "Logudoro" Blackshirt (CCNN) Legion** (later renamed **359ᵗʰ Infantry Regiment**):

32ⁿᵈ "Marche" Infantry Division (reduced) (pre-war; named for in region in Italy; 04/05/41, part of the XVII Army Corps, Ninth Army; Greece and Yugoslavia; Russia; 09/08/43, surrendered and disbanded by the Germans): /39 MG Count Fernando Gelich (Commanding General, 1ˢᵗ "Superga" Assault & Landing (Mountain) Infantry Division) 06/10/40? MG Riccardo Pentimalli (/43, Commanding General, XIX Army Corps) /41 MG Giuseppe Amico (executed by the Germans) 09/08/43 disbanded.
A. **Chief of Staff, 32ⁿᵈ "March" Infantry Division**: /4? Col. Carlo Cinti (Chief of Staff, 47ᵗʰ "Bari" Infantry Division) /42 unknown? 09/08/43 dissolved.
B. *Components - 32ⁿᵈ "Marche" Infantry Division (reduced)* (06/10/40)
   1. **55ᵗʰ "Marche" Infantry Regiment**:
   2. **56ᵗʰ "Marche" Infantry Regiment**:
   3. **32ⁿᵈ Artillery Regiment**:
   4. **49ᵗʰ "San Marco" Blackshirt (CCNN) Legion**:
C. **Infantry, 32ⁿᵈ "Marche" Infantry Division (reduced)**: unknown? /43 Col. Fortunato Mauro (to /45, German prisoner-of-war) 09/08/43 dissolved.

33ʳᵈ "Acqui" (Mountain) Infantry Division (reduced) (pre-war; has mountain equipment in it's TO&E; 06/40, France; 12/40, Balkans, Aegean; 10/43, destroyed and disbanded by the Germans): /39 MG Renato Coturri (Commanding General, 54ᵗʰ "Napoli" Infantry Division) /39 MG Adamo Mariotti (/41, Chief of Staff, Sixth Army) /39? MG Luigi Mazzini (retired?) 06/10/40? MG Francesco Sartoris (?   ) 01/01/43? MG Ernesto Chiminelli (Commanding General, 151ˢᵗ "Perugia" Garrison Division) /43 MG Antonio Gandin (Deputy Chief of the Army General Staff) /43 unknown? 10/43 disbanded.
A. **Chief of Staff, 33ʳᵈ "Acqui" (Mountain) Infantry Division**: /39? Col. Ferrante Gonzga del Vodice (Artillery Commander, XIII Army Corps) 06/10/40 unknown? 09/08/43 dissolved.
B. *Components - 33ʳᵈ "Acqui" (Mountain) Infantry Division (reduced)* (06/10/40)
   1. **17ᵗʰ "Acqui" Infantry Regiment**: /38? LCol. Gino Piccini (Commanding Officer, 45ᵗʰ "Reggio" Infantry Regiment) /39? Col. Gualtiero Gabutti (Commanding General, 51ˢᵗ "Siena" Infantry Division) 06/10/40? Col. Amedeo Pederzini (Deputy Commander, 132ⁿᵈ "Ariete" Armored Division) /42 Col. Angiolo Tosi (Commanding General, 213ᵗʰ Coastal Division) 01/01/43? unknown? 09/08/43 dissolved.
   2. **18ᵗʰ "Acqui" Infantry Regiment**:
   3. **317ᵗʰ Infantry Regiment**:
   4. **33ʳᵈ Artillery Regiment**:
   5. **27ᵗʰ "Fanfulla" Blackshirt (CCNN) Legion** (later renamed **343ʳᵈ Infantry Regiment**):

C. **Infantry, 33rd "Acqui" Infantry Division**: /43 BG Luigi Gherzi (executed by the Germans) /43 unknown? 09/08/43 dissolved.

37th "Modena" (Mountain) Infantry Division (reduced) (pre-war; has mountain equipment in it's TO&E; 06/40, France Alpine Front; 11/40, Balkans; 09/08/43, surrendered and disbanded by the Germans): /39 MG Carlo Rossi (I) (Commanding General, XVI Army Corps) 07/40? MG Giovanni Magli (Vice Chief of the Supreme General Staff) /40 MG Marquis Luigi Trionfi (/41, discharged from the Army; /44 to /45, imprisoned by the Germans) /40 MG Alessandro Gloria (Commanding General, XXVI Army Corps) /41 MG Marlo Guassardo (09/43, joins the Social Republic of Italy; 10/43, Commanding General, 210th Regional Military Command Genova [Genoa]) 01/01/43? MG Italo Caracciolo (Commanding General, Argolide Sector, Greece) /43 BG Ettore Carossini (to /45, German prisoner-of-war) /43 BG Erberto Papini (to /45, German prisoner-of-war) 09/08/43 disbanded.
   A. ***Components*** - **37th "Modena" (Mountain) Infantry Division (reduced)** (06/10/40)
      1. **41st "Modena" Infantry Regiment**:
      2. **42nd "Modena" Infantry Regiment**:
      3. **341st Infantry Regiment**:
      4. **29th "Cosseria" Artillery Regiment**:
      5. **36th "Christoforo Colombo" Blackshirt (CCNN) Legion**:

38th "Pulgie" Infantry Division (reduced) (pre-war; named for in region in Italy; 0341, part of XIV Army Corps, Ninth Army; Greece and Yugoslavia; 09/08/43, surrendered and disbanded by the Germans): /39 MG Mario Marghinotti (Deputy Commander, VIII Army Corps) /40 unknown? 04/05/41? MG Alberto D'Aponte (?) /41 MG Federico d'Arle (Commanding General, Argolide-Kossovo Sector) 04/43 MG Carlo Baudino (German prisoner-of-war) or MG Luigi Clerico (German prisoner-of-war) 09/08/43 disbanded.
   A. ***Components*** - **38th "Pulgie" Infantry Division (reduced)** (06/10/40)
      1. **71st "Pulgie" Infantry Regiment**:
      2. **72nd "Pulgie" Infantry Regiment**:
      3. **15th "Montenero" Artillery Regiment** (named for a mountain):
      4. **115th Blackshirt (CCNN) Legion**:

40th "Cacciatori d'Africa" Division [Africa Light Division] (06/10/40, part of Eastern Sector, Italian East African Armed Forces; 03/41 to 05/41, destroyed): 06/10/40? MG Giovanni Varda (British prisoner-of-war) 05/41 destroyed.
   A. ***Components*** - **40th "Cacciatori d'Africa" Division [Africa Light Division]** (06/10/40)
      1. **210th "Bisagno" Infantry Regiment**:
      2. **211th "Pescara" Infantry Regiment**
      3. **10th "Monto Bello" Blackshirt (CCNN) Legion**:

41st "Firenzi [Florence]" Infantry Division (reduced) (pre-war; 06/40, France; 04/05/41, part of Librazhd Sector, Ninth Army; Greece and Yugoslavia; 09/08/43, surrendered and disbanded by the Germans): /39 MG Paride Negri (/41, Commanding General, 154th "Murge" Garrison Division) /40 BG Guido Boselli (01/01/43?, Commanding General, 9th "Pasubio" Semi-Motorized Infantry Division) /41 MG Arnaldo Azzi (/44, Commanding

General, Lazio, Umbria & Abruzzi Military Command) /43 BG Gino Piccini (acting Commanding General, 30th " Sabauda" Infantry Division) /43 unknown? 09/08/43 disbanded.
- A. **Deputy Commander, 41st "Firenzi [Florence]" Infantry Division**: /40 BG Emilio Giglioli (Commanding General, Italian Troops in Zara; /42, Chief of Staff, Commander-in-Chief, North Africa) /41 unknown? 09/08/43 dissolved.
- B. **Components - 41st "Firenzi [Florence]" Infantry Division (reduced)** (06/10/40)
    1. **127th "Firenzi" Infantry Regiment**:
    2. **128th "Firenzi" Infantry Regiment**:
    3. **41st Artillery Regiment**:
    4. **92nd "Francesco Ferrucci" Blackshirt (CCNN) Legion**:
- C. **Infantry, 41st "Firenzi" Infantry Division** (06/10/40): unknown? /42? Col. Gino Piccini (acting Commanding General, 41st "Firenzi [Florence]" Infantry Division) /43 unknown? 09/08/43 dissolved.

44th "Cremona" Infantry Division (reduced) (pre-war; 06/40, France; Italy; 11/41, Sardinia, Corsica; 09/08/43, surrendered to Allies): /39? MG Nino Sozzani (/42, Commanding General, 136th "Giovanni Fascisti" Armored Division) 06/10/40? MG Umberto Mondino (Commanding General, XXX Army Corps) /42 MG Giaocchino Solinas (Commanding General, 21st "Granatieri di Sardegna" Infantry Division) /43 unknown? 09/08/43 surrendered to Allies.
- A. **Components - 44th "Cremona" Infantry Division (reduced)** (06/10/40)
    1. **21st "Cremona" Infantry Regiment**: /40? Col. Giorgio Masina (Commanding Officer, 84th "Venezia" Infantry Regiment) /41? unknown? 09/08/43 dissolved.
    2. **22nd "Cremona" Infantry Regiment**: /41? Col. Giovanni Grassi (President, Regional Commission Albanian Frontier, General Headquarters Albania) 03/42 unknown? 09/08/43 dissolved.
    3. **7th "Curtatone e Montanara" Artillery Regiment** (named for towns and a location of battles): Col. Alberto Cordero di Montezemolo (British prisoner-of-war) /41 Col. Mario Martorrelli (Artillery Commander, II Army Corps) 08/08/42? unknown? 09/08/43 dissolved.
    4. **90th "Pisa" Blackshirt (CCNN) Legion** (later renamed **321st Infantry Regiment**):
- B. **Infantry, 44th "Cremona" Infantry Division**: /43 BG Arnaldo Bonelli (Commanding General, 3rd Blackshirt (CCNN) Zone) /43 BG Giacomo Zanussi (Deputy Chief of the Army General Staff) /43 unknown? 09/08/43 dissolved.

45th "Bersaglieri (sharpshooter) d'Africa" Division (formed by the **5th Bersaglieri Cyclist Regiment**, the **8th Bersaglieri Cyclist Regiment**, and the **136th Armored Regiment 5th Bersaglieri Cyclist Regiment**):

47th "Bari" Infantry Division (reinforced) (pre-war; 06/40, Corfu; 11/40, Balkans; 03/43, Sardinia; 09/08/43, surrendered to Allies): /39 MG Ernesto Zaccone (?) /40 MG Achille D'Havet (Commanding General, 206th Coastal Division) 12/41 BG Matteo Negro (acting Commanding General, VIII Army Corps) /42 MG Ismaele Di Nisio (Commanding General, IX Army Corps) 01/01/43? MG Ernesto Ferone (?) /43 BG Enrico Bianco di San Secondo (?) /43 MG Giuseppe Cortese (acting) /43 MG Carlo Petra di Caccuri

(Commanding General, Bari Division) 09/08/43 surrendered to Allies.
- A. **Chief of Staff, 47th "Bari" Infantry Division**: /42 BG Carlo Cinti (?) 09/08/43 dissolved.
- B. ***Components - 47th "Bari" Infantry Division (reinforced)*** (06/10/40)
    1. **139th "Bari" Infantry Regiment**:
    2. **140th "Bari" Infantry Regiment**:
    3. **47th Artillery Regiment**:
    4. **152nd "Acciasta" or "Salentina I" Blackshirt (CCNN) Legion** (later renamed **340th Infantry Regiment**):

48th "Taro" Infantry Division (reinforced) (pre-war; named for a river; 06/40, France; 11/40, Balkans; Vichy France; 03/43, Sardinia; 09/08/43, disbanded): /39 MG Luigi Chiolini (/42, Commandant, Central Military School) 06/10/40? MG Gino Pedrazzoli (to /45, German prisoner-of-war) /43 BG Alberto Trevissio (to /45, German prisoner-of-war) 09/08/43 disbanded.
- A. ***Components - 48th "Taro" Infantry Division (reinforced)*** (06/10/40)
    1. **207th "Taro" Infantry Regiment**:
    2. **208th "Taro" Infantry Regiment**:
    3. **48th Artillery Regiment**:
    4. **164th "Eroclino Scalfaro" Blackshirt (CCNN) Legion**:

49th "Parma" Infantry Division (pre-war; 10/40, Balkans; 09/08/43, disbanded): /37? BG Ugo Adami (in reserves) /39 MG Attilio Grattarola (Commanding General, I Territorial Defense Command) /41 MG Emillio Battisti (Commanding General, 4th "Cuneense" Alpini Division) 01/42 BG Luigi Podio (acting; special duties, Inspector of Artillery) 01/42 MG Paolo Micheletti (Commandant, Argyrocastron) 01/43 BG Ezio Vegni (acting; /45, Commanding General, Piceno Division) /43 BG Enrico Lugli (to /45, German prisoner-of-war) 09/08/43 disbanded.
- A. ***Components - 49th "Parma" Infantry Division*** (06/10/40)
    1. **49th "Parma" Infantry Regiment**:
    2. **50th "Parma" Infantry Regiment**:
    3. **49th Artillery Regiment**:
    4. **109th " Filippo Corridoni" Blackshirt (CCNN) Legion**:
- B. **Infantry, 49th "Parma" Infantry Division**: /42 BG Luigi Clerico (Commanding General, 38th "Puglie" Infantry Division) /42 unknown? 09/08/43 dissolved.

50th "Regina" Infantry Division (pre-war; named for the word "Queen"; 06/40, Aegean, Italian Dodecanese Islands; 10/43, surrendered and disbanded by the Germans): /37 MG Marquis Ettore Manca di Mores (Inspector of Artillery) /39 MG Pietro Pietracaprina (retired?) 40 BG Alessandro Piazzoni (Commanding General, 101st "Trieste" Motorized Division) /41 MG Michele Giocomo Scaroina (to /45, German prisoner-of-war) 10/43 disbanded.
- A. ***Components - 50th "Regina" Infantry Division*** (06/10/40)
    1. **9th "Regina" Infantry Regiment**: /37? Col. Gino Cristiani /38? Col. Furio Monticelli (acting Commanding General, 2nd "Emanuele Filiberto Testa di Ferro" Cavalry (Celere) Division) /39? Col. Raffaello Calzini (/43, Military-

Governor, Rhodes) /41? unknown? 09/08/43 dissolved.
2. **10th "Regina" Infantry Regiment**:
3. **309th Infantry Regiment**:
4. **50th "Regina" Artillery Regiment**:
5. **201st "Conte Verde" then "Egeo [Rhodes]" Blackshirt (CCNN) Legion**:
6. **331st "Avellino" Infantry Regiment** (from **11th "Brennero" Infantry Division**):

B. **Artillery, 50th "Regina" Infantry Division**: unknown? /43 Col. Giuseppe Consoli (Artillery Commander, Aegean Islands) /43 unknown? 09/08/43 dissolved.

51st "Siena" Infantry Division (pre-war; 10/40, Balkans, Aegean; 09/08/43, disarmed and disbanded by the Germans): /39 MG Ercole Caligian (?) 06/10/40? BG Gualtiero Gabutti (?) /40 MG Guilo Perugi (Commanding General, 26th "Assietta" Mountain Infantry Division) 02/07/41 unknown? 01/01/43? MG Angelico Carta (Commanding General, XIII Army Corps) /43 BG Luigi Chatrian (Commanding General, 227th Coastal Division) 07/43 unknown? 09/08/43 disbanded.

A. **Chief of Staff, 51st "Siena" Infantry Division** (06/10/40): Col. Marquis Alberto Trionfi (Chief of Staff, 57th "Lombardia" Infantry Division) /41 unknown? 09/08/43 dissolved.
B. *Components - 51st "Siena" Infantry Division* (06/10/40)
   1. **31st "Siena" Infantry Regiment**:
   2. **32nd "Siena" Infantry Regiment**:
   3. **51st Artillery Regiment**:
   4. **141st "Capuano" or "Volturno" Blackshirt (CCNN) Legion**:
C. **Infantry Commander, 51st "Siena" Infantry Division**: /43 BG Enrico Andreini (German prisoner-of-war) 09/08/43 dissolved.

53rd "Arezzo" Infantry Division (pre-war; 10/40, Balkans; 04/05/41?, part of Librazhd Sector, Ninth Army; Greece and Yugoslavia; Montenegro; 09/08/43, disarmed and disbanded by the Germans): /39 MG Michele Molinari (?) /40 BG Ernesto Ferone (Commanding General, 47th "Bari" Infantry Division) 10/42? BG Ernesto Rerone (acting) 01/01/43? BG Salavatore d'Arminio Monforte (?) /43 MG Carlo Rivolta (acting Commanding General, IV Army Corps) /43 MG Alessandro Piazzoni (Commanding General, VI Army Corps) /43 MG Arturo Torriano (to /45, German prisoner-of-war) 09/08/43 disbanded.

A. *Components - 53rd "Arezzo" Infantry Division* (06/10/40)
   1. **225th "Arezzo" Infantry Regiment**: /40? Col. Egisto Conti (Commanding General, 8th "di Marcia" (Training) Infantry Division) /42 unknown? 09/08/43 dissolved.
   2. **226th "Arezzo" Infantry Regiment**:
   3. **53rd Artillery Regiment**:
   4. **80th "Alessandro Farnese" Blackshirt (CCNN) Legion**:
B. **Infantry, 53rd "Arezzo" Infantry Division** (06/10/40): unknown? /42 Col. Eugenio Peirolo (Infantry Commander, 6th "Cuneo" Infantry Division) /43 unknown? 09/08/43 dissolved.

54th "Napoli [Naples]" Infantry Division (reinforced) (pre-war; 06/40, Italy, Sicily; 08/43 destroyed): /39 MG Renato Coturri (Commanding General, XXX Army Corps) /42 unknown? 01/01/43? MG Count Guillo Cesare Gotti-Porcinari (Allied prisoner-of-war) 08/43 destroyed.
- A. **Components - 54th "Napoli [Naples]" Infantry Division (reinforced)** (06/10/40)
  1. **75th "Napoli [Naples]" Infantry Regiment**: /39? Col. Marcello Piccone (Commanding Officer, Frontier Guards, XIV Army Corps) /40? Col. Francesco Bruno /41? Col. Francesco Mazzerelli (Commanding General, 4th Royal Carabinieri Brigade) /42 unknown? 09/08/43 dissolved.
  2. **76th "Napoli [Naples]" Infantry Regiment**:
  3. **54th Artillery Regiment**:
  4. **173rd "Salso" Blackshirt (CCNN) Legion**:

55th "Savona" Infantry Division (pre-war; North Africa Model Division: semi-motorized with special TO&E; 01/17/42, destroyed at Alam Halfa): /39 BG Feruccio Paganuzzi (acting; 05/42?, President, War Tribunal, Albania) /40 MG Pietro Maggiani (Commanding General, 25th "Bologna" Semi-Motorized Infantry Division) /41 MG Fedele De Giorgis (British prisoner-of-war) 01/17/42 destroyed.
- A. **Components - 55th "Savona" Infantry Division** (06/10/40)
  1. **15th "Savona" Infantry Regiment**:
  2. **16th "Savona" Infantry Regiment**:
  3. **12th "Sila" Artillery Regiment** (named for a mountain):

56th "Casale" Infantry Division (reduced) (pre-war; 03/41, Balkans; 09/08/43, disbanded): /39 MG Enea Navarini (Commanding General, XXI Army Corps) /41 MG Pietro Maggiani (Commanding General, IV Army Corps) /42 MG Italo Caracciolo (acting; Commanding General, 37th "Modena" Infantry Division) 01/01/43? MG Mario Maggiani (?) 09/08/43 disbanded.
- A. **Components - "Casale" Infantry Division** (06/10/40)
  1. **11th "Casale" Infantry Regiment**: /37? Col. Agostino Cinti (/43, Commanding General, XVI Army Corps) /39? unknown? 09/08/43 dissolved.
  2. **12th "Casale" Infantry Regiment**:
  3. **311th Infantry Regiment**:
  4. **56th Artillery Regiment**:
  5. **23rd "Bersaglieri del Mincio" Blackshirt (CCNN) Legion**:
- B. **Infantry, 56th "Casale" Infantry Diviison**: /42 BG Eugenio Gatti (to /45, German prisoner-of-war) 09/08/43 dissolved/

57th "Lombardia" Infantry Division (reinforced) (pre-war; named for in region in Italy; (04/05/41?, part of V Army Corps, Second Army; Greece and Yugoslavia; 09/08/43, disbanded by the Germans): /39 MG Giovanni Esposito (Commanding General, 5th "Pusteria" Alpine Division) 04/05/41? MG Vittorio Zatti (?) /41 BG Pietro Scipioni (German prisoner-of-war; 10/43, joins Social Republic of Italy) /43 BG Beniamino Pittau (to /45, German prisoner-of-war) 09/08/43 disbanded.
- A. **Chief of Staff, 57th "Lombardia" Infantry Division** (06/10/40): unknown? /41 Col. Marquis Alberto Trionfi (Chief of Staff, VIII Territorial Defense Command) /41 unknown? 09/08/43 dissolved.

B. ***Components - 57th "Lombardia" Infantry Division*** (06/10/40)
   1. **73rd "Lombardia" Infantry Regiment**:
   2. **74th "Lombardia" Infantry Regiment**:
   3. **57th Artillery Regiment**:
   4. **137th "Monte Maiella" Blackshirt (CCNN) Legion**:

58th "Legnano" Infantry Division (reduced) (pre-war as **"Legnano" Infantry Division**; 06/40, France; 01/41, Balkans; 11/42, France; 07/43, Italy; 09/08/43, surrendered to Allies): **"Legnano" Infantry Division** /39? BG Giovanni Marciani (Commanding General, 208th Coastal Division) /39 BG Ettore Baldassare (acting Commanding General, Armored Corps) /40 redesignated **58th "Legnano" Infantry Division** /40 MG Edoardo Scala (?) /41 MG Vittorio Ruggero (Commanding General, 22nd "Cacciatori delle Alpi" Infantry Division) /41 MG Amedeo De Cia (?) 01/01/43? MG Roberto Olmi (?) /43 BG Vincenzo Dapino (Commanding General, 1st Italian Motorized Group) 09/08/43 surrendered to Allies.
   A. ***Components - 58th "Legnano" Infantry Division (reduced)*** (06/10/40)
      1. **67th "Palermo" Infantry Regiment**: /37? Col. Emilio Bancale (Commanding General, 21st "Brennero" Infantry Brigade) /39? unknown? 09/08/43 dissolved.
      2. **68th "Palermo" Infantry Regiment**: Col. Luigi Gherzi /39? Col. Emillio Bisson (acting Commanding General, 2nd Infantry Brigade) /39? Col. Luigi Gherzi (Chief of Staff, 26th "Assieta" Mountain Infantry Division) /39 unknown? 09/08/43 dissolved.
      3. **58th "Legnano" Artillery Regiment** (named for a town and a location of a battle):
   B. **Infantry, 58th "Legnano" Infantry Division**: unknown? /42 Col. Vincenzo Dapino (Commanding General, 58th "Legnano" Infantry Division) /43 unknown? 09/08/43 dissolved.

59th "Cagliari" (Mountain) Infantry Division (reduced) (pre-war; has mountain equipment in it's TO&E; 06/40, France; 091/41, Balkans; 09/08/43, surrendered and disbanded by the Germans): /39 MG Ruggero Tracchia (acting Commanding General, 102nd "Trento" Motorized Infantry Division) /40 MG Antonio Scuero (Undersecretary of War, War Ministry) /41 MG Giuseppe Gianni (Artillery Commander, Second Army) /41 MG Paolo Angioj (German prisoner-of-war) 09/08/43 disbanded.
   A. ***Components - 59th "Cagliari" (Mountain) Infantry Division (reduced)*** (06/10/40)
      1. **63rd "Cagliari" Infantry Regiment**:
      2. **64th "Cagliari" Infantry Regiment**:
      3. **363rd Infantry Regiment**:
      4. **59th Artillery Regiment**:
      5. **28th "Randaccio" Blackshirt (CCNN) Legion**:
   B. **Infantry, 59th "Cagliari" (Mountain) Infantry Division (reduced)** (06/10/40): unknown? /42 BG Marquis Alberto Trionfi (to /45, German prisoner-of-war; /45, executed by the Germans) 09/08/43 dissolved.

60th "Sabratha" Infantry Division (pre-war; named for a Libyan town; 06/40, North Africa Model Division: semi-motorized with special TO&E; 11/42, destroyed at El Alamein; 12/42, disbanded): /37 MG Guiseppe Tellera (Chief of Staff, Commander-in-Chief, North Africa)

/39 MG Guido Della Bona (Commanding General, XXVI Army Corps) /41 MG Mario Soldarelli [+ in /41, acting Commanding General, Tripolitania Command; + in /41, acting Commanding General, XX Army Corps] (Commanding General, 6th "Cuneo" Infantry Division) 11/42 destroyed 12/42 disbanded.
- A. **Components - 60th "Sabratha" Infantry Division** (06/10/40)
    1. **85th "Verona" Infantry Regiment**:
    2. **86th "Verona" Infantry Regiment**: /36 LCol. Dino Parri (Commandant, Tripoli Fortress) /39 unknown? 09/08/43 dissolved.
    3. **42nd "Sabratha" Artillery Regiment**:
    4. **3rd "Articelere" Heavy Artillery Regiment**: Col. Antonio Cozzolino 09/08/43 dissolved.

61st "Sirte" Infantry Division (pre-war; named for a Libyan town; 06/40, 06/40, North Africa Model Division: semi-motorized with special TO&E; 01/41, destroyed at Tobruk): /37 BG Alberto Barbieri (Commanding General, 131st "Centauro" Armored Division) /38? MG Valentino Babini (Commanding General, 28th "Aosta" Infantry Division) 06/10/40? BG Vincenzo Della Mura (British prisoner-of-war) 01/41 destroyed.
- A. **Components - 61st "Sirte" Infantry Division** (06/10/40)
    1. **69th "Ancona" Infantry Regiment**:
    2. **70th "Ancona" Infantry Regiment**:
    3. **43rd "Sirte" Artillery Regiment**:

62nd "Marmarica" Infantry Division (pre-war; named for a Libyan region; 06/40, North Africa Model Division: semi-motorized with special TO&E; 12/40, destroyed at Bardia): /37 MG Angelo Rossi (Commanding General, III Army Corps) /38 MG Armando Pescatori (Commanding General, 2nd Libyan "Pescator" Infantry Division) /39 MG Francesco Lavinao (?) 06/10/40? MG Ruggero Tracchia (British prisoner-of-war; captured at Bardia) 01/05/41 destroyed.
- A. **Components - 62nd "Marmarica" Infantry Division** (06/10/40)
    1. **115th "Treviso" Infantry Regiment**:
    2. **116th "Treviso" Infantry Regiment**:
    3. **44th "Marmarica" Artillery Regiment**:

63rd "Cirene" Infantry Division (pre-war; named for a Libyan town; 06/40, North Africa Model Division: semi-motorized with special TO&E; 12/40, destroyed at Bardia): /37 MG Carlo Spatocco (Commanding General, XXI Army Corps) /40 BG Alessandro De Guidi (British prisoner-of-war) 12/40 destroyed.
- A. **Components - 63rd "Cirene" Infantry Division** (06/10/40)
    1. **157th "Liguria" Infantry Regiment** (named for in region in Italy): /39 Col. Ugo Pizzarello /40 Col. Paolo Angioj (Commanding General, 59th "Cagliari" Infantry Division) /41 Col. Manlio Mora (Commanding General, Italian Troops in Zara) /42 unknown? 09/08/43 dissolved.
    2. **158th "Liguria" Infantry Regiment** (named for in region in Italy):
    3. **45th "Cirene" Artillery Regiment**:

64th "Catanzaro" Infantry Division (pre-war; 06/40, North Africa Model Division: semi-motorized with special TO&E; 12/40, destroyed at Buq Buq): /39? BG Lorenzo Mugnai (

?) 06/10/40? MG Giuseppe Stefanelli (?) /40 MG Nicola Spinelli (10/01/41, Judge, Supreme Military Tribunal) /40 MG Giuseppe Amico (Commanding General, 32nd "Marche" Infantry Division) 12/40 destroyed.
- A. **Components - 64th "Catanzaro" Infantry Division** (06/10/40)
    1. **141st "Catanzaro" Infantry Regiment**:
    2. **142nd "Catanzaro" Infantry Regiment**:
    3. **203rd Artillery Regiment**:

65th "Granatieri di Savoia" Infantry Division (pre-war; named after the Grenadiers of Savoy; 06/10/40, part of Eastern Sector, Italian East African Armed Forces; 05/41, destroyed and surrendered in Ethiopia): /38? MG Ettore Scala (/41, British prisoner-of-war) /40? MG Enrico Armando (acting; /41, Commanding General, XX Army Corps) /40? Col. Antonio Callierno (acting; /42? Commanding General, 207th Coastal Division) /41 MG Amadeo Liberati (British prisoner-of-war) 05/41 destroyed.
- A. **Components - 65th "Granatieri di Savoia" Infantry Division** (06/10/40)
    1. **10th "Granatieri di Savoia" Infantry Regiment**:
    2. **11th "Granatieri di Savoia" Infantry Regiment**:
    3. **60th Artillery Regiment**:
    4. **11th "Monteferato" Blackshirt (CCNN) Legion**:

130th "Sabauda II" Infantry Division (/37, from **"Sabauda II" Infantry Brigade**; /39?, disbanded): BG Carlo Bracco (Commanding General, 5th "Cosseria" Infantry Division) /39? disbanded.

D'Antoni Division (1943): BG Giovanni D'Antoni (Prefect of Milano [Milan], III Territorial Defense Command) /43 disbanded.

"Egeo" Independent Division
- A. **Components - "Egeo" Independent Division** (06/10/40)
    1. **Infantry Regiment**:
    2. **Infantry Regiment**

Italian Troops in Zara (/36, Spain; 04/05/41?, part of the Ninth Army; Greece and Yugoslavia): /36 Col. Carlo Rivolta (/41, Commanding General, Littoral Group, Greece; /43,Commanding General, 53rd "Arezzo" Infantry Division) /38 BG Ubaldo Scanagatta (Commanding General, "Sabauda" Infantry Brigade) /38 BG Luigi Zo (09/42?, attached to VIII Territorial Defense Command) 04/04/41? BG E. Gilioli (?) /42 BG Ruggiero Cassata (?) /42 BG Manlio Mora (Commanding General, 204th Coastal Division) /43 unknown? 09/08/43 dissolved.
- A. **Components - Italian Troops in Zara** (04/05/41):
    1. **Zara Army Corps Artillery Regiment**
    2. **"Fronte a Terra" Infantry Regiment** (temporary unit): 04/05/41? Col. E. Morra 09/08/43 dissolved.

V Corps Border Guard Division (04/05/41?, part of V Army Corps, Second Army; Greece and Yugoslavia): 04/05/41? MG Arturo Torriano (Commanding General, 17th "Pavia" Semi-

Motorized Infantry Division) /42 unknown? 09/08/43 disbanded.
A. **Components - V Corps Border Guard Division** (04/05/41)
1. **25th Border Guard Sector Regiment**: Col. O. Franchini Timavo 09/08/43 dissolved.
2. **26th Border Guard Sector Regiment**: 04/05/41? Col. Lorenzo Brovarone Carnaro (Commanding General, Bolzano Border Guards) /43 unknown 09/08/43 dissolved.
3. **27th Border Guard Sector Regiment**: Col. P. Fioretti Fiume 09/08/43 dissolved.
4. **10th Border Guard Artillery Regiment**

XI Corps Border Guard Division (04/05/41?, part of XI Army Corps, Second Army; Greece and Yugoslavia): 04/05/41? BG Carlo Viale (Commanding General, 152nd "Piceno" Garrison Division) /42 unknown? 09/08/43 disbanded.
A. **Components - XI Corps Border Guard Division** (04/05/41)
1. **17th Border Guard Sector Regiment**
2. **21st Border Guard Sector Regiment**
3. **22nd Border Guard Sector Regiment**
4. **23rd Border Guard Sector Regiment**
5. **9th Border Guard Artillery Regiment**
6. **17th Border Guard Artillery Regiment**

Garrison Divisions

151st "Perugia" Garrison Division (08/41; 12/41, Balkans; 10/43, disbanded by the Germans): /39 MG Riccardo Pentimalli (Commanding General, 32nd "Marche" Infantry Division) 06/10/40? BG Antonio Luridiana (Deputy Commander, 3rd "Principe Amedeo Duce D'Aosta" Cavalry (Celere) Civision) 12/12/42 MG Ernesto Chiminelli (killed by the Germans) 10/43 disbanded.
- A. **Components - 151st "Perugia" Garrison Division (08/41)**
    1. **129th "Perugia" Infantry Regiment**:
    2. **130th "Perugia" Infantry Regiment**:
    3. **151st Artillery Regiment**:
    4. **29th "Chinotto" Blackshirt (CCNN) Legion**:
- A. **Infantry Commander, 151st "Perugia" Garrison Division**: /42 BG Domenico Canistrà (acting Commanding General, 152nd "Piceno" Garrison Division) /42 BG Guiseppe Adami (?) 10/43 dissolved.

152nd "Piceno" Garrison Division (04/41, Italy; named for in region in Italy; 09/08/43, surrendered and disbanded by the Allies): BG Giovanni Battista Guiccione (/43, Artillery Commander, Seventh Army) /42 BG Domenico Canistrà (Commanding General, 5th "Calabria" Internal Security Brigade) /42 BG Carlo Viale (Commanding General, 158th "Zara" Garrison Division) /42 MG Emilio Coronati (Commanding General, XXXI Army Corps) /43 unknown? 09/08/43 disbanded.
- A. **Components - 152nd "Piceno" Garrison Division (04/41)**
    1. **235th "Piceno" Infantry Regiment**:
    2. **236th "Piceno" Infantry Regiment**:
    3. **336th Infantry Regiment**:
    4. **152nd Artillery Regiment**:

153rd "Macerata" Garrison Division (12/41; 06/42, Balkans; 09/08/43, disbanded by the Germans): MG Eduardo Quarra-Sito (/43, Commanding General, 154th "Murge" Garrison Division) /42 MG Vincenzo Giardina (09/43, joins Social Republic of Italy; /43, Commanding General, 1st "Italia" Infantry Division) /43 BG Antonio Cesaretti (/44, Commanding General, 1st "Sabauda" Internal Security Brigade) 09/08/43 disbanded.
- A. **Components - 153rd "Macerata" Garrison Division (12/41)**
    1. **121st "Macerata" Infantry Regiment**:
    2. **122nd "Macerata" Infantry Regiment**
    3. **153rd Artillery Regiment**:

154th "Murge" Garrison Division (04/42; named for in region in Italy; 05/42, Balkans; 09/08/43, disbanded by the Germans): /41 MG Paride Negri (acting Commanding General, VI Army Corps) /43 MG Eduardo Quarra-Sito (?) 09/08/43 disbanded.
- A. **Components - 154th "Murge" Garrison Division (04/42)**
    1. **259th "Murge" Infantry Regiment**:
    2. **260th "Murge" Infantry Regiment**
    3. **154th Artillery Regiment**:
- B. **Infantry, 154th "Murge" Garrison Division (04/42)**: BG Luigi Gherzi (Infantry

Commander, 33rd "Acqui" Infantry Division) /43 unknown? 09/08/43 dissolved.

155th "Emilia" Garrison Division (12/41; named for in region in Italy; 03/42, Balkans; 09/08/43, disbanded by the Germans): MG Giuseppe Romano (Commanding General, 28th "Aosta" Infantry Division) 01/01/43? BG Ugo Butta (?   ) /43 BG Livio Negro (?   ) 09/08/43 disbanded.
- A. *Components - 155th "Emilia" Garrison Division* (12/41)
    1. **119th "Emilia" Infantry Regiment**:
    2. **120th "Emilia" Infantry Regiment**
    3. **155th Artillery Regiment**:
- B. **Infantry, 155th "Emilia" Garrison Division** (12/41): /41? Col. Livio Negro (Commanding General, 155th "Emilia" Garrison Division) /43 unknown? 09/08/43 dissolved.

156th "Vicenza" Garrison Division (01/42; 07/42, part of Eighth Army; Soviet Union; 01/43, destroyed at Stalingrad): 08/08/42? BG Etelvoldo Pascolini (to /50, Russian prisoner-of-war) 01/15/43 MG Enrico Broglia (Commanding General, 205th Military Region Command) 01/43 destroyed.
- A. *Components - 156th "Vicenza" Garrison Division* (01/42)
    1. **277th "Vicenza" Infantry Regiment** (01/42): Col. Giulio Cesare Salvi 09/08/43 dissolved.
    2. **278th "Vicenza" Infantry Regiment** (01/42): Col. Gaetano Romeres 09/08/43 dissolved.
    3. **156th Artillery Regiment**:

157th "Novara" Garrison Division (03/42, Italy; 06/43, absorbed by **2nd "Sforzesca" Infantry Division**): MG Vincenso Paolini (?   ) 06/43 absorbed by **2nd "Sforzesca" Infantry Division** - see **2nd "Sforzesca" Infantry Division**.
- A. *Components - 157th "Novara" Garrison Division* (03/42)
    1. **153rd "Novara" Infantry Regiment**:
    2. **154th "Novara" Infantry Regiment**
    3. **157th Artillery Regiment**:

158th "Zara" Garrison Division (03/42; 03/42, Balkans; 09/08/43, surrendered and disbanded by the Germans): MG Carlo Viale (?   ) 09/08/43 disbanded.
- A. *Components - 158th "Zara" Garrison Division* (03/42)
    1. **291st "Zara" Infantry Regiment**:
    2. **292nd "Zara" Infantry Regiment**:
    3. **158th Artillery Regiment**:
    4. **107th Blackshirt (CCNN) Legion**:
- B. **Infantry, 158th "Zara" Garrison Division**: /43 BG Francesco Giangreco (to /45, German prisoner-of-war) 09/08/43 dissolved.

159th "Veneto" Garrison Division (1942, Italy; named for in region in Italy; 06/43, merged with **52nd "Torino [Turin]" Semi-Motorized Infantry Division**): MG Luigi Krall (?   ) 06/43 merged with **52nd "Torino [Turin]" Semi-Motorized Infantry Division** - see **52nd**

"Torino [Turin]" Semi-Motorized Infantry Division.
A.   *Components* - **159th "Veneto" Garrison Division** (1942)
     1.   **255th "Veneto" Infantry Regiment**:
     2.   **256th "Veneto" Infantry Regiment**
     3.   **159th Artillery Regiment**:

Commanding General, Dodecanese Islands: /35 BG Ettore Manca di Mores (Commanding General, 50th "Regina" Infantry Division) /37 BG Pietro Pietracaprina (Commanding General, 50th "Regina" Infantry Division) /39 BG Count Cesare Maria de Vecchi di Val Cismon (retired?; 07/42, Commanding General, 215th Coastal Division) /40 disbanded.

Coastal Defense Divisions

201st Coastal Division (/39, as a militia division; 12/41, reorganized as a coastal division; France; 09/08/43, disbanded): /42 MG Enrico Gazzale (Commanding General, 5th "Cosseria" Infantry Division) 08/08/42? 01/01/43? MG Constantino Salvi (German prisoner-of-war; died in prison) 09/08/43 idsbanded.
- A. **Components - 201st Coastal Division (12/41)**
    1. **55th Coastal Defense Regiment**:
    2. **131st Coastal Defense Regiment**:
    3. **201st Coastal Defense Artillery Regiment**:

202nd Coastal Division (/39, as a militia division; 12/41, reorganized as a coastal division; France; Italy, Sicily; 07/43, disbanded): /41 BG Mario Badino-Rossi (Commanding General, 2nd "Emanuele Filiberto Testa di Ferro" Celere Division) 01/01/43? MG Ascanio Sibilla (?) or MG Luigi Sibille (?) /43 BG Gino Ficalbi (?) 07/43 disbanded.
- A. **Components - 202nd Coastal Division (12/41)**
    1. **120th Coastal Defense Regiment**:
    2. **124th Coastal Defense Regiment**:
    3. **142nd Coastal Defense Regiment**:
    4. **43rd Coastal Defense Artillery Regiment**:

203rd Coastal Division (/39, as a militia division; 05/43, reorganized as a coastal division; Sardinia; 09/08/43, surrendered to the Allies): unknown? 09/08/43 surrendered.
- A. **Components - 203rd Coastal Division (12/41)**
    1. **126th Coastal Defense Regiment**:
    2. **174th Coastal Defense Regiment**:
    3. **203rd Coastal Defense Artillery Regiment**:

204th Coastal Division (/39, as a militia division; 12/41, reorganized as a coastal division; Sardinia; 09/08/43, surrendered to Allies): 01/01/43? MG Manlio Mora (?) 09/08/43 surrendered.
- A. **Components - 204th Coastal Division (12/41)**
    1. **19th Coastal Defense Regiment**:
    2. **130th Coastal Defense Regiment**:
    3. **149th Coastal Defense Regiment**:
    4. **204th Coastal Defense Artillery Regiment**:

205th Coastal Division (/39, as a militia division; 12/41, reorganized as a coastal division; Sardinia; 09/08/43, surrendered to the Allies): 01/01/43? BG (Res.) Giovanni Manildo (?) 09/08/43 surrendered.
- A. **Components - 205th Coastal Division (12/41)**
    1. **127th Coastal Defense Regiment**:
    2. **128th Coastal Defense Regiment**:
    3. **129th Coastal Defense Regiment**:

206th Coastal Division (12/41, Italy, Sicily; 07/43, disbanded): MG Achille D'Havet (Allied

prisoner-of-war; /44, released; /45, retired) 07/43 disbanded.
- A.   ***Components*** - **206th Coastal Division** (12/41)
    1.   **122nd Coastal Defense Regiment**:
    2.   **123rd Coastal Defense Regiment**:
    3.   **146th Coastal Defense Regiment**:
    4.   **44th Coastal Defense Artillery Regiment**:

207th Coastal Division (12/41, Italy, Sicily; 07/43, disbanded): /41 BG Giuseppe Romano (Commanding General, 155th "Emilia" Garrison Division) 12/41 MG Antonio Callierno (?) /42? BG Umberto Marchesi (Commanding General, 6th "Calabria" Internal Security Brigade) 01/01/43? MG Ottorino Schreiber (Commanding General, 26th "Assietta" Mountain Infantry Division) /43 BG Augusto de Laurentis (Allied prisoner-of-war) 07/43 disbanded.
- A.   ***Components*** - **207th Coastal Division** (12/41)
    1.   **138th Coastal Defense Regiment**:
    2.   **139th Coastal Defense Regiment**:
    3.   **12th Coastal Defense Artillery Regiment**:

208th Coastal Division (12/41, Italy, Sicily; 07/43, disbanded): MG Gastano Binacchi (Commanding General, Como Province) 07/43 disbanded.
- A.   ***Components*** - **208th Coastal Division** (12/41)
    1.   **133rd Coastal Defense Regiment**:
    2.   **147th Coastal Defense Regiment**:
    3.   **28th Coastal Defense Artillery Regiment**:

209th Coastal Division (07/43, Pulgia, Italy; 09/08/43, surrendered to Allies): /43 BG Luigi Arnato (?) 09/08/43 surrendered.
- A.   ***Components*** - **209th Coastal Division** (07/43)
    1.   **15th Coastal Defense Regiment**:
    2.   **112th Coastal Defense Regiment**:
    3.   **41st Coastal Defense Artillery Regiment**:

210th Coastal Division (07/43, Taranto, Italy, Sicily; 09/08/43, surrendered and disbanded by the Allies): unknown? 09/08/43 disbanded.
- A.   ***Components*** - **210th Coastal Division** (07/43)
    1.   **113th Coastal Defense Regiment**:
    2.   **114th Coastal Defense Regiment**:
    3.   **164th Coastal Defense Regiment**:

211th Coastal Division (12/41, Calabria, Italy; 09/08/43, disbanded): MG Francesco La Ferla (Commanding General, 101st "Trieste" Motorized Infantry Division) /41 MG Felice Gonnella [+ in /42, acting Commanding General, XXXI Army Corps] (?) 09/08/43 disbanded.
- A.   ***Components*** - **211th Coastal Division** (12/41)
    1.   **53rd Coastal Defense Regiment**:
    2.   **118th Coastal Defense Regiment**:
    3.   **143rd Coastal Defense Regiment**:

    4.   **49th Coastal Defense Artillery Regiment**:

212th Coastal Division (12/41, Calabria, Italy; 09/08/43, disbanded): 01/01/43? BG Ugo Medori 09/08/43 disbanded.
- A. ***Components - 212th Coastal Division*** (12/41)
    1. **115th Coastal Defense Regiment**:
    2. **144th Coastal Defense Regiment**:
    3. **45th Coastal Defense Artillery Regiment**:

213th Coastal Division (12/41, Messina, Sicily; 07/43, destroyed): MG Nazzaromo Scattaglia (Commanding General, 17th "Pavia" Semi-Motorized Infantry Division) /42 BG Ugo Butta (sent to North Africa; /43, Commanding General, 155th "Emilia" Garrison Division) 11/42 MG Carlo Gotti (Commanding General, IX Territorial Defense Command) 01/01/43? BG Angiolo Tosi (?) 07/43 destroyed.
- A. ***Components - 213th Coastal Division*** (12/41)
    1. **139th Coastal Defense Regiment**:
    2. **140th Coastal Defense Regiment**:
    3. **22nd Coastal Defense Artillery Regiment**:

214th Coastal Division (12/41, Italy; 09/08/43, disbanded): BG Carlo Laina (?) 09/08/43 disbanded.
- A. ***Components - 214th Coastal Division*** (12/41)
    1. **103rd Coastal Defense Regiment**:
    2. **148th Coastal Defense Regiment**:

215th Coastal Division (07/42, Tuscany, Italy; 09/08/43, disbanded): BG [Retired '40?] Count Cesare Maria de Vecchi di Val Cismon (retired?) 09/08/43 disbanded.
- A. ***Components - 215th Coastal Division*** (07/42)
    1. **6th Coastal Defense Regiment**:
    2. **14th Coastal Defense Regiment**:
    3. **108th Coastal Defense Regiment**:
    4. **27th Coastal Defense Artillery Regiment**:

216th Coastal Division (07/42, Pisa, Italy; 09/08/43, disbanded): unknown? /43 BG Carlo Magneri (?) 09/08/43 disbanded.
- A. ***Components - 216th Coastal Division*** (07/42)
    1. **12th Coastal Defense Regiment**:
    2. **13th Coastal Defense Regiment**:

220th Coastal Division (07/42, Lazio, Italy; 09/08/43, disbanded): unknown? 01/01/43? MG Creste Sant' Andrea (?) 09/08/43 disbanded.
- A. ***Components - 220th Coastal Division*** (07/42)
    1. **111th Coastal Defense Regiment**:
    2. **152nd Coastal Defense Regiment**:

221st Coastal Division (07/42, Lazio, Italy; 09/08/43, disbanded): MG Eduardo Minaja (

?) 09/08/43 disbanded.
A. **Components - 221ˢᵗ Coastal Division** (07/42)
1. **4ᵗʰ Coastal Defense Regiment**:
2. **8ᵗʰ Coastal Defense Regiment**:

222ⁿᵈ Coastal Division (07/42, Nappli [Naples], Italy; Salerno, Italy; 09/08/43, surrendered to Allies): 01/01/43? MG Antoniazzi /43 MG Ferrante Gonzga del Vodice (killed in action) 09/08/43 surrendered .
A. **Components - 222ⁿᵈ Coastal Division** (07/42)
1. **74ᵗʰ Coastal Defense Regiment**:
2. **89ᵗʰ Coastal Defense Regiment**:
3. **151ˢᵗ Coastal Defense Regiment**:
4. **163ʳᵈ Coastal Defense Regiment**:

223ʳᵈ Coastal Division (France; 09/08/43, disbanded): 01/01/43? MG Amedeo De Cia (joins Social Republic of Italy; /43, Commanding General, 210ᵗʰ Regional Military Command Gebova [Genoa]) 09/08/43 disbanded.
A. **Components - 223ʳᵈ Coastal Division** (09/43)
1. **82ⁿᵈ Coastal Defense Regiment**:
2. **112ᵗʰ Coastal Defense Regiment**:

224ᵗʰ Coastal Division (01/43, Corsica; 09/08/43, surrendered to the Allies): 01/01/43? vacant /43 MG Mario Badino-Rossi 09/08/43 surrendered.
A. **Components - 224ᵗʰ Coastal Division** (01/43)
1. **80ᵗʰ Coastal Defense Regiment**:
2. **81ˢᵗ Coastal Defense Regiment**:

225ᵗʰ Coastal Division (01/43, Corsica; 09/08/43, surrendered to the Allies): /42 BG Bartolomeo Pedrotti (Deputy Commander, Friuli Division) 09/08/43 surrendered.
A. **Components - 225ᵗʰ Coastal Division** (01/43)
1. **172ⁿᵈ Coastal Defense Regiment**:
2. **173ʳᵈ Coastal Defense Regiment**:
4. **52ⁿᵈ Coastal Defense Artillery Regiment**:

226ᵗʰ Coastal Division (04/43; also known as **Group Ajaccio**; Corsica; 09/08/43, surrendered to the Allies): /42 BG Attilo Lazzarini (/45, Commanding General, Internal Security Division "Sabauda") 09/08/43 surrendered.
A. **Components - 226ᵗʰ Coastal Division** (04/43)
1. **170ᵗʰ Coastal Defense Regiment**:
2. **171ˢᵗ Coastal Defense Regiment**:
3. **181ˢᵗ Coastal Defense Regiment**:
4. **53ʳᵈ Coastal Defense Artillery Regiment**:

227ᵗʰ Coastal Division (07/43, Calabria, Italy; 09/08/43, disbanded): BG Luigi Chatrian (?) 09/08/43 disbanded.
A. **Components - 227ᵗʰ Coastal Division** (07/43)

1. **141st Coastal Defense Regiment**:
2. **145th Coastal Defense Regiment**:

230th Coastal Division (04/43, from Headquarters, **3rd Brigade**; Sicily; 07/43, destroyed by the Allies): MG Egisto Conti (Allied prisoner-of-war) 07/43 destroyed.

Motorized and Semi-Motorized Divisions
Motorized Divisions

1st "Trento" Motorized Infantry Division (/35,; /36, redesiganted **32nd "Trento" Motorized Infantry Division**; /39, redesignated **101st "Trentoi" Motorized Infantry Division**): **1st "Trento" Motorized Infantry Division**: /35 BG Antonio Tissi (Commanding General, 32nd "Trento" Infantry Division) /36 redesignated **32nd "Trento" Motorized Infantry Division** /36 BG Antonio Tissi (retired) /39 redesignated **101st "Trento" Motorized Infantry Division** -see **101st "Trento" Motorized Infantry Division**.

10th "Piave" Motorized Infantry Division (pre-war; named after a World War I battlefield; 06/40, France; 07/40, France/Italy; 10/43, disbanded by the Germans): /37 MG Francesco Zingales (Commanding General, Truck Borne Corps) /40 BG Ercole Roncaglia (Commanding General, Special Army Corps) /41 BG Guido Bologna (Commanding General, 104th "Mantova" Semi-Motorized Infantry Division) /42 MG Ugo Tabellini (to /45, German prisoner-of-war) 10/43 disbanded.
  A. **Deputy Commander, 10th "Piave" Motorized Infantry Division** (06/10/40): unknown? /41 Col. Dino Parri (Deputy Commander, 27th "Brescia" Semi-Motorized Infantry Division) /42 unknown? 09/08/43 dissolved.
  B. *Components* - **10th "Piave" Motorized Infantry Division** (06/10/40)
    1. **57th "Abruzzi" Infantry Regiment** (named for in region in Italy):
    2. **58th "Abruzzi" Infantry Regiment** (named for in region in Italy):
    3. **20th "Piave" Artillery Regiment**:

16th "Pistoia" Motorized Infantry Division (reduced) (pre-war; 06/40, French Alpine Front; 07/42, North Africa; 10/23/42?, part of the Cyrenaica Defense Command; Libya; 04/43, destroyed in Tunisia): /39 MG Mario Priore (/41, Commanding General, VII Army Corps) /40 MG Egidio Levis (/42, Commanding General, Tirana) /41 MG Guglielmo Negro (assigned to special duties, VIII Army Corps) 07/20/42 BG Giuseppe Falugi (Allied prisoner-of-war) 04/43 destroyed.
  A. **Deputy Commander, 16th "Pistoia" Motorized Infantry Division**: BG Giovanni D'Antoni (Commanding General, D'Antoni Division) /43 unknown? 09/08/43 dissolved.
  B. *Components* - **16th "Pistoia" Motorized Infantry Division** (06/10/40)
    1. **35th "Pistoia" Infantry Regiment**:
    2. **36th "Pistoia" Infantry Regiment**:
    3. **3rd "Fossalta" Artillery Regiment** (named for a town and a location of a battle):

101st "Po" Motorized Infantry Division (pre-war as **"Po" Motorized Infantry Division**; /39, redesignated **101st "Po" Motorized Infantry Division**; /39, disbanded): **"Po" Motorized Infantry Division** /37? MG Emilio Garavelli (Commanding General, 101st "Po" Motorized Infantry Division) /38 redesignated **101st "Po" Motorized Infantry Division** /39 MG Emilio Garavelli (Commanding General, 101st "Trieste" Motorized Infantry Division) /39

disbanded.
A. **Artillery, "Po" Motorized Infantry Division**: /36 Col. Mario Zanotti (retired?; 03/43, attached to, III Territorial Defense Command) /38? unknown? 09/08/43 dissolved.

101st "Trieste" Motorized Infantry Division (pre-war as **32nd "Trento" Motorized Infantry Division**; 06/40, France; 11/40, Balkans; 08/41, North Africa; 04/43, destroyed in Tunisia)**:** 04/01/39 MG Emilio Garavelli 08/09/39 BG Vito Ferroni (Commanding General, 19th "Venezia [Venice]" Infantry Division) 09/10/40 BG Arnaldo Azzi (Commanding General, 41st "Firenze [Florence]" Infantry Division) /41 BG Alessandro Piazzoni (acting Commanding General, XX Army Corps) 12/11/41 MG Francesco La Ferla (Allied prisoner-of-war) 04/43 destroyed.
[NOTE: /43 MG Francesco Ronco [acting; + Commanding General, 184th "Nembo" Airborne Division]**]**
A. **Deputy Commander, 101st "Trieste" Motorized Infantry Division**: /40? BG Carlo Ticchioni (acting Commanding General, 2nd "Emanuele Filiberto Testa di Ferro" Cavalry (Celere) Division) /42 unknown? 04/43 dissolved.
B. *Components* - **101st "Trieste" Motorized Infantry Division** (06/10/40)
   1. **65th "Valtellina" Infantry Regiment** (named for in region in Italy):
   2. **66th "Valtellina" Infantry Regiment** (named for in region in Italy):
   3. **21st "Po" Artillery Regiment** (named for a river):
   4. **101st "Trieste" Artillery Regiment**:

102nd "Trento" Motorized Infantry Division (pre-war, as **32nd "Trento" Motorized Infantry Division**; /39, redesignated **102nd "Trento" Motorized Infantry Division**; 06/40, France; 01/41, North Africa; 11/42, destroyed at EL Alamein): **102nd "Trento" Motorized Infantry Division** /37? BG Francesco Lombardi (?) /38? MG Luigi Nuvoloni (Commanding General, 102nd "Trento" Motorized Infantry Division) /39 redesignated **102nd "Trento" Motorized Infantry Division** /39 MG Luigi Nuvoloni (Commanding General, X Army Corps) /41 MG Giuseppe de Stefanis (Commanding General, 132nd "Ariete" Armored Division) /41 MG Francesco Scotti (/43, Commanding General, 26th "Assietta" Mountain Infantry Division) /41 MG Stampioni (?) /41 MG Carlo Gotti (Commanding General, 213th Coastal Division) /42 BG Giorgio Masina (British prisoner-of-war) 11/42 destroyed.
[NOTED: also listed in /40 MG Ruggero Tracchia (acting; 62nd "Marmarcia" Infantry Division0 06/10/40?**]**
A. **Deputy Commander, 102nd "Trento" Motorized Infantry Division** (06/10/40): unknown? /41? BG Arturo Kellner (Allied prisoner-of-war) 11/42 dissolved.
B. *Components* - **102nd "Trento" Motorized Infantry Division** (06/10/40)
   1. **61st "Sicilia" Infantry Regiment** (named for in region in Italy):
   2. **62nd "Sicilia" Infantry Regiment** (named for in region in Italy):
   3. **102nd Artillery Regiment**:
C. **Infantry, 102nd "Trento" Motorized Infantry Division** (06/10/40): Col. Arturo Kellner (Deputy Commander, 102nd "Trento" Motorized Infantry Division) /41? unknown? 11/42 dissolved.

Semi-Motorized Divisions

9th **"Pasubio" Semi-Motorized Infantry Division** (pre-war, from **"Pasubio" Infantry Division**; named after a World War I battlefield; 06/40, France; 08/40, Yugoslavia; 04/05/41?, part of Truck Borne Corps; Second Army; Greece and Yugoslavia; 07/41, part of Eighth Army; Soviet Union; 01/43, virtually destroyed; 01/43, Italy for reforming and refitting; 09/08/43, surrendered to Allies): **"Pasubio" Infantry Division** /35 MG Ezio Babbini (Commanding General, IV (East African) Army Corps) /36 MG Domenico Rossi (retired?) /37 MG Count Sebastiano Murari della Corte Brà (Inspector-General of Cavalry (Celere)) /38 MG Umberto Somma (Commanding General, XXII Army Corps) /39 redesignated **9th "Pasubio" Semi-Motorized Infantry Division** 06/10/40? MG Vittorio Giovannelli (?) /42 BG Gerolamo Pittagula (acting) /42 MG Cesare Gandini (acting; /43, Chief of Staff, Eleventh Army) /42 MG Carlo Biglioni (07/44, Commanding General, Piceno Division) /42 BG Roberto Olmi (Commanding General, 58th "Legnano" Infantry Division) 01/01/43? MG Guido Boselli (Commanding General, 136th "Giovani Fascisti" Motorized Infantry Division) 09/08/43 surrendered to Allies.

- A. **Components** - 9th **"Pasubio" Semi-Motorized Infantry Division** (06/10/40)
    1. **79th "Roma" Infantry Regiment**: 08/05/41? Col. Rocco Biasioli 12/10/42? Col. Armandi Mazzocchi 09/08/43 dissolved.
    2. **80th "Roma" Infantry Regiment**: 08/05/41? Col. Epifanio Chiaramonti (Commandant, Milan Military School) 08/08/42? Col. Eugenio Peirolo (Infantry Commander, 53rd "Arezzo" Infantry Division) /42? LCol. G. B. Casassa 09/08/43 dissolved.
    3. **8th "Pasubio" Artillery Regiment**: /38? LCol. Pier Giulio Properzj (06/43, Depot Commander, IX Army Corps Artillery Regiment) /39? Col. Edoardo Nebbia (Commanding General, 104th "Mantova" Semi-Motorized Infantry Division) 08/05/41? Col. Alfredo Reginella 09/08/43 dissolved.
    4. **1st "Sabauda" Blackshirt (CCNN) Legion**:
- A. **Infantry Commander, 9th "Pasubio" Semi-Motorized Infantry Division**: /40 BG Cesare Gandini (/42, acting Commanding General, 9th "Pasubio" Semi-Motorized Infantry Division) 08/05/41? BG Aldo Princivalle 12/10/41? BG Davide Borghini (?) 08/08/42? BG Roberto Olmi (acting Commanding General, 9th "Pasubio" Semi-Motorized Infantry Division) /42 unknown? 09/08/43 dissolved.

17th **"Pavia" Semi-Motorized Infantry Division** (/39, from **17th "Rubicone" Infantry Division**; 10/39, Libya; 06/40, North Africa Model Division: semi-motorized with special TO&E; 11/42, destroyed at El Alamein): /39 MG Pietro Zaglio (Commanding General, 26th "Assietta" Mountain Infantry Division) /41 MG Antonio Franceschini*Commanding General, 23rd "Ferrara" Infantry Division) /42 MG Arturo Torriano (/43, Commanding General, 53rd "Arezzo" Infantry Division) /42 MG Nazzarono Scattaglia (British prisoner-of-war) 11/42 destroyed.

- A. **Components - 17th "Pavia" Semi-Motorized Infantry Division** (06/10/40)
    1. **27th "Pavia" Infantry Regiment**:
    2. **28th "Pavia" Infantry Regiment**: /41? Col. Francesco Montagna [MVSN]

(Commanding Officer, 59th "Calabria" Infantry Regiment; /43?, Commandant, Central School of Infantry) /42? Col. Giuseppe Vallerini (Infantry Commander, 30th "Sabauda" Infantry Division) /43 unknown? 09/08/43 dissolved.
   3. **26th "Rubicone" Artillery Regiment** (named for a river):

25th "Bologna" Semi-Motorized Infantry Division (/39, from **25th "Volturno" Infantry Division**; 12/40, North Africa Model Division: semi-motorized with special TO&E; 11/42, destroyed at El Alamein): MG Giuseppe Pafundi (Commanding General, XVII Army Corps) 06/10/40? MG Roberto Lerici (08/08/42, Commanding General, 52nd "Torino" Infantry Division) /41 MG Carlo Gotti (acting Commanding General, 102nd "Trento" Motorized Infantry Division) /41 MG Pietro Maggiani (Commanding General, 6th "Cuneo" Infantry Division) /41 MG Mario Marghinotti (/42, Commanding General, VIII Army Corps) /41 MG Alessandro Gloria (acting Commanding General, XXI Army Corps) 11/42 destroyed.

A. **Components - 25th "Bologna" Semi-Motorized Infantry Division** (06/10/40)
   1. **39th "Bologna" Infantry Regiment**: /42? Col. Guido Manardi (joins the Social Republic of Italy; /44 Commanding General, 1st "Italia" Infantry Division, Social Republic of Italy) 11/42 dissolved.
   2. **40th "Bologna" Infantry Regiment**: /37 Col. Riccardo di Belfiore Mattioli (/43, Infantry Commander, 29th "Piemonte" Infantry Division) /39? unknown? 11/42 dissolved.
   3. **10th "Volturno" Artillery Regiment** (named for a river):
   4. **205th Artillery Regiment** (added:

27th "Brescia" Semi-Motorized Infantry Division (pre-war; 06/40, North Africa Model Division: semi-motorized with special TO&E; 11/42, destroyed at El Alamein): /39 BG Giuseppe Cremascuoli (died of illness) /40 MG Bortolo Zambon (07/42?, special duties, Inspectorate of Infantry) /41 BG Giacomo Lombardi (?) /42 MG Brunetto Brunetti (British prisoner-of-war; /45, acting Commanding General, General Headquarters Sardina) 08/42 MG Giovanni Battista Oxilia (/43, Commanding General, 19th "Venezia" Infantry Division) 09/42 unknown? 11/42 destroyed.

A. **Deputy Commander, 27th "Brescia" Semi-Motorized Infantry Division** (06/10/40): unknown? /42 BG Dino Parri (Commander, Rear Troops, X Army Corps) 11/42 dissolved.
B. **Components - 27th "Brescia" Semi-Motorized Infantry Division** (06/10/40)
   1. **19th "Brescia" Infantry Regiment**:
   2. **20th "Brescia" Infantry Regiment**:
   3. **55th Semi-Motorized Artillery Regiment**:

52nd "Torino [Turin]" Semi-Motorized Infantry Division (pre-war; 06/40, Army Reserve; Yugoslavia; 04/05/41?, part of Truck Borne Corps; Second Army; Greece and Yugoslavia; 07/41, part of Eighth Army; Soviet Union; 01/43, virtually destroyed; 06/43, merged with **159th "Veneto" Garrison Division**; 0943, disbanded by the Germans): **"Torino [Turin]"**

Infantry Division /39 MG Mario Priore (Commanding General, 16th "Pistolia" Infantry Division) /39 MG Mario Arisio (Commanding General, 52nd "Torino [Turin]" Infantry Division) /40 redesignated **52nd "Torino [Turin]" Semi-Motorized Infantry Division** /40 MG Mario Arisio (Commanding General, III Army Corps) 06/10/40? MG Luigi Manzi (/42, Commanding General, 28th "Aosta" Infantry Division) /41 MG Francesco Du Pont (Commanding General, 104th "Mantova" Semi-Motorized Infantry Division) /42 MG Luigi Krall (Commanding General, 159th "Veneto" Garrison Division) /42 BG Cesare Rossi (/43?, Commanding General, Liguria Military Area) 08/08/42? MG Roberto Lerici (Commanding General, IX Army Corps) 12/42 BG Bruno Malaguti (?) 09/08/43 disbanded.

A. ***Components*** - **52nd "Torino [Turin]" Semi-Motorized Infantry Division** (06/10/40)
   1. **81st "Torino [Turin]" Infantry Regiment**: 08/05/41? Col. Carlo Piccinini 08/08/42? Col. Biagio Santini 09/08/43 dissolved.
   2. **82nd "Torino [Turin]" Infantry Regiment**: /38 Col. Gaetano Cantaluppi (Commandant, Royal Academy of Infantry & Cavalry) /39? unknown? 08/05/41? LCol. Evaristo Fioravanti 09/08/43 dissolved.
   3. **52nd "Torino [Turin]" Artillery Regiment**: /39? Col. Luigi Podio (acting Commanding General, 49th "Parma" Infantry Division) 08/05/41? Col. Giuseppe Ghiringhelli 09/08/43 dissolved.
B. **Infantry Commander, 52nd "Torino [Turin]" Semi-Motorized Infantry Division**: 08/05/41? Col. Ugo De Carolis (killed in action) 12/12/41 unknown? 08/08/42? BG Ottorino Schreiber (Commanding General, 207th Coastal Division) 12/10/42? BG Cesare Rossi (?) 09/08/43 dissolved.

103rd "Piacenza" Semi-Motorized Infantry Division (03/42, Italy; 09/08/43, destroyed and disbanded by the Germans): MG Carlo Rossi (II) (?) 09/08/43 destroyed and disbanded.
A. ***Components*** - **103rd "Piacenza" Semi-Motorized Infantry Division** (03/42)
   1. **111th "Piacenza" Infantry Regiment**:
   2. **112th "Piacenza" Infantry Regiment**:
   3. **37th Artillery Regiment**:
   4. **29th "Cosseria" Artillery Regiment** (named for a town and a location of a battle; to 37th "Modena" Artillery Regiment):

104th "Mantova" Semi-Motorized Infantry Division (03/42, Italy; Sicily; 09/08/43, surrendered to Allies): /40 BG Edoardo Nebbia (Commanding General, 3rd "Ravenna" (Mountain) Infantry Division) /40 BG Aldo Rossi (Assistant Chief of the Army General Staff) /42 BG Guido Bologna (/44, Commanding General, Mantova Division) /42 MG Francesco Du Pont (Commanding General, 3rd "Ravenna" (Mountain) Infantry Division) 10/03/42 BG Marcello Piccone (?) /43 MG Manilo Capizzi (?) 09/08/43 surrendered to Allies.
A. ***Components*** - **104th "Mantova" Semi-Motorized Infantry Division** (03/42)
   1. **113th "Mantova" Infantry Regiment**:
   2. **114th "Mantova" Infantry Regiment**:
   3. **11th "Monferrato" Artillery Regiment**: /35 Col. Giuseppe Jacopetti 09/08/42 dissolved.

105th "Rovigo" Semi-Motorized Infantry Division (03/42, Italy; 09/08/43, surrendered to the Germans): BG Ottorino Battista Dabbeni (acting) /42 MG Pietro Belletti (Artillery

Commander, First Italo-German Army) 01/01/43? MG Erminio Rovida (to /45, German prisoner-of-war) 09/08/43 surrendered.
- A. **Components - 105th "Rovigo" Semi-Motorized Infantry Division** (03/42)
    1. **227th "Rovigo" Infantry Regiment**:
    2. **228th "Rovigo" Infantry Regiment**:
    3. **117th Motorized Artillery Regiment**:

136th "Giovanni Fascisti" Motorized Infantry Division (05/16/43 to 05/22/43, Sicily, from **136th "Giovani Fascisti Armored Division**; a hybird unit composed of German and Italian units; 05/22/43, captured and disbanded): /42 MG Nino Sozzani (Commanding General, 30th "Sabauda" Infantry Division) /43 MG Guido Boselli (Allied prisoner-of-war; /43, acting Commanding General, General Headquarters Sardinia) /43 captured and disbanded.
- A. **Components - 136th "Giovani Fascisti Armored Division** (05/43)
    1. **Giovani Fascisti Infantry Regiment**:
    2. **136th Armored Regiment**

Armored Divisions

131st "Centauro" Armored Division (04/20/39; Albania, Greece, Yugoslavia; 06/40, France; 01/41, North Africa; 04/05/41?, part of the XVII Army Corps, Ninth Army; Greece and Yugoslavia; /41, North Africa; 03/43, virtually destroyed with remnants absorbed into the **134th Division**; 09/08/43, disbanded by the Germans): BG Alberto Barbieri (Commanding General, XX Army Corps) /39 MG Giovanni Magli (acting Commanding General, 37th "Modena" Infantry Division 07/40? MG Count Giorgio Calvi di Bergolo (Italian Liaison Officer to German Field Marshal Erwin Rommel) 04/05/41? MG Gavino Pizzolato (Commanding General, 80th "La Spezia" Air Landing Division) /42 MG Count Giorgio Calvi di Bergulo (07/25/43, Commanding General, 134th "Centauro" Armored Division) /43 BG Ettore Pettinau (acting; /45, Commanding General, 2nd "Sabauda" Internal Security Brigade) 03/43 virtually destroyed with remnants absorbed into the **134th "Centauro" Armored Division** - see **134th "Centauro" Armored Division**.

A. **Deputy Commander, 131st "Centauro" Armored Division**: unknown? /43 BG Giuseppe Costa (?) 03/43 dissolved.
B. *Components* - **131st "Centauro" Armored Division** (04/20/39)
   1. **31st Tank Regiment**:
   2. **131st Tank Regiment**
   3. **5th Bersaglieri (sharpshooter) Cyclist** (later **Motorized**) **Regiment**
   4. **131st Armored Artillery Regiment**

132nd "Ariete" Armored Division (02/01/39, Northern Italy; 06/40, Balkans; 01/41, Northern Italy; 11/42, Libya; virtually destroyed at El Alamein; 02/43, redesignated **132nd "Ariete" Light Armored Division (I)**; 04/43, destroyed and surrendered in Tunisia): /39 MG Carlo de Simone (Commanding General, 102nd Colonial Infantry Division) /39 MG Carlo Vecchiarelli (Commanding General, V Army Corps) /39 MG Ettore Baldassare (/42, Commanding General, XX Army Corps) 07/21/41 BG Mario Balotta (acting; acting Commanding General, X Army Corps) /41 MG Giuseppe de Stefanis (Commanding General, XX Army Corps) 10/23/42 MG Ismaele Di Nisio (acting; Commanding General, 136th "Giovani Fascists" Armored Division) /42 MG Francesco Antonio Arena (Commanding General, 36th "Forlì" Infantry Division) /42 MG Adolfo Infante (Commanding General, 24th "Pinerolo" Infantry Division) 11/42 virtually destroyed 02/43 redesignated **132nd "Ariete" Light Armored Division (I)** 02/43 MG Raffaele Cadorna (Commanding General, 135th "Ariete II" Armored Division) 04/43, destroyed.

A. **Deputy Commander, 132nd "Ariete" Armored Division** (02/01/39): unknown? /42 BG Amedeo Pederzini (?) 04/43 dissolved.
A. *Components* - **132nd "Ariete" Armored Division** (02/01/39)
   1. **132nd Tank Regiment** (removed by 02/43)
   2. **8th Bersaglieri (sharpshooter) Cyclist Regiment** (removed by 11/42)
   3. **132nd Armored Artillery Regiment** (removed by 02/43)
   4. **32nd Tank Regiment** (added 11/42; removed by 02/43)

5. **3rd Armored Group Nizza Cavalry** (from **"Nizza Cavalleria" Cavalry Regiment**; added 11/42; removed by 02/43): **"Nizza Cavalleria" Cavalry Regiment** /36 Col. Count Giorgio Calvi di Bergolo (Commanding General, 131st "Centauro" Armored Division) /40 unknown? /42? Col. Achille Maffei (Commanding General, "Pantelleria" Mixed Brigade) 04/43 dissolved.

B. *Components* - **132nd "Ariete" Light Armored Division (I)** (02/43)
   1. **8th "Montabello" Armored Regiment**
   2. **10th "Lancieri Vittorio Emanuele II" Armored Regiment**
   3. **16th "Lucca" Armored Cavalry Regiment**
   4. **135th Armored Artillery Regiment**
   5. **9th Lancieri di Firenze [Florence] Regiment**: /37? Col. Emanuelle Beraudo di Pralorme (Commandant, Central School for Cavalry Troops) /39? Col. Carlo Ticchioni (Deputy Commander, 101st "Trieste" Motorized Infantry Division) /40? unknown? 09/08/43 dissolved.

133rd "Littorio" Armored Division (/37, Spain as **Italian Volunteer Division [C. T. V.]**; /39, on French Alpine Front; 04/05/41?, part of Truck Borne Corps; Second Army; Greece and Yugoslavia; 01/42, North Africa; 11/42, destroyed at El Alamein): /38 MG Gervasio Bitossi (Commanding General, II Army Corps) /41? MG Count Carlo Ceriana-Mayneri (Commanding General, 2nd "Emanuele Filiberto Testa di Ferro" Cavalry (Celere) Division) 04/05/41? unknown? /42 BG Emilio Becuzzi (acting; Commanding General, 15th "Bergamo" Infantry Division) 11/42 destroyed.

A. *Components* - **133rd "Littorio" Armored Division** (1939)
   1. **33rd Armored Regiment**:
   2. **133rd Armored Regiment**:
   3. **12th Bersaglieri (sharpshooter) Cyclist Regiment**
   4. **133rd Armored Artillery Regiment**

134th "Centauro" Armored Division (07/25/43, Italy, from **M (MUSSOLINI Blackshirt (CCNN) Division**; 09/08/43, crushed by the Germans and disbanded): MG Count Giorgio Calvi di Bergolo (to /45, German prisoner-of-war) 09/08/43 disbanded.

   A. *Components* - **134th "Centauro" Armored Division**
      1. **10th Lancieri di Vittorio Emanuele II Armored Regiment**:
      2. **134th Armored Regiment**:
   3. **1st Bersaglieri (sharpshooter) Cyclist Regiment**
   4. **133rd Armored Artillery Regiment**

135th "Frecchia" Light Armored Division (05/42, by converting the **2nd "Emanuele Filiberto Testa di Ferro" Cavalry (Celere) Division** into an armored division; served as a training and reserve unit; 01/43, disbanded after the decision to reform the **Ariete Armored Division**): unknown? 01/43 disbanded.

A. *Components* - **135th "Frecchia" Light Armored Division** (1939)

135th "Ariete II" Light Armored Division (04/43, Rome, Italy, from original **"Ariete" Armored Division**, as a Armor-Cavalry Division; 09/08/43, fought against the Germans after the armistice with the Allies; 09/08/43, overtaken and disbanded by the Germans): MG Raffele Cadorna (/44, Commanding General, Italian Liberation Corps) 09/08/43 disbanded.
- A. *Components* - **135th "Ariete II" Light Armored Division** (05/43)
    1. **10th "Lancieri di Vittorio Emanuele II" Armored Regiment**:
    2. **16th "Cavalleggeri di Lucca" Motorized Cavalry Regiment**:
3. **8th "Lancieri de Montebello" or "Reparto Explorante Corazzato" Armored Car Regiment**:
4. **135th Armored Regiment**:
5. **235th Armored Regiment**:

136th "Giovani Fascisti" Armored Division (in name only; also known as **Cacciatori d'Africa Division**; in Tunisia was renamed a Motorized Infantry Division; /43 redesignated **136th "Giovani Fascisti Motorized Infantry Division**): /42 MG Ismaele Di Nisio (Commanding General, 47th "Bari" Infantry Division) /42 MG Nino Sozzani (Commanding General, 136th "Giovani Fascisti" Motorized Infantry Division) /43 redesignated **136th "Giovani Fascisti" Motorized Infantry Division** see - **136th "Giovani Fascisti" Motorized Infantry Division**.
:

Mountain & Alpini Divisions

[Mountain Divisions are not to be confused with the Alpini Divisions, which are highly specialized mountain troops. These divisions had pack-horse artillery instead of the usual towed type, and some other small differences in TO&E from the "standard" Infantry Divisions.]

Mountain Divisions

26th "Assietta" Mountain Infantry Division (reduced) (pre-war; named for the War of the Austrian Succession (1741) battle against the French; has mountain equipment in it's TO&E; 06/40, Italy; 04/05/41?, part of VI Army Corps, Second Army; Greece and Yugoslavia; /42, Sicily; 08/43, destroyed by the Allies): /35 MG Count Enrico Riccardi (retired?; 06/42?, Administrator, Torino [Turin] Military District) /36? MG Enrico Boscardi (?) /38? MG Camillo Mercalli (Commanding General, IV Army Corps) /39 unknown? 06/10/40? MG Emanuele Girlando (Commanding General, 28th "Aosta" Infantry Division) 02/07/41 MG Pietro Zaglio (11/42, special duties, XV Territorial Defense Command) /41 MG Giulio Perugi 11/01/41 BG Guido Piacenza (acting; Artillery Commander, XX Army Corps) /42 MG Giulio Perugi (Commanding General, XI Territorial Defense Command) 01/01/43? MG Pietro Zaglio /43 BG Erberto Papini (acting; Commanding General, 37th "Modena" Infantry Division) /43 MG Francesco Scotti (?) /43 MG Ottorino Schreiber (?) 08/43 destroyed.
  - A. **Chief of Staff, 26th "Assietta" Mountain Infantry Division**: /40 Col. Luigi Gherzi (assigned to XIV Territorial Defense Command) /42
  - B. *Components - 26th "Assietta" Mountain Infantry Division (reduced)* (06/10/40)
    1. **29th "Pisa" Infantry Regiment**:
    2. **30th "Pisa" Infantry Regiment**:
    3. **25th "Assietta" Artillery Regiment**:
    4. **17th "Cremona" Blackshirt (CCNN) Legion**:
  - C. **Infantry, 26th "Assietta" Mountain Infantry Division** (06/10/40): unknown? /43 BG Mario Vece (/46, Commanding General, "Aosta" Infantry Brigade) 09/08/43 dissolved.

36th "Forlì" Mountain Infantry Division (reduced) (pre-war as **39th "Forlì" Infantry Division**; has mountain equipment in it's TO&E; 06/40, France; 01/41, Balkans; 09/08/43, surrendered to and disbanded by the Germans): **36th "Forlì" Infantry Division** /39 MG Giulio Perugi (Commanding General, 36th "Forlì" Mountain Infantry Division) /40 redesignated **36th "Forlì" Mountain Infantry Division (reduced)** /40 MG Giulio Perugi (Commanding General, 51st "Siena" Infantry Division) /40 MG Antonio Franceschini (Commanding General, 17th "Pavia" Semi-Motorized Infantry Division) or MG Giunio Ruggiero (Commanding General, 21st "Granatieri di Sardegna" Infantry Division) /41 BG Guglielmo Morgari (acting; Commanding General, 24th "Pinerolo" Infantry Division) /42 MG Francesco Antonio Arena (German prisoner-of-war; /45, killed by the Russians in unknown circumstances) 09/08/43 surrendered to the Germans and disbanded.
  - A. *Components - 36th "Forlì" Mountain Infantry Division (reduced)* (06/10/40)
    1. **43rd "Forlì" Infantry Regiment**:

2. **44th "Forli" Infantry Regiment**
3. **36th Artillery Regiment**:

B. **Infantry, 36th "Forli" Mountain Infantry Division** (06/10/40): unknown? /43 BG Guglielmo Morgari (to /45, German prisoner-of-war) 09/08/43 dissolved.

Alpine Divisions
[High Mountain Divisions]

1st "Taurinense" Alpini Division (pre-war; 06/60, France; 01/42, Balkans; 09/08/43, surrendered to and disbanded by the Germans): /37? BG Luigi Nuvoloni (Commanding General, 32nd "Trento" Motorized Infantry Division) /38? unknown? 06/10/40? MG Paolo Micheletti (/42, Commanding General, 49th "Parma" Infantry Division) /41 MG Giovanni Maccario (?) /42 BG Lorenzo Vivalda (?) 09/08/43 surrendered to the Germans and disbanded.
    A.   ***Components* - 1st "Taurinense" Alpini Division** (06/10/40)
        1.   **3rd Alpini Regiment**: /39 Col. Emilio Faldella (Chief, Training Officer, General Staff) 04/05/41? Col. A. Bruzzone
    2.   **4th Alpini Regiment**: /42? Col. Emilio Magliano (acting Commanding General, 5th "Pusteria" Alpini Division) /43
    3.   **1st "Taurinense" Alpini Artillery Regiment**:

2nd "Tridentina" Alpini Division (pre-war; 06/40, France; 11/40, Balkans; 08/42, part of the Eighth Army; Soviet Union; 01/43, virtually destroyed on the Don; 02/43, Balkans): /35 MG Gabrielle Nasci (Commanding General, Alpine Troops) /38 MG Ugo Santovito (Commanding General, XXVI Army Corps) /41 BG Luigi Reverberi (to /45, German prisoner-of-war) 09/08/43 disbanded.
    A.   ***Components* - 2nd "Tridentina" Alpini Division** (06/10/40)
        1.   **5th Alpini Regiment**: /39? Col. Franco Testi (on staff, XVI Army Corps; /43, Commanding General, 3rd "Julia" Alpini Division) /41 Col. Lorenzo Vivaldi (Commanding General, 1st "Taurinense" Alpini Division) 08/08/42? Col. Guiseppe Adami (Infantry Commander, 151st "Perugia" Garrison Division) /43
    2.   **6th Alpini Regiment**: 08/08/42? Col. Paolo Signorini
    3.   **2nd "Tridentina" Alpini Artillery Regiment**: /41? Col. Carlo Filippi (Artillery Commander, Alpine Corps) 08/08/42? Col. Federico Moro /42 Col. Armando Lubrano (acting Commanding General, XI Army Corps) /43

3rd "Julia" Alpini Division (pre-war; 10/39, Albania; 10/40 Balkans; 08/42, part of the Eighth Army; Soviet Union; 01/43, virtually destroyed; 01/43, Italy, for reforming and refitting; 09/08/43, disbanded): /35 BG Carlo Rossi (I) (Commanding General, 37th "Modena" Infantry Division) /38 BG Fedele De Giorgis (Commanding General, 55th "Savona" Infantry Division) /40 MG Mario Girotti (Commanding General, 6th "Alpi Graie" Alpini Division) 11/41 BG Umberto Ricagno (to /50, Russian prisoner-of-war) /43 MG Franco Testi (to /45, German prisoner-of-war) 09/08/43 disbanded.

A.   ***Components* - 3rd "Julia" Alpini Division** (06/10/40)
    1.   **8th Alpini Regiment**: /39 Col. Giacomo Lombardi (Commandant, Central Military School of Mountaineering [Alpinism]) /40? Col. Antonia Grazioci (British prisoner-of-war) /41 Col. Vincenzo Dapino (Infantry Commander, 58th

"Legnano" Infantry Division) 08/08/42? Col. Armando Cimolino
2. **9th Alpini Regiment:** 08/08/42? Col. Fausto Lavizzari
3. **3rd "Julia" Alpini Artillery Regiment**: /36 Col. Enrico Carlino /38 unknown? /40 Col. Luigi Jalla (Artillery Commander, Italian Expeditionary Corps) 08/08/42? Col. Pietro Gay

4th "Cuneense" Alpini Division (pre-war; 06/40, France; 12/40, Balkans; 04/05/41, part of XIV Army Corps, Ninth Army; Greece and Yugoslavia; 08/42, part of the Eighth Army; Soviet Union; 01/43, virtually destroyed on the Don; 01/43, Italy, for reforming and refitting; 09/08/43, disbanded): **4th "Cuneense" Alpini Division (#1)** /37? MG Umberto Testa (/40, Commanding General, Alpine [Alpini] Corps) /39 BG Achille D'Havet (at dispostion of the Army General Staff) 06/10/40? BG Alberto Ferrero (Chief of Staff, General Headquarters Albania) /41 MG Giovanni Maccario (Commanding General, 1st "Taurinense" Alpini Division) /41 MG Alberto Ferrero (Commandant, Supreme Institute of War) 08/08/42? MG Emilio Battisti (Russian prisoner-of-war; /45? Commanding General, VI Territorial Command) 01/43 destroyed; rebuilding **4th "Cuneense" Alpini Division (#2)** 01/43 MG Carlo Fassi (to /45, German prisoner-of-war) 09/08/43 disbanded.

A. **Chief of Staff, 4th "Cuneense" Alpini Division** (06/10/40): Col. Umberto Ricagno (Chief of Staff, General Headquarters, Albania) /41
B. *Components - 4th "Cuneense" Alpini Division* (06/10/40)
1. **1st Alpini Regiment**: 08/08/42? Col. Luigi Manfredi
2. **2nd Alpini Regiment:** Col. Lazzaro Maurizio de Castiglione (Comnmanding General, 5th "Pusteria" Alpini Division) 08/08/42? Col. Luigi Serimin
3. **4th "Cuneense" Alpini Artillery Regiment**: 08/08/42? Col. Enrico Orlandi
   a. **Attached to 4th "Cuneense" Alpini Artillery Regiment**: 07/05/42 BG Flaminio [MVSN]

5th "Pusteria" Alpini Division (pre-war; 06/40, France; 11/40, Balkans; 08/42, Italy-France; 09/08/43, disbanded): /36 MG Luigi Negri Cesi (Commanding General, Alpine Corps) 12/39 MG Amedeo De Cia (Commanding General, 58th "Legnano" Infantry Division) /41 MG Giovanni Esposito (/43, Inspector of Alpine Troops) /41 BG Vincenso Paolini (Commanding General, 157th "Novara" Garrison Division) /42 MG Lazzaro Maurizio de Castiglione (/45, Commanding General, XI Territorial Defense Command) /43 BG Emilio Magliano (Commanding General, 4th "Cremona" Infantry Division) 09/08/43 disbanded.

A. **Chief of Staff, 5th "Pusteria" Alpini Division**: /39 Col. Guilio Martinat (Chief of Staff, XVI Army Corps) /40
B. *Components - 5th "Pusteria" Alpini Division* (06/10/40)
1. **7th Alpini Regiment**: /38? Col. Carlo Danioni /39? Col. Emillio Battisti (Chief of Staff, Army Group West) /40 Col. Vincenso Paolini (Commanding General, 5th "Pusteria" Alpini Division) /41
2. **11th Alpini Regiment**: /37 LCol. Guilio Martinat (Chief of Staff, 5th "Pusteria" Alpini Division) /39 Col. Giovanni Varda (Commanding General, 40th "Cacciatori d'Africa" Division) /40

3. **5th "Pusteria" Alpini Artillery Regiment**:

6th "Alpi Graie" Alpini Division (11/41, Italy; 03/42, Balkans; 12/42, Italy; 09/08/43, surrendered and disbanded): MG Mario Girotti (?) /42 MG Mario Gorlier (?) 09/08/43 surrendered and disbanded.
- A. *Components - 6th "Alpi Graie" Alpini Division* (11/41)
  1. **10th Alpini Regiment**:
     a. **Deputy Commander, 10th Alpini Regiment**: /37? LCol. Alessandro Tarabin $_{[MSVN]}$ (04/43, Association of Alpine Veterans) /39?
  2. **12th Alpini Regiment**:
3. **6th "Alpi Graie" Alpini Artillery Regiment**:

Celeri (Fast) Divisions
[Celeri Divisions are a mixed Cavalry-Motor unit. All named after famous generals of the House of Savoy.]

1st "Eugenio di Savoia" Celere Division (pre-war, as **1st "Eugenio di Savoia" Celere Brigade**; /39, redesignated **1st "Eugenio di Savoia" Celere Division**; part of Celere [Fast] Corps; 04/05/41?, Greece and Yugoslavia; 09/08/43, disbanded): **1st "Eugenio di Savoia" Celere Brigade** /35 MG Mario Caracciolo di Feroleto (/37, Commanding General, Libya & Commanding General, XXI Army Corps) /36 BG Umberto Vaccari (/42, Head, Fiume Military Tribunal, V Territorial Defense Command) /37 BG Federico Ferrari Orsi (Commanding General, 1st "Eugenio di Savoia" Celere Division) /39 redesignated **1st "Eugenio di Savoia" Celere Division** /39 MG Federico Ferrari Orsi (Commanding General, Celere [Fast] Corps) /40 BG Giuseppe Lombardi (acting) /40 MG Cesare Lomaglio (?) 09/08/43 disbanded.

A. *Components* - 1st "Eugenio di Savoia" Celere Division (06/10/40)
1. **12th "Cavalleggeri di Saluzzo" Cavalry Regiment**:
2. **14th "Cavalleggeri di Alesszndria" Cavalry Regiment**: 12/10/42? LCol. Egon Zitnik
3. **11th Bersaglieri (sharpshooter) Cyclist Regiment**:
4. **1st "Eugenio di Savoia" (Articlere) Artillery Regiment**:

2nd "Emanuele Filiberto Testa di Ferro" Cavalry (Celere) Division (pre-war; 06/40, France; part of Celere [Fast] Corps; 04/05/41?, Greece and Yugoslavia; late-/41, Italy/France; 05/42, began the conversion process into the **Freccia Armored Division**, but was converted into a light mechanized division; 09/43, returned to Italy and disbanded): **2nd "Emanuele Filiberto Testa di Ferro" Cavalry (Celere) Brigade**: MG Count Gerolamo Majnoni D'Intignano [MVSN] (retired?) /37 BG Gervasio Bitossi (Commanding General, 133rd "Littorio" Armored Division) /38 BG Enrico Armando (acting Commanding General, 65th "Granatieri di Savoia" Infantry Division) /39? redesignated **2nd "Emanuele Filiberto Testa di Ferro" Cavalry (Celere) Division**: /39 MG Sebastiano Visconti Prasca (Commanding General, III Army Corps) /39 BG Furio Monticelli (acting; /41, Commanding General, 12th "Sassari" Infantry Division) 06/10/40? MG Gavino Pizzolato (Commanding General, 131st "Centauro" Armored Division) 04/05/41? MG Count Carlo Ceriana-Mayneri (Inspector of Cavalry Troops) /42 BG Carlo Ticchioni (acting; /43, Commanding General, South Group, Sardinia) /42 BG Enrico Kellner (acting Commanding General, 134th "Emanuele Filiberto Testa di Ferro" Armored Division) /42 redesignated **134th "Emanuele Filiberto Testa di Ferro" Armored Division** /42 BG Enrico Kellner (acting Commanding General, 134th "Emanuele Filiberto Testa di Ferro" Cavalry (Celere) Division) /42 redesignated **2nd "Emanuele Filiberto Testa di Ferro" Cavalry (Celere) Division** /42 BG Enrico Kellner (?) 01/01/43? MG Mario Badino-Rossi (Inspector of Celere Troops) /43 BG Giuseppe Andreoli (German prisoner-of-war; /45, executed by the Germans) 09/08/43 disbanded.

A. *Components* 2nd "Emanuele Filiberto Testa di Ferro" Cavalry (Celere) Division (06/10/40)
1. **9th "Lancieri di Firenze [Florence]" Cavalry Regiment**:
2. **10th "Lancieri di Vittorio Emenuele II" Cavalry Regiment**: /42 Col.

Dardano Fenulli (joins the Resistance; /44, arrested and executed by the Germans) /43
3. **6th Bersaglieri (sharpshooter) Cyclist Regiment**: /41? Col. Giulio Brunelli (British prisoner-of-war) /41 unknown? 12/10/42? Col. Mario Carloni (Commanding Officer, 1st "Italia" Infantry Division, Social Republic of Italy) /43
4. **2nd Artillery (Articlere) Regiment**:

3rd "Principe Amedeo Duca d'Aosta" Cavalry (Celere) Division (pre-war, from **3rd "Principe Amedeo Duca d'Aosta" Cavalry (Celere) Brigade**; part of Celere [Fast] Corps; 06/40, French Alpine Front; 04/05/41?, Greece and Yugoslavia; 07/41, Eastern Front; /42, part of the Eighth Army; Soviet Union; 01/43, virtually destroyed; 01/43, Italy, for reforming and refitting; 09/08/43, disbanded by the Germans): **3rd "Principe Amedeo Duca d'Aosta" Cavalry (Celere) Brigade** /36 BG Riccardo Massone (?) /37? BG Umberto di Giorgio (/42, Commanding General, VIII Territorial Defense Command) /38 redesignated **3rd "Principe Amedeo Duca d'Aosta" Cavalry (Celere) Division** /38 unknown? /39 MG Giovanni Messe (Deputy Commander, General Headquarters Albania) 04/39 BG Mario Marazzani (Inspector of Cavalry (Celere) Troops) /41 MG Ettore de Blasio (to /45, German prisoner-of-war) 09/08/43 disbanded.

A. **Deputy Commander, 3rd "Principe Amedeo Duca d'Aosta" Cavalry (Celere) Division**: /38 BG Mario Marazzani (Commanding General, 3rd "Principe Amedeo Duca d'Aosta" Cavalry (Celere) Division) /39 unknown? 06/10/40? BG Gioacchino Solinas (Commanding General, 44th "Cremona" Infantry Division) /42 BG Carlo Lombardi (?) 12/12/42 BG Antonio Luridiana
B. *Components* - **3rd "Principe Amedeo Duca d'Aosta" Cavalry (Celere) Division** (06/10/40)
    1. **3rd "Savoia Cavalleria" Cavalry Regiment**: see under **"Barbò" Cavalry Brigade**.
    2. **5th "Lancieri di Novara" Cavalry Regiment**: see under **"Barbò" Cavalry Brigade**.
    3. **3rd Bersaglieri (sharpshooter) Cyclist Regiment**: 08/05/41? Col. Aminto Carette 12/10/42? Col. Ercole Felici
    4. **3rd "Principe Amedeo Duca d'Aosta" (Articlere) Artillery Regiment**: /39 Col. Giovanni Carlo Re (Military Attaché, Croatia & Head, Military Mission to Croatia) 08/05/41? Col. Cesare Colombo
    5. **120th Artillery Regiment** (added by 08/08/42): LCol. Ugo de Simone

Celere Column A. O. (/35, Eritrea): BG Achille Starace [MVSN] [+ Secretary-General, National Fascist Party] /37?

Airborne Divisions

80th "La Spezia" Airlanding Division (11/41, Italy; 10/42, North Africa; 10/43, part of Tripolitania Defense Command; Libya; 04/43, destroyed): BG Alessandro Maccario (Commanding General, 14th "Isonzo" Infantry Division) /41 MG Quirino Armellini (Commanding General, XVIII Army Corps) /42 MG Gavino Pizzolato (killed in action in Tunesia) 04/43 destroyed.

A. **Deputy Commander, 80th "La Spezia" Airlanding Division** (11/41): BG Arturo Scattini (Allied prisoner-of-war, captured in Tunisia; /45, Commanding General, "Friuli" Combat Group) 04/43 dissolved.
B. *Components - 80th "La Spezia" Airlanding Division* (11/41)
   1. **125th "La Spezia" Infantry Regiment**:
   2. **126th "La Spezia" Infantry Regiment**:
   3. **80th Artillery Regiment**:

183rd "Ciclone" Airborne Division (still forming 09/08/43; never fully formed):
A. *Components - 183rd "Ciclone" Airborne Division*
   1. **Infantry Regiment**:
   2. **Infantry Regiment**

184th "Nembo" Airborne Division (12/42, fought with the Germans; 01/0143, Italy; units of this division were assigned to Yugoslavia, Italy, Sardinia; 09/08/43, surrendered to Allies): MG Francesco Ronco [+ in /43, acting Commanding General, 101st "Trieste" Motorized Infantry Division] (?) 09/08/43 surrendered.
A. *Components - 184th "Nembo" Airborne Division* (12/42)
   1. **183rd Parachutist Infantry Regiment**:
   2. **184th Parachutist Infantry Regiment**:
   3. **185th Parachutist Infantry Regiment**:
   4. **184th "Nembo" Parachutist Artillery Regiment**:

185th "Folgore" Airborne Division (09/41, North Africa, from **1st "Folgore" Airborne Division**; 11/42, virtually destroyed at El Alamein; 04/43, remnants of the division destroyed in Tunisia): 08/41 **1st "Folgore" Airborne Division** 08/41? MG Enrico Frattini (Commanding General, 185th "Folgore" Airborne Division) 09/41 redesignated **185th "Folgore" Airborne Division** MG Enrico Frattini (acting Commanding General, XXX Army Corps) /41 BG Francesco Sapienza (acting) /42 MG Alberto Aliberti (acting Commanding General, IX Territorial Defense Command) /42 MG Gaetano Cantaluppi (?) /42 BG Riccardo Bignami (Allied prisoner-of-war) 04/43 destroyed.
A. **Deputy, 185th "Folgore" Airborne Division**: unknown? /42 BG Riccardo Bignami (Commanding General, 185th "Folgore" Airborne Division) /42 unknown? 04/43 dissolved.
B. *Components - 185th "Folgore" Airborne Division* (09/41)

1. **186th Parachutist Infantry Regiment:**
2. **187th Parachutist Infantry Regiment:**
3. **184th "Folgore" Parachutist Artillery Regiment:**

Assault & Landing Divisions

1st "Superga" Assault & Landing (Mountain) Infantry Division (reduced) (pre-war, as "Superga" Assault & Landing (Mountain) Infantry Division; named after a small mountain near Torino [Turin]; has mountain equipment in it's TO&E; 6/40, French Alpine campaign; 08/41, moved to Naples; 03/43, converted to Assault and landing division for possible Malta invasion; 11/42, sent to Tunisia; 05/43, destroyed): <u>**1st "Superga" Assault & Landing (Mountain) Infantry Division**</u> /39 MG Count Curio Barbasetti di Prun (Commanding General, I Army Corps) /40 MG Count Fernando Gelich /40 MG Dante Lorenzelli (Commanding General, XXX Army Corps) /41 MG Conte Fernando Gelich (Allied prisoner-of-war) 05/43 destroyed.
- A. **Components - 1st "Superga" Assault & Landing (Mountain) Infantry Division**
    1. **91st "Basilicata" Infantry Regiment** (named for in region in Italy):
    2. **92nd "Basilicata" Infantry Regiment** (named for in region in Italy):
    3. **5th "Superga" Artillery Regiment**: /39? Col. Alberto Roda (Chief of Staff, 7th "Lupi di Toscana" Infantry Division) /40? unknown?
- B. **Infantry Commander, 1st "Superga" Assault & Landing (Mountain) Infantry Division**: /41 BG Arturo Benigni (Commanding General, 2nd March Brigade) /42 unknown? 05/43 dissolved.

4th "Livorno" Assault & Landing (Mountain) Infantry Division (reduced) (pre-war; has mountain equipment in it's TO&E; 06/40, France; 07/40, Italy; 02/43, Sicily; 07/43, virtually destroyed; 09/08/43, surrendered): /39 MG Antero Canale (Commanding General, XI Army Corps) /39 unknown? /40 MG Benvenuto Gioda (Commanding General, X Army Corps) /41 MG Domenico Chirieleison (?) 07/43 virtually destroyed. 09/08/43 surrendered
- A. **Components - 4th "Livorno" Assault & Landing (Mountain) Infantry Division** (06/10/40)
    1. **33rd "Livorno" Infantry Regiment**:
    2. **34th "Livorno" Infantry Regiment**:
    3. **28th "Monviso" Artillery Regiment** (named for a mountain):

20th "Friuli" Assault & Landing Infantry Division (reinforced) (pre-war; named for in region in Italy; 06/40, France; 07/40, Italy; 04/05/41?, part of VI Army Corps, Second Army; Greece and Yugoslavia; /42?, Corsica; 09/08/43, surrendered to Allies): /37 MG Luigi Frusci (Commanding General, XX Army Corps) /38 BG Biagio Russo (acting; 07/41?, attached to VIII Army Corps) /39 BG Luigi Chiolini (Commanding General, 48th "Taro" Infantry Division) /39 MG Vittorio Sogno (Commanding General, VII Army Corps) /40 BG Ettore Cotronei (/42, Commanding General, 20th "Friuli" Assault & Landing Infantry Division) /41 MG Ugo Fongoli (British prisoner-of-war) /41 BG Vito Ferrari (acting) /41 MG Giacomo Carboni (Commanding General, VII Army Corps) /42 MG Ettore Cotronei (?) /43 MG Ugo de Lorenzis (Commanding General, Friuli Division, Italian Co-Belligerent Army) 09/08/43 surrendered to Allies.
- A. **Components - 20th "Friuli" Assault & Landing Infantry Division** (06/10/40)
    1. **87th "Friuli" Infantry Regiment**:
    2. **88th "Friuli" Infantry Regiment**: /38? Col. Guglielmo Negro (/40, Chief of

Staff, Army Group East) /39? Col. Giuseppe Fraticelli (Commanding General, 2nd Territorial Zone) /40 unknown?

3. **35th Artillery Regiment**:
4. **88th "A. Cappellini" Blackshirt (CCNN) Legion** (later renamed **359th Infantry Regiment**):

Colonial Divisions

1st Libyan "Sibelle" Infantry Division (pre-war; 06/40, Libya; 01/09/41, destroyed at Meiltila): /36 MG Guglielmo Ciro Nasi (Italian Governor of Harrar) 06/01/36 unknown? 06/10/40? MG Luigi Sibille (/43, possible Commanding General, 202nd Coastal Division) 01/09/41 destroyed.
A. *Components*
    1. **1st Libyan Infantry Regiment**:
    2. **2nd Libyan Infantry Regiment**:
    3. **1st Libyan Artillery Regiment**:

2nd Libyan "Pescator" Infantry Division (pre-war; 06/40, Libya; 01/41, destroyed at Tumar): /39 MG Armando Pescatori (British prisoner-of-war, captured at Alam el Tumar) /40 unknown? 01/41 destroyed.
A. *Components*
    1. **3rd Libyan Infantry Regiment**:
    2. **4th Libyan Infantry Regiment**:
    3. **2nd Libyan Artillery Regiment**:

3rd Libyan "Gruppo Maletti" Infantry Division (pre-war; 06/40, Libya; 12/40, destroyed): **3rd Libyan Infantry Division** /40 MG Pietro Maletti (Commanding General, Libyan Group) /40 redesignated **Libyan Group** /40 MG Pietro Maletti (Commanding General, Group Maletti) /40 redesignated **Group Maletti** MG Pietro Maletti (killed in action) 12/40 destroyed.
A. *Components*
    1. **5th Libyan Infantry Regiment**:
    2. **6th Libyan Infantry Regiment**:
    3. **3rd Libyan Artillery Regiment**:

1st (Eritrean) Colonial Infantry Division (pre-war; 06/40, East Africa; 05/17/41, destroyed in Gondar area of Ethiopia): /35 MG Gustavo Pesenti (Governor of Italian Somaliland) /40 unknown? 05/17/41 destroyed.

2nd (Eritrean) Colonial Infantry Division (pre-war; 06/40, East Africa; 05/17/41, destroyed): /35 MG Lorenzo Dalmazzo /40 MG Nicolangelo Carnimeo (Commanding General, X Territorial Defense Command) 05/17/41 destroyed.

4th (Eritrean) Colonial Infantry Division (pre-war; 06/40, East Africa; 05/17/41, destroyed): 06/40 MG Luigi Frusci [+ Governor of Amhara, Ethiopia; Governor of Eritrea; & Commanding General, Eritrea Corps] 05/17/41 destroyed.

101st (Somalian) Colonial Infantry Division (pre-war; 06/40, East Africa; 05/17/41, destroyed in the Soddu region): unknown? /40 MG Pietro Gazzera [+ Commanding General, Southern Sector, Italian East Africa] (Victory of Ethiopia) /40 BG Alfredo Baccari (British prisoner-of-war) 05/17/41 destroyed.
A. *Components* - **101st (Somalian) Colonial Infantry Division**

1. **13th Infantry Brigade**
2. **14th Infantry Brigade**
3. **15th Infantry Brigade**

102nd (Somalian) Colonial Infantry Division (pre-war; 06/40, East Africa; 03/41, destroyed): /39 MG Carlo de Simone (Governor of Italian Somaliland & Commanding General, Italian Somaliland Corps) 11/40 BG Amedeo Liberati (Commanding General, 65th "Granatieri di Savoia" Infantry Division) 03/10/41 destroyed.

A. *Components* - **102nd (Somalian) Colonial Infantry Division**
1. **21st Infantry Brigade**
2. **25th Infantry Brigade**

Harar Division (1940, Italian Somaliland Army)

"Sahariano" Department (06/10/40, part of General Headquarters North Africa reserves): 06/10/40? LG Sebastiano Gallina (British prisoner-of-war; captured at Sidi Barrani; /45, killed in an Allied bombing of the town Orbassano) 12/10/40 disbanded

A. *Components* - **Sahariano Department** (06/10/40)
1. **Gadames Sector**
2. **Cufra Sector**
3. **Seredeles Sector**

Agedabia-Jalo Sector, Cyrenaica Defense Command (10/23/42?; division status; Libya)

Barce Sector, Cyrenaica Defense Command (10/23/42?; division status; Libya)

Garian Sector, Tripolitania Defense Command (10/23/42?; division status; Libya)

Ghat Sector, Libyan Sahara Defense Command (10/23/42)

Homs Sector, Tripolitania Defense Command (10/23/42?; division status; Libya)

Hon Sector, Libyan Sahara Defense Command (10/23/42)
A. **34th Coastal and Anti-Aircraft Regiment**

Jarabub-Siwa Sector, Cyrenaica Defense Command (10/23/42?; division status; Libya)

Sebha Sector, Libyan Sahara Defense Command (10/23/42)

Sirte Sector, Tripolitania Defense Command (10/23/42?; division status; Libya)

Zuara Sector, Tripolitania Defense Command (10/23/42?; division status; Libya)

Derna Fortress (10/23/42?, Cyrenaica Defense Command; division status; Libya)

Tobruk Fortress (10/23/42?, Cyrenaica Defense Command; division status; Libya):

unknwon?
A. *Components* - **Tobruk Fortress** (10/23/42):
1. **Tobruk Garrison Brigade**
2. **Bardia Garrison Brigade**
3. **Mersa Matruh Garrison Brigade**
4. **350th "March" Infantry Regiment**
5. **2nd Anti-Aircraft Regiment**: /39? Col. Achille Rosica (assigned to Inspectorate, Technical Services) /41 unknown?
6. **37th Anti-Aircraft Regiment**

Benghazi Fortress (10/23/42?, Cyrenaica Defense Command; division status; Libya): MG Camillo Zarri (Artillery Commander, Eleventh Army) 05/43 disbanded.

Unknown? Colonial Division (/40?, East Africia): BG Emanuelle Beraudo di Pralorme (British prisoner-of-war; /44, Commanding General, 152nd "Piceno" Division) /44

Territorial Zones

1st Territorial Zone (part of I Territorial Defense Command; HQ: Torino [Turin], Italy; division status): 06/42? LG [Retired '36?] Count Enrico Riccardi (retired) /43 MG Vittorio Asinari di Bernezzo

2nd Territorial Zone (part of II Territorial Defense Command; HQ: Alessandria, Italy; division status): /40 BG Giuseppe Fraticelli

3rd Territorial Zone (part of III Territorial Defense Command; HQ: Milano [Milan], Italy; division status): MG [Retired] Francesco Barberis (retired) /43 MG Michele Ricciuti (to ./45, German prisoner-of-war) 09/08/43 dissolved.

4th Territorial Zone (part of I Territorial Defense Command; HQ Novara, Italy; division status): unknown? /43 MG Amedeo Sorrentino (to /45, German prisoner-of-war) 09/43 dissolved.
    A.   **At Disposal of, Attached to, or on Special Duties with 4th "Novara" Territorial Zone**:
        11/15/41 (attached to) BG Ferrucio Bondi

5th Territorial Zone (part of IV Territorial Defense Command; HQ: Verona, Italy; division status): unknown? /43 BG Guglielmo Orengo (to /45, German prisoner-of-war) 09/08/43 dissolved.

6th Territorial Zone (part of XIV Territorial Defense Command; HQ: Trieste, Italy; division status):

7th Territorial Zone (part of IV Territorial Defense Command; HQ: Trento, Italy; division status):

8th Territorial Zone (part of VI Territorial Defense Command; HQ: Bologna, Italy; division status; 09/08/43, disbanded by the Germans): /41 BG Carlo Racca (?) 04/42? BG Enrico Muttini (?) /43 BG Luigi Barbara (German prisoner-of-war) 09/43 BG (Res.) Umberto Ricci [+ to 02/11/44, Interior Minister; + attached to VI Territorial Defense Command]

9th Territorial Zone (part of VI Territorial Defense Command; HQ: Ravenna, Italy; division status): /41 MG Nicola Bellomo (/43, Allied prisoner-of-war; /45, condemned to death and executed as war criminal) 12/42 BG Gennaro Carraba

10th Territorial Zone (part of V Territorial Defense Command; HQ: Trieste, Italy; division status): /43 BG Enrico Giorgetti (to /45, German prisoner-of-war) 09/08/43 dissolved.

11th Territorial Zone (part of V Territorial Defense Command; HQ: Piacenza, Italy; division status):

12th Territorial Zone (part of XI Territorial Defense Command; HQ: Gorizia, Italy; division status): /41 BG Giuseppe Beato

13th Territorial Zone (part of VII Territorial Defense Command; HQ: Firenze [Florence], Italy; division status): unknown? /42 BG Carlo Barrilis

14th Territorial Zone (part of XV Territorial Defense Command; HQ: Genova [Genoa], Italy; division status): 06/42? LG [Retired 11/40] Gustavo Pesenti

15th Territorial Zone (part of VI Territorial Defense Command; HQ: Pola, Italy; division status): /42 MG Rosario Assanti
A. **At Disposal of, Attached to, or on Special Duties with 15th Territorial Zone**:
    /43 (at disposal) BG Giacomo Florio (to /45, German prisoner-of-war) 09/08/43 dissolved.

16th Territorial Zone (part of VIII Territorial Defense Command; HQ: Rome, Italy; division status): unknown? /43 BG Luigi Paolocci

17th Territorial Zone (part of VII Territorial Defense Command; HQ: Livorno, Italy; division status):

18th Territorial Zone (part of IX Territorial Defense Command; HQ: Perugia, Italy; division status): 07/41? BG Luigi Renzoni (?) /42 BG Ettore Del Totto (/44, Condemned to 20 years imprisonment for misconduct of the defense of Naples; /45, died in prison) 10/43

19th Territorial Zone (part of X Territorial Defense Command; HQ: Napoli [Naples], Italy; division status):

20th Territorial Zone (part of X Territorial Defense Command; HQ: Salerno, Italy; division status):

21st Territorial Zone (part of XII Territorial Defense Command; HQ: Catanzaro, Italy; division status): /42 BG Attilio de Michelis

22nd Territorial Zone (part of IX Territorial Defense Command; HQ: Bari, Italy; division status):
A. **Medical Inspector, 22nd Territorial Zone**: /41 Col. Carlo de Porcellinis

23rd Territorial Zone (part of IX Territorial Defense Command; HQ: Chieti, Italy; division status):

24th Territorial Zone (part of IX Territorial Defense Command; HQ: Ancona, Italy; division status): /43 MG Massimo Asteriti (German prisoner-of-war) 09/08/43 disbanded.
A. **Attached to 24th Territorial Zone**
    /43 BG Rodolfo Piazzi (to /45, German prisoner-of-war) 09/08/43 dissolved.

25th Territorial Zone (part of XII Territorial Defense Command; HQ: Palermo, Sicily; division status): 01/40 BG Federico Magri (/43, joins the Social Republic of Italy; /43, Commanding General, 200th Regional Military Command Roma) /42 BG Ildebrando Fiocca

26th Territorial Zone (part of XII Territorial Defense Command; HQ: Messina, Sicily; division status):

27th Territorial Zone (part of XIII Territorial Defense Command; HQ: Cagliari, Sardina; division status):

Royal Navy Squadrons (division status)

1st Heavy Cruiser Squadron [Commando 8a Divisione] (HQ: Taranto, Italy; Flagship: RIN heavy cruiser *Zara*; part of 1st Fleet): 01/13/40 RA Pellegrino Matteucci [RIN] (Commanding Officer, 9th Battleship Squadron) 12/13/40 RA Carlo Cattaneo [RIN] (?) 03/29/41 unknown? 01/12/42 Adm. Angelo Jachino [RIN] [+ Commander-in-Chief, Italian Royal Naval Fleet Afloat & Commanding Officer, 2nd Light Cruiser Squadron] 01/07/43
- A. *Components - 1st Heavy Cruiser Squadron* (06/10/40)
    1. **RIN heavy cruiser Zara**
    2. **RIN heavy cruiser Gorizia**
    3. **RIN heavy cruiser Fiume**
    4. **Destroyer Division 9**

2nd Light Cruiser Squadron [Commando 2a Divisione] (HQ: La Spezia, Italy; Flagship: RIN light cruiser *Giovanni dalle Bande Nere*; part of 2nd Fleet): 05/24/40 RA Ferdinando Casardi [RIN] (Commanding Officer, 7th Light Cruiser) 07/25/40 VA Angelo Jachino [RIN] [+ 12/09/40, Commander-in-Chief, Italian Royal Naval Fleet Afloat; + 01/12/42, Commanding Officer, 1st Heavy Cruiser Squadron] 01/07/43
- A. *Components - 2nd Light Cruiser Squadron* (06/10/40)
    1. **RIN light cruiser Giovanni dalle Bande Nere**
    2. **RIN light cruiser Bartolomeo Colleoni**
    3. **Destroyer Division 10**

3rd Heavy Cruiser Squadron [Commando 3a Divisione] (HQ: La Spezia, Italy; Flagship: RIN heavy cruiser *Trento*; part of 2nd Fleet): 05/26/40 RA Carlo Cattaneo (Commanding Officer, 6th Battleship Squadron) 08/28/40 RA Luigi Sansonetti [RIN] (Vice Chief of Naval Operations 04/24/41 RA Bruno Brivonesi [RIN] [+ Commanding Officer, Libya Naval Command] 11/13/41 RA Angelo Parona [RIN] (?) 07/25/43 VA Luigi Sansonetti [RIN]
- A. *Components - 3rd Heavy Cruiser Squadron* (06/10/40)
    1. **RIN heavy cruiser Trento**
    2. **RIN heavy cruiser Bolzano**
    3. **RIN heavy cruiser Trieste**
    4. **Destroyer Division 11**

4th Light Cruiser Squadron [Commando 4a Divisione] (HQ: Taranto, Italy; Flagship: RIN light cruiser *Alberico da Barbiano*; part of 1st Fleet): 05/30/39 Commo. Alberto Da Zara [RIN] (/40, Commander, Venice Arsenal; 09/06/40, Commander, RIN light cruiser *Emanuele Filiberto Duca d'Aosta* Battle Group) 05/24/40 RA Alberto Marenco di Moriondo [RIN] (?) 10/03/41 RA Guido Porzio Giovanola [RIN] (?) 01/12/42 VA Antonino Toscano [RIN]
- A. *Components - 4th Light Cruiser Squadron* (06/10/40)
    1. **RIN light cruiser Alberico da Barbiano**
    2. **RIN light cruiser Luigi Cadorna**
    3. **RIN light cruiser Alberto da Giussano**
    4. **RIN light cruiser Armando Diaz**

5th Battleship Squadron [Comando 5a Divisione] (HQ: Taranto, Italy; Flagship: RIN battleship *Giulio Casare*; part of 1st Fleet): 08/01/39 RA Carlo Bergamini [RIN] (Commander, 9th Battleship Squadron) 04/25/40 RA Bruto Brivonesi [RIN] (?) 11/07/41 RA Carlo Bergamini [RIN] [Flag: RIN battleship *Caio Duilio*] [+ to 12/09/41, Commander, 9th Battleship Squadron; + 01/12/42, Commander-in-Chief, 2nd Fleet & Deputy Commander, 1st Fleet] (Commander-in-Chief, 1st Fleet) 01/01/43 RA Giuseppe Fioravanzo [RIN] [+ 03/14/43, Commanding Officer, 8th Light Cruiser Squadron] 04/08/43 RA Emilio Brenta [RIN] (?) 09/21/43 RA Alberto Da Zara [RIN] [+ Commander, Superior Naval Force] (surrender to Allies; 03/10/44, Inspector of Naval Forces)

- A. **Components - 5th Battleship Squadron** (06/10/40)
  1. **RIN battleship *Giulio Casare***
  2. **RIN battleship *Conte di Cavour***
  3. **Destroyer Division 7**
  4. **Destroyer Division 8**

6th Battleship Squadron [Commando 6a Divisione] (HQ: La Spezia, Italy; Flagship: RIN battleship *Andrea Doria* ; part of 2nd Fleet): 06/10/40? vacant 08/30/40 RA Carlo Cattaneo [RIN] (Commanding Officer, 1st Heavy Cruiser Squadron) 12/09/40 unknown? 08/11/41 RA Ferdinando Casardi [RIN]

- A. **Components - 6th Battleship Squadron** (06/10/40)
  1. **RIN battleship *Andrea Doria***
  2. **RIN battleship *Caio Duilio***
  3. **Destroyer Division 12**

7th Light Cruiser Squadron [Comando 7a Divisione] (HQ: La Spezia, Italy; Flagship: RIN light cruiser *Eugenio di Savoia*; part of 2nd Fleet): 08/03/39 RA Luigi Sansonetti [RIN] (Commanding Officer, 3rd Heavy Cruiser Squadron) 08/27/40 RA Ferdinando Casardi [RIN] (Commanding Officer, 6th Battleship Squadron) 08/01/41 RA Raffaele de Courten [RIN] (01/01/43, Commanding Officer, 8th Light Cruiser Squadron) 03/07/42 RA Alberto Da Zara [RIN] (09/21/43, Commander, 5th Battleship Squadron) 04/25/43 RA Romeo Oliva [RIN]

- A. **RIN light cruiser *Emanuele Filiberto Duca d'Aosta* Battle Group**: 09/06/40 Commo. Alberto Da Zara [RIN] (Flag Officer, Anti-Submarine Inspectorate) 08/41
- B. **Components - 7th Light Cruiser Squadron** (06/10/40)
  1. **RIN light cruiser *Eugenio di Savoia***
  2. **RIN light cruiser *Emanuele Filiberto Duca d'Aosta***
  3. **RIN light cruiser *Muzio Attendolo***
  4. **RIN light cruiser *Raimondo Montecuccoli***
  5. **Destroyer Division 13**

8th Light Cruiser Squadron [Commando 8a Divisione] (HQ: Taranto, Italy; Flagship: RIN light cruiser *Duca degli Abruzzi*; part of 1st Fleet): 08/05/39 RA Antonio Legnani [RIN] (Commanding Officer, Submarine Fleet) 06/21/41 RA Giuseppe Lombardi [RIN] [+ 10/21/42?, Commanding Officer, Libya Naval Command] 01/01/43 RA Raffaele de Courten [RIN] (Navy Minister & Chief of Staff, Royal Italian Navy) 03/14/43 RA Giuseppe Fioravanzo [RIN] [+ to 04/08/43, Commanding Officer, 5th Battleship Squadron] (?) 09/21/43 VA Luigi Bianchieri [RIN]

- A. **Components - 8th Light Cruiser Squadron** (06/10/40)

1. **RIN light cruiser *Duca deghi Abruazzi***
2. **RIN light cruiser *Giuseppe Garibaldi***
3. **Destroyer Division 16**

9th Battleship Squadron [Comando 9a Divisione] (HQ: Taranto, Italy; Flagship: RIN battleship *Littorio* ; part of 1st Fleet): 05/07/40 RA Carlo Bergamini [RIN][Flag: RIN battleship *Vittorio Veneto*] [+ 11/07/41, Commander, 5th Battleship Squadron] 12/09/41 RA Pellegrino Matteucci [RIN](?) 02/01/41 unknown? 04/07/43 RA Enrico Accoretti [RIN]

A. *Components - 9th Battleship Squadron* (06/10/40)
1. **RIN battleship *Littorio***
2. **RIN battleship *Vittorio Veneto***
3. **Destroyer Division 14**
4. **Destroyer Division 15**

Anti-Submarine Division: 09/21/43 RA Amadeo Nomis di Pallone [RIN]

Albania Naval Command (HQ: Tirana, Albania): /39 Commo Alberto Da Zara [RIN] (Commander, 4th Light Cruiser Squadron) 05/30/39 unknown? 06/10/40? RA Vittorio Tur [RIN]

Taranto Naval Command (I Naval District):

Naples Naval Command (II Naval District):

Sicily Naval Command (III Naval District; part of Lower Tyrrenhian Sea Department): 06/10/40? RA Barone [RIN]
A. *Components - Sicily Naval Command* (06/10/40)
1. **1st Torpedo Boat Squadron**
2. **2nd Torpedo Boat Squadron**
3. **2nd Fast Torpedo Boat [MAS] Squadron**
4. **Torpedo Boat Division 5**

Syracuse-Palerno-Tripoli Naval Command (IV Naval District):

Sardinia Naval Command (V Naval District; part of Lower Tyrrenhian Sea Department): 06/10/40? RA Sportiello [RIN]
A. *Components - Sardinia Naval Command* (06/10/40)
1. **Torpedo Boat Division 2**
2. **Torpedo Boat Division 9**
3. **Fast Torpedo Boat [MAS] Division 4**

Aegean Sea Naval Command (VI Naval District; HQ: Rhodes, Dodecanese): 06/10/40? RA Luigi Bianchieri [RIN] (Commanding Officer, 8th Light Cruiser Squadron) 09/21/43
A. *Components - Aegean Sea Naval Command* (06/10/40)
1. **3rd Fast Torpedo Boat [MAS] Squadron**
2. **5th Submarine Squadron**

  3. **Destroyer Division 4**
  4. **Torpedo Boat Division 8**

Tobruk Naval Command (VII Naval District):

Libya Naval Command (VIII Naval District; HQ: Tripoli, Libya): 06/10/40? RA Bruno Brivonesi [RIN] [+ 04/24/41 to 11/13/41, Commanding Officer, 3rd Heavy Cruiser Division] (?) 10/21/42? RA Giuseppe Lombardi [RIN] [+ to 01/01/43, Commanding Officer, 8th Light Cruiser Squadron]

A. ***Components* - Libya Naval Command** (06/10/40)
  1. **RIN heavy cruiser *San Giorgio***
  2. **6th Submarine Squadron**
  3. **Destroyer Division 1**
  4. **Torpedo Boat Division 11**

Pola Naval Command (IX Naval District; part of Upper Adriatic Sea Department)

Brindisi Naval Command (X Naval District; part of Ionian and Lower Adriatic Sea Department)

A. ***Components* - Brindisi Naval Command** (06/10/40)
  1. **Torpedo Boat Division 7**
  2. **Fast Torpedo Boat [MAS] Division 3**

Spezia Naval Command (XI Naval District):

Italian East Africa Naval Command (XII Naval District; HQ: unknown?) 06/10/40? RA Balsamo [RIN]

A. ***Components* - Italian East Africa Naval Command** (06/10/40)
  1. **8th Submarine Squadron**
  2. **Destroyer Division 3**
  3. **Destroyer Division 5**
  4. **Fast Torpedo Boat [MAS] Division 21**

Naval Fleet Train (supplies for the Italian Fleets): 06/10/40? unknown?

Royal Air Force Commands (division status)

1st "Aquila" Fighter Command (part of 2nd Air Force; Base: Palermo Sicily):
A. *Components - 1st "Aquila" Fighter Command* (06/10/40):
    1. **1st CT Fighter Group** (Base: Palermo, Sicily; regiment status)

2nd "Borea" Fighter Command (part of 1st Air Force; Base: Torino [Turin]-Caselle, Italy):
A. *Components - 2nd "Borea" Fighter Command* (06/10/40):
    1. **3rd "Caccia" Fighter Group** (Base: Novi Ligure, Italy; regiment status)
    2. **53rd "Caccia" Fighter Group** (Base: Torino [Turin]-Caselle, Italy; regiment status)
    3. **54th "Caccia" Fighter Group** (Base: Airasca, Italy; regiment status)

3rd "Centauro" Bomber Command (part of 2nd Air Force; Base: Palermo, Sicily):
A. *Components - 3rd "Centauro" Bomber Command* (06/10/40):
    1. **11th Bombardment Group** (Base: Cosmiso, Sicily; regiment status)
    2. **34th Bombardment Group** (Base: Cantania-Fontanarossa, Sicily; regiment status)

4th "Drago" Bomber Command (part of 1st Air Force; Base: Novara, Italy):
A. *Components - 4th "Drago" Bomber Command* (06/10/40):
    1. **7th Bombardment Group** (Base: Lonate Pozzolo, Italy; regiment status)
    2. **13th Bombardment Group** (Base: Piacenza, Italy; regiment status)
    3. **43rd Bombardment Group** (Base: Cameri, Italy; regiment status)

6th "Falco" Bomber Command (part of 1st Air Force; Base: Padova, Italy):
A. *Components - 6th "Falco" Bomber Command* (06/10/40):
    1. **16th Bombardment Group** (Base: Vicezia [Venice], Italy; regiment status)
    2. **18th Bombardment Group** (Base: Aviano, Italy; regiment status)
    3. **47th Bombardment Group** (Base: Ghedi, Italy; regiment status)

8th "Astore" Bomber Command (part of 3rd Air Force; Base: Viterbo, Italy):
A. *Components - 8th "Astore" Bomber Command* (06/10/40):
    1. **9th Bombardment Group** (Base: Viterbo, Italy; regiment status)
    2. **12th Bombardment Group** (Base: Orvieto, Italy; regiment status)
    3. **46th Bombardment Group** (Base: Pisa-S. Giustro, Italy; regiment status)

13th "Pegaso" Bomber Command (06/10/40?, part of 1st Air Force; HQ: El Adem, Libya; 05/20/41?, HQ: Misurate, Libya):
A. *Components - 13th "Pegaso" Bomber Command* (06/10/40):
    1. **10th Bombardment Group** (Base: Benina, Libya; regiment status)
    2. **14th Bombardment Group** (El Adem, Libya; regiment status)

1st Air Force Support Command (part of 1st Air Force; HQ: Milano [Milan], Italy):

2nd Air Force Support Command (part of 2nd Air Force; HQ: Palermo, Italy):

3rd Air Force Support Command (part of 3rd Air Force; HQ: Rome, Italy):

4th Air Force Support Command (part of 4th Air Force; HQ: Bari, Italy):

Eastern Air Sector (Settore Est), Libya Air Command (part of Libya Air Command; HQ: Benghasi, Libya Base: Fulka, Egypt; division status): /40 MG Fernando Silvestri [RIAF] (?) 02/25/42 Col. Carlo Drago [RIAF] 10/23/42? Col. Girandinetti [RIAF] 08/42? BG Venceslao D'Aurelio [RIAF]
- A. *Components - Eastern Sector, Libya Air Command* (06/10/40):
    1. **Libyan Eastern Support Sector** (division status)
    2. **13th "Pegaso" Bomber Command** (division status)
    3. **14th "Rex" Fighter Wing** (brigade status)
- B. *Components - Eastern Sector, 5th Air Force* (10/23/42):
    1. **3rd CT Fighter Group** (Base: Bu Amud; regiment status)
    2. **4th CT Fighter Group** (Base: Benghazi; regiment status)
    3. **50th Fighter-Bomber Group** (Base: Barce; regiment status)

Central Air Sector (Settore Centrale) (part of Libya Air Command; HQ Sidi Califa; part of 5th Air Force; Base: Cyrenaica; later **Northern Sector**; division status): 08/42? BG Augusto Bacchiani [RIAF]
- A. *Components - Central Sector, 5th Air Force* (10/23/42):
    1. **2nd CT Fighter Group** (Base: Bu Amud; regiment status)
    2. **15th Assalto Fighter-Bomber Group** (Base: Benghazi; regiment status)
    3. **35th BT Fighter Group** (Base: Barce; regiment status)

Western Air Sector (Settore Ovest), Libya Air Command (part of Libya Air Command; HQ: Tripoli, Libya): /40 BG Raul da Barberino [RIAF] (?) 08/42? BG Mario Boschi [RIAF] (?) /43 BG Ruggero Bonomi (/44, Undersecretary of the Air Force) 05/43
- A. *Components - Western Sector, Libya Air Command* (06/10/40):
    1. **Libyan Western Support Sector** (division status)
    2. **2nd CT Fighter Group** (Base: Castelbenito, Libya; regiment status)
    3. **15th Bombardier Group** (Base: Trahuna T18, Libya; regiment status)
    4. **33rd Bombardier Group** (Base: Bir El Bherao, Libya; regiment status)
    5. **50th "Assalto" Dive-Bomber Ground Support Attack Group** (Base: Sorman, Libya; regiment status)

Southern Air Sector: 03/43 Col. V. Biani [RIAF]

Libyan Eastern Sector Support Command (part of Eastern Sector, Libya Air Command; HQ: Benghasi, Libya):

Libyan Western Sector Support Command (part of Western Sector, Libya Air Command; HQ: Tripoli, Libya):

Tunisia Air Command [Aeronautica Della Tunisia (ATUN)] (11/42; also known as **Tripolitania Air Command**; (part of 5th Air Force; Base: Tripoli, Libya; division status; Sicily and Tunisia; 05/43, surrendered): **Aeronautica Della Tunisia (#1)** 08/23/42? BG Mario Boschi [RIAF] 11/42 BG G. Gaeta [RIAF] (?) 02/43 disbanded; reformed **Aeronautica Della Tunisia (#2)** 02/43 MG Mario Boschi [RIAF] (?) 05/43 surrendered.

Eastern Front Air Command [Aeronautica Fronte Orientale] (07/10/41, from **Air Assets, Italian Expeditionary Corps**; Italian Expeditionary Corps; Eighth Army, Soviet Union):07/10/41): **Air Assets, Italian Expeditionary Corps** 07/10/41 Col. Carlo Drago [RIAF] (Commanding Officer, Eastern Air Sector, Libya Air Command) 02/25/42 BG Enrico Pezzi [RIAF] (missing in action, Russia) /42

Greece Air Command [Aeronautica Della Grecia (AGRE)] (08/41, HQ: Araxos? Greece mainland): 08/42? Col. Umberto Chiesa [RIAF] (?) 09/08/43 disbanded.

Slovenia-Dalmazia Air Command [Aeronautica Della Slovenia-Dalmazia (ASloDa)] (HQ: Sussak): 08/42? BG Mario Piccini [RIAF] (?) 09/08/43 disbanded.

Provence Air Command [Aeronautica Della Provence (APRO)] (04/43; southern France):

Albania Air Support Command (part of Albania Air Command; HQ: Tirana, Albania):

Eastern Africa Air Support Command (part of Eastern Africa Air Command; HQ: Addis Ababa, Abyssinia [Ethiopia]):

Sardinia Air Support Command (part of Sardinia Air Command; HQ: Cagliari, Sardinia):

Fascist Militia (division status)
Blackshirt (CCNN) Divisions

1st "Dio lo Vuole [God wants it]" Blackshirt (CCNN) Division (/37, Spanish Civil War; 10/37, consolidated with the **2nd "Fiamme Nere [Black Flames]" Blackshirt (CCNN) Division** to form **1st "23 Marzo" Blackshirt (CCNN) Division**): unknown? 10/37 consolidated with the **2nd "Fiamme Nere [Black Flames]" Blackshirt (CCNN) Division** to form **1st "23 Marzo" Blackshirt (CCNN) Division** - see **1st "23 Marzo" Blackshirt (CCNN) Division**.

2nd "Fiamme Nere [Black Flames]" Blackshirt (CCNN) Division (/37, Spanish Civil War; 04/37, **3rd "Penne Nere [Black Feathers]" Blackshirt (CCNN) Division** consolidated into it; 10/37, consolidated with the **1st "Dio lo Vuole [God wants it]" Blackshirt (CCNN) Division** to form **1st "23 Marzo" Blackshirt (CCNN) Division**): unknown? 10/37 consolidated with the **1st "Dio lo Vuole [God wants it]" Blackshirt (CCNN) Division** to form **1st "23 Marzo" Blackshirt (CCNN) Division** - see **1st "23 Marzo" Blackshirt (CCNN) Division**.

3rd "Penne Nere [Black Feathers]" Blackshirt (CCNN) Division (/37, Spanish Civil War; 04/37, consolidated into **2nd "Fiamme Nere [Black Flames]" Blackshirt (CCNN) Division** and disbanded): unknown? 04/37 consolidated into **2nd "Fiamme Nere [Black Flames]" Blackshirt (CCNN) Division** and disbanded.

"Africa" Blackshirt (CCNN) Division (1940; 03/41, East Africa; 05/41 destroyed): unknown? 05/41 destroyed.

"Cacchatorie d'Africa" Blackshirt (CCNN) Division (1941; 01/42, North Africa; 05/43, destroyed at Bardia): unknown? 05/43 destroyed.

1st "23 Marzo" Blackshirt (CCNN) Division (10/37, from consolidation of **1st "Dio lo Vuole [God wants it]" Blackshirt (CCNN) Division** and **2nd "Fiamme Nere [Black Flames]" Blackshirt (CCNN) Division**; 06/40, North Africa; 12/40, destroyed at Bardia; reformed; /42, Soviet Union; part of the II Army Corps, Eighth Army): **1st "23 Marzo" Blackshirt (CCNN) Division (#1)** /35 MG Ettore Bastico (Commanding General, III Army Corps) /35 MG Count Alberto Galamini [MVSN] (/43, Commandant, Anti-Aircraft Militia) /36 MG Domenico Siciliani (Commanding General, Roma Corps) /38 unknown? 06/10/40? MG Francesco Antonelli [MVSN] (01/06/41, British prisoner-of-war; captured at Bardia) 12/40 destroyed; reformed **1st "23 Marzo" Blackshirt (CCNN) Division (#2)** /42 MG Luigi Martinesi [MVSN] (?) 08/08/42? MG Enrico Francisci [MVSN] (killed in action in Sicily) /43

A. **Components - 1st "23 Marzo" Blackshirt (CCNN) Division**
    1. **219th "23 Marzo" Blackshirt (CCNN) Legion** (Tagliamento Group): /36 Col. Carlo Rastrelli [MVSN] (Commanding Officer, 238th "28 Ottobre" Blackshirt (CCNN) Legion) /39 unknown? /40 BG Morsero [MVSN]
    2. **233rd "23 Marzo" Blackshirt (CCNN) Legion** (Tagliamento Group):

3. **201st Artillery Regiment**:

2nd "28 Ottobre" Blackshirt (CCNN) Division (pre-war; 06/40, North Africa; 12/40, destroyed at Bardia): /35 MG Umberto Somma (Commanding General, 9th "Pasubio" Semi-Motorized Infantry Division) /38? unknown? 06/10/40? MG Francesco Argentino (01/09/41, captured at Tobruk, British prisoner-of-war) 12/40 destroyed.
A. *Components - 2nd "28 Ottobre" Blackshirt (CCNN) Division*
    1. **231st "28 Ottobre" Blackshirt (CCNN) Legion**:
    2. **238th "28 Ottobre" Blackshirt (CCNN) Legion**: /39 Col. Carlo Rastrelli [MVSN] (Commanding General, 33rd Blackshirt (CCNN) Group) /40
    3. **202nd Artillery Regiment**:

3rd "21 Aprile" Blackshirt (CCNN) Division (#1) (05/40, disbanded and redesignated **64th "Catanzaro" Infantry Division**; /43, reformed; 09/08/43, disbanded): **3rd "21 Aprile" Blackshirt (CCNN) Division (#1)** /35 MG Giacomo Appiotti (Member, Commission of Affairs of Italian Africa, Senate) /39 unknown? 05/40 disbanded and redesignated **64th "Catanzaro" Infantry Division** - see **64th "Catanzaro" Infantry Division**, reformed **3rd "21 Aprile" Blackshirt (CCNN) Division (#2)** /43 MG Renzo Montagna [MVSN] (joins Social Republic of Italy; 10/43, Commanding General, National Republican Guard, Social Republic of Italy) /43 MG Niccolò Nicchiarelli [MVSN] (joins Social Republic of Italy; 10/43, Chief of Staff, National Republican Guard, Social Republic of Italy) 09/08/43 disbanded.
A. *Components - 3rd "21 Aprile" Blackshirt (CCNN) Division*
    1. **181st "Arborea" Blackshirt (CCNN) Legion**:
    2. **203rd "21 Aprile" Blackshirt (CCNN) Legion**:
    3. **203rd Artillery Regiment**:

4th "3 Gennaio" Blackshirt (CCNN) Division (pre-war; 03/41, East Africa; 12/10/40, destroyed at Sidi Barrani): /35 MG Alessandro Traditi (?) /40 MG Fabio Merzari (captured at Sidi Barrani; British prisoner-of-war) 12/10/40 destroyed.
A. *Components - 4th "3 Gennaio" Blackshirt (CCNN) Division*
    1. **250th "3 Gennaio" Blackshirt (CCNN) Legion**:
    2. **270th "3 Gennaio" Blackshirt (CCNN) Legion**:
    3. **204th Artillery Regiment**:

5th "1 Febbraio" Blackshirt (CCNN) Division: /35 MG Attillo Teruzzi [MVSN] (Undersecretary of Ministry of Italian Africa) /37? inactivated during World War II.

6th "Tevere" Blackshirt (CCNN) Division: /35 MG Enrico Boscardi (Commanding General, 26th "Assietta" Infantry Division) /3? inactivated during World War II.

7th "Cirene" Blackshirt (CCNN) Division:

M (MUSSOLINI) Blackshirt (CCNN) Division (07/25/43, was still forming at the fall of Fascism; converted to a regular army unit and renamed the **134th "Centauro II" Armor Division**): still forming at the fall of Fascism 07/25/43 renamed the **134th "Centauro II" Armor Division** - see **134th "Centauro II" Armor Division**.

A. ***Components* - M (MUSSOLINI) Blackshirt (CCNN) Division**
 1. "Leonessa" Armored Regiment:
 2. 10th "Montebello" Blackshirt (CCNN) Legion:
 3. 63rd "Tagliamento" Blackshirt (CCNN) Legion:
 4. "Valle Scrivia" Artillery Regiment:

Other Blackshirt (CCNN) Units with Division Status

1st Blackshirt [CCNN (Camicie Nere)] Zone (Piemonte Area; HQ: Torino [Turin], Italy): 06/10/40? MG Piero Brandimarte [MVSN] (?) /43 MG Niccolò Nicchiarelli [MVSN] (Commanding General, 3rd "21 Aprile" Blackshirt (CCNN) Division (#2)) /43 unknown? 09/08/43 disbanded.
- A. **Components - 1st Blackshirt [CCNN (Camicie Nere)] Zone** (06/10/40)
  1. **1st Blackshirt (CCNN) Group** (HQ: Torino [Turin], Italy; brigade status)
  2. **2nd Blackshirt (CCNN) Group** (HQ: Novara, Italy; brigade status)
  3. **Other Regiments**
     - a. **18th Fiat Factory Blackshirt Legion**

2nd Blackshirt [CCNN (Camicie Nere)] Zone (Liguria Area; HQ: Genova [Genoa], Italy): 06/10/40? unknown? 04/43 MG Italo Romegialli [MVSN] (joins Social Republic of Italy; /43, Deputy Commander, National Republican Guard) 09/08/43 disbanded.
- A. **Components - 2nd Blackshirt [CCNN (Camicie Nere)] Zone** (06/10/40)
  1. **3rd Blackshirt (CCNN) Group** (HQ: Alessandria, Italy; brigade status)
  2. **4th Blackshirt (CCNN) Group** (HQ: Imperia, Italy; brigade status)
  3. **36th "Christoforo Colombo" Blackshirt Legion** (Genova [Genoa], Italy)
- B. **At Disposal of, Attached to, or on Special Duties with 2nd Blackshirt [CCNN (Camicie Nere)] Zone**:
  07/41 BG (Res.) Luigi Rossi [MVSN]

3rd Blackshirt [CCNN (Camicie Nere)] Zone (Lombardi Area; HQ: Milano [Milan], Italy): 06/10/40? unknown? /43 BG Angelo Cesare Bracci [MVSN] (?) /43 BG Arnaldo Bonelli (to /45, German prisoner-of-war) /43
- A. **Components - 3rd Blackshirt [CCNN (Camicie Nere)] Zone** (06/10/40)
  1. **5th Blackshirt (CCNN) Group** (HQ: Milano [Milan], Italy; brigade status)
  2. **6th Blackshirt (CCNN) Group** (HQ: Como, Italy; brigade status)
  3. **8th Blackshirt (CCNN) Group** (HQ: Cremona, Italy; brigade status)
  4. **30th Blackshirt (CCNN) Group** (HQ: Pavia, Italy; brigade status)

4th Blackshirt [CCNN (Camicie Nere)] Zone (Emilia and Romagna Areas; HQ: Bologna, Italy): 06/10/40? unknown? /41 BG Dino Zauli [MVSN] (?) /43 MG Mario Borghi [MVSN]
- A. **Components - 4th Blackshirt [CCNN (Camicie Nere)] Zone** (06/10/40)
  1. **9th Blackshirt (CCNN) Group** (HQ: Bologna, Italy; brigade status)
  2. **10th Blackshirt (CCNN) Group** (HQ: Ferrara, Italy; brigade status)
  3. **11th Blackshirt (CCNN) Group** (HQ: Piacenza, Italy; brigade status)
  4. **12th Blackshirt (CCNN) Group** (HQ: Ravenna, Italy; brigade status)
- B. **Inspector, 4th Blackshirt Zone**: /41 BG Giovanni D'Oro [MVSN] (Regional Inspector of National Republican Guard Emilia, Social Republic of Italy) 10/43

5th Blackshirt [CCNN (Camicie Nere)] Zone (Venezia Tridenta Area; HQ: Bolzano, Italy): 06/10/40? unknown? /43? BG Giovanni Martini [MVSN] (?) /43 MG Alberto Vasarri (to /45,

German prisoner-of-war) 09/08/43 disbanded.
- A.   ***Components - 5th Blackshirt [CCNN (Camicie Nere)] Zone*** (06/10/40)
  1.   **7th Blackshirt (CCNN) Group** (HQ: Treviso, Italy; brigade status)
  2.   **13th Blackshirt (CCNN) Group** (HQ: Verona, Italy; brigade status)
  3.   **14th Blackshirt (CCNN) Group** (HQ: Venezia [Venice], Italy; brigade status)

6th Blackshirt [CCNN (Camicie Nere)] Zone (Venezia Guilia Area; HQ: Trieste, Italy): 06/10/40? unknown? /43 MG Eduardo Preti [MVSN]
- A.   ***Components - 6th Blackshirt [CCNN (Camicie Nere)] Zone*** (06/10/40)
  1.   **15th Blackshirt (CCNN) Group** (HQ: Udine, Italy; brigade status)
  2.   **16th Blackshirt (CCNN) Group** (HQ: Trieste, Italy; brigade status)

7th Blackshirt [CCNN (Camicie Nere)] Zone (Tuscany Area; HQ: Firenze [Florence], Italy): 06/10/40? unknown? /42 MG Adolfo Mozzoni [MVSN] (?) /43 MG Mario Marino [MVSN] (joins Social Republic of Italy; Commandant, National Republican Guard Non-Commissioned Officers School, Social Republic of Italy) 10/43
- A.   ***Components - 7th Blackshirt [CCNN (Camicie Nere)] Zone*** (06/10/40)
  1.   **17th Blackshirt (CCNN) Group** (HQ: Firenze [Florence], Italy; brigade status)
  2.   **18th Blackshirt (CCNN) Group** (HQ: Livorno, Italy; brigade status)

8th Blackshirt [CCNN (Camicie Nere)] Zone (Umbria and Marche Areas; HQ: Ancona, Italy): 06/10/40? MG Antonio La Corte [MVSN] (?) /43 MG Alessandro Biscaccianti [MVSN]
- A.   ***Components - 8th Blackshirt [CCNN (Camicie Nere)] Zone*** (06/10/40)
  1.   **19th Blackshirt (CCNN) Group** (HQ: Perugia, Italy; brigade status)
  2.   **20th Blackshirt (CCNN) Group** (HQ: Ancona, Italy; brigade status)

9th Blackshirt [CCNN (Camicie Nere)] Zone (Luzio Area; HQ: Rome, Italy): 06/10/40? BG Ugo Colizza [MVSN]
- A.   ***Components - 9th Blackshirt [CCNN (Camicie Nere)] Zone*** (06/10/40)
  1.   **21st Blackshirt (CCNN) Group** (HQ: Rome, Italy; brigade status)
  2.   **31st Blackshirt (CCNN) Group** (HQ: Rome, Italy; brigade status)
  3.   **Other Regiments**
     - a.   **Rome Permanent Blackshirt Garrison** (Rome, Italy)
     - b.   **War Disabled Blackshirt Legion** (Rome, Italy)

10th Blackshirt [CCNN (Camicie Nere)] Zone (Abruzzi-Molise Area; HQ: L'Aquila, Italy): 06/10/40? unknown? /41 MG Silvio Masciocchi [MVSN]
- A.   ***Components - 10th Blackshirt [CCNN (Camicie Nere)] Zone*** (06/10/40)
  1.   **22nd Blackshirt (CCNN) Group** (HQ: Chieti, Italy; brigade status)
  2.   **32nd Blackshirt (CCNN) Group** (HQ: L'Aquila, Italy; brigade status)

11th Blackshirt [CCNN (Camicie Nere)] Zone (Camania and Calabria Areas; HQ: Napoli [Naples], Italy): 06/10/40? unknown? /43 MG Umberto Chiappe [MVSN]
- A.   ***Components - 11th Blackshirt [CCNN (Camicie Nere)] Zone*** (06/10/40)
  1.   **23rd Blackshirt (CCNN) Group** (HQ: Napoli [Naples], Italy; brigade status)
  2.   **26th Blackshirt (CCNN) Group** (HQ: Reggio Calabria, Italy; brigade status)

3.   **33rd Blackshirt (CCNN) Group** (HQ: Salerno, Italy; brigade status)

12th Blackshirt [CCNN (Camicie Nere)] Zone (Puglia and Basilicata Areas; HQ: Bari, Italy): 06/10/40? MG Luigi Martinesi [MVSN] (Commanding General, Blackshirt (CCNN) "23 Marzo" Division (#2))
A.   *Components - 12th Blackshirt [CCNN (Camicie Nere)] Zone* (06/10/40)
1.   **24th Blackshirt (CCNN) Group** (HQ: Bari, Italy; brigade status)
2.   **25th Blackshirt (CCNN) Group** (HQ: Lecce, Italy; brigade status)

13th Blackshirt [CCNN (Camicie Nere)] Zone (Sicily Area; HQ: Palermo, Sicily): 06/10/40?
A.   *Components - 3rd Blackshirt [CCNN (Camicie Nere)] Zone* (06/10/40)
1.   **27th Blackshirt (CCNN) Group** (HQ: Palermo, Sicily; brigade status)
2.   **28th Blackshirt (CCNN) Group** (HQ: Messina, Sicily; brigade status)

14th Blackshirt [CCNN (Camicie Nere)] Zone (Sardinia Area; HQ: Cagliari, Sardinia): 06/10/40?
A.   *Components - 3rd Blackshirt [CCNN (Camicie Nere)] Zone* (06/10/40)
1.   **29th Blackshirt (CCNN) Group** (HQ: Milano [Milan], Italy; brigade status)

Forest Militia [Milizia Forestale] (HQ: Rome, Italy): /35 Col. Augusto Agostini [MVSN] (joins Italian Social Republic; Commanding General National Republican Mountain & Forest Guard) /43 MG Guido Felici [MVSN] (Regional Inspector of National Republican Guard Marche, Social Republic of Italy) /44
A.   *Components - Forest Militia* (06/10/40) [All Forest Legions similar to regiments]
1.   **1st Forest Legion** (HQ: Udine, Italy): 06/10/40?
2.   **2nd Forest Legion** (HQ: Trento, Italy): 06/10/40?
3.   **3rd Forest Legion** (HQ: Brescia, Italy): 06/10/40?
4.   **4th Forest Legion** (HQ: Torino [Turin], Italy): 06/10/40?
5.   **5th Forest Legion** (HQ: Bologna, Italy): 06/10/40?
6.   **6th Forest Legion** (HQ: Firenze [Florence], Italy): 06/10/40?
7.   **7th Forest Legion** (HQ: L'Aquila, Italy): 06/10/40?
8.   **8th Forest Legion** (HQ: Napoli [Naples], Italy): 06/10/40?
9.   **9th Forest Legion** (HQ: Reggio Calabria, Italy): 06/10/40?
10.   **10th Forest Legion** (HQ: Tripoli, Libya): 06/10/40?
11.   **11th Forest Legion** (HQ: Addis Abeba, East Africa): 06/10/40?
12.   **12th Forest Legion** (HQ: Tirana, Albania): 06/10/40?

Railway Militia [Milizia Ferroviaria] (HQ: Rome, Italy): /32 Col. Vittorio Raffaldi [MVSN] (joins Social Republic of Italy; 09/43, Head, Inspectorate of National Republican Railway Guard, Social Republic of Italy) 09/08/43 disbanded.
A.   *Components - Railway Militia* (06/10/40) [All Railway Legions similar to regiments]
1.   **1st Railway Legion** (HQ: Torino [Turin], Italy): 06/10/40?
2.   **2nd Railway Legion** (HQ: Milano [Milan], Italy): 06/10/40?
3.   **3rd Railway Legion** (HQ: Genova [Genoa], Italy): 06/10/40?
4.   **4th Railway Legion** (HQ: Verona, Italy): 06/10/40?

5. **5ᵗʰ Railway Legion** (HQ: Trieste, Italy): 06/10/40?
6. **6ᵗʰ Railway Legion** (HQ: Bologna, Italy): 06/10/40?
7. **7ᵗʰ Railway Legion** (HQ: Firenze [Florence], Italy): 06/10/40?
8. **8ᵗʰ Railway Legion** (HQ: Ancona, Italy): 06/10/40?
9. **9ᵗʰ Railway Legion** (HQ: Roma, Italy): 06/10/40?
10. **10ᵗʰ Railway Legion** (HQ: Napoli [Naples], Italy): 06/10/40?
11. **11ᵗʰ Railway Legion** (HQ: Bari, Italy): 06/10/40?
12. **12ᵗʰ Railway Legion** (HQ: Reggio Calabria, Italy): 06/10/40?
13. **13ᵗʰ Railway Legion** (HQ: Palermo, Italy (Sicily)): 06/10/40?
14. **14ᵗʰ Railway Legion** (HQ: Cagliari, Italy (Sardinia)): 06/10/40?

Harbor or Port Militia [Milizia Portuaria] (HQ: Rome, Italy): 06/10/40? unknown? 03/43 BG Giuseppe Visconti [MVSN]

A. **Components - Harbor Militia** (06/10/40) [All Harbor Legions similar to regiments]
1. **1ˢᵗ Harbor Legion** (HQ: Genova [Genoa], Italy): 06/10/40?
2. **2ⁿᵈ Harbor Legion** (HQ: Napoli [Naples], Italy): 06/10/40?
3. **3ʳᵈ Harbor Legion** (HQ: Trieste, Italy): 06/10/40?
4. **4ᵗʰ Harbor Legion** (HQ: Bari, Italy): 06/10/40?
5. **Harbor Legion** (HQ: Genova [Genoa], Italy): 06/10/40?

University Militia [Milizia Universitaria] (HQ: Rome, Italy): 06/10/40? unknown?

A. **Components - University Militia** (06/10/40) [All University Legions similar to regiments]
1. **1ˢᵗ "Principe di Piemonte" University Legion** (HQ: Torino [Turin], Italy): 06/10/40?
2. **2ⁿᵈ "Arnaldo Mussolini" University Legion** (HQ: Milano [Milan], Italy): 06/10/40?
3. **3ʳᵈ "Dante Alighieri" University Legion** (HQ: Florence, Italy): 06/10/40?
4. **4ᵗʰ "Benito Mussolini" University Legion** (HQ: Rome, Italy): 06/10/40?
5. **5ᵗʰ "Goffredo Mameli" University Legion** (HQ: Napoli [Naples], Italy): 06/10/40?
6. **6ᵗʰ "San Georgio" University Legion** (HQ: Genova [Genoa], Italy): 06/10/40?
7. **7ᵗʰ "Guglielmo Marconi" University Legion** (HQ: Bologna, Italy): 06/10/40?
8. **8ᵗʰ "E. Ingravelle" University Legion** (HQ: Bari, Italy): 06/10/40?
9. **9ᵗʰ "Michele Marrone" University Legion** (HQ: Palermo, Italy (Sicily)): 06/10/40?

Frontier Militia [Milizia Confinaria] (HQ: Rome, Italy): 06/10/40? unknown? /43 BG Antonio Cobianchi

A. **Components - Frontier Militia** (06/10/40) [All Frontier Legions similar to regiments]
1. **1ˢᵗ "Monviso" Frontier Legion** (HQ: Torino [Turin], Italy): 06/10/40?
2. **2ⁿᵈ "Monte Rosa" Frontier Legion** (HQ: Como, Italy): 06/10/40?
3. **3ʳᵈ "Vetta d'Italia" Frontier Legion** (HQ: Bolzano, Italy): 06/10/40?
4. **4ᵗʰ "Monte Nevoso" Frontier Legion** (HQ: Trieste, Italy): 06/10/40?

Post and Telegraph Militia [Milizia Postelegrafica] (HQ: Rome, Italy; responsible for military censorship of the Field Postal Service including telephones): 06/10/40? unknown? /43 MG Rodolfo Tanese [MSVN] (joins Social Republic of Italy; 10/43, Commanding General, Republican Harbor Gurad, Social Republic of Italy) 09/08/43 disbanded.

Roads Militia [Milizia Stradadle] (HQ: Rome, Italy; responsible for road police duties) /39 MG Ugo Leonardi [MVSN] (Commanding General, National Republican Roads Guard, Social Republic of Italy) 09/08/43

Royal Carabinieri (CCRR) Units

Administration Divisions

1st Pastrengo Carabinieri Division (Milan): /40 BG Gilberto De Marinis (?) 03/43 BG (Res.) Nicolol Giani or BG Umberto Giani

2nd Podaga Carabinieri Division (Rome):
A. **Autonomous Group of Carabinieri. Aegean Islands**:

3rd Ogaden Carabinieri Division (Naples):

Brigades

1st Royal Carabinieri Brigade (Torino [Turin]: 10/42 BG Guiseppe Paglieri

2nd Royal Carabinieri Brigade: /41 BG Francesco Guala (?) 08/10/41 unknown? /43 BG Erminio Bocchi

4th Royal Carabinieri Brigade: /41 BG Francesco Mazzerelli (Commanding Officer, Royal Carabinieri, Eleventh Army) /43

Brigades

Infantry Brigades

"Alessandria" Infantry Brigade:
A. *Components* - "Alessandria" Infantry Brigade
 1. 155th "Alessandria" Infantry Regiment:
 2. 156th "Alessandria" Infantry Regiment:

"Aquila" Infantry Brigade:
A. *Components* - "Aquila" Infantry Brigade
 1. 269th Aquila" Infantry Regiment:
 2. 270th Aquila" Infantry Regiment:

"Arno" Infantry Brigade:
A. *Components* - "Arno" Infantry Brigade
 1. 213th "Arno" Infantry Regiment:
 2. 214th "Arno" Infantry Regiment:

"Barlette" Infantry Brigade:
A. *Components* - "Barlette" Infantry Brigade
 1. 137th "Barlette" Infantry Regiment:
 2. 138th "Barlette" Infantry Regiment:

"Belluno" Infantry Brigade:
A. *Components* - "Belluno" Infantry Brigade
 1. 274th "Belluno" Infantry Regiment:
 2. 275th "Belluno" Infantry Regiment:
 3. 276th "Belluno" Infantry Regiment:

"Benevento" Infantry Brigade:
A. *Components* - "Benevento" Infantry Brigade
 1. 133rd "Benevento" Infantry Regiment:
 2. 134th "Benevento" Infantry Regiment:

"Bisagno" Infantry Brigade:
A. *Components* - "Bisagno" Infantry Brigade
 1. 209th "Bisagno" Infantry Regiment:
 2. 210th "Bisagno" Infantry Regiment:

"Cacciatori della Alpi" Infantry Brigade (pre-war; /39, disbanded): /37 BG Giacomo Carboni (Chief, Military Intelligence Service) /39 disbanded.

"Caltanissetta" Infantry Brigade:
A. *Components*- "Caltanissetta" Infantry Brigade

1. **147th "Caltanissetta" Infantry Regiment:**
2. **148th "Caltanissetta" Infantry Regiment:**

"Campania" Infantry Brigade:
A. *Components* - **"Campania" Infantry Brigade**
1. **135th "Campania" Infantry Regiment:**
2. **136th "Campania" Infantry Regiment:**

"Campobasso" Infantry Brigade:
A. *Components* - **"Campobasso" Infantry Brigade**
1. **229th "Campobasso" Infantry Regiment:**
2. **230th "Campobasso" Infantry Regiment:**

"Caserta" Infantry Brigade:
A. *Components* - **"Caserta" Infantry Brigade**
1. **267th "Caserta" Infantry Regiment:**
2. **268th "Caserta" Infantry Regiment:**

"Catania" Infantry Brigade:
A. *Components* - **"Catania" Infantry Brigade**
1. **145th "Catania" Infantry Regiment:**
2. **146th "Catania" Infantry Regiment:**

"Chieti" Infantry Brigade:
A. *Components* - **"Chieti" Infantry Brigade**
1. **123rd "Chieti" Infantry Regiment:**
2. **124th "Chieti" Infantry Regiment:**

"Cosenza" Infantry Brigade:
A. *Components* - **"Cosenza" Infantry Brigade**
1. **243rd "Cosenza" Infantry Regiment:**
2. **244th "Cosenza" Infantry Regiment:**

"Del Timavo" Infantry Brigade (pre-war; /39, disbanded): /37 BG Roberto Lerici (06/10/40?, Commanding General, 25th "Bologna" Infantry Division) /38 BG Michele Giacomo Scaroina (Commanding General 12th "Sassari" Infantry Division) /39 disbanded.

"Elba" Infantry Brigade: unknown? /43 BG Achille Gilardi (to /45, German prisoner-of-war) 09/08/43 disbanded.
A. *Components* - **"Elba" Infantry Brigade**
1. **261st "Elba" Infantry Regiment:**
2. **262nd "Elba" Infantry Regiment:**

"Etna" Infantry Brigade:
A. *Components* - **"Etna" Infantry Brigade**
1. **223rd "Etna" Infantry Regiment:**

2.   224th "Etna" Infantry Regiment:

"Foggia" Infantry Brigade:
A.   *Components - "Foggia" Infantry Brigade*
  1.   280th "Foggia" Infantry Regiment:
  2.   281st "Foggia" Infantry Regiment:
  3.   282nd "Foggia" Infantry Regiment:

"Fossaita" Infantry Brigade: BG Giovanni Cerio (06/10/40, Commanding General, 29th "Piemonte" Infantry Division) /39 disbanded.

"Gaeta" Infantry Brigade:
A.   *Components - "Gaeta" Infantry Brigade*
  1.   263rd "Gaeta" Infantry Regiment:
  2.   264th "Gaeta" Infantry Regiment:

"Gavinana" Infantry Brigade (pre-war; /39, disbanded): /38? BG Emanuele Girlando (/40, Commanding General, 26th "Assietta" Mountain Infantry Division) /39 disbanded.

"Genova [Genoa]" Infantry Brigade:
A.   *Components - "Genova [Genoa]" Infantry Brigade*
  1.   97th "Genova [Genoa]" Infantry Regiment:
  2.   98th "Genova [Genoa]" Infantry Regiment:

"Girgenti" Infantry Brigade:
A.   *Components - "Girgenti" Infantry Brigade*
  1.   247th "Girgenti" Infantry Regiment:
  2.   248th "Girgenti" Infantry Regiment:

"Granatieri di Sardegna" Infantry Brigade (pre-war, named after the Sardinia Grenadiers, the Royal Guards; /39, upgraded to **21st "Granatieri di Sardegna" Infantry Division**): /37? MG Ezio Rosi (Commanding General, VI Army Corps) /39 BG Giunio Ruggiero (Commanding General, 21st "Granatieri di Sardegna" Infantry Division) /39 upgraded to **21st "Granatieri di Sardegna" Infantry Division** - see **21st "Granatieri di Sardegna" Infantry Division**.

"Grosseto" Infantry Brigade:
A.   *Components - "Grosseto" Infantry Brigade*
  1.   237th "Grosseto" Infantry Regiment:
  2.   238th "Grosseto" Infantry Regiment:

"Isonzo" Infantry Brigade (/39, upgraded to **14th "Isonzo" Infantry Division (reinforced)**): BG Giovanni Cocconi (Commanding General, 14th "Isonzo" Infantry Division) /39 upgraded up **14th "Isonzo" Infantry Division (reinforced)** - see **14th "Isonzo" Infantry Division**.

"Ivrea" Infantry Brigade:
A. *Components - "Ivrea" Infantry Brigade*
   1. **161st "Ivrea" Infantry Regiment:**
   2. **162nd "Ivrea" Infantry Regiment:**

"Jonio" Infantry Brigade:
A. *Components - "Jonio" Infantry Brigade*
   1. **221st "Jonio" Infantry Regiment:**
   2. **222nd "Jonio" Infantry Regiment:**

"Lambro" Infantry Brigade:
A. *Components - "Lambro" Infantry Brigade*
   1. **205th "Lambro" Infantry Regiment:**
   2. **206th "Lambro" Infantry Regiment:**

"Lario" Infantry Brigade:
A. *Components - "Lario" Infantry Brigade*
   1. **233rd "Lario" Infantry Regiment:**
   2. **234th "Lario" Infantry Regiment:**

"Lazio" Infantry Brigade:
A. *Components - "Lazio" Infantry Brigade*
   1. **131st "Lazio" Infantry Regiment:**
   2. **132nd "Lazio" Infantry Regiment:**

"Lecce" Infantry Brigade:
A. *Components - "Lecce" Infantry Brigade*
   1. **265th "Lecce" Infantry Regiment:**
   2. **266th "Lecce" Infantry Regiment:**

"Lucca" Infantry Brigade:
A. *Components - "Lucca" Infantry Brigade*
   1. **163rd "Lucca" Infantry Regiment:**
   2. **164th "Lucca" Infantry Regiment:**

"Manferrato" Infantry Brigade (pre-war; /39, disbanded): /37? BG Natale Pentimalli (/40?, special duties, VIII Army Corps) /38 BG Alessandro Gloria (/40, Commanding General, 37th "Modena" Infantry Division) /39 BG Luigi Carini (?) /39 disbanded.

"Massa Carrara" Infantry Brigade:
A. *Components = "Massa Carrara" Infantry Brigade*
   1. **251st "Massa Carrara" Infantry Regiment:**
   2. **252nd "Massa Carrara" Infantry Regiment:**

"Metauro" Infantry Brigade (prewar; /39, disbanded): /37? BG Angelo Stirpe (acting Commanding General, "Metauro" Infantry Division) /38? BG Egidio Levis (/40?,

Commanding General, 16th "Pistoia" Motorized Infantry Division) /39 Col. Orazio Mariscalco (acting; /43, Commanding General, 18th Coastal Brigade) disbanded.

"Milano [Milan]" Infantry Brigade:
A. *Components* - **"Milano [Milan]" Infantry Brigade**
1. **159th "Milano [Milan]" Infantry Regiment**:
2. **160th "Milano [Milan]" Infantry Regiment**:

"Montenero" Infantry Brigade (prewar; /39, disbanded): /37? BG Gino Pedrazzoli (Commanding General, 48th "Taro" Infantry Division) /39 disbanded.

"Monviso" Infantry Brigade (/39, upgraded to **4th "Monviso" Infantry Division (reinforced)**): BG Renato Coturri (Commanding General, 33rd "Acqui" Infantry Division) /39 BG Giuseppe Cortese (acting; /43, acting Commanding General, 47th "Bari" Infantry Division) /39 upgraded up **4th "Monviso" Infantry Division** - see **4th "Monviso" Infantry Division**.

"Murge" Infantry Brigade (pre-war; 04/42, upgraded to **154th "Murge" Garrison Division**): /38 BG Licurgo Zannini (Commanding General, 23rd "Murge" Infantry Division) /39 BG Giorgio Cristani (?) 04/42 upgraded up **154th "Murge" Garrison Division** - see **154th "Murge" Garrison Division**.

"Padova" Infantry Brigade:
A. *Components* - **"Padova" Infantry Brigade**
1. **117th "Padova" Infantry Regiment**:
2. **118th "Padova" Infantry Regiment**:

"Pallanza" Infantry Brigade:
A. *Components* - **"Pallanza" Infantry Brigade**
1. **249th "Pallanza" Infantry Regiment**:
2. **250th "Pallanza" Infantry Regiment**:

"Pasubo" Infantry Brigade (pre-war; /41 disbanded): /40? BG Enrico Broglia (Commanding General, "Sabauda" Infantry Brigade" /41? disbanded.

"Pesaro" Infantry Brigade:
A. *Components* - **"Pesaro" Infantry Brigade**
1. **239th "Pesaro" Infantry Regiment**:
2. **240th "Pesaro" Infantry Regiment**:

"Pescara" Infantry Brigade:
A. *Components* - **"Pescara" Infantry Brigade**
1. **211th "Pescara" Infantry Regiment**:
2. **212th "Pescara" Infantry Regiment**:

"Piave" Infantry Brigade (pre-war, /40, disbanded): /39 BG Quirino Armellini (Vice Chief of the Supreme General Staff) /40 disbanded.

"Porto Maurizio" Infantry Brigade:
A. ***Components - "Porto Maurizio" Infantry Brigade***
    1.   253rd **"Porto Maurizio" Infantry Regiment**:
    2.   254th **"Porto Maurizio" Infantry Regiment**:

"Potenza" Infantry Brigade:
A. ***Components - "Potenza" Infantry Brigade***
    1.   271st **"Potenza" Infantry Regiment**:
    2.   272nd **"Potenza" Infantry Regiment**:
    3.   273rd **"Potenza" Infantry Regiment**:

"Sabauda" Infantry Brigade: /38? BG Ubaldo Scanagatta (/40, Commanding General, 30th "Sabauda" Infantry Division) /40 BG Enrico Broglia (Commanding General, 156th "Vincenza" Garrison Division) 01/01/43?

"Sele" Infantry Brigade:
A. ***Components = "Sele" Infantry Brigade***
    1.   219th **"Sele" Infantry Regiment**:
    2.   220th **"Sele" Infantry Regiment**:

"Sesia" Infantry Brigade:
A. ***Components - "Sesia" Infantry Brigade***
    1.   201st **"Sesia" Infantry Regiment**:
    2.   202nd **"Sesia" Infantry Regiment**:

"Sila II" Infantry Brigade (pre-war; /39 disbanded): /37? BG Giulio Scavazzi (?) /39 disbanded.

"Siracusa" Infantry Brigade:
A. ***Components - "Siracusa" Infantry Brigade***
    1.   245th **"Siracusa" Infantry Regiment**:
    2.   246th **"Siracusa" Infantry Regiment**:

"Superga" Infantry Brigade (pre-war; /39, disbanded): /37 MG Mario Gamaleri (Commanding General, Bolzano Army Corps) /38 BG Dante Lorenzelli (Commanding General, 22nd "Cacciatori delle Alpi" Infantry Division) /39 disbanded.

"Tanaro" Infantry Brigade:
A. ***Components - "Tanaro" Infantry Brigade***
    1.   203rd **"Tanaro" Infantry Regiment**:
    2.   204th **"Tanaro" Infantry Regiment**:

"Taranto" Infantry Brigade:
A. ***Components - "Taranto" Infantry Brigade***

1. **143rd "Taranto" Infantry Regiment**:
2. **144th "Taranto" Infantry Regiment**:

"Teramo" Infantry Brigade:
A. *Components=* **"Teramo" Infantry Brigade**
   1. **241st "Teramo" Infantry Regiment**:
   2. **242nd "Teramo" Infantry Regiment**:

"Tevere" Infantry Brigade:
A. *Components -* **"Tevere" Infantry Brigade**
   1. **215th "Tevere" Infantry Regiment**:
   2. **216th "Tevere" Infantry Regiment**:

"Tortona" Infantry Brigade:
A. *Components -* **"Tortona" Infantry Brigade**
   1. **257th "Tortona" Infantry Regiment**:
   2. **258th "Tortona" Infantry Regiment**:

"Trapani" Infantry Brigade:
A. *Components -* **"Trapani" Infantry Brigade**
   1. **149th "Trapani" Infantry Regiment**:
   2. **150th "Trapani" Infantry Regiment**:

"Treviso" Infantry Brigade:
A. *Components -* **"Treviso" Infantry Brigade**
   1. **99th "Treviso" Infantry Regiment**:
   2. **100th "Treviso" Infantry Regiment**:

"Udine" Infantry Brigade:
A. *Components -* **"Udine" Infantry Brigade**
   1. **95th "Udine" Infantry Regiment**:
   2. **96th "Udine" Infantry Regiment**:

"Vicenza" Infantry Brigade:
A. *Components -* **"Vicenza" Infantry Brigade**
   1. **279th "Vicenza" Infantry Regiment**:

"Volturno" Infantry Brigade:
A. *Components -* **"Volturno" Infantry Brigade**
   1. **217th "Volturno" Infantry Regiment**:
   2. **218th "Volturno" Infantry Regiment**:

1st "Cosseria" Infantry Brigade: /37 BG Giovanni Magli (Commanding General, 131st "Centauro" Armored Division) /39 BG Educardo Quarra-Sito (11/25/41, Commanding General, 153rd "Macerata" Garrison Division) /40 BG Luigi Manzi (Commanding General, 52nd "Torino [Turin]" Semi-Motorized Infantry Division) /40

1st Infantry (March) Brigade (03/43, redesignated **28th Coastal Defense Brigade**): /42 BG Giuseppe Vitelli (?) 03/43 redesignated **28th Coastal Defense Brigade** - see **28th Coastal Defense Brigade**.

2nd Infantry (March) Brigade (03/43, redesignated **29th Coastal Defense Brigade**): BG Armellini Chiappi (Commanding General, 29th "Piemonte" Infantry Division) /39? Col. Attilio Amato (acting Commanding General, 18th "Messina" Infantry Division) /39? BG Pietro Maggiani (Commanding General, 55th "Savona" Infantry Division) 06/10/40? BG Emilio Bisson (British prisoner-of-war) /41 BG Arturo Benigni /43 BG Luigi Fazzini (?) 03/43 BG Arturo Benigni (Allied prisoner-of-war, captured in Tunisia) 05/43 redesignated **29th Coastal Defense Brigade** - see **29th Coastal Defense Brigade**.

3rd Infantry (March) Brigade (03/43, assigned anti-partisan duty in Yugoslavia; 04/43, headquarters used to form **230th Coastal Defense Division**): /42 BG Carlo Baudino (Commanding General, 38th "Puglia" Infantry Division) /43 BG Luigi Masini (?) 04/43 disbanded; used to form **230th Coastal Defense Division** - see **230th Coastal Defense Division**.

8th "Cuneo" Infantry Brigade: /39 BG Cesare Amé (Chief, Military Information Service) /40

13th Infantry Brigade (1940, part of the 101st (Somalian) Colonial Infantry Division):

14th Infantry Brigade (1940, part of the 101st (Somalian) Colonial Infantry Division):

15th Infantry Brigade (1940, part of the 101st (Somalian) Colonial Infantry Division):

20th Infantry Brigade: /36? BG Giovanni Majoli (Commanding General, 15th "Carnaro" Infantry Division) /37? BG Luigi Chiolini (acting Commanding General, 20th "Friuli" Assault & Landing Infantry Division) /39 BG Biagio Russo (acting Commanding General, 20th "Friuli" Assault & Landing Infantry Division) /39

21st "Brennero" Infantry Brigade (1940, part of the 102nd (Somalian) Colonial Infantry Division): /38? BG Gustano Reisoli-Matthieu (/42, Commanding General, 7th "Lupi di Toscana" Infantry Division) /39

24th "Brennero" Infantry Brigade: /39? BG Emilio Bancale (Commanding General, VIII Army Corps) /40

24th "Gran Sasso" Infantry Brigade: /37? BG Mario Zaccone (07/41, attached to, I Army Corps) /39

25th Infantry Brigade (1940, part of the 102nd (Somalian) Colonial Infantry Division): /38? BG Mario Marghinotti (Commanding General, 38th "Puglie" Infantry Division) /39

28th "Vespri" Infantry Brigade: /37? BG Giovanni Esposito (Commanding General, 57th "Lombardia" Infantry Division) /39 BG Mario Arisio (Commanding General, 28th "Aosta"

Infantry Division) /39

39th Infantry Brigade: BG Attilo Grattarola (Commanding General, 49th "Parma" Infantry Division) /39 Col. Americo Coppi (Commanding General, 2nd Armored Brigade) /39

50th Special Brigade: 01/01/43? BG Giavanni Imperiali de Franscavilla (?) 09/08/43 disbanded.

51st Special Brigade: /43 BG Mario Matteucci (to /45, German prisoner-of-war) 09/08/43 disbanded.

100th Infantry (March [Marcia]) Brigade (Italy): /42 BG Mario Roveda (?) 01/01/43? BG Domenico Peroglio (?) /43 BG Mario Russo (?) 09/08/43 disbanded.

110th Infantry (March [Marcia]) Brigade: /42 BG Guido Froio (Commanding General, 110th "March [Marcia]" Artillery Brigade) /43 BG Ettore Benvenutti (?) 09/08/43 disbanded.

"Pantelleria" Mixed Brigade (/43, Pantelleria): BG Achille Maffei (prisoner-of-war) /43 disbanded.

110th "March [Marcia]" Artillery Brigade (Italy): 01/01/43? BG Guido Froio (Commanding General, 5th "Calabria" Internal Security Brigade) /44

Banghazi Fortress (06/10/40, part of Tenth Army; brigade status): unknown? 05/43 disbanded.

1st Alpini Brigade: 06/10/40? BG Giovanni Maccario (Commanding General, 4th "Cuneense" Alpini Division) /41

2nd "Varalta-Po" Alpine Brigade (06/10/40, France): /40 MG Paolo Berardi (Commanding General, 11th "Brennero" Infantry Division) /40 disbanded.

"Alto Isonzo" Alpini Brigade (06/10/40?):

"Levanna" Alpini Brigade (/39?): BG Mario Girotti (Commanding General, 3rd "Julia" Alpini Division) /40

4th Coastal Defense Brigade (Sardina, part of XXX Army Corps; 09/08/43, surrendered to the Allies): 01/01/43? BG Berteno Bulbo (?) 09/08/43 surrendered to the Allies.

9th Coastal Defense Brigade (Italy): 01/01/43? BG Luigi Amato (?) 09/08/43 disbanded.

10th Coastal Defense Brigade (Italy; 10/43, disbanded): 01/01/43? BG Raffaele Colonna (Commanding General, 210th Coastal Division) 10/43 disbanded.

11th Coastal Defense Brigade (Italy): 01/01/43? BG Felice Pellegrini (?) 09/08/43 disbanded.

13th Coastal Defense Brigade (Sardinia): 01/01/43? BG Provanzano (?) 09/08/43 disbanded.

14th Coastal Defense Brigade (Balkans, part of V Army Corps): 01/01/43 BG Attilio Amato (Commanding General, 18th "Messina" Infantry Division) /43 unknown? 09/08/43 disbanded.

15th Coastal Brigade: /43 BG Oscar Gritti (?) 09/08/43 disbanded.

16th Coastal Brigade: 01/01/43? BG Giuseppe Maestrelli (?) 09/08/43 disbanded.

17th Coastal Brigade (Yugoslavia): /42 BG Alfonso Cigala-Fulgosi (Commanding General, 15th "Bergamo" Infantry Division) /43 unknown? 09/08/43 disbanded.

18th Coastal Defense Brigade (Sicily, part of XVI Army Corps): /43 BG Orazio Mariscalco (?) 08/43 disbanded.

19th Coastal Defense Brigade (Sicily, part of XVI Army Corps): /43 BG Giovanni Bocchetti (?) or BG Aldo De Ferrari (?) 08/43 disbanded.

28th Coastal Defense Brigade (03/43, from **1st Brigade**; Balkans, part of VI Army Corps):

29th Coastal Defense Brigade (03/43, from **2nd Infantry (March) Brigade**): BG Luigi Fazzini (?) 09/08/43 disbanded.

31st Coastal Defense Brigade (Italy, part of IX Army Corps; 09/08/43, surrendered to the Allies): unknown? 09/08/43 surrendered to the Allies.

32nd Coastal Defense Brigade (Italy, part of XIX Army Corps; 09/08/43, surrendered to the Allies): unknown? 09/08/43 surrendered to the Allies.

33rd Coastal Defense Brigade (Sardina, part of XIII Army Corps):

34th Coastal Defense Brigade (Italy, part of XVII Army Corps):

13th Border Artillery Brigade

"Barbò" Cavalry Brigade (/42, part of Eighth Army; Soviet Union): 08/08/42? BG Count Guglielmo Barbò di Caselmorano (Commandant, School of Application of Cavalry) /43 unknown? 09/08/43 disbanded.
   A.   ***Components - "Barbo" Cavalry Brigade** (08/08/42)*
        1.   **3rd "Savoia Cavalleria" Cavalry Regiment**: /39? Col. Raffele Cadorna (Commandant, School of Application of Cavalry) /40 Col. Ottorino Battista Dabbeni (Commanding General, 13th "Re" Infantry Division 08/05/41? Col.

        Weiss Poccetti 08/08/42? Col. Alessandro Bettoni Cazzago 09/08/43 disbanded.
2. **5th "Lancieri di Novara" Cavalry Regiment**: /35 Col. Cesara Lomaglio [+ /38, acting Commanding Officer, 7th "Lancieri di Milano [Milan]" Cavalry Regiment] (/40, Commanding General, 1st "Principe Eugenio di Savoia" Cavalry (Celere) Division) /39 Col. Carlo Lombardi (12/10/42, Deputy Commander, 3rd "Principe Amedeo Duca D'Aosta" Cavalry Division) 08/05/41? Col. Egidio Giuliana /41 Col. Count Guglielmo Barbò di Caselmorano (Commanding Officer, Barbò Cavalry Group) 08/08/42? Col. U. Salvatores or Col. Carlo Pagliano 09/08/43 disbanded.

Armored Infantry Brigade: /38? BG Giuseppe Stefanelli (Commanding General, 64th "Catanzaro" Infantry Division) /40

2nd Armored Brigade: /39 BG Americo Coppi (/42, Commanding General, XV Territorial Defense Command) /39

Bardia Garrison Brigade: unknown? 05/43 disbanded.

Mersa Matruh Garrison Brigade (10/23/42): BG Alpinoio Paoletti (at disposal of VI Territorial Defense Command):

Tobruk Garrison Brigade: unknown? 05/43 disbanded.

Grosseto Forces: 04/43? BG Paolo Marchini (?) 09/08/43 disbanded.

Division Depots (brigade status)

1st "Superga" Infantry Division Depot (part of 1st Territorial Zone; brigade status):

2nd "Sforzesca" Division Depot (part of 1st Territorial Zone; brigade status):

2nd Division Depot (part of 16th Territorial Zone):

3rd "Ravenna" Infantry Division Depot (part of 2nd Territorial Zone; brigade status):

4th Division Depot (part of 16th Territorial Zone):

5th Division Depot (part of 14th Territorial Zone):

6th "Cuneo" Infantry Division Depot (part of 3rd Territorial Zone; brigade status):

7th "Lupidi Toscana" Infantry Division Depot (part of 3rd Territorial Zone; brigade status):

9th "Pasubio" Infantry Division Depot (part of 5th Territorial Zone; brigade status):

10th "Piave" Infantry Division Depot (part of 5th Territorial Zone; brigade status):

11th "Brennero" Infantry Division Depot (part of 7th Territorial Zone; brigade status):

12th "Sassari" Infantry Division Depot (part of 10th Territorial Zone; brigade status):

13th Division Depot (part of 12th Territorial Zone):

14th Division Depot (part of 12th Territorial Zone):

15th "Bergamo" Infantry Division Depot (part of 11th Territorial Zone; brigade status):

16th "Pistoia" Infantry Division Depot (part of 8th Territorial Zone; brigade status):

17th "Pavia" Infantry Division Depot (part of 9th Territorial Zone; brigade status):

18th Division Depot (part of 24th Territorial Zone):

19th Division Depot (part of 13th Territorial Zone):

20th Division Depot (part of 17th Territorial Zone):

22nd Division Depot (part of 18th Territorial Zone):

23rd Division Depot (part of 22nd Territorial Zone):

24th Division Depot (part of 23rd Territorial Zone):

25th Division Depot (part of 19th Territorial Zone):

26th "Assietta" Infantry Division Depot part of 2nd Territorial Zone; (brigade status):

27th Division Depot (part of 21st Territorial Zone):

28th Division Depot (part of 25th Territorial Zone):

29th Division Depot (part of 26th Territorial Zone):

30th Division Depot (part of 27th Territorial Zone):

31st Division Depot (part of 27th Territorial Zone):

32nd Division Depot (part of 6th Territorial Zone):

33rd "Acqui" Infantry Division Depot (part of 7th Territorial Zone; brigade status):

36th "Forli" Infantry Division Depot (part of 1st Territorial Zone; brigade status):

37th "Modena" Infantry Division Depot (part of 1st Territorial Zone; brigade status):

38th Division Depot (part of 12th Territorial Zone):

41st Division Depot (part of 13th Territorial Zone):

43rd Division Depot (part of 22nd Territorial Zone):

44th Division Depot (part of 17th Territorial Zone):

47th Division Depot (part of 22nd Territorial Zone):

48th Division Depot (part of 18th Territorial Zone and 21st Territorial Zone):

49th Division Depot (part of 24th Territorial Zone):

51st Division Depot (part of 19th Territorial Zone):

52nd Division Depot (part of 16th Territorial Zone):

54th Division Depot (part of 25th Territorial Zone):

55th Division Depot (part of 20th Territorial Zone):

56th "Casale" Infantry Division Depot (part of 9th Territorial Zone; brigade status)**:**

57th "Lombardia"" Infantry Division Depot (part of 11th Territorial Zone; brigade status):

58th "Legnano" Infantry Division Depot (part of 3rd Territorial Zone; brigade status):

59th "Cagliari" Infantry Division Depot (part of 3rd Territorial Zone; brigade status):

60th Division Depot (part of 19th Territorial Zone):

61st Division Depot (part of 18th Territorial Zone and 21st Territorial Zone):

62nd Division Depot (part of 23rd Territorial Zone):

63rd Division Depot (part of 14th Territorial Zone):

64th Division Depot (part of 18th Territorial Zone and 21st Territorial Zone):

101st "Trieste" Infantry Division Depot (part of 15th Territorial Zone; brigade status)**:**

102nd "Trento" Infantry Division Depot (part of 7th Territorial Zone; brigade status):

131st Division Depot (part of 13th Territorial Zone):

133rd "Littorio" Armor Division Depot (part of 15th Territorial Zone; brigade status)**:**

1st "Taurineense" Mountain Division Depot (part of 1st Territorial Zone; brigade status):

2nd "Tridentina" Mountain Division Depot (part of 7th Territorial Zone; brigade status):

3rd Mountain Division Depot (part of 12th Territorial Zone):

4th "Cuneense" Mountain Division Depot (part of 2nd Territorial Zone; brigade status):

9th "Pusteria" Mountain Division Depot (part of 7th Territorial Zone; brigade status):

132nd "Ariete" Armor Division Depot (part of 5th Territorial Zone; brigade status):

1st Celere [Fast] Division Depot (part of 12th Territorial Zone):

2nd Celere [Fast] Division Depot (part of 9th Territorial Zone; brigade status):

3rd Celere [Fast] Division Depot (part of 5th Territorial Zone; brigade status):

Central Depot, Colonial Troops, Naples (brigade status) /42 BG Giuseppe Milocco

Territorial Districts (brigade status)

1st Territorial District (part of 2nd Territorial Zone; HQ: Alessandria, Italy; brigade status):

2nd Territorial District (part of 15th Territorial Zone; HQ: Piacenza, Italy; brigade status): 07/41? BG (Res.) Luigi Pinto

6th Territorial District (part of 8th Territorial Zone; HQ: Bologna, Italy; brigade status): 05/42 MG (Res.) Mario Moreno

7th Territorial District (part of 5th Territorial Zone; HQ: Parma, Italy; brigade status):

8th Territorial District (part of 9th Territorial Zone; HQ: Ravenna, Italy; brigade status):

23rd Territorial District (part of 3rd Territorial Zone; HQ: Milano [Milan], Italy; brigade status): /41 BG Giuseppe Molinero (Commandant, Palermo, XII Territorial Defense Command) /42 BG Count Antonio Barni

24th Territorial District (part of 1st Territorial Zone; HQ: Novara, Italy; brigade status):

40th Territorial District (part of 1st Territorial Zone; HQ: Cuneo, Italy; brigade status): unknown? /43 MG Alberto Vasarri (Commanding General, V Blackshit [CCNN] Zone) /43
- A. **At Disposal of, Attached to, or on Special Duties with 40th Territorial District**: /43 (at disposal) Col. (Res.) Renzo Vaccari (to /45, German prisoner-of-war) 09/08/43 dissolved.

42nd Territorial District (part of 3rd Territorial Zone; HQ: Bergamo, Italy; brigade status):

44th Territorial District (part of 3rd Territorial Zone; HQ: Cremona, Italy; brigade status):

45th Territorial District (part of 5th Territorial Zone; HQ: Verona, Italy; brigade status):

47th Territorial District (part of 8th Territorial Zone; HQ: Modena, Italy; brigade status):

54th Territorial District (part of 3rd Territorial Zone; HQ: Pavia, Italy; brigade status):

55th Territorial District (part of 9th Territorial Zone; HQ: Ferrara, Italy; brigade status):

56th Territorial District (part of 9th Territorial Zone; HQ: Forli, Italy; brigade status):

57th Territorial District (part of 15th Territorial Zone; HQ: Reggio Emilia, Italy; brigade status):

61st Territorial District (part of 5th Territorial Zone; HQ: Mantova, Italy; brigade status; 09/08/43, disbanded by the Germans): unknown? /43 BG Cesare Bartolotta (German prisoner-of-war) 09/08/43 disbanded.

62nd Territorial District (part of 5th Territorial Zone; HQ: Vicenza, Italy; brigade status):

63rd Territorial District (part of 5th Territorial Zone; HQ: Rovigo, Italy; brigade status):

65th Territorial District (part of 3rd Territorial Zone; HQ: Lodi, Italy; brigade status):

67th Territorial District (part of 3rd Territorial Zone; HQ: Ivrea, Italy; brigade status):

68th Territorial District (part of 3rd Territorial Zone; HQ: Lecco, Italy; brigade status):

73rd Territorial District (part of 3rd Territorial Zone; HQ: Varese, Italy; brigade status):

75th Territorial District (part of 3rd Territorial Zone; HQ: Vercelli, Italy; brigade status):

76th Territorial District (part of 3rd Territorial Zone; HQ: Monza, Italy; brigade status):

77th Territorial District (part of 7th Territorial Zone; HQ: Belluno, Italy; brigade status):

86th Territorial District (HQ: part of 2nd Territorial Zone; Casale Monferrato, Italy; brigade status):

88th Territorial District (part of 7th Territorial Zone; HQ: Sulmona, Italy; brigade status):

89th Territorial District (part of 7th Territorial Zone; HQ: Sondrio, Italy; brigade status):

90th Territorial District (part of 7th Territorial Zone; HQ: Treviglio, Italy; brigade status):

91st Territorial District (part of 7th Territorial Zone; HQ: Bassano, Italy; brigade status):

92nd Territorial District (part of 7th Territorial Zone; HQ: Trento, Italy; brigade status):

93rd Territorial District (part of 7th Territorial Zone; HQ: Bolzano, Italy; brigade status):

94th Territorial District (part of 10th Territorial Zone; HQ: Trieste, Italy; brigade status): unknown? 03/43 BG Marquis Francesca Navarra-Viggiani [+ Commanding General, Trieste Garrison]

97th Territorial District (part of 11th Territorial Zone; HQ: Pola, Italy; brigade status):

Border Guard Sectors (brigade status)

XI Border Guard Sector (part of III Territorial Defense Command; HQ: Varese, Italy; brigade status):

XII Border Guard Sector (part of III Territorial Defense Command; HQ: Sondrie, Italy; brigade status):

XIII Border Guard Sector (part of IV Territorial Defense Command; HQ: Merano, Italy; brigade status):

XIV Border Guard Sector (part of IV Territorial Defense Command; HQ: Bressanone, Italy; brigade status):

XV Border Guard Sector (part of IV Territorial Defense Command; HQ: Brunico, Italy; brigade status):

XVI Border Guard Sector (part of XIV Territorial Defense Command; under control of the Italian Army; brigade status):

XVII Border Guard Sector (part of XIV Territorial Defense Command; HQ: Vinadio, Italy; brigade status):

XXVIII Border Guard Sector (06/10/40, part of Fifth Army; HQ: Zuara; brigade status):

XXIX Border Guard Sector (06/10/40, part of Fifth Army; HQ: Nalut; brigade status):

XXX Border Guard Sector (06/10/40, part of Tenth Army; HQ: Berdia; brigade status):

XXXIII Border Guard Sector (part of Tripoli Fortress; HQ: Tripoli; brigade status):

XXXIV Border Guard Sector (part of Tripoli Fortress; HQ: Tripoli; brigade status):

XXXV Border Guard Sector (part of Tripoli Fortress; HQ: Tripoli; brigade status):

South East Border Guard Sector (part of Tripoli Fortress; HQ: Tripoli; brigade status):

Miscellaneous Units (brigade status)

Gadames Sector (06/10/40, part of "Sahariano" Department):

Cufra Sector (06/10/40, part of "Sahariano" Department):

Seredeles Sector (06/10/40, part of "Sahariano" Department):

Ogaden Border Region Command (/35, Somaliland): Col. Luigi Frusci (Inspector of Infantry)

Sultan Olol Dinke Column (/35, Somaliland): Sultan of Sciavelli, Olol Dinke [Somalian]

Ajacco Fortified Area: /42 BG Guglielmo Bazzarello (Commanding General, Pula Fortified Area) /43 unknown? 09/08/43 disbanded.

Pula Fortified Area: /43 BG Guglielmo Bazzarello (German prisoner-of-war, Camp 64-Z, Poland) 09/08/43 disbanded.

Dalmatia Coastal Defense: /43 BG Emilio Becuzzi (?   ) 09/08/43 disbanded.

14th Frontier Guards (09/08/43, disbanded): /43 BG Ludovico Castellani (to /45, German prisoner-of-war) 09/08/43 disbanded.

25th Frontier Guards (09/08/43, disbanded): /43 BG Ruggero Cessari (to /45, German prisoner-of-war) 09/08/43 disbanded.

Frontier Guards Albania (09/08/43, disbanded): /43 BG Enrico Lugli (Commanding General, 49th "Parma" Infantry Division) /43 unknown? 09/08/43 disbanded.

Foreign Volunteers in the Italian Military

[Compagnia Autocarrata Tedesca (Deutsche Motorisierte Kompanie)]: (07/01/40, a company of 150 German volunteers who had flee from Kenya and Tanganyika; 09/40, part of the Italian East African Army): LCol. Gustan Hamel [German]

Raggruppamento Frecee Rosse (07/42, as **Raggruppamento Centri Militari**, from Prisoners-of-war and foreign nationals living in Italy; 08/42, redesignated **Raggruppamento Frecee Rosse**): <u>Raggruppamento Centri Militari</u> 07/42 Col. Massimo Invrea (Commanding Officer, Raggruppamento Frecee Rosse) 08/42, redesignated <u>**Raggruppamento Frecee Rosse**</u> 08/42 Col. Massimo Invrea

Colonial Brigades

1st Colonial Brigade (06/10/41, part of Southern Sector, Italian East African Armed Forces): 06/10/40? Col. Guido Pialorsi (Commanding General, 22nd "Cacciatori delle Alpi" Infantry Division) /41

2nd Colonial Brigade (06/10/41, part of Eastern Sector, Italian East African Armed Forces): 06/10/40? BG Orlando Lorenzini (killed in action) /41

3rd Colonial Brigade (06/10/41, part of Northern Sector, Italian East African Armed Forces): /36 BG Sebastiano Gallina (06/10/40, Commanding General, Sahariano Department) 06/10/40? Col. Saverio Maraventano

4th Colonial Brigade (06/10/41, part of Northern Sector, Italian East African Armed Forces): 06/10/40? Col. Livio Bonelli

5th Colonial Brigade (06/10/41, part of Northern Sector, Italian East African Armed Forces): 06/10/40? BG Angelo Bergonzi (British prisoner-of-war) /41

6th Colonial Brigade (06/10/41, part of Northern Sector, Italian East African Armed Forces): 06/10/40? LCol. Agostino Magrini

7th Colonial Brigade (06/10/41, part of Eastern Sector, Italian East African Armed Forces): 06/10/40? Col. Tiburzio Rean

8th Colonial Brigade (06/10/41, part of Northern Sector, Italian East African Armed Forces): 06/10/40? Col. Antonio Rizzo (Italian Governor of Gimma; /04/01/41 to /43, British prisoner-of-war, captured at Asmara) /41

9th Colonial Brigade (06/10/41, part of Southern Sector, Italian East African Armed Forces): /37 Col. Orlando Lorenzini (Commanding General, 2nd Colonial Brigade) 06/10/40? Col. Flaminio Orrigo

10th Colonial Brigade (06/10/41, part of Southern Sector, Italian East African Armed Forces): 06/10/40? Col. Giuseppe Cloza

11th Colonial Brigade (06/10/41, part of Eastern Sector, Italian East African Armed Forces): 06/10/40? Col. Francesco Prina

12th Colonial Brigade (06/10/41, part of Northern Sector, Italian East African Armed Forces): 06/10/40? Col. Ugo Tabellini (/42, Commanding General, 10th "piave" Motorized Infantry Division) /40

13th Colonial Brigade (06/10/41, part of Eastern Sector, Italian East African Armed Forces): 06/10/40? BG Cesare Nam (British prisoner-of-war) /41

14th Colonial Brigade (06/10/41, part of Eastern Sector, Italian East African Armed Forces): 06/10/40? Col. Gioegio Siliprandi (?) /41 BG Carlo Tosti (British prisoner-of-war) 05/41

15th Colonial Brigade (06/10/41, part of Eastern Sector, Italian East African Armed Forces): 06/10/40? Maj. Luigi Romano

16th Colonial Brigade (06/10/41, part of Northern Sector, Italian East African Armed Forces): 06/10/40? Col. Manlio Manetti

17th Colonial Brigade (06/10/41, part of Eastern Sector, Italian East African Armed Forces): 06/10/40? Col. Ettore Focanti

18th Colonial Brigade (06/10/41, part of Southern Sector, Italian East African Armed Forces): 06/10/40? Col. Bartolomeo Minola

19th Colonial Brigade (06/10/41, part of Northern Sector, Italian East African Armed Forces): 06/10/40? Col. Enrico Durante

20th Colonial Brigade (06/10/41, part of Giuba Sector, Italian East African Armed Forces): 06/10/40? unknown?

21st Colonial Brigade (06/10/41, part of Northern Sector, Italian East African Armed Forces; /41, disbanded): 06/10/40? Col. Ignazio Angelini (British prisoner-of-war) /41 disbanded.

22nd Colonial Brigade (06/10/41, part of Northern Sector, Italian East African Armed Forces): 06/10/40? Col. Adriano Torelli

23rd Colonial Brigade (06/10/41, part of Southern Sector, Italian East African Armed Forces): 06/10/40? unknown?

25th Colonial Brigade (06/10/41, part of Southern Sector, Italian East African Armed Forces): 06/10/40? LCol. Giorgio Rolandi

41st Colonial Brigade (06/10/41, part of Northern Sector, Italian East African Armed Forces): 06/10/40? BG Ugo Fongoli (Commanding General, "Friuli" Infantry Division) /41

42nd Colonial Brigade (06/10/41, part of Northern Sector, Italian East African Armed Forces): 06/10/40? unknown?

43rd Colonial Brigade (06/10/41, part of Northern Sector, Italian East African Armed Forces): 06/10/40? unknown?

70th Colonial Brigade (06/10/41, part of Eastern Sector, Italian East African Armed Forces): 06/10/40? unknown?

85th Colonial Brigade (06/10/41, part of Southern Sector, Italian East African Armed Forces): 06/10/40? Col. Sebastiano Lannuti

86th Colonial Brigade (06/10/41, part of Southern Sector, Italian East African Armed Forces): 06/10/40? unknown?

91st Colonial Brigade (06/10/41, part of Giuba Sector, Italian East African Armed Forces): 06/10/40? Col. Pietro Bivona

92nd Colonial Brigade (06/10/41, part of Giuba Sector, Italian East African Armed Forces): 06/10/40? Col. Carlo Garino

Royal Navy Squadrons (brigade status)

Far East Naval Command (HQ: Tientsin, China): Commo. or Cdr. Galletti [RIN]

1st Submarine Squadron (HQ: La Spezia, Italy; part of the Submarine Fleet)
A. *Components - 1st Submarine Squadron* (06/10/40)
 1. **Submarine Division 11**
 2. **Submarine Division 12**
 3. **Submarine Division 13**
 4. **Submarine Division 14**
 5. **Submarine Division 15**
 6. **Submarine Division 16**
 7. **Submarine Division 17**

2nd Submarine Squadron (HQ: Napoli [Naples], Italy; part of the Submarine Fleet)
A. *Components - 2nd Submarine Squadron* (06/10/40)
 1. **Submarine Division 21**
 2. **Submarine Division 22**

3rd Submarine Squadron (HQ: Messina, Sicily; part of the Submarine Fleet)
A. *Components - 3rd Submarine Squadron* (06/10/40)
 1. **Submarine Division 31**
 2. **Submarine Division 33**
 3. **Submarine Division 34**
 4. **Submarine Division 35**
 5. **Submarine Division 37**

4th Submarine Squadron (HQ: Taranto, Italy; part of the Submarine Fleet)
A. *Components - 4th Submarine Squadron* (06/10/40)
 1. **Submarine Division 40**
 2. **Submarine Division 41**
 3. **Submarine Division 42**
 4. **Submarine Division 43**
 5. **Submarine Division 44**
 6. **Submarine Division 45**
 7. **Submarine Division 46**
 8. **Submarine Division 47**
 9. **Submarine Division 48**
 10. **Submarine Division 49**

5th Submarine Squadron (HQ: Rhodes, Dodecanese; part of Aegean Sea Naval Command)
A. *Components - 5th Submarine Squadron* (06/10/40)
 1. **Submarine Division 51**
 2. **Submarine Division 52**

6th Submarine Squadron (HQ: Tripoli, Libya; part of Libya Naval Command)
A. *Components - 6th Submarine Squadron* (06/10/40)
  1. **Submarine Division 61**
  2. **Submarine Division 62**

7th Submarine Squadron (HQ: Cagliari, Sardinia; part of the Submarine Fleet)
A. *Components - 7th Submarine Squadron* (06/10/40)
  1. **Submarine Division 71**
  2. **Submarine Division 72**

8th Submarine Squadron (HQ: unknown?; part of Italian East Africa Naval Command)
A. *Components - 8th Submarine Squadron* (06/10/40)
  1. **Submarine Division 81**
  2. **Submarine Division 82**

1st Fast Torpedo Boat [MAS] Squadron (part of Upper Tyrrenhian Sea Department):
A. *Components - 1st MAS Squadron* (06/10/40)
  1. **MAS Division 1**
  2. **MAS Division 5**
  3. **MAS Division 12**
  4. **MAS Division 13**
  5. **MAS Division 15**

2nd Fast Torpedo Boat [MAS] Squadron (part of Sicily Naval Command)
A. *Components - 2nd MAS Squadron* (06/10/40)
  1. **MAS Division 2**
  2. **MAS Division 9**
  3. **MAS Division 10**
  4. **MAS Division 15**

3rd Fast Torpedo Boat [MAS] Squadron (HQ: Rhodes, Dodecanese; part of Aegean Sea Naval Command)
A. *Components - 23rd MAS Squadron* (06/10/40)
  1. **MAS Division 7**
  2. **MAS Division 11**
  3. **MAS Division 16**
  4. **MAS Division 22**

1st Torpedo Boat Squadron (part of Sicily Naval Command)
A. *Components - 2nd MAS Squadron* (06/10/40)
  1. **Torpedo Boat Division 13**
  2. **Torpedo Boat Division 14**

2nd Torpedo Boat Squadron (part of Sicily Naval Command)
A. *Components - 2nd MAS Squadron* (06/10/40)
  1. **Torpedo Boat Division 1**

2. **Torpedo Boat Division 12**

Fascist Militia (brigade status)

"Diamanti" Blackshirt (CCNN) Brigade (04/05/41?, temporary unit; part of the XVII Army Corps, Ninth Army; Greece and Yugoslavia; 08/08/42?, disbanded): 04/05/41? MG Filippo Diamanti [MVSN] (Commanding General, "3 Gennaio" Blackshirt (CCNN) Brigade) 08/08/42? disbanded.
- A. *Components - "Diamanti" Blackshirt (CCNN) Brigade* (04/05/41)
    - a. 28th "Randaccio" Blackshirt (CCNN) Legion
    - b. 108th "Stamita" Blackshirt (CCNN) Legion
    - c. 109th "Acciaiata" Blackshirt (CCNN) Legion
    - d. 115th "Del Cimino" Blackshirt (CCNN) Legion
    - e. 136th "Tre Monti" Blackshirt (CCNN) Legion

"3 Gennaio" Blackshirt (CCNN) Brigade (/42, Soviet Union; part of the II Army Corps, Eighth Army): 08/08/42? MG Filippo Diamanti [MVSN] (joins Social Republic of Italy; 10/43, Commanding General, 210th Regional Military Command Genova [Genoa]) 09/08/43
- A. *Components - "3 Gennaio" Blackshirt (CCNN) Brigade* (08/08/42)
    1. 63rd "Tagliamento" Blackshirt (CCNN) Legion: 08/08/42? Col. Domenico Mittica [MVSN] (joins Social Republic of Italy; /43, Regional Inspector of Natioonal Republican Guard Piemonte, Social Republic of Italy) 09/08/43 dissolved.
    2. 10th "Montebello" Blackshirt (CCNN) Legion: 08/08/42? Col. I. Vianini [MVSN]

"23 Marzo" Blackshirt (CCNN) Brigade (/42, Soviet Union; part of the II Army Corps, Eighth Army; 08/08/42, redesignated **1st "23 Marzo" Blackshirt (CCNN) Division (#2)**): BG Enrico Francisci [MVSN] (Commanding General, 1st "23 Marzo" Blackshirt (CCNN) Division (#2)) 08/08/42 redesignated **1st "23 Marzo" Blackshirt (CCNN) Division (#2)** - see **1st "23 Marzo" Blackshirt (CCNN) Division**.
- A. *Components - "23 Marzo" Blackshirt (CCNN) Brigade* (08/08/42)
    1. 15th "Leonessa" Blackshirt (CCNN) Legion: 08/08/42? Col. G. Sardu [MVSN]
    2. 5th "Valle Scrivia" Blackshirt (CCNN) Legion: 08/08/42? Col. Mario Bertoni [MVSN] (Regional Inspector, National Republican Guard Liguria, Social Republic of Italy) /44

1st Blackshirt (CCNN) Group (HQ: Torino [Turin], Italy; brigade status; 09/08/43, disbanded by the Germans): /41 BG Gino Giusfredi [MVSN] (?) /43 BG Michele Baratono (German prisoner-of-war) 09/08/43 disbanded.
- A. *Components - 1st Blackshirt (CCNN) Group* (06/10/40)
    1. 1st "Sabauda" Blackshirt (CCNN) Legion (Torino [Turin], Italy)
    2. 12th "Monte Bianco" Blackshirt (CCNN) Legion (Aosta, Italy)

2nd Blackshirt (CCNN) Group (HQ: Novara, Italy; brigade status)
- A. *Components - 2nd Blackshirt (CCNN) Group* (06/10/40)
    1. 11th "Monferrato" Blackshirt (CCNN) Legion (Casale Monferrato, Italy)
    2. 28th "Randaccio" Blackshirt (CCNN) Legion (Vercelli, Italy)
    3. 29th "Chinotto" Blackshirt (CCNN) Legion (Arona, Italy)

    4.   **30th "Rovberto Forni" Blackshirt (CCNN) Legion** (Novara, Italy)

3rd Blackshirt (CCNN) Group (HQ: Alessandria, Italy; brigade status)
A.   *Components - 3rd Blackshirt (CCNN) Group* (06/10/40)
    1.   **3rd "Monviso" or "Subalpina" Blackshirt (CCNN) Legion** (Cureo, Italy)
    2.   **4th "Santarosa" Blackshirt (CCNN) Legion** (Alessandria, Italy)
    3.   **5th "Valle Scrivia" Blackshirt (CCNN) Legion** (Tortona, Italy): 08/08/42? Col. Mario Bertoni [MVSN] (Regional Inspector, National Republican Guard Liguria, Social Republic of Italy) /44
    4.   **10th "Monte Bello" Blackshirt (CCNN) Legion** (Voghera, Italy): /41 BG Fedele Maugliam [MVSN] (?) /42 BG Guido Felici [MVSN] (Commanding General, Forest Militia) /43
    5.   **38th "N. Alfieri" Blackshirt (CCNN) Legion** (Asti, Italy)

4th Blackshirt (CCNN) Group (HQ: Imperia, Italy; brigade status)
A.   *Components - 4th Blackshirt (CCNN) Group* (06/10/40)
    1.   **33rd "Gen. Giovanni Gandolfo" Blackshirt (CCNN) Legion** (Imperia, Italy)
    2.   **34th "Premuda" Blackshirt (CCNN) Legion** (Savona, Italy)
    3.   **36th "Christoforo Colombo" Blackshirt (CCNN) Legion** (Genova [Genoa], Italy)

5th Blackshirt (CCNN) Group (HQ: Milano [Milan], Italy; brigade status)
A.   *Components - 5th Blackshirt (CCNN) Group* (06/10/40)
    1.   **14th "Garibaldina" Blackshirt (CCNN) Legion** (Bergamo, Italy)
    2.   **15th "Leonessa" Blackshirt (CCNN) Legion** (Brescia, Italy):
    3.   **24th "Carroccio" Blackshirt (CCNN) Legion** (Milano [Milan], Italy)
    4.   **25th "Ferrera" Blackshirt (CCNN) Legion** (Monza, Italy)

6th Blackshirt (CCNN) Group (HQ: Como, Italy; brigade status)
A.   *Components - 6th Blackshirt (CCNN) Group* (06/10/40)
    1.   **8th "Cacciatori delle Alpi" Blackshirt (CCNN) Legion** (Varese, Italy)
    2.   **9th "Cacciatoni della Valtelina" Blackshirt (CCNN) Legion** (Sondrio, Italy)
    3.   **16th "Alpina" Blackshirt (CCNN) Legion** (Como, Italy)

7th Blackshirt (CCNN) Group (HQ: Treviso, Italy; brigade status): BG Carlo Malavasi [MVSN]
A.   *Components - 7th Blackshirt (CCNN) Group* (06/10/40)
    1.   **42nd "Berica" Blackshirt (CCNN) Legion** (Vicenza, Italy)
    2.   **43rd "Piave" Blackshirt (CCNN) Legion** (Belluno, Italy)
    3.   **44th "Pasubio" Blackshirt (CCNN) Legion** (Schio, Italy)
    4.   **50th "Trevigiana" Blackshirt (CCNN) Legion** (Treviso, Italy)

8th Blackshirt (CCNN) Group (HQ: Cremona, Italy; brigade status): /43 MG Giuseppe Moretti [MVSN]
A.   *Components - 8th Blackshirt (CCNN) Group* (06/10/40)
    1.   **6th "Sforzesca" Blackshirt (CCNN) Legion** (Vigevano, Italy)
    2.   **17th "Cremona" Blackshirt (CCNN) Legion** (Cremona, Italy)

3. **19th "Fedelissima" Blackshirt (CCNN) Legion** (Casalmaggiore, Italy)

9th Blackshirt (CCNN) Group (HQ: Bologna, Italy; brigade status)
A. *Components - 9th Blackshirt (CCNN) Group* (06/10/40)
    1. **67th "Volontari del Reno" Blackshirt (CCNN) Legion** (Bologna, Italy)
    2. **72nd "Farini" Blackshirt (CCNN) Legion** (Modena, Italy)
    3. **73rd "Boiardo" Blackshirt (CCNN) Legion** (Mirandola, Italy)
    4. **79th "Cispadana" Blackshirt (CCNN) Legion** (Reggio Emilia Italy)

10th Blackshirt (CCNN) Group (HQ: Ferrara, Italy; brigade status)
A. *Components - 10th Blackshirt (CCNN) Group* (06/10/40)
    1. **68th "Riario Sforza" Blackshirt (CCNN) Legion** (Imola, Italy)
    2. **75th "Italo Balbo" or "20 Dicembre" Blackshirt (CCNN) Legion** (Ferrara, Italy)
    3. **76th "Estense" Blackshirt (CCNN) Legion** (Este, Italy)

11th Blackshirt (CCNN) Group (HQ: Piacenza, Italy; brigade status): /40 BG Giovanni Zanella [MVSN]
A. *Components - 11th Blackshirt (CCNN) Group* (06/10/40)
    1. **74th "Taro" Blackshirt (CCNN) Legion** (Fidenza, Italy)
    2. **80th "Alessandro Farnese" Blackshirt (CCNN) Legion** (Parma, Italy)
    3. **83rd "Sant'Antonio" Blackshirt (CCNN) Legion** (Piacenza, Italy)

12th Blackshirt (CCNN) Group (HQ: Ravenna, Italy; brigade status)
A. *Components - 12th Blackshirt (CCNN) Group* (06/10/40)
    1. **71st "Manfreda" Blackshirt (CCNN) Legion** (Faenza, Italy)
    2. **81st "Alberico Da Barbiano" Blackshirt (CCNN) Legion** (Ravenna, Italy)
    3. **82nd "Bonito Mussolini" Blackshirt (CCNN) Legion** (Forli, Italy)

13th Blackshirt (CCNN) Group (HQ: Verona, Italy; brigade status): /40 BG Santi Quasimodo [MVSN] (Commanding General, Blackshirt Battalion Group M; /43, in France; /43, arrested by the Germans; /43 released at the request of Marshal Graziani; /43, joind Social Republic of Italy) /41
A. *Components - 13th Blackshirt (CCNN) Group* (06/10/40)
    1. **20th "Po" Blackshirt (CCNN) Legion** (Suzzara, Italy)
    2. **23rd "Bersaglieri del Mincio" Blackshirt (CCNN) Legion** (Mantova, Italy)
    3. **40th "Scaligera" Blackshirt (CCNN) Legion** (Verona, Italy)
    4. **41st "Battisti" Blackshirt (CCNN) Legion** (Trento, Italy)
    5. **45th "Alto Adige" Blackshirt (CCNN) Legion** (Bolzano, Italy)

14th Blackshirt (CCNN) Group (HQ: Venezia [Venice], Italy; brigade status)
A. *Components - 14th Blackshirt (CCNN) Group* (06/10/40)
    1. **49th "San Marco" Blackshirt (CCNN) Legion** (Venezia [Venice], Italy)
    2. **52nd "Polesana II" Blackshirt (CCNN) Legion** (Rovigo, Italy)
    3. **53rd "Patavina" Blackshirt (CCNN) Legion** (Padova, Italy)
    4. **54th "Euganea" Blackshirt (CCNN) Legion** (Este, Italy)

15th Blackshirt (CCNN) Group (HQ: Udine, Italy; brigade status)
- A. *Components - 15th Blackshirt (CCNN) Group* (06/10/40)
    1. **55th "Alpina Friulana" Blackshirt (CCNN) Legion** (Gemona, Italy)
    2. **62nd "Isonzo" Blackshirt (CCNN) Legion** (Gorizia, Italy)
    3. **63rd "Tagliamento" Blackshirt (CCNN) Legion** (Udine, Italy)

16th Blackshirt (CCNN) Group (HQ: Trieste, Italy; brigade status): 10/40? BG Nunzio Luna [MVSN]
- A. *Components - 16th Blackshirt (CCNN) Group* (06/10/40)
    1. **58th "San Giusto" Blackshirt (CCNN) Legion** (Trieste, Italy)
    2. **59th "Del Carso" Blackshirt (CCNN) Legion** (Sesana, Italy)
    3. **60th "Istria" Blackshirt (CCNN) Legion** (Pola, Italy)
    4. **61st "Carnaro" Blackshirt (CCNN) Legion** (Fiume, Italy)

17th Blackshirt (CCNN) Group (HQ: Firenze [Florence], Italy; brigade status)
- A. *Components - 17th Blackshirt (CCNN) Group* (06/10/40)
    1. **89th "Etrusca" Blackshirt (CCNN) Legion** (Volterra, Italy)
    2. **92nd "Francesco Ferrucci" Blackshirt (CCNN) Legion** (Firenze [Florence], Italy)
    3. **93rd "Gigilo Rosso" Blackshirt (CCNN) Legion** (Empoli, Italy)
    4. **94th "Fedele" Blackshirt (CCNN) Legion** (Pistoia, Italy)
    5. **95th "Sante Ceccherini" or "Marzocco" Blackshirt (CCNN) Legion** (Firenze [Florence], Italy)
    6. **96th "Petrarca" Blackshirt (CCNN) Legion** (Arezzo, Italy)
    7. **97th "Senese" Blackshirt (CCNN) Legion** (Siena, Italy)

18th Blackshirt (CCNN) Group (HQ: Livorno, Italy; brigade status)
- A. *Components - 18th Blackshirt (CCNN) Group* (06/10/40)
    1. **35th "Indomita" Blackshirt (CCNN) Legion** (La Spezia, Italy)
    2. **85th "Apuana" Blackshirt (CCNN) Legion** (Massa, Italy)
    3. **86th "Intrepida" Blackshirt (CCNN) Legion** (Lucca, Italy)
    4. **88th "A. Cappellini" Blackshirt (CCNN) Legion** (Livorno, Italy)
    5. **90th "Pisa" Blackshirt (CCNN) Legion** (Pisa, Italy)

19th Blackshirt (CCNN) Group (HQ: Perugia, Italy; brigade status)
- A. *Components - 19th Blackshirt (CCNN) Group* (06/10/40)
    1. **102nd "Cacciatori di Tevere" Blackshirt (CCNN) Legion** (Perugia, Italy)
    2. **103rd "Clitunno" Blackshirt (CCNN) Legion** (Foligno, Italy)
    3. **104th "Trotti" Blackshirt (CCNN) Legion** (Terni, Italy)
    4. **105th "Benito Mogioni" Blackshirt (CCNN) Legion** (Orvieto, Italy)

20th Blackshirt (CCNN) Group (HQ: Ancona, Italy; brigade status)
- A. *Components - 20th Blackshirt (CCNN) Group* (06/10/40)
    1. **107th "F. Rismondo" Blackshirt (CCNN) Legion** (Zara, Yugoslavia)
    2. **108th "Stamita" Blackshirt (CCNN) Legion** (Ancona, Italy)
    3. **109th "F. Corridoni" Blackshirt (CCNN) Legion** (Macerata, Italy)

4. **110th "Picena" Blackshirt (CCNN) Legion** (Ascoli, Italy)
5. **111th "F. Michelini Tocci" Blackshirt (CCNN) Legion** (Pesaro, Italy)

21st Blackshirt (CCNN) Group (HQ: Rome, Italy; brigade status): 01/42 BG Virgilio Nurchis [MVSN]
A. *Components - 21st Blackshirt (CCNN) Group* (06/10/40)
1. **112th "Dell'Urbe" Blackshirt (CCNN) Legion** (Rome, Italy)
2. **114th "G. Veroli" Blackshirt (CCNN) Legion** (Tivoli, Italy)
3. **118th "Volsca" Blackshirt (CCNN) Legion** (Velletri, Italy)
4. **119th "Caio Mario" or "N. Ricciotti" Blackshirt (CCNN) Legion** (Frosinone, Italy)
5. **120th "Giulio Cesare" Blackshirt (CCNN) Legion** (Rome, Italy)

22nd Blackshirt (CCNN) Group (HQ: Chieti, Italy; brigade status): /40 BG Carlo Rastrelli [MVSN] (?) /43
A. *Components - 22nd Blackshirt (CCNN) Group* (06/10/40)
1. **129th "Adriatica" Blackshirt (CCNN) Legion** (Pesscara, Italy)
2. **133rd "Lupi di Matese" Blackshirt (CCNN) Legion** (Campobasso, Italy)
3. **134th "Monte Mauro" Blackshirt (CCNN) Legion** (Chieti, Italy)
4. **136th "Tre Monti" Blackshirt (CCNN) Legion** (Lanciano, Italy)
5. **137th "Monte Majella" Blackshirt (CCNN) Legion** (Corna, Italy)

23rd Blackshirt (CCNN) Group (HQ: Napoli [Naples], Italy; brigade status)
A. *Components - 23rd Blackshirt (CCNN) Group* (06/10/40)
1. **138th "R. Padovani" or "Partenopeaa" Blackshirt (CCNN) Legion** (Napoli [Naples], Italy)
2. **141st "Capuano" or "Volturnio" Blackshirt (CCNN) Legion** (Caserta, Italy)
3. **144th "Irpina" Blackshirt (CCNN) Legion** (Avellino, Italy)

24th Blackshirt (CCNN) Group (HQ: Bari, Italy; brigade status)
A. *Components - 24th Blackshirt (CCNN) Group* (06/10/40)
1. **148th "Tavoliere" Blackshirt (CCNN) Legion** (Foggia, Italy)
2. **150th "G. Carli" Blackshirt (CCNN) Legion** (Barletta, Italy)
3. **151st "Domenico Pipca" Blackshirt (CCNN) Legion** (Bari, Italy)
4. **155th "Val Bradano" Blackshirt (CCNN) Legion** (Matera, Italy)

25th Blackshirt (CCNN) Group (HQ: Lecce, Italy; brigade status)
A. *Components - 25th Blackshirt (CCNN) Group* (06/10/40)
1. **152nd "Acciaiata" or "Salentina I" Blackshirt (CCNN) Legion** (Lecce, Italy)
2. **9153rd "Salentina II" Blackshirt (CCNN) Legion** (Brindisi, Italy)
3. **154th "D. Mastronuzzi" Blackshirt (CCNN) Legion** (Potenza, Italy)
4. **156th "Lucana" Blackshirt (CCNN) Legion** (Lodi, Italy)

26th Blackshirt (CCNN) Group (HQ: Reggio Calabria, Italy; brigade status)
A. *Components - 26th Blackshirt (CCNN) Group* (06/10/40)
1. **162nd "Luigi Settino" Blackshirt (CCNN) Legion** (Cosenza, Italy)

2. **163rd "Tonimaso Gulli" Blackshirt (CCNN) Legion** (Reggio Calabria, Italy)
3. **164th "Ercolino Scalfaro" Blackshirt (CCNN) Legion** (Catanzaro, Italy)

27th Blackshirt (CCNN) Group (HQ: Palermo, Sicily; brigade status)
A. *Components - 27th Blackshirt (CCNN) Group* (06/10/40)
   1. **168th "Ibla" Blackshirt (CCNN) Legion** (Ragusa, Sicily)
   2. **170th "Agrigentum" Blackshirt (CCNN) Legion** (Agrigento, Sicily)
   3. **171st "Vespri" Blackshirt (CCNN) Legion** (Palermo, Sicily)
   4. **172nd "Enna" Blackshirt (CCNN) Legion** (Enna, Sicily)
   5. **174th "Segesta" Blackshirt (CCNN) Legion** (Trapani, Sicily)

28th Blackshirt (CCNN) Group (HQ: Messina, Sicily; brigade status)
A. *Components - 28th Blackshirt (CCNN) Group* (06/10/40)
   1. **166th "Peloro" Blackshirt (CCNN) Legion** (Messina, Sicily)
   2. **167th "Etna" Blackshirt (CCNN) Legion** (Catania, Sicily)
   3. **169th "Syracusae" Blackshirt (CCNN) Legion** (Siracuse, Sicily)
   4. **173rd "Salso" Blackshirt (CCNN) Legion** (Caltanissetta, Sicily)

29th Blackshirt (CCNN) Group (HQ: Milano [Milan], Italy; brigade status)
A. *Components - 29th Blackshirt (CCNN) Group* (06/10/40)
   1. **175th "Salvaterra" Blackshirt (CCNN) Legion** (Iglesias, Sardinia)
   2. **176th "Sant'Efisio" Blackshirt (CCNN) Legion** (Cagliari, Sardinia)
   3. **177th "Logudoro" Blackshirt (CCNN) Legion** (Sassari, Sardinia)
   4. **178th "Gennargentu" Blackshirt (CCNN) Legion** (Nuoro, Sardinia)

30th Blackshirt (CCNN) Group (HQ: Pavia, Italy; brigade status): BG Brancati [MVSN]
A. *Components - 30th Blackshirt (CCNN) Group* (06/10/40)
   1. **7th "Cairoli" Blackshirt (CCNN) Legion** (Pavia, Italy)
   2. **18th "Costantissima" Blackshirt (CCNN) Legion** (Crema, Italy)
   3. **26th "Alberto da Giussano" Blackshirt (CCNN) Legion** (Legnano, Italy)
   4. **27th "Fanfulla" Blackshirt (CCNN) Legion** (Lodi, Italy)

31st Blackshirt (CCNN) Group (HQ: Rome, Italy; brigade status)
A. *Components - 31st Blackshirt (CCNN) Group* (06/10/40)
   1. **98th "Maremmana" Blackshirt (CCNN) Legion** (Grosseto, Italy)
   2. **115th "Del Cimino" Blackshirt (CCNN) Legion** (Viterbo, Italy)
   3. **116th "Sabina" Blackshirt (CCNN) Legion** (Rieti, Italy)
   4. **117th "Del Mare" Blackshirt (CCNN) Legion** (Civitavecchia, Italy)
   5. **121st "Coriolano" Blackshirt (CCNN) Legion** (Littoria, Italy): /42 BG Eugenio Coselschi [MVSN]

32nd Blackshirt (CCNN) Group (HQ: L'Aquila, Italy; brigade status): 06/42 BG Griffini [MVSN]
A. *Components - 32nd Blackshirt (CCNN) Group* (06/10/40)
   1. **130th "L'Aquila" or "Monte Sirente" Blackshirt (CCNN) Legion** (L'Aquila, Italy)
   2. **131st "Monte Morrone" or "G. Paolini" Blackshirt (CCNN) Legion**

(Sulmona, Italy)
3. **132ⁿᵈ "Monte Velino" Blackshirt (CCNN) Legion** (Avezzano, Italy)
4. **135ᵗʰ "Gran Sasso" Blackshirt (CCNN) Legion** (Teramo, Italy)

33ʳᵈ Blackshirt (CCNN) Group (HQ: Salerno, Italy; brigade status): /40 BG Carlo Rastrelli [MVSN] (Commanding General, 22ⁿᵈ Blackshirt (CCNN) Group) /40
A. *Components - 33ʳᵈ Blackshirt (CCNN) Group* (06/10/40)
    1. **140ᵗʰ "Aquilia" Blackshirt (CCNN) Legion** (Salerno, Italy)
    2. **143ʳᵈ "Clino Ricci" Blackshirt (CCNN) Legion** (Benevento, Italy)
    3. **145ᵗʰ "Pisacane" or "Sorrentina" Blackshirt (CCNN) Legion** (Castellamare, Italy)
    4. **146ᵗʰ "Alburnina" Blackshirt (CCNN) Legion** (Sala Consilina, Italy)

Unknown? Blackshirt (CCNN) Group: 01/41 BG Evandro Talinucci [MVSN]

1ˢᵗ DICAT Blackshirt (CCNN) Legion Group (HQ: Torino [Turin], Italy): 06/10/40?
A. *Components - 1ˢᵗ DICAT Blackshirt (CCNN) Legion Group* (06/10/40)
    1. **1ˢᵗ DICAT Blackshirt (CCNN) Legion** (Torino [Turin], Italy; also listed under I Territorial Defense Command)
    2. **2ⁿᵈ DICAT Blackshirt (CCNN) Legion** (Savona, Italy; also listed under XV Territorial Defense Command)
    3. **3ʳᵈ DICAT Blackshirt (CCNN) Legion** (Genova [Genoa], Italy; also listed under XV Territorial Defense Command)
    4. **4ᵗʰ DICAT Blackshirt (CCNN) Legion** (Alessandria, Italy; also listed under II Territorial Defense Command)

2ⁿᵈ DICAT Blackshirt (CCNN) Legion Group (HQ: Milano [Milan], Italy): 06/10/40?
A. *Components - 2ⁿᵈ DICAT Blackshirt (CCNN) Legion Group* (06/10/40)
    1. **5ᵗʰ DICAT Blackshirt (CCNN) Legion** (Milano [Milan], Italy; also listed under III Territorial Defense Command)
    2. **6ᵗʰ DICAT Blackshirt (CCNN) Legion** (Piacenza, Italy; also listed under VI Territorial Defense Command)
    3. **7ᵗʰ DICAT Blackshirt (CCNN) Legion** (Brescia, Italy; also listed under III Territorial Defense Command)
    4. **8ᵗʰ DICAT Blackshirt (CCNN) Legion** (Verona, Italy; also listed under IV Territorial Defense Command)

3ʳᵈ DICAT Blackshirt (CCNN) Legion Group (HQ: Bologna, Italy): 06/10/40?
A. *Components - 3ʳᵈ DICAT Blackshirt (CCNN) Legion Group* (06/10/40)
    1. **9ᵗʰ DICAT Blackshirt (CCNN) Legion** (Padova, Italy; also listed under XIV Territorial Defense Command)
    2. **10ᵗʰ DICAT Blackshirt (CCNN) Legion** (Udine, Italy; also listed under XI Territorial Defense Command)
    3. **11ᵗʰ DICAT Blackshirt (CCNN) Legion** (Trieste, Italy; also listed under V Territorial Defense Command)
    4. **12ᵗʰ DICAT Blackshirt (CCNN) Legion** (Bologna, Italy; also listed under VI Territorial Defense Command)

5. **15ᵗʰ DICAT Blackshirt (CCNN) Legion** (Ancona, Italy; also listed under IX Territorial Defense Command)

4ᵗʰ DICAT Blackshirt (CCNN) Legion Group (HQ: Rome, Italy): 06/10/40?
A. *Components - 4ᵗʰ DICAT Blackshirt (CCNN) Legion Group* (06/10/40)
    1. **13ᵗʰ DICAT Blackshirt (CCNN) Legion** (Livorno, Italy; also listed under VII Territorial Defense Command)
    2. **14ᵗʰ DICAT Blackshirt (CCNN) Legion** (Firenze [Florence], Italy; also listed under VII Territorial Defense Command)
    3. **16ᵗʰ DICAT Blackshirt (CCNN) Legion** (Terni, Italy; also listed under VIII Territorial Defense Command)
    4. **17ᵗʰ DICAT Blackshirt (CCNN) Legion** (Cagliani, Sardinia; also listed under XIII Territorial Defense Command)
    5. **18ᵗʰ DICAT Blackshirt (CCNN) Legion** (Rome, Italy; also listed under VIII Territorial Defense Command)

5ᵗʰ DICAT Blackshirt (CCNN) Legion Group (HQ: Napoli [Naples], Italy): 06/10/40?
A. *Components - 5ᵗʰ DICAT Blackshirt (CCNN) Legion Group* (06/10/40)
    1. **19ᵗʰ DICAT Blackshirt (CCNN) Legion** (Napoli [Naples], Italy; also listed under X Territorial Defense Command)
    2. **20ᵗʰ DICAT Blackshirt (CCNN) Legion** (Bari, Italy; also listed under IX Territorial Defense Command)
    3. **21ˢᵗ DICAT Blackshirt (CCNN) Legion** (Catanzaro, Italy; also listed under XII Territorial Defense Command)
    4. **22ⁿᵈ DICAT Blackshirt (CCNN) Legion** (Palermo, Sicily; also listed under XII Territorial Defense Command)

1ˢᵗ MILMART Blackshirt (CCNN) Legion Group (HQ: Messina, Sicily): 06/10/40?
A. *Components - 1ˢᵗ MILMART Blackshirt (CCNN) Legion Group* (06/10/40)
    1. **6ᵗʰ MILMART Blackshirt (CCNN) Legion** (Messina, Sicily)
    2. **7ᵗʰ MILMART Blackshirt (CCNN) Legion** (Augusta, Sicily)
    3. **8ᵗʰ MILMART Blackshirt (CCNN) Legion** (Trapani, Sicily)
    4. **9ᵗʰ MILMART Blackshirt (CCNN) Legion** (Pantelleria Island)
    5. **14ᵗʰ MILMART Blackshirt (CCNN) Legion** (Reggio Calabria, Italy)

2ⁿᵈ MILMART Blackshirt (CCNN) Legion Group (HQ: La Spezia, Italy): 06/10/40?
A. *Components - 2ⁿᵈ MILMART Blackshirt (CCNN) Legion Group* (06/10/40)
    1. **1ˢᵗ MILMART Blackshirt (CCNN) Legion** (Venezia [Venice], Italy)
    2. **2ⁿᵈ MILMART Blackshirt (CCNN) Legion** (La Spezia, Italy)
    3. **3ʳᵈ MILMART Blackshirt (CCNN) Legion** (La Maddalena, Sardinia)
    4. **4ᵗʰ MILMART Blackshirt (CCNN) Legion** (Cagliari, Sardinia)
    5. **5ᵗʰ MILMART Blackshirt (CCNN) Legion** (Taranto, Italy)

Royal Air Force Brigades

9th Air Brigade: /41 BG Enrico Pezzi [RIAF] (Commanding General, Air Force Command, Eighth Army) 08/01/42?

Royal Air Force Wings (brigade status)

8th "Astore" Fighter Wing (part of 3rd Air Force; Base: Rome-Ciampino, Italy): 06/10/40?
A. *Components - 8th "Astore" Fighter Wing* (06/10/40):
   1. **51st "Caccia" Fighter Group** (Base: Rome-Ciampino, Italy regiment status)
   2. **52nd "Caccia" Fighter Group** (Base: Pontedera, Italy regiment status)

10th Bombardment Wing (part of Sardinia Air Command; HQ: Cagliani, Sardinia): 06/10/40?
A. *Components - 10th Bombardment Wing* (06/10/40):
   1. **8th Bombardier Group** (Base: Villacidro, Sardinia regiment status)
   2. **31st Bombardier Group** (Base: Cagliani-Elmas, Sardinia regiment status)
   3. **32nd Bombardier Group** (Base: Decimomannu, Sardinia regiment status)

11th "Nibbio" Bombardment Wing (part of 2nd Air Force; HQ: Castelvetrano, Italy): 06/10/40?
A. *Components - 11th "Nibbio" Bombardment Wing* (06/10/40):
   1. **30th Bombardier Group** (Base: Sciacca, Italy regiment status)
   2. **36th Bombardier Group** (Base: Castelvetrano, Italy regiment status)

14th "Rex" Fighter Wing (06/10/40?, part of Eastern Sector, Libya Air Command; HQ: Tobruk T2, Libya; 05/20/41?, HQ: Tripoli, Libya): 06/10/40?

Naval Garrisons (brigade status)

Naval Garrison, Tobruk: RA Vietina [RIN]

The Military of the Italian Social Republic
(October 28, 1943)

National Republican Army
[Esercito Nazionale Repubblicano (ENR)]

Army

Italo-German Army Group Liguria {XLVII "Liguria" Army [Battle Group Ligurien]} (07/03/44; also known as **Italian Fascist Army Italy**): Gen. Alfredo Guzzoni (?) 02/11/45 dissolved.

A.   *Components* - Italo-German Army Group Liguria (04/30/45)
    1.   **German LXXV Army Corps**
        a.   **German 5th Mountain Division**:
        b.   **2nd "Littorio" Infantry Division**:
        c.   **German 34th Infantry Division**:
    2.   **Lombardia Corps**
        a.   **3rd "San Marco" Marine Division**
        b.   **German 134th Infantry Brigade**
        c.   **4th "Monte Rosa" Alpine Division**

[NOTE: 1st "Italia" Infantry Division - attached to German Fourteenth Army**.**

Divisions (National Republican Army)

1st "Italia" Infantry Division (10/43): MG Vincenzo Giardina (?) /43 Col. Mario Carloni (Commanding General, 4th "Mount Rosa" Alpine Division) /44 BG Guido Manardi (?) /45 MG Mario Carloni.

2nd "Littorio" Infantry Division (/44): MG Tito Agosti (arrested; /46, committed suicide in prison) /45 disbanded.

3rd San Marco" Marine Division (10/43): MG Aldo Princivalle (?) /44 MG Amilcare Farina

4th "Monte [Mount] Rosa" Alpine Division (/44): MG Goffredo Ricci (Commandant, Center of Mobilization of Major Units, Social Republic of Italy) /44 BG Mario Carloni (Commanding General, 1st "Italia" Infantry Division) /45

"Decima" Infantry Division (/44): BG Uberto Corrado.

National Republican "Etna" Guard Division (10/43): BG Giuseppe Volante [MVSN] (?) /45 BG Giovanni Bocchio [MVSN].

National Republican "Emilia" Guard Division: /43? BG Bruno Calzolari [MVSN].

National Republican Mountain & Forest Guard (10/28/43): MG Augusto Agostini [MVSN] (?) /44 BG Mario Candelori [MVSN].

National Republican Harbor Guard (10/28/43): MG Rodolfo Tanese [MVSN] (?) /44 BG August Bastianon [MVSN].

National Republican Customs Guard (10/28/43): MG Filippo Crimi (member of the Resistance; /44, Commanding General, Rome Special Customs Guard Zone Inspectorate) /43 MG Arturo Cerrato [MVSN].

National Republican Roads Guard (10/28/43): MG Ugo Leonardi [MVSN] (?) /43 BG Pietro Grillo [MVSN]

Inspectorate of National Republican Railway Guard (10/28/43): MG Vittorio Raffaldi [MVSN].

Brigades (National Republican Army)

National Republican Guard Brigade "Nere" (09/23/43): MG Alessandro Pavolini [+ Leader of the Republican Fascist Party] (executed by Partisans) /45

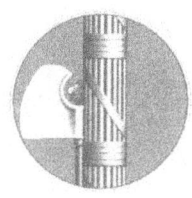

National Republican Air Force
[Aeronautica Nazionale Repubblicano (ANR)]

Very little of the Royal Air Force chose to side with the Italian Social Republic in the North.
The only units they had were:

3 - fighter groups
1 - air torpedo bomber group
1 - bomber group

National Republican Navy
[Marina Nazionale Repubblicano (MNR)]

Very little of the Royal Navy chose to side with the Italian Social Republic in the North.
The only units they had were:
- 4 - motor Torpedo boats (MAS)
- 2 - anti-submarine vessels
- 5 - submarines
- various light vessels

MAS Division 10 [Decima Flottiglia Motoscafo Anti-Sommergibile (MAS)]: Cdr. Prince Junio Valerio Borghese [RIN]

The Military of the Royal Italian Government
(September 8, 1943)

Italian Co-Belligerent Army
[Esercito Cobelligerante Italiano]
or
Army of the South
[Esercito del Sud]

After Italy's surrender to the Allies on September 8, 1943, Germany moved quickly to disarm and take into custody the Italian Army in north of Rome. Very few of the major Italian Army formations fell into Allies hands. The following units were able to because they were beyond the German grasp. These units are best viewed as a mass of trained men and available manpower. Many of these units were disbanded and their troops absorbed into those divisions designated by the new Italian government as the core of the new Italian Army.

Friuli Division from Corsica
Cremona Division from Corsica
Pasubio Division found in Campania
222nd Coastal Division found in Campania
32nd Coastal Brigade found in Campania
Piceno Division found in Lucania
209th Coastal Division found in Lucania
210th Coastal Division found in Lucania
31st Coastal Brigade found in Lucania
Legnano Division found in Lucania
Mantova Division found in Calabria
XXX Army Corps from Sardinia
Calabria Division from Sardinia
204th Coastal Division from Sardinia
4th Coastal Brigade from Sardinia
XII Army Corps
Nembo Division
Bari Division
Sabaudo Division

Inspector-General of the Army (09/08/43): Gen. Vittorio Ambrosio (retired) /44

Corps (Italian Co-Belligerent Army)

LI Army Corps (09/08/43): MG Giovanni Battista Guiccione (acting) 09/43 LG Giuseppe de Stefanis
A. *Components - LI Army Corps* (09/43)
   1. "Piceno" Division
   2. "Legnano" Division
   3. "Emilia" Division
   4. 231st Coastal Division

Italian Liberation Corps [Corpo Italiano di Liberaziono (CIL)] (04/03/44): MG Umberto Utili (Commanding General, Combat Group Legnano) /44 LG Raffele Cadorna.
A. *Components - Italian Liberation Corps* (04/03/44; 09/24/44, disbanded):
   1. "Nembo" Division
   2. "Utili" Division
   3. 2nd Motorized Battle Group [II Ragruppamento Motorizzato]
   4. 3rd Brigade
   5. 4th Brigade
   6. 11th Artillery Regiment (04/03/44): BG Alessandro Albert (Commandant, School of Arms Applications) /45

Campania Military Command (09/43): LG Antonio Basso (?) /44 MG Mario Soldarelli.

Lazio, Umbria & Abruzzi Military Command (1944): LG Arnaldo Azzi (Commanding General, VIII Territorial Defense Command) /45 disbanded.

Divisions (Italian Co-Belligerent Army)

Garibaldi Division (09/08/43, from **19th "Venezia" Infantry Division**, who joined the Yugoslav Partisans and fought the Axis powers): MG Giovanni Battista Oxilia (Deputy Chief of the General Staff & Undersecretary of War) /44 unknown?

09/44 Battle Groups [Gruppi di Combattimento] were formed around Infantry Divisions and corps were not used until after the war.

> **Cremona Division**
> **Fruili Division**
> **Folgore Division**
> **Legnano Division**
> **Mantova Division**
> **Piceno Division**

1st Motorized Battle Group [I Ragruppamento Motorizzato] (09/23/43, Italy; 04/03/44, upgraded to **Italian Liberation Corps**): BG Vincenzo Dapino (?) 04/03/44, upgraded to **Italian Liberation Corps** - see **Italian Liberation Corps**.
A. *Components* - **1st Motorized Battle Group** (09/28/43)
   1. **67th (Motorized) Infantry Regiment**
   2. **11th (Motorized) Artillery Regiment**
   3. **68th Infantry Regiment** (added 02/25/44)

2nd Motorized Battle Group [II Ragruppamento Motorizzato] (1943):

Nembo Division (12/43, Italy (Airborne unit); 04/03/44, part of Italian Liberation Corps; 10/44, disbanded and redesignated **Nembo Regiment** and assigned to newly formed **Folgore Division**): BG Giorgi Morigi (Commanding General, Folgore Division) 10/44 disbanded.
A. *Components* - **Nembo Division** (04/18/44)
   1. **183rd Parachute Regiment** (10/44, disbanded and redesignated **1st Battalion, Nembo Regiment**)
   2. **184th Parachute Regiment** (10/44, disbanded and redesignated **2nd Battalion, Nembo Regiment**)
   3. **184th Artillery Regiment** (10/44, disbanded and redesignated **Folgore Artillery Regiment**)

Utili Division (1944, Italy; also known as **I Motorized Group**; 08/44, disbanded): MG Umberto Utili [+ 04/03/44, Commanding General, Italian Liberation Corps] 08/44 disbanded.

Cremona Division (07/44, Italy; from the **44th "Cremona" Infantry Division**): <u>Cremona Division</u>: /43 MG Emilio Magliano (Commanding General, II Territorial Defense Command) /43 MG Clemente Primieri (Commanding General, Cremona Combat Group) 07/44

Cremona Combat Group 07/44 MG Clemente Primieri (Commanding General, Cremona Division) /45 redesignated **Cremona Division** /45 MG Clemente Primieri (?) /45 MG Giacomo Zanussi.
- A. **Components - Cremona Division (07/44)**
    1. **21st Infantry Regiment**
    2. **22nd Infantry Regiment**
    3. **7th Artillery Regiment**

Friuli Division (07/44, Italy; from the **20th "Fruili" Assault and Landing Division**): 09/08/43 MG Ugo de Lorenzis (Commanding General, 2nd Internal Security Brigade) 07/44 MG Carlo Ticchioni (?) /44 designated **Friuli Combat Group** /44 BG Bartolomeo Pedrotti (?) /45 MG Arturo Scattini.
- A. **Deputy Commander, Friuli Division** (09/08/43): BG Bartolomeo Pedrotti (Commanding General, Friuli Combat Group) .44
- B. **Components - Fruili Division (07/44)**
    1. **87th Infantry Regiment**
    2. **88th Infantry Regiment**
    3. **35th Artillery Regiment**

Mantova Division (07/44, Italy; from original division): MG Guido Bologna (Commanding General, Mantova Combat Group) 07/44 redesignated **Mantova Combat Group** 07/44 MG Guido Bologna (Commanding General, Mantova Division) /45 redesignated **Mantova Division** /45 MG Guido Bologna.
- A. **Deputy Commander, Mantova Division**: /43 BG Ettore Monacci.
- B. **Components - Mantova Division (07/44)**
    1. **76th Infantry Regiment**
    2. **114th Infantry Regiment**
    3. **155th Artillery Regiment**

Piceno Division (07/44, Italy; from the **152nd "Piceno" Garrison Division**): MG Carlo Biglioni (?) /44 MG Emanuelle Beraudo di Pralorme (Commanding General, Piceno Combat Group) /44 redesignated **Piceno Combat Group** /44 MG Emanuelle Beraudo di Pralorme (Commanding General, Piceno Division) /45 redesignated **Piceno Division** /45 BG Ercole Ronco (acting; Assistant Chief of the Army General Staff) /45 MG Emanuelle Beraudo di Pralorme.
- A. **Components - Piceno Division (07/44)**
    1. **235th Infantry Regiment**
    2. **336th Infantry Regiment**
    3. **152nd Artillery Regiment**

Legnano Division (09/44, Italy; from the **58th "Legnano" Infantry Division**): **Legnano Division** /43 BG Silvio Brisotto (?) /43 MG Gino Granata (Commanding General, V Territorial Defense Command) 09/44 redesignated **Combat Group Legnano** 09/44 MG Umberto Utili (Commanding General, Legnano Division) /45 redesignated **Legnano Division** /45 MG Umberto Utili (/50, Commanding General, III Territorial Defense Command) /45 MG Giovanni Carlo Re.

A. ***Components* - Legnano Division (09/44)**
   1. **67th Infantry Regiment**
   2. **68th Infantry Regiment**
   3. **58th Artillery Regiment**

Folgore Division (10/44, Italy; from the **185th "Folgore" Airborne Division**): MG Giorgio Morigi (?) /44 MG Guido Pialorsi.
A. ***Components* - Folgore Division (10/44)**
   1. **San Marco Marine Regiment**
   2. **Nembo Regiment**
   3. **Folgore Artillery Regiment**

Sabauda Internal Security Division (12/43, from the **30th "Sabauda" Infantry Division** as a territorial division in Sicily): BG Ercole Ronco (Commanding General, Piceno Division) /44 MG Ugo de Lorenzis
A. ***Components* - Sabauda Division (12/43)**
   1. **45th Infantry Regiment**
   2. **46th Infantry Regiment**
   3. **16th Field Artillery Regiment**

Aosta Division (01/44, from the **28th "Aosta" Infantry Division** as a territorial division in Sicily): MG Valentino Babini (Inspector of Infantry; /52, killed in a car accident) /45 redesignated **Security Division Aosta** /45 BG Giulio Vanden Heuvet.
A. **Security, Aosta Division (01/44)**: BG Giuseppe Castellano

Calabria Internal Security Division (01/44, from the **31st "Calabria" Infantry Division** as a territorial division in Sardina): /43 BG Antonio Garelli (5th "Calabria" Internal Security Brigade) /44 MG Giovanni Casula (?) /44? MG Alessandro Maccario
A. ***Components* - Calabria Division (01/44)**
   1. **59th Infantry Regiment**
   2. **60th Infantry Regiment**
   3. **355th Infantry Regiment**
   4. **40th Artillery Regiment**

Bari Division (01/44, from the **47th "Bari" Infantry Division** as a territorial division in Sardina): MG Carlo Petra di Caccuri (acting Commanding General, Headquarters, Sardinia) /44
A. ***Components* - Bari Division (01/44)**
   1. **139th Infantry Regiment**
   2. **140th Infantry Regiment**
   3. **340th Infantry Regiment**
   4. **47th Artillery Regiment**

203rd Coastal Division (12/43, from the remnants of the **203rd Coastal Division**):
A. ***Components* - 203rd Coastal Division (02/18/44)**
   1. **526h Infantry Regiment**

2. **574th Infantry Regiment**
3. **595th Infantry Regiment**
4. **570th Artillery Regiment**

204th Coastal Division (12/43, from the remnants of the **204th Coastal Division**):
A. *Components - 204th Coastal Division* (02/18/44)
1. **530th Infantry Regiment**
2. **549th Infantry Regiment**
3. **546th Artillery Regiment**

205th Coastal Division (12/43, from the remnants of the **205th Coastal Division**):
A. *Components - 205th Coastal Division* (02/18/44)
1. **528th Infantry Regiment**
2. **529th Infantry Regiment**

209th Coastal Division (12/43, from the remnants of the **209th Coastal Division**):
A. *Components - 209th Coastal Division* (02/18/44)
1. **515th Infantry Regiment**
2. **522nd Infantry Regiment**
3. **541st Infantry Regiment**

210th Coastal Division (12/43, from the remnants of the **210th Coastal Division**): BG Raffaele Colonna
A. *Components - 210th Coastal Division* (02/18/44)
1. **512th Infantry Regiment**
2. **513th Infantry Regiment**
3. **545th Infantry Regiment**

211th Coastal Division (12/43, from the remnants of the **211th Coastal Division**):
A. *Components - 211th Coastal Division* (02/18/44)
1. **516th Infantry Regiment**
2. **518th Infantry Regiment**
3. **543rd Infantry Regiment**

212th Coastal Division (12/43, from the remnants of the **212th Coastal Division**):
A. *Components - 212th Coastal Division* (02/18/44)
1. **503rd Infantry Regiment**
2. **525th Infantry Regiment**
3. **544th Infantry Regiment**
4. **545th Artillery Regiment**

225th Coastal Division (12/43, from the remnants of the **225th Coastal Division**):
A. *Components - 225th Coastal Division* (02/18/44)
1. **527th Infantry Regiment**
2. **572nd Infantry Regiment**
3. **582nd Infantry Regiment**

        4. **553rd Artillery Regiment**

226th Coastal Division (12/43, from the remnants of the **226th Coastal Division**):
A. *Components - **226th Coastal Division** (02/18/44)*
        1. **570th Infantry Regiment**
        2. **571st Infantry Regiment**
        3. **581st Infantry Regiment**
        4. **552nd Artillery Regiment**

227th Coastal Division (12/43, from the remnants of the **227th Coastal Division**):
A. *Components - **227th Coastal Division** (02/18/44)*
        1. **523rd Infantry Regiment**
        2. **345th Infantry Regiment**
        3. **512th Infantry Regiment**

228th Coastal Division (01/44, from the remnants of the **228th Coastal Division**):
A. *Components - **228th Coastal Division** (02/18/44)*
        1. **514th Infantry Regiment**

230th Coastal Division (11/20/44):

231st Coastal Division (11/20/44, from the remnants of the **231st Coastal Division**):
A. *Components - **231st Coastal Division** (12/16/44)*
        1. **402nd Engineer Regiment**
        2. **412th Engineer Regiment**
        3. **417th Engineer Regiment**

Brigades (Italian Co-Belligerent Army)

1st Brigade (04/03/44, as **3rd Brigade**; part of Italian Liberation Corps; 07/01/44, renamed **1st Brigade**): **3rd Brigade** 04/03/44 unknown? 07/01/44 redesignated **1st Brigade** 07/01/44
A. *Components - 3rd Brigade* (04/03/44)
  1. **4th Bersaglieri Regiment**
  2. **3rd Alpini Regiment**

2nd Brigade (04/03/44, as **4th Brigade**; part of Italian Liberation Corps; 07/01/44, renamed **2nd Brigade**): **4th Brigade** 04/03/44 unknown? 07/01/44 redesignated **2nd Brigade** 07/01/44
A. *Components - 4th Brigade & 2nd Brigade* (04/03/44 & 07/01/44)
  1. **68th Artillery Regiment**
  2. **Bafile Naval Regiment** (removed by 07/01/44)
  3. **San Marco Marine Regiment** (added 07/01/44)
  4. **9th Assault Regiment** (added 07/01/44)

4th Brigade (Sardinia): BG Del Pante
A. *Components - 4th Brigade* (01/44)
  1. **535th Infantry Regiment**
  2. **580th Infantry Regiment**

33rd Brigade (Sardinia): BG De Benedettis
A. *Components - 4th Brigade* (01/44)
  1. **519th Infantry Regiment**
  2. **532nd Infantry Regiment**

Maiella Brigade (01/44, Sicily; also known as **410th Infantry Regiment**): LCol. Ettoro Troilo

Sassari Brigade (01/44?): BG Antonio Rizzo

1st "Sabauda" Internal Security Brigade: /44 BG Antonio Cesaretti

2nd "Sabauda" Internal Security Brigade: 07/44 MG Ugo de Lorenzis (acting Commanding General, "Sabuda" Internal Security Division) /45? BG Ettore Pettinau

5th "Calabria" Internal Security Brigade: /43? BG Domenico Canistrà (?) /44 BG Antonio Garelli (?) /44 BG Guido Froio (?) /44 BG Augusto Ferrari

6th "Calabria" Internal Security Brigade: /43? BG Umberto Marchesi.

Italian Co-Belligerent Air Force
[Aviazione Cobelligerante Italiano (ACI)]
or
Air Force of the South
[Aeronautical del Sud]

Formed 10/43; never operated over Italian Territory. Objectives were always in the Balkans. This was to avoid any possible encounters between Italian-manned aircraft fighting for the Italian Social Republic. There are no records showing that any battle took place between the two Italian Air Forces from 09/08/43 to 05/08/45. Most of the Italian Air Force remained loyal to the king and stayed with the Italian Co-Belligerent Air Force.

Naval Ensign

Italian Co-Belligerent Navy
[Marina Cobelligerante Italiano (MCI)]
or
Navy of the South
[Marina del Sud]

Formed 09/28/43; most of the Italian Navy remained loyal to the king and stayed with the Italian Co-Belligerent Navy. The Italian Co-Belligerent Navy consisted of:

> 5 - battleships
> 8 - cruisers
> 33 - destroyers
> 39 - submarines
> 12 motor torpedo boats
> 20 - escorts
> 3 - mine-layers
> numerous smaller vessels

Superior Naval Force: 09/21/43 VA Alberto Da Zara [RIN] (surrendered to the Allies)

Inspector of Naval Forces: 03/10/44 VA Alberto Da Zara [RIN].

Part 3

SAN MARINO

San Marino
(Area: 24 sq. mi.)

Ever since the times of Giuseppe Garibaldi, San Marino has maintained strong ties with the Italian state. San Marino joined Italy in declaring war on Great Britain in 1940. Following the Italian surrender, San Marino immediately declared its neutrality. On June 26, 1944, it was bombed by the British Royal Air Force which mistakenly believed it had been overrun by German forces and was being used to amass stores and ammunition. The railway was destroyed, but 63 civilians died during the operation. The British government later admitted the bombing had been executed on receipt of erroneous information.

On September 21, 1944 San Marino declared war on Germany, which eventually occupied the nation while retreating northward. San Marino was a refuge for over 100000 civilians who sought safety on the passing of Allied forces over the Gothic Line during the Battle of Rimini. Allied troops occupied San Marino after that, but only stayed for two months before returning the Republic's sovereignty.

San Marino Government

Executive Branch

Captains Regent [Head of State] (Capitani Reggenti la Repubblica di San Marino) (Every six months the Grand and General Council elects two Captains Regent to be the head of state. They serve a six month term. The term starts April 1 and October 1, each year):

Date	Captains Regent
04/01/37	GIULIANO GOZI (4th time) & SETTIMIO BELLUZZI (2nd time)
10/01/37	MARINO ROSSI (4th time) & GIOVANNI LONFERNINI (2nd time)
04/01/38	MANLIO GOZI (3rd time) & LUIGI MULARONI
10/01/38	CARLO BALSIMELLI (2nd time) & CELIO GOZI
04/01/39	POMPEO RIGHI (3rd time) & MARINO MORRI (4th time)
10/01/39	MARINO MICHELOTTI (2nd time) & ORLANDO REFFI
04/01/40	ANGELO MANZONI BORGHESI (6th time) & FILIPPO MULARONI (3RD time)
10/01/40	FEDERICO GOZI (2nd time) & SALVATORE FOSCHI (2nd time)
04/01/41	GINO GOZI (4th time) & SECONDO MENICUCCI
10/01/41	GIULIANO GOZI (5th time) & GIOVANNI LONFERNINI (3rd time)
04/01/42	SETTIMIO BELLUZZI (3rd time) & CELIO GOZI
10/01/42	CARLO BALSIMELLI (3rd time) & RENATO MARTELLI
04/01/43	MARINO MICHELOTTI (3rd time) & BARTOLOMEO MANZONI BORGHESI
10/01/43	MARINO DELLA BALDA & SANTE LONFERNINI
04/01/44	FRANCESCO BALSIMELLI & SANZIO VALENTINI
10/01/44	TEODORO LONFERNINI & LEONIDA SUZZI VALLI
04/01/45	ALVARO CASALI & VITTORIO VALENTINI
10/01/45	etc.

The State Congress (composed of 10 Secretaries, which wields executive powers):
A. **Secretary of State for Foreign and Political Affairs (has assumed many of the duties of a Prime Minister or Head of Government):**
B. **Secretary of State for Internal Affairs and Civil Defense:**
C. **Secretary of State for Finance, Budget and Programming, Information and Relations with the State Philatelic and Numismatic Office:**
D. **Secretary of State for Education, Culture, University and Justice:**
E. **Secretary of State for Territory, Environment and Agriculture:**
F. **Secretary of State for Health and Social Security:**
G. **Secretary of State for Trade and Relations with the Town Council:**
H. **Secretary of State for Communications, Transport, Relations with the Azienda Autonoma di Stato for Services, Tourism and Sport:**
I. **Secretary of State for Industry and Crafts:**
J. **Secretary of State for Labor and Cooperation:**

Legislative Branch

Grand and General Council (Consiglio grande e generale) (a unicameral legislature with 60 members elected very 5 years from 9 administrative districts (castelli); has the power to ratify treaties with other countries).
A. **Advising Commissions** (There are 5 advising Commissions consisting of 15 councilors which examine, propose, and discuss the implementation of new laws to be presented on the floor of the Council):

Judical Branch

Counsel of Twelve (Consiglio dei XII) (serves as the supreme tribunal of the republic; elected by the Grand and General Council, and remain in office until the next general election; it has appellate jurisdiction; two government inspectors represent the State in financial and patrimonial concerns):

German Occupation of San Marino
[August 10, 1944 to September 21, 1944]

Commander of German Troops (278th Infantry Division) (08/10/44): MG Henry Hoppe [German] (evacuated San Marino) 09/21/44 disbanded.

Allied Occupation of San Marino
[September 21, 1944 to October 20, 1944]

Commander of the Allied Forces (British Eighth Army, 11th Indian Infantry Brigade) (09/21/44): Brig. Henry Cuthbert Partridge [British] (no longer on occupation duty) 10/20/44 disbanded.

San Marino Military Forces

San Marino has one of the smallest military forces in the world. Its different branches have varied functions including: performing ceremonial duties, patrolling borders, mounting guards at government buildings, and assisting police in major criminal cases. There is also a Gendarmerie which is technically part of the military forces of the republic. **The National Defense of San Marino in the face of an aggressive world power is, by arrangement, the responsibility of Italy's Armed Forces.**

The Crossbow Guard (once the heart of the Army, it is now a ceremonial force of 80 volunteer soldiers; led by a Commander (rank of Captain)):

The Guard of the Rock (front-line military unit of San Marino; also known as the "Fortress" Guards; patrols the borders and defends them; also responsible for guarding the Palazzo Pubblico, the seat of the national Government; led by a Commander (rank of Captain)):

The Guard of the Council Great and General (also known as the "Guard of Nobles", composed mostly of volunteers; its duties are largely ceremonial; the functions are to protect the Captains Regent, and to defend the Great and General Council during its formal sessions; led by a Commander (rank of Captain)):

The Army Militia (the basic fighting force of San Marino, but largely ceremonial; led by a Commander (rank of Captain)):

The Military Ensemble (formally part of the Army Militia; it is a ceremonial military band, composed of about 50 musicians; led by a Bandmaster):

The Gendarmerie (full-time militarized police service and have the responsibility for the protection of its citizens and their property, and for the preservation of law and order; led by a Commander (rank of Lieutenant Colonel); does not include the Municipal Police, which is not part of the armed forces of San Marino):
A. **Criminal Police Division**:
B. **Flying Squad Division**:

Part 4

VATICAN CITY

Vatican City State & The Holy See
(Area: 108.7 acres)

Vatican City (a landlocked sovereign city-state whose territory consisted of a walled enclave within the city of Rome, Italy): It refers to the framework of an absolute theocratic monarchy (sometimes referred to as a papacy), in which the head of the Roman Catholic Church, the Pope, exercises ex officio supreme legislative, executive, and power over the State of the Vatican City, a rare case of non-hereditary monarchy.

Holy See (the central government of the Roman Catholic Church): It refers to the composition of the authority, jurisdiction, and sovereignty vested in the Pope and his advisers to direct the worldwide Roman Catholic Church. The Holy See has a legal personality that allows it to enter into treaties as juridical equal of a state and to send and receive diplomatic representatives.

Vatican City State

Head of State (the Pope; elected in the Conclave of Cardinals, composed of all the Cardinal Electors): 02/06/22 POPE PIUS XI (Cardinal Achille Ambrogio Damiano Ratti) 02/10/39 Cardinal EUGENIO MARIA GIUSEPPE GIOVANNI RASCELLI [Pope's Chamberlain] (acting) 03/02/39 POPE PIUS XII (Cardinal Eugenio Maria Giuseppe Giovanni Rascelli).

Government of Vatican City State

Executive Branch

Governor of Vatican City (Governatore dello Stato della Città del Vaticano) (to 1952 when it was dissolved, when the functions of this office was taken over by the Pontifical Commission for Vatican City State): 06/07/29 Marquis [Marchese] CAMILLO SERAFINI.
- A. **Legal Office**:
- B. **Office for Personnel**:
- C. **Office for Civil Records**:
- D. **Archives**:
- E. **Accounting Office**:
- F. **Numismatic and Philatelic Office**:
- G. **Post and Telegraph Office**:
- H. **Shipping Office**:
- I. **Police Department**:
- J. **Tourist Information Office**:
- K. **Department of Museums and Galleries**:
  - 1. **Vatican Museum**:
- L. **Department of Economic Services**:

M. **Department of Technical Services**:
N. **Vatican Observatory**:
O. **Department of Pontifical Villas**:
    1. **Castel Gandolfo**:
P. **Office for Archeological Research**:
Q. **Corpo della Gendarmeria**:

Legislative Branch

Pontifical Commission for Vatican City State (operatives as a unicameral legislative branch, proposing law and policy to the pope; it consists of Cardinals appointed to five-year terms by the Pope; prior to taking effect, the laws and policies passed by the commission must be approved by the pope, through the Secretariat of State.

A. **President of the Pontifical Commission for Vatican City State** (is a senior member of the Roman Curia, and normally a Cardinal of the Roman Catholic Church; appointed to a five-year term by the Pope; who after 1952, is also *ex officio* President of the Governorate; appointed by the Pope for a five-year term, and may be removed any time by the Pope or a vacancy in the Holy See): 03/20/39 Cardinal NICOLA CANALI.

Judicial Branch

Prefect of the Supreme Tribunal of the Apostolic Signatura (The Pope's judicial authority is exercised through this body, as the Pope customarily serves as **President of the Cassation Court of Vatican City**, and the **Dean of the Sacra Rota** as **President of the Appellate Court of Vatican City;** most crimes in Vatican City are prosecuted by and handled in the courts of the Republic of Italy, by agreement between the Vatican and the Italian government):

The Holy See

Roman Curia (Court of Rome) (the administrative apparatus of the Holy See and the central governing body of the entire Roman Catholic Church, together with the Pope. It coordinates and provides the necessary central organization for the correct functioning of the Church and the achievement of its goals**):**

Secretariat of State (oldest dicastery in the Roman Curia; It is headed by a Cardinal, and performs all the political and diplomatic functions of Vatican City and the Holy See): 02/09/30 Cardinal EUGENIO MARIA GIUSEPPE GIOVANNI RASCELLI (Pope's Chamberlain) 02/10/39 Cardinal LUIGI MAGLIONE 08/22/44 vacant 11/29/52

A. **Sacred Congregation for the Extraordinary Ecclesiastical Affairs**:
B. **Sacred Congregation for the Ordinary Ecclesiastical Affairs**:
C. **The Chancery of Apostolic Beliefs (duty of preparing and dispatching pontifical Briefs)**:

Military Forces

Vatican City lies entirely within Rome, Italy. **Therefore, its military defense is provided by Italy.** Vatican City does have a mercenary unit of Swiss Guard as well as other military units.

Vatican City Military Forces

The Noble Guard (Guardia Nobile) (1801; will be abolished in 1970; the papal horse guard; volunteers; only appeared in public when the Pope took part in public functions):

Corps of the Pontifical Swiss Guard (Pontificia Cohors Helvetica or Cohors Pedestris Helvetiorum a Sacra Custodia Pontificis) (1506; a small force, approximately 135, responsible for the safety of the Pope, including the security of the Apostolic Palace; it serves as the military of the Vatican City (Commanded by a Commandant (Colonel)): /35 Cmdt. Georg von Sury d'Aspremont [Swiss] /42 Cmdt. Heinrich Pfyffer von Altishofen [Swiss].

The Palatine Guard (Guardia Palatina d'Onore) (1850; will be abolished in 1970; the papal militia; volunteers):

Corps of Gendarmerie of Vatican City (Corpo della Gendarmeria dello Stato della Città del Vaticano) (1816; the police or security force; responsible for security, public order, border control, traffic control, criminal investigation, and other general police duties; will be abolished in 1970):
:

APPENDIX

FOR

SECTION A

ITALY

Appendix A
Table of Equivalent

Italian Army, Air Force & MVSN
Primo Maresciallo dell'Impero

Maresciallo d'Italia (Army)
Maresciallo dell Aria (Air Force)

Generale d'Armata (Army)
Generale d'Armata Aerea (Air Force)
Comandante Generale (MVSN)
    (Commander-in-Chief)

Generale designato d'armata (Army)
Generale di Corpo d'Armata (Army)
Generale di Corpo d'Armata Aerea (Air Force)
Generale di Squadra Aerea (Air Force)
Luogotenente Generale Capo di Stato Maggiore (MVSN)
    (Chief of Staff)

Generale di Divisione (Army)
Generale di Divisione Aerea (Air Force)
Luogotenente Generale (MVSN)

Generale di Brigata (Army)
Generale di Brigata Aerea (Air Force)
Console Generale (MVSN)

Colonnello
Console (MVSN)

Tenente Colonnello
Primo Seniore (MVSN)

Maggiore
Seniore (MVSN)

Primo Tenente
Centurione (MVSN)

Capitano (Junior Captain)

Primo Tenente
Capo Manipolo (MVSN)

United States & British Army
NO EQUIVALENT

Field Marshal [Brit.]
General of the Army [U. S.]

General

Lieutenant General

Major General

Brigadier [Brit.]
Brigadier General [U. S.]

Colonel

Lieutenant Colonel

Major

Captain

NO EQUIVALENT

First Lieutenant

Tenente   NO EQUIVALENT

Sottotenente   Second Lieutenant
Soto Capo Manipolo (MVSN)

Table of Equivalent Ranks

Italian Navy	United States & British Navy
Grande Ammiraglio	Admiral of the Fleet [Brit] Fleet Admiral [U. S.]
Ammiraglio d'Armata	Admiral
Ammiraglio designato d'Armata Ammiraglio di Squadra	Vice Admiral
Ammiraglio di Divisione	Rear Admiral
Contrammiraglio	Commodore
Capitano di Vascello	Captain
Capitano di Fregata	Commander
Capitano di Corvetta	Lieutenant Commander
Primo Tenente di Vascello	Lieutenant
Tenente di Vascello	Lieutenant (Junior Grade)
Sottotenente di Vascello	Ensign

Appendix B
Senior Commanders

First Marshal of the Empire
His Royal Highness King VICTOR EMMANUEL III
BENITO AMILCARE ANDREA MUSSOLINI
Badoglio, Pietro, Duke of Addis Abeba, Marquis of Sabotino 1943

	Marshal
Caviglia, Enrico	06/25/26
Balbo, Italo (Air Force)	1933
De Bono, Emilio	11/16/35
Graziani, Rodolfo, Marquis of Neghelli	05/09/36
Cavallero, Count Ugo	07/02/42
Bastico, Ettore	08/12/42
HRH Humberto Principe di Piemonte	10/28/42
Messe, Giovanni	05/12/43

	General/Admiral
Mambretti, Gen. Ettore	02/01/33
Zoppi, Gen. Ottavio (des)	03/01/28
Ago, Gen. Pietro (des)	01/29/32
Baistrocchi, Gen. Count Federico	04/15/36
Pirzio-Biroli, Gen. Alessandro	04/15/36
Pariani, Gen. Alberio (des)	06/15/36
Tua, Gen. Angelo (des)	05/09/37
Vacca-Maggiolini, Gen. Arturo (des)	05/14/37
Grossi, Gen. Camillo (des)	10/01/37
Ambrosio, Gen. Vittorio	12/10/38
Guidi, Gen. Francesco (des)	01/23/39
Maravigna, Gen. Pietro (des)	03/14/39
Santini, Gen. Ruggero	1939
Bobbio, Gen. Valentino	prior to 1940
Gabba, Gen. Melchiade	05/15/40
Soddu, Gen. Ubaldo	11/29/40
Pintor, Gen. Ben Pietro	1940
Nasi, Gen. Gugllelmo Ciro	11/41
Guzzoni, Gen. Alfredo	1941
Marinetti, Gen. Adriano	1941
Rosi, Gen. Ezio (des)	1941
Gariboldi, Gen. Italo	10/28/42
Geloso, Gen. Carlo	10/28/42
Vercellino, Gen. Mario	10/28/42
Caracciolo di Feroleto, Gen. Mario	11/42
HRH Adalberto, Gen. Duke of Bergamo	unknown?
HRH Prince Amadeo, Gen. Duke of Aosta	unknown?

Gazzera, Gen. Pietro	unknown?
Grazioli, Gen. Francesco (des)	unknown?
HRH Filiberto, Gen. Duke of Pistoia	unknown?
Riccardi, Adm. Arturo	unknown?
Bergamini, Adm. Carlo	unknown?
Jachino, Adm. Angelo	unknown?
Gambara, Gen. Gastone	10/28/43

Appendix C

Military units in Selected Campaigns

Italian Army Peacetime Organization

I Army Corps
    1st "Superga" Infantry Division (reduced)
    2nd "Sfòrzesca" Infantry Division (reduced)
    26th "Assietta" Infantry Division (reduced)
    59th "Cagliari" Infantry Division (reduced)

II Army Corps
    3rd "Ravenna" Infantry Division (reduced)
    4th "Livorno" Infantry Division (reduced)
    36th "Forli" Infantry Division (reduced)

III Army Corps
    6th " Cuneo" Infantry Division (reduced)
    7th "Lupi di Toscana" Infantry Division (reduced)
    58th "Legnano" Infantry Division (reduced)

IV Army Corps
    11th "Brennero" Infantry Division (reduced)
    33rd "Acqui" Infantry Division (reduced)

V Army Corps
    12th "Sassari" Infantry Division (reinforced)
    15th "Bergamo" Infantry Division (reinforced)
    57th "Lombardia" Infantry Division (reinforced)

VI Army Corps
    16th "Pistoia" Infantry Division (reduced)
    17th "Pavia" Infantry Division
    18th "Messina" Infantry Division (reduced)
    56th "Casale" Infantry Division (reduced)

VII Army Corps
    20th "Friuli" Infantry Division (reinforced)
    41st "Firenzi" Infantry Division (reduced)
    44th "Cremona" Infantry Division (reduced)

VIII Army Corps
    21st "Granatieri di Sardegna" Infantry Division (reduced)
    22nd "Cacciatori della Alpi" Infantry Division (reduced)
    52nd "Torino [Turin]" Infantry Division

IX Army Corps
    24th "Pinerolo" Infantry Division (reinforced)
    47th "Bari" Infantry Division (reinforced)
    49th "Parma" Infantry Division

X Army Corps
    25th "Bologna" Infantry Division

    27th "Brescia" Infantry Division
    51st "Siena" Infantry Division (also listed with XX Army Corps)
    55th "Savona" Infantry Division

XI Army Corps
    13th "Rè" Infantry Division (reinforced)
    14th "Isonzo" Infantry Division (reinforced)

XII Army Corps
    28th "Aosta" Infantry Division (reinforced)
    29th "Piemonte" Infantry Division
    54th "Napoli [Naples]" Infantry Division (reinforced)

XIII Army Corps
    30th "Sabauda" Infantry Division (reinforced)
    31st "Calabria" Infantry Division (reinforced)
    48th "Taro" Infantry Division (reinforced)

XIV Army Corps
    32nd "Marche" Infantry Division (reduced)
    38th "Pulgie" Infantry Division (reduced)

XV Army Corps
    5th "Cosseria" Infantry Division (reduced)
    37th "Modena" Infantry Division (reduced)

XX Army Corps
    60th "Sabratha" Infantry Division
    51st "Siena" Infantry Division (also listed with X Army Corps)

XXI Army Corps
    62nd "Marmarica" Infantry Division
    63rd "Cirene" Infantry Division

XXVI Army Corps
    19th "Venezia [Venice]" Infantry Division
    23rd "Ferrara" Infantry Division
    53rd "Arezzo" Infantry Division
    131st "Centauro" Armored Division
    3rd "Julia" Alpini Division

Fast (Cavalry) Corps
    1st Fast Division "Eugenio di Savoia"
    2nd Fast Divison "Eugenio Filiberto"
    3rd Fast Division "Prinicipe Amendeo, Duca d'Aosta"

Armored Corps
    101st "Trieste" Motorized Infantry Division
    102nd "Trento" Motorized Infantry Division
    132nd "Ariete" Armored Division
    133rd "Littorio" Armored Division

Truck Born Corps
    9th "Pasubio" Infantry Division
    10th "Piave" Infantry Division
    "Egeo" Independent Division
    50th "Regina" Infantry Division

Alpine Corps

1st "Taurinense" Alpini Division
2nd "Tridentina" Alpini Division
4th "Cuneense" Alpini Division
5th "Pusteria" Alpini Division
6th "Alpi Graie" Alpini Division

The Italian Army in Albania, October 28, 1940

Eleventh Army
    Tsamouia Corps [in Epirus]
        23rd "Ferrara" Infantry Division
        51st "Siena" Infantry Division
        131st "Centauro" Armored Division
        Coastal Group
    XXVI Army Corps [in Macedonia]
        29th "Piemonte" Infantry Division
        49th "Parma" Infantry Division
    Eleventh Army reserve
        19th "Venezia [Venice]" Infantry Division [on Yugoslavian border]
        53rd "Arezzo" Infantry Division [on Yugoslavian border]
        3rd "Julia" Alpini Division [in eastern Epirus]

Between 11/40 and 01/41 the following divisions arrived in Albania/Greece

    November 1940
        37th "Modena" Infantry Division
        47th "Bari" Infantry Division
        48th "Taro" Infantry Division
        2nd "Tridentina" Alpini Division
        5th "Pusteria" Alpini Division
        101st "Trieste" Motorized Infantry Division

    December 1940
        6th " Cuneo" Infantry Division
        11th "Brennero" Infantry Division
        33rd "Acqui" Infantry Division
        4th "Cuneense" Alpini Division

    January 1941
        7th "Lupi di Toscana" Infantry Division
        22nd "Cacciatori della Alpi" Infantry Division
        24th "Pinerolo" Infantry Division
        36th "Forli" Infantry Division
        58th "Legnano" Infantry Division
        59th "Cagliari" Infantry Division

In early 03/41 the following divisions had also arrived in Albania/Greece
        2nd "Sfòrzesca" Infantry Division
        38th "Pulgie" Infantry Division
        41st "Firenzi" Infantry Division
        56th "Casale" Infantry Division

The Italian Army in Libya, December 1940

Commander-in-Chief Libya
    Fifth Army [in Tripolitania]
        X Army Corps
            25th "Bologna" Infantry Division
            27th "Brescia" Infantry Division
            55th "Savona" Infantry Division
        XX Army Corps Infantry Division
            17th "Pavia" Infantry Division [in Benghazi]
            60th "Sabratha" Infantry Division [in Derna]
            61st "Sirte" Infantry Division [in Tobruk]
    Tenth Army [in Cyrenaica]
        XIII Army Corps
            62nd "Marmarica" Infantry Division [in Sidi Omar]
            63rd "Cirene" Infantry Division [in Sofafi/Rabia]
            1st "23 Marzo" Blackshirt [CCNN] Infantry Division [Bardia]
        XXII Army Corps
            64th "Catanzaro" Infantry Division [in Buq Buq]
            2nd "28 Ottobre" Blackshirt [CCNN] Infantry Division [in Sollum/Halfaya]
            4th "3 Gennaio" Blackshirt [CCNN] Infantry Division [in Sidi Barrani]

Italian Army for the East African Campaign January 19, 1941

General Headquarters, Italian East Africa [A. O. I.]
    Northern Army [in Eritrea]
        1st Colonial Infantry Division
        2nd Colonial Infantry Division
        4th Colonial Infantry Division
    Commander-in-Chief, Somalia [in Somaliland]
        102nd Colonial Infantry Division
        104th Colonial Infantry Division
    General Headquarters, Italian East Africa [A. O. I.] reserves
        65th "Granatieri di Savoia Infantry Division [in Addis Ababa]
        Cacciatori d'Africa [in Addis Ababa]

Colonial Divisions formed after the British invasion
        21st Colonial Infantry Division
        26th Colonial Infantry Division

The Italian Army in Albania, April 1941

Army Group East
  Ninth Army
    III Army Corps
      19th "Venezia [Venice]" Infantry Division
      36th "Forli" Infantry Division
      48th "Taro" Infantry Division
    XXVI Army Corps
      29th "Piemonte" Infantry Division
      49th "Parma" Infantry Division
      2nd "Tridentina" Alpini Division
  Eleventh Army
    IV Army Corps
      5th "Pusteria" Alpini Division
      22nd "Cacciatori della Alpi" Infantry Division
    VIII Army Corps
      24th "Pinerolo" Infantry Division
      51st "Siena" Infantry Division
      59th "Cagliari" Infantry Division
    XXV Army Corps
      2nd "Sfòrzesca" Infantry Division
      7th "Lupi di Toscana" Infantry Division
      11th "Brennero" Infantry Division
      23rd "Ferrara" Infantry Division
      58th "Legnano" Infantry Division
      3rd "Julia" Alpini Division
    Special Army Corps
      6th " Cuneo" Infantry Division
      33rd "Acqui" Infantry Division
    Eleventh Army reserve
      47th "Bari" Infantry Division
      56th "Casale" Infantry Division

Also present on the Albania-Yugoslavia frontier
    41st "Firenzi" Infantry Division
    53rd "Arezzo" Infantry Division

Axis Forces at the Battle of El Alamein October 24, 1942

German Panzer Group Africa
    German Africa Panzer Corps
        German 15th Panzer Division
        German 21st Panzer Division
    German 90th Light Infantry Division
    German 164th Light Infantry Division
    German Ramcke Parachute Brigade
    X Army Corps
        17th "Pavia" Infantry Division
        27th "Brescia" Infantry Division
        185th "Foligore" Parachute Division
    XX Armor Corps
        132nd "Ariete" Armored Division
        133rd "Littorio" Armored Division
        101st "Trieste" Motorized Infantry Division
    XXI Army Corps
        25th "Bologna" Infantry Division
        102nd "Trento" Motorized Infantry Division
    German Panzer Group Africa reserve
        16th "Pistoia" Infantry Division
        G. F. Infantry Division

Italian Army - November 20, 1942

Army General Staff
    XIX Army Corps (in Bozen)

Assignment Unknown?
    XXII Army Corps (in Triest)
        152nd "Piceno" Garrison Division (in Chieti)
        157th "Novara" Garrison Division (in Triest)
        159th "Veneto" Garrison Division (in Udine)
        103rd "Piacenza" Infantry Division (in Genoa)
        104th "Mantova" Infantry Division (southwest of Turin)
        105th "Rovigo" Infantry Division (southwest of Savona)
        21st "Granatieri di Sardegna" Infantry Division (enroute to Dalmatia)
        220th Coastal Division (location not known)
        221st Coastal Division (location not known)
        222nd Coastal Division (location not known)

Middle & Southern Italian Army Group
  Fifth Army
    XIII Army Corps (in Florence)
        30th "Sabauda" Infantry Division (in Cagloiari, Sardinia)
        31st "Calabria" Infantry Division (in Sassari, Sardinia)
    XVII Army Corps (in Rome)
        4th "Livorno" Infantry Division (enroute to Tunis)
        47th "Bari" Infantry Division (Livorno)
  Sixth Army
    XII Army Corps (in Enna, Sicily)
        28th "Aosta" Infantry Division (in Palermo, Sicily)
        54th "Napoli [Naples]" Infantry Division (in Palermo, Sicily)
    XVI Army Corps (in Catania, Sicily)
        26th "Assietta" Infantry Division
    Assignment Unknown?
        202nd Coastal Division (in Castelvetrano, Sicily)
        206th Coastal Division (in Modica, Sicily)
        207th Coastal Division (in Agrigento, Sicily)
        208th Coastal Division (in Monreale, Sicily)
        213th Coastal Division (in Paterno, Sicily)
  Seventh Army
    IX Army Corps (in Bari)
        units unknown?
    XXX Army Corps
        1st "Superga" Infantry Division
        204th Coastal Division (in Sassari, Sardinia)
        205th Coastal Division (in Carbonia, Sardinia)
    XXXI Army Corps
        211th Coastal Division (in Cittanuvoa)
        212th Coastal Division (in Catanzaro)

Balkans
- **Supreme Command Slovenia-Dalmatia**
  - **V Army Corps** (in Crikvenica)
    - 13th "Rè" Infantry Division (in Gospic)
    - 57th "Lombardia" Infantry Division (in Delinice)
    - 1st "Eugenio di Savoia" Cavalry (Celere) Division (in Karlovac)
  - **VI Army Corps** (in Ragusa)
    - 18th "Messina" Infantry Division (in Metkovic)
    - 32nd "Marche" Infantry Division (in Dubrovnik)
    - 154th "Murge" Garrison Division (in Mostar)
    - 155th "Emilia" Garrison Division (in Cattero)
  - **XI Army Corps** (in Laibach)
    - 14th "Isonzo" Infantry Division (in Rudolfswerth)
    - 22nd "Cacciatori della Alpi" Infantry Division (in Grosuplje)
    - 153rd "Macerata" Garrison Division
  - **XVIII Army Corps** (in Spalato)
    - 12th "Sassari" Infantry Division (in Knin)
    - 15th "Bergamo" Infantry Division (in Spalato)
    - 158th "Zara" Garrison Division (in Zara)
- **Supreme Command Albania** (in Tirana)
  - **IV Army Corps** (in Berat)
    - 23rd "Ferrara" Infantry Division (in Elbasan)
    - 49th "Parma" Infantry Division
    - 53rd "Arezzo" Infantry Division (in Korica)
- **Governor of Montenegro**
  - **XIV Army Corps**
    - 19th "Venezia [Venice]" Infantry Division (in Berane)
    - 38th "Pulgie" Infantry Division (in Gegend Prizren)
    - 41st "Firenzi" Infantry Division (in Debar)
    - 1st "Taurinense" Alpini Division
    - 6th "Alpi Graie" Alpini Division
    - 151st "Perugia" Garrison Division
- **Senior Command in Greece**
  - **III Army Corps** (in Volos)
    - 11th "Brennero" Infantry Division (in Athens)
    - 24th "Pinerolo" Infantry Division (in Tricala)
    - 36th "Forli" Infantry Division (in Larissa)
  - **VIII Army Corps** (in Zylokastron)
    - 29th "Piemonte" Infantry Division (in Patras)
    - 59th "Cagliari" Infantry Division (in Triocala)
  - **XXVI Army Corps**
    - 33rd "Acqui" Infantry Division (in Corfu)
    - 37th "Modena" Infantry Division (in Jannina)
    - 56th "Casale" Infantry Division (in Agrinion)
    - 6th " Cuneo" Infantry Division (in Samos, Aegean)
- **Supreme Command Aegean Islands**
  - 50th "Regina" Infantry Division (in Rhodes)

51st "Siena" Infantry Division (in Crete)

In France
- **Fourth Army**
  - **I Army Corps**
    - 10th "Piave" Motorized Infantry Division (in Aix-Brignoles)
    - 5th "Pusteria" Alpini Division (west of Avignon)
  - **XV Army Corps**
    - 2nd "Emanuele Filiberto Testa di Ferro" Cavalry (Celere) Division (near Fréjus)
    - 58th "Legnano" Infantry Division (near Nizza)
  - **XXII Army Corps**
    - 7th "Lupi di Toscana" Infantry Division (near Marseilles)
    - 48th "Taro" Infantry Division (near Hyéres)

In Corisica
- **Fifth Army**
  - **VII Army Corps**
    - 20th "Friuli" Infantry Division
    - 44th "Cremona" Infantry Division

In North Africa
- **X Army Corps**
  - 17th "Pavia" Infantry Division
  - 27th "Brescia" Infantry Division
  - 85th "Folgore" Airborne Division
- **XX Army Corps**
  - 101st "Trieste" Motorized Infantry Division
  - 132nd "Ariete" Armored Division
  - 133rd "Littorio" Armored Division
- **XXI Army Corps**
  - 102nd "Trento" Motorized Infantry Division
  - 25th "Bologna" Infantry Division
- **Other**
  - 16th "Pistoia" Infantry Division
  - 136th Giovanni Fascisti" Motorized Infnatry Division
  - 80th "La Spezia" Air Landing Division
  - 131st "Centauro" Armored Division

In Soviet Union
- **Eighth Army**
  - **II Army Corps**
    - 2nd "Sfòrzesca" Infantry Division
    - 3rd "Ravenna" Infantry Division
    - 5th "Cosseria" Infantry Division
  - **XXXV Army Corps**
    - 9th "Pasubio" Infantry Division
    - 52nd "Torino [Turin]" Infantry Division
    - 3rd "Prinicipe Amendeo, Duca d'Aosta" Cavalry (Celere) Division
  - **Alpine Corps**
    - 2nd "Tridentina" Alpini Division

3rd "Julia" Alpini Division
4th "Cuneense" Alpini Division
Other
156th "Vicenza" Garrison Division
"Barbo" Cavalry Brigade

Italian Army - January 1, 1943

Army Group South (Gruppo Armate Sud)
    Fifth Army
- 12th "Sassari" Infantry Division
- 184th "Nembo" Airborne Division

        VII Army Corps
- 20th "Friuli" Infantry Division
- 44th "Cremona" Infantry Division

        XIII Army Corps
- 30th "Sabauda" Infantry Division
- 31st "Calabria" Infantry Division
- 204th Coastal Division
- 205th Coastal Division
- 4th Coastal Brigade
- 13th Coastal Brigade

        XVII Army Corps
- 21st "Granatieri di Sardegna" Infantry Division
- 47th "Bari" Infantry Division
- 220th Coastal Division
- 221st Coastal Division

    Sixth Army
- 4th "Livorno" Infantry Division

        XII Army Corps
- 26th "Assietta" Infantry Division
- 28th "Aosta" Infantry Division
- 202nd Coastal Division
- 207th Coastal Division
- 208th Coastal Division

        XVI Army Corps
- 54th "Napoli [Naples]" Infantry Division
- 206th Coastal Division
- 213th Coastal Division

    Seventh Army
        IX Army Corps
- 152nd "Piceno" Garrison Division
- 9th Coastal Brigade
- 10th Coastal Brigade

        XXXI Army Corps
- 104th "Mantova" Infantry Division
- 211th Coastal Division (in Cittanuvoa)
- 212th Coastal Division (in Catanzaro)

S.M.R.E
- 100th "Marcia" Infantry Brigade
- 110th "Marcia" Artillery Brigade

        XIX Army Corps

    8th "Marcia" (Training) Infantry Division
  XXIII Army Corps
    157th "Novara" Garrison Division
    159th "Veneto" Garrison Division
Naples
  222nd Coastal Division
Firenze [Florence]
  15th Coastal Brigade
  16th Coastal Brigade
Balkans
  Supreme Command Albania
    IV Army Corps
      38th "Pulgie" Infantry Division
      41st "Firenzi" Infantry Division
    XXV Army Corps
      49th "Parma" Infantry Division
      53rd "Arezzo" Infantry Division
  Supreme Command in Greece
    33rd "Acqui" Infantry Division (in Corfu)
    51st "Siena" Infantry Division (in Crete)
    51st Infantry Brigade
  III Army Corps
    11th "Brennero" Infantry Division
    24th "Pinerolo" Infantry Division
    36th "Forli" Infantry Division
  VIII Army Corps
    29th "Piemonte" Infantry Division
    59th "Cagliari" Infantry Division
  XXVI Army Corps
    37th "Modena" Infantry Division (in Jannina)
    56th "Casale" Infantry Division (in Agrinion)
  Supreme Command Aegean Islands
    6th " Cuneo" Infantry Division
    50th "Regina" Infantry Division
  Supreme Command Slovania (Second Army)
    V Army Corps
      13th "Rè" Infantry Division
      57th "Lombardia" Infantry Division
      14th Coastal Brigade
    VI Army Corps (in Ragusa)
      18th "Messina" Infantry Division
      22nd "Cacciatori della Alpi" Infantry Division
      32nd "Marche" Infantry Division
      154th "Murge" Garrison Division
      155th "Emilia" Garrison Division
    XI Army Corps
      14th "Isonzo" Infantry Division

                153rd "Macerata" Garrison Division
        XVIII Army Corps
                15th "Bergamo" Infantry Division
                158th "Zara" Garrison Division
                1st "Eugenio di Savoia" Cavalry (Celere) Division
                17th Coastal Brigade
Italian Troop Command in Montenegro
    XIV Army Corps
                19th "Venezia [Venice]" Infantry Division
                23rd "Ferrara" Infantry Division
                151st "Perugia" Garrison Division
                1st "Taurinense" Alpini Division
Supreme Command in Libya
    XX Army Corps
                16th "Pistoia" Infantry Division
                80th "La Spezia" Air Landing Division
                101st "Trieste" Motorized Infantry Division
    XXI Army Corps
                131st "Centauro" Armored Division
                136th Giovanni Fascisti" Motorized Infnatry Division
    XXX Army Corps
                1st "Superga" Infantry Division
                50th Special Brigade
Occupation of France
    Fourth Army
                5th "Pusteria" Alpini Division
        I Army Corps
                58th "Legnano" Infantry Division
                2nd "Emanuele Filiberto Testa di Ferro" Cavalry (Celere) Division
                224th Coastal Division
        XV Army Corps
                103rd "Piacenza" Infantry Division
                105th "Rovigo" Infantry Division
                6th "Alpi Graie" Alpini Division
                201st Coastal Division
        XXII Army Corps
                7th "Lupi di Toscana" Infantry Division
                10th "Piave" Motorized Infantry Division
                48th "Taro" Infantry Division
                223rd Coastal Division
Occupation of Soviet Union
    Eighth Army
        II Army Corps
                3rd "Ravenna" Infantry Division
                5th "Cosseria" Infantry Division
        XXXV Army Corps
                9th "Pasubio" Infantry Division

XXIX Army Corps
    2nd "Sfòrzesca" Infantry Division
    52nd "Torino [Turin]" Infantry Division
    3rd "Prinicipe Amendeo, Duca d'Aosta" Cavalry (Celere) Division

Alpine Corps
    156th "Vicenza" Garrison Division
    2nd "Tridentina" Alpini Division
    3rd "Julia" Alpini Division
    4th "Cuneense" Alpini Division

The Axis Forces in Tunisia, April 1943

German-Italian Army Group Africa
    German Fifth Panzer Army
        German 1st Infantry Division
        German 334th Infantry Division
        German 999th Infantry Division
        German Hermann Goering [Göring] Panzer Division
        Imperiali Brigade
    German-Italian Army Group Africa reserve
        German 10th Panzer Division
        German 21st Panzer Division
First Army
    German Africa Corps
        German 15th Panzer Division
        131st "Centauro" Armored Division
        German Ramcke Parachute Brigade
    XX Armor Corps
        German 90th Light Infantry Division
        101st "Trieste" Motorized Infantry Division
        G. F. Infantry Division
    XXI Armor Corps
        German 164th Light Infantry Division
        16th "Pistoia" Infantry Division
        80th "La Speczia" Infantry Division

Italian Army - September 8, 1943

Army Group South (Gruppo Armate Sud)
    Eighth Army
        XXIII Army Corps
            2nd "Sfòrzesca" Infantry Division
        XXIV Army Corps
            52nd "Torino [Turin]" Infantry Division
            3rd "Prinicipe Amendeo, Duca d'Aosta" Cavalry (Celere) Division
        XXXV Army Corps
            2nd "Tridentina" Alpini Division
            4th "Cuneense" Alpini Division
        In Lombardi
            5th "Cosseria" Infantry Division
            3rd Besaglieri Regiment
        In Emilia & Romagna
            3rd "Prinicipe Amendeo, Duca d'Aosta" Cavalry (Celere) Division
    Fifth Army
        XVI Army Corps
            105th "Rovigo" Infantry Division
            6th "Alpi Graie" Alpini Division
        II Army Corps
            3rd "Ravenna" Infantry Division
            215th Coastal Division
    Seventh Army
        XIX Army Corps
            9th "Pasubio" Infantry Division
            222nd Coastal Division
            32nd Coastal Brigade
        IX Army Corps
            152nd "Piceno" Garrison Division
            209th Coastal Division
            210th Coastal Division
            31st Coastal Brigade
    In Sardina
        XIII Army Corps
            30th "Sabauda" Infantry Division
            203rd Coastal Division
            205th Coastal Division
            33rd Coastal Brigade
        XXX Army Corps
            31st "Calabria" Infantry Division
            204th Coastal Division
            4th Coastal Brigade
        Reserve
            47th "Bari" Infantry Division

                184th "Nembo" Airborne Division
                1st Armored Raggruppamento
        Defense of Rome
                Motorized Army Corps
                        21st "Granatieri di Sardegna" Infantry Division
                        10th "Piave" Motorized Infantry Division
                        131st "Centauro" Armored Division
                        132nd "Ariete" Armored Division
                XVII Army Corps
                        103rd "Piacenza" Infantry Division
                        220th Coastal Division
                        221st Coastal Division
                        34th Coastal Brigade
                Rome Army Corps
                        12th "Sassari" Infantry Division
                        7th "Lupi di Toscana" Infantry Division
                        13th "Rè" Infantry Division
                        58th "Legnano" Infantry Division
Army of the East
        In
                IV Army Corps
                        11th "Brennero" Infantry Division
                        49th "Parma" Infantry Division
                XXV Army Corps
                        41st "Firenzi" Infantry Division
                        53rd "Arezzo" Infantry Division
                Reserve
                        151st "Perugia" Garrison Division
        In Herzegovina
                VI Army Corps
                        18th "Messina" Infantry Division
                        32nd "Marche" Infantry Division
                        27th Coastal Brigade
        In Montenegro
                XIV Army Corps
                        19th "Venezia [Venice]" Infantry Division
                        23rd "Ferrara" Infantry Division
                        155th "Emilia" Garrison Division
                        1st "Taurinense" Alpini Division
Second Army (In Greece & on Ionian Islands)
        III Army Corps
                24th "Pinerolo" Infantry Division
                36th "Forli" Infantry Division
        VIII Army Corps
                33rd "Acqui" Infantry Division (in Corfu)
                56th "Casale" Infantry Division (in Agrinion)
        XXVI Army Corps

                37th "Modena" Infantry Division (in Jannina)
            LVIII Army Corps
                29th "Piemonte" Infantry Division
                59th "Cagliari" Infantry Division
        In Crete
                51st "Siena" Infantry Division (in Crete)
                51st Special Brigade
        Aegean Islands
                6th " Cuneo" Infantry Division
                50th "Regina" Infantry Division
Occupation of France
    Fourth Army
        I Army Corps
                223rd Coastal Division
                224th Coastal Division
        XII Army Corps
                48th "Taro" Infantry Division
                5th "Pusteria" Alpini Division
                2nd "Emanuele Filiberto Testa di Ferro" Cavalry (Celere) Division
        XV Army Corps
                201st Coastal Division
    On Corsica
        VII Army Corps
                20th "Friuli" Infantry Division
                44th "Cremona" Infantry Division
In Slovenia, Croatia & Dalmatia
    Second Army
        V Army Corps
                153rd "Macerata" Garrison Division
                154th "Murge" Garrison Division
                5th Frontier Guard Raggruppamento
        XI Army Corps
                14th "Isonzo" Infantry Division
                22nd "Cacciatori della Alpi" Infantry Division
                57th "Lombardia" Infantry Division
        XVIII Army Corps
                15th "Bergamo" Infantry Division
                158th "Zara" Garrison Division
                16th Coastal Brigade
                4th Bersaglieri Regiment
        Reserve
                1st "Eugenio di Savoia" Cavalry (Celere) Division

Appendix D

The Fleet

of the

Royal Italian Navy

Aircraft Carriers [CV]

Aquila [Eagle] (ex-passenger ***Roma***; Builder: Arsenale di La Spezia; Laid Down: unknown?; Launched: 1926; Completed: 10/27; 1941, turned over to Royal Navy for conversation to carrier; 09/08/43, conversation never completed nor commissioned for Royal Navy; 04/45, scuttled by Germans): NEVER FOUGHT IN WORLD WAR II.

Sparviero [Sparrowhawk] (ex-merchant ***Augustus***; ex-***Falco [Falcon]***; Builder: Arsenale di La Spezia; Laid Down: unknown?; Launched: 12/26; Completed: 1927; 1939, turned over to Royal Navy for conversation to carrier; 09/08/43, conversation never completed nor commissioned for Royal Navy; 10/05/44, hull of ship scuttled by Germans): NEVER FOUGHT IN WORLD WAR II.

Seaplane Carriers/Tenders

Giuseppe Miraglia (ex-merchant ***Citta de Messina***; Builder: Arsenale di La Spezia; Laid Down: 03/05/21; Launched: 12/20/23; Completed: 1927; 1930's, designated a seaplane carrier; 1940, redesignated a transport ship):

Battleships [BB]

Andrea Doria (Builder: Arsenale Navale, La Spezia; Laid Down: 04/01/37; Launched: 10/26/40; Commissioned: 10/26/40; Duilio Class; part of 6th Battleship Squadron):

Caio Duilio (Builder: Navalmeccanica, Castellammare; Laid Down: 04/08/37; Launched: 07/15/40; Commissioned: 07/15/40; Duilio Class; part of 6th Battleship Squadron):

Conte di Cavour (Builder: Cantieri Riuniti dell'Adriatico, Trieste; Laid Down: 10/01/33; Launched: 06/01/37; Commissioned: 10/01/37; Cavour Class; part of 5th Battleship Squadron): unknown? 11/40 sunk.

Giulio Cesare (Builder: Cantieri del Tirreno (C.T.), Genoa-Riva-Trigoso; Laid Down: 10/01/33; Launched: 10/01/37; Commissioned: 06/02/37; Cavour Class; part of 5th Battleship Squadron; 02/15/45, scrapped): unknown? 02/15/45 scraped.

Impero (Builder: Ansaldo, Genoa; Laid Down: 05/14/38; Launched: 11/15/40; Class: Littorio): NOT COMPLETED.

Littorio (ex-*Italia*; Builder: Ansaldo, Genoa; Laid Down: 10/28/34; Launched: 08/22/37; Commissioned: 05/06/40; Class: Littorio; part of 9th Battleship Squadron): unknown? 11/40 sunk.

Roma (Builder: Cantieri Riuniti dell'Adriatico, Trieste; Laid Down: 09/18/38; Launched: 06/09/40; Commissioned: 06/14/42 Class: Littorio; sunk 09/09/43): unknown? 09/09/43 sunk.

Vittorio Veneto (Builder: Cantieri Riuniti dell'Adriatico, Trieste; Laid Down: 10/28/34; Launched: 07/25/37; Commissioned: 04/28/40 Class: Littorio; part of 9th Battleship Squadron):

Heavy Cruisers [CA]

Bolzano (Builder: Ansaldo, Genoa; Laid Down: 06/11/30; Launched: 08/31/32; Commissioned: 08/19/33; Class Bolzano; part of 4th Heavy Cruiser Squadron; converted to an aviation and transport cruiser; 06/22/44, sunk): unknown? 06/22/44 sunk.

Fiume (Builder: Stabilimento Tecnico Triestino, Trieste; Laid Down: 04/29/29; Launched: 04/27/30; Commissioned: 11/23/31; Class Zara; part of 1st Heavy Cruiser Squadron; 03/28/41, sunk): unknown? 03/28/41 sunk.

Gorizia (Builder: Odero-Terni-Orlandi (O.T.O.), Livorno; Laid Down: 03/17/30; Launched: 12/28/30; Commissioned: 12/23/31; Class Zara; part of 1st Heavy Cruiser Squadron; 09/08/43, captured): unknown? 09/08/43 captured.

Pola (Builder: Odero-Terni-Orlandi (O.T.O.), Livorno; Laid Down: 03/17/31; Launched: 12/05/31; Commissioned: 12/21/32; Class: Zara; flagship of 2nd Fleet; 03/28/41, sunk): unknown? 03/28/41 sunk.

San Giorgio (Builder: unknown?; Laid Down: unknown?; Launched: 05/27/1908; Commissioned: 1910; part of Libya Naval Command; 01/22/41, scuttled at Tobruk): unknown? 01/22/41 scuttled.

Trento (Builder: Odero-Terni-Orlandi (O.T.O.), Livorno; Laid Down: -2/08/25; Launched: 10/04/27; Commissioned: 04/03/29; Class: Zara; part of 4th Heavy Cruiser Squadron; 06/15/42): unknown? 06/15/42 sunk.

Trieste (Builder: Stabilimento Tecnico Triestino, Trieste; Laid Down: 06/22/25; Launched: 10/24/26; Commissioned: 12/21/28; Class: Zara; part of 4th Heavy Cruiser Squadron; 04/10/43, sunk): unknown? 04/10/43 sunk.

Zara (Builder: Odero-Terni-Orlandi (O.T.O.), La Spezia; Laid Down: 07/04/29; Launched: 04/27/30; Commissioned: 10/20/31; Class: Zara; part of 1st Heavy Cruiser Squadron; 03/28/41, sunk): unknown? 03/28/41 sunk.

Light Cruisers [CL]

Alberico da Barbiano (Builder: Ansaldo, Genoa; Laid Down: 04/16/28; Launched: 08/23/30; Commissioned: 06/09/31; Class: Condottieri tipo Di Giussano; part of 4th Light Cruiser Squadron; 12/13/41, sunk): unknown? 12/13/41 sunk.

Alberto da Giussano (Builder: Ansaldo, Genoa; Laid Down: 03/29/28; Launched: 04/27/30; Commissioned: 02/05/31; Class: Condottieri tipo Di Giussano; part of 4th Light Cruiser Squadron; 12/31/41, sunk): unknown? 12/31/41 sunk.

Armando Diaz (Builder: Odero-Terni-Orlandi (O.T.O.), La Spezia; Laid Down: 07/28/30; Launched: 07/10/32; Commissioned: 04/29/33; Class: Condottieri tipo Cadorna; part of 4th Light Cruiser Squadron; 02/25/41, sunk): unknown? 02/25/41 sunk.

Attilio Regolo (Builder: Odero-Terni-Orlandi (O.T.O.), Livorno; Laid Down: 09/28/39; Launched: 08/28/40; Commissioned: 05/14/42; Class: Capitani Romani; used as a mine layer until seriously damaged by a torpedo in 11/43): unknown? 11/43 damaged.

Bari (1914, ex-Russian *Muraviev Amurski*; ex-German *Pillau*; Builder: Schichau, Danzig; Laid Down: 04/13; Launched: 1914; Commissioned: 12/15; seized by Germany on outbreak of World War I against Russia in 1914; 1920, taken over by Italy; part of Ionian and Lower Adriatic Sea Department; sunk 06/28/43): unknown? 06/28/43 sunk.

Bartolomeo Colleoni (Builder: Ansaldo, Genoa; Laid Down: 06/21/28; Launched: 12/21/30; Commissioned: 02/10/32; Class: Condottieri tipo Di Giussano; part of 2nd Light Cruiser Squadron; 07/19/40, sunk): unknown? 07/19/40 sunk.

Caio Mario (Builder: Odero-Terni-Orlandi (O.T.O.), Livorno; Laid Down: /39; Launched: 08/17/41; Class: Capitani Romani; 09/08/43, captured in La Spezia by the Germans, with only hull completed; used as a floating oil tank and scuttled in /44): unknown? 09/08/43 captured by the Germans /44 scuttled.

Claudio Druso (Builder Cantieri del Tirreno (C.T.), Genoa-Riva-Trigoso; Laid Down: /39;

Class: Capitani Romani; 06/40, construction cancelled; 11/41 to 02/42, scrapped): SCRAPPED - NEVER COMPLETED.

Claudio Tiberio (Builder: Odero-Terni-Orlandi (O.T.O.), Livorno; Laid Down: /39; Class: Capitani Romani; 06/40, construction cancelled; 11/41 to 02/42, scrapped): SCRAPPED - NEVER COMPLETED.

Cornelio Silla (Builder: Ansaldo Genoa; Laid Down: /39; Launched: 06/28/41; Class: Capitani Romani; 09/08/43, captured in Genoa by the Germans while fitting out; never completed; 07/44, sunk in an air raid): unknown? 09/08/43 captured by the Germans 07/44 sunk.

Emanuele Filiberto Duca d'Aosta (Builder: Odero-Terni-Orlandi (O.T.O.), Livorno; Laid Down: 10/29/32; Launched: 04/22/34; Commissioned: 03/17/35; Class: Condottieri tipo Duca di Aosta; part of 7th Light Cruiser Squadron): unknown?

Etna (ex-Thai ***Taksin***; Builder: Cantieri Riuniti dell'Adriatico, Trieste; Laid Down: 09/23/39; Launched: 05/28/42; Commissioned: not commissioned 53% completes in 09/08/43; Class: Etna; ordered by the Thai Navy in 1938 and subsequently requisitioned by the Italian Navy at the outbreak of World War II; 09/08/43, scuttled): 53% completed when scuttled in 09/08/43.

Eugenio di Savoia (Builder: Ansaldo, Genoa; Laid Down: 07/16/33; Launched: 03/16/35; Commissioned: 01/16/36; Class: Condottieri tipo Duca di Aosta; part of 7th Light Cruiser Squadron): unknown?

FR 11 (ex-French ***Jean de Vienne***; Builder: Arsenal de la Marine, Lorient; Laid Down: 12/20/31; Launched: 07/31/35; Commissioned: 02/10/37; Class: La Galissoniere; 11/27/42, scuttled by Vichy France in Toulon; 02/18/43, raised by Italy, renamed ***FR 11***; 11/24/43, damaged bu incendiary bombs): 02/18/43 raised by Italy 02/18/43 unknown? 11/24/43 damaged bu incendiary bombs. NEVER USED BY ITALY IN WORLD WAR II.

FR 12 (ex-French ***La Galissoniere***; Builder: Arsenal de la Marine, Lorient; Laid Down: 12/15/31; Launched: 11/18/33; Commissioned: 01/01/36; Class: La Galissoniere; 11/27/42, scuttled by Vichy France in Toulon; 03/03/43, raised by Italy, renamed ***FR 12***; 08/18/44, sunk): 03/03/43 raised by Italy 03/03/43 unknown? 08/18/44 sunk.

Giovanni delle Bande Nere (Builder: Navalmeccanica, Castellammare; Laid Down: 10/31/28; Launched: 04/27/30; Commissioned:04/01/31; Class: Condottieri tipo Di Giussano; part of 2nd Light Cruiser Squadron; 04/01/42, sunk): unknown? 07/40 Capt. Franco Maugeri [RIN] (Director General of Naval Intelligence) /41 unknown? 04/01/42 sunk.

Giulio Germanico (Builder: Navalmeccanica, Castellammare; Laid Down: 04/03/39; Launched: 07/20/41; Class: Capitani Romani; 09/08/43, captured in Castellammare di Stabia by the Germans almost completed; 09/28/43, scuttled by the Germans; raised and completed by the Italian Navy after the war): ALMOST COMPLETED 09/28/43 scuttled.

Giuseppe Garibaldi (Builder: Cantieri Riuniti dell'Adriatico, Trieste; Laid Down: 01/12/33; Launched: 04/21/36; Commissioned: 12/20/37; Class: Condottieri tipo Duca degli Abruzzi; part of 8th Light Cruiser Squadron): unknown?

Luigi Cadorna (Builder: Cantieri Riuniti dell'Adriatico, Trieste; Laid Down: 09/19/30; Launched: 09/30/31; Commissioned: 08/11/33; Class: Condottieri tipo Cadorna; part of 4th Light Cruiser Squadron): unknown?

Luigi di Savoia Duca deghi Abruazzi (Builder: Odero-Terni-Orlandi (O.T.O.), La Spezia; Laid Down: 12/28/33; Launched: 04/21/36; Commissioned: 12/01/37; Class: Condottieri tipo Duca degli Abruzzi; part of 8th Light Cruiser Squadron): unknown?

Muzio Attendolo (Builder: Cantieri Riuniti dell'Adriatico, Trieste; Laid Down: 04/10/33; Launched: 09/09/34; Commissioned: 08/07/35; Class: Condottieri tipo Montecuccoli; part of 7th Light Cruiser Squadron; 12/04/42, sunk): unknown? 12/04/42 sunk.

Ottaviano Augusto (Builder: Riuniti, Ancona; Laid Down: /39; Launched: 05/31/42; Class: Capitani Romani; 09/08/43, captured in Ancona by the Germans while being completed; 11/01/43, sunk in an air attack): 09/08/43 by the Germans 11/01/43 sunk.

Paolo Emilio (Builder: Ansaldo Genoa; Laid Down: /39; Class: Capitani Romani; 06/40, construction cancelled; 10/41 to 02/42, scrapped): SCRAPPED - NEVER COMPLETED.

Pompeo Magno (Builder: Odero-Terni-Orlandi (O.T.O.), Livorno; Laid Down: 09/23/39;

Launched: 08/24/41; Commissioned: 06/04/43; Class: Capitani Romani): unknown?

Raimondo Montecuccoli (Builder: Ansaldo, Genoa; Laid Down: 10/01/31; Launched: 08/02/34; Commissioned: 06/30/35; Class: Condottieri tipo Montecuccoli; part of 7th Light Cruiser Squadron): unknown?

Scipione Africano (Builder: Odero-Terni-Orlandi (O.T.O.), Livorno; Laid Down: 09/28/39; Launched: 01/12/41; Commissioned: 04/23/43; Class: Capitani Romani): unknown?

Taranto (ex-***Strassburg***; Builder: Wilhelmshaven, Germany; Laid Down: 04/10; Launched: 1911; Commissioned: 12/12; 1920, taken over by Italy; part of Ionian and Lower Adriatic Sea Department): unknown?

Ulpio Traiano (Builder: Riuniti, Palermo; Laid Down: 10/39; Launched: 1941; Commissioned: not commissioned, not completed when sunk in 1943; Class: Capitani Romani): 1943 not completed when sunk.

Vesuvio (ex-Thai ***Naresuan***; Builder: Cantieri Riuniti dell'Adriatico, Trieste; Laid Down: 08/26/39; Launched: 08/06/41; Commissioned: not commissioned 53% completes in 09/08/43; Class: Etna; ordered by the Thai Navy in 1938 and subsequently requisitioned by the Italian Navy at the outbreak of World War II; 09/08/43, scuttled): 53% completed when scuttled in 09/08/43.

Vipsanio Agrippa (Builder: Cantieri del Tirreno (C.T.), Genoa-Riva-Trigoso; Laid Down: /39; Class: Capitani Romani; 06/40, construction cancelled; 10/41 to 02/42, scrapped): SCRAPPED - NEVER COMPLETED.

Destroyer Divisions

Destroyer Division 1 (HQ: Tripoli, Libya; part of Libya Naval Command)

Destroyer Division 2 (HQ: Taranto, Italy; part of Ionian and Lower Adriatic Sea Department):

Destroyer Division 3 (part of Italian East Africa Naval Command)

Destroyer Division 4 (part of Aegean Sea Naval Command)

Destroyer Division 5 (part of Italian East Africa Naval Command)

Destroyer Division (HQ: Taranto, Italy; part of Ionian and Lower Adriatic Sea Department):

Destroyer Division 7 (part of 5th Battleship Squadron)

Destroyer Division 8 (part of 5th Battleship Squadron)

Destroyer Division 9 (part of 1st Heavy Cruiser Squadron)

Destroyer Division 10 (part of 2nd Light Cruiser Squadron)

Destroyer Division 11 (part of 4th Heavy Cruiser Squadron)

Destroyer Division 12 (part of 6th Battleship Squadron)

Destroyer Division 13 (part of 7th Light Cruiser Squadron)

Destroyer Division 14 (part of 9th Battleship Squadron)

Destroyer Division 15 (part of 9th Battleship Squadron)

Destroyer Division 16 (part of 8th Light Cruiser Squadron)

Submarine Divisions

Submarine Division 11 (part of 1st Submarine Squadron)

Submarine Division 12 (part of 1st Submarine Squadron)

Submarine Division 13 (part of 1st Submarine Squadron)

Submarine Division 14 (part of 1st Submarine Squadron)

Submarine Division 15 (part of 1st Submarine Squadron)

Submarine Division 16 (part of 1st Submarine Squadron)

Submarine Division 17 (part of 1st Submarine Squadron)

Submarine Division 21 (part of 2nd Submarine Squadron)

Submarine Division 22 (part of 2nd Submarine Squadron)

Submarine Division 31 (part of 3rd Submarine Squadron)

Submarine Division 33 (part of 3rd Submarine Squadron)

Submarine Division 34 (part of 3rd Submarine Squadron)

Submarine Division 35 (part of 3rd Submarine Squadron)

Submarine Division 37 (part of 3rd Submarine Squadron)

Submarine Division 40 (part of 4th Submarine Squadron)

Submarine Division 41 (part of 4th Submarine Squadron)

Submarine Division 42 (part of 4th Submarine Squadron)

Submarine Division 43 (part of 4th Submarine Squadron)

Submarine Division 44 (part of 4th Submarine Squadron)

Submarine Division 45 (part of 4th Submarine Squadron)

Submarine Division 46 (part of 4th Submarine Squadron)

Submarine Division 47 (part of 4th Submarine Squadron)

Submarine Division 48 (part of 4th Submarine Squadron)

Submarine Division 49 (part of 4th Submarine Squadron)

Submarine Division 51 (part of 5th Submarine Squadron)

Submarine Division 52 (part of 5th Submarine Squadron)

Submarine Division 61 (part of 6th Submarine Squadron)

Submarine Division 62 (part of 6th Submarine Squadron)

Submarine Division 71 (part of 7th Submarine Squadron)

Submarine Division 72 (part of 7th Submarine Squadron)

Submarine Division 81 (part of 8th Submarine Squadron)

Submarine Division 82 (part of 8th Submarine Squadron)

Fast Torpedo Boat [MAS] Divisions [Decima Flottiglia Motoscafo Anti-Sommergibile]

MAS Division 1 (part of 1st Fast Torpedo Boat [MAS] Squadron)

MAS Division 2 (part of 2nd Fast Torpedo Boat [MAS] Squadron)

MAS Division 3 (part of Brindisi Naval Command)

MAS Division 4 (part of Sardinia Naval Command)

MAS Division 5 (part of 1st Fast Torpedo Boat [MAS] Squadron)

MAS Division 6 (part of Upper Adriatic Sea Department)

MAS Division 7 (part of 3rd Fast Torpedo Boat [MAS] Squadron)

MAS Division 9 (part of 2nd Fast Torpedo Boat [MAS] Squadron)

MAS Division 10 (part of 2nd Fast Torpedo Boat [MAS] Squadron; 09/08/43, disbanded): 08/40 Cdr. Vittorio Moccagatta [RIN] /42 Cdr. Prince Junio Valerio Borghese [RIN] 09/08/43 disbanded.

MAS Division 11 (part of 3rd Fast Torpedo Boat [MAS] Squadron)

MAS Division 12 (part of 1st Fast Torpedo Boat [MAS] Squadron)

MAS Division 13 (part of 1st Fast Torpedo Boat [MAS] Squadron)

MAS Division 14 (part of 1st Fast Torpedo Boat [MAS] Squadron)

MAS Division 15 (part of 2nd Fast Torpedo Boat [MAS] Squadron)

MAS Division 16 (part of 3rd Fast Torpedo Boat [MAS] Squadron)

MAS Division 21 (part of Italian East Africa Naval Command)

MAS Division 22 (part of 3rd Fast Torpedo Boat [MAS] Squadron)

Torpedo Boat Divisions

Torpedo Boat Division 1 (part of 2nd Torpedo Boat Squadron and/or Libya Naval Command; HQ: Tripoli, Libya)

Torpedo Boat Division 2 (part of Sardinia Naval Command)

Torpedo Boat Division 3 (part of Lower Tyrrenhian Sea Department)

Torpedo Boat Division 4 (part of Lower Tyrrenhian Sea Department)

Torpedo Boat Division 5 (part of Sicily Naval Command)

Torpedo Boat Division 7 (part of Brindisi Naval Command)

Torpedo Boat Division 8 (part of Aegean Sea Naval Command)

Torpedo Boat Division 9 (part of Sardinia Naval Command)

Torpedo Boat Division 10 (part of Upper Tyrrenhian Sea Department)

Torpedo Boat Division 11 (HQ: Tripoli, Libya; part of Libya Naval Command)

Torpedo Boat Division 12 (part of 2nd Torpedo Boat Squadron)

Torpedo Boat Division 13 (part of 1st Torpedo Boat Squadron)

Torpedo Boat Division 14 (part of 1st Torpedo Boat Squadron)

Torpedo Boat Division 15 (part of Upper Adriatic Sea Department)

Torpedo Boat Division 16 (part of Upper Tyrrenhian Sea Department)

SECTION B

FRANCE

MONACO

&

ANDORRA

Part 1

THE FRENCH GOVERNMENT AND THE ORGANIZATION AND STRUCTURE OF THE FRENCH MILITARY HIGH COMMAND

Government of France
(Third Republic)

President: 05/06/32 ALBERT FRANÇOIS LEBRUN [+ Co-Regent of Andorra] (fled France after surrender to Germany and replaced as President) 07/10/40 see **Vichy France**.
    1.   **Head, Military Household to the President**: /31 Col. Joseph-Eugène-Charles Braconnier (retired) 07/10/40 dissolved.

Prime Minister: 06/04/36 LÉON-ANDRÉ BLUM (Vice Premier) 06/22/37 CAMILLE CHAUTEMPS (Vice Premier) 03/13/38 LÉON-ANDRÉ BLUM [+ Finance Minister] 04/10/38 ÉDOUARD DALADIER [+ President of the Army Council, Chairman of the Superior Council of National Defense, & Commander-in-Chief, Armed Forces; + 09/13/39, Foreign Minister; + 06/04/39, Minister of National Defense and War] 03/21/40 PAUL REYNAUD [+ President of the Army Council, Chairman of the Superior Council of National Defense, & Commander-in-Chief, Armed Forces; + to 05/18/40, Foreign Minister; + 06/05/40, Foreign Minister] 06/16/40 Marshal Henri-Philippe-Benoni-Omar-Joseph Pétain [+ President, Council of Ministers] 07/10/40 see **Vichy France**.

  A. **Vice Premier:** 06/04/36 ÉDOUARD DALADIER (01/18/38, Vice Premier) 06/22/37 LÉON-ANDRÉ BLUM (03/13/38, Prime Minister & Finance Minister) 01/18/38 ÉDOUARD DALADIER (Prime Minister, President of the Army Council, Chairman of the Superior Council of National Defense, & Commander-in-Chief, Armed Forces) 04/10/38 CAMILLE CHAUTEMPS 06/16/40 PIERRE LAVAL [+ Chief of Staff & Vice-President Council of Ministers] 07/10/40 see **Vichy France**.

  B. **Foreign Minister**: 01/24/36 PIERRE-ÉTIENNE FLANDIN (12/13/40, Chief of State [Vice Premier], Vichy France & Foreign Minister, Vichy France) 06/04/36 YVON DELBOS (09/13/40, Education Minister) 03/13/38 AUGUSTIN-ALFRED-JOSEPH-PAUL BONCOUR 04/10/38 GEORGES-ÉTIENNE BONNET (Justice Minister) 09/13/39 EDOUARD DALADIER [+ Prime Minister, Minister of National Defense and War, President of the Army Council, Chairman of the Superior Council of National Defense, & Commander-in-Chief, Armed Forces] 03/21/40 PAUL REYNAUD [+ Prime Minister, President of the Army Council, Chairman of the Superior Council of National Defense, & Commander-in-Chief, Armed Forces] 05/18/40 EDOUARD DALADIER 06/05/40 PAUL REYNAUD [+ Prime Minister, President of the Army Council, Chairman of the Superior Council of National Defense, & Commander-in-Chief, Armed Forces] 06/16/40 PAUL BAUDOUIN (Foreign Minister, Vichy France) 07/10/40 see **Vichy France**.

  C. **Finance Minister**: 06/04/36 JULES-VINCENT AURIOL 06/22/37 GEORGES-ÉTIENNE BONNET (04/10/38, Foreign Minister) 01/18/38 PAUL MARCHANDEAU 03/13/38 LÉON-ANDRÉ BLUM [+ Prime Minister] 04/10/38 PAUL MARCHANDEAU (Minister of Justice) 11/01/38 PAUL REYNAUD (Prime Minister & Foreign Minister) 03/21/40 LUCIEN LAMOUREUX 06/05/40 YVES BOUTHILIER [+ Minister of Commerce and Industry] (Finance Minister, Vichy France] 07/10/40 see **Vichy France**.

  D. **Minister of National Defense and War**: 06/04/39 EDOUARD DALADIER [+ to

03/21/40, Prime Minister, President of the Army Council, Chairman of the Superior Council of National Defense, & Commander-in-Chief, Armed Forces; + 09/13/39 to 03/21/40, Foreign Minister] (Foreign Minister) 05/18/40 PAUL REYNAUD [+ Prime Minister, President of the Army Council, Chairman of the Superior Council of National Defense, & Commander-in-Chief, Armed Forces; + 06/05/40, Foreign Minister] 06/16/40 separated into **Minister of National Defense** and **Minister of War**.

    1.   **Undersecretary of National Defense**: 06/05/40 BG Charles-André-Joseph-Marie de Gaulle (fled to England; 06/18/40, Commander-in-Chief, Free French Forces) 06/16/40

    2.   **Director, Intendant [Quartermaster] Service, Ministry of National Defense**: /38 MG Joseph-Frédéric-Ange-Désiré Bernard

        a.   **Inspector-General of Clothing**: /38 BG Joseph-Jean-Louis Boissel

    3.   **Technical Adviser to the Minister of War**: /36 MG Marie-Joseph-Paul-Laurent Jacomet

E.   **Minister of National Defense** (06/16/40): Gen. Louis-Antoine Colson (Minister of National Defense, Vichy France) 07/10/40 see **Vichy France**.

F.   **Minister of War** (06/16/40): Gen. [Retired '35] Maxime Weygand [+ Commander-in-Chief, Allied Forces in France; + Commander-in-Chief, Land Forces; & Chief of the Army General Staff] (Vichy France Minister of War; Delegate-General of the Vichy Government to North Africa; Commander-in-Chief, North Africa Land Forces) 07/16/40 dissolved - see **Vichy France**.

G.   **Air Minister**: 01/24/36 MARCEL d'EAT 06/04/36 PIERRE COT (Minister of Commerce and Industry) 01/18/38 GUY LA CHAMBRE 03/21/40 LAUENT EYNAC 06/16/40 BERTRAND PUJO (Minister of Air, Vichy France) 07/10/40 see **Vichy France**.

H.   **Minister of Military Marine**: /36 LOUIS de CHAPPEDELAINE (04/10/38, Minister of Merchant Marine) 06/22/37 CÉSAR CAMPINCHI (Justice Minister) 01/18/38 WILLIAM BERTRAND 03/13/38 CÉSAR CAMPINCHI 06/16/40 Adm. of the Fl. Jean-Louis-Xavier-François Darlan [FN] [+ Chief of the General Staff for Naval Operations & Commander-in-Chief, Navy; + 06/16/40, Minister of Merchant Marine; + 06/22/40, Commander-in-Chief, Vichy France Armed Forces] 07/10/40 see **Vichy France**.

I.   **Minister of Merchant Marine**: 06/04/36 ALPHONSE GASHIER-DUPARC 01/18/38 PAUL ELBEL 04/10/38 LOUIS de CHAPPEDELAINE 09/13/39 ALPHONSE RIO 06/16/40 Adm. of the Fl. Jean-Louis-Xavier-François Darlan [FN] [+ Chief of the General Staff for Naval Operations & Commander-in-Chief, Navy & Minister of Military Marine; + 06/22/40, Commander-in-Chief, Vichy France Armed Forces] 07/10/40 see **Vichy France**.

J.   **Minister for Colonies (Overseas France)**: 03/13/38 THÉODORE STEEG 04/10/38 MARIUS MOUTET 05/18/40 GEORGES MANDEL [+ Interior Minister] 06/16/40 LOUIS ROLLIN 07/12/40 see **Vichy France**.

K.   **Interior Minister**: 01/24/36 ALBERT-PIERRE SARRAUT 06/04/36 ROGER-HENRI-CHARLES SALENGRO (committed suicide) 11/18/36 MARX DORMOY 01/18/38 ALBERT-PIERRE SARRAUT 03/13/38 MARX DORMOY 04/10/38 ALBERT-PIERRE SARRAUT (Education Minister) 03/21/40 HENRI ROY 05/18/40 GEORGES MANDEL [+ Minister for Colonies (Overseas France)] 06/16/40

CHARLES POMARET [+ Minister of Labor] 06/26/40 ADRIEN MARQUET 07/10/40 see **Vichy France**.

L. **Minister of Information**: 03/13/38 LUDOVIC-OSCAR FROSSARD (Minister of Transport and Public Works) 04/10/38 vacant 03/21/40 LUDOVIC-OSCAR FROSSARD (Minister of Transport and Public Works) 06/05/40 JEAN PROUVOST 06/16/40 vacant 07/10/40 see **Vichy France**.

M. **Minister of Commerce and Industry**: 06/04/36 PAUL BASTID 06/22/37 FERNAND CHAPSAL (Minister of Agriculture) 01/18/38 PIERRE COT 04/10/38 FERNAND GENLIN 03/21/40 LOUIS ROLLIN (Minister for Colonies (Overseas France)) 05/18/40 LÉON BARÉTY 06/05/40 ALBERT CHICHERY Minister of Agriculture) 06/16/40 YVES BOUTHILIER [+ Finance Minister] (Finance Minister, Vichy France) 07/10/40 did not exist in **Vichy France** Cabinet.

N. **Minister of Justice**: 01/18/38 CËSAR CAMPINCHI (Minister of Military Marine [Navy]) 03/13/38 MARC RUCAST (Minister of Health) 04/10/38 PAUL REYNAUD (Finance Minster) 11/01/38 PAUL MARCHANDEAU 09/13/39 GEORGES-ÉTIENNE BONNET 03/40 ALBERT SÉROL 06/40 CHARLES FRÉMICOURT 07/12/44 see **Vichy France**.

O. **Minister of Agriculture**: 06/04/36 GEORGES MONNET 01/18/38 FERNAND CHAPSAL 03/13/38 GEORGES MONNET 04/10/38 HENRI QUEUILLE 03/21/40 PAUL THELLIER 06/16/40 ALBERT CHICHERY 07/12/40 see **Vichy France**.

P. **Minister of Transport and Public Works**: 06/22/37 HENRI QUEUILLE (Minister of Agriculture) 03/13/38 JULES MOCH (03/11/45, Minister of Transport and Public Works) 04/10/38 LUDOVIC-OSCAR FROSSARD (03/21/40, Minister of Information) 08/23/38 ANATOLE de MONZIE 06/05/40 LUDOVIC-OSCAR FROSSARD 07/12/40 did not exist in **Vichy France** Cabinet.
   1. **Chief of Cabinet, Ministry of Public Works**: /37 Col. Louis-Lazare Kahn (Director, Center of Construction of Naval Arms)

Q. **Minister of Health**: 01/24/36 LOUIS NICOLLE 06/04/36 HENRI SELLIER 06/22/37 MARC RUCAST (Justice Minister) 03/13/38 FERNAND GENLIN (Minister of Commerce and Industry) 04/10/38 MARC RUCAST 03/21/40 MARCEL HÉRAUD 06/05/40 GEORGES PERNOT 06/16/40 JEAN YBARNEGARAY 07/12/40 see **Vichy France**.

R. **Education Minister**: 01/24/36 HENRI GUERNUT 06/04/36 JEAN ZAY 09/10/39 vacant 09/13/39 YVON DELBOS 03/21/40 ALBERT-PIERRE SARRAUT 06/05/40 YVON DELBOS 06/16/40 ALBERT RIVAUD 07/12/40 becomes **Minister of Public Instruction** in **Vichy France** Government - see **Vichy France**.

S. **Minister of Labor**: 06/04/37 JEAN-BAPTISTE LEBAS (03/13/38, Minister of Posts, Telegraphs & Telephones) 06/22/37 ANDRÉ FÉVRIER (06/27/40, Minister of Posts, Telegraphs and Telephones) 01/18/38 ALBERT SÉROL (03/40, Minister of Justice) 04/10/38 PAUL RAMADIER 08/23/38 CHARLES POMARET [+ 06/16/40 to 06/26/40, Minister of Interior] 07/12/40 see **Vichy France**.

T. **Minister of Posts, Telegraphs and Telephones**: 01/18/38 FERNAND GENLIN (Minister of Health) 03/13/38 JEAN-BAPTISTE LEBAS 04/10/38 ALFRED JULES-JULIEN 06/16/40 vacant 06/27/40 ANDRÉ FÉVRIER 07/12/40 see **Vichy France**.

U. **Minister of Armaments** (09/13/39): RAOUL DAUTRY
   1. **Department of Armaments Manufacture [Direction des Fabrications d'Armaments]** (09/06/39 moved from Ministry of War): /36 MG Paul-

George Happich (?) 06/25/40
2. **Powder and Chemical Service [Service de Poudres et Products Chimiques]**: 09/06/39 moved from Ministry of War.
3. **Inspector of Armament Manufacturing**: /38 Col. Marie-François-Joseph Laffon
4. **Inspector-General of Powder**: /38 BG Louis-Philippe-Henri Rausch
5. **Inspector of Protection Material**: /38 Col. Félix-Étienne Pognon
6. **Inspector-General of Machines**: /38? Col. Albert Coulon
7. **Inspector-General of Provisions**: /38 unknown?
   a. **Assistant Inspector-General of Provisions**: /38 Col. Jean-Marie-Louis Verret

French Senate
A. **Military Commandant of the French Senate**: /38 BG Delphin-Joseph-Théodore Michel

Minister of National Defense and War

Minister of National Defense and War: 06/04/39 EDOUARD DALADIER [+ to 03/21/40, Prime Minister, President of the Army Council, Chairman of the Superior Council of National Defense, & Commander-in-Chief, Armed Forces; + 09/13/39 to 03/21/40, Foreign Minister] (Foreign Minister) 05/18/40 PAUL REYNAUD [+ Prime Minister, President of the Army Council, Chairman of the Superior Council of National Defense, & Commander-in-Chief, Armed Forces; + 06/05/40, Foreign Minister] 06/16/40 separated into **Minister of National Defense** and **Minister of War**.

A. **The Ministerial Cabinet**: /37 MG Jules-Philippe-Octave Decamp (Army Vice Chief of the General Staff) 06/25/40 dissolved.
   1. **1st Bureau (Administration)**:
   2. **2nd Bureau (Military Decoration)**:
   3. **3rd Bureau (Posting of General officers & general correspondence)**:
   4. **4th Bureau (Military works - books, manuals, other publications)**:
   5. **Civil Cabinet (Civil Affairs)**:

B. **Central Administration (Secrétariat Général)**: Controller General of the Army Robert Jacomet
   1. **Cabinet**
   2. **Administrative Section** (main tasks of office)
   3. **Legislative Section** (civilian workers)
   4. **Materials & Land Service**

C. **Chief of Staff of the Army and Interior (État-Major de l'Armée]**: 01/08/40 Gen. Louis-Antoine Colson [+ 06/16/40, Minister of National Defense] (Vichy France Minister of National Defense) 07/10/40
   1. **Deputies Chief of Staff** (three):
      01/08/40? BG Marie-Martin-Jean-Alfred de Charry
      01/08/40? BG Pierre-Jean Raymond Granboulan
      01/08/40? BG Émile-Pierre-Edouard Ricard
   2. **1st Bureau (Organization and manpower)**:
      a. **Deputy Chief for Organization, Manpower, & Reinforcement**:
      b. **Deputy Chief for running the Bureau, Military Justice, & Administration**:
      c. **Section 1 (General Organization)**:
      d. **Section 2 (Infantry, Armor, Cavalry, & Gendarmes)**:
         i. **Director of Infantry, Ministry of National Defense**: /38 BG Charles-Jean-Baptiste Stehlé
      e. **Section 3 (Artillery, Horse and Motor Transport, Engineers, & Signals)**:
         i. **Director of Engineers, Ministry of National Defense**: /38 BG Georges-Gabriel Métrot
         ii. **Director of Signals, Ministry of War**: /38 BG Léon Jullien
      f. **Section 4 (Anti-Aircraft and Camouflage)**:
      g. **Section 5 (Service Troops - Medical, Quartermaster, etc.)**:
      h. **Section 6 (Manpower and Order of Battle)**:
      i. **Section 7 (Current service matters, including promotions, leave,

        & discipline):
- j. **Section 8 (Military Justice)**:
- k. **Section 9 (Relations with Civilian Authorities)**:
- l. **Section 10 (Courier Section [Sécretariat-Courrier])**:

3. **2nd Bureau (Intelligence)**:
   a. **Espionage**:
   b. **Counter-Espionage**:
   c. **Overseas Territories**:
   d. **Radio Intercept/Direction Finding Stations**:
   e. **Aerial Photography Analysis**:

4. **3rd Bureau (Army Operations)**: /35 LCol. Louis-Léon-Marie-André Buisson (05/16/40, Commanding Officer, 3rd Armored Division) /39

5. **4th Bureau (Army Transport & Logistics)**:

6. **5th Bureau (Overseas Intelligence)** (10/03/39, from **Secret Intelligence Service [Service de Renseignements]**): Col. Pierre-Louis Rivet (Chief of Security, Army of Armistice [no entry]) 06/25/40

7. **Administrative Section**:
   a. **Personnel Section**:
   b. **Statistical Section**:
   c. **Historical Section**:
   d. **Overseas Section**:
   e. **Armaments Section**:
   f. **Chemical Warfare Section**:
   g. **Shipping Section**:

8. **Department for Personnel & Material Services [Direction des Services du Personnel et du Matériel]**:

9. **Audit Department [Direction du Contrôle]**:

10. **Department of Infantry [Direction de l'Infanterie]**:
    a. **Infantry Technical Section**: /38 Col. André-Pierre Hillairet

11. **Department of Cavalry & Transport [Direction de la Cavalerie et du Train]**: /36 BG René-Jacques-Adolphe Prioux (Commanding General, Military District VII) /38 BG Paul-Jean Rupied

12. **Department of Artillery [Direction de l'Artillerie]**: /36 MG Odilon-Léonard-Théophile Picquendar (Commanding General, Military District IX) /40
    a. **Commander-in-Chief, Anti-Aircraft Defenses**: 01/13/40 MG Darius-Paul Bloch-Dassault (Deputy, Coordination of Air Defense Operations) /40
    b. **Artillery Technical Section**:
       i. **Deputy, Artillery Technical Section**: /38 LCol. Germain-Charles-Henri Périer

13. **Department of Engineers [Direction du Genie]**:

14. **Quartermaster Department [Direction de l'Intendance]**:

15. **Department of the Medical Service [Direction du Service du Santé]**: /40 BG Justin-François-Bertrand-Marcel-Angéli-Gustavé Fontan (retired) 06/25/40 dissolved.
    a. **Assistant Director, Medical Services, Ministry of National**

    Defense: /38 Col. Ferdinand-Émile-Casimir Coudray
  b. **Director of Provisioning & Manufacturing of the Medical Services**: BG Pierre-Anselme-Léon Lannes-Dehore
  c. **Consultative Committee on Health**:
    i. **Members**:
      /38 BG Robert-Eugène-Hippolyte-Alexandre Mancier
16. **Department of Colonial Troops [Direction des Troupes Coloniales]**: /35 MG Jean-Joseph-Guillaume Barrau (Commanding General, 3rd Colonial Division) /38 BG Maurice-Émile Falvy (Commanding General, 3rd Colonial Infantry Division) 04/09/40
  a. **Service Colonial Forces in France**: /38 MG Blasie-Henry-Donatien Barbe
17. **Legal, Military Justice and Police Department [Direction du Contentiaux, de la Justice Militaire et de la Gendarmerie]**:
  a. **Director-General of Gendarmerie**: MG Clément Martin (?) /?? René-Romain-Marie-Robert Meunier
18. **Army Geographical Service [Service Geographique d'Armée]**: /37 Col. Louis-Aristide-Alexandre Hurault (in reserve; /44, Director Army Geographical Service) 06/22/40 dissolved.
  [NOTE: also found but no dates available BG Pierre-Charles-Joseph Penel]
19. **Department of Armaments Manufacture [Direction des Fabrications d'Armaments]**: 09/06/39 moved to Ministry of Armaments.
20. **Powder and Chemical Service [Service de Poudres et Products Chimiques]**: 09/06/39 moved to Ministry of Armaments.
  a. **Director, Powder Service**: /38 Col. André-Jean-Marie Blanchard
D. **At Disposal of the Minister of National Defense and War**:
  /40 LG [Retired '35] Ferréol-François-Gabriel Lefort (retired) /40

Minister of National Defense (06/16/40): Gen. Louis-Antoine Colson (Vichy France Minister of National Defense) 07/10/40 see **Vichy France**.
A. **Chief-of-Staff to the Minister of National Defense**: /38 Gen. Maurice-Gustavé Gamelin [+ to 09/39?, Inspector-General of the Army & Vice President of the Army Council; + 09/39?, Commander-in-Chief, Land and Air Forces; Chief of the Army General Staff; & Commander-in-Chief, Allied Forces in France] (retired; /42, arrested and accused in Rion Trail, which was an attempt by Vichy France to prove the leaders of the French Third Republic had been responsible for France's defeat by Germany in 06/40; /43 to /45, imprisoned by Vichy France at Fort du Portaleb in the Pyrennes, then later deported by the Germans to Itter Castle in Tyrol) 05/18/40

Minister of War (06/16/40): Gen. [Retired '35] Maxime Weygand [+ Commander-in-Chief, Allied Forces in France; + Commander-in-Chief, Land Forces; & Chief of the Army General Staff; (Vichy France Minister of War; Delegate-General of the Vichy Government to North Africa; Commander-in-Chief, North Africa Land Forces) 07/16/40 dissolved - see **Vichy France**.

The Army Council
[Conseil Supérieur de la Guerre]

The Army Council (Supreme War Council) [Conseil Supérieur de la Guerre] (The Army Council had the task of preparing the Army for war. The counsel was made up of Generals who were expected to command the Army Groups and Armies after mobilization for war.]

A. **President of Army Council**: 04/10/38 Prime Minister EDOUARD DALADIER [+ Chairman of the Superior Council of National Defense, & Commander-in-Chief, Armed Forces; + 06/04/39, Minister of National Defense and War; + 09/13/39, Foreign Minister] 03/21/40 PAUL REYNAUD [+ Chairman of the Superior Council of National Defense, & Commander-in-Chief, Armed Forces; + to 05/18/40, Foreign Minister; + 06/05/40, Foreign Minister] 06/16/40 disbanded.

B. **Vice President of Army Council**: /35 Gen. Maurice-Gustavé Gamelin [+ Inspector-General of the Army; + /38, Deputy Chairman of Supreme National Defense Council] (Commander-in-Chief, Land and Air Forces; Chief of the Army General Staff; & Commander-in-Chief, Allied Forces in France) 09/39?

C. *Members of the Army Council*:

/32 LG Alphonse-Joseph Georges [+/35, Chief of the French Empire General Staff] (Deputy Commander-in-Chief, Land Forces) 09/39?

/33 LG Gaston-Henri-Gustavé Billotte [+ /36 to /38, President, Consultative Committee for Colonial Affairs; + /37, Military-Governor of Paris & Commanding General, Paris Military District] (Commander-in-Chief, 1st Army Group) 10/01/39

/34 LG André-Gaston Prételat (Commander-in-Chief, 2nd Army Group) 08/27/39

/35 LG Antoine-Jules-Joseph Huré [+ to /36, Commander-in-Chief, Morocco; +/36, Inspector-General of Engineers & President, Committee of Engineering Techniques] (retired; /40, Vichy France Inspector-General of the Military Regions) /38

/35 LG Pierre Héring (retired; 10/01/39, Commanding General, Paris Military District; Military-Governor, Paris; & President, Consultative Committee for Colonial Defense) /39

/36 LG Louis-Antoine Colson (01/08/40, Chief of Staff of the Army and Interior) /39

/36 LG Charles-Marie Condé [+ Inspector-General of Artillery] (Commander-in-Chief, Third Army) 08/27/39

/36 LG Edmond-Lois Dosse (retired; /39, Inspector of Military Formations of the Interior except Colonial Forces) /39

/36 LG Charles-Auguste-Paul Noguès [+ Resident-General of Morocco & Commander-in-Chief, Morocco]
Chief of Staff to LG Noguès as Member, The Army Council: /37 Col. Alphonse-Pierre Juin (Chief of Staff, North Africa Theater) /39

/37 LG Antoine-Marie-Benoit Besson (Commander-in-Chief, Sixth Army) 09/02/39
Chief of Staff to LG Besson as Member, The Army Council: /38 Col. Louis-Albert-Pierre Robert de Saint-Vincent (Chief of Staff, Sixth Army) 09/02/39

/38 LG Georges-Maurice-Jean Blanchard [+ Director, Higher Military Study Centers

& Inspector-General, Higher Military Education] (Commander-in-Chief, First Army) 08/27/39

/38 LG Jules-Antoine Bührer [+ Inspector-General of Colonial Forces & Member, Consultative Committee of Colonial Defense & Chief of Staff, Colonial Forces] /39

/38 Gen. Jeanny-Jules-Marcel Garchèry [+ Inspector-General of Infantry] (Commander-in-Chief, Eighth Army) 08/27/39

/38 LG Charles-Léon-Clément Huntziger (Commander-in-Chief, Second Army) 08/27/39

Chief of Staff to LG Huntziger as Member, The Army Council: /38 Col. Alphonse-Pierre Juin (Chief of Staff, Second Army) 08/27/39

/38 LG Edouard-Jean Réquin [+ Commandant, Higher Studies of National Defense College] (Commander-in-Chief, Fourth Army) 08/27/39

/39 Gen. Victor Bourret (Commander-in-Chief, Fifth Army) 08/27/39

/39 Gen. Henri-Honoré Giraud (Commander-in-Chief, Seventh Army) 09/02/39

12/39 Gen. Joseph-Edouard-Aimé Doumenc [+ Deputy Chief of the General Staff & Inspector-General, Anti-Aircraft Defenses] (Chief of the Army General Staff, Vichy France) 07/40

D. **Attached to The Army Council**

/39 Col. Jean-Marie-Léon Etcheberrigaray (Vice Chief of Staff, First Army Group) /39

The Superior Council of National Defense [Conseil Supérieur de la Défense Nationale]

The Superior Council of National Defense [Conseil Supérieur de la Défense Nationale] (1936, set up for national defense policy could be coordinated between the army, navy, and air force.]

A. **Chairman of Superior Council of National Defense**: 04/10/38 Prime Minister EDOUARD DALADIER [+ President of the Army Council & Commander-in-Chief, Armed Forces; + 09/13/39, Foreign Minister; + 06/04/39, Minister of National Defense and War] 03/21/40 PAUL REYNAUD [+ President of the Army Council & Commander-in-Chief, Armed Forces; + to 05/18/40, Foreign Minister; + 06/05/40, Foreign Minister] 06/16/40 disbanded.

B. **Deputy Chairman of Superior Council of National Defense**: /38 Gen. Maurice-Gustavé Gamelin [+ to 09/39?, Inspector-General of the Army & Vice President of the Army Council; + 09/39?, Commander-in-Chief, Land and Air Forces; Chief of the Army General Staff; & Commander-in-Chief, Allied Forces in France] (retired; /42, arrested and accused in Rion Trail, which was an attempt by Vichy France to prove the leaders of the French Third Republic had been responsible for France's defeat by Germany in 06/40; /43 to /45, imprisoned by Vichy France at Fort du Portaleb in the Pyrennes, then later deported by the Germans to Itter Castle in Tyrol) 05/18/40

C. ***Members of the Superior Council of National Defense***:
   1. **Secretariat of the Superior Council of National Defense**: /36 BG Louis-Marie Jamet (Commanding General, Military District XIII) /40 LG Henri-Léon Caillault [+ /40, Chief of the General Staff] 06/25/40 dissolved.
   2. **Minister of Foreign Affairs**: 01/24/36 PIERRE-ÉTIENNE FLANDIN (12/13/40, Chief of State [Vice Premier], Vichy France & Foreign Minister, Vichy France) 06/04/36 YVON DELBOS (09/13/40, Education Minister) 03/13/38 AUGUSTIN-ALFRED-JOSEPH-PAUL BONCOUR 04/10/38 GEORGES-ÉTIENNE BONNET (Justice Minister) 09/13/39 EDOUARD DALADIER [+ Prime Minister, Minister of National Defense and War, President of the Army Council, Chairman of the Superior Council of National Defense, & Commander-in-Chief, Armed Forces] 03/21/40 PAUL REYNAUD [+ Prime Minister, President of the Army Council, Chairman of the Superior Council of National Defense, & Commander-in-Chief, Armed Forces] 05/18/40 EDOUARD DALADIER 06/05/40 PAUL REYNAUD [+ Prime Minister, President of the Army Council, Chairman of the Superior Council of National Defense, & Commander-in-Chief, Armed Forces] 06/16/40 PAUL BAUDOUIN (Foreign Minister, Vichy France).
   3. **Minister of Air**: 01/24/36 MARCEL d'EAT 06/04/36 PIERRE COT (Minister of Commerence and Industry) 01/18/38 GUY LA CHAMBRE 03/21/40 LAUENT EYNAC 06/16/40 BERTRAND PUJO (Minister of Air, Vichy France) 07/10/40 see **Vichy France**.
   4. **Minister of the Navy**: /36 LOUIS de CHAPPEDELAINE (04/10/38, Minister of Merchant Marine) 06/22/37 CÉSAR CAMPINCHI (Justice Minister) 01/18/38 WILLIAM BERTRAND 03/13/38 CÉSAR CAMPINCHI 06/16/40

Adm. of the Fl. Jean-Louis-Xavier-François Darlan [FN] [+ Chief of the General Staff for Naval Operations & Commander-in-Chief, Navy & Minister of Military Marine & Minister of Merchant Marine; + 06/22/40, Commander-in-Chief, Vichy France Armed Forces] 06/25/40 dissolved.

5. **Commander-in-Chief, Navy**: /39 Adm. of the Fl. Jean-Louis-Xavier-François Darlan [FN] [+ Chief of the General Staff for Naval Operations; + 06/16/40, Minister of Military Marine & Minister of Merchant Marine; + 06/22/40, Commander-in-Chief, Vichy France Armed Forces] 07/40 see **Vichy France**.

6. **Chief of the General Staff for Naval Operations**: /36 Adm. of the Fl. Jean-Louis-Xavier-François Darlan [FN] [+ /39, Commander-in-Chief, Navy; + 06/16/40, Minister of Military Marine & Minister of Merchant Marine; + 06/22/40, Commander-in-Chief, Vichy France Armed Forces] 07/40 see **Vichy France**.

7. **Commander-in-Chief, Air Force**: 10/15/36 Gen. Philippe Féquant [FAF] 02/21/38 LG Joseph Vuillemin [FAF] [+ Vice Chairman, Supreme Air Council & Inspector-General, Home Air Defense] (06/24/40, Inspector-General of the Air Force) 07/04/40 vacant - see **Vichy France**.

Armed Forces High Command

Commander-in-Chief Armed Forces: 04/10/38 Prime Minister EDOUARD DALADIER [+ President of the Army Council & Chairman of the Superior Council of National Defense; + 09/13/39, Foreign Minister; + 06/04/39, Minister of National Defense and War] 03/21/40 Prime Minister PAUL REYNAUD [+ President of the Army Council & Chairman of the Superior Council of National Defense; + to 05/18/40, Foreign Minister; + 06/05/40, Foreign Minister] 06/16/40 disbanded.

A. **Senior Generals on the Active List but no employment**:
/39 Mar. Louis-Félix-Marie-François Franchet d'Esperey (died) /42
/39 Gen. Marie-Louis-Adolphe Guillaumat (died) /40
/39 Gen. Edmund-Just-Victor Boichut (died) /41
/39 Gen. Marie-Eugène Debeney.
/39 Gen. Henri-Joseph-Eugène Gouraud.

B. **Commandant, Higher Studies of National Defense Institute [l'Institut des Hautes Études de la Défense Nationale]**: /36 VA Raoul-Victor-Patrice Castex $_{[FN]}$ (retired) 12/38 LG Edouard-Jean Réquin [+ Member, The Army Council] (Commander-in-Chief, Fourth Army) 08/27/39

General Headquarters [Army High Command] [Grand Quartier Général (GQG)]

Commander-in-Chief, Land Forces [Commandant-en-Chef des Forces Terrestres] (actual title, **Commander-in-Chief, Land and Air Forces**): /35 Gen. Maurice-Gustavé Gamelin [+ Deputy Chairman of Supreme National Defense Council; Chief of the Army General Staff; & Commander-in-Chief, Allied Forces in France] (retired; /42, arrested and accused in Rion Trail, which was an attempt by Vichy France to prove the leaders of the French Third Republic had been responsible for France's defeat by Germany in 06/40; /43 to /45, imprisoned by Vichy France at Fort du Portaleb in the Pyrennes, then later deported by the Germans to Itter Castle in Tyrol) 05/18/40 Gen. [Retired '35] Maxime Weygand [+ Commander-in-Chief, Allied Forces in France & Chief of the Army General Staff; + 06/16/40, Minister of War] (Vichy France Minister of War; Delegate-General of the Vichy Government to North Africa; Commander-in-Chief, North Africa Land Forces) 07/16/40 dissolved - see **Vichy France**.

A. **Deputy Commander-in-Chief, Land Forces [Général Adjoint au Général Commandant en Chef]**: 09/39? Gen. Alphonse-Joseph Georges [+ 01/40, Commander-in-Chief, North Eastern Theater of Operations] (Inspector-General of Land Forces) 05/17/40

B. **Consultative Committee for Colonial Defense**:
   1. **President, Consultative Committee for Colonial Defense**: /36 LG Gaston-Henri-Gustavé Billotte [+ Member, the Army Council; + /37, Military-Governor of Paris & Commanding General, Paris Military District] (Commander-in-Chief, 1st Army Group) 10/01/39 Gen. [Retired '39] Pierre Héring [+ Commanding General, Paris Military District & Military-Governor, Paris] (Commander-in-Chief, Army of Paris) 06/40 Gen. Jules-Antoine Bührer [+ Inspector-General of Colonial Forces & Inspector of Colonel Forces in France] (retired) /41
   2. **Member, Consultative Committee for Colonial Defense**:
      /36 Col. Maurice Viant [+ Artillery Commander, 3rd Colonial Infantry Division; + /37, Member, Engineering Technical Committee] /39
      /37 MG Paul-Louis-François Villain (at disposal Commander-in-Chief, Armed Forces; /38 retired; /39, recalled; 09/02/39, Commanding General, Military District VIII) /38
      /37 MG Jules-Antoine Bührer [+ Inspector-General of Colonial Forces; + /38 to /39, Member, the Army Council; + /38, Chief of Staff, Colonial Forces] (President, Consultative Committee for Colonial Defense & Inspector of Colonial Forces in France) 06/40
      /37 MG René-Paul Dubuisson [+ Commander-in-Chief, French West Africa] (Commanding General, 2nd Colonial Infantry Division) /38
      /38 MG Maxime-Jean-Vincent Germain (Commanding General, 1st Colonial Infantry Division) /38
      /38 BG Étienne Bonnet (Assistant Director, General Office of Military Recruitment) /39
      /38 MG Pierre-André-Antoine Marquis (Commanding General, 16th Infantry Division) 09/02/39

C. **Inspector-General of Land Forces**: 05/17/40 Gen. Alphonse-Joseph Georges (retired; /42, Member, French Committee for National Liberation) 06/25/40 dissolved.
   1. **Inspector-General, Anti-Aircraft Defenses**: 12/39 Gen. Joseph-Edouard-Aimé Doumenc [+ Member, the Army Council & Deputy Chief of the General Staff] (Chief of the Army General Staff, Vichy France) 07/40 dissolved.
   2. **Inspector of Military Formations of the Interior (except Colonial Forces)**: /39 Gen. [Retired '39] Edmond-Lois Dosse (retired) /40
   3. **Inspector-General of Colonial Forces**: /37 MG Jules-Antoine Bührer [+ to 06/40, Member, Consultative Committee of Colonial Defense; + /38 to /39, Member, The Army Counsel; + 38 to 06/40, Chief of Staff, Colonial Forces; + 06/40, President, Consultative Committee of Colonial Defense & Inspector of Colonial Forces in France] (retired) /41
      a. **Inspector of Colonial Forces in France**: 06/40 Gen. Jules-Antoine Bührer [+ Inspector-General of Colonial Forces & President, Consultative Committee of Colonial Defense]
      b. **Technical Assistant to the Inspector-General of Colonial Forces**: /39 BG Henrich-Camille-Constant-Arthur Rinck (Artillery Commander, Colonial Army Corps) 09/02/39
   4. **Inspector of Gendarmes of the Interior**: /39 MG Louis-Eugène-Fernand Bucheton (retired) 06/25/40 dissolved.
      a. **Inspector of Gendarmes 3rd District**: /38 Col. Pierre-Émile-Gabriel Piquet
D. **Attached to Grand Quartier Générale**:
   /39 Gen. [Retired] Eugène-Désité-Antoine Mittlehauser (retired; Head, Military Mission to the Netherlands) /40
E. **At disposal of the Commander-in-Chief**:
   /39 MG Joseph-Jules-Marie Legendre (Commanding General, Depots of Colonial Forces in France) /39

Chief of the Army General Staff [Chef d'État-Major Général]: /35 Gen. Maurice-Gustavé Gamelin [+ Deputy Chairman of Supreme National Defense Council; Commander-in-Chief, Land and Air Forces; & Commander-in-Chief, Allied Forces in France] (retired) 05/18/40 LG Henri-Léon Caillault (retired; /42, arrested and accused in Rion Trail, which was an attempt by Vichy France to prove the leaders of the French Third Republic had been responsible for France's defeat by Germany in 06/40; /43 to /45, imprisoned by Vichy France at Fort du Portaleb in the Pyrennes, then later deported by the Germans to Itter Castle in Tyrol) 05/18/40 Gen. [Retired '35] Maxime Weygand [+ Commander-in-Chief, Allied Forces in France & Commander-in-Chief, Land Forces; + 06/16/40, Minister of War] (Vichy France Minister of War; Delegate-General of the Vichy Government to North Africa; Commander-in-Chief, North Africa Land Forces) 07/16/40 dissolved - see **Vichy France**.
   1. **Chief of Special Cabinet, Chief of the Army General Staff**: /38 LCol. Jean-Louis-Paul-Marie Petibon (Infantry Commander, 20th Infantry Division) /40 unknown? 07/40 dissolved - see **Vichy France**.
A. **Deputy Chief of the Army General Staff [Général Major Général des Armée]**: /37 MG Henri-Fernand Dentz (Assistant Chief of the General Staff for Intelligence)

or BG Jean-Baptiste Limasset (Commanding General, 5th Motorized Infantry Division) /39 MG [Retired '38] Henri-Marie-Auguste Bineau (retired) 12/39 Gen. LG Joseph-Edouard-Aimé Doumenc [+ Member, the Army Council & Inspector-General, Anti-Aircraft Defenses] (Chief of the Army General Staff, Vichy France) 07/40 dissolved.

    [NOTE: also found but no dates of service BG François-Louis Paquin**]**

B. **Assistant Chief of the General Staff [Aides-Majors Gïnïeraux des Armïe] for Personnel:** BG Halbwachs
C. **Assistant Chief of the General Staff [Aides-Majors Gïnïeraux des Armïe] for Intelligence**: /39 LG Henri-Fernand Dentz (Commanding General, XV Army Corps) 10/19/39
D. **Assistant Chief of the General Staff [Aides-Majors Gïnïeraux des Armïe] for Operations**: BG Gaston-René-Eugène Roton (Chief of Staff, Northwestern France) 12/39 BG Marie-Louis Koëltz (Director, Armistice Service, Vichy France Ministry of War) /40
E. **Assistant Chief of the General Staff [Aides-Majors Gïnïeraux des Armïe] for Logistics:** BG Pierre-Louis-Charles-Constance Hanoteau (Commanding General, 7th Military Division) /41
F. **Assistant Chief of the General Staff [Aides-Majors Gïnïeraux des Armïe] for Transport** (02/27/40): Col. François-Jean Kergoat [+ Director, Department of Railway Service] (Artillery Commander, XIX Army Corps) /40 unknown? 06/25/40 dissolved.
G. **Assistant Chief of the General Staff [Aides-Majors Gïnïeraux des Armïe] for Medical Services [Service de Santé]** (02/27/40): Méd.-Col. Marcel Liégeois 06/25/40 dissolved.
H. **1st Bureau (Administration)**: LCol. Robert-Henri-Eugène Dromard (/43, Engineers Commander, French Expeditionary Corps in Italy) 06/25/40 dissolved.
    1. **Director, General Office of Military Recruitment**:
        a. **Assistant Director, General Office of Military Recruitment**: /39 BG Étienne Bonnet (Commanding General, 24th Infantry Division) 02/25/40 unknown? 06/25/40 dissolved.
    2. **Director, Armaments & Technical Studies Section**: /38 BG Charles-Eugène Rinderneck (?) 06/25/40 dissolved.
I. **2nd Bureau (Intelligence)**: /35 Col. Maurice-Henri Gauché (Head, 5th Bureau) /40 unknown? 06/25/40 dissolved.
J. **3rd Bureau (Operations)**: LCol. Lagarde
K. **4th Bureau (Supply)**: Col. Beau /40? Col. Jean-Clément Blanc (Commanding Officer, 63rd Moroccan Artillery Regiment; /43, Deputy Chief of the General Staff) /40?
L. **5th Bureau**: /40 BG Maurice-Henri Gauché (?) 06/25/40 dissolved.
M. **Personnel Bureau**: /40 Col. André-Marie-Martial d'Anselme (Commanding Officer, Vichy, 18th Infantry Regiment) 06/25/40 dissolved.
N. **Courier Bureau**:
O. **Inspector General of the Army [Inspecteur Général de l'Armée]**: /35 Gen. Maurice-Gustavé Gamelin [+ Vice President, The Army Council; + /38, Deputy Chairman of Supreme National Defense Council] (Commander-in-Chief, Land and Air Forces; Chief of the Army General Staff; & Commander-in-Chief, Allied Forces

in France) 09/39?
1. ***Inspector-Generals [Inspecteurs Généraux]***:
    a. **Inspector-General of Infantry [Infanterie]**: /38 Gen. Jeanny-Jules-Marcel Garchèry [+ Member, The Army Council] (Commander-in-Chief, Eighth Army) 08/27/39 MG [Retired] Jean-Baptiste-François-Paul Dufour (Commanding General, Military District III & Commanding General, Group Dufour) 05/25/40
        i. **Assiatant Inspector-General of Infantry**: /37 BG Julien-François-René Martin [+ Inspector of Armored] (Commanding General, Military District XI) /39
        ii. **Chief of Staff, Inspector-General of Infantry**: /39 Col. Marie-Louis Koëltz (Chief of Staff, Eighth Army) /39
    b. **Inspector-General of Cavalry**: /36 BG Charles-Gabriel-Renaud Massiet (retired) /39 MG René-Jacques-Adolphe Prioux (Commanding General, Cavalry Corps) 09/02/39
    c. **Inspector-General of Remount**: /36 MG Jean-Charles-Edmond Wattel (retired?) /38
    d. **Inspector-General of Armor Troops [Chars]**: /37 BG Julien-François-René Martin [+ Assistant Inspector-General of Infantry] (Commanding General, Military District XI) /39 MG Louis-Marie-Joseph-Ferdinand Keller (Commanding General, I Armored Group) /40
        i. **Assistant Inspector of Armored Forces**: /40 BG [Retired '39] Charles-Georges-Antoine Delestraint (Commanding General, 2nd Cavalry Division) /40
    e. **Inspector-General of Artillery [Artillerie]**: /36 LG Charles-Marie Condé [+ Member, Army Council] (Commander-in-Chief, Third Army) 08/27/39 MG [Retired '35] Hippolyte-Maurice-René Jeanpierre (retired) /39 LG [Retired '36] Jean-Jacques Carence (retired) 01/14/40 LG Pierre-Louis-André Boris (retired) 06/25/40 dissolved.
        i. **Assistant Inspector-General of Artillery**: /38 Col. René-Théodre-Marie Ract-Madoux (Director, Department of Artillery Service) 02/27/40
    f. **Inspector-General of Engineers [Génie]**: /36 LG Antoine-Jules-Joseph Huré [+ Member, The Army Council & President, Committee of Engineering Techniques] (retired; /40 Vichy France, Inspector-General of the Military Regions) /38 LG Louis-Auguste-Julien Philippe (retired) /40
        i. **Assistant Inspector-General of Engineers**: /38 Col. Georges-Joseph Froment /39? Col. Paul-Ernest Dumont-Fillon 06/25/40 dissolved.
        ii. **Inspector of Engineering Works**: /38 BG Edouard Bertière
        iii. **Inspector of Technical Engineering Work**: /38 BG Charles Frossard
    g. **Inspector-General of Signals [Transmissions]**:
    h. **Inspector-General of Intendance [Quartermaster] Services**: Int-Gen. 1st Class Théry

- i. **Representative of the Colonial Forces in the Intendant Inspection**: /38 BG Émile-Ange-Marie Fichet
- i. **Inspector-General of Medical Services [Service de Santé]**: MG [Méd-Gen.] Lucien-Georges-Émile-Félicien Plisson
- j. **Inspector-General of the Transportation Service [Train]**:
- k. **Inspector-General of Fortifications & Military Engineering**: /38 BG Charles Griveaud (Commanding General, Military District II) /39
- l. **Inspector-General of Rear Areas**: /39 Gen. [Retired '38] Julien-Claude-Marie-Sosthène Dufieux (retired; /40, President, Special Court-Martial of Gannet) 06/25/40 dissolved.
- m. **Inspector-General, Higher Military Education**: /38 LG Georges-Maurice-Jean Blanchard [+ Member, The Army Council & Director, Higher Military Study Centers] (Commander-in-Chief, First Army) 08/27/39

P. **Department of Artillery Service [Artillerie]**: 02/27/40? BG René-Théodre-Marie Ract-Madoux
1. **Self-Propelled Material Service**: 02/27/40? BG Paul Maisons
2. **Armaments Material Service**: 02/27/40? Col. Rozan
3. **Munitions Service**: 02/27/40? LCol. Ruot
4. **Fuel Service**:
5. **Gas Service**: 02/27/40? LCol. Milliau

Q. **Department of Engineer Service [Génie]**: 02/27/40? BG Henri-Zéphir-Clément Mouflard
1. **Deputy, Department of Engineer Service**: 02/27/40? LCol. Tresoul
2. **Material**: 02/27/40? Col. Stockel
3. **Material & Concrete Materials**: 02/27/40? Maj. Hermil
4. **Billing Quarters**: 02/27/40? LCol. Châlon
5. **Roads**: 02/27/40? LCol. Lipman
6. **Electrical Service**: 02/27/40? Col. Petit
7. **Water Service**: 02/27/40? Maj. Boudier
8. **Forestry Service**: 02/27/40? Conservateur Perrin
9. **Historical Monuments**: 02/27/40? Capt. [Army] Prieur
10. **Camouflage Service**: 02/27/40? Col. Chambon

R. **Department of Signal Service [Transmission]**: 38 MG Louis-Auguste-Julien Philippe (Inspector-General of Engineers) /39 BG Joseph-Charles-Eugène Goetschy (Vichy Inspector of Signal Service) 06/25/40 LCol. Baussac (Head, Department of Signal Service, Chief of the Vichy French General Staff) see **Vichy France**.

S. **Department of Railway Service [Chemin de Fer]**: 02/27/40? Col. François-Jean Kergoat [+ Assistant Chief of the General Staff for Transport] (Artillery Commander, XIX Army Corps) /40 Maj. Gainsette

T. **Department of Road Transpost Service [Transport sur Route]**: 02/27/40? LCol. Ardouin-Dumazet

U. **Department of Waterway Transport Service [Voies Navigables]**: 02/27/40? LCol. Huet

V. **Department of Quartermaster Service [Intendance]**: 02/27/40? Int-Gén 2nd Class Marcel-Auguste Riand

1. **Chief of the Cabinet**: 02/27/40? Int-Mil 3rd Class Bouche
2. **Deputy Director, Department of Quartermaster Service**: 02/27/40? Int-Mil. 1st Class Moreau
3. **Chief of Bureaus**: 02/27/40? LCol. Meillier
4. **Rear Area Zones, General Headquarters**: 02/25/40 MG Étienne Bonnet (retired) /40

W. **Department of Medical Service [Santé]**: /38? Col. Gustavé Worms (Medical Services, Fourth Army) /39 02/27/40? Méd-Col. Bouisson
   1. **1st Section**: 02/27/40? Méd-LCol. Lassaie
   2. **2nd Section**: 02/27/40? Pharmacien-Maj. Velluz
   3. **3rd Section**: 02/27/40? Pharmacien-Maj. Rey

X. **Department of Remount Service [Remontes]**: 02/27/40? MG Henry-Joseph-Gaston Choderlos de Laclos (German prisoner-of-war) 06/22/40

Y. **Department of Veterinary Service [Vétérinaire]**: 02/27/40? BG Pierre-Jules-Joseph Rebeu

Z. **Depart of Army Treasury Service [Trésorie]**: 02/27/40? Pay-Gén. Raynaud

AA. **Department of Army Postal Service [Poste]**: 02/27/40? Ins-Gén. Girodet

AB. **Department of Army Civil Service [État Civil]**: 02/27/40? Int-Mil. 1st Class Jeanrot

AC. **Department of Geographic Service [Géographique]**: 02/27/40? LCol. Jacquinet

AD. **Department of Telegraphic Communication Service [Service de la Correspondance Télégraphique]**: 02/27/40? Maj. Chautant

AE. **Director, Higher Military Study Centers**: /38 LG Georges-Maurice-Jean Blanchard [+ Member, The Army Council & Inspector-General, Higher Military Education] (Commander-in-Chief, First Army) 08/27/39
   1. **Commandant, Mobile Combat School [l'École des Chars de Combat]**: /38 Col. Albert-Charles-Émile Bruché (Commanding General, 2nd Armored Division) 01/16/40
   2. **Director, Artillery Training Course**: /38 Col. Charles-Eugène-Ladisias-Louis Pellion (Artillery Commander, III Army Corps) 09/02/39
   3. **Commandant, Signal Corps School [l'École de Liaison et de Transmissions]**: /38 Col. Henri-Alexandre Calvel (Engineers Officer, X Army Corps) 09/02/39

AF. **Department of Military Chaplains**:
   1. **Catholic**: 02/27/40? Monseigneur Sudour
   2. **Protestant**: 02/27/40? Monsieur le Pasteur Monod
   3. **Jewish**: 02/27/40? Monsieur le Rabbin Liebert

AG. **Recruiting, Organization & Training of Norwegian Forces in French Territories**: /40 LG [Retired '36] Paul-Jean-Louis Azan

AH. *Military Attachés*
   1. **Military Attaché Belgian (Brussels)**: /37 Col. Edmond-Camille-Jean-Bapiste Laurent 06/40 dissolved.
   2. **Military Attaché Germany (Berlin)**: /38 BG Henri-Antoine Didelet (Commanding General, Seine-et-Oise Department, Paris Military District) /39
   3. **Military Attaché Italy (Rome)**: /38 Col. Jean-Benigne-Auguste-Francis Toussaint (Commanding General, 19th Infantry Division) 12/28/39 unknown?

02/01/40 MG Henri Parisot (Deputy Commander, Military District XV) 06/40
4. **Military Attaché Poland (Warsaw)**: /38 Col. Félix-Joseph Musse (Commanding General, 4th Infantry Division) 09/39 dissolved.
5. **Military Attaché Romania (Bucharest)**: /39 BG Victor-Eugène-Lucien-Gabriel Petin (?) 05/40 dissolved.
6. **Military Attaché Turkey (Ankara)**: /39 Col. Paul-Albert Voirin (Commandijng General, 24th Infantry Division) 02/25/40
7. **Military Attaché United Kingdom (London)**: /36 BG Albert Lelong (?) /40

AI. **French Delegation to Moscow**: 10/39? LG Joseph-Edouard-Aimé Doumenc (Deputy Chief of the General Staff, Inspector-General of Anti-Aircraft Defenses, & Member, Supreme Defense Council) 12/39

AJ. *Military Missions*
1. **French Military Mission to Belgian**: 05/11/40 MG Pierre-Louis-Célestin-Michel Champon (Commanding General, XII Army Corps) 06/04/40
2. **French Military Mission to the Netherlands**: /40 Gen. [Retired] Eugène-Désité-Antoine Mittlehauser (Commander-in-Chief, Eastern Mediterranean Theater of Operations) /40
3. **French Military Mission to Paraguay**: /38 Col. Ernest-Émile Petit (Chief of Staff, Commander-in-Chief Free French Forces) /40 MG Paul-Émile Angénot
4. **French Military Mission to Poland**: /39 MG Louis-Augustin-Joseph Faury (retired) /39 Gen. [Retired] Eugène-Désité-Antoine Mittlehauser (in reserve; /39, attached to Grand Quartier Générale) 09/39 dissolved.
5. **French Military Mission to Turkey**: 12/28/39 MG Charles-Henri-Paul d'Arbonneau (retired) /40
6. **French Military Mission to the Dutch Army**: /40 BG Georges-Eugène-Joseph Lascroux [+ Commanding General, 17th Infantry Division (#1] 05/40

AK. **French Liaison Officer to Polish General Staff in Exile**: /39 MG [Retired] Louis-Pierre-Henri Demain (retired) /40

AL. *Commissions or Committees*
1. **Commission for the Studies of Fortified Zones**
   a. **Members**
      /39 LG [Retired '35] Ferréol-François-Gabriel Lefort (at disposal of the Ministry of War) /40
2. **Interdepartmental Commission of Control & Revision of the Special Assignments**: /39 BG [Retired '34] Philippe-Paul Matter (/42, retired; /44, recalled; /44, Chairman, Commission of Purification of Rehabilitation of Military Personnel) 06/25/40 dissolved.
3. **President, Executive Committee of Friendship to Africa**: /39 LG Henri-Albert Niessel (retired) /39

AM. **At Disposal of Chief of the Army General Staff**:
/39 BG Émile-Jean-Gabriel Carlès (Commanding General, Colonial Group South East; /39, Commanding General, 6th Colonial Division) 12/03/39
/39 BG Louis-Eugène Faucher **[NOTE:** used to organize a Czechoslovakian Legion**]** (/43, entered the Resistance; /43 Head, Resistance Bordeaux Region; /44, arrested by the Germans; /44 to /45, deported) 06/25/40

dissolved.

Colonial Forces

Chief of the French Empire [Colonial Forces] General Staff: /35? LG Alphonse-Joseph Georges (Deputy Commander-in-Chief, Land Forces) 09/39?
/40 Gen. Jules-Antoine Bührer [+ Inspector-General of Colonial Forces & Inspector of Colonial Forces in France & President, Consultative Committee of Colonial Defense] (retired) /41
/40 LG Émile-Jean-Gabriel Carlès (retired) /41 - see **Vichy France**.
A.   **Colonial Forces in France**: see **Corps** section.

Air Force Headquarters
[Armée de l'Air Headquarters]

Supreme Air Council [Conseil Supérieur de l'Air]:
A. **Vice Chairman, Supreme Air Council**: 02/21/39 LG Joseph Vuillemin [FAF] [+ Commander-in-Chief, Air Force & Inspector-General, Home Air Defense] (Inspector-General of the Air Force) 06/24/40

Commander-in-Chief, Air Force [Chefs d'État-Major Général de l'Armée de l'Air]:
10/15/36 Gen. Philippe Féquant [FAF] 02/21/38 LG Joseph Vuillemin [FAF] [+ Vice Chairman, Supreme Air Council & Inspector-General, Home Air Defense] (06/24/40, Inspector-General of the Air Force) 07/04/40 vacant - see **Vichy France**.
A. **Inspector, Medico-Physiological Services of the Air Force**: /38 BG Pierre-Jules-Émile Beyne

Navy High Command

Minister of Military Marine [Navy]: /36 LOUIS de CHAPPEDELAINE (04/10/38, Minister of Merchant Marine) 06/22/37 CÉSAR CAMPINCHI (Justice Minister) 01/18/38 WILLIAM BERTRAND 03/13/38 CÉSAR CAMPINCHI 06/16/40 Adm. of the Fl. Jean-Louis-Xavier-François Darlan [FN] [+ Chief of the General Staff for Naval Operations & Commander-in-Chief, Navy; + 06/16/40, Minister of Merchant Marine; + 06/22/40, Commander-in-Chief, Vichy France Armed Forces] 07/10/40 see **Vichy France**.
- A. **Major General assistant to the Minister**: 09/01/39? RA François-Félix Michelier [FN] (Commanding Officer, Casablanca [Morocco] Naval Force) 11/08/42?
    1. **1st Bureau - Administration**:
    2. **4th Bureau - Supply**
- B. **Engineer-General of Maritime Engineering**: /44 MG Louis-Lazare Kahn.
    1. **Director, Centre of Construction of Naval Arms**: /43 BG Louis-Lazare Kahn (Engineer-General of Maritime Engineering) /44

Commander-in-Chief, Navy: /39 Adm. of the Fl. Jean-Louis-Xavier-François Darlan [FN] [+ Chief of the General Staff for Naval Operations; + 06/16/40, Minister of Marine {Military & Merchant}; + 06/22/40, Commander-in-Chief, Vichy France Armed Forces] 07/40 see **Vichy France**.
- A. **Chief of Staff, Commander-in-Chief, Navy**: 09/01/39? RA Maurice-Athanase le Luc [FN] 07/40 see **Vichy France**.
    1. **2nd Bureau - Intelligence**:
    2. **3rd Bureau - Operations**
- B. **Naval General Staff**
- C. **Naval Commands**
    1. **High Seas Force**
    2. **Raiding Force**
    3. **Admiral North**
    4. **Admiral West**
    5. **Admiral South**
    6. **Admiral Antilles**
    7. **Admiral Africa**
    8. **Admiral Far East (Indochina)**

Naval General Staff

Chief of the General Staff for Naval Operations: /36 Adm. of the Fl. Jean-Louis-Xavier-François Darlan [FN] [+ /39, Commander-in-Chief, Navy; + 06/16/40, Minister of Marine {Military & Merchant}; + 06/22/40, Commander-in-Chief, Vichy France Armed Forces] 07/40 07/40 see **Vichy France**.

A. **Naval Attaché London**: 09/01/39? VA Odend'hal [FN] [+ Head, French Naval Mission to London] (?) /40 RA A. Sala [FN]
B. **Naval Mission to London**: 09/01/39? VA Odend'hal [FN] [+ Naval Attaché London]
C. **Naval Liaison Officer to British Royal Navy in Egypt**: /39? Capt. Philippe Auboyneau [FN] (07/20/40, fled to England and joins Free French Movement; /40, Commanding Officer, Free French Pacific Naval Forces) 06/22/40

Military Districts

Military District of France, November 1939
Military District XIX is Algeria in North Africa
Military Districts X and XII was disbanded in 1939

Paris Military District [Région Militaire de Paris]: /36 LG Antoine-Marie-Benoit Besson (The Army Council) /36 /36 LG Victor Bourret (Member, The Army Council) /39 /37 LG Gaston-Henri-Gustavé Billotte [+ Member, the Army Council; + Military-Governor of Paris; + to /38, President, Consultative Committee for Colonial Affairs] (Commander-in-Chief, 1st Army Group) /39 /39 LG Alfred-Marie-Joseph-Louis Montagne (Commanding General, XII Army Corps) 09/02/39 Gen. [Retired '39] Pierre Héring [+ Military-Governor of Paris & President, Consultative Committee for Colonial Defense] 11/39? MG [Retired '38] Octave-Charles Lanoix (Assistant Military Governor of Paris) 06/04/40 LG Henri-Fernand Dentz (Commanding General, Vichy Military District XV) 06/25/40 disbanded; reformed /44 MG Georges-Marie-Joseph Revers.

A. **Assistant Commander, Paris Military District**: /34 MG Octave-Charles Lanoix (retired) /38 BG Pierre-Joseph Herbillon (Commandant of Paris) /39
B. **Chief of Staff, Paris Military District**: /36 Col. Ernest-André Daudin /38 Col. Louis-Michel-Marie-Joseph Michel (Commanding General, Rhône Defense Sector) /39
C. *Components* - **Paris Military District**
    1. **Seine Department**: /35 BG Pierre-Joseph Herbillon (Assistant Commander, Paris Military District) /38 BG Joseph-Antoine-Jacques-Louis Baudet (09/03/39, Commanding General, 71st Infantry Division) /38 BG Georges-Auguste Schmidlin
        a. **Commandant of Paris**: 11/39? BG Pierre-Joseph Herbillon (in reserve/retired) /40
    2. **Seine-et-Oise Department**: /39 BG Henri-Antoine Didelet (Commanding General, 9th Motorized Infantry Division) 11/13/39 BG [Retired '38 & '39] Gaston-Marie-Joseph de Chomereau, Count of Saint-André (retired) /40
    3. **Seine-et-Marne Department**: /38 BG Paul-Eugène-Maurice Drôme (retired) /38 unknown? 11/39? BG Mignon
D. **Military Preparation Services, Paris Military District**: /36 Col. Pierre-Nicolas-Louis Decharme (Commanding General, 35th Infantry Division) 09/02/39
E. **Assistant Director of Military Training, Paris Military District**: /38 BG Jules-Henri Watrin (retired; /39, recalled; 10/39?, General Officer Commanding, Dunkerque Subdivision Group, Military District I)
F. **Artillery, Paris Military District**: /38 BG Gaston-Ernest Renondeau (Commanding General, 2nd Infantry Division) 09/02/39
G. **Intendant [Quartermaster] Service, Paris Military District**: /38 Col. Henri-Charles Thomassin
H. **Medical Services, Paris Military District**: /36 BG Charles-Yriex-Jean-Bernard Gay-Bonnet (?) /38 BG Antoine-Jean Fayet (?) 06/22/40 dissolved; reformed /44 Col. Lucien-Eugène-Paul-Gabriel Jame.
I. **Gendarmerie [Military Police], Paris Military District**: /38 MG Théodre-Benoit-Honoré-Louis Gest

Military District I [Ie Région Militaire] (Nord & Pas de Calais Departments; HQ: Lille): /37 MG Joseph-Edouard-Aimé Doumenc (Head, French Delegation in Moscow) /39 MG Théodore-Marcel Sciard (Commanding General, I Motorized Army Corps) 08/27/39 LG [Retired '37] Eugène-Henri-Jaques Pagézy (General Officer Commanding, Military District VIII) /40 unknown? 06/25/40 disbanded.

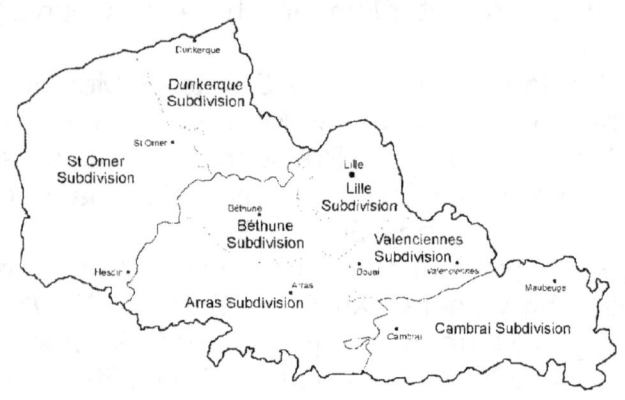

A. **Components - Military District I**
1. **Dunkerque Subdivision Group**: 10/39? MG [Retired '38] Jules-Henri Watrin (retired) /40
    a. **Dunkerque Subdivision**:
    b. **St-Omer Subdivision**:
2. **Lille Subdivision Group**: 10/39? BG Hardoun de Grosville
    a. **Lille Subdivision**:
    b. **Béthune Subdivision**:
    c. **Arras Subdivision**:
    d. **Valenciennes Subdivision**:
3. **Independent Subdivision**
    a. **Cambrai Independent Subdivision**:

B. **Engineers, Military District I**: /38 Col. André-Pierre Nicolle
C. **Intendant [Quartermaster] Services, Military District I**: /36 Col. Émile-Jules-Pierre Le Loarer
D. **Medical Services, Military District I**: /39? Col. Henri-Ernest-Christophe Lortholary
E. **Military-Governor, Dunkerque**: /38 BG Julian-Maurice Tencé [+ Commanding General, Flandres Defense Sector] (Commanding General, Northern Group; 12/27/39, Commanding General, Belfort Fortified Region) 08/31/39

Military District II [IIe Région Militaire] (Somme, Oise, Aisne, & Ardennes Departments;

HQ: Amiens): /36 LG André-Georges Corap (Commanding General, Ardennes Army Detachment) /39 MG Charles Griveaud (09/12/40, Commanding General, 11th Military Division; /40, retired) 09/39 MG [Retired] Marie-François-Armand-Roger Barbeyrac de Saint-Maurice [+ to 01/01/40, Commanding General, 57th Infantry Division & to 05/25/40, Commanding General, 87th African Infantry Division] (retired) 06/01/40 LG Marcel-Charles-Joseph Lamson (?) 06/25/40 disbanded.

A. *Components* - **Military District II**
   1. **Amiens Subdivision Group**: 10/39? BG Gondy
      a. **Amiens Subdivision**:
      b. **Beauvais Subdivision**:
      c. **Laon Subdivision**:
      d. **Mézières Subdivision**: /39 Col. Rocca
B. **Artillery, Military District II**: 05/18/40 BG [Retired '38] Joseph-Armand-Victor Gain (retired) 06/25/40 dissolved.

Military District III [IIIe Région Militaire] (Seine, Inférieure, Eure, Calvados, & Manche Departments; HQ: Rouen): /37 MG Aubert-Achille-Jules Frère (Commanding General, Military District X) 08/23/39 MG Léon-Benoit de Fornel de La Laurencie (Commanding General, III Army Corps) 09/02/39 MG Issaly (?) /40 MG Pierre-Jean-Marie Pégay [Commanding General, Group Dufour] (retired) 05/25/40 LG [Retired] Jean-Baptiste-François-Paul Dufour [+ Commanding General, Group Dufour] (retired) 06/25/40 disbanded; reformed /44 LG Paul-Louis-Victor-Marie Legentilhomme.

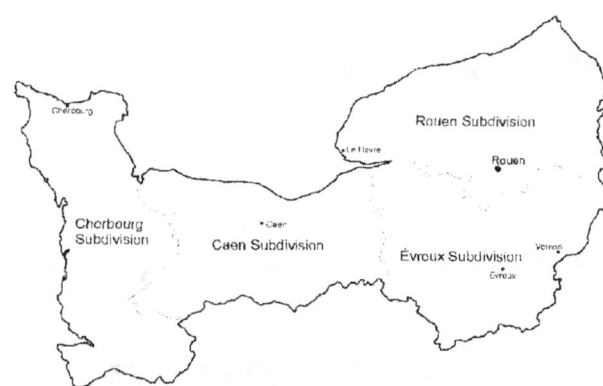

A. *Components* - **Military District III**
   1. **Rouen Subdivision Group**: /38 Col. Elophe-Jean Larcher (Chief of Staff, XVII Army Corps) 09/02/39 BG Lallement
      a. **Rouen Subdivision**:
      b. **Evreux Subdivision**:
      c. **Cherbourg Subdivision**:
      d. **Caen Subdivision**:
   2. **Cherbourg Subdivision Group** (10/39, dissolved).
      a. **Cherbourg Subdivision** (10/39, incorporated into Rouen Subdivision Group)
      b. **Havre Subdivision** (10/39, absorbed by other subdivisions)
      c. **St Lô Subdivision** (10/39, absorbed by other subdivisions)
B. **Artillery, Military District III**: /38 BG Gabriel-Léopard Glück
C. **Engineering, Military District III**: unknown?
   1. **Engineering, Havre Department**: /38 Col. Calixte-Louis-François Roussel
D. **Intendant [Quartermaster] Service, Military District III**: /38 Col. Gustavé-Bruno-Henri Cavailher /39 Col. Félix-François-Maurice Cuq
E. **Medical Services, Military District III**: /39 Col. Maurice-Louis-Étienne Pilod (Director, Medical Services, Eighth Army) /40

Military District IV [I^{VE} Région Militaire] (Eure-et-Loir, Orne, Sarthe, Mayenne, Ille-et-Vilaine & Côtes-de Nord (less Guingamp District) Departments; HQ: Le Mans): /36 MG Pierre-Louis-André Boris (Commanding General, IV Army Corps) 09/02/39 LG Étienne (?) 06/04/40 MG Coudanne (?) 06/25/40 disbanded.

   A.   *Components* - **Military District IV**
       1.   **Rennes Subdivision Group**: 10/39? MG Bazoche
          a.   **Rennes Subdivision**:
          b.   **St-Brieux Subdivision**:
       2.   **Mans Subdivision Group**: 10/39? MG Arguerolle
          a.   **Le Mans Subdivision**:
          b.   **Chartres Subdivision**:
          c.   **Alençon Subdivision**:
          d.   **Laval Subdivision**:
   B.   **Intendent [Quartermaster] Service, Military District IV**: /36 BG Marie-Philippe Robinet-Marcy

Military District V [Ve Région Militaire] (Loiret, Loir-et-Cher, Cher & Nièvre Departments; HQ: Orléans): /38 MG Darius-Paul Bloch-Dassault (Commanding General, V Motorized Army Corps) 10/39? LG [Retired '38] Pierre Michelin (retired) 06/25/40 disbanded.

   A.   *Components* - **Military District V**
       1.   **Orléans Subdivision Group**: 10/39? unknown?
          a.   **Orléans Subdivision**:
          b.   **Blois Subdivision**:
          c.   **Bourges Subdivision**:
          d.   **Nevers Subdivision**:
   B.   **Intendant [Quartermaster] Service, Military District V**: /36 Col. Auguste-Marie-Maurice Le Quintrec
   C.   **Inspector of Gendarmerie, Military District V**: /38 Col. Pierre-Léon Nicolet

Military District VI [VIᵉ Région Militaire] (Meuse & Marne Departments, Thionville & Briey District of Meuthe et Moselle & Moselle Departments; HQ: Châlons-sur-Marne): /36 LG Henri-Honoré Giraud [+ Military-Governor, Metz] (Member, The Army Council) 08/23/39 MG Lucien Loizeau [+ Military Governor, Metz] (Commanding General, VI Army Corps) 08/31/39 LG [Retired '39] Charles-Gabriel-Renaud Massiet (Commanding General, Levant Mobile Force) 10/23/39 MG Pierre-Paul-Jacques Cabotte (retired) 06/25/40 disbanded.

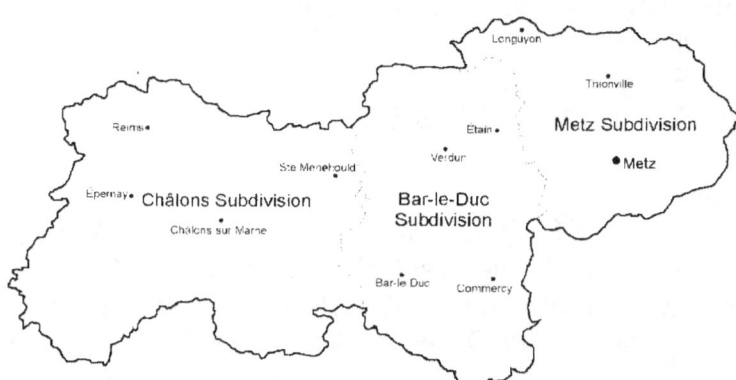

A. **Deputy Commander, Military District VI**: /38 BG Joseph-Antoine-Sylvain-Raoul de Verdillac (Commanding General, 6th North African Infantry Division) 11/01/39
B. *Components* - **Military District VI**
   1. **Châlons Subdivision Group**: 10/39? BG Foisy
      a. **Châlons Subdivision**:
      b. **Bar-le-Duc Subdivision**:
      c. **Metz Subdivision**: /35 MG Louis-Eugène Hubert [+ Commanding General, Metz Fortified Region] (Commanding General, Military District XX)
C. **Engineers, Military District VI**: /38 Col. Henry-François Vernillat (Commanding General, 43rd Infantry Division) 08/23/39
D. **Intendent [Quartermaster] Service, Military District VI**: /36 Col. René Lévy
E. **Governor-General of Verdun** (09/20/39): LG René-Paul Dubuisson [+ 06/13/40, Commanding General, Group Dubuisson] (to /45, German prisoner-of-war; /49 condemned to 4 years imprisonment for collaboration with the enemy) /06/25/40 disbanded.
F. **Military-Governor, Metz**: /36 LG Henri-Honoré Giraud [+ Commanding General, Military District VI] (Member, The Army Council) 08/23/39 MG Lucien Loizeau [+ Commanding General, Military District VI] (Commanding General, VI Army Corps) 08/31/39 BG [Retired] Paulin-André-Jean Le Bleu (Commanding General, Vannes Subdivision, Military District XI) /40 MG Edouard-Octave-Jules Brussaux

Military District VII [VIIᵉ Région Militaire] (Haute-Marne, Haute-Saône, Haut-Rhin, Doubs, Jura & Belfort Departments; HQ: Besançon): /35 MG Georges-Maurice-Jean Blanchard (Member, The Army Council) /38 MG René-Jacques-Adolphe Prioux (Inspector-General of Cavalry) /39 MG Marius Daille [+12/16/39 to 02/09/40, Commanding General, Army Corps du Jura; + 02/09/40, Commanding General, XLV Fortress Army Corps] (interned in Switzerland) 06/25/40 LG /39 MG Onésime-Paul Noël (?) /40 MG Marie-Alphonse-Théodore-René-Adrian Desmazes (Commanding General, 7th Military Division) 09/12/40 disbanded.

307

A. ***Components* - Military District VII**
   1. **Besançon Subdivision Group**: 10/39? BG Duhesme
      a. **Besançon Subdivision**:
      b. **Lons-le-Saulnier Subdivision**:
   2. **Chaumont Subdivision Group**: 10/39? MG Bret
      a. **Chaumont Subdivision**:
      b. **Vesoul Subdivision**:
   3. **Belfort Subdivision Group**: 08/30/39 BG Louis-Germain Girol [+ Commanding General, Belfort Defense Sector] (Commanding General, Altkirch Fortified Sector) 10/29/39 unknown? 03/15/40 MG Louis-Germain Girol [+ Commanding General, Belfort Defense Sector] (?) 06/22/40 disbanded
      a. **Belfort Subdivision**:
      b. **Mulhouse Subdivision**:
   4. **Independent Subdivision**
      a. **Colmar Independent Subdivision**: /38 BG Louis-Gustavé-Adolphe Coradin [+ Commanding General, Colmar Fortified Sector] (Commanding General, 54th Infantry Division) 11/27/39
B. ***Components* - Military District VII (07/40)**
   1. **Jura Department**
   2. **Saône-et-Loire Department**
C. **Engineers, Military District VII**: /36 Col. Maurice-Jules-Zacharie Grenet (Engineers Commander, Eighth Army) 08/27/39 unknown? /40 BG Maurice-Jules-Zacharie Grenet (retired) /40
D. **Military-Governor, Belfort**: /37 BG Jean Guillemont [+ Commanding General, Belfort Fortified Region] (acting Commanding General, XLIV Fortress Army Corps) 12/22/39

Military District VIII [VIIIe Région Militaire] (Yonne, Aube, Côte-d'Or & Saône-et-Loir Departments; HQ: Dijon): /33 LG Eugène-Henri-Jaques Pagézy (retired) /37 MG Victor-Henri Schweizguth (retired; /40 recalled; /40 Commanding General, Military District VIII) 08/39 MG Pierre-Paul-Jacques Grandsard (Commanding General, X Army Corps) 09/02/39 LG [Retired '38] Paul-Louis-François Villain (retired) /40 LG [Retired '37] Eugène-Henri-Jaques Pagézy (retired) /40 MG [Retired '39] Victor-Henri Schweizguth (Head, Prisoner-of-War Services, Army General Staff) 06/25/40 disbanded; reformed /44

A. ***Components* - Military District VIII**
   1. **Dijon Subdivision Group**: 10/39? BG Févre
      a. **Dijon Subdivision**:
      b. **Châlons-sur-Saône Subdivision**:
      c. **Auxerre Subdivision**:
      d. **Troyes Subdivision**:
B. **Engineers, Military District VIII**: BG Ernest-Alidor Planche
C. **Intendent [Quartermaster] Services, Military District VIII**: /38 BG Mario-Olivier Galmiche

D. **Medical Services, Military District VIII**: /38 Col. Xavier-Marie Cristau (Director, Medical Services, Ninth Army) 11/05/39 unknown? 06/25/40 dissolved; reformed /44 Col. Georges-André Hugonot.

Military District IX [IXᵉ Région Militaire] (Indre-et-Loire, Maine-et-Loire, Deux-Sèvres, Vienne, Indre, Haute-Vienne, Charente & Dordogne Departments; HQ: Tours): /38 MG Auguste-Marie-Émile Laure (Commanding General, IX Army Corps) 09/05/39 MG Henri-Louis Vary (retired) 07/40 LG Odilon-Léonard-Théophile Picquendar (Chief of the Vichy Army General Staff) /40 MG Alfred-Marie-Joseph-Louis Montagne (Commanding General, 9th Military Division) 09/12/40 redesignated **9th Military Division** - see **Vichy France 9th Military Division**.

A. *Components - Military District IX*
1. **Tours Subdivision Group**: 10/39? BG Herlant
   a. **Tours Subdivision**:
   b. **Angers Subdivision**:
   c. **Poitiers Subdivision**:
   d. **Niort Subdivision** (10/25/39):
2. **Limoges Subdivision Group**: 10/39? BG Michet de la Baume (Commanding Officer, Savoie Fortified Sector) 01/01/40
   a. **Limoges Subdivision**:
   b. **Châteauroux Subdivision**: /39 BG [Retired '38] Gaston-Marie-Joseph de Chomereau, Count of Saint-André (retired) /39 vacant /39 BG [Retired '38 & '39] Gaston-Marie-Joseph de Chomereau, Count of Saint-André (General Officer Commanding, Seine-et-Oise Department, Paris Military District) 11/39?
   c. **Angoulême Subdivision**:
   d. **Périgueux Subdivision**:
B. *Components - Military District IX* (07/40, Vichy France)
   1. **Dordogne Department**: 07/40 BG Georges-Edmond-Lucien Barré (Head, French Delegation to the Italian Sub-Commission for Demilitarization of the Libyan Border Zone) /40
   2. **Indre Department**
   3. **Vienne Department**: /40 MG Georges-Eugène-Joseph Lascroux (Commanding General, Fez Territorial Division) /40
   4. **Haute-Vienne Department**
C. **Engineers, Military District IX**: /36 Col. Anne-Baltbazar Suchet
D. **Medical Services, Military District IX**: /36 LCol. Auguste Schneider (Medical Services, Third Army) 08/27/39

Military District X [Xᵉ Région Militaire] (pre-war; /39 abolished; 05/10/40 was in the beginning stages of reforming from Military District XX, when France was invaded): /39 LG Aubert-Achille-Jules Frère (Military-Governor of Strasbourg, Military District XX) /39 LG [Retired '37] Marie-Robert Altmayer (retired) /39 abolished; reformed 05/10/40 LG [Retired '36] Jean-Marcel-Robert Guitry (to /41, German prisoner-of-war; /41, died in a Prisoner-of-War

Camp) /40 disbanded; reformed /44 MG Jacques-Fernand Schwartz

Military District XI [XIᵉ Région Militaire]: Loire-Inférieure, Vendée, Finistère, Morbihan Departments & Guingamp District of Côtes du Nord Department; HQ: Nantes): /35 MG Henri-Joseph-Léon Herscher (at disposal of the Chief of the Army General Staff; /39, retired) /39 MG Debailleul (?) /39 MG Julien-François-René Martin (at disposal of the Minister of War) 06/25/40 disbanded.

- A. **Components - Military District XI**
  1. **Nantes Subdivision Group**: /39? BG [Retired '36] Gaëtan-Louis-Elie [Georges-Louis] Germain (Commanding General, French Somaliland) 07/25/40
     - a. **Nantes Subdivision**: /38 Col. Pierre-Louis-Arthur-Marie Beziers-Lafosse (Infantry Commander, 22ⁿᵈ Infantry Division) 08/23/39
     - b. **La Roche-sur-Yon Subdivision**:
     - c. **Vannes Subdivision**: /40 BG [Retired] Paulin-André-Jean Le Bleu (retired) 06/25/40 dissolved.
     - d. **Lorient Subdivision**:
  2. **Brest Subdivision Group**: /38 Col. André-Georges-Louis Tranchant (Infantry Commander, 4ᵗʰ Colonial Infantry Division) 10/39? unknown?
     - a. **Brest Subdivision**:
       - i. **Commandant, Brest**: /40 BG Jean-Eugène-Marie Charbonneau (Commanding General, Oran Territorial Division) /40
     - b. **Quimper Subdivision**:
     - c. **Guingamp Subdivision**:
- B, **Artillery, Military District XI**: /38 Col. Joseph-Armand-Victor Gain (retired; /39, Artillery Officer, 22ⁿᵈ Infantry Division) /38 Col. Jean-Marie-Léon Etcheberrigaray (attached to The Army Council) /39 Col. Paul-Gilbert-Eugène Frénal (Artillery Commander, XI Army Corps) /39
- C. **Intendant [Quartermaster] Service, Military District XI**: /38 Col. Pierre-Auguste Bravais

Military District XII [XIIᵉ Région Militaire] (/34 abolished; 05/10/40 was in the beginning stages of reforming from Military District VI, when France was invaded): /39 MG Jean-Adolphe-Louis-Robert Flavigny (Commanding General, XXI Army Corps) 08/26/39 unknown? 06/22/40 LG Aubert-Achille-Jules Frère (Commanding General, Military District XIV) /40 MG [Retired '37] Marie-Robert-Guy Marin de Montmarin (retired) 07/40 MG Joseph-Charles-Robert Jeannel (Commanding General, 12ᵗʰ Military District) 09/12/40 redesignated **12ᵗʰ Military Division** - see **Vichy France 12ᵗʰ Military Division**.
- A. **Deputy Commander, Military District XII** (05/10/40): unknown? 06/25/40 MG Joseph-Charles-Robert Jeannel (Commanding General, Military District XII) 07/40
- B. **Chief of Staff, Military District XII** (05/10/40): Col. Paul-Arsène-Gérard Devinck (Chief of Staff, Commander-in-Chief, North Africa) 05/23/40 Col. Marcel Rime-

Bruneau (Commanding Officer, 4th Zouaves Infantry Regiment) 06/25/40 dissolved.

Military District XIII [XIIIᵉ Région Militaire] (Allier, Creuse, Puy-de-Dôme, Corrèze, Cantal, Loire & Haute-Loire Departments; HQ: Clermont Ferrand): /36 MG Eugène-Georges Ducasse (at disposal of the Commander-in-Chief, Armed Forces; /39, retired) /39 MG Georges-Henri-Jean-Baptiste Misserey (Commanding General, XIII Aqrmy Corps) 08/21/39 MG [Retired '38] Gaspard-Henri-Marie-Gaston d'Humières (retired) 10/39? LG [Retired '37] Charles-Joseph Chedeville (retired) 06/22/40 LG Louis-Marie Jamet (at disposal, Commander-in-Chief, Vichy France Land Forces; /40, retired) /40 LG Pierre-Paul-Jacques Grandsard (Commanding General, 13th Military Division) 09/12/40 redesignated **13th Military Division** - see **Vichy France 13th Military Division**.

A. **Deputy Commander, Military District XIII**: 06/25/40 MG Jean-Léon-Albert Langlois (Head of the Reorganization of Cavalry Supervision; /40, Inspector of Cavalry) /40
B. *Components - Military District XIII*
   1. **Clermont Ferrand Subdivision Group**: /38 Col. René-Jules Troublé (Commanding General, 26th Infantry Division) 09/02/39? BG Henry-Joseph-Gaston Choderlos de Laclos (Department of Remount Services, General Staff) 02/27/40?
      a. **Clermont Ferrand Subdivision**:
         i. **Rhône-Alps Department**
            A. **Engineers, Rhône-Alps Department**: /38 Maj. Roger-Charles-Marcel Guérithault
      b. **Tulle Subdivision**:
      c. **Aurillac Subdivision**:
   2. **Moulins Subdivision Group**: 10/39? unknown?
      a. **Moulins Subdivision**:
      b. **Gueret Subdivision**:
   3. **St-Étienne Subdivision Group**: 10/39? MG de Gérault de Langalene
      a. **St-Étienne Subdivision**:
      b. **Le Puy Subdivision**:
C. *Components - Military District XIII* (07/40, Vichy France)
   1. **Allier Department**: 07/40 BG Louis-Gustavé Bérard (Deputy Commander, 17th Military Division) /41
   2. **Cantal Department**: 07/40 BG Jean-Marie-Léon Etcheberrigaray (Commanding General, 2nd Military Division) /40
   3. **Corrèze Department**
   4. **Creuse Department**
   5. **Loire Department**
   6. **Haute-Loire Department**: 07/40 MG Maurice Viant (Commanding General, Dakar Defense Position, French West Africa) /40
   7. **Puy-de-Dôme Department**: 07/40 BG Jean-Joseph-Marie-Gabriel de Lattre

    de Tassigny (Deputy Commander, 13th Military Division) /41
D. **Intendant [Quartermaster] Service, Military District XIII**:
  1. **Assistant Head, Intendant [Quartermaster] Service, Military District XIII**: /38 Col. Jean-Jacques-Alexandre Cumin

Military District XIV [XIVᵉ Région Militaire] (Haute-Savoie, Ain, Rhône, Isère, Savoie, Hautes-Alpes & Drômes Departments; HQ Lyon): /38 MG Robert-Auguste Touchon [+ Military-Governor, Lyon] (Commanding General, XIV Army Corps) 09/02/39 MG Hartung (?) 07/40 LG Robert-Auguste Touchon (retired) /40 MG Paul-André Doyen (acting; Deputy Commander, Military District XIV) /40 LG Aubert-Achille-Jules Frère (Military-Governor of Lyon, Military District XIV & Commanding General, 14th Military District) 09/12/40 redesignated **14th Military Division** - see **Vichy France 14th Military Division**.

 A. **Deputy Commander, Military District XIV**: /40 MG Paul-André Doyen (Head, French Mission, Armistice Commission, Wiesbaden) 09/12/40 dissolved.
 B. *Components* - **Military District XIV**
  1. **Lyon Subdivision Group**: 10/39? BG Jean-Joseph-Marie de Mesmay
   a. **Lyon Subdivision**:
   b. **Bourg Subdivision**:
  2. **Grenoble Subdivision Group**: 10/39? BG Jean-Auguste-Velentin Coste
   a. **Grenoble Subdivision**:
   b. **Valence Subdivision**:
   c. **Gap Subdivision**:
  3. **Chambéry Subdivision Group**: 10/39? unknown?
   a. **Chambéry Subdivision**:
   b. **Annecy Subdivision**:
C. *Components* - **Military District XIV** (07/40, Vichy France)
 1. **Ain Department**
 2. **Haute-Alps Department**: 07/40 BG Henri-Louis-Léon Cyvogt (Deputy Commander, 12th Military Division) /41
 3. **Drôme Department**
 4. **Isère Department**
 5. **Rhône Department**
 6. **Savoie Department**
 7. **Haute-Savoie Department**: 07/40 BG Marie-Cyrille-Victor Debeney (Infantry Commander, 7th Military Division) /40 MG Fernand-Zacharie-Joseph Lenclud (Deputy Commander, 7th Military Division) /41
  a. **Haute-Savoie Subdivision**: 07/40 unknown? /40 BG Fernand-

Zacharie-Joseph Lenclud (Commanding General, Haute-Savoie Department, Military District XIV) /40
- D. **Engineers, Military District XIV**: /38 BG Barthélémy-Joseph-Alexandre Piraud
- E. *Military-Governors*
    1. **Military-Governor of Lyon**: /38 MG Robert-Auguste Touchon [+ Commanding General, Military District XIV] (Commanding General, XIV Army Corps) 09/02/39 unknown? 09/12/40 LG Aubert-Achille-Jules Frère [+ Commanding General, 14th Military Division] (Commanding General, II Group of Military Divisions) /41 LG Louis-Albert-Pierre Robert de Saint-Vincent [+ Commanding General, 14th Military Division] (retired) 11/42
    2. **Military-Governor of Grenoble**: /39? MG Charles-Victor-André Laffargue

Military District XV [XVe Région Militaire] (Gard, Vauduse, Bassees-Alps, Alpes-Maritimes, Var, Ardèche & Bouches-du-Rhône Departments and Corsica (Corse); HQ: Marseille): /37 MG René-Henri Olry (Commanding General, XV Army Corps) 09/02/39 MG Clére (?) /40 LG Henri-Fernand Dentz (Commanding General, 15th Military Division) 09/12/40 redesignated **15th Military Division** - see **Vichy France 15th Military Division**.

- A. **Deputy Commander, Military District XV**: /39 BG Amédée Duron (Commanding General 30th Alpine Infantry Division) 08/22/39 unknown? 06/40 MG Henri Parisot (at disposal, Vichy France Commander-in-Chief, Armed Forces; 09/12/40, Vice-President, French Delegation to the Italian Armistice Committee) 07/40 MG Jules-Philippe-Octave Decamp (Commanding General, 8th Military Division) and/or MG Paul-Henry Gérodias (at disposal of the Vichy Minister of National Defense; /40, Head, Secretary-General of National Defense) 09/12/40 dissolved.
- B. *Components* - **Military District XV**
    1. **Marseille Subdivision Group**: 10/39? BG Jeanpert
        - a. **Marseille Subdivision**:
            - i. **Commandant, Marseille**: /38 Col. Pierre-Désiré-Robert Didio (Infantry Commander, 30th Alpine Infantry Division) /39
        - b. **Toulon Subdivision**:
    2. **Avignon Subdivision Group**: 10/39? BG Octave-Georges-Alexandre Desprez (retired) 06/25/40 dissolved.
        - a. **Avignon Subdivision**:
        - b. **Nimes Subdivision**:

              c.   **Privas Subdivision**:
       3.   **Nice Subdivision Group**: /38 BG René-Alphonse-Joseph Magnien (Deputy Commander, Alps-Maritime Fortified Sector) /38 BG Lemoine
              a.   **Nice Subdivision**:
              b.   **Digne Subdivision**:
       4.   **Independent Subdivision**
              a.   **Bastia Independent Subdivision** (Corsica): /38 Col. Amédée-Jean-Joseph-Jules-Stanislas Mollard (/41, Head of Resistance on Corsica; /42, fled to Algeria; Military-Governor of Corsica) /40
C.   *Components* - **Military District XV** (07/40, Vichy France)
       1.   **Alpes-de-Haute Province**
       2.   **Alpes-Maritime Department**
       3.   **Ardèche Department**
       4.   **Bouches-du-Rhône Department**: 07/11/40 MG Paul-Hippolyte Arlabosse (Deputy Commander-in-Chief, Levant) /40
       5.   **Gard Department**
       6.   **Var Department**: 07/40 MG Joseph-Louis-François Hassler
       7.   **Vaucluse Department**: 07/40 MG Louis-Albert-Pierre Robert de Saint-Vincent (Commanding General, 7th Military Division) /40
       8.   **Corsica**: 07/40 BG Agathon-Jules-Joseph Deligne (/42, Commanding General, Division Algiers) /40 Col. Jacques-Émile-Louis-Léon Humbert
D.   **Engineers, Military District XV**: /38 Col. Paul-Alphonse-Léon Gaglio /39 Col. Jacob-Raoul El Ghozi (Engineers Commander, Army Corps du Jara) 12/16/39
E.   **Medical Services, Military District XV**: /38? Col. Henri-Ernest-Christophe Lortholary (Medical Services, Military District I) /39?
F.   **Military-Governor of Corsica** (/43): MG Amédée-Jean-Joseph-Jules-Stanislas Mollard (retired) /45

Military District XVI [XVIᵉ Région Militaire] (Tarn, Lozère, Aveyron, Hérault, Pyrénées Orient & Aude Departments; HQ: Montpellier; 07/40?, reformed as Vichy **16th Military Division**): /36 MG Victor-Nicolae Goudot (retired) /38 MG Marie-Bertrand-Alfred Fagalde (Commanding General, XVI Army Corps) 08/27/39 LG [Retired '38] Charles-Gustavé Hanote (retired; /40, entered the resistance) /40 LG Léon-Benoit de Fornel de La Laurencie (Head, French Delegation for the Occupied Territories) /40 MG Félix-René Altmayer (Commanding General, Vichy 16th Military Division) 09/12/40 redesignated **16th Military Division** - see **Vichy France 16th Military Division**.

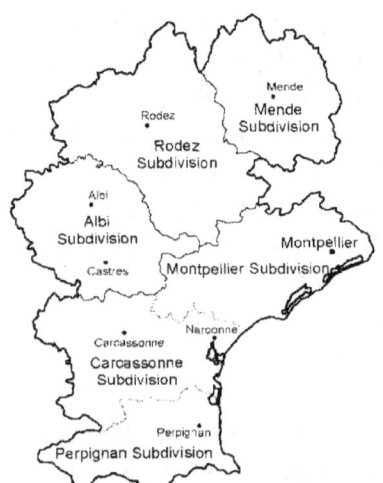

A.   *Components* - **Military District XVI**
       1.   **Montpellier Subdivision Group**: /38 Col. Marie-Joseph-André Saint-Julien (Commanding General, 65th Infantry Division) 10/39? BG Murat
              a.   **Montpellier Subdivision**:
              b.   **Carcassone Subdivision**:
              c.   **Perpignan Subdivision**:

        2.   **Independent Subdivision**
              a.   **Albi Independent Subdivision**:
              b.   **Rodez Independent Subdivision**:
              c.   **Mende Independent Subdivision**:
B.   *Components* - **Military District XVI** (07/40)
      1.   **Aude Department**
      2.   **Aveyron Department**
      3.   **Hérault Department**
      4.   **Lozère Department**
      5.   **Pyrénées-Orientales Department**
      6.   **Tarn Department**
C.   **Artillery, Military District XVI**: /37 Col. Jean-François-Marie-Joseph-Béranfer de Curières de Castelnau (Artillery Commander, XVI Army Corps) /39
D.   **Intendant [Quartermaster] Service, Military District XVI**: BG Marie-Fernand Aymé
E.   **Medical Services, Military District XVI**: /38 BG Adolphe-Charles Mathieu
F.   **At Disposal of Commanding General, Military District XVI**:
      06/25/40 BG Jean-François-Marie-Joseph-Béranfer de Curières de Castelnau (retired) /40

Military District XVII [XVIIe Région Militaire] (Ariège, Haute Garonne, Gers, Tarn-et-Garonne, Lot, & Lot-et-Garonne Departments; HQ: Toulouse): /39 MG Onésime-Paul Noël (Commanding General, XVII Army Corps) 09/02/39 LG [Retired '37] Saint-Cyr-Étienne Mussel (retired) 07/40 LG Théodore-Marcel Sciard (Commanding General, 17th Military Division) 09/12/40 redesignated **17th Military Division** - see **Vichy France 17th Military Division**.

      A.   **Deputy Commander, Military District XVII**: 06/25/40 MG Maxime-Jean-Vincent Germain **(in reserve; 09/12/40, Commanding General, 7th Military Division)** /40
      B.   *Components* - **Military District XVII**
            1.   **Toulouse Subdivision Group**: 10/39? BG Riedinger
                  a.   **Toulouse Subdivision**:
                  b.   **Foix Subdivision**:
                  c.   **Auch Subdivision**:
            2.   **Montauban Subdivision Group**: 10/22/39 BG [Retired '37] Eugène-Henri-Étienne-Auguste Penavayre (retired) 06/25/40 dissolved.
                  a.   **Montauban Subdivision**:
                  b.   **Agen Subdivision**:
                  c.   **Cahors Subdivision**:
      C.   *Components* - **Military District XVII** (07/40)
            1.   **Ariège Department**
            2.   **Haute-Garonne Department**
            3,   **Gers Department**

4. **Lot Department**: 07/11/40 BG Fernand-Zacharie-Joseph Lenclud (Commanding General, Haute-Savoie Subdivision, Military District XIV) /40
5, **Lot-et-Garonne Department**
6. **Hautes-Pyrénées Department**
7. **Tarn-et-Garonne Department**

D. **Artillery, Military District XVII**: /38 Col. Jean-Ernest-Anne Sainctavit (Artillery Commander, XVII Army Corps) 09/02/39

E. **Intendant [Quartermaster] Service, Military District XVII**: /38 Col. Paul-Charles-Joseph Hugot

F. **Medical Services, Military District XVII**: /38 Antoine-Marie-Gabriel Goursolas (Director, Medical Services, Eighth Army) 08/27/39

G. **Military-Governor, Toulouse**: /44 MG Philibert Collet [+ Commanding General, Division Mèknès].

Military District XVIII [XVIIIᵉ Région Militaire] (Haute Pyrénées, Basses Pyrénées, Landes & Gironde Departments; HQ: Bordeaux): /38 MG Alfred-Marie-Joseph-Louis Montagne (Commanding General, Paris Military District) /39 MG Eugène-Jules Rochard (Commanding General, XVIII Army Corps) 09/02/39 LG [Retired '38] Ange-Marie-Léon Chauvin (retired) 06/05/40 LG [Retired '39] Michel-Laurent-Marie-Joseph Lafont (retired) 06/25/40 disbanded.

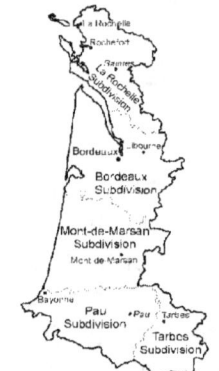

A. **Deputy Commander, Military District XVIII**: 06/25/40 MG Félix-René Altmayer (Commanding General, Military District XVI) 07/40?

B. *Components* - **Military District XVIII**
1. **Bordeaux Subdivision Group**: 10/39? BG Bret
    a. **Bordeaux Subdivision**:
    b. **Mont de Marsan Subdivision** (04/40, switched to Pau Subdivision Group):
    c. **Pau Subdivision** (04/40, switched to Pau Subdivision Group):
    d. **Tarbes Subdivision** (04/40, switched to Pau Subdivision Group):
    e. **La Rochelle Subdivision**:
2. **Pau Subdivision Group** (04/40): unknown?
    a. **Pau Subdivision** (04/40):
    b. **Tarbes Subdivision** (04/40):
    c. **Mont de Marsan Subdivision** (04/40):

C. *Components* - **Military District XVIII** (07/40)
1. **Landes Department**: 07/40 BG Marcel-Georges François (Infantry Commander, 2ⁿᵈ Military District) /40

D. **Medical Services, Military District XVIII**: /38 Col. Pierre-Jean-Joseph Causeret (Director, Medical Service, Second Army) 08/27/39

Military District XIX [XIXᵉ Région Militaire] (Algeria; HQ: Algiers): /39 LG [Retired '38] Victor-Nicolae Goudot (retired) 06/25/40 LG Raymond-Jules-Émile Poupinel (retired) /40 MG Étienne-Paul-Émile-Marie Beynet (Head, French Delegation to Armistice Commission) /41 BG Marie-Louis Koëltz (Commanding General, XIX Army Corps) /41 BG Jean-Paul Bergeron (Commanding General, Sub-Division Tunis) 11/08/42 BG Jean-Sylvain-Louis

Roubertie (acting) /42 MG Yves-Marie-Jacques-Guillaume de Boisboissel (Commander-in-Chief, French West Africa) /43
- A. **Deputy Commander, Military District XIX**: unknown? 09/12/40 MG Étienne-Paul-Émile-Marie Beynet (Commanding General, Military District XIX) /40 unknown? /41 BG Yves-Marie-Jacques-Guillaume de Boisboissel (Commanding General, Military District XIX) /42
- B. **Chief of Staff, Military District XIX**: /38 Col. Maurice-Paul-Raoul Barbeyrac de Saint-Maurice /40 BG Georges-Edmond-Lucien Barré (Commander-in-Chief, Tunisia) 11/08/42?
- C. **Artillery, Military District XIX**: /35 Col. Jacques-Albert Apffel (Artillery Commander, North Africa) /3?

Military District XX [XXe Région Militaire] (Vosages, Bas-Rhin, Meuthe-et-Moselle (less the Briey District) & Moselle (less the Thionville District); HQ: Nancy): /38 MG Louis-Eugène Hubert (Commanding General, XX Army Corps) 08/22/39 MG Servet (?) /40 MG [Retired '39] Henri Fournier (to /45, German prisoner-of-war; /45, died in a Prisoner-of-War camp) 06/25/40 disbanded; reformed /44 BG Aimable-Adrien-Fernand Allemandet

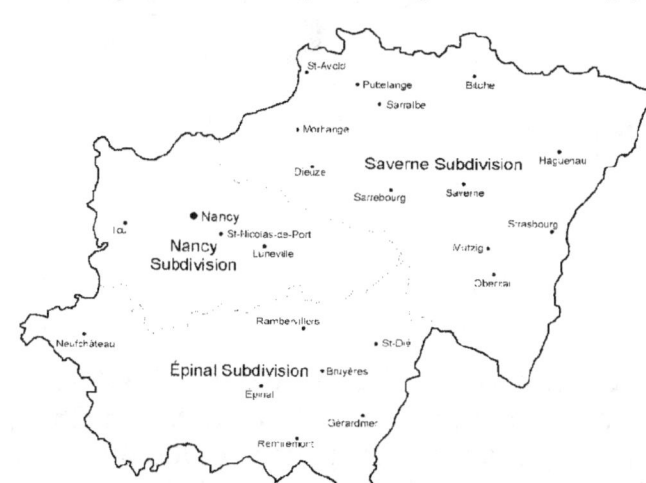

- A. **Deputy Commander, Military District XX**: /38 BG Roger-Gaston-Marie-Joseph Villers
- B. **Chief of Staff, Military District XX**: /38 Col. Léon-Eugène Serant
- C. *Components* - **Military District XX**
  1. **Nancy Subdivision Group**: 10/39? BG Tassel
     - a. **Nancy Subdivision**:
     - b. **Épinal Subdivision**:
     - c. **Saverne Subdivision**:
- D. **Artillery, Military District XX**: /36 Col. Henri Fournier (retired; /39 Artillery Commander, Fifth Army) /39
- E. **Medical Service, Military District XX**: /36 Col. Marie-Joseph-Antoine Schickele
- F. **Military-Governor, Strasbourg**: /35 LG Pierre Héring [+ Member, The Army Council] (retired; /39 Commanding General, Paris Military District) /39 LG Aubert-Achille-Jules Frère (Commanding General, VIII Army Corps) 09/02/39

Military District XXI [XXIe Région Militaire] (/44, Free France): LG André-Marie-François Dody [+ Military-Governor, Metz].
- A. **Military-Governor, Metz**: /44 LG André-Marie-François Dody [+ Commanding General, Military District XXI].

Overseas Colonies and Protectorates
[Under Minister of War]

French North Africa [L'Afrique Française du Nord]:

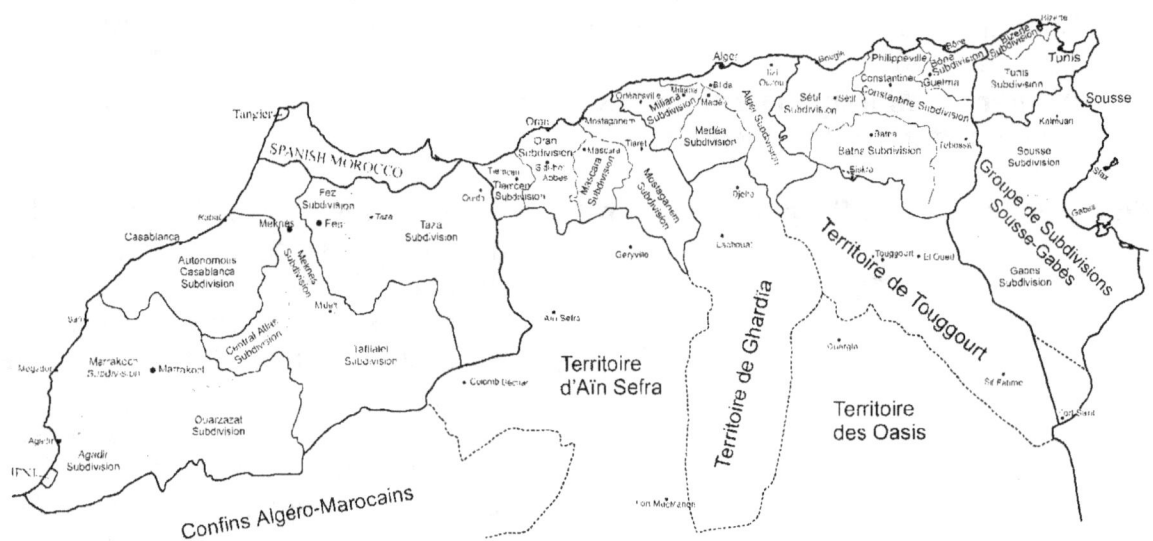

Delegate-General Commissioner of the Government for North Africa: 10/39? Gen. Charles-Auguste-Paul Noguès (Resident-General of Morocco & Commander-in-Chief, Morocco) 06/26/40 dissolves 07/16/40 Gen. [Retired '35] Maxime Weygand [+ 09/06/40, Vichy France Minister of War; + Commander-in-Chief, Land and Air Forces North Africa Land] (Governor-General of Algeria) 07/16/41 unknown? 09/08/44 Gen. [Retired '39] Georges-Albert-Julien Catroux [+ Minister of North Africa].

A. **Components - French North Africa**
1. **Governor-General, Algeria** (Capital: Algiers): 09/21/35 GEORGES LE BEAU 07/20/40 Adm. Jean-Marie-Charles Abrial [FN] (Minister of Marine, Vichy Government) 07/16/41 Gen. [Retired '35] Maxime Weygand [+ Commander-in-Chief, Land and Air Forces North Africa] (to /45, Free French prisoner-of-war; after war held as a collaborator at Val-de-Grâce; 05/46, released; /48, cleared) 11/20/41 LG Yves-Charles Châtel (retired) 01/20/43 MARCEL PEYROUTON (resigned; 10/44, arrested by the French Provisional Government) 06/03/43 Gen. [Retired '39] Georges-Albert-Julien Catroux [+ to /44, State Commissioner for Muslim Affairs] (Delegate-General Commissioner of the Government for North Africa & Minister of North Africa) 09/08/44 YVES CHATAIGNEAU.
    a. **Chief of Staff, Governor-General of Algeria**: /43 Col. Moïse-Germain-Louis Jousse (Chief of Staff, Chairmen of the French Committee of National Liberation) 11/09/43
    b. **Oran Territory Division**: see **Divisions in Overseas Colonies and Protectorates** Section.
    c. **Algiers Territory Division**: see **Divisions in Overseas Colonies and Protectorates** Section.

        d. **Constantine Territory Division**: see **Divisions in Overseas Colonies and Protectorates** Section.
        e. **Aïn Sefra Territory [Territoire d'Aïn Sefra]**
        f. **Ghardia Territory [Territoire de Ghardin]**
        g. **Oasis Territory [Territoire des Oasis]**
        h. **Touggourt Territory [Territoire de Touggourt]**
        i. **Director, Engineers, Algeria**: /40 Col. Pierre-Marie Braconnier (retired) /40 unknown? /42 BG [Retired '40] Pierre-Marie Braconnier (Director, Engineers, Morocco) /44

2. **Tunisia** (Capital: Tunis): **Resident-General of Tunisia**: 04/17/36 ARMAND GUILLON 10/18/38 EIRIK LABONNE 06/03/40 MARCEL PEYROUTON (Vichy France Minister of the Interior) 07/22/40 vacant 07/26/40 VA Jean-Pierre Estéva [FN] (return to Vichy France; 09/22/44, arrested by Free French; 03/15/45, sentenced to solitary confinement for life for treason; 04/11/50, pardoned) 05/10/43 LG Alphonse-Pierre Juin (Commanding General, Free French Expeditionary Corps in Italy) 09/43 MG Charles Emmanuel Mast.
        i. **Chief of Military Cabinet**: /43 Col. André-Eugène Navereau (Artillery Commander, 4th Moroccan Mountain Infantry Division) 10/01/43
        a. **Commander of the Troops & Territory of Tunisia**:
            i. **Tunis Territory Division**: see **Divisions in Overseas Colonies and Protectorates** Section.
            ii. **Sousse Territory Division**: see **Divisions in Overseas Colonies and Protectorates** Section.
        b. **Official Representative at the French Residence in Tunis**: /43 BG Marcel Rime-Bruneau.

3. **Morocco** (Captial: Rabat): **French Resident-General**: 09/16/36 Gen. Charles-Auguste-Paul Noguès [+ /39 to /40 Commander-in-Chief, French North Africa] (relieved; 10/20/43, arrested by French Committee of Liberation) 06/21/43 **Resident-Governor**: GABRIEL PUAUX.
        a. **Deputy Resident-General, Morocco**: /36 BG Marie-Jules-Victor-Léon François [+ Commander-in-Chief, Morocco] /39
        b. **Military Secretary to Resident-General, Morocco**: /43 BG Raymond-Francis Duval (Chief of Staff, III Free French Army Corps) /44
        c. **Commander-in-Chief, Morocco**: see **Morocco Army Corps**.
            i. **Fèz Territory Division**: see **Divisions in Overseas Colonies and Protectorates** Section.
            ii. **Marrakech Territory Division**: see **Divisions in Overseas Colonies and Protectorates** Section.
            iii. **Meknès Territory Division**: see **Divisions in Overseas Colonies and Protectorates** Section.
            iv. **Casablanca (Independent) Territory Division**: see **Divisions in Overseas Colonies and Protectorates** Section.
        d. **Colonial Troops Morocco**

The Levant (was made up of two French mandates Syria and Lebanon; Capital: Beirut):

French High Commissioner: 07/16/33 DAMIEN de MARTEL, Count de Martel 01/39 GABRIEL PUAUX (06/21/43, Resident-Governor Morocco) 11/24/40 JEAN CHIAPPE (did not take office) 11/27/40 LG Henri-Fernand Dentz [+ Commander-in-Chief, Levant Forces] (President, Commission of Conferment of Awards 1939 to 1940) 02/01/42 **Delegate-General**: Gen. [Retired '39] Georges-Albert-Julien Catroux [+ Commander of Free French Forces in Levant] (State Commissioner for Foreign Affairs) 06/07/43 JEAN HELLEU 11/23/43 YVES CHATAIGNEAU (09/09/44, Governor-General, Algeria) 01/23/44 LG Étienne-Paul-Émile-Marie Beynet [+ High Commissioner of Levant].

A. **Commander-in-Chief, Levant Forces [Commandant Supérieur Troupes du Levant]** (Middle East; HQ: Beirut): /34 MG Charles-Léon-Clément Huntziger (Member, The Army Council) /38 MG Henri-Léon Caillault (Secretary-General of the Supreme Council of National Defense) /40 MG Louis-Gabriel Lepetit (retired) 07/40 MG François-Marie-Jacques Fougère (Deputy Commander-in-Chief, Levant) 11/27/40 LG Henri-Fernand Dentz [+ High Commissioner for Levant - supervising repatriation of the French Forces in Levant] /41 Gen. [Retired '39] Georges-Albert-Julien Catroux [+ 02/01/42, High Commissioner, Levant] (State Commissioner for Foreign Affairs) /43 MG Georges-Jean-Emile-René Chadebec de Lavelade

B. **Deputy Commander-in-Chief, Levant**: 11/27/40 MG François-Marie-Jacques Fougère (retired) /41 unknown? /43 BG Marcel-Georges François (at disposal of the Chief of the General Staff; /44, retired) /44 BG Charles-Raoul Magrin-Vernerey dit Monclar.

C. *Components*
   1. **Levant Mobile Force**: see **Levant Mobile Force** in **Army Corps** Section.
   2. **Commander of Troops, North Syria [Général Commandant Troupes de Territorie Nord-Syrie et Euphrates]** (Middle East): see **Commands equivalant to Divisions** Section.
   3. **Commander of Troops, South Syria [Général Commandant Troupes de Territorie Sud-Syrie]** (Middle East): see **Commands equivalant to Divisions** Section.
   4. **Commander of Troops, Lebanon [Général Commandant Troupes de Territorie Liban]** (Middle East): see **Commands equivalant to Divisions** Section.

D. **Military-Governor of Damascus**: BG François-Fernand-Michel Olivie dit Oliva-Rogel

Overseas Colonies and Protectorates
[Under Minister of Colonies]

French West Africa [Afrique Occidentale Française (AOF)] (Capital: Dakar, Senegal):

Governor-General, French West Africa: 10/29/38 PIERRE-FRANÇOIS BOISSON 08/10/39 LÉON-HENRI-CHARLES CAYLA (Governor-General, Madagascar, French East Africa) 06/25/40 PIERRE-FRANÇOIS BOISSON [+ Vichy High Commissioner for all French Africa which did not rally to the Free French] (resigned; 10/44, arrested by the French Provisional Government; + to 08/28/40, Governor-General, French Equatorial Africa] 07/13/43 PIERRE-CHARLES-ALBERT COURNARIE.

A. **Commander-in-Chief, French Troops in French West Africa [Supérieur des Troupes d'Afrique Occidentale Française]** (HQ: Dakar, Senegal): /34 BG René-Paul Dubuisson [+ /37, to /38, Member, Consultative Committee of Colonial Defense; + /38 to 09/02/39, Commanding General, 2nd Colonial Infantry Division] (Governor-General of Verdun) /37 MG Joseph-Jules-Marie Legendre (on leave; /39, at disposal of the Commander-in-Chief) 09/20/39 MG Jean-Joseph-Guillaume Barrau (Member, The Army Council) /41 unknown? /41 LG Jean-Joseph-Guillaume Barrau (retired) /42 LG Maurice Viant (retired) /43 LG Yves-Marie-Jacques-Guillaume de Boisboissel (retired) /45 MG Joseph-Abraham-Auguste-Pierre-Edouard Magnan.
    1. **Dakar, Senegal, and Mauritanian Military District**: /41 MG Maurice Viant (Commander-in-Chief, French West Africa) /42

B. *Areas of French West Africa*:
    1. **Mauritania [Mauritanie]** (Capital: Nouakchott): **Governor**: 08/07/38 CHARLES-ANDRÉ DUMAS (acting) 11/38 JEAN-LOUIS BEYRIES 05/04/44 CHRISTIAN-ROBERT-ROGER LAIGRET 07/31/45 RENÉ BABIN.
    [NOTE: acting for Beyries from 04/42 JEAN-VICTOR-LOUIS-JOSEPH CHALVET (French Governor, French Somaliland, French East Africa) 05/01/44**]**
    2. **Senegal [Sénégal]** (Capital: Dakar): **Governor**: 10/25/38 JEAN-PAUL PARISOT /40 unknown? 01/01/41 GEORGES-PIERRE REY [+ 09/29/42, Governor, Ivory Coast] 12/22/42 HUBERT-JULES DESCHAMPS 12/02/43 CHARLES-JEAN DEGAIN 06/45 PIERRE-LOUIS MAESTRACCI
        a. **Dakar Defense Position** (/40): MG Maurice Viant [+ Artillery Commander, French West Africa] (Commanding General, Dakar,

Sebegal, and Mauritanian Military District) /41

3. **French Guinea [Guinée Français] {the country of Guinea today}** (Capital: Conakry): **Governor**: 03/07/36 LOUIS-PLACIDE BLACHER 02/12/40 ANTOINE-FÉLIX GIACOBBI 08/42 HORACE-VALENTIN CROCICCHIA 03/25/44 JACQUES-GEORGES FOURNEAU.
[NOTE: acting for Blacher from 09/04/37 to 01/26/38 PIERRE TAP and from 06/10/39 to 10/01/39 FÉLIX MARTINE]

4. **Ivory Coast [Côte d'Ivoire]** (Capital: Yamoussoukro): **Governor**: 07/16/38 LOUIS-HENRI-FRANÇOIS-DENIS BRESSOLES (acting; /40, French Governor, Martinique, French Antilles) 01/27/39 HORACE-VALENTIN CROCICCHIA (08/42, French Governor, French Guinea) 01/01/41 HUBERT-JULES DESCHAMPS (12/22/42, French Governor, Senegal) 09/29/42 GEORGES-PIERRE REY [+ to 12/22/42, French Governor, Senegal] 08/03/43 JEAN-FRANÇOIS TOBY [+ Lieutenant-Governor, Niger] 08/26/43 ANDRÉ-JEAN-GASTON LATRILLE 08/16/45 HENRY-JEAN-MARIE de MAUDUIT.

5. **Dahomey {the country of Benin today}** (Capital: Porto-Novo): **Lieutenant-Governor**: 06/01/38 ARMAND-LÉON ANNET (04/11/41, Governor-General, Madgascar, French East Africa) 08/27/40 PIERRE-JEAN-ANDRÉ PALICETI (acting) 09/18/40 LÉON-HIPPOLYTE TRUITARD 08/26/43 CHARLES-ANDRÉ MAURICE ASSIER de POMPIGNAN.

6. **Upper Volta [Côte d'Ivoire du Nord] {the country of Burkina Faso today}** (Capital: Ouagadougou): **Resident-Superior**: 01/01/38 EDMOND LOUVEAU (imprisoned by Boisson, for proclaiming adhesion to Free France) 07/29/40 direct rule by Ivory Coast 09/06/47.

7. **Niger** (Niamey): **Lieutenant-Governor**: 04/29/38 JEAN-BAPTISTE-VICTOR CHAZELAS (acting) 02/18/39 JEAN-ALEXANDRE-LÉON RAPENNE 11/07/40 LÉON SOLOMIAC (acting) 12/08/40 LG Maurice-Émile Falvy (?) 03/04/42 JEAN-FRANÇOIS TOBY [+ 08/03/43 to 08/26/43, Governor, Ivory Coast].

8. **French Sudan [Soudan Français] {the country of Mali today}** (Capital: Bamako): **Governor**: 03/28/38 JEAN DESANTI 04/17/42 AUGUSTE CALVEL.
   a. **Medical Services, French Sudan**: /36 Col. Marie-Eugène-Adolphe Sicé (Medical Services, XV Army Corps) 09/02/39

9. **Togo** (Capital: Lomé): **Commissioner**: 09/25/36 MICHEL-LUCIEN MONTAGNÉ 01/01/41 LÉONCE-JOSEPH DELPECH 11/19/41 JEAN-FRANÇOIS de SAINT-ALARY 04/12/42 PIERRE SALCETI 08/31/43 ALBERT MERCADIER (acting) 01/10/44 JEAN NOUTARY.

French Equatorial Africa [Afrique Equatoriale Française (AEF)] (Capital: Brazzaville, Moyan Congo): **Governor-General**: 04/05/36 DIEUDONNÉ-FRANÇOIS-JOSEPH-MARIE RESTE 04/21/39 LÉON SOLOMIAC (acting; acting Lieutenant Governor, Niger, French West Africa) 09/03/39 PIERRE-FRANÇOIS BOISSON [+ 06/25/40, Governor-General, French West Africa] 07/17/40 BG [Retired '36] Paul-Louis Husson [acting for Boisson] (retired) 08/28/40 both Vichy France and Free France placed Governor-Generals in French Equatorial Africa.
[NOTE: for **Vichy France** (Libreville, Gabon): 08/29/40 Gen. Marcel Têtu [FAF] (surrenders

to Free French forces, and imprisoned) 11/09/40]

[NOTE: for Free French Capital: Brazzaville, Moyan Congo): 08/28/40 BG René-Marie-Edgar de Larminat [acting; + High Commissioner, Free French Colonies in Africa & Member, Council for the Defense of the Empire] (Commanding General, Free French Oriental Brigade) 11/12/40 BG (Chief Doctor) Marie-Eugène-Adolphe Sicé [acting; + Director, Medical Services, French Equatorial Africa; + Council for the Defense of the Empire] 12/30/40 ADOLPHE-FÉLIX-SYLVESTRE ÉBOUÉ 05/17/44; 02/15/44 ANGE-MARIE-CHARLES-ANDRÉ RAYARDELLE.]

A. **Commander-in-Chief, French Troops in French Equatorial Africa [Supérieur des Troupes d'Afrique Equatoriale Française]** (HQ: Brazzaville, Moyan Congo): /37 BG Émile-Jean-Gabriel Carlès (at disposal of Commander-in-Chief, Land Forces) /39 BG [Retired '36] Paul-Louis Husson (acting Governor-General, French Equatorial Africa) 07/17/40 unknown? 08/29/40 /41 BG Philippe-François-Marie-Jacques Leclerc de Hauteclocque, Count of Hauteclocque [+ Commanding General, Column Leclerc] (08/24/43, Commanding General, 2nd Free French Armored Division) /42

B. *Areas of French Equatorial Africa*:
   1. **Chad [Tchad]** (Capital: N'Djamena): **Governor**: 12/14/38 CHARLES DAGAIN (acting) 01/04/39 ADOLPHE-FÉLIX-SYLVESTRE ÉBOUÉ (Governor-General, French Equatorial Africa) 12/10/40 Col. Philippe-François-Marie-Jacques Leclerc de Hauteclocque, Count of Hauteclocque (acting; Commander-in-Chief, French Equatorial Africa) 01/21/41 PIERRE-OLIVIER LAPIE 12/12/42 ANDRÉ-JEAN-GASTON LATRILLE 09/05/43 JACQUES-CAMILLE-MARIE ROGUÉ 10/13/46

   [NOTE: filling in for Rogué 01/44 to 02/44 FRANÇOIS CASAMATTE; and from 08/28/45 to 10/45 AUGUSTE-LÉON-VALENTIN ÉVEN]

   a. **Commandant, Fort Archambault, Chad**: /40 Col. François-Joseph-Jean Ingold (Military Commander, Cameroon) /40

   2. **Middle Congo [Congo-Moyen] {the country of Republic of the Congo today}** (Capital: Brazzaville): 11/21/32 Administration by French Equatorial Africa Governor-General 02/10/41 GABRIEL-ÉMILE FORTUNE 08/20/45 Administration by French Equatorial Africa Governor-General

   [NOTE: acting for Fortune, for a short time in 1942 JEAN-CHARLES-ANDRÉ CAPAGORRY(12/01/42, French Governor, Réunion, French East Africa)]

   3. **Gabon** (Capital: Libreville): **Governor-Delegate**: 10/24/36 LOUIS-ALEXIS-ÉTIENNE BONVIN (09/26/38, Governor of Pondicherry, India) 09/11/37 GEORGES-HUBERT PARISOT (01/45, Governor of Martinique) 08/29/38 GEORGES-PIERRE MASSON (committs suicide) 11/12/40 unknown? 03/15/41 **Governor**: 03/26/41 VICTOR-VALENTIN SMITH 05/30/42 CHARLES-ANDRÉ MAURICE ASSIER de POMPIGNAN (Lieutenant Governor, Dahomey) 08/26/43 PAUL VUILLAUME 11/19/44 NUMA-HENRI-FRANÇOIS SADOUL.

   4. **Ubangi-Shari [Oubangui-Chari] {the country of Central African Republic today}** (Capital: Banqul): **Governor**: 12/31/37 MAX de MASSON de SAINT-FÉLIX 03/28/39 PIERRE de SAINT-MART (05/03/43, Governor-Resident, Madagascar) 05/30/42 ANDRÉ-JEAN-GASTON LATRILLE (12/12/42, French Governor, Chad) 07/30/42 HENRI-CAMILLE SAUTOT.

5. **Cameroons [Cameroun]** (Capital: Douala): **French Commissioner**: 01/37 PIERRE-FRANÇOIS BOISSON [+ 10/29/38, Governor-General, French West Africa] 11/16/38 RICHARD-EDMOND-MAURICE-ÉDOUARD BRUNOT (06/18/41, French Governor, French Polynesia) 08/27/40 **Governor**: 08/27/40 Col. Philippe-François-Marie-Jacques Leclerc de Hauteclocque, Count of Hauteclocque (Military-Governor of Chad) 11/20/40 PIERRE-CHARLES-ALBERT COURNARIE (Governor-General, French West Africa) 07/13/43 vacant 07/20/43 HUBERT-EUGÈNE-PAUL CARRAS 11/15/44 HENRI-PIERRE NICOLAS.
[**NOTE:** acting for Boisson from 10/07/37 to 03/09/38 PIERRE-ÉMILE AUBERT (French Governor, Réunion, French East Africa)]
    a. **Military Commander, Cameroon**: /40 BG Marie-Joseph-Pierre-François Kœnig (Chief of Staff, 1st Free French Division, Syria) /40 BG François-Joseph-Jean Ingold (Director, Overseas Troops) /44

C. **Medical Service, French Equatorial Africa**: /39 BG Franck-Jules-Léon Cazanove (?) /40 BG Marie-Eugène-Adolphe Sicé [+ 11/12/40 to 12/30/40, acting Governor-General, French Equatorial Africa] (High Commissioner of Free French in Africa) 08/41

French East Africa [L'Afrique Oriental Française]
A. *Areas of French East Africa*:
1. **French Somaliland {the country of Djibouti today}** (Capital: Djibouti): **Governor**: 04/27/38 HUBERT-JULES DESCHAMPS (01/01/41, French Governor, Ivory Coast, French West Africa) 07/25/40 BG [Retired '36] Gaëtan-Louis-Elie [Georges-Louis] Germain (retired) 09/02/40 PIERRE-MARIE-ELIE-LOUIS NOUAILHETAS 10/21/42 TRUFFERT 12/04/42 EDMOND-GUSTAVÉ DUPONT (acting) 12/30/42 ANGE-MARIE-CHARLES-ANDRÉ BAYARDELLE 06/22/43 MICHEL-RAPHAËL-ANTOINE SALLER 05/01/44 JEAN-VICTOR-LOUIS-JOSEPH CHALVET.
2. **Réunion** (Capital: Saint-Denis): **Governor**: 10/28/38 JOSEPH-URBAIN COURT 12/29/39 PIERRE-ÉMILE AUBERT 12/01/42 JEAN-CHARLES-ANDRÉ CAPAGORRY.
3. **Madagascar** (Capital: Antananarivo): **Governor-General**: 05/01/30 LÉON-HENRI-CHARLES CAYLA (Governor-General, French West Africa) 10/29/38 unknown? 04/22/39 LÉON-MAURICE-VALENTIN RÉALLON (acting) 06/10/39 JULES-MARCEL de COPPET 07/30/40 LÉON-HENRI-CHARLES CAYLA 04/11/41 ARMAND-LÉON ANNET 09/30/42 09/30/42 V. BECH (acting) 01/07/43 MG Paul-Louis-Victor-Marie Legentilhomme [+ Free French War Commissioner; + Commanding General, Madagascar] (Deputy Commissioner of National Defense) 05/03/43 PIERRE de SAINT-MART
    a. **Comoros** (Capital: Moroni): 02/23/14 province of Madagascar 10/13/46
    b. **Mayotte** (Capital: Mamoutzou): 07/25/12 part of Comoros 07/21/75

French Antilles (Capital: Fort-de-France, Martinque): **Governor-General**: 09/01/39? Adm. Georges-Achille-Marie-Joseph Robert [FN] [+ Admiral Antilles] retired) 07/14/43 HENRI HOPPENOT
A. *Areas of French Antilles*:

1. **French Guyana** (Capital: Cayenne): **Governor**: /38 ROBERT-PAUL CHOT-PLASSOT /42 RENÉ VEBER 03/18/43 JEAN-ALEXANDRE-LÉON REPENNE /44 JULES-EUCHER SURLEMONT.
2. **Guadeloupe** (Capital: Basse-Terre): **Governor**: 11/29/38 MARIE-FRANÇOIS-JULIEN PIERRE-ALYPE 02/21/40 unknown? 04/30/40 CONSTANT-LOUIS-SYLVAIN SORIN 07/15/43 PERRIER (acting) 08/43 MAURICE-PIERRE-EUGÈNE BERTAUT.
   a. **St. Martin** (Capital: Marigot): **Mayor**: /28 LOUIS-CONSTANT FLEMING.
   b. **St. Batthélémy** (Capital: Gustavia): **Mayor**: /33 RUBEN DÉRAVIN /41 CLÉMENT LÉDÉE /42 JEAN LÉDÉE /43 CLÉMENT LÉDÉE /44 RAYNAL ROSEY
3. **Martinique** (Capital: Fort-de-France): **Governor**: /38 MAURICE-XAVIER-JOSEPH DECHARTRE /39 GEORGES-AIMÈ SPITZ /40 LOUIS-HENRI-FRANÇOIS-DENIS BRESSOLES 03/41 YVES-MAURICE NICOL 07/43 LOUIS-GEORGES-ANDRÉ PONTON 07/31/44 ANTOINE-MARIE ANGELINI 01/45 GEORGES-HUBERT PARISOT.

French Oceania [the Pacific]:
A. *Areas of French Oceania*:
1. **French Polynesia** (Capital: Papeete, Tahiti; 130 islands in 5 archipelagos): **Governor**: FRÉDÉRIC-MARIE-JEAN-BAPTISTE CHASTENET de GÉRY 09/04/40 **Provisional Government** (ÉDOUARD AHNNE, GEORGES LAGARDE, ÉMILE MARTIN, GEORGES BAMBRIDGE) 09/12/40 **Governor**: 09/12/40 EDMOND MANSARD 11/05/40 ÉMILE de CURTON 06/18/41 RICHARD-EDMOND-MAURICE-ÉDOUARD BRUNOT 11/41 GEORGES-LOUIS-JOSEPH ORSELLI /45 JEAN-CAMILLE HAUMANT.
   a. **Society Islands**
      i. **Windward Islands**
         A. **Tahiti** (Papeete)
      ii. **Leeward Islands**
   b. **Marquesas Islands**
   c. **Tuamotu Archipelago**
   d. **Gambier Islands**
   e. **Austral Islands**
2. **New Caledonia [Nouvelle Calédonie]** (Capital: Nouméa): **Governor**: 07/38 LÉONCE-ALPHONSE-NOËL-HENRI JORE 08/07/39 RENË-VICTOR-MARIE BARTHÈS 09/20/39 unknown? 10/20/39 MARIE-MARC-GEORGES PELICIER 09/04/40 DENIS (acting) 09/19/40 HENRI-CAMILLE SAUTOT (Governor of Ubangi-Shari, French Equatorial Africa) 05/06/42 MARIE-HENRI-FERDINAND-AUGUSTE MONTCHAMP 06/23/43 unknown? 09/15/43 CHRISTIAN-ROBERT-ROGER LAIGRET (05/14/44, Governor of Mauritania, French West Africa) 02/14/44 JACQUES-VICTOR-FRANÇOIS TALLEC.

St. Pierre and Miquelon (islands off Newfoundland, north Atlantic Ocean; Capital: St. Pierre): **Administrators**: 12/17/36 GILBERT de BOURNAT 12/24/41 VA Émile-Henri Muselier [FN] [acting; + Commander of Free French Forces] 12/25/41 ALAIN SAVARY

02/25/43 PIERRE-MARIE-JACQUES-FRANÇOIS GARROUSTE.

French Settlements in India (Pondicherry, India): **Governor**: 09/26/38 LOUIS-ALEXIS-ÉTIENNE BONVIN.

French Indochina:
Governor-General, French Indochina: (Capital: Saigon, Indochina): 09/36 JOSEPH-JULES BRÉVIÉ (03/26/43, Vichy France Minister for Colonies [Overseas France]) 08/23/39 Gen. [Retired '39] Georges-Albert-Julien Catroux (acting; replaced) 06/27/40 VA Jean d'Decoux [FN] (ousted by the Japanese; arrested and tried after the war for collaboration with the Japanese, but not convicted) 03/09/45 Japanese Governor Generals 08/15/45 vacant 09/23/45 redesignated **High Commissioner, French Indochina** 09/23/45 JEAN-MARIE-ARSÈNE CÉDILE.

A. **Commander-in-Chief, Troops in French Indochina [Commandant Supérieur de Troupes du Groupe l'Indochine]** (HQ: Saigon, Indochina): /38 LG Maurice-Paul-Auguste Martin (retired) /40 LG Eugène Mordant (retired; /44, Head, Military Resistance Indochina & Delegate-General, Provisional Government, Indochina) /44 MG Camille-Ange-Gabriel Sabattier

B. *Areas of French Indochina*:
   1. **Tonkin {part of Vietnam today}** (Capital: Hanoi): **French Resident-Superior**: /37 MG Yves-Charles Châtel (11/20/41, Governor-General of Algeria) /40 ÉMILE-LOUIS-FRANÇOIS GRANDJEAN [+ French Resident-Superior, Annam] /41 EDOUARD-ANDRÉ DELSALLE /42 JEAN-MAURICE-NORBERT HAELEWYN (French Resident-Superior of Annam) /44 CAMILLE AUPELLE 03/45 **Japanese Resident**: NISHIMURA KUMAO [Japanese] 08/45 **French Commissioner**: 08/18/45 PIERRE MESSMER (acting) 08/22/45 JEAN-ROGER SAINTENY.
   2. **Annam {part of Vietnam today}** (Capital: Hué): **French Resident-Superior**: MAURICE-FERNAND GRAFFEUIL /40 ÉMILE-LOUIS-FRANÇOIS GRANDJEAN [+ to /41, French Resident-Superior, Tonkin] /44 JEAN-MAURICE-NORBERT HAELEWYN 03/45 **Japanese Resident**: YOKOYAMA MASAYUKI [Japanese] 08/45 under the **French Commissioner of Tonkin**.
   3. **Cochin Chine {part of Vietnam today}** (Capital: Saigon): **French Governor**: /39 RENÉ VEBER (/42, Governor, French Guyana) /40 HENRI-GEORGES RIVOAL /42 ERNEST-THIMOTHÉE HOEFFEL 03/45 **Japanese Governor**: MINODA FUJIO [Japanese] 08/15/45 **Imperial Delegate**: NGUYEN VAN SAM [Vietnamese]
   4. **Laos** (Capital: Vientiane): **French Resident-Superior**: EUGÈNE-HENRI-

ROGER EUTROPE 04/38 ANDRÈ TOUZET 11/40 ADRIEN-ANTHONY-MAURICE ROQUES 12/41 LOUIS-ANTOINE-MARIE BRASEY 04/05/45 **Japanese Resident in Vientiane**: 03/45 MASANORI SAKO [Japanese] 08/45 and **Japanese Supreme Counselor in Luang Prabang**: 04/05/45 ISHIBASHI [Japanese] 08/22/45 **French Commissioner**: 08/25/45 HANS IMFELD.

5. **Cambodia [Cambodge]** (Capital: Phnom Penh): **French Resident-Superior**: 12/12/36 LÉON-EMMANUEL THIBAUDEAU 12/29/41 JEAN de LENS 03/02/43 GEORGES-ARMAND-LÉON GAUTHIER 11/44 ANDRÉ-JOSEPH BERJOAN 03/09/45 **Japanese Sepreme Advisor**: 03/14/45 KUBO [Japanese] 08/45 **French Resident-Superior**: 08/45 ANDRÉ-JOSEPH BERJOAN.

    A. **Commanding General, Cambodia**: /40 BG Yves-Marie-Jacques-Guillaume de Boisboissel (Deputy Commander, Military District XIX) /41

C. **Military-Governor, Hanoi**: 07/40 BG Camille-Ange-Gabriel Sabattier (Commanding General, Cochinchine Brigade, Indochina) 12/08/41

Japanese Military Commanders in Indochina

Japanese Military Commanders in Indochina: 09/07/40 MG Takuma Nishimura [Japanese] [+ Commanding General, Japanese Indochina Expeditionary Force; + 06/26/41, Commanding General, Imperial Guards Division & Commanding General, 21st Independent Mixed Brigade (see Volume IV)] 07/05/41 LG Shojiro Iida [Japanese] [+ Commanding General, Japanese 15th Army (see Volume IV)] /41 unknown? 11/10/42 LG Viscount Kazumoto Machijiri [Japanese] [+ Commanding General, Japanese 38th Army (see Volume IV)] 11/22/44 LG Yuitsu Tsuchihashi [Japanese] [+ Commanding General, Japanese 38th Army (see Volume IV)] 08/15/45 disbanded.

German Occupied France (Frankreich) (May 10, 1940 - March 9, 1945)

German Military Governors for France (HQ: Paris, 05/10/40): CG (Heinrich Alfred Hermann) Walther von Brauchitsch [German] [+ Commander-in-Chief, Army High Command] 10/25/40 GdI Otto von Stuelpnagel [Stülpnagel] [German] (retired) 11/25/41 GdI Karl Heinrich von Stuelpnagel [Stülpnagel] [German] (arrested) 07/21/44 GdFl Karl Kitzinger [German-Luft] (?) FM (Otto Moritz) Walter Model [German] [+ to 09/04/44, Commander-in-Chief [Oberbefehlshaber (OB)] West; + (Commander-in-Chief, Army Group "B" (France #2); + Commander-in-Chief, Army Group "D"] 09/04/44 FM Karl Rudolf Gerd von Runstedt [German] [Commander-in-Chief [+ Oberbefehlshaber (OB)] West] 05/09/45

A. **Chief of Staff, France**: /44 LG Dr. Hans Speidel [German]
B. **Chief, Command Staff, Military Commander, France** 06/40 MG Helge Arthur Auleb [German] (Commanding General, 72nd Infantry Division) 07/25/40
C. **Military Districts**:
   1. **Regional Commander Northern France** (05/29/40, HQ: Paris): Gen. Johannes Blaskowitz [German] (officer reserve pool; 10/26/40, Commander-in-Chief, First Army) 07/40 LG Alfred Streccius [German] (Commander-in-Chief, Wehrkreis [Military District] XVII) 10/25/40 disbanded, command now falls under **Belgium-North France Command** with **Greater Paris** becoming it's own command area.
      a. **Chief, Command Staff, Military Commander, Northern France**: 05/40 MG Helge Arthur Auleb [German] (Chief, Command Staff, Military Commander, France) /40
   2. **Commander Greater Paris** (07/01/40): LG Ernst Schaumburg [German] (retired) 06/42 LG Hans Wilhelm Freiherr [Baron] von Boineburg-Langsfeld [German] [+ 08/26/42 to 12/26/42, Commanding General, 23rd Panzer Division; + 05/01/43, Commanding General, 325th Sicherungs [Security] Division] 07/03/44 LG Dietrich von Choltitz [German] [+ Commanding General, LXXXIV Army [Infantry] Corps] (Allied prisoner-of-war) 07/30/44 disbanded.
   3. **Regional Commander Northwestern France** (HQ: Angers): 03/07/42 LG Karl-Ulrich Newmann-Neurode [German] (reserve officer pool) 07/01/43 GdI Dipl. Ing. Erwin Vierow [German] (Commanding General, Corps Somme) 06/44 MG Vilsow [German] (Allied prisoner-of-war) 07/44 disbanded
      a. **Chief of Staff, Northwest France**: LCol. Oelsner-Woller [German] 05/19/41 Col. d. Res. Hubertus von Auloch [German] (Commanding Officer, Battle Group "Von Auloch"/Allied prisoner-of-war) 08/15/44
   4. **Regional Commander Northeastern France** (HQ: Dijon): 01/11/43 LG Wilhelm Hans Hederich [German] (?) 09/20/44 LG Heinrich Ritter [Knight] von Fuechtbauer [Füchtbauer] [German]
   5. **Regional Commander Southwestern France** (HQ: Bordeaux): 03/01/42 LG Freiherr [Baron] von Rotberg [German] (?) 01/11/43 LG Kurt Feldt [German] (Regional Commander, Section III [Corps "Feldt"]) 08/10/44 redesignated **Regional Commander Section III** - - see **Corps "Feldt"**.
   6. **Regional Commander Southern France**: 12/29/41 MG Heinrich Ritter [Knight] von Fuechtbauer [Füchtbauer] [German] (09/20/44, Regional

Commander Northeastern France) 11/11/42 Alexander Freiherr [Baron] von Neubronn von Eisenburg [German] 12/15/42 LG Johannes Niehoff [German] [+ 04/01/43, Commanding General, 371st Infantry Division] 06/10/44 GdA Theodor Geib [German] (?) 07/30/44 GdA Edgar Theissen [Theißen] [German] (?) 08/05/44 disbanded.

7. **Regional Commander Southeast France** (08/15/43): GdI Hans-Gustav Felber [German] (Commanding General, Army Detachment "Serbia") 09/26/44 disbanded.

8. **Administrative Headquarters**:
   a. OFK Laon (592nd):
   b. La Roche-sur Yon (505th): MG von Kurnatowski [German]
   c. FK Channel Islands (515th) (08/28/40): MG Robert Graf [Count] von Schmettow [German] /41 Col. Mueller [Müller] [German] (acting) /41 MG Robert Graf [Count] von Schmettow [German] (Commanding General, 319th Infantry Division) 02/27/45 VA Friedrich Hueffmeier [Hüffmeier] [German-GN].
   d. FK Rouen (517th):
   e. FK Bordeaux (529th): 06/40 LG Moritz von Faber du Faur [German]
   f. FK Chalons-sur-Marne (531st):
   g. FK Epinal (532nd):
   h. FK Biarritz (541st): MG Claus Sigurd Boie [German]
   i. FK Rennes (549th): 10/25/41 MG Alfred Jacobi [German] (Commanding General, 201st Sicherungs [Security] Division) 05/20/42
   j. FK Besancon (560th):
   k. FK Saint-Dizier (563rd):
   l. FK Paris (575th):
   m. FK Amiens (580th): 12/02/42 MG Friedemund von Arnim [German] (Commanding General, 602nd Administrative Area) 08/22/43
   n. FK Le Mans (588th): Col. Ernst Adolph [German] (Commandant, Dnepropetrovsk) 02/01/42
   o. FK Bar-le-Duc (590th):
   p. FK Nancy (591st): MG Franz Karl von Bock [German]
   q. FK Angers (595th): 06/20/42 MG Juergen [Jürgen] Baarth [German] (Commandant, Remount School at Beeskow, Wehrkreis [Military District] III) 08/26/43
   r. FK Laon (602nd): 08/22/43 MG Friedemund von Arnim [German] (reserve officer pool) 09/05/44
   s. FK Dijon (622nd):
   t. FK Beauais (638th): 12/01/42 MG Friedemund von Arnim [German] (Commanding General, 580th Administrative Area) 12/01/42
   u. FK Niort (651st):
   v. FK Poitiers (677th):
   w. FK Arras (678th):
   x. FK Melun (680th): Col. Rudolf Ritter [Knight] und Elder [Noble] von Xylander [German] (09/44, Chief of Staff, Army Group "A" (Russia #2))
   y. FK Cherleville (684th):
   z. FK Saint-Lo (722nd):
   aa. FK Caen (723rd):

ab. FK Paris area (734th):
ac. FK Montdidier (746th):
ad. FK Vannes (750th):
ae. FK Chartrese (751st):
af. FK Quimper? (752nd):
ag. FK Flers (754th):
ah. FK Marseille (758th): 08/16/40 Col. Alfred Beckmann [German] (Commanding General, 199th Administrative Area) 07/17/41 MG Gustav von Bartenwerffer [German] (reserve officer pool/retired) 09/01/42 MG Botho Elster [German] (Allied prisoner-of-war) 08/44
ai. FK Tours (788th):
aj. FK Evreux (801st):
ak. KK Belfort (554th):
al. KK Dijon (563rd):
am. KK Cherbourg? (583rd):
an. KK Nancy (593rd):
ao. KK Sedan (612th):
ap. KK Brest (623rd): 09/08/43 MG (Hermann) Bernhard Ramcke [German-Luft] (Commanding General, 2nd Parachute Division) 06/01/44
aq. KK Abbeville (626th):
ar. KK Le Havre (637th):
as. KK Verdun (672nd):
at. KK Marseille (704th):
au. KK Boulogne? (713th):
av. KK Lorient (735th):
aw. KK Fontainebleau (781st):
ax. KK Amiens (800th):
ay. KK Longevy (892nd):

D. **Area (Corps Commands)**
1. **Normandy East Area** (HQ: Rouen, 06/40; **XXXII Corps Command;** formed 10/39, Wehrkreis [Military District] ?; converted to **LXXXI Army [Infantry] Corps**, 06/42): LG Fritz Buechs [Büchs] [German] (staff, Wehrkreis [Military District] VI) 01/10/40 LG Alfred Boehm-Tettelbach [Böhm-Tettelbach] [German] (Commanding General, XXXVII Corps Command) 03/01/40 GdK Guenther [Günther] von Pogrell [German] (?) 04/01/42 GdPzTr Adolf Kuntzen [German] (Commanding General, LXXXI Army [Infantry] Corps) 06/10/42 converted to **LXXXI Army {Infantry] Corps** - see **LXXXI Army [Infantry] Corps**.
2. **Normandy West Area** (HQ: Caen; **LX Corps Command**; converted to **LXXXIV Army [Infantry] Corps**; 05/15/42):11/01/40 GdK Rudolf Koch-Erpach [German] (Commanding General, XXXV Corps Command) 03/01/41 GdI Max von Viebahn [German] (Chief of Staff, Army Group "D") 12/15/41 GdA Hans Behlendorff [German] (Commanding General, LXXXIV Army [Infantry] Corps) 05/15/42 converted to **LXXXIV Army [Infantry] Corps** - see **LXXXIV Army [Infantry] Corps**.
3. **Brittany Area** (HQ: Angers; **? Corps Command**):
4. **Guyenne-Gascony Area** (HQ: Bordeaux; **? Corps Command**):
5. **Burgundy Area** (HQ: Dijon; **XXXXV [XLV] Corps Command**, upgraded to **LXXXII Army [Infantry] Corps** 06/42): 03/10/40 GdI Kurt von Greiff [German]

330

(officer reserve pool) 04/01/42 GdI Hans-Gustav Felber [German] (Commanding General, LXXXII Army [Infantry] Corps) 05/26/42 upgraded to **LXXXII Army [Infantry] Corps** - - see **LXXXII Army [Infantry] Corps**.
6. **Unknown Corps Commands will go with either "3" or "4" above**
   a. **LXIV Corps Command** (Wehrkreis [Military District] ?; either in **Brittany Area** or **Guyenne-Gascony Area**, France; converted into **LXIV Reserve Army [Infantry] Corps** 09/42): unknown? 09/42 converted to **LXIV Reserve Army [Infantry] Corps** - - see **LXIV Reserve Army [Infantry] Corps**.
   b. **LXVII Corps Command** (1940, Wehrkreis [Military District] ?; either in **Brittany Area** or **Guyenne-Gascony Area**, France; converted into **LXVII Reserve Army [Infantry] Corps** 09/42): unknown? 09/42 converted to **LXVII Reserve Army [Infantry] Corps** - see **LXVII Reserve Army [Infantry] Corps**.

Pas-de-Calais and Nord 1940 - 1944

[The departments of Pas-de-Calais and Nord were occupied by Germany and attached to Belgian military administration; but normally under the authority of Vichy France. Both deapartments were liberated by the allies in 09/44.]

German Military Governors [OFK Lille (670th)] (06/22/40, subordinated to Military Governor of Belgium): GdI Johannes Niehoff [German] (German Commander of the Army Territory of Southern Vichy France) 12/15/42 LG Wilhelm Daser [German] (02/01/44, Commanding General, 165th Reserve Infantry Division) /43 MG George Bertram [German] (?) 09/44

Regional Prefect of Lille: /41 FERNAND CARLES /44
A. **Prefect, Department du Nord**: /36 FERNAND CARLES [+ /41, Regional Prefect of Lille]
   1. **Delegate** (/41): HENRI-JOSEPH DARROUY
B. **Prefect, Department of Pas-de-Calais**: /33 GABRIËL-AUGUSTA-LÉON ROCHARD /40 AMÉDÉE-FÉLIX BUSSIÈRE /42 JEAN-MAECEL DAUGY /43 ANDRÉ-PAUL SADON /44 ANDRÉ-ALEXANDRE PUJES

Territory of Southern Vichy France [Südfrankreich] (November 11, 1942 to August 5, 1944)

German Commander of Vichy France: 12/29/41 MG Heinrich Ritter [Knight] von Fuechtbauer [Füchtbauer] [German] (09/20/44, Regional Commander Northeastern France) 11/11/42 disbanded.

German Commander of the Army Territory of Southern Vichy France (11/11/42): LG Alexander Freiherr von Neubronn von Eisenburg [German] 12/15/42 LG Johannes Niehoff [German] [+ 04/01/43, Commanding General, 371st Infantry Division] 06/10/44 GdA Theodor Geib [German] (?) 07/30/44 GdA Edgar Theissen [Theißen] [German] (?) 08/05/44 disbanded.

Italian Occupied French Zone (June 22, 1940 to September 8, 1943)
[The eight French departments west of the Rhone River]

Italian Commander, Fourth Army: 06/40 Gen. Alfredo Guzzoni [Italian] (Italian Undersecretary of War & Deputy Chief of the Supreme General Staff) 06/40 Gen. Mario Vercellino [Italian] (Commander-in-Chief, Italian Ninth Army) 11/40 Gen. Mario Caracciolo di Feroleto [Italian] (Commander-in-Chief, Italian Fifth Army) 05/41 Gen. Mario Vercellino [Italian] (?) 09/08/43 taken over by German forces.

Government of Vichy France (June 22, 1940 - August 17, 1944)

After the signing of the armistice with Germany on June 22, 1940, the French Government and national Assembly moved down to Vichy and in July the Assembly voted to give full powers to Marshal Pétain as head of state, thus ending the Third Republic. But Marshal Pétain was very much a figurehead and the real power was exercised by the Vice-President of the Council of Ministers or, from April 1942 the Chief of Government.

Chief of State [Vice Premier] (06/16/40): PIERRE LAVAL [+ Vice Premier & Vice-President Council of Ministers; + 10/28/40, Foreign Minister] (04/18/42, Chief of Staff; Vice Premier; President of the Council of Ministers; Foreign Minister; Minister of the Interior; & Minister of Information) 12/13/40 PIERRE-ÉTIENNE FLANDIN [+ Foreign Minister, Vichy France] 02/09/41 Adm. of the Fl. Jean-Louis-Xavier-François Darlan [FN] [+ Commander-in-Chief, Vichy France Armed Forces; Commander-in-Chief, Navy; Chief of the General Staff for Naval Operations; Minister of Marine; + 02/01/41, Foreign Minister; + 02/14/41 to 07/18/41, Minister of the Interior; + 08/11/41, Minister of National Defense and War] 04/18/42 PIERRE LAVAL [+ Vice Premier; + President of Council of Ministers; + Foreign Minister; + Minister of the Interior; + Minister of Information] (arrested by the Germans and moved to Belfort; 09/07/44, moved to Sigmaringen Castle, Germany; 04/45, imprisoned by the French; tried for treason and collaboration; 10/15/45, executed) 08/17/44 see **French Provisional Government**.

A. **Secretary-General to the Head of State, Vichy** (07/40): Gen. Auguste-Marie-Émile Laure (retired; /43 to /45, arrested by the Germans) /42

President, Vichy Government (Prime Minister) (07/10/40): Marshal Henri-Philippe-Benoni-Omar-Joseph Pétain [+ to 04/18/42, President, Council of Ministers] (forcibly moved to Sigmaringen, Germany as Vichy France Government-in-Exile; /45, condemned to death as a traitor, but commuted to life imprisonment) 08/20/44 see **French Provisional Government**.

A. **Vice Premier** (07/10/40): PIERRE LAVAL [+ Chief of Staff & Vice-President Council of Ministers; + 10/28/40, Foreign Minister] (04/18/42, Chief of Staff; Vice Premier; President of the Council of Ministers; Foreign Minister; Minister of the Interior; & Minister of Information) 12/13/40 PIERRE-ÉTIENNE FLANDIN [+ Chief of State, Vichy France & Foreign Minister, Vichy France] 02/09/41 Adm. of the Fl. Jean-Louis-Xavier-François Darlan [RN] [+ Commander-in-Chief, Vichy France Armed Forces; Commander-in-Chief, Navy; Chief of the General Staff for Naval Operations; Minister of Marine; + 02/01/41, Foreign Minister; + 02/14/41 to 07/18/41, Minister of the Interior; + 08/11/41, Minister of National Defense and War] 04/18/42 PIERRE LAVAL [+ Chief of State; + President of Council of Ministers; + Foreign Minister; + Minister of the Interior; + Minister of Information] (arrested by the Germans and moved to Belfort; 09/07/44, moved to Sigmaringen Castle, Germany; 04/45, imprisoned by the French; tried for treason and collaboration; 10/15/45, executed) 08/17/44 see **French Provisional Government**.

B. **Chief of Military Cabinet to Marshal Pétain**: /40? BG Jacques-Marie-Joseph-François Campet

C. **Military Secretary to Marshal Pétain**: /44 MG [Retired '42] Marie-Cyrille-Victor Debeney (/46, retired).

President Council of Ministers, Vichy Government: 06/16/40 Marshal Henri-Philippe-Benoni-Omar-Joseph Pétain [+ Vichy France President or Vichy Prime Minster] 04/18/42 PIERRE LAVAL [+ Chief of State; + Vice Premier; + Foreign Minister; + Minister of the Interior; + Minister of Information] (arrested by the Germans and moved to Belfort; 09/07/44, moved to Sigmaringen Castle, Germany; 04/45, imprisoned by the French; tried for treason and collaboration; 10/15/45, executed) 08/17/44 see **French Provisional Government**.

A. **Vice-President Council of Ministers** (06/16/40): PIERRE LAVAL [+ to 12/13/40, Chief of State; + 10/28/40 to 12/13/40, Foreign Minister] (Chief of Staff; Vice Premier; President of the Council of Ministers; Foreign Minister; Minister of the Interior; & Minister of Information) 04/18/42 disbanded.

B. **Secretary-General of the Cabinet**: 07/40 VA Fernet [FN] (?) /40 Gen. Charles-Théodore Brécard

C. **Foreign Minister, Vichy Government** (07/10/40): PAUL BAUDOUIN (Minister of Information, Vichy France) 10/28/40 PIERRE LAVAL [+ Chief of Staff; + Vice Premier; + Vice-President of the Council of Ministers] (04/18/42, Chief of Staff; Vice Premier; President of the Council of Ministers; Foreign Minister; Minister of the Interior; & Minister of Information) 12/13/40 PIERRE-ÉTIENNE FLANDIN [+ 12/13/40 to 02/09/41, Chief of State [Vice Premier], Vichy France] 02/09/41 Adm. of the Fl. Jean-Louis-Xavier-François Darlan [FN] [+ Chief of State [Vice Premier]; Commander-in-Chief, Vichy France Armed Forces; Commander-in-Chief, Navy; Chief of the General Staff for Naval Operations; Minister of Marine; + 02/14/41 to 07/18/41, Minister of the Interior; + 08/11/41, Minister of National Defense and War] 04/18/42 PIERRE LAVAL [+ Chief of State; + Vice Premier; + President of Council of Ministers; + Minister of the Interior; + Minister of Information] (arrested by the Germans and moved to Belfort; 09/07/44, moved to Sigmaringen Castle, Germany; 04/45, imprisoned by the French; tried for treason and collaboration; 10/15/45, executed) 08/20/44 see **French Provisional Government**.

D. **Finance Minister** (07/10/40): YVES BOUTHILIER 04/18/42 PIERRE CATHALA [+ 01/06/44, Minister of Agriculture, Vichy France] 08/20/44 see **French Provisional Government**.

E. **Minister of National Defense** (07/10/40): Gen. Louis-Antoine Colson (retired) 09/06/40 redesignated **Minister of National Defense and War**.
   1. **Director, Medical Service, Ministry of National Defense**: /40 BG Pierre-Joseph-Félix-Romuald Maisonnet

F. **Minister of War** (07/10/40): Gen. [Retired '35] Maxime Weygand [+ Delegate-General of the Vichy Government to North Africa; + Commander-in-Chief, Land and Air Forces North Africa] 09/06/40 redesignated **Minister of National Defense and War**.
   1. **At disposal of Minister of War**:
      /40 LG Julien-François-René Martin (Commander-in-Chief, Foreign Legion) /40

G. **Minister of National Defense and War** (09/06/40): Gen. Charles-Léon-Clément Huntziger (killed in an air crash) 08/11/41 Adm. of the Fl. Jean-Louis-Xavier-François Darlan [FN] [+ Chief of State [Vice Premier]; Commander-in-Chief, Vichy France Armed Forces; Commander-in-Chief, Navy; Chief of the General Staff for Naval Operations; Minister of Marine; + 02/01/41, Foreign Minister; + 02/14/41 to 07/18/41, Minister of the Interior] 04/18/42 MG Eugène-Marie-Louis Bridoux (/45, arrested by the Americans; fled to Spain; /48, condemned to death in absentia) 08/20/44 see **French Provisional Government**.
  1. **Head, Military Secretary, Minister of National Defense and War** (09/12/40): vacant 09/40 MG Paul-Henry Gérodias (Vichy Inspector-General of Infantry) /40
     a. **Military Secretary, Minister of National Defense and War** (09/06/40): BG Henri Lacaille (Deputy Commander, Military District XVII) 08/11/41 unknown? /42 MG Joseph-Dominique-Victor-Robert Delmotte
  2. **Director of Infantry, Ministry of War**: /41 MG Marie-Cyrille-Victor Debeney (Inspector of the Army) /42
  3. **Director, Armistice Service, Ministry of War**: /40 BG Marie-Louis Koëltz (Commanding General, Military District XIX) /41
H. **Minister of Air** (07/10/40): BERTRAND PUJO 09/06/40 Gen. Jean-Marie-Joseph Bergeret [FAF] (11/13/42, Chief of Staff to Adm. Darlan) 04/18/42 MG Jean-François Jannekeyn [FAF] [to 02/27/43, Chief of the Air Force General Staff] 08/20/44 see **French Provisional Government**.
I. **Minister of Marine (Military and Merchant)** (07/10/40): Adm. of the Fl. Jean-Louis-Xavier-François Darlan [FN] [+ to 04/18/42, Chief of State [Vice Premier]; + Commander-in-Chief, Vichy France Armed Forces; + Commander-in-Chief, Navy; + Chief of the General Staff for Naval Operations; + 02/01/41, Foreign Minister; + 02/14/41 to 07/18/41, Minister of the Interior; + 08/11/41, Minister of National Defense and War] (talked with Allies in North Africa about French troops laying down their weapons; changed sides and assisted the Allies; through his deal he becomes High Commissioner of French North Africa and West Africa; dismissed from the Vichy government and for his actions, Vichy Southern France was 'invaded' by the German Army and it's armed forces demobilized) 04/42 VA Gabriel-Paul Auphan [FN] (resigned) 11/18/42 Adm. Jean-Marie Charles Abrial [FN] (retired?) /43 HENRI BLÉHAUT
  1. **Chief of Cabinet, Minister of Marine**: /41 RA Gabriel-Paul Auphan [+ Chief of Staff, Commander-in-Chief, Navy] (Minister of Marine) 04/42
J. **Minister for Colonies [Overseas France]** (07/12/40): ALBERT RIVIÈRE 09/06/40 HENRY LÉMERY 04/18/42 RA Charles Platon [FN] 03/26/43 JOSEPH-JULES BRÉVIÉ 08/20/44 see **French Provisional Government**.
  1. **Secretary, Ministry of Colonies**: 07/40 RA Charles Platon [FN] (Minister for Colonies) 04/18/42
  2. **Director, Ministry of Colonies**: /40 BG Henri-Frédéric-Paul Casseville 08/20/44 see **French Provisional Government**.
  3. **Director of Military Services, Ministry of Colonies**: /38 BG Louis-Émile Noiret (Commanding General, 7th Colonial Infantry Division) 09/01/39
K. **Minister of the Interior** (07/12/40): ADRIEN MARQUET 09/06/40 MARCEL PEYROUTON [+ Governor-General of Algeria] 02/14/41 Adm. of the Fl. Jean-

Louis-Xavier-François Darlan [FN] [+ Chief of State [Vice Premier]; Commander-in-Chief, Vichy France Armed Forces; Commander-in-Chief, Navy; Chief of the General Staff for Naval Operations; Minister of Marine; Foreign Minister; Minister of National Defense and War] 07/18/41 PIERRE PUCHEAU (08/10/43, arrested by the French Provisional Government; 03/22/44, tried and shot to death for collaboration) 04/18/42 PIERRE LAVAL [+ Chief of State; + Vice Premier; + President of Council of Ministers; + Foreign Minister; + Minister of Information] (arrested by the Germans and moved to Belfort; 09/07/44, moved to Sigmaringen Castle, Germany; 04/45, imprisoned by the French; tried for treason and collaboration; 10/15/45, executed) 08/20/44 see **French Provisional Government**.

L. **Minister of Information** (07/12/40; also known as **Ministry of Propaganda**): vacant 12/40 PAUL BAUDOUIN 01/02/41 vacant 02/25/41 PAUL MARION 04/18/42 PIERRE LAVAL [+ Chief of State; + Vice Premier; + President of Council of Ministers; + Foreign Minister; + Minister of the Interior] (arrested by the Germans and moved to Belfort; 09/07/44, moved to Sigmaringen Castle, Germany; 04/45, imprisoned by the French; tried for treason and collaboration; 10/15/45, executed) 08/20/44 see **French Provisional Government**.

M. **Minister of Industrial Production and Labor** (07/12/40): RENÉ BELIN (Minister of Labor, Vichy France) 02/25/41 separates into **Ministry of Labor** and **Ministry of Industrial Production**.

N. **Minister of Industrial Production** (02/25/41): PIERRE PUCHEAU [+ 07/18/41, Minister of Interior, Vichy France] 08/12/41 FRANÇOIS LEHIDEUX 04/18/42 JEAN BICHELOONE [+ 11/18/42, Minister of Posts, Telegraphs and Telephones, Vichy France] 08/20/44 see **French Provisional Government**.

O. **Minister of Justice** (07/10/40): RAPHAËL ALIBERT /41 JOSEPH BARTHÉLÉMY /43 MAURICE GABOLDE 08/20/44 see **French Provisional Government**.

P. **Minister of Agriculture** (07/12/40): PIERRE CAZIOT, 04/18/42 JACQUES LE ROY LADURIE 09/11/42 MAX BONNAFOUS 01/06/44 PIERRE CATHALA 08/20/44 see **French Provisional Government**.

Q. **Minister of Transport and Public Works**: did not exist in **Vichy France** Cabinet.

R. **Minister of Health** (07/12/40): JEAN YBARNEGARAY 09/06/40 vacant 02/25/41 JACQUES CHEVALIER 08/12/41, SERGE HUARD 04/18/42 EDMOND GRASSET 08/20/44 see **French Provisional Government**.

S. **Minister of Public Instruction [Education Minister]** (07/12/40): ÉMILE MIRAUD 09/06/40 GEORGES RIPERT 12/13/40 JACQUES CHEVALIER (Minister of Health, Vichy France) 02/23/41 becomes **Education Minister**.

T. **Education Minister** (02/23/41): JÉRÔME CARCOPINO 04/18/42 ABEL BONNARD 08/20/44 see **French Provisional Government**.

U. **Minister of Labor** (02/25/41): RENÉ BELIN 04/18/42 HUBERT LAGARDELLE 08/20/44 see **French Provisional Government**.

V. **Minister of Social Affairs** (11/09/43): ADRIEN TIXIER (09/20/44, Interior Minister, Provisional Government) 08/20/44 see **French Provisional Government**.

W. **Minister of Posts, Telegraphs and Telephones** (07/12/40): FRANÇOIS PIÉTRI 09/06/40 JEAN BERTHLOT 04/18/42 ROBERT GIBRAT 11/18/42 JEAN BICHELOONE 08/20/44 see **French Provisional Government**.

X. **Minister of Family & Youth** (07/12/40):
   1. **Commissioner-General of Strengthening the Youth**: /41 MG Paul-Marie-

Joseph de la Porte du Theil (arrested by the Germans) /44

Vichy Armed Forces High Command

General Headquarters [Army High Command] [Grand Quartier Général (GQG)]

Commander-in-Chief, Vichy Armed Forces (06/22/40): Adm. of the Fl. Jean-Louis-Xavier-François Darlan [FN] [+ Commander-in-Chief, Navy; Chief of the General Staff for Naval Operations; Minister of Marine; + 02/01/41 to 04/18/42, Foreign Minister; + 02/09/41 to 04/18/42, Chief of State [Vice Premier]; + 02/14/41 to 07/18/41, Minister of the Interior; + 08/11/41 to 04/18/42, Minister of National Defense and War] (talked with Allies in North Africa about French troops laying down their weapons; changed sides and assisted the Allies; through his deal he becomes High Commissioner of French North Africa and West Africa; dismissed from the Vichy government and for his actions, Vichy Southern France was 'invaded' by the German Army and it's armed forces demobilized) 11/42 demobilized.

    1. **Chief of Staff to the Commander-in-Chief**: BG Georges-Marie-Joseph Revers (Chief of the Military Cabinet to Admiral Darlan) /42
- A. **Chief of Military Cabinet**: /42 BG Georges-Marie-Joseph Revers (Commander-in-Chief, l'Organization de Résistance de l'Armée) /43
- B. **Commander-in-Chief, Vichy France Land Forces** (09/06/40): see below.
- C. **Chief of the Vichy Army General Staff**: see below.
- D. **Commander-in-Chief, Vichy Navy** (07/04/40): see below
- E. **Chief of the General Staff for Naval Operations** (07/04/40): see below.
- F. **Commander-in-Chief, Vichy Air Force [Chefs d'État-Major Général de l'Armée de l'Air]** (07/04/40): see below.
- G. **Chief of the Air Force General Staff [Chef d'État-Major des Forces Aériennes]**: see below.
- H. **Commander-in-Chief, Foreign Legion**: see below.

The Army Council [Supreme War Council]
- A. *Members*:
    - /40 MG Jean-Joseph-Guillaume Barrau (Commander-in-Chief, French West Africa) /40
    - /40 Gen. René-Henri Olry (Inspector of Military Districts VII, XIV, & XV) /40
    - /40 Gen. Joseph-Edouard-Aimé Doumenc [+ to /40, Chief of the Army General Staff; + /40 to /40, General-Commissioner of National Reconstruction; + /40, President, Commission for Investigation Suspicious Retreats] (at disposal of Commander-in-Chief, Armed Forces; /42, retired) /42
    - /41 LG Jean-Joseph-Guillaume Barrau (Commander-in-Chief, French West Africa) /41
    - /41 LG Aubert-Achille-Jules Frère [+ Commanding General, II Group of Military Divisions] (retired; /42, President, Investigating Commission of War Events) /42
    - /41 MG Maxime-Jean-Vincent Germain [+ Inspector of Colonial Forces] (on leave; /42, retired; /44 to /45, arrested by the Germans and deported) /42

Commander-in-Chief, Vichy France Land Forces (09/06/40): Gen. Charles-Léon-Clément Huntziger [+ Minister of National Defense and War] (killed in an air crash) 08/11/41
A.   **Consultative Committee for Colonial Defense**:

Chief of the Vichy Army General Staff: /40 Gen. Joseph-Edouard-Aimé Doumenc (General-Commissioner of National Reconstruction) /40 LG Odilon-Léonard-Théophile Picquendar (Commanding General, I Group of Military Divisions) /42 MG /41 BG Jean-Edouard Verneau (joins Resistance; Commander-in-Chief, Résistance de l'Armée) /43 MG Roger-Alexander-Louis Leyer
- A.   **Deputy Chief of the Army General Staff**: 06/25/40 MG Jules-Philippe-Octave Decamp (Deputy Commander, Military District XV) 07/40 MG Pierre-Jules-André-Marie de La Font Chabert (/42, Inspector of Cavalry) /41 BG Jean-Edouard Verneau (Chief of the Vichy General Staff) /42 MG Pierre-Armand-Marie-Robert Olleris (Chief of Staff, Organisation de Résistance de l'Armée) 11/29/42 dissolved.
  [NOTE: also found but no dates MG Georges-Jean-Eugène Pfister (Director of Infantry) /4?]
- B.   **1st Bureau (Administration)**:
- C.   **2nd Bureau (Intelligence)**:
- D.   **3rd Bureau (Operations)**:
- E.   **4th Bureau (Supply)**:
- F.   **Personnel**: /42 BG André-Marie-Martial d'Anselme (retired) /43
- G.   **Counter-Espionage**: /40? BG Emmanuel-Auguste-Abel Ronin
- H.   **Inspector-General of the Army**: /42 MG Marie-Cyrille-Victor Debeney (retired) /42
  1.   **Inspector-General of the Military Districts** (/40): Gen. [Retired '38] Antoine-Jules-Joseph Huré (retired) /40 Gen. [Retired] Camille Walch (retired) /40
     - a.   **Inspector, Military Districts VII, XIV, and XV**: 07/40 Gen. René-Henri Olry (Commanding General, I Group of Military Divisions) 09/12/40
     - b.   **Inspector, Military Districts IX and XII**: 07/40 Gen. Georges-Maurice-Jean Blanchard (retired) 09/12/40
     - c.   **Inspector, Military Districts XIII and XVI**: 07/40 Gen. Antoine-Marie-Benoit Besson (Director, Prisoner-of-War Service) 09/12/40
     - d.   **Inspector, Military District XVII and XVIII**: 07/40 Gen. Edouard-Jean Réquin (Commanding General, II Group of Military Divisions) 09/12/40
       - i.   **Chief of Staff, Inspector, Military Districts XVII and XVIII**: 07/40 LCol. Paul-Henri Dumas (Chief of Staff, II Group of Military Divisions) /40
  2.   **Inspector of Colonial Forces**: /41 MG Maxime-Jean-Vincent Germain [+ Member The Army Council] (on leave; /42, retired; /44 to /45, arrested by the Germans and deported) /42 LG Guillaume-Charles Roucaud (retired) /42
  3.   **Inspector-General of Infantry**: /40 LG Paul-Henry Gérodias (retired) /42
  4.   **Inspector of Cavalry**: /40 MG Jean-Léon-Albert Langlois (Commanding General, 9th Military Division) /42 MG Pierre-Jules-André-Marie de La Font Chabert (Commanding General, 7th Military Division) /42

5. **Inspector-General, Anti-Aircraft Artillery in France & North Africa** (07/40): LG Darius-Paul Bloch-Dassault (retired; /42, in resistance movement; /44, Military-Governor of Paris) /42
6. **Inspector of Signal Services** (06/25/39): /39 BG Joseph-Charles-Eugène Goetschy (in reserve; /43 to /45, German prisoner-of-war; /45, retired) 11/18/42 dissolved.
7. **Inspector-General of Education and Experimental Techniques**: /40? BG Paul-Gabriel Arnaud (Head, Disarmament of Germany Commission) /44?

I. **Department of Infantry**: /4? MG Georges-Jean-Eugène Pfister
J. **Department of Artillery**
   1. **Coordination of Air Defense Operations**:
      a. **Deputy, Coordination of Air Defense Operations**: /40 MG Darius-Paul Bloch-Dassault (Inspector-General, Anti-Aircraft Artillery in France & North Africa) /40
K. **Department of Engineer Service**:
L. **Department of Signal Service [Transmission]**: 06/25/40 LCol. Baussac
M. **Department of Transport**:
N. **Department of Intendent [Quartermaster] Service**:
O. **Department of Medical Service**:
P. **Army Social Service**: /42 LG [Retired '41] Louis-Eugène Hubert (retired) /43
Q. **Commandant, Technical Information Center**: 07/01/40? BG Jean-Baptiste-Henri Baurés
R. **Director, Prisoner-of-War Service**: /40 Gen. Antoine-Marie-Benoit Besson (retired) /40 LG [Retired '39] Victor-Henri Schweizguth (retired) /40
S. *Schools*
   1. **Director, Military Reconstruction School**: /41 Col. Raymond-Francis Duval (Military Attaché Ankara) /42?
   2. **Deputy Commandant, Lyon Medical School**: /42 LCol. Georges-André Hugonot (Director, Medical Services, Tunisia) /42
T. *Military Attaché*
   1. **Military Attaché Ankara (Turkey)**: /42? Col. Raymond-Francis Duval (Military Secretary to the Resident-General, Morocco) /43
U. *Commissions*
   1. **General-Commissioner of National Reconstruction**: /40 Gen. Joseph-Edouard-Aimé Doumenc (President, Commission for Investigation Suspicious Retreats) /40
   2. **Commission for Investigation Suspicious Retreats**:
      a. **President**: /40 Gen. Joseph-Edouard-Aimé Doumenc (st disposal of the Commander-in-Chief, Armed Forces; /42, retired) /42
   3. **Commission Reviewing Citations**:
      a. **President**: /40 MG Robert-Marie-Eduardo Petiet (retired) /42
   4. **Commission in Charge of granting Rewards in the War**:
      a. **Chairman**: 02/01/42 LG Henri-Fernand Dentz (01/45, arrested and condemned to death as a collaborator; /45, sentence changed to life imprisonment; /45, died in prison) /43 LG Paul-Hippolyte Arlabosse (at disposal of Commander-in-Chief of the Army; /45, retired) /44
      b. **Members**:

                    /43 MG Paul-Hippolyte Arlabosse (Chairman, Committee in charge of granting rewards in the war) /43
5. **Investigating Commission of War Events**
    a. **President**: /42 Gen. [Retired '42] Aubert-Achille-Jules Frère (retired; /43, Commander-in-Chief, l'Organisation de Réeistance de l'Armée) /43
6. **Commission for the Studies of Fortified Zones**
    a. **Member**
        /40 BG Maurice-Jules-Zacharie Grenet (Engineers Commander, Military District VII) /40

V. *French Delegations*:
1. **French Delegation to the Italian Sub-Commission for Demilitarization of the Libyan Border Zone**: /40 BG Georges-Edmond-Lucien Barré (Chief of Staff, Military District XIX) /40
2. **French Delegation to the Franco-German Armistice Commission** (Wiesbaden, Germany):
    a. **Head** (06/22/40): Gen. Charles-Léon-Clément Huntziger (Commander-in-Chief, Vichy France Land Forces & Vichy France Minister of National Defense and War) 09/06/40 LG Paul-André Doyen (retired; /42, arrested) /40 BG Jean-Edouard Verneau (Deputy Chief of the Vichy Army General Staff) /41BG Jean-Louis-Auguste Humbert (Commanding General, Unknown? Mountain Demi-Brigade; /42, Commanding General, 15th Military Division) /41 unknown? 08/42 VA Landriau [FN]
    b. **Members**
        /41 MG Étienne-Paul-Émile-Marie Beynet (retired; /42, fled to England; /43, joined the Free French; /43, Head, French Military Mission to Washington, D. C.) /42
        /43 MG Louis-Gustavé Bérard (at disposal of Commander-in-Chief of the Army; /45 retired) /44
3. **French Delegation to the Franco-Italian Armistice Commission** (Turin, Italy):
    a. **President** (09/12/40): VA E. A. H. Duplat [FN]
    b. **Vice President** (09/12/40): MG Henri Parisot (retired) /43
4. **French Delegation for the Occupied Territories**: /40 LG Léon-Benoit de Fornel de La Laurencie (retired; /42 to /44, interned by the Vichy Government) /40

Chief of the French Empire [Colonial Forces] General Staff:
/40 Gen. Jules-Antoine Bührer [+ Inspector-General of Colonial Forces & Inspector of Colonial Forces in France & President, Consultative Committee of Colonial Defense] (retired) /41
/40 LG Émile-Jean-Gabriel Carlès (retired) /41
/41 MG Guillaume-Charles Roucaud (Inspector of Colonial Troops) /42

Commander-in-Chief, Vichy Navy (07/04/40): Adm. Of the Ft. Jean-Louis-Xavier-François Darlan [FN] [+ Commander-in-Chief, Vichy Armed Forces; Chief of the General Staff for Naval Operations; Minister of Marine; + 02/01/41 to 04/18/42, Foreign Minister;

+ 02/09/41 to 04/18/42, Chief of State [Vice Premier]; + 02/14/41 to 07/18/41, Minister of the Interior; + 08/11/41 to 04/18/42, Minister of National Defense and War] (talked with Allies in North Africa about French troops laying down their weapons; changed sides and assisted the Allies; through his deal he becomes High Commissioner of French North Africa and West Africa; dismissed from the Vichy government and for his actions, Vichy Southern France was 'invaded' by the German Army and it's armed forces demobilized) 11/42 demobilized.

- A. **Chief of Staff, Commander-in-Chief, Navy**: 09/01/39? RA Maurice-Athanase le Luc [FN] 09/41 RA Gabriel-Paul Auphan [+ /41, Chief of Cabinet, Minister of Marine] (Minister of Marine) 04/42 unknown? 11/42 VA Maurice-Athanase le Luc [FN] (02/25/50, condemned to 2 years imprisonment for collarboration; /51, released) 11/42 dissolved.
    1. **2nd Bureau - Intelligence**:
    2. **3rd Bureau - Operations**
- B. **Deputy Chief of Staff, Commander-in-Chief, Navy** (responsible for Merchant Marine): Capt. Gabriel-Paul Auphan (Chief of Staff, Commander-in-Chief, Navy) /41
- C. **Naval General Staff**
- D. **Naval Commands** (07/40)
    1. **High Seas Fleet**
    2. **Maritime Perfect and Governor of Toulon**
    3. **Algiers Naval Force**
    4. **Oran Naval Force**
    5. **Bizerte Naval Force**
    6. **Casablanca Naval Force**
    7. **Levant Naval Station**
    8. **West Africa Naval Station**
    9. **Admiral Antilles**
    10. **Admiral Far East [Indochina]**

Chief of the General Staff for Naval Operations (07/04/40): Adm. Of the Ft. Jean-Louis-Xavier-François Darlan [FN] [+ Commander-in-Chief, Vichy Armed Forces; Commander-in-Chief, Vichy Navy; ; Minister of Marine; + 02/01/41 to 04/18/42, Foreign Minister; + 02/09/41 to 04/18/42, Chief of State [Vice Premier]; + 02/14/41 to 07/18/41, Minister of the Interior; + 08/11/41 to 04/18/42, Minister of National Defense and War] (talked with Allies in North Africa about French troops laying down their weapons; changed sides and assisted the Allies; through his deal he becomes High Commissioner of French North Africa and West Africa; dismissed from the Vichy government and for his actions, Vichy Southern France was 'invaded' by the German Army and it's armed forces demobilized) 11/42 demobilized.

Commander-in-Chief, Vichy Air Force [Chefs d'État-Major Général de l'Armée de l'Air] (07/04/40): vacant 09/10/40 LG Robert Odic [FAF] 09/23/40 MG Jean-Charles Romatet [FAF] (?) 12/21/42 disbanded.
- A. **Inspector-General of the Air Force**: 06/24/40 Gen. Joseph Vuillemin [FAF] (retired) 11/40

Chief of the Air Force General Staff [Chef d'État-Major des Forces Aériennes]: 03/19/42 MG Jean-François Jannekeyn [FAF] [+ Air Minister [Vichy Government] 02/27/43 disbanded.

Commander-in-Chief, Foreign Legion: /40 LG Julien-François-René Martin (retired) /41

Vichy France in North Africa

Committee of Five (01/42):
A. **Members:**
      HENRI d'ASTIER de la VIGERIE
      JEAN RIGAULT
      JACQUES LEMAIGRE-DUBREUIL
      JACQUES TARBÉ de SAINT-HARDOUIN
      Col. Van Hecke

[The term "Free French" is used only by individuals or groups of individuals that joined BG Charles-André-Joseph-Marie de Gaulle before July 31, 1943 inclusive. This is to distinguish between those who joined de Gaulle in the early stages of the war and those who became "resistants" after the landings of United States troops in North Africa and after the end of the North African campaign in May 1943.]

National Committee of the Free French

Head, French National Committee (F. N. C.) (09/24/41): BG Charles-André-Joseph-Marie de Gaulle [+ to 01/43, Commander-in-Chief, Free French Armed Forces; + 12/26/42, one of the Co-Chairman of French Committee of National Liberation] 06/03/43 disbanded.

A. **Assistant to BG de Gaulle**: 12/42 LG François d'Astier de la Vigerie $_{[FAF]}$ [Member, Free French Supreme War Council; + 01/01/43 to /43, Commanding General, French Troops in Great Britain].

Civil Affairs

A. **Administration and Finances** (06/22/40): ARISTIDE ANTONINE (alias Fontaine or Colonel Roland) /40 PIERRE DENIS (alais Rauzan) /40? Maj. Étienne Hirsch /41? Maj. Menguy 09/24/41 becomes Finance Commission, National Committee of Free French and disbanded.

B. **Armament** (06/22/40): Maj. Étienne Hirsch (Administration and Finances, French National Committee) /40 ANDRÉ LABARTHE (fired) 09/40

   [NOTE: Fired from the Free French in September 1940 after it was discovered that he had a phony diploma and was not a scientist he claimed to be. The recent declassified American NSA files in the Verona project prove he was a communist spy, who together with his secretary, provided valuable military information to the Russian Embassy in London for money.]

C. **Economy and Colonies** (06/22/40): PIERRE-OLIVIER LAPIE (01/21/40, Governor of Chad, French Equatorial Africa) /40 RENÉ PLEVEN (Head, Finance Commission, National Committee of Free French &Head, Colonies Commission, National Committee of Free French) 09/24/41 becomes Finance Commission, National Committee of Free French & Colonies Commission, National Committee of Free French and disbanded.

   1. **Information and Press** (06/22/40): ÉTIENNE DENNERY /40? ROBERT MARJOLIN /40? Col. Jean Massip /41? JACQUES SOUSTELLE (07/28/42, Head, Information Commission, National Committee of Free French) 09/24/41 becomes Information Commission, National Committee of Free French and disbanded.

D. **Merchant Navy (Sea Transport)** (06/22/40): JACQUES INGEN /41? PIERRE de MALGLAIVE 09/24/41 becomes Navy and Merchant Navy Commission, National Committee of Free French and disbanded.

E. **Politics** (06/22/40): GASTON PALEWSKI /40 MAURICE DEJEAN (Head, Foreign Affairs Commission, National Committee of Free French) 09/24/41 JOSEPH

HACKIN 09/24/41 becomes Foreign Affairs Commission, National Committee of Free French) and disbanded.

French National Committee (Commissions)
A. **Foreign Affairs Commission** (09/24/41): MAURICE DEJEAN 10/17/42 RENÉ PLEVEN (09/10/44, Head, Colonies (Overseas France) Commission, National Committee of Free French) 02/05/43 RENÉ MASSIGLI 09/10/44 see **French Provisional Government**.
   [NOTE: acting in /43 Gen. [Retired '39] Georges-Albert-Julien Catroux (Commissioner for Coordination of Muslim Affairs) /43**]**
B. **Finance Commission** (09/24/41): RENÉ PLEVEN [+ Head, Colonies (Overseas France) Commission, National Committee of Free French] (Head, Foreign Affairs Commission, National Committee of Free French)10/17/42 ANDRÉ DIETHELM (Head, Commerce and Industry Commission, National Committee of Free French) 06/07/43 MAURICE COUVE de MURVILLE 11/09/43 PIERRE MENDÈS-FRANCE 09/04/44 see **French Provisional Government**.
C. **National Defense Commission**: 11/09/43 LG Paul-Louis-Victor-Marie Legentilhomme (/44, Commanding General, Military District III) /43 unknown? 04/04/44 ANDRÉ DIETHELM [+ Head, War Commission, National Committee of Free French] (Minister of National Defense and War, French Provisional Government) 09/10/44 see **French Provisional Government**.
   1. **Deputy, National Defense Commission**: 05/03/43 MG Paul-Louis-Victor-Marie Legentilhomme [+ Head, War Commission, National Committee of Free French] (Commissioner of National Defense, National Committee of Free French) 11/09/43
D. **War Commission** (09/24/41): MG Paul-Louis-Victor-Marie Legentilhomme [+ /42 to 01/07/43, High Commissioner, French Possessions, Indian Ocean; + 01/07/43 to 05/03/43, Governor-General, Madagascar & Commanding General, Madagascar; + 05/03/43, Deputy Commission to National Defense] 11/09/43 ANDRÉ Le TROQUET (Head, Air Commission, National Committee of Free French) 04/04/44 ANDRÉ DIETHELM [+ Head, National Defense Commission, National Committee of Free French] (Minister of National Defense and War, French Provisional Government) 09/10/44 see **French Provisional Government**.
E. **Air Commission** (09/24/41): BG Martial Valin [FAF] [+ Commandant of Free French Air Force] 06/07/43 ANDRÉ Le TROQUET 04/04/44 FERNAND GRENIER 09/10/44 see **French Provisional Government**.
F. **Navy and Merchant Navy Commission** (09/24/41): VA Émile-Henri Muselier [FN] [+ Member, Council for the Defense of the Empire & Commander-in-Chief, Free French Navy] (resigned) 04/42 RA Philippe Auboyneau [FN] [+ Commander-in-Chief, Free French Navy]
G. **Colonies (Overseas France) Commission** (09/24/41): RENÉ PLEVEN [+Head, Finance Commission, National Committee of Free French] (Head, Foreign Affairs Commission, National Committee of Free French)10/17/42 HERVÉ ALPHAND 09/10/44 RENÉ PLEVEN (Finance Minister, French Provisional Government & Minister for Colonies (Overseas France), French Provisional Government) 11/16/44 see **French Provisional Government**.
H. **Interior Commission** (09/24/41): ANDRÉ DIETHELM [+Information Commission,

National Committee of Free French & Labor Commission, National Committee of Free French] (10/17/42, Finance Minister, National Committee of Free French) 07/28/42 ANDRÉ PHILIP [Head, Labor Commission, National Committee of Free French] 11/09/43 EMMANUEL d'ASTIER de la VIGERIE 09/10/44 see **French Provisional Government**.

I. **Information Commission** (09/24/41): ANDRÉ DIETHELM [+ Head, Interior Commission, National Committee of Free French & Head, Labor Commission, National Committee of Free French] (10/17/42, Head, Finance Minister, National Committee of Free French) 07/28/42 JACQUES SOUSTELLE (09/10/44, Minister of Information, French Provisional Government) 06/07/43 HENRI BONNET 09/10/44 see **French Provisional Government**.

J. **Commerce and Industry Commission** (06/07/43): ANDRÉ DIETHELM (04/04/44, Head, War Commission, National Committee of Free French & Head, National Defense Commission, National Committee of Free French) 11/09/43 disbanded.

K. **Justice Commission** (09/24/41): RENÉ CASSIN [+ Head, Education Commission, National Committee of Free French] 06/43 JULES ABADIE [+ Head, Health, Commission, National Committee of Free French] 09/43 FRANÇOIS de MENTHON (Minister of Justice, French Provisional Government) 09/10/44 see **French Provisional Government**.

L. **Transport and Public Works Commission** (11/09/43): RENÉ MAYER (Minister of Transport and Public Works, French Provisional Government) 09/10/44 see **French Provisional Government**.

M. **Health Commission** (06/07/43): JULES ABADIE [+ to 09/43, Head, Justice Commission, National Committee of Free French] 11/09/43 disbanded.

N. **Education Commission** (09/24/41): RENÉ CASSIN [+ to 06/43, Head, Justice Commission, National Committee of Free French] 09/10/44 see **French Provisional Government**.

O. **Labor Commission** (09/24/41): ANDRÉ DIETHELM [+Information Commission, National Committee of Free French & Interior Commission, National Committee of Free French] (10/17/42, Finance Minister, National Committee of Free French) 07/28/42 ANDRÉ PHILIP [+ to 11/09/43, Head, Interior Commission, National Committee of Free French] 09/10/44 see **French Provisional Government**.

P. **Commissioner for Coordination for Muslim Affairs**: /43 Gen. [Retired '39] Georges-Albert-Julien Catroux (Governor-General of Algeria) /43

Q. **Minister of State (No Portfolios)**:
/40 Gen. [Retired '39] Georges-Albert-Julien Catroux (Commander-in-Chief, Free French Forces, Middle East) /40
/40 RA Georges Thierry d'Argenlieu [FN]

Free French Armed Forces

Council for the Defense of the Empire (formed in French Equatorial Africa)
    RENÉ CASSIN
    Gen. [Retired '39] Georges-Albert-Julien Catroux
    Governor ADOLPHE-FÉLIX-SYLVESTRE ÉBOUÉ [Governor of Chad]
    MG René-Marie-Edgar de Larminat [+ High Commissioner of Free French Colonies in Africa & Commanding General, Free French Forces in Equatorial Africa] (Commanding General, Free French Oriental Brigade) 11/12/40
    Col. Philippe-François-Marie-Jacques Leclerc de Hauteclocque, Count of Hauteclocque [+ 08/27/40 to 11/20/39, Military Governor, Cameroon; + 12/10/39 to 01/21/40, Military Governor, Chad; + 01/21/41, Commander-in-Chief, French Equatorial Africa; + /41, Commanding General, Column Leclerc] (08/24/43, Commanding General, 2nd Free French Armored Division) /42
    VA Émile-Henri Muselier [FN] [+ Navy and Merchant Navy Commission & Commander-in-Chief, Free French Navy] (resigned) 04/42
    BG (Chief Doctor) Marie-Eugène-Adolphe Sicé [+ Director, Medical Service, French Equatorial Africa; + 11/12/40 to 12/30/40 acting Governor-General of French Equatorial Africa; + 08/41 to 07/42, High Commissioner of Free French in Africa] (Inspector-General of Medical Services, Free French Forces) /42
    Governor HENRI-CAMILLE SAUTOT [French Governor, New Caladonia] (French Governor, Ubangi-Shari, French Equatorial Africa) 05/06/42
    RA Georges Thierry d'Argenlieu [FN] [High French Commissioner in the Pacific]

Commander-in-Chief, Free French Armed Forces (06/18/40): see **Provisional Government of France** section.

Chief of Staff, Free French Armed Forces: see **Provisional Government of France** section.

Free French in North Africa

High Commissioner of North Africa (11/13/42) Adm. of the Fl. Jean-Louis-Xavier-François Darlan [FN] [+ Chairmen, French Empire Council & Commander-in-Chief, Free French Naval Fleet] (assassinated) 12/24/42 Gen. Henri Honoré Giraud [+ to 11/09/43, Member, Empire Council; + 12/26/42 to 11/09/43, one of the Co-Chairman of the French Committee of National Liberation & Military and Civilian Commander-in-Chief; + 01/43, Commander-in-Chief, Free French Army] 04/04/44

- A. **Chief of Staff, High Commissioner North Africa** (11/13/42): Gen. Jean-Marie-Joseph Bergeret [FAF] (11/44, arrested by the Provisional Government)
- B. **Foreign Affairs** (11/13/42): JACQUES TARBÉ de SAINT-HARDOUIN
- C. **Interior** (11/13/42): JEAN RIGAULT
    - 1. **Assistant Director, Interior** (11/13/42): HENRI d'ASTIER de la VIGERIE [+ Head, South Liberation Resistance Movement]
- D. **Commander-in-Chief, Land & Air Forces, North Africa**: 07/16/40 Gen. [Retired '35] Maxime Weygand [+ Vichy France Minister of War; + to 07/16/41, Delegate-General of the Vichy Government to North Africa; + 07/16/41, Governor, Algeria] (to /45, Free French prisoner-of-war; after war held as a collaborator at Val-de-Grâce; 05/46, released; /48, cleared) 11/20/41 unknown? 11/13/42 Gen. Henri Honoré Giraud (Military and Civilian Commander-in-Chief) 12/26/42 disbanded.
- E. **Commander-in-Chief, Free French Naval Fleet** (11/13/42): Adm. of the Fl. Jean-Louis-Xavier-François Darlan [FN] [+ Chairmen, French Empire Council; High Commissioner of North Africa and French West Africa] (assassinated) 12/24/42
- F. **Military and Civilian Commander-in-Chief** (12/26/42, North Africa): Gen. Henri Honoré Giraud [+ High Commissioner, North Africa, one of the Co-Chairman of the French Committee of National Liberation; + to 11/09/43, Member, Empire Council; + 01/43, Commander-in-Chief, Free French Army] (Inspector-General of the Army) 04/04/44 dissolved.
- G. **Chief of the Free French Army General Staff** (12/26/42): Gen. René-Jacques-Adolphe Prioux (removed) /43
- H. **Chief of The Free French Navy General Staff** (12/26/42): VA François-Félix Michelier [FN] (removed) /43
- I. **Official Representative for the French at Allied Forces Headquarters in Algeria** (12/26/42): BG Marcel Rime-Bruneau (Official Representative at the French Residence in Tunis) /43

Empire Council (12/07/42)
- A. **Chairman, Empire Council** (12/07/42): Adm. of the Fl. Jean-Louis-Xavier-François Darlan [FN] [+ High Commissioner of North Africa and French West Africa; Commander-in-Chief, Free French Naval Fleet] (assassinated) 12/24/42
- B. **Members, Empire Council** (12/07/42):
    12/07/42 Gen. Jean-Marie-Joseph Bergeret [FAF] [+ Chief of Staff, High

Commissioner North Africa]
12/07/42 Gen. Henri Honoré Giraud [+ to 12/26/42, Commander-in-Chief, Land & Air Forces, North Africa; + 12/24/42, High Commissioner, North Africa; + 12/26/42, one of the Co-Chairman of the French Committee of National Liberation & Military and Civilian Commander-in-Chief; + 01/43, Commander-in-Chief, Free French Army] 11/09/43
12/07/42 Gen. Charles-Auguste-Paul Noguès [+ Resident-General, Tunisia] (relieved) 06/21/43
12/07/42 LG Yves-Charles Châtel [+ Governor-General of Algeria] (retired) 01/20/43
12/07/42 PIERRE-FRANÇOIS BOISSON [+ Governor-General of French West Africa] (resigned) 05/43

Resistance Organizations

[There were many resistance groups that were formed in France. The ones listed below are the largest or best known of these resistance groups.]

Musée de l'Homme [Museum of Man] (formed in 07/40, by group of Paris academics and lawyers, calling for the French to resist the Germans; the group was infiltrated by a supporter of the French Vichy Government and virtually all of the members arrested): GERMAINE TILLON (concentration camp - survived the war), PIERRE BROSSOLETTE (escaped and joined Socialist Action Committee), JEAN PAULHAM (unknown?), BORIS WILDE (executed), YVONNE ODDON (concentration camp - survived the war), PIERRE WALTER (executed), JULES ANDRIEU (executed), LÉON-MAURICE NORDMANN (executed), ALICE SIMMONET (concentration camp - survived the war), GEORGE ITHIER (executed), SYLVETTE LELEU (concentration camp - survived the war), ANATOLE LEWITSKY (executed), VALENTIN FELDMAN (executed), CLAUDE AVELINE (unknown?), and JEAN CASSOU (unknown?) /40 disbanded.

Défense de la France [Defense of France] (07/40, a group of students at the Sorbonne; besides publishing a newspaper encouraging resistance, they also established an intelligence and escape network): HELENE VIANNAY [nee MORDKOVITCH].

Comité d'Action Socialiste [Socialist Action Committee] (formed in 01/41, in the French Socialist Party; 05/43, joins forces with Combat, Franc-Tireur, the National Front, South Liberation, and the Secret Army to form the **National Resistance Council [Conseil National de la Resistance]**): DANIEL MAYER and in 03/41 PIERRE BROSSOLETTE 05/43 helps forms the **National Resistance Council [Conseil National de la Resistance]**.

Liberation-Sud [South Liberation] (formed in 07/41; 05/43, joins forces with Combat, Franc-Tireur, the National Front, Socialist Action Committee, and the Secret Army to form the **National Resistance Council [Conseil National de la Resistance]**): EMMANUEL d'ASTIER de la VIGERIE [+ 11/13/42, Assistant Director, Interior for North Africa] LUCIE AUBRAC, and RAYMOND AUBRAC 05/43 helps forms the **National Resistance Council [Conseil National de la Resistance]**.

Combat (formed in 11/41, around Lyon; 05/43, joins forces with South Liberation, Franc-Tireur, the National Front, Socialist Action Committee, and the Secret Army to form the **National Resistance Council [Conseil National de la Resistance]**): HENRY FRENAY 05/43 helps forms the **National Resistance Council [Conseil National de la Resistance]**.

Franc-Tireur [French irregular rifleman] (formed in 11/41, by socialist, communist, and liberals, around Lyon; 05/43, joins forces with Combat, South Liberation, the National Front, Socialist Action Committee, and the Secret Army to form the **National Resistance Council [Conseil National de la Resistance]**): JEAN-PIERRE LÉVY 05/43 helps forms the **National Resistance Council [Conseil National de la Resistance]**.

Franc-Tireur et Partisans (FTP) [the **French Partisan irregular rifleman**] (formed in 1941, mainly from the French Communist Party): CHARLES TILLON (09/10/44, Minister of Air, French Provisional Government) and PIERRE FABIEN [Col. Fabien] (arrested, but in 06/43, escaped).

Front National [National Front] (formed in 05/42; 05/43, joins forces with Combat, Franc-Tireur, the South Liberation, Socialist Action Committee, and the Secret Army to form the **National Resistance Council [Conseil National de la Resistance]**): PIERRE VILLON [ROGER GINSBURGER took the pseudonym PIERRE VILLON] 05/43 helps forms the **National Resistance Council [Conseil National de la Resistance]**.

Armée secrète [Secret Army] (/42; 05/43, joins forces with Combat, Franc-Tireur, the National Front, Socialist Action Committee, and South Liberation to form the **National Resistance Council [Conseil National de la Resistance]**): JEAN MOULIN (President, National Resistance Council) 03/24/43 MG [Retired '39 & '40] Charles-Georges-Antoine Delestraint (to /45, German prisoner-of-war; /45, died in Struthoff Concentration Camp; /45, posthumously promoted to Lieutenant General) /43 BG Pierre-Marie-Philippe Dejussieu-Pontcarrel (Chief of Staff, French Forces of the Interior) 06/23/44 disbanded.
[NOTE: 05/43 helps forms the **National Resistance Council [Conseil National de la Resistance]**].

Maquis (04/42?, communist militants acting independently of the French Communist Party, around Limousine and Puy-de-Dôm):
A. **Leader, Limousine Maquis**: 05/42 GEORGES GUINGOUIN

l'Organisation de Résistance de l'Armée [Army Resistance Organization]: /43 Gen. [Retired '42 & '43] Aubert-Achille-Jules Frère (to /44, German prison; /44, died in Struthoff Concentration Camp) /43 MG /41 BG Jean-Edouard Verneau (arrested by the Germans; /44, died in Buchenwald Concentration Camp) /44 BG Georges-Marie-Joseph Revers (Commanding General, Paris Military District) /44
A, **Deputy, l'Organisation de Réeistance de l'Armée**: /43 BG [Retired '43] André-Marie-Martial d'Anselme (Deputy Commander, French Forces in the West) /44
B. **Chief of Staff, Army Resistance Organization**: /42 MG Pierre-Armand-Marie-Robert Olleris (?) /44 Col. Pierre-Salomon-Isaac Brisac
C. *Regions, Army Resistance Organization*
    1. **5th Region, Army Resistance Organization**: /41 Col. Jacques-Pierre-Louis de Grancey (arrested and deported by the Germans) /44
    2. **6th Region, Army Resistance Organization**: /41 Col. Pierre-Marie-Philippe Dejussieu-Pontcarrel (/43, Commanding General, Secret Army, Southern France) /42
    3. **Alpine Resistance Zone**: /44 Col. Henri Zeller (Deputy Chief of the Free French General Staff) /45

National Resistance Council [Conseil National de la Resistance (CNR)] (05/43, from the following resistance groups: **Socialist Action Committee**, **Liberation**, **Combat**, **Franc-Tireur**, **National Front**, and the **Secret Army**):
A. **President, National Resistance Council** (05/27/43): JEAN MOULIN (arrested and

351

tortured to death by the Germans) 06/43 GEORGES BIDAULT (Foreign Minister, French Provisional Government) 09/10/44 dissolved.

French Committee of National Liberation [F. C. N. L.]

Co-Chairmen of the French Committee of National Liberation (F. C. N. L.) (12/26/42, in London; from 06/03/43 in Algiers): BG Charles-André-Joseph-Marie de Gaulle [+ to 01/43, Commander-in-Chief, Free French Armed Forces & to 06/03/43, Head, French National Committee; + 04/43 to 04/08/43, Commander-in-Chief, Free French Army] and Gen. Henri Honoré Giraud [+ High Commissioner, North Africa; + Member, Empire Council; + Military and Civilian Commander-in-Chief; + 01/43 to 04/43, Commander-in-Chief, Free French Army] 11/09/43 redesignated **Chairmen of the French Committee of National Liberation (F. C. N. L.)** 11/09/43 BG Charles-André-Joseph-Marie de Gaulle 06/03/44 redesignated Chairman and Prime Minister of the Provisional Government.

A. **Chief of Staff, Chairmen of the French Committee of National Liberation**: BG Moïse-Germain-Louis Jousse
B. **Committee for National Defense**:
   1. **Chief, National Defense Staff**: /43 MG Marie-Emil-Antoine Béthouart (Commanding General, I French Army Corps) 07/44 LG Alphonse-Pierre Juin [+ Chief of the Army General Staff].
      a. **Deputy Chief, National Defense Staff**: 05/13/43 MG Marie-Joseph-Pierre-François Kœnig (French Liaison Officer to Supreme Headquarters Allied Expeditionary Forces [see Volume III] & Commanding General, French Forces in Great Britain) /44 MG François-Adolphe-Laurent Sevez.
   2. **Secretary, Committee for National Defense**: /43 BG Jean Breuillac (/44, Commanding General, Algier Division) /43 BG Pierre-Armand-Gaston Billotte (Deputy Commander, 2nd Free French Armored Division) /44
C. **High Commission for the Levant**: 01/23/44 LG Étienne-Paul-Émile-Marie Beynet [+ Commander-in-Chief, the Levant].
D. **Members, French Committee of National Liberation**
   /42 Gen. Alphonse-Joseph Georges /45

Commander-in-Chief, Free French Army (01/43): Gen. Henri-Honoré Giraud [+ High Commissioner, North Africa; + to 11/09/43, Member, Empire Council; + to 11/09/43, one of the Co-Chairman of the French Committee of National Liberation; + Military and Civilian Commander-in-Chief] (Inspector-General of the Army) 04/04/44 BG Charles-André-Joseph-Marie de Gaulle [+ Head, French National Committee] 04/08/44 abolished.
A. **Chief of the Free French Army General Staff** (/43): MG René-Marie-Edgar de Larminat (Commanding General, II Free French Army Corps) 08/31/44 see under **Provisional Government** Section.

Provisional Government of France

Chairman and Prime Minister of the Provisional Government (06/03/44): BG Charles-André-Joseph-Marie de Gaulle [+ 07/44, Commander-in-Chief, French Army] 01/26/46 FÉLIX GOUIN.

Prime Minister (10/01/44): FERNAND de BRINON (acting) 05/09/45 BG Charles-André-Joseph-Marie de Gaulle [+ Minister of National Defense].
- A. **Foreign Minister** (09/10/44): GEORGES BIDAULT.
- B. **Finance Minister** (09/04/44): AIMÉ LEPERCQ 11/09/44 RENÉ PLEVEN [+ 11/16/44, Minister for Colonies (Overseas France), French provisional Government].
- C. **Minister of National Defense and War** (09/04/44): ANDRÉ DIETHELM 11/21/45 EDMOND MICHELET.
    1. **Bureau of French Forces of the Interior (FFI) [Forces Françaises l'Intérieur], Commissariat of Defense**: /44 BG Pierre de Bénouville (Commanding General, Moroccan Light Infantry, Italy) /44
- D. **Minister of Air** (09/10/44): CHARLES TILLON 11/21/45 vacant 01/22/47 ANDRÉ MAROSELLI.
- E. **Minister of Navy** (09/10/44): M. LOUIS JACQUINOT
- F. **Minister for Colonies (Overseas France)**: 11/16/44 RENÉ PLEVEN [+ Finance Minister, French provisional Government]..
    1. **Director, Ministry of Colonies** (08/20/44): BG Henri-Frédéric-Paul Casseville.
    2. **Director, Overseas Troops** (/44): BG François-Joseph-Jean Ingold.
- G. **Interior Minister** (09/10/44): ADRIEN TIXIER.
- H. **Minister of Information** (09/10/44): PIERRE-HENRI TEITGEN (Minister of Justice, French Provisional Government) 05/30/45 JACQUES SOUSTELLE 11/21/45 ANDRÉ MALRAUX.
- I. **Minister of Commerce and Industry**: not did exist until 01/22/47.
- J. **Minister of Justice** (09/10/44): FRANÇOIS de MENTHON /45 PIERRE-HENRI TEITGEN.
- K. **Minister of Agriculture** (09/04/44): FRANÇOIS TANGUY-PRIGENT.
- L. **Minister of Transport and Public Works** (09/10/44): RENÉ MAYER 11/21/45 JULES MOCH.
- M. **Minister of Health** (09/10/44): FRANÇOIS BILLOUX 11/21/45 ROBERT PRIGENT.
- N. **Education Minister** (08/20/44): RENÉ CAPITANT 11/21/45 PAUL GIACOBBI.
- O. **Minister of Social Affairs (Labor)**: not did exist until 10/22/47.
- P. **Minister of Posts, Telegraphs and Telephones** (09/10/44): AUGUSTIN LAURENT 06/27/45 EUGÈNE THOMAS.
- Q. **Minister of North Africa** (09/08/44): Gen. [Retired '39] Georges-Albert-Julien Catroux [+ Delegate-General Commissioner of the Government for North Africa].

Provisional Government Armed Forces

Commander-in-Chief, Free French Armed Forces (06/18/40): BG Charles-André-Joseph-Marie de Gaulle [+ 09/24/41 to 12/26/42, Head, French National Committee; + 12/26/42, one of the Co-Chairmen of the French Committee of National Liberation] 01/43
    1. **Chief of Staff to BG Charles de Gaulle**: /40 Col. Diégo-Charles-Jospeh Brosset (Head, French Military Mission to Ethiopia) /41
    2. **Deputy Chief of Staff to BG Charles de Gaulle**: /41 LCol. Achille-Fernand-Hector Dassonville (Chief of Staff, Free French Forces, Libya) /42
A. **Commander-in-Chief, French Army**
B. **Chief of Staff, Free French General Staff**:
C. **Commandant of the Navy**
D. **Commandant of Free French Air Force [Forces Aériennes François Libres (FAFL)]**
E. **Chief of the General Staff, Navy and Air Force [Chefs d'État-Major des FAFL]**

Commander-in-Chief, French Army (07/44): BG Charles-André-Joseph-Marie de Gaulle
    1. **Inspector of Finances**: /43 Col. Jacques-Pierre-Michel Chaban-Dalmas (Chief Inspectorate-General of the Army) /44
A. **French Forces in the West**:
    1. **Deputy Commander, French Forces in the West**: /44 MG [Retired '43] André-Marie-Martial d'Anselme.
B. **French Forces of the Interior (FFI) [Forces Françaises l'Intérieur]** (06/23/44, placed the resistance fighter under one command; 10/44, disbanded and were amalgamated into the French regular forces): MG Marie-Joseph-Pierre-François Kœnig [+ Military-Governor of Paris] 10/44 disbanded.

Chief of the French Army General Staff (06/40): MG Ernest-Émile Petit (/42, Head, Free French Military Mission to Soviet Union) /41 MG Raymond Tissier /42 BG Pierre-Armand-Gaston Billotte (Secretary, Committee for National Defense) /43 MG René-Marie-Edgar de Larminat (Commanding General, II Free French Army Corps) /43 LG Alphonse-Pierre Juin [+ Chief of National Defense Staff].
A. **Deputy Chief of the General Staff** (06/40): LCol. Moïse-Germain-Louis Jousse (Chief of Staff, Governor-General of Algeria) /43 BG Jean-Clément Blanc (?) /45 Col. Henri Zeller
B. ***Army Commands***:
    1. **Commander-in-Chief, French Land Forces, North Africa** (01/43): see **Commander-in-Chief, North Africa Theater** 05/10/43 disbanded.
    2. **Commander-in-Chief, French Expeditionary Corps in Italy** (09/43): LG Alphonse-Pierre Juin (Chief of the Free French General Staff) 07/44 disbanded.
    3. **Commander-in-Chief, Army B** (12/43): LG Jean-Joseph-Marie-Gabriel de Lattre de Tassigny (Commander-in-Chief, First Free French Army) 08/44 redesignated **First French Army** - see **First French Army**.
B. **1st Bureau (Administration)**:
C. **2nd Bureau (Intelligence)**: Cdr. Andre Dewavrin (alais Passy)

D. **3rd Bureau (Operations)**:
E. **4th Bureau (Supply)**:
F. **Inspector-General of the Army [Inspecteur Général de l'Armée]** (04/04/44): BG Jacques-Pierre-Michel Chaban-Dalmas (?   ) /44 Gen. Henri Honoré Giraud.
   1. **Inspector of Artillery** (/43): BG Marie-Antoine-Arthur-Olivier Poydenot (Artillery Commander, 2nd Moroccan Infantry Division) /44
   2. **Inspector-General of Army Medical Services**: /41 MG Maurice-Louis-Étienne Pilod (?   ) 07/42 BG Marie-Eugène-Adolphe Sicé.
G. *Directors*
   1. **Director of Artillery**: /45 BG André-Marie Zeller.
   2. **Director, Colonial Forces**: /43 BG Jean-Étienne Valluy (Chief of Staff, Free French First Army) /44
H. **Army Geographical Service [Service Geographique d'Armée]**: /44 MG Louis-Aristide-Alexandre Hurault
I. *High Commissioners*:
   1. **High Commissioner of Free French for Middle East**: 02/01/42 Gen. [Retired '39] Georges-Albert-Julien Catroux [+ Commander-in-Chief, Levant] **[NOTE: was in fact senior and superior to de Gaulle]** (State Commissioner for Foreign Affairs) /43
   2. **High Commissary of Free French in Africa**: 08/28/40 BG René-Marie-Edgar de Larminat [+ Commanding General, Free French Forces in Equatorial Africa & Member, Council for the Defense of the Empire] (Commanding General, Free French Oriental Brigade) 11/12/40 unknown? 08/41 BG (Chief Doctor) Marie-Eugène-Adolphe Sicé [+ Council for the Defense of the Empire] (Inspector-General of Medical Services, Free French Forces) 07/42
   3. **High Commissioner, French Possessions Indian Ocean**: /42 MG Paul-Louis-Victor-Marie Legentilhomme [+ Free French War Commissioner] (Governor-General, Madagascar & Commander-in-Chief, Madagascar) 01/07/43
   4. **High Commissioner, French Possession Pacific Ocean**: RA Georges Thierry d'Argenlieu [FN]
J. *Schools*
   1. **Commandant, Poly-Technical School**: /38 Col. Maurice-Henri Dumontier (Engineers Commander, Fifth Army) 08/27/39 unknown? /44 MG Pierre-Nicolas-Louis Decharme (retired) /45.
K. *Military Attachés*
   1. **Military Attaché Soviet Union (Moscow)**: /44 MG Ernest-Émile Petit.
L. *Military Missions*:
   1. **French Military Mission to Moscow** (/41): BG Pierre-Armand-Gaston Billotte (/42, Chief of Staff to BG Charles de Gaulle) /41 unknown? /42 MG Ernest-Émile Petit (Military Attache, Soviet Union) /44
   2. **French Military Mission to Ethiopia** (/41): Col. Diégo-Charles-Jospeh Brosset (Chief of Staff, Free French Forces, Middle East) /41
   3. **French Military Mission to Washington, D. C.** (/42): MG Marie-Emil-Antoine Béthouart (Chief, National Defense Staff) /43 LG Étienne-Paul-Émile-Marie Beynet (Commander-in-Chief, the Levant & High Commissioner

of Levant) 01/23/44 MG Auguste-Marie Brossin de Saint-Didier.
4. **French Military Mission to Syria & Egypt** (06/09/43): MG Charles-Emmanuel Mast (Resident-General of Tunisia) 09/43
5. **French Military Mission for German Affairs**: /44 LG Marie-Louis Koëltz.

M. *Commissions, Services, Etc.*
1. **Disarmament of Germany Commission**: /44? MG Paul-Gabriel Arnaud.
2. **Commission of Purification of Rehabilitation of Military Personnel: Chairman**: /44 BG [Retired '34] Philippe-Paul Matter.
3. **Head, Preservation of War Material Service**: /42 LG Odilon-Léonard-Théophile Picquendar (retired) /43
4. **Director, Bureau of Armistice Studies**: /44 LG Marie-Louis Koëltz (Head, Military Mission for German Affairs) /44

N. *Liaison Officers*
1. **French Liaison Officer, Supreme Headquarters Allied Expeditionary Force [SHAEF]** (01/44): MG Marie-Joseph-Pierre-François Kœnig [+ Commanding General, French Forces in Great Britain] (Commander-in-Chief, French Forces of the Interior) 06/23/44 BG Paul-Henri-Romuald Ely.
2. **French Liaison Officer to United States Fifth Army** (1943): BG Georges-Jacques-Frédéric Beucler
3. **French Liaison Officer to United States Seventh Army**: /44 BG René de Hesdin (Deputy Chief of Staff, United States Sixth Army Group [see Volume III]; /44, Commanding General, 4th Moroccan Mountain Division) /44

O. *Other Missions*
1. **French Transportation Mission to Belgian**: /44 BG André-Marie Zeller (Director of Artillery) /45

Commander-in-Chief, Free French Naval Forces (07/40, London; 09/24/41; /42, includes Free French naval forces in French Equatorial Africa, the Levant, Djibouti, and Madagascar): (09/24/41): **Commandant of the Navy** 07/40 VA Émile-Henri Muselier [FN] [Flag: submarine *Surcouf*] [+ Member, Council for the Defense of the Empire & Head, Navy and Merchant Navy Commission; + to 07/10/41, Commandant of Free French Air Force] (resigned) 04/42 RA Philippe Auboyneau [FN] [+ Head, Navy and Merchant Navy Commission] (Commanding Officer, 3rd Cruiser Division) 08/44
[NOTE: In /40, VA Émile-Henri Muselier [FN] the Vichy Government sentenced him to death in absentia and confiscated all of his possessions; /41, the Vichy Government forfeited his French citizenship]
A. *Components*
1. **Free French Pacific Naval Forces** (brigade status)

Chief of the General Staff, Navy and Air Force [Chefs d'État-Major des FAFL] (London; 07/01/40): Capt. Eugène-Marcel Chevrier [FN] 12/25/40 vacant 01/13/41 LCol. Charles-Félix Pijaud [FAF] 03/31/41 BG Martial Valin [FAF] (Commandant Navy and Air Force) 07/10/41 LCol. Charles-Félix Pijaud [FAF] 12/01/41 Col. Charles Luguet [FAF] 04/13/42 Col. Pierre Coustey [FAF] 03/43 vacant 04/13/43 Col. Georges Audrieu [FAF] 11/44 dissolved.

Chief of the General Naval Staff (06/06/43): VA André G. Lemonnier [FN].
A. **Vice-Chief of Navy Staff**: VA Jaugard [FN]

B.   **Deputy Chief of Navy Staff**: RA Deramond [FN]

Commandant of Free French Air Force [Forces Aériennes François Libres (FAFL)] (London; 07/40): VA Émile-Henri Muselier [FN] [+ Commandant of the Navy] 06/41 vacant 07/10/41 BG Martial Valin [FAF] [+ 09/41 to 06/07/43, Head, Air Commission, National Committee of Free French] (10/31/44, Commander-in-Chief, Air Force, French Provisional Government) 06/44 disbanded.

Commander-in-Chief, Air Force [Chefs d'État-Major Général de l'Armée de l'Air], French Provisional Government (07/01/43): Gen. René Bouscat [FAF] 10/31/44 Gen. Martial Valin [FAF].

Part 2

FRANCE'S ORDER OF BATTLE 1939 - 1945

Theater

Commander-in-Chief Allied Armies in France: Gen. Maurice-Gustavé Gamelin [+ Deputy Chairman of Supreme National Defense Council; Commander-in-Chief, Land and Air Forces; & Chief of the Army General Staff] (retired; /42, arrested and accused in Rion Trail, which was an attempt by Vichy France to prove the leaders of the French Third Republic had been responsible for France's defeat by Germany in 06/40; /43 to /45, imprisoned by Vichy France at Fort du Portaleb in the Pyrennes, then later deported by the Germans to Itter Castle in Tyrol) 05/18/40 unknown? 06/25/40 disbanded.
- A. *Components* - **Supreme Headquarters Reserve** (05/10/40)
    1. **XXI Army Corps**
    2. **XXIII Army Corps**
    3. **I Armored Group (Groupement Cuirassé)**
- B. **Deputy Chief of Staff, Commander-in-Chief Allied Armies in France**: /39 Col. René de Hesdin (/41, Commanding Officer, 68th Artillery Regiment) 06/25/40 dissolved.

Commander-in-Chief, North-Eastern Theater of Operations (01/40): Gen Alphonse-Joseph Georges [+ Deputy Commander-in-Chief, Land Forces] (Inspector-General of Land Forces) 05/17/40 unknown? 06/22/40 disbanded.
- A. **Chief of Staff, North-Eastern Theater of Operations** (01/40): BG Gaston-René-Eugène Roton (/41, Deputy Commander, Vichy 13th Military Division) 06/22/40 dissolved.
- B. **Deputy Chief of Staff, North-Eastern Theater of Operations** (01/40): Col. Du Mazel 06/22/40 dissolved.
- C. **1st Bureau (Administration), North-Eastern Theater of Operations** (01/40): LCol. Jean-Louis-Auguste Humbert (/41, Head, French Mission, Armistice Commission, Wiesbaden) 06/22/40 dissolved.
    1. **Deputy, 1st Bureau, North-Eastern Theater of Operations** (01/40): LCol. Chevrier 06/22/40 dissolved.
    2. **Organization Section**:
    3. **Manpower Section**:
    4. **Order-of-Battle Section**:
    5. **Material Section**:
    6. **Administration Section**:
    7. **Courier Sécretariat**:
- D. **2nd Bureau (Intelligence), North-Eastern Theater of Operations** (01/40): Maj. Louis Baril (/43, killed in action) 06/22/40 dissolved.
    1. **Section NE**:
    2. **Fortifications Section**:
    3. **Air Liaison Section**:
    4. **Cyphers Section**:
    5. **Cryptography Section**:
    6. **Mission Section**:
    7. **Translation Section**:
    8. **Mission C Attachments Section**:

E. **3rd Bureau (Operations), North-Eastern Theater of Operations** (01/40): Col. Marie-Henri-Pierre Préaud (09/40, Commanding General, 9th Military Division) 06/22/40 dissolved.
   1. **Deputy, 3rd Bureau, North-Eastern Theater of Operations** (01/40): LCol. Charles-Jean-Roger Noiret 06/22/40 dissolved.
   2. **Operations Section**:
   3. **Operations Sub-Office Section**:
   4. **Liaison Sub-Section**:
   5. **Training & Study of Matériels Section**:
   6. **Training Sub-Office Section**:
   7. **Study of Matériels Sub-Office Section**:
   8. **Sécretariat**:

Eastern Mediterranean Theater of Operations [Théâtre d'Opérations de la Méditerranée Orientale (T. O. M. O.)] (08/26/39, Syria): Gen. [Retired '35] Maxime Weygand (+ Commander-in-Chief, Allied Forces in France; + Commander-in-Chief, Land Forces; & Chief of the Army General Staff) 05/17/40 Gen. [Retired] Eugène-Désité-Antoine Mittlehauser (Commander-in-Chief, Levant) /40

A. **Deputy Commander, Eastern Mediterranean Theater of Operations** (08/26/39): LCol. Lavilléon
B. **Chief of Staff, Eastern Mediterranean Theater of Operations** (08/26/39): Col. Paul-Alexandre-Pierre Bourget or Col. René-Marie-Edgar de Larminat (Chief of Staff, Levant) /40
C. **1st Bureau (Administration), Eastern Mediterranean Theater of Operations** (08/26/39): Maj. Cherrière [+ 4th Bureau, Eastern Mediteranean Theater of Operations] (10/01/43, Commanding Officer, 6th Morocco Tirailleurs (Infantry) Regiment)
D. **2nd Bureau (Intelligence), Eastern Mediterranean Theater of Operations** (08/26/39): Maj. Lelaquet
E. **3rd Bureau (Operations), Eastern Mediterranean Theater of Operations** (08/26/39): Capt. [Army] Marion
F. **4th Bureau (Supply), Eastern Mediterranean Theater of Operations** (08/26/39): Maj. Cherrière [+ 1st Bureau, Eastern Mediteranean Theater of Operations] (10/01/43, Commanding Officer, 6th Morocco Tirailleurs (Infantry) Regiment)
G. **Transport and Service, Eastern Mediterranean Theater of Operations** (08/26/39): Col. Coudrain
H. **Director, Medical Services, Eastern Mediterranean Theater of Operations** (08/26/39): BG [Méd.-Gen.] Paul-Louis-Malie-Félix Corbel (?) /40

Army Groups

1st Army Group (10/01/39): Gen. Gaston-Henri-Gustavé Billotte (car accident; died two days later) 05/22/40 Gen. Georges-Maurice-Jean Blanchard (German prisoner-of-war; /40, Inspector, Vichy Military Districts IX & XII) 06/22/40 disbanded.
- A. **Chief of Staff, 1st Army Group** (10/01/39): unknown? 10/39 BG Jean-Marie-Léon Etcheberrigaray (Commander, Artillery, V Motorized Army Corps) 12/13/39 LCol. Jacques-Émile-Louis-Léon Humbert (Commanding Officer, Corsica) 06/22/40 dissolved.
- B. *Components* - **1st Army Group** (05/10/40)
    1. First Army
    2. Second Army
    3. Seventh Army
    4. Ninth Army
- C. **Vice Chief of Staff, 1st Army Group** (10/01/39): Col. Jean-Marie-Léon Etcheberrigaray (Chief of Staff, 1st Army Group) 10/39

2nd Army Group (08/27/39): Gen. Andre-Gaston Prételat (retired) 06/40 Gen. Charles-Marie Condé (to /45, German prisoner-of-war; /45, retired) 06/22/40 disbanded.
- A. **Chief of Staff, 2nd Army Group** (08/27/39): Col. Louis-Gustavé Bérard (Commanding General, Allier Department, Military District XIII) 06/22/40 dissolved.
- B. *Components* - **2nd Army Group** (05/10/40)
    1. Third Army
    2. Fourth Army
    3. Fifth Army

3rd Army Group (10/20/39): Gen. Antoine-Marie-Benoit Besson (Inspector, Vichy France Military Districts XIII & XVI) 06/22/40 disbanded.
- A. **Chief of Staff, 3rd Army Group** (10/20/39): BG Louis-Albert-Pierre Robert de Saint-Vincent (Commanding General, 64th Alpine Infantry Division) 11/25/39 Col. Louis-Ernest-Henri-Robert Bailly 06/22/40 dissolved.
- B. *Components* - **3rd Army Group** (05/10/40)
    1. Eighth Army
    2. 3rd Army Group Reserve
        a. XLV Fortress Army Corps

4th Army Group (06/04/40): Gen. Charles Léon-Clement Huntziger (Head, Franco-German Armistice Commission to Weisbaden) 06/22/40 disbanded.
- A. **Chief of Staff, 4th Army Group** (06/04/40): Col. Henri Lacaille (09/06/40, Military Secretary, Minister of National Defense and War) 06/22/40 dissolved.

Commander-in-Chief, French North Africa [L'Afrique Française du Nord]: 10/39? Gen. Charles-Auguste-Paul Noguès [+ Resident-General of Morocco] /40 unknown? 11/08/42 LG Alphonse-Pierre Juin (Resident-General, Tunisia) 05/10/43
- A. **Chief of Staff, French North Africa**: 10/39? BG Alphonse-Pierre Juin (Commanding General, 15th Motorized Infantry Division) /40 Col. Paul-Arsène-

Gérard Devinck (Chief of Staff, Méknes Territorial Division) 02/01/40 BG Marcel-Maurice Carpentier (/43, Chief of Staff, French Expeditionary Corps in Italy) /41 unknown? /42 BG François-Adolphe-Laurent Sevez (Commanding General, 4th Moroccan Infantry Division (Free French))

- B. **Components**
  1. **Algeria**: see **XIX Army Corps**.
  2. **Morocco**: see **Morocco Army Corps**.
  3. **Commander of the Troops & Territory of Tunisia**
- C. **1st Deputy Chief of Staff, French North Africa**: 10/39? Col. Jean-Edouard Verneau (Head, French Delegation Armistice Commission, Weisbaden) /40
- D. **2nd Deputy Chief of Staff, French North Africa**: 10/39? LCol. Royer
- E. **3rd Deputy Chief of Staff, French North Africa**: 10/39? LCol. Jean-Charles-Marie-Joseph Gross (Director, Armistice Service, North Africa) 07/40
- F. **National Defense Secretary, French North Africa**: 10/39? LCol. Cordier
- G. **Chief of Cabinet, French North Africa**: 10/39? Maj. René-Gabriel-Henri Bertrand
- H. **Aide-de-Camp, French North Africa**: 10/39? Maj. Pique-Aubrun (/44, Commanding Officer, 3rd Morocco Spahis (Cavalry) Regiment)
- I. **Indigenous Affairs, French North Africa**: 10/39? LCol. Augustin-Léon Guillaume (assigned to Morocco; /43, Commanding General, Moroccan Tabors) /40
- J. **1st Bureau (Administration), French North Africa**: 10/39? LCol. Jourdan
- K. **2nd Bureau (Intelligence), French North Africa**: 10/39? LCol. Maurice-Yves-Seraphin-Joseph Vanlande 11/42 Col. Chrétien /43 Col. Raoul-Albert-Louis Salan (Commanding Officer, 6th Senegalese Infantry Regiment) /44
- L. **3rd Bureau (Operations), French North Africa**: 10/39? Maj. Moise-Germain-Louis Jousse (Deputy Chief of Staff, Commander-in-Chief, Free French Armed Forces) 06/40
- M. **4th Bureau (Supply), French North Africa**: 10/39? Maj. Baufine-Ducrocq
- N. **Artillery Commander, French North Africa**: 10/39? MG Jacques-Albert Apffel (retired) /40
- O. **Engineer Commander, French North Africa**: /38 MG Émile-Auguste-Marie Doizelet
- P. **Intendant [Quartermaster] Supplies, French North Africa**: /36 BG Henri Jacques (?) 10/39? Int-Gen. 1st Class Cahuzac /4? BG Pierre-Emannuel-André Dario (/44, Commanding General, I Free French Armored Corps) /4?
- Q. **Medical, French North Africa**: /38 Med-Gen. Insp. Maurice-Alphonse-Joseph-Marie Potet
- R. **Armistice Services, North Africa**: 07/40 LCol. Jean-Charles-Marie-Joseph Gross (Commanding Officer, 1st Zouaves Regiment) /40

French Armies (pre-July 1940)

Military-Governor of Paris: /37 LG Gaston-Henri-Gustavé Billotte [+ Member, the Army Council; + Commanding General, Paris Military District; + to /38, President, Consultative Committee for Colonial Affairs] (Commander-in-Chief, 1st Army Group) 10/01/39 Gen. [Retired '39] Pierre Héring [+ Commanding General, Paris Military District & President, Consultative Committee for Colonial Defense] (Commander-in-Chief, Army of Paris) 06/22/40 disbanded; reformed /44 LG Darius-Paul Bloch-Dassault (?) /44 LG Marie-Joseph-Pierre-François Kœnig [+ to 10/44, Commander-in-Chief, French Forces of the Interior].

A. **Assistant Military Governor of Paris**: /40 MG [Retired '38] Octave-Charles Lanoix (retired) 05/15/40 MG Joseph-Louis-François Hassler (Commanding General, Department of Var, Military District XV) 06/22/40 dissolved.

B. **Chief of Staff, Military-Governor, Paris**: /37 LCol. René de Hesdin (Deputy Chief of Staff, Allied Forces, Northwestern France) /39

First Army (08/27/39, assigned to General Headquarters; 10/01/39, assigned to 1st Army Group; 06/22/40, disbanded): Gen. Georges-Maurice-Jean Blanchard (Commander-in-Chief, 1st Army Group) 05/24/40 Gen. René-Jacques-Adolphe Prioux (to /42, German prisoner-of-war; 12/26/42, Chief of the Free French Army General Staff) 06/22/40 disbanded.

A. **Chief of Staff, First Army** (08/27/39): Col. Pierre-Paul-Étienne Alombert-Goget 06/22/40 dissolved.

B. *Components - First Army* (05/10/40)
   1. **III Army Corps**
   2. **IV Army Corps**
   3. **V Motorized Army Corps**
   4. **Cavalry Corps**

C. **Artillery, First Army** (08/27/39): Col. Claude-Philippe-Armand Chaillet (09/43, Artillery Commander, French Expeditionary Corps in Italy) 06/22/40 dissolved.

Second Army (08/27/39, assigned to General Headquarters; 10/01/39, assigned to 1st Army Group; 05/14/40, assigned to North East Headquarters; 05/17/40, transferred to 2nd Army Group; 06/06/40, assigned to 4th Army Group; 06/15/40, transferred back to 2nd Army Group; 06/22/40, disbanded): Gen. Charles-Léon-Clément Huntziger (Commander-in-Chief, 4th Army Group) 06/04/40 MG [Retired '38] Henri Freydenberg (retired) 06/22/40 disbanded.

A. **Chief of Staff, Second Army** (08/27/39): BG Jean-Léon-Albert Langlois (Commanding General, 3rd Light Mechanized Division) 05/40 Col. Henri Lacaille (Chief of Staff, 4th Army Group) 06/40 Col. Edmund-Auguste Ruby 06/22/40 dissolved.

B. *Components - Second Army* (05/10/40)
   1. **X Army Corps**
   2. **XVIII Army Corps**

C. **Artillery, Second Army** (08/27/39): unknown? /40 BG Maurice Viant (Commanding General, XVIII Army Corps) /40

D. **Armored, Second Army** (08/27/39): BG Louis-Ferdinand Bourguignon (?) 06/22/40 dissolved.
E. **Medical Service, Second Army** (08/27/39): BG Pierre-Jean-Joseph Causeret (?) 06/22/40 dissolved.

Third Army (08/27/39, assigned to 2nd Army Group; 06/22/40, disbanded): Gen. Charles-Marie Condé (Commander-in-Chief, 2nd Army Group) 06/22/40 disbanded.
A. **Chief of Staff, Third Army** (08/27/39): Col. Raymond-Jules-Paul-Henri Tessier or Col. Raymond-Francis Duval (/41, Director, Military Reconstruction School) 06/22/40 dissolved.
B. *Components* - **Third Army** (05/10/40)
    1. **VI Army Corps**
    2. **XXIV Army Corps**
    3. **Colonial Army Corps**
    4. **XLII Fortress Army Corps**
C. **Armored, Third Army** (08/27/39): Col. Marie-Germain-Christian Bruneau (Commanding General, 1st Armored Division) 01/15/40 unknown? 06/22/40 dissolved.
D. **Medical Services, Third Army** (08/27/39): Col. Auguste Schneider 06/22/40 dissolved.

Fourth Army (08/27/39, assigned to 2nd Army Group; 06/06/40, assigned to 4th Army Group; 06/22/40, disbanded): Gen. Edouard-Jean Réquin (Inspector, Vichy XVII & XVIII Military Regions) 06/22/40 disbanded.
A. **Chief of Staff, Fourth Army** (08/27/39): Col. Pierre Dame (Commanding General, 2nd North African Infantry Division) 12/31/39 Col. Codechevre /40 Col. Auguste-Jean Gilliot (/43 to /45, German prisoner-of-war) 06/22/40 dissolved.
B. *Components* - **Fourth Army** (05/10/40)
    1. **IX Army Corps**
    2. **XX Army Corps**
C. **Deputy Chief of Staff, Fourth Army** (08/27/39): unknown? /39 LCol. Paul-Henri Dumas 06/22/40 dissolved.
D. **3rd Department, Staff, Fourth Army** (08/27/39): LCol. Paul-Henri Dumas (Deputy Chief of Staff, Fourth Army) /39 unknown? 06/25/40 dissolved.
E. **Armored, Fourth Army** (08/27/39): unknown? /40 Col. Jean-Gaston Guillot 06/22/40 dissolved.
F. **Medical Services, Fourth Army** (08/27/39): BG Lucien-Meyer Lévy (?) /40 Col. Gustavé Worms 06/22/40 dissolved.

Fifth Army (08/27/39, assigned to 2nd Army Group; 06/22/40, disbanded.): Gen. Victor Bourret (to /45, German prisoner-of-war; /45, retired) 06/22/40 disbanded.
A. **Chief of Staff, Fifth Army** (08/27/39): BG Jean-Joseph-Marie-Gabriel de Lattre de Tassigny (Commanding General, 14th Infantry Division) 01/04/40 unknown? 06/22/40 dissolved.

B. **Components - First Army** (05/10/40)
   1. **VIII Army Corps**
   2. **XII Army Corps**
   3. **XVII Army Corps**
   4. **XLIII Fortress Army Corps**
C. **Armored, Fifth Army** (08/27/39): Col. Charles-André-Joseph-Marie de Gaulle (Commanding Officer, 4th Armored Division) 05/15/40 unknown? 06/25/40 dissolved.
D. **Artillery, Fifth Army** (08/27/39): BG [Retired '39] Henri Fournier (Commanding General, Military District XX) /40 unknown? 06/25/40 dissolved.
E. **Engineers, Fifth Army** (08/27/39): BG Maurice-Henri Dumontier (?) 06/22/40 dissolved.
F. **Medical Services, Fifth Army** (08/27/39): BG Pierre-Joseph-Félix-Romuald Maisonnet (Director, Medical Services, Ministry of National Defense) 06/25/40 dissolved.

Sixth Army (09/02/39, assigned to General Headquarters; 12/05/39, transferred to General Headquarters Reserve; 05/20/40, assigned to 3rd Army Group; 06/11/40, assigned to 4th Army Group; 06/15/40, transferred back to 3rd Army Group; 06/22/40, disbanded): Gen. Antoine-Marie-Benoit Besson (Commander-in-Chief, 3rd Army Group) 10/20/39 Gen. René-Henri Olry (Commander-in-Chief, Army of the Alps) 12/05/39 LG Robert-Auguste Touchon (Commanding General, Military District XIV) 06/22/40 disbanded.
A. **Chief of Staff, Sixth Army** (09/02/39): Col. Louis-Albert-Pierre Robert de Saint-Vincent (Chief of Staff, 3rd Army Group) 10/20/39 Col. Henri Mainié 06/22/40 dissolved.
B, **Armor, Sixth Army** (09/02/39): unknown? 05/17/40 MG Marie-Joseph-Edmond Welvert [+ Commanding General, 1st Armored Division & to 06/02/40, Commanding General, I Armored Group or Welvert Mechanized Group] (11/08/42, Commanding General, Constantine Territory Division) 06/25/40 dissolved.
C. **Medical Services, Sixth Army** (09/02/39): Col. Roger-Albert-Firmin Morisson
D. **Lines of Communication [Rear Area], Sixth Army** (09/02/39): unknown? 12/02/39 MG Georges-Eugène-Alphonse Cartier (Commanding General, Group Cartier) 06/03/40 MG Eugène-Prosper-Joseph Sisteron (at disposal Commander-in-Chief, Armed Forces; /40, retired) 06/22/40 dissolved.

Seventh Army (09/02/39, assigned to General Headquarters Reserve; 11/11/39, assigned to 1st Army Group; 05/15/40, transferred back to General Headquarters Reserve; 05/20/40, assigned to 3rd Army Group; 06/22/40, disbanded): Gen. Henri-Honoré Giraud (Commander-in-Chief, Ninth Army) 05/15/40 MG Marie-Bertrand-Alfred Fagalde [acting; + Commanding General, XVI Army Corps] 05/16/40 Gen. André-Georges Corap (retired) 05/18/40 Gen. Aubert-Achille-Jules Frère (Commanding General, Military District XII) 06/22/40 disbanded.
A. **Chief of Staff, Seventh Army** (09/02/39): Col. Jean-Baptiste-Henri Baurés (Commandant, Technical Information Center) 06/22/40 dissolved.
B. **Components - Seventh Army** (05/10/40)
   1. **I Motorized Army Corps**

2. **XVI Army Corps**
C. **Armored Forces, Seventh Army** (09/02/39): BG [Retired '39] Charles-Georges-Antoine Delestraint (Assistant Inspector of Armored Forces) /40
D. **Medical Services, Seventh Army** (09/02/39): BG Pierre-Philippe Hornus (?) 06/22/40 dissolved.

Eighth Army (08/27/39, assigned to General Headquarters Reserve; 05/19/40, assigned to 2nd Army Group; 06/22/40, disbanded): Gen. Jeanny-Jules-Marcel Garchèry (at disposal of Commander-in-Chief, Land and Air Forces; /40, retired) 05/22/40 Gen. Auguste-Marie-Émile Laure (German prisoner-of-war; /40, released; /40, Secretary-General to the Head of State, Vichy) 06/22/40 disbanded.
A. **Chief of Staff, Eighth Army** (08/27/39): Col. Marie-Louis Koëltz (Vice Chief of Operations) /39 Col. Jacques-Marie-Joseph-François Campet (Chief of the Military Cabinet to Marshal Pétain) 06/22/40 dissolved.
B. *Components* - **Eighth Army** (05/10/40)
    1. **VII Army Corps**
    2. **XIII Army Corps**
    3. **XLIV Fortress Army Corps**
C. **Engineers, Eighth Army** (08/27/39): BG Maurice-Jules-Zacharie Grenet (Member, Commission for the Studies of Fortified Zones) 06/22/40 dissolved.
D. **Medical Services, Eighth Army** (08/27/59): BG Antoine-Marie-Gabriel Goursolas (?) /40 BG Maurice-Louis-Étienne Pilod (/41, Inspector-General of Army Medical Services) 06/22/40 dissolved.

Ninth Army (11/05/39, assigned to 1st Army Group; 06/22/40, disbanded): Gen. André-Georges Corap (Commander-in-Chief, Seventh Army) 05/15/40 Gen. Henri-Honoré Giraud (German prisoner-of-war at Königstein Castle near Dresden; 04/17/42, escaped; 11/13/42, Commander-in-Chief, Free French Land and Air Forces & Member, Empire Council) 06/22/40 disbanded.
A. **Chief of Staff, Ninth Army** (11/05/39): Col. Olivier-Charles-Marie Thierry d'Argenlieu (killed in action) 06/22/40 dissolved.
B. *Components* - **First Army** (05/10/40)
    1. **II Motorized Army Corps**
    2. **XI Army Corps**
    3. **XLI Fortress Army Corps**
C. **Deputy Chief of Staff, Ninth Army** (11/05/39): LCol. Jean-Émile-Louis Véron 06/22/40 dissolved.
D. **Operations, Ninth Army** (11/05/39): Col. André-Paul Vallet 06/22/40 dissolved.
E. **Medical Services, Ninth Army** (11/05/39): BG Xavier-Marie Cristau (?) 06/22/40 dissolved.
F. **Lines of Communications [Rear Area], Ninth Army** (11/05/39): Col. Marcel-Émile Deslaurens (Commanding General, 60th Infantry Division) 01/01/40

Tenth Army (05/40, from **Altmayer Group**; 05/31/40, redsignated **Tenth Army** and

assigned to General Headquarters; 06/03/40, assigned to 3rd Army Group; 06/11/40, transferred back to General Headquarters; 06/13/40, assigned to North East Front Headquarters; 06/22/40, disbanded): **Altmayer Group** 05/40 LG [Retired '37 & '39] Marie-Robert Altmayer (Commander-in-Chief, Tenth Army) 05/31/40 redesignated **Tenth Army** 05/31/40 LG [Retired '37 & '39] Marie-Robert Altmayer (German prisoner-of-war; .41, released; /42 retired) 06/22/40 disbanded.
A. **Chief of Staff, Army** (05/31/40): Maj. de Petitville 06/22/40 dissolved.

Army of the Alps (12/05/39, assigned to General Headquarters; southwestern France along border with Italy; 06/20/40, North East Front Headquarters; 06/22/40 disbanded): Gen. René-Henri Olry (Member, The Vichy French Army Council) 06/22/40 disbanded.
A. **Chief of Staff, Army of the Alps** (12/05/39): BG Jean Mer (/41, Commanding General, 14th Military Division) 06/22/40 dissolved.
B. *Components - Army of the Alps* (05/10/40)
    1. **XIV Army Corps**
    2. **XV Army Corps**
C. **Deputy Chief of Staff, Army of the Alps** (12/05/39): Col. Jacques-Pierre-Louis de Grancey (09/12/40, Chief of Staff, I Vichy Army Corps) 06/22/40 dissolved.
D. **Director, Medical Services, Army of the Alps** (12/05/39): BG Jules-Marie-Antoine-Joseph Botreau-Roussel (?) 06/22/40 dissolved.

Army of Paris [Armée de Paris]: 06/40 Gen. [Retired '39] Pierre Héring (retired) 06/22/40 disbanded.

Commander-in-Chief, Levant Forces [Commandant Supérieur Troupes du Levant] (Middle East; the Levant was made up of two French mandates Syria and Lebanon): /34 MG Charles-Léon-Clément Huntziger (Member, The Army Council) /38 MG Henri-Léon Caillault (Secretary-General of the Supreme Council of National Defense) /40 Gen. [Retired] Eugène-Désité-Antoine Mittlehauser (retired) 11/27/40 LG Henri-Fernand Dentz [+ High Commissioner for Levant - supervising repatriation of the French Forces in Levant] /41 Gen. [Retired '39] Georges-Albert-Julien Catroux [+ 02/01/42, High Commissioner, Levant] (State Commissioner for Foreign Affairs) /43 MG Georges-Jean-Emile-René Chadebec de Lavelade.
A. **Deputy Commander-in-Chief, Levant**: /40 MG Paul-Hippolyte Arlabosse (Commanding General, French Troops Lebanon): /41 MG Joseph-Antoine-Sylvain-Raoul de Verdillac
B. **Chief of Staff, Free French Forces Middle East**: /40 Col. René-Marie-Edgar de Larminat (arrested by Vichy France; /40, fled and joins the Free French; 08/26/40, High Commissioner of Free French Colonies in Africa & Commanding General, Free French Forces in Equatorial Africa) /40 unknown? /41 Col. Diégo-Charles-Jospeh Brosset (Commanding Officer, Eastern Syria; /43, Commanding General, 2nd Colonial Infantry Brigade) /41
C. *Components*
    1. **Levant Mobile Force**: see **Levant Mobile Force** in **Army Corps** Section.

2. **Commander of Troops, North Syria [Général Commandant Troupes de Territorie Nord-Syrie et Euphrates]** (Middle East): see **Commands equivalant to Divisions** Section.
3. **Commander of Troops, South Syria [Général Commandant Troupes de Territorie Sud-Syrie]** (Middle East): see **Commands equivalant to Divisions** Section.
4. **Commander of Troops, Lebanon [Général Commandant Troupes de Territorie Liban]** (Middle East): see **Commands equivalant to Divisions** Section.

Army Detachments

Ardennes Army Detachment [Détachement d'Armée des Ardennes (DAA)] (09/39; 10/15/39, redesignated **Ninth Army**): Gen. André-Georges Corap (Commander-in-Chief, Ninth Army) 10/15/39 redesignated **Ninth Army** - see **Ninth Army**.

Pyrenees Army Detachment [Détachement d'Armée des Pyrénées] (09/39; 12/12/39, disbanded): LG [Retired '37] Auguste-Edouard-Maurice Moyrand (retired) 12/12/39 disbanded.

Air Forces

First Air Army: Gen. Mouchard [FAF] 02/40 redesignated **Cooperation Air Force**
A. *Components* - First Air Army
    1. **Northern Zone of Air Operation**
    2. **Eastern Zone of Air Operation**

Cooperation Air Force [Forces Aériennes de Coopération du Nord-Est] (02/40, from **First Air Army**; set up on the North-Eastern Front and was in chanrge of the Northern and Eastern Zones of Air Operations): Gen. Marcel Têtu [FAF] (08/29/40, Governor-General, Vichy French Equatorial Africa) 06/25/40 disbanded.
A. *Components* - Cooperation Air Force
    1. **Northern Zone of Air Operation**
    2. **Eastern Zone of Air Operation**

Northern Zone of Air Operations [Zone d' Opérations Aériennes Nord (Z. O. A. N.)] (formed to operate in conjunction with 1st Army Group): Gen. François d'Astier de la Vigerie [FAF] (Commanding General, French's Air Forces, Morocco) 06/22/40
A. *Components* - Northern Zone of Air Operations (05/10/40)
    1. **1st Air Division [1re Division Aérienne]**:
        a. **6th Bomber Group [Groupement de Bombardement 6]**:
        b. **9th Bomber Group [Groupement de Bombardement 9]**:
        c. **18th Assault Bomber Group [Groupement de Bombardement d'Assaut 18]**:
    2. **21st Fighter Group [Groupement de Chasse 21]**: 05/10/40? BG Armand Pinsard [FAF] (after fall of France, fought with Nazi Germany on Eastern Front; after war, convicted of collaboration and sentence to life imprisonment)
    3. **23rd Fighter Group [Groupement de Chasse 23]**: 05/10/40? BG Jean-Charles Romatet [FAF] (Commander-in-Chief, Vichy Air Force) 09/25/40
    4. **25th Fighter Group [Groupement de Chasse 25]**: 05/10/40? LCol. De Moussac [FAF]
    5. **Night Fighter Group [Groupement de Nuit]**: 05/10/40? LCol. Dordilly [FAF]

Eastern Zone of Air Operations [Zone d' Opérations Aériennes Est (Z. O. A. E.)] (formed to operate in conjunction with 2nd Army Group): Gen. Pennès [FAF] (Commanding General, North African Zone of Air Operations) 10/39 Gen. Marcel Têtu [FAF] (Commanding General, Cooperation Air Force) 02/40 Gen. René Bouscat [FAF]
A. *Components* - Eastern Zone of Air Operations (05/10/40)
    1. **3rd Air Division [3e Division Aérienne]**:
        a. **10th Bomber Group [Groupement de Bombardement 10]**:
        b. **15th Bomber Group [Groupement de Bombardement 15]**:
    2. **22nd Fighter Group [Groupement de Chasse 22]**: 05/10/40? Col. Dumèmes [FAF]

Southern Zone of Air Operations [Zone d' Opérations Aériennes Sud. (Z. O. A. S.)]: LG Robert Odic [FAF]

A. ***Components* - Southern Zone of Air Operations** (05/10/40)
   1. **6ᵗʰ Air Division [6e Division Aérienne]**:
   2. **24ᵗʰ Fighter Group [Groupement de Chasse 24]**: 05/10/40? LCol. Lamon [FAF]

Alpine Zone of Air Operations [Zone d' Opérations Aériennes des Alps (Z. O. A.)] (02/40, from **Third Air Army**; formed to operate in conjunction with 3ʳᵈ Army Group): Gen. Houdemon [FAF] 05/10/40? Gen Laurens [FAF]

A. ***Components* - Alpine Zone of Air Operations** (05/10/40)
   1. **South Eastern Bomber Training Command [Groupement d'Instruction de l'Aviation de Bombardement du Sud-Est (G. I. A. B. S. E.)]**:
      a. **1ˢᵗ Bomber Group [Groupement de Bombardement 1]**: 05/10/40? Unknown?
      b. **6ᵗʰ Bomber Group [Groupement de Bombardement 6]**: 05/10/40? Unknown?
      c. **7ᵗʰ Bomber Group [Groupement de Bombardement 7]**: 05/10/40? Unknown?
      d. **9ᵗʰ Bomber Group [Groupement de Bombardement 9]**: 05/10/40? Unknown?
      e. **11ᵗʰ Bomber Group [Groupement de Bombardement 11]**: 05/10/40? Unknown?
      f. **19ᵗʰ Assault Bomber Group [Groupement de Bombardement d'Assaut 19]**: 05/10/40? Unknown?

North African Zone of Air Operations (02/40, from **Fifth Air Army**): Gen. René Bouscat [FAF] 10/39 Gen. Pennès [FAF] (?   ) 06/25/40 redesignated **North African Air Army** [downgraded to division status] - see **North African Air Army**.

A. ***Components* - North African Zone of Air Operations** (05/10/40)
   1. **1ˢᵗ Bomber Group [Groupement de Bombardement 1]**: 05/10/40? Unknown?
   2. **2ⁿᵈ Bomber Group [Groupement de Bombardement 2]**: 05/10/40? Unknown?
   3. **3ʳᵈ Bomber Group [Groupement de Bombardement 3]**: 05/10/40? Unknown?
   4. **8ᵗʰ Bomber Group [Groupement de Bombardement 8]**: 05/10/40? Unknown?

Major Naval Commands and Fleets

High Seas Force (HQ: Oran, Algeria): 09/01/39? VA Emmanuel L. H. Ollive [FN.] [Flag: BB *Provence*] [+ Commander-in-Chief, III Naval Region & Commander-in-Chief, 2nd Flotilla] (Admiral Africa) 12/20/39 VA Marcel-Bruno Gensoul [FN.] (?) 07/40 Adm. Count Jean J. de Laborde [FN.] [Flag: 06/40, DD *Hardi*] (after war sentenced to death for treason and for failing to save the fleet; sentence was converted to a life sentence; 06/09/47, pardoned) 11/27/42 scuttled.

- A. ***Components*** - High Seas Force (09/01/39)
    1. **2nd Flotilla [Squadron]**
        - a. **2nd Battle Division**
            - i. BB *Lorraine*
            - ii. BB *Bretagne*
        - b. **1st Light Destroyer Squadron**
            - i. **1st Light Destroyer Division**
            - ii. **3rd Light Destroyer Division**
            - iii. **7th Light Destroyer Division**
    2. **3rd Flotilla [Squadron]**
        - a. **1st Cruiser Squadron**
            - i. **1st Cruiser Division**
                - A. CA *Algérie*
                - B. CA *Foch*
                - C. CA *Dupeix*
            - ii. **2nd Cruiser Division**
                - A. CA *Colbert*
                - B. CA *Duquesne*
                - C. CA *Tourville*
        - b. **3rd Light Squadron**
            - i. **5th Destroyer Division**
            - ii. **7th Destroyer Division**
            - iii. **9th Destroyer Division**
- A. ***Components*** - High Seas Force (07/40, at Toulon, France)
    1. BC *Strasbourg*
    2. BB *Provence*
    3. CA *Algérie*
    4. CA *Colbert*
    5. CA *Dupeix*
    6. CL *Jean de Vienne*
    7. CL *Marseillaise*
    8. 13 Destroyers
    9. 6 Submarines

Raiding Force (HQ: Brest, France): 09/01/39? VA Marcel-Bruno Gensoul [FN] [Flag: battleship *Dunkerque*] [+ Commander-in-Chief, 1st Flotilla & Commander, 1st Battle Division] (Commanding Officer, High Seas Force) 12/20/39
- A. ***Components*** - Raiding Force (09/01/39)

1. **1st Flotilla [Squadron]**
   a. **1st Battle Division**
      i. BC *Dunkerque*
      ii. BC *Strasbourg*
   b. **4th Cruiser Division**
      i. CL *Georges Leygues*
      ii. CL *Glorie*
      iii. CL *Montcalm*
   c. **CV Béarn**
   d. **2nd Light Squadron**
      i. **6th Large Destroyer Division**
      ii. **8th Large Destroyer Division**
      iii. **10th Large Destroyer Division**

Admiral North (HQ: Dunkerque, France): 09/01/39? Adm. Raoul Victor Patrice Castex [FN] (?) 11/17/39 VA J. J. G. M. La Bigot [FN] (?) 12/20/39 Adm. Jean-Marie-Charles Abrial [FN] (Governor-General of Algeria) 06/22/40 disbanded.

A. *Components - Admiral North* (09/01/39)
   1. **I Naval Region**
      a. **11th Light Destroyer Division**
      b. **16th Submarine Division**
      c. **1st Sloop Squadron**
      d. **CM [minelayer] *Pollux***
      e. **Dunkirque**
      f. **Pas-de-Calais**

Admiral West (HQ: Brest, France): 09/01/39? VA Count Jean J. J. de Laborde [FN] (Commanding Admiral, High Seas Force) 06/18/40 disbanded.

A. *Components - Admiral West* (09/01/39)
   1. **II Naval Region**
      a. **3rd Battle Division**
         i. BB *Paris*
         ii. BB *Courbet*
      b. **2nd Destroyer Division**
      c. **2nd Light Destroyer Squadron**
         i. **2nd Light Destroyer Division**
         ii. **4th Light Destroyer Division**
         iii. **5th Light Destroyer Division**
         iv. **6th Light Destroyer Division**
      d. **4th Submarine Squadron**
         i. **2nd Submarine Division**
         ii. **4th Submarine Division**
         iii. **6th Submarine Division**
         iv. **8th Submarine Division**
      e. **2nd Sloop Squadron**
   2. **V Naval Region**
      a. **14th Light Destroyer Division**

  b. **5ᵗʰ Sloop Squadron**

Admiral South (HQ: Toulon, France): 09/01/39? VA Jean-Pierre Estéva [FN] (Resident-General of Tunisia) 07/26/40 disbanded.
- A. *Components* - **Admiral South** (09/01/39)
  1. **III Naval Region**:
     - a. **4ᵗʰ Destroyer Division**
     - b. **13ᵗʰ Light Destroyer Division**
     - c. **1ˢᵗ Submarine Flotilla**
       - i. **3ʳᵈ Submarine Squadron**
         - A. **1ˢᵗ Submarine Division**
         - B. **3ʳᵈ Submarine Division**
         - C. **5ᵗʰ Submarine Division**
       - ii. **5ᵗʰ Submarine Squadron**
         - A. **13ᵗʰ Submarine Division**
         - B. **15ᵗʰ Submarine Division**
     - d. **Toulon Submarine Base**
       - i. **7ᵗʰ Submarine Division**
       - ii. **19ᵗʰ Submarine Division**
       - iii. **21ˢᵗ Submarine Division**
     - e. **3ʳᵈ Sloop Squadron**
     - f. **Torpedo Bomber Seaplane Group**:
  2. **IV Naval Region**
     - a. **Light Attack Forces**
       - i. **3ʳᵈ Cruiser Division**
         - A. **CL *Marseillaise***
         - B. **CL *Jean de Vienne***
         - C. **CL *La Galisonniere***
       - ii. **Bizerte Destroyers [4ᵗʰ Light Squadron]**
         - A. **1ˢᵗ Destroyer Division**
         - B. **3ʳᵈ Destroyer Division**
         - C. **11ᵗʰ Destroyer Division**
         - D. **CM [minelayer] *Émile Bertin***
     - b. **Bizerte Submarine Base**
       - i. **6ᵗʰ Submarine Squadron** (
         - A. **9ᵗʰ Submarine Division**
         - B. **10ᵗʰ Submarine Division**
         - C. **17ᵗʰ Submarine Division**
         - D. **20ᵗʰ Submarine Division**
       - ii. **AS [submarine tender] *Castor*.**
     - c. **Oran Naval Force [6ᵗʰ Light Squadron]**
       - i. **8ᵗʰ Light Destroyer Division**
       - ii. **2ⁿᵈ Submarine Squadron**
         - A. **12ᵗʰ Submarine Division**
         - B. **14ᵗʰ Submarine Division**
         - C. **18ᵗʰ Submarine Division**
       - iii. **CVS *Commandant Teste***

                iv.   **AS [submarine tender]** *Jules Verne*:
        d.   **Casablanca Naval Station [Morocco Naval Force]**
                i.   **9th Light Destroyer Division**
                ii.   **4th Submarine Division**
        e.   **12th Light Destroyer Division**
        f.   **4th Sloop Squadron**
    3.   **Levant Naval Station**
        a.   **11th Submarine Division**

Admiral Antilles (09/14/39; HQ: Fort de France, Matinique, Antilles, Caribbean): 09/01/39? Adm. Georges-Achille-Marie-Joseph Robert [FN] [+ Military-Governor, Antilles]
A.   *Components - Admiral Antilles* (09/40)
    1.   **CV** *Béarn* (at Port-de-France, Martinique)
    2.   **CL [minelayer]** *Émile Bertin* (at Port-de-France, Martinique)
    3.   **CL [training cruiser]** *Jeanne d'Arc* (at Guadeloupe)

Admiral Africa (12/20/39; HQ: Casablanca, Morocco; the command covers the sea area from Gibraltar to Dakar, westward to include the Azores, Madeira, the Canaries, and Cape Verde Islands): VA Emmanuel L. H. Ollive [FN]
A.   *Components - Admiral Africa* (12/20/39)
    1.   **West Africa Naval Station**
        a.   **5th Light Squadron**
                i.   **6th Cruiser Division**
                        A.   **CL** *Duguay-Trouin*
                        B.   **CL** *Primauguet*
                ii.   **7th Cruiser Division**
                        A.   **CL** *Jeanne de Arc*
                        B.   **CL** *La Tour d'Auvergne [Pluton]*
        b.   **SS [submarine]** *Surcouf*: 09/01/39? Cdr. P. M. H. Martin [FN]
    2.   **Madagascar**: 09/40 Capt. P. Maertan [FN]

Admiral Far East [Indochina]: 09/01/39 VA Jean d'Decoux [FN] [+ Commanding Officer, Far East Naval Forces] (Governor-General, French Indochina) 06/25/40 VA Jules E. M. A. Terraux [FN] [+ Commanding Officer, Far East Naval Forces] (?   ) /45 VA Philippe Auboyneau [FN] [+ Commanding Officer, Far East Naval Forces].
A.   **Deputy Admiral Far East**: /39 Capt. Philippe Auboyneau [FN] (Naval Liaison Officer to British Royal Navy in Egypt) /39
B.   *Components - Admiral Far East [Indochina]* (09/01/39)
    1.   **Far East Naval Forces**
        a.   **5th Cruiser Division**
                i.   **CL** *Lamotte Picquett*
                ii.   **CA** *Suffren*
        b.   **Yanztse Gunboats**
        c.   **West River [Si Kiang] Gunboat**
        d.   **Indochina Gunboats**
        e.   **Sloops**
        f.   **SS [submarine]** *l'Espoir*

2. **Indian Ocean Naval Station**
3. **Pacific Ocean Naval Station**

Army Corps [Corps d'Armée] (pre-July 1940)

Each Military District mobilized an Army Corps carrying the same number as the district. The exceptions were the Paris Military District who mobilized XXI Army Corps and the Colonial Army Corps. The X and XII Military Districts did not exist but whose corps were mobilized by other districts. The I, II, and V Army Corps were motorized army corps.

I Motorized Army Corps (08/27/39, in Military District I, and assigned to First Army; 09/03/39, assigned to General Headquarters Reserve; 09/13/39, assigned to Seventh Army; 11/20/39, transferred to Seventh Army Reserve; 05/10/40, assigned to Seventh Army): MG Théodore-Marcel Sciard (Commanding General, Military District XVII) 06/25/40 disbanded.
  A. **Chief of Staff, I Motorized Army Corps** (08/27/39): Col. Paul-Constant-Amédée Gastey (Commanding Officer, 12th Light Mechanized Brigade) 12/03/39 Col. Maurice-Noël-Eugène Mathenet (11/42, Commanding General, 1st Moroccan Infantry Division) 06/2540 dissolved.
  B. **Artillery, I Motorized Army Corps** (08/27/39): Col. Jacques-Marie-Joseph-Edmond-Ignace Trancart 06/25/40 dissolved.

II Motorized Army Corps (08/26/39, in Military District II; 08/27/39, assigned to Ardennes Army Detachment; 09/12/39, assigned to General Headquarters Reserve; 09/16/39, transferred to Third Army Zone; 01/14/40, assigned to Ninth Army; 01/30/40, assigned to General Headquarters Reserve; 04/01/40, transferred to Ninth Army Zone; 05/10/40, assigned to Ninth Army): MG Marcel-Charles-Joseph Lamson (06/01/40, Commanding General, Military District II) 01/06/40 MG Jean-Gabriel Bouffet (killed in action) 05/25/40 BG Georges-Edgar Boucher (acting) 06/25/40 disbanded.
  A. **Chief of Staff, II Motorized Army Corps** (08/27/39): Col. Georges-Jean-Eugène Pfister (/4?, Deputy Chief of the Army General Staff) 05/40 LCol. Auguste-Émile Barbier 06/25/40 dissolved.
  B. **Artillery, II Motorized Army Corps** (08/27/40): BG [Retired '38] Maurice Parmentier (retired) 06/25/40 dissolved.
  C. **Engineers, II Motorized Army Corps** (08/27/39): unknown? /39 Col. Gaston Gimpel 06/25/40 dissolved.

III Army Corps (09/02/39, in Military District III; 09/08/39, assigned to First Army; 06/09/40, assigned to Tenth Army; 06/19/40, assigned to 3rd Army Group; 06/20/40, assigned to Army of Paris): LG Léon-Benoit de Fornel de La Laurencie (Commanding General, Military District XVI) 06/25/40 disbanded.
  A. **Chief of Staff, III Army Corps** (09/02/39): Col. Maurice-Marie-Joseph Gauthier 05/10/40 Col. Camille-Roger Salland 06/25/40 dissolved.
  B. **Artillery, III Army Corps** (09/02/39): Col. Charles-Eugène-Ladisias-Louis Pellion /40 Col. Jean-Baptiste-François Voisin 06/25/40 dissolved.
  C. **Intendent [Quartermaster], III Army Corps** (09/02/39): Col. Firmin-Philippe-Edouard Fagot 06/25/40 dissolved.

IV Army Corps (09/02/39, in Military District IV, and assigned to Military District V; 09/10/39, assigned to Ardennes Army Detachment; 10/15/39, assigned to Ninth Army; 01/12/40, assigned to First Army Reserve; 05/10/40, transferred to First Army): LG Pierre-Louis-André Boris (Inspector-General of Artillery) 01/14/40 MG Henri-Marie-Joseph Aymes (German prisoner-of-war; /41, released on the grounds of health; /42, retired) 05/29/40 disbanded.
- A. **Chief of Staff, IV Army Corps** (09/02/39): Col. Greot 04/15/40 Col. de Vanssay (German prisoner-of-war) 05/29/40 dissolved.
- B. **Artillery, IV Army Corps** (09/02/39): unknown? /40 Col. Charles-Marie-François-Joseph Mazen 05/29/40 dissolved.
- C. **Engineers, IV Army Corps** (09/02/39): Col. Gaston Gimpel (Engineers Commander, II Motorized Army Corps) /39 unknown? 05/29/40 dissolved.

V Motorized Army Corps (08/26/39, in Military District V; 09/02/39, assigned to Third Army Zone; 09/05/39, assigned to Fourth Army; 09/25/39, assigned to Fifth Army; 09/39/39, transferred to First Army; 05/30/40, assigned to XVI Army Corps; 06/09/40, assigned to Zone "A"; 06/10/40, assigned to Military District X): LG Darius-Paul Bloch-Dassault (Commander-in-Chief, Anti-Aircraft Defense) 01/13/40 MG Félix-René Altmayer (Deputy Commander, Military District XVIII) 06/25/40 disbanded.
- A. **Chief of Staff, V Motorized Army Corps** (08/26/39): Col. Lucien-Émile-Eugéne Monniot [+ Chief of Staff, 83rd African Infantry Division] 10/15/39 LCol. Guedeney 06/25/40 dissolved.
- B. **Artillery, V Motorized Army Corps** (08/26/39): unknown? 12/13/39 BG Jean-Marie-Léon Etcheberrigaray (Commanding General, 53rd Infantry Division) 06/01/40 Col. Albert-Joseph Daine 06/25/40 dissolved.

VI Army Corps (08/31/39, in Military District VI, and assigned to Third Army): MG Lucien Loizeau (to /45, German prisoner-of-war; /45, retired) 06/25/40 disbanded.
- A. **Chief of Staff, VI Army Corps** (08/31/39): BG Joseph-Antoine-Sylvain-Raoul de Verdillac 10/10/39 LCol. Thouvenin de Villaret 06/40 BG Joseph-Antoine-Sylvain-Raoul de Verdillac (/41, Commanding General, Southern Syria) 06/25/40 dissolved.
- B. **Artillery, VI Army Corps** (08/31/39): unknown? /40 BG Géraud-Maurice-Marie-Joseph de Fontanges (to /45, German Prisoner-of-war) 06/25/40 dissolved.
- C. **Engineers, VI Army Corps** (08/31/39): Col. Georges-Henri-Auguste Beaumont 06/25/40 dissolved.

VII Army Corps (08/27/39, in Military District VII; 08/30/39, assigned to Eighth Army; 09/02/39, transferred to Eighth Army Reserve; 10/05/39, assigned to Eighth Army; 05/21/40, assigned to Sixth Army): MG Pierre-Louis-Célestin-Michel Champon (Head, French Military Mission to Belgian) 05/11/40 MG Paul-Marie-Joseph de la Porte du Theil [+ to 06/11/40, Commanding General, 42nd Infantry Division] (at disposal of the Ministry of Family & Youth; /41, at disposal of the Secretary-General of Youth; /41, Comissioner-General of Strengthing the Youth) 06/25/40 disbanded.
- A. **Chief of Staff, VII Army Corps** (08/27/39): Col. Pierre-Henri-Marie Coudret 06/25/40 dissolved.
- B. **Artillery, VII Army Corps** (08/27/39): Col. Eugène-Jules-Octave Balourdet 06/25/40 dissolved.

VIII Army Corps (08/27/39, in Military District VIII; 08/28/39, assigned to Fifth Army; 09/02/39, transferred to Fifth Army; 06/02/40, assigned to 2nd Army Group Reserve; 06/08/40, assigned to Fourth Army; 06/23/40, assigned to 2nd Army Group): vacant 09/02/39 LG Aubert-Achille-Jules Frère (Commander-in-Chief, Seventh Army) 05/19/40 MG Marie-Alphonse-Théodore-René-Adrian Desmazes (Commanding General, Vichy Military District VII) 06/25/40 disbanded.

A. **Chief of Staff, VIII Army Corps** (09/02/39): Col. Fernand-Zacharie-Joseph Lenclud (Infantry Commander, 11th Infantry Division) 01/15/40 LCol. Tourret 06/25/40 dissolved.

B. **Artillery, VIII Army Corps** (09/02/39 BG [Retired '38] Charles-Amédée Thiébeauid (retired) 06/25/40 dissolved.

IX Army Corps (09/05/39, in Military District IX; 09/16/39, assigned to Fourth Army; 06/01/40, assigned to Tenth Army): LG Auguste-Marie-Émile Laure (Commander-in-Chief, Eighth Army) 05/22/40 LG Marcel Ihler (to /45, German prisoner-of-war; /45, retired) 06/25/40 disbanded.

A. **Chief of Staff, IX Army Corps** (09/05/39): Col. Henri-Jules-Jean Martin (05/25/40, Commanding General, 87th African Infantry Division) 02/12/40 Col. Joseph-Vincent-Félix Fonsagrive 05/12/40 Col. Guérin 06/25/40 dissolved.

B. **Artillery, IX Army Corps** (09/05/39): Col. Pierre-Servais Durand (Infantry Commander, 68th Infantry Division) 01/16/40

X Army Corps (09/02/39, in Military District IV; 09/17/39, assigned to Second Army Reserve; 10/12/39, transferred to Second Army; 05/13/40, assigned to Grpt. Touchon; 05/15/40, transferred back to Second Army; 05/19/40, assigned to Seventh Army; 05/23/40, assigned to Group "A"; 05/30/40, assigned to Tenth Army; 06/08/40, transferred back to Seventh Army, 06/10/40, assigned to Army of Paris): LG Pierre-Paul-Jacques Grandsard (Commanding General, Military District XIII) 06/25/40 disbanded.
[NOTE: also found, acting Commanding General, but no dates, in 06/40 MG Louis-Ernest Gillier [+ Commanding General, 8th Light Colonial Infantry Division] 06/40**]**

A. **Chief of Staff, X Army Corps** (09/02/39): Col. Linder 02/15/40 Col. Charles-Emmanuel Mast (Commanding Officer, 3rd North African Infantry Division) 05/23/40 LCol. Badel 06/25/40 dissolved.

B. **Artillery, X Army Corps** (09/02/39): BG Louis-Joseph Duhautois (?) 06/25/40 dissolved.

C. **Engineers, X Army Corps** (09/02/39): BG Henri-Alexandre Calvel (?) 06/25/40 dissolved.

XI Army Corps (09/02/39, in Military District XI; 09/17/39, assigned to Ardennes Army Detachment; 10/15/39, assigned to Ninth Army; 05/19/40, assigned to First Army): LG Julien-François-René Martin (at disposal of the Minister of War) 06/25/40 disbanded.

A. **Chief of Staff, XI Army Corps** (09/02/39): Col. Parent 04/40 Col. Pierre-Marie-Charles de Lorme [+ to 06/10/40, Chief of Staff, XXV Army Corps] 06/25/40 dissolved.

B. **Artillery, XI Army Corps** (09/02/39): Col. Paul-Gilbert-Eugène Frénal (to /41, German prisoner-of-war; /41, released) 06/25/40 dissolved.

XII Army Corps (09/02/39, in Military District ??; 09/12/39, assigned to Fifth Army Reserve; 10/08/39, assigned to Fifth Army): LG Alfred-Marie-Joseph-Louis Montagne (Commanding General, XV Army Corps) 11/11/39 MG Joseph-Charles-Robert Jeannel [+ Commanding General, 23rd Infantry Division] 11/14/39 LG Henri-Fernand Dentz (Commanding General, Paris Military District) 06/04/40 LG Pierre-Louis-Célestin-Michel Champon (German prisoner-of-war; /40, died in prisoner-of-war camp in Germany) 06/25/40 disbanded.
- A. **Chief of Staff, XII Army Corps** (09/02/39): Col. Hermann-Françis-Denis Delsuc (Infantry Commander, 8th Colonial Infantry Division) 11/15/39 Col. Hautcœur 06/25/40 dissolved.
- B. **Artillery, XII Army Corps** (09/02/39): Col. Jean-Charles-Louis Regnault de Premesnil /40 BG Louis-Léon Dechaux (German prisoner-of-war; /40, released; /40, retired) 06/25/40 dissolved.
- C. **Engineers, XII Army Corps** (09/02/39): BG [Retired '38] Constant-André Tétevuide (retired) 06/25/40 dissolved.

XIII Army Corps (08/21/39, in Military District XIII; 08/23/39, assigned to Eighth Army): LG Georges-Henri-Jean-Baptiste Misserey (to /45, German prisoner-of-war; /45, retired) 06/25/40 disbanded.
- A. **Chief of Staff, XIII Army Corps** (08/21/39): Col. Félix-Marie-Étienne Boudet 06/25/40 dissolved
- B. **Artillery, XIII Army Corps** (08/21/39): Col. Laurent-Maurice Berquet 06/25/40 dissolved.

XIV Army Corps (08/27/39, in Military District XIV, and assigned to Sixth Army; 02/06/40, assigned to Army of the Alps): vacant 09/02/39 MG Robert-Auguste Touchon (Commander-in-Chief, Sixth Army) 12/05/39 MG Étienne-Paul-Émile-Marie Beynet (09/12/40, Deputy Commander, Military District XIX) 06/25/40 disbanded.
- A. **Chief of Staff, XIV Army Corps** (08/27/39): vacant 09/02/39 Col. François-Jacques-André Duchemin (Commanding General, 3rd Light Infantry Division) 04/13/40 vacant 05/10/40 LCol. Pierre-Félix Conne (/43, Commanding General, Group Conne) 06/25/40 dissolved.

XV Army Corps (09/02/39, in Military District XV, and assigned to Sixth Army; 12/06/39, assigned to Army of the Alps): LG René-Henri Olry (Commander-in-Chief, Sixth Army) 10/19/39 LG Henri-Fernand Dentz (Commanding General, XII Army Corps) 11/14/39 LG Alfred-Marie-Joseph-Louis Montagne (in reserve; Commanding General, Military District IX) 06/25/40 disbanded.
- A. **Chief of Staff, XV Army Corps** (09/02/39): LCol. Granier (07/43, Deputy Commander, 1st Armored Division) 01/15/40 Col. Marie-Henri-Charles Raoux 06/25/40 dissolved.
- B. **Artillery, XV Army Corps** (09/02/39): Col. Gaston-Auguste-Paul Lemière /39 Col. Georges-Marie Vermiel du Conchard 06/25/40 dissolved.
- C. **Medical Services, XV Army Corps** (09/02/39): Col. Marie-Eugène-Adolphe Sicé (Medical Services, French Equatorial Africa) /40

XVI Army Corps (08/27/39, in Military District XVI, and assigned to Sixth Army Reserve; 09/15/39, transferred to Sixth Army; 09/28/39, assigned to First Army; 10/06/39, assigned

to 1st Army Group; 10/11/39, assigned to Seventh Army; 05/18/40, transferred back to 1st Army Group; 05/21/40, assigned to Belgian General Headquarters; 05/24/40, assigned to Admiral North; 06/07/40, assigned to Zone "A"; 06/13/40, transferred to General Headquarters; 06/15/40, assigned to Tenth Army): MG Marie-Bertrand-Alfred Fagalde [+ 05/15/40 for 1 day, acting Commanding General, Seventh Army] (to /45, German prisoner-of-war; /49, condemned to five years in prison, with loss of Military rank and properties) 06/25/40 disbanded.
- A. **Chief of Staff, XVI Army Corps** (08/27/39): Col. Estremé 06/25/40 dissolved.
- B. **Artillery, XVI Army Corps** (08/27/39): Col. Jean-François-Marie-Joseph-Béranfer de Curières de Castelnau (at disposal of Commanding General, Military District XVI) 06/25/40 dissolved.

XVII Army Corps (09/02/39, in Military District XVII; 09/24/39, assigned to Fourth Army; 10/04/39, assigned to Fifth Army; 05/16/40, assigned to Sixth Army): LG Onésime-Paul Noël (Commanding General, Military District VII) 06/25/40 disbanded.
- A. **Chief of Staff, XVII Army Corps** (09/02/39): Col. Elophe-Jean Larcher (Infantry Officer, 53rd Infantry Division) 11/06/39 Col. Mulot 06/25/40 dissolved.

XVIII Army Corps (09/02/39, in Military District XVIII; 09/14/39, assigned to Third Army; 10/15/39, assigned to Second Army): LG Eugène-Jules Rochard (retired) 05/18/40 MG Paul-André Doyen (Commanding General, Military District XIV) 06/25/40 MG Maurice Viant (Commanding General, Haute-Loire Department, Military District XIII) 07/40 disbanded.
- A. **Chief of Staff, XVIII Army Corps** (09/02/39): Col. Benson 03/15/40 Col. Duche 06/25/40 dissolved.
- B. **Artillery, XVIII Army Corps** (09/02/39): Col. Jean-Ernest-Anne Sainctavit /40 Col. Georges-Léon-Gustavé Mouton 06/25/40 dissolved.

XIX Army Corps (comprised of Algeria; HQ: Algiers): /36 LG Georges-Albert-Julien Catroux (retired; 08/23/39, Governor-General of French Indochina) /39 MG Raymond-Jules-Émile Poupinel [+ /40, Commanding General, South Tunisian Front] (Commanding General, Military District XIX) 06/25/40 unknown? 11/08/42? MG Marie-Louis Koëltz (Director, Free French Bureau of Armistice Studies) /44 LG Henri-Jules-Jean Martin.
- A. **Chief of Staff, XIX Army Corps**: /39 BG Georges-Edmond-Lucien Barré (Chief of Staff, Southern Tunisia Front) /39 unknown? /42 BG Charles-Emmanuel Mast (Commanding General, Territorial Division) 11/08/42?
- B. *Components* - **XIX Army Corps** (08/39)
    1. **Algiers Division [Division d'Alger]**
    2. **Oran Division [Division d'Oran]**
    3. **Constantine Division [Division de Constantine]**
    4. **East Saharian Front [Front Est Saharien]**
- C. *Components* - **XIX Army Corps** (05/10/40)
    1. **85th African Infantry Division**
    2. **181st African Infantry Division**
    3. **182nd African Infantry Division**
    4. **183rd African Infantry Division**
    5. **East Saharian Front [Front Est Saharien]**
- D. **Infantry, XIX Army Corps**: /44 BG Henri-Gustavé-André Borgnis-Desbordes.

E.   **Artillery, XIX Army Corps**: /40 Col. François-Jean Kergoat /42 Col. René de Hesdin (Artillery Commander, 3rd Algerian Infantry Division) /43

XX Army Corps (08/22/39, in Military District XX; 08/25/39, assigned to Fourth Army; 05/31/40, assigned to 2nd Army Group; 06/14/40, assigned to Third Army): LG Louis-Eugène Hubert (to /41, German prisoner-of-war; /41, retired, /42, Head, Army Social Service) 05/17/40 LG Frainot 06/25/40 disbanded.
A.   **Chief of Staff, XX Army Corps** (08/22/39): Col. Joseph-Charles-Gaëtan Andreï 05/17/40 unknown? 06/25/40 dissolved.

XXI Army Corps (08/26/39, in Paris Military District, and assigned to Second Army; 12/17/39, assigned to Third Army; 03/27/40, assigned to General Headquarters; 04/14/40, transferred back to Third Army; 05/05/40, assigned to General Headquarters Reserve; 05/15/40, assigned to Second Army; 06/17/40, assigned to Third Army): LG Jean-Adolphe-Louis-Robert Flavigny (to /45, German prisoner-of-war; /45, retired) 06/25/40 disbanded.
A.   **Chief of Staff, XXI Army Corps** (08/26/39): Col. Marcel-Louis-Lucien Trinquand /40? Col. Charles-Marte-Jules Tassin 06/25/40 dissolved.

XXIII Army Corps (02/05/40, in Military District XIV; 03/20/40, assigned to General Headquarters; 05/15/40, assigned to Army Detachment Touchon; 05/16/40, assigned to Sixth Army; 06/06/40, transferred to Fourth Army; 06/23/40, assigned to 2nd Army Group): vacant 04/01/40 MG Maxime-Jean-Vincent Germain (Deputy Commander, Military District XVII) 06/25/40 disbanded.
A.   **Chief of Staff, XXIII Army Corps** (02/05/40): vacant 04/01/40 Col. Camille-Ange-Gabriel Sabattier (Military-Governor, Hanoi, Indochina) 06/25/40 dissolved.
B.   **Artillery, XXIII Army Corps** (02/05/40): BG [Retired] Edouard-Joseph Arnaud (retired) 06/25/40 dissolved.

XXIV Army Corps (#1) (11/20/39, from **Fortress Army Corps**; 01/20/40, disbanded to form **XLI Fortress Army Corps [Ardennes Army Corps]**): unknown? 01/20/40 disbanded to form **XLI Fortress Army Corps** - see **XLI Fortress Army Corps**.
A.   **Chief of Staff, XXIV Army Corps (#1)** (11/20/39): unknown? 01/20/40 dissolved.

XXIV Army Corps (#2) (01/08/40; 02/28/40, assigned to General Headquarters Reserves; 04/15/40, assigned to Third Army; 05/18/40, assigned to Seventh Army): vacant 02/25/40 MG François-Marie-Jacques Fougère (Commander-in-Chief, Levant) 06/25/40 disbanded.
A.   **Chief of Staff, XXIV Army Corps (#2)** (01/08/40): Col. Marie-Joseph-Charles-François Brenet 06/25/40 dissolved.
B.   **Artillery, XXIV Army Corps (#2)** (01/08/40): Col. Léon-Joseph-Louis Saint-Paul de Sinçay 06/25/40 dissolved.

XXV Army Corps (05/28/40; 06/01/40 assigned to Tenth Army; 06/10/40, assigned to the Army of Paris): vacant 06/01/40 MG Sylvestre-Gérard Audet (in reserve; /40, Resident-General of Tunisia) 06/09/40 LG Emmanuel-Urbain Libaud [+ Commanding General, XLI Fortress Army Corps] (at disposal of the Minister of War; /40, retired) 06/25/40 disbanded.
A.   **Chief of Staff, XXV Army Corps** (05/28/39): Col. Pierre-Marie-Charles de Lorme [+ 04/40, Chief of Staff, XI Army Corps] 06/10/40 LCol. de Roucy 06/40? Col. de

Froissard Broissia 06/25/40 dissolved.
B. **Artillery, XXV Army Corps** (05/28/39): unknown? /40 Col. Michel-Alexandre-Maximilien Hanck 06/25/40 dissolved.

Colonial Army Corps (09/02/39, in Paris Military District; 09/11/39, assigned to Third Army; 05/22/40, assigned to Second Army; 06/18/40, assigned to Group Flavigny): MG [Retired '38] Henri Freydenberg 06/05/40 MG Émile-Jean-Gabriel Carlès (German prisoner-of-war; /40, released; /40, Chief of Staff, Colonial Forces) 06/25/40 disbanded.
A. **Chief of Staff, Colonial Army Corps** (09/02/39): Col. Edgard-Marie-Julien Cornet 04/40 LCol. David Laffitte 06/25/40 dissolved.
B. **Artillery, Colonial Army Corps** (09/02/39): BG Henrich-Camille-Constant-Arthur Rinck (to /45, German prisoner-of-war; /45, retired) 06/25/40 dissolved.
C. **Engineers, Colonial Army Corps** (09/02/39): BG [Retired '38] Paul-Eugène-Maurice Drôme (retired) 06/25/40 dissolved.

Metz Fortified Region (Région Fortifiée de Metz) (Mobilized on 08/21/39; 08/21/39, Military District VI; 08/26/39, Third Army; 03/18/40, disbanded and with **Crusnes Fortified Sector** formed **XLII Fortress Army Corps**): /35 MG Louis-Eugène Hubert [+ Commanding General, Metz Group of Subdivisions] (Commanding General, Military District XX) /38 unknown? 08/21/39? MG Désiré-Louis Sivot 03/18/40 disbanded and with **Crusnes Fortified Sector** forms **XLII Fortress Army Corps** - see **XLII Fortress Army Corps**.
A. **Chief of Staff, Metz Fortified Region** (08/21/39): LCol. Hème de la Cotte 03/18/40 dissolved.
B. **Artillery, Metz Fortified Region** (08/21/39): /38 Col. Henri-Jules-Alexis-Marie Menjaud 08/21/39 Col. Maurice-Eugène-Marcel-Joseph Hanly (Artillery Commander, XLII Fortress Army Corps) 03/18/40 dissolved.
C. **Engineers, Metz Fortified Region**: /38 Col. Adolphe-Pierre-Henri Séron 03/18/40 dissolved.

Lauter Fortified Region (Région Fortifiée de la Lauter) (Mobilized on 08/21/39; 08/21/39, Military District XX; 08/26/39, Fifth Army; 03/05/40, disbanded and with **Vosges Fortified Sector** forms **XLIII Fortress Army Corps**): Col. Aldophe-François Vieillard (Commanding General, Vosges Fortified Sector) 08/27/39 BG Bastidon 01/07/40 MG Maurice-Charles-Gabriel Lucas [+ Commanding General, 32nd Infantry Division] 03/05/40 disbanded and with **Vosges Fortified Sector** forms **XLIII Fortress Army Corps** - see **XLIII Fortress Army Corps**.
A. **Chief of Staff, Lauter Fortified Region** (08/27/39): LCol. Joseph-Louis-Justin Vidal (Chief of Staff, XLIII Fortress Army Corps) 03/05/40 dissolved.
B. **Engineers, Lauter Fortified Region**: /38 Col. Léon-Charles-Victor Cussenot 08/27/39 Col. Joseph-Guillaume Verdier 03/05/40 dissolved.

Belfort Fortified Region (Région Fortifiée de Belfort) (Mobilized on 08/21/39; 08/21/39, Military District VII; 09/02/39, Eighth Army; 11/06/39, XIII Army Corps; 11/20/39. Eighth Army; 02/09/40, disbanded and used to form **XLIV Fortress Army Corps**): /36 BG Jean Guillemont [+ /37, Military Governor, Belfort] (acting Commanding General, XLIV Fortress Army Corps) 12/22/39 BG Henri-Aimé Boutignon [+ Commanding General, 67th Infantry Division] 12/27/39 MG Julian-Maurice Tencé (Commanding General, XLIV Fortified Army

Corps) 02/09/40 disbanded and used to form **XLIV Fortress Army Corps**.
- A. **Chief of Staff, Belfort Fortified Region** (08/21/39): Maj. Perrin (04/40, Chief of Staff, Altkirch Fortified Sector) 12/22/39 LCol. Plagnol (Chief of Staff, XLIV Fortress Army Corps) 02/09/40 dissolved.
- B. **Artillery, Belfort Fortified Sector** (08/21/39): Col. Charles-Léon-Ferdinand Menu (Artillery Commander, XLIV Fortified Army Corps) 03/16/40 dissolved.

Sarre Fortified Region (Région Fortifiée de la Sarre) (09/01/39, under control of Military District XX; 09/25/39 redesignated **Fourth Army Fortified Region**; 10/27/39, disbanded): **Sarre Fortified Region** 09/01/39 BG Henri-Aimé Boutignon [+ Commanding General, Rohrbach Fortified Sector] (Commanding General, Fourth Army Fortified Region) 09/25/39 redesignated **Fourth Army Fortified Region** 09/25/39 BG Henri-Aimé Boutignon [+ Commanding General, Rohrbach Fortified Sector] (Commanding General, 67th Infantry Division) 10/20/39 vacant 10/27/39 disbanded.
- A. **Chief of Staff, Sarre Fortified Region** (09/01/39): LCol. Gras (Chief of Staff, 6th Infantry Division) 10/30/39 dissolved.

Fortress Army Corps (09/02/39, by the Military Governor of Paris, and assigned to General Headquarters Reserves; 09/10/39, assigned to Second Army; 11/15/39, assigned to First Army; 11/20/39, dissolved to form **XXIV Army Corps**): 09/02/39 LG $_{[Retired]}$ Jean-Baptiste-François-Paul Dufour (05/25/40, Commanding General, Military District III) 11/20/39 dissolved to form **XXIV Army Corps** - see **XXIV Army Corps**.
- A. **Chief of Staff, Fortress Army Corps** (09/02/39):

XLI Fortress Army Corps (01/20/40, from **XXIV Army Corps (#1)**; 01/11/40, Ninth Army; 05/17/40, General Headquarters): 01/15/40 MG Emmanuel-Urbain Libaud [+ 06/09/40, Commanding General, XXV Army Corps] (at disposal of the Minister of War; /40, retired) 06/25/40 disbanded.
- A. **Chief of Staff, XLI Fortress Army Corps** (01/15/40): Col. Jean-Sylvain-Louis Roubertie (/42, Commanding General, Casablanca Territory Division) 06/25/40 dissolved.
- B. *Components - XLI Fortress Army Corps*
    1. **41st Fortress Army Corps Artillery Park**

XLII Fortress Army Corps (03/16/40, from **Metz Fortified Region** and **Crusnes Fortified Sector**; 03/16/40, Third Army; 06/21/40, Group Dubuisson): MG Désiré-Louis Sivot (?) 05/27/40 MG Gaston-Ernest Renondeau (to /45, German prisoner-of-war; /45, retired) 06/25/40 disbanded.
- A. **Chief of Staff, XLII Fortress Army Corps** (03/16/40): vacant 03/20/40 LCol. Roederer 06/25/40 dissolved.
- B. *Components - XLII Fortress Army Corps*
    1. **128th Fortress Infantry Regiment**
    2. **139th Fortress Infantry Regiment**
    3. **149th Fortress Infantry Regiment**
    4. **46th Fortress Artillery Regiment**
    5. **152nd Static Artillery Regiment**
    6. **42nd Fortress Army Corps Artillery Park**

C. **Artillery, XLII Fortress Army Corps** (03/16/40): Col. Maurice-Eugène-Marcel-Joseph Hanly 06/25/40 dissolved.

XLIII Fortress Army Corps (03/05/40, from **Lauter Fortified Region** and **Vosges Fortified Sector**; 03/05/40, Fifth Army; 06/13/40, disbanded and used to create **Senselme March Division**): MG Fernand-Joseph-Louis Lescanne (to /45, German prisoner-of-war; /45, retired) 06/13/40 disbanded and used to create **Senselme March Division**.
- A. **Chief of Staff, XLIII Fortress Army Corps** (03/05/40): Col. Joseph-Louis-Justin Vidal 06/25/40 dissolved.
- B. *Components - XLIII Fortress Army Corps*
  1. **154th Fortress Infantry Regiment**
  2. **165th Fortress Infantry Regiment**
  3. **60th Fortress Artillery Regiment**
  4. **168th Static Artillery Regiment**
  5. **43rd Fortress Army Corps Artillery Park**

XLIV Fortress Army Corps (03/16/40, from **Belfort Fortified Region**; 03/05/40, Fifth Army): BG Jean Guillemont (acting) 03/16/40 MG Julian-Maurice Tencé (to /45, German prisoner-of-war) 06/25/40 disbanded.
- A. **Chief of Staff, XLIV Fortress Army Corps** (03/16/40): LCol. Plagnol 06/25/40 dissolved.
- B. **Artillery, XLIV Fortress Army Corps** (03/16/40): Col. Charles-Léon-Ferdinand Menu (retired) 06/25/40 dissolved.

XLV Fortress Army Corps (02/09/40, from **Jura Army Corps**; 02/09/40, 3rd Army Group; 05/19/40, Eighth Army): LG Marius Daille [+ Commanding General, Military District VII] (interned in Switzerland) 06/25/40 disbanded.
- A. **Deputy Commander, XLV Fortress Army Corps** (02/09/40): MG Edouard-Octave-Jules Brussaux (Military-Governor, Metz) 06/25/40 dissolved.
- B. **Chief of Staff, XLV Fortress Army Corps** (02/09/40): LCol. Rimaud 06/25/40 dissolved.
- C. *Components - XLV Fortress Army Corps*
  1. **45th Fortress Army Corps**
- D. **Artillery, XLV Fortress Army Corps** (02/09/40): BG Marie-Paul-Vincent Grollemund (retired) 06/25/40 dissolved.
- E. **Engineers, XLV Fortress Army Corps** (02/09/40): Col. Jacob-Raoul El Ghozi (retired) 06/25/40 dissolved.

French Scandinavian Expeditionary Force [Corps Expéditionnaire Français en Scandinavie (CEFS)] (02/16/40, to help the Finns fight the Soviet Union; 03/17/40, redesignated "Group [Groupement] A"; 04/15/40, redesignated back to **French Scandinavian Expeditionary Force**): French Scandinavian Expeditionary Force (#1) 02/16/40 MG Sylvestre-Gérard Audet (Commanding General, Group A) 03/17/40 redesignated **Group A** 03/17/40 MG Sylvestre-Gérard Audet (Commanding General, French Scandinavin Expeditionary Force) 04/15/40 redesignated **French Scandinavian Expeditionary Force (#2)** 04/15/40 LG Sylvestre-Gérard Audet (Commanding General, XXV Army Corps) 06/01/40 disbanded.

A. **Chief of Staff, French Scandinavian Expeditionary Force** (02/26/40): Maj. Goybet 06/01/40 dissolved.
B. *Components* - **French Scandinavian Expeditionary Force** (03/17/40)
   1. **1st Light Division [Division Légère de Chasseurs]**
   2. **2nd Light Division [Division Légère de Chasseurs]**
   3. **3rd Light Division [Division Légère de Chasseurs]**
   4. **Polish Highland Brigade [Brigade Polonaise or Samodzielna Brygada Strzelcow Podhalanskich]**
   5. **13th Foreign Legion March Half-Brigade [13ᵉ Demi-Brigade de Marche de Légion Étranger]**: /40 Col. Charles-Raoul Magrin-Vernerey dit Monclar (/41, Commanding Officer, Free French Oriental Brigade) /40 Col. Alfred-Maurice Cazaud [+ /41, acting Commanding General, 2nd Free French Light Division] (Commanding General, 2nd Free French Infantry Brigade) /42

Colonial Forces in France: /42 MG Jean-Eugène-Marie Charbonneau
A. **Chief of Staff, Colonial Forces in France**: /38 Col. Edmond-Edouard Husson
B. **Artillery, Colonial Forces in France**: /37 Col. Henrich-Camille-Constant-Arthur Rinck (Technical Assistant to the Inspector-General of Colonial Troops) /39
C. **Depots of Colonial Forces in France**: /39 MG Joseph-Jules-Marie Legendre (?) /40

Levant Mobile Force [Groupement des Forces Mobiles du Levant] (10/01/39, as **Army Corps "L" [Corps d'Armée "L"]**; 10/23/39, redesignated **Levant Mobile Force**): **Army Corps L** /39 BG François-Pierre-Louis Keller (Commanding General, Troops in Southern Syria) 10/23/39 redesignated **Levant Mobile Force** 10/23/39 LG _[Retired '39] Charles-Gabriel-Renaud Massiet (retired) /40
A. **Chief of Staff, Levant Mobile Force** (10/01/39): /37 LCol. Marcel-Maurice Carpentier (/40, Chief of Staff, Commander-in-Chief, North Africa) /37 unknown? 10/01/39? Col. Amédée-Paul-Georges-Joseph Keime (Commanding Officer, Cavalry, Levant; /41, Commander of French Troops, South Syria) /41
B. *Components* - **Levant Mobile Force**
   1. **86th African Infantry Division**
   2. **191st African Infantry Division**
   3. **192nd African Infantry Division**
C. **Deputy Chief of Staff, Levant Mobile Force**: 04/40? LCol. Lenglet
D. **1st Bureau (Administration), Levant Mobile Force**: 04/40? Maj. Magnillat
E. **2nd Bureau (Intelligence), Levant Mobile Force**: 04/40? Capt. _[Army] Leridon
F. **3rd Bureau (Operations), Levant Mobile Force**: 04/40? LCol. Guilbaud
G. **4th Bureau (Supply), Levant Mobile Force**: 04/40? Capt. _[Army] Dulac /?? Capt. _[Army] Guichard /?? Capt. _[Army] Odry
H. **Commands & Services, Levant Mobile Force**: 04/40? BG Thierry

Army Corps du Jura (12/16/39, temporary corps; 02/09/40, disbanded): MG Marius Daille [+ Commanding General, Military District VII] (Commanding General, XLV Fortress Army Corps) 02/09/40 disbanded.
A. **Engineers, Army Corps du Jara** (12/16/39): BG Jacob-Raoul El Ghozi (Engineers Commander, XLV Fortress Army Corps) 02/09/40 dissolved.

Morocco Army Corps [Commander-in-Chief, Morocco] (North Africa; HQ: Rabat, Morocco): /36 Gen. Charles-Auguste-Paul Noguès [+ Resident-General of Morocco] /36 BG Marie-Jules-Victor-Léon François [+ to /39, Deputy Resident-General of Morocco] (Infantry Commander, 5th Colonial Infantry Division) /40 MG Bernard-Marie-Alexis Vergès (retired) /41 MG Alphonse-Pierre Juin (Commander-in-Chief, North Africa) 12/41 MG Georges-Eugène-Joseph Lascroux [+ to /42, General Officer Commanding, Fèz Division] (/44, retired) /43 MG Raymond-Charles-Émile Desre.

- A. **Deputy Commander-in-Chief, Morocco**: unknown? /41 MG Alphonse-Pierre Juin (Commander-in-Chief, Morocco) /41
- B. **Chief of Staff, Morocco Army Corps**: /38 Col. François-Antoine-Charles Chevallier (Commanding General, 81st African Infantry Division) 02/05/39
- C. *Components* - Morocco Army Corps
    1. **Casablanca Territorial Division**: see **Divisions in Overseas Colonies and Protectorates** Section.
    2. **Fèz Territorial Division**: see **Divisions in Overseas Colonies and Protectorates** Section.
    3. **Marrakech Territorial Division**: see **Divisions in Overseas Colonies and Protectorates** Section.
    4. **Meknès Territorial Division**: see **Divisions in Overseas Colonies and Protectorates** Section.
- D. *Components* - Morocco Army Corps
    1. **2nd Moroccan Infantry Division**
    2. **3rd Moroccan Infantry Division**
- E. **Vice Chief of Staff, Morocco**: /41 Col. Paul-Arsène-Gérard Devinck (Commanding Officer, 62nd Anti-Aircraft Artillery Regiment; /44, Deputy Commander, 5th Free French 5th Armored Division) /42
- F. **Cavalry, Morocco**: /38 Col. Antoine-Charles Lefèvre /38 Col. Jean-Joseph-Lucien Mordacq (Commanding General, 3rd Moroccan Infantry Division & Commanding General, Méknes Territorial Division) 09/02/39
- G. **Engineers, Morocco**: /38 Col. Paul-Ernest Dumont-Fillon (Assistant Inspector-General, Engineers) /39? unknown? /44 BG $_{[Retired '40]}$ Pierre-Marie Braconnier.
- H. **French Air Forces, Morocco**: 06/22/40 LG François d'Astier de la Vigerie $_{[FAF]}$ (joined Resistance; 11/42, joins BG de Gaulle in London, 12/01/42, Assistant to BG Charles de Gaulle) 08/40

Commander of the Troops & Territory of Tunisia [État-Major des Troupes de Tunisie et du Territorie] (also known as **Commander-in-Chief of Tunisia Forces [Commandant Supérieur de Troupes de Tunisia]**; redesignated **Tunisian Front [Commandant des Fronts Tunisiens]** (North Africa): **Commander of the Troops & Territory of Tunisia** /38 LG Amédée-Ferdinand-Auguste Blanc (Commanding General, Tunisian Front) /40 redesignnated **Tunisian Front** /40 LG Amédée-Ferdinand-Auguste Blanc (retired) 07/40 LG Sylvestre-Gérard Audet (Commanding General, Military District XVII) /41 LG Jean-Joseph-Marie-Gabriel de Lattre de Tassigny (arrested; /43, escapes to London; 12/43, Commander-in-Chief, Army B) 11/08/42? LG Georges-Edmond-Lucien Barré (at disposal of Commander-in-Chief of the Army; /45, retired) /43

- A. **Chief of Staff, Commander of the Troops & Territory of Tunisia**: Col. Maurice-Charles-Henri-Félicien Jurion /40 Col. Jean Breuillac (arrested by Vichy

Government; /43, escaped; Cabinet-Secretary to Ministry of National Defense) /41
- B. ***Components*** - **Commander of the Troops & Territory of Tunisia** (pre-'39)
    1. **Tunis Territory Division**: see **Divisions in Overseas Colonies and Protectorates** Section.
    2. **Sousse Territory Division**: see **Divisions in Overseas Colonies and Protectorates** Section.
- C. ***Components*** - **Tunisia Front** (05/40)
    2. **North Tunisian Front**: see **Overseas Infantry Divisions** Section.
    3. **South Tunisian Front**: see **Miscellaneous Units** Section.
    4. **Territory of Tunisia**: see **Miscellaneous Units** Section.
- D. **Artillery, Commander of the Troops & Territory of Tunisia**: /38 BG Louis-Clitus-Honoré Delègue (?) /?? BG Pierre-Émile-Henri Moreau
- E. **Engineers, Commander of the Troops & Territory of Tunisia**: /39 Col. Charles-Eugène Morin /38 Col. Jacob-Raoul El Ghozi (Engineers Commander, Military District XV) /39 Col. Pierre-Marie Braconnier (Director, Engineers, Algeria) /40
- F. **Medical Services, Commander of the Troops & Territory of Tunisia**: /42 Col. Georges-André Hugonot (Director, Medical Services, Free French Expeditionary Corps in Italy) 09/43
- G. **Director of the Tunisian Front Rear Zone [Directeur des Étapes des Fronts Tunisiens]** (also Commanding Officer, Territory of Tunisia): MG de Lescales /43 MG Jean-Paul Bergeron

Indochina Army Corps or **Commander-in-Chief, Troops in French Indochina [Commandant Supérieur de Troupes du Groupe l'Indochine]** (HQ: Saigon, Indochina): /38 LG Maurice-Paul-Auguste Martin (retired) /40 LG Eugène Mordant (retired; /44, Head, Military Resistance Indochina & Delegate-General, Provisional Government, Indochina) /44 MG Camille-Ange-Gabriel Sabattier
- A. **Chief of Staff, Indochina Army Corps**: /39 Col. Marcel-Jean-Marie Alessandri (Commanding Officer, 5th Foreign Legion Infantry Regiment) 12/08/41?
- B. ***Components*** - **Indochina Army Corps**
    1. **Tonkin Division**: see **Divisions in Overseas Colonies and Protectorates** Section.
    2. **Cochinchine-Cambodge Division**: see **Divisions in Overseas Colonies and Protectorates** Section.
    3. **Annam Brigade**: see **Infantry Brigades** in **Brigades** Section.
    4. **Indochina Independent Air Force Wing**
- C. **Deputy Chief of Staff, Indochina Army Corps**: /39 LCol. Marcel-Jean-Marie Alessandri (Chief of Staff, Indochina Army Corps) /39
- D. **Artillery, Indochina Army Corps**: /38 BG Joseph-Edouard-Henri-Marie-André Bourély
- E. **Signals, Indochina Army Corps**: /39 Maj. Callin
- F. **Intendant [Quartermaster; Logistics] Services, Indochina Army Corps**: /38 BG Fernand-Georges Gaucher (?) /39 BG Blanc
- G. **Medical Director, Indochina Army Corps**: /38 BG Frédéric-François-Marie Heckenroth (?) /38 BG Marie-Camille-Henri Gravellat (?) /39 Méd-Gen. Millour
- H. ***Military Territories***

1. **I Military Territory, Indochina Army Corps**: /39 LCol. Carles
2. **II Military Territory, Indochina Army Corps**: /39 LCol. Lapy
3. **III Military Territory, Indochina Army Corps**: /39 unknown? 04/40 Maj. de Montegny
4. **IV Military Territory, Indochina Army Corps**: /39 Capt. [Army] Emblanc

I. **French Liaison Officer, Allied Commander-in-Chief, Southeast Asia**: /43 BG Roger-Charles-André-Henri Blaizot

French West Africa [Afrique Occidentale Française (AOF)] (HQ: Dakar, Senegal): /34 BG René-Paul Dubuisson [+ /37, to /38, Member, Consultative Committee of Colonial Defense; + /38 to 09/02/39, Commanding General, 2nd Colonial Infantry Division] (Governor-General of Verdun) 09/20/39 MG Jean-Joseph-Guillaume Barrau (Member, The Army Council) /41 unknown? /41 LG Jean-Joseph-Guillaume Barrau (retired) /42 LG Maurice Viant (retired) /43 LG Yves-Marie-Jacques-Guillaume de Boisboissel (retired) /45 MG Joseph-Abraham-Auguste-Pierre-Edouard Magnan.

A. *Components*
   1. **1st Brigade, French West Africa**
   2. **2nd Brigade, French West Africa**
   3. **3rd Brigade, French West Africa**
B. **2nd Bureau (Intelligence), French West Africa**: /41 LCol. Raoul-Albert-Louis Salan (Head, 2nd Bureau, North Africa) /43
C. **Artillery, French West Africa**: /38 Col. Gauthier-Léon Niollet (Artillery Commander, 65th Alpine Infantry Division) 09/02/39 BG Jean-Jules-Ernest Picard (?) /40 MG Maurice Viant [+ Commanding General, Dakar Defense Position] (Commanding General, Dakar, Senegal, and Mauritanian Military District) /41
D. **Medical Services, French West Africa**: /36 BG Louis-Eugène-Benoit-Léon Couvy (?) /38

Commander-in-Chief, French Troops in French Equatorial Africa [Supérieur des Troupes d'Afrique Equatoriale Française (AEF)] (HQ: Brazzaville, Moyan Congo): /37 BG Émile-Jean-Gabriel Carlès (at disposal of Commander-in-Chief, Land Forces) /39 BG [Retired '36] Paul-Louis Husson (acting Governor-General, French Equatorial Africa) 07/17/40

Cavalry Corps and Armored Group

Cavalry Corps [Corps de Cavalerie] (08/27/39, and assigned to General Headquarters; 11/10/39, assigned to 1st Army Group; 05/10/40, assigned to First Army; 06/09/40, transferred to Zone "A"; 06/10/40, assigned to Tenth Army; 06/20/40, assigned to the Army of Paris): vacant 09/02/39 LG René-Jacques-Adolphe Prioux (Commander-in-Chief, First Army) 05/25/40 MG Jean-Léon-Albert Langlois (Deputy Commander, Military District XIII) 06/25/40 disbanded.
- A. **Chief of Staff, Cavalry Corps** (08/27/39): LCol. Pierre-Georges Arlabosse 04/40 LCol. Pierre-Armand-Marie-Robert Olleris (/42, Deputy Chief of the Vichy French Army General Staff) 06/25/40 dissolved.
- B/ **3rd Bureau, Cavalry Corps** (08/27/39): unknown? /40 Col. Jean-Louis-Alai Touzet du Vigier (Commanding Officer, 2nd Armored Regiment) /41?

I Armored Group (Groupement Cuirassé) (01/16/40, from the **Training Group**, and assigned to General Headquarters Reserve; 05/14/40, under control of the Inspector-General of Tanks; 05/15/40, assigned to Ninth Army; 05/17/40, assigned to Sixth Army; 05/23/40, assigned to Seventh Army; 06/02/40, transferred to North East Headquarters; 06/12/40, assigned to the Army of Paris): BG Louis-Marie-Joseph-Ferdinand Keller (Commanding General, 7th Military Division) 05/17/40 MG Marie-Joseph-Edmond Welvert [temporary; + Armor Commander, Sixth Army & Commanding General, 1st Armored Division] 06/02/40 BG [Retired '39] Charles-Georges-Antoine Delestraint (retired; 03/24/43, Commander-in-Chief, Secret Army) 06/25/40 disbanded
- A. **Chief of Staff. 1st Armored Group** (01/06/40): LCol. Bourcart 06/04/40 Maj. Cardin
- B. *Components* - **1st Armored Group** (01/06/40)
    1. **1st Reserve Armored Division** (01/06/40)
    2. **2nd Reserve Armored Division** (01/06/40)
    3. **3rd Reserve Armored Division** (03/20/40)

II Armored Group (06/07/40, a temporary formation; disbanded, 06/11/40): BG Louis-Léon-Marie-André Buisson (Commanding General, 3rd Armored Division) 06/11/40 disbanded.

Miscellaneous Units: Fronts, Groups [Groupement] (Corps sized units)

South Tunisian Front [Commandant de Front Sud Tusisien] (North Africa, subordinate to Tunisian Front; had the authority equivalent to an army corps commander): LG Raymond-Jules-Émile Poupinel [+ Commanding General, XIX Army Corps] (Commanding General, Military District XIX) 06/25/40
- A. **Chief of Staff, South Tunisian Front**: /39 BG Georges-Edmond-Lucien Barré (Commanding General, 7th North African Infantry Division) 03/16/40
- B. *Components* - **South Tunisian Front**
    1. 83rd **African Infantry Division**
    2. 84th **African Infantry Division**
- C. *Components* - **South Tunisian Front** (05/10/40)
    1. 81st **African Infantry Division**
    2. 180th **African Infantry Division**
    3. 6th **DLC**

Territory of Tunisia [Commandant de Territorie du Tunisie] (North Africa, subordinate to Tunisian Front; equivalent to a commander of a Military District and responsible for the rear areas of the two Tunisian Fronts with the title **Director of the Tunisian Front Rear Zone**]: MG de Lescales (?) /43 MG Jean-Paul Bergeron

Group Dubuisson (06/13/40, by the Maj. Supérieur de la Défense de Verdun): LG René-Paul Dubuisson [+ Governor-General of Verdun] (to /45, German prisoner-of-war; /49 condemned to 4 years imprisonment for collaboration with the enemy) /06/25/40 disbanded.

Group Dufour (from **Basse-Seine Defense Sector [Secteur Défensif de la Basse-Seine]**: MG Pierre-Jean-Marie Pégay [+ Commanding General, Military District III] (retired) 05/25/40 LG $_{[Retired]}$ Jean-Baptiste-François-Paul Dufour [+ Commanding General, Military District III] (retired) 06/25/40 disbanded

Group Molinié (05/28/40; 05/31/40, surrendered): MG Jean-Baptiste-Emmanuel Molinié 05/31/40 surrendered.

Naval Commands (Corps equivalent)

1st Flotilla [Squadron] (HQ: Brest, France; 09/01/39, assigned to Raiding Force): 09/01/39? VA Marcel-Bruno Gensoul [FN] [Flag: battleship *Dunkerque*] [+ Commander-in-Chief, Raiding Force & Commander, 1st Battle Division] (Commanding Officer, High Seas Force) 12/20/39
- A. **Components - 1st Flotilla [Squadron]** (09/01/39)
  1. **1st Battle Division**
     - a. BC *Dunkerque*
     - b. BC *Strasbourg*
  2. **4th Cruiser Division**
     - a. CL *Georges Leygues*
     - b. CL *Glorie*
     - c. CL *Montcalm*
  3. **CV Béarn**
  4. **2nd Light Destroyer Squadron**
     - a. 6th Destroyer Division
     - b. 8th Destroyer Division
     - c. 10th Destroyer Division

2nd Flotilla [Squadron] (HQ: Oran, Algeria; 09/01/39, assigned to High Seas Force): 09/01/39? VA Emmanuel. L. H. Ollive [FN] [Flag: BB *Provence*] [+ Commander-in-Chief, High Seas Force & Commander-in-Chief, III Naval Region] (Admiral Africa) 12/22/39 RA J. F. E. Bouxin [FN] [Flag: BB *Provence*]
- A. **Components - 2nd Flotilla [Squadron]** (09/01/39)
  1. **2nd Battle Division**
     - a. BB Lorraine
     - b. BB Bretagne
  2. **1st Light Destroyer Squadron**
     - a. 1st Light Destroyer Division
     - b. 3rd Light Destroyer Division
     - c. 7th Light Destroyer Division

3rd Flotilla [Squadron] (HQ: Toulon, France; 09/01/39, assigned to High Seas Force): 09/01/39? VA E. A. H. Duplat [FN] [Flag: heavy cruiser *Algérie*] [+ Commander-in-Chief, 1st Cruiser Squadron & Commander, 1st Cruiser Division] (Head, French Delegation to the Franco-Italian Armistice Commission) 09/12/40 disbanded.
- A. **Components - 3rd Flotilla [Squadron]** (09/01/39)
  1. **1st Cruiser Squadron**
     - a. **1st Cruiser Division**
       - i. CA *Algérie*
       - ii. CA *Foch*
       - iii. CA *Dupeix*
     - b. **2nd Cruiser Division**

            i.   **CA *Duquesne***
            ii.   **CA *Colbert***
            iii. **CA *Tourville***
    2. **3rd Light Squadron**
        a. **5th Destroyer Division**
        b. **7th Destroyer Division**
        c. **9th Destroyer Division**

Force X (06/40, Eastern Mediterranean; 07/03/40, interned by the British at Alexandria, Egypt): VA René-Émile Godfroy [FN] [Flag: CA *Duquesne*] (interned by the British) 07/03/40 interned.
A. ***Components* - Force X** (06/40)
    1. **BB *Lorraine***
    2. **CA *Duquesne***
    3. **CA *Tourville***
    4. **CA *Suffren***
    5. **CL *Duguay-Trouin***

I Naval Region (HQ: Cherbourg, France; 09/01/39, assigned to Admiral North): 09/01/39? Adm. Jean-Marie-Charles Abrial [FN] [+ Admiral North] (Governor-General of Algeria) 06/18/40 disbanded.
A. ***Components* - I Naval Region** (09/01/39)
    1. **11th Light Destroyer Division**
    2. **16th Submarine Division**
    3. **1st Sloop Squadron** (HQ: Cherbourg, France; sloops *Amiral Mouchez, Arras, Gaston Rivier, Quentin Roosevelt*)
       [stationed in Dunkirque; sloops *Belfort, Diligente*]
    4. **CM [minelayer] *Pollux***
B. **Dunkirque**: RA Charles Platon [FN] (Secretary, Minister for Colonies [Overseas France]) 06/18/40 dissolved,
C. **Pas-de-Calais**: RA Landriau [FN] (09/40, Commanding Officer, West Africa Naval Station) 06/18/40 dissolved.

II Naval Region (HQ: Brest, France; 09/01/39, assigned to Admiral West): 09/01/39? VA M. E. F. Traub [FN] (?) 06/18/40 disbanded.
A. ***Components* - II Naval Region** (09/01/39)
    1. **3rd Battle Division**
        a. **BB *Paris***
        b. **BB *Courbet***
    2. **2nd Destroyer Division**
    3. **2nd Light Destroyer Squadron**
        a. **2nd Light Destroyer Division**
        b. **4th Light Destroyer Division**
        c. **5th Light Destroyer Division**

        d.   **6th Light Destroyer Division**
    4.   **4th Submarine Squadron**
        a.   **2nd Submarine Division**
        b.   **4th Submarine Division**
        c.   **6th Submarine Division**
        d.   **8th Submarine Division**
    5.   **2nd Sloop Squadron** (HQ: Brest, France; sloops *Élan, Coucy, Épinal, Somme, Suippe, Vauquois*):
        [stationed at Lorient; sloops *Commandant Duboc, Commandant Rivière*]

III Naval Region (HQ: Toulon, France; 09/01/39? assigned to Admiral South): 09/01/39? VA Emmanuel L. H. Ollive [FN] [Flag: BB *Provence*] [+ Commander-in-Chief, High Seas Forces] (Admiral Africa) 12/20/39 disbanded.
    A.   *Components* - **III Naval Region** (09/01/39)
        1.   **4th Destroyer Division**
        2.   **13th Light Destroyer Division**
        3.   **1st Submarine Flotilla**
            a.   **3rd Submarine Squadron**
                i.   **1st Submarine Division**
                ii.   **3rd Submarine Division**
                iii.   **5th Submarine Division**
            b.   **5th Submarine Squadron**
                i.   **13th Submarine Division**
                ii.   **15th Submarine Division**
        4.   **Toulon Submarine Base [Submarine Center at Toulon]**
            a.   **7th Submarine Division**
            b.   **19th Submarine Division**
            c.   **21st Submarine Division**
        5.   **3rd Sloop Squadron** (HQ: Toulon, France; sloops *Amiens, Dédaigneuse, Lassigny, Les Éparges*):
        6.   **Torpedo Bomber Seaplane Group**: 09/01/39? LCdr. Guillard [FN]

IV Naval Region (HQ: Bizerte, Tunisia): 09/01/39? VA E. L. Rivet [FN] [Flag: CL *Marseillaise*]
    A.   **Light Attack Forces**
        1.   **3rd Cruiser Division**
            a.   **CL *Marseillaise***
            b.   **CL *Jean de Vienne***
            c.   **CL *La Galisonniere***
        2,   **Bizerte Destroyers [4th Light Squadron]** (becomes **Tunis Naval Force**)
            a.   **1st Destroyer Division**
            b.   **3rd Destroyer Division**
            c.   **11th Destroyer Division**
            d.   **CL [minelayer] *Émile Bertin***
    B.   **Bizerte Submarine Base**

1. **6th Submarine Squadron**
   a. **9th Submarine Division**
   b. **10th Submarine Division**
   c. **17th Submarine Division**
   d. **20th Submarine Division**
2. **AS [submarine tender]** *Castor*

C. **Oran Naval Force [6th Light Squadron]**
1. **8th Light Destroyer Division**
2. **2nd Submarine Squadron**
   a. **12th Submarine Division**
   b. **14th Submarine Division**
   c. **18th Submarine Division**
3. **CVS** *Commandant Teste*
4. **AS [submarine tender]** *Jules Verne*

D. **Casablanca Naval Station [Morocco Naval Force]**
1. **9th Light Destroyer Division**
2. **4th Submarine Division**

E. **12th Light Destroyer Division**

F. **4th Sloop Squadron** (HQ: Toulon, France; sloops *Engageante, Tapageuse, Ypres*):

V Naval Region (HQ: Lorient, France; 09/01/39, assigned to Admiral West): VA H. L. M. de Penfentyo de Kervereguin [FN] (?) 06/18/40 disbamded.
A. *Components - V Naval Region* (09/01/39)
1. **14th Light Destroyer Division**
2. **5th Sloop Squadron** (HQ: Lorient, France; sloops *Chamois, Commandant Bory, Le Chevreuil, Ailette, Dubourdieu, Luronne*)

Tunis Naval Force (HQ: Tunis, Tunisia; subordinated to IV Naval Region): 11/08/42? VA E. H. H. N. Derrien [FN] [+ Commanding Admiral, Bizerta Naval Base] (German prisoner-of-war; 10/44, arrested; condemned to death and executed) 12/07/42 surrendered.
A. *Components - Tunis Naval Force* (11/08/42)
1. **Bizerta Naval Base**

Algiers Naval Force (HQ: Oran, Algeria): 09/40 VA J. H. C. F. Moreau [FN]
A. *Components - Oran Naval Force* (11/08/42)

Casablanca [Morocco] Naval Force (HQ: Casablanca, Morocco): 11/08/42? VA François-Félix Michelier [FN] (Chief of the Free French Navy General Staff) 12/26/42
A. *Components - Morocco Naval Force* (11/08/42)
1. **BB** *Jean Bart*
2. **CL** *Primauguet*
3. **2nd Light Destroyer Division**
4. *a Submarine Division*

Maritime Perfect and Governor of Toulon (HQ: Toulon, France): 09/40? VA André A. A. Marquis [FN]
- A. *Components* - **Toulon Naval Base** (11/18/42)
    1. **BC** *Dunkerque*
    2. **CVS** *Commandant Teste*
    3. **CA** *Foch*
    4. **CL** *La Galissonniére*
    5. **13 Destroyers**
    6. **6 Submarines**
    7. **18 Sloops**

Divisions

Motorized Infantry Divisions
[Divisions d'Infanterie Motorisée]

1st Motorized Infantry Division (05/23/39, organized; 08/31/39, First Army Covering Force; 09/16/39, General Headquarters Reserve;05/10/40, III Army Corps; 05/17/40, First Army Reserve; 05/18/40, III Army Corps; 05/29/40, Group Moliné; 06/06/40, Regrouping Zone D; 06/10/40, disbanded): /38 BG Paul-René Malivoire-Filhol de Camas (Commanding General, 1st Light Infantry Division) 06/10/40 disbanded.
- A. **Chief of Staff, 1st Motorized Infantry Division** (05/23/39): Col. Weischinger (Chief of Staff, 1st Light Infantry Division) 06/10/40 dissolved.
- B. *Components - 1st Motorized Infantry Division* (08/23/39)
    1. **1st Motorized Infantry Regiment**
    2. **43rd Motorized Infantry Regiment**
    3. **110th Motorized Infantry Regiment**
    4. **15th Divisional Artillery Regiment**
    5. **215th Divisional Heavy Artillery Regiment**
- C. **Infantry, 1st Motorized Infantry Division** (05/23/39): unknown? /40 Col. Charles-Léon Jenoudet (German prisoner-of-war) 06/10/40 dissolved.

3rd Motorized Infantry Division (08/25/39, organized; 08/28/39, Second Army Covering Force; 09/10/39, General Headquarters Reserve; 12/01/39, IX Army Corps; 01/25/40, General Headquarters Reserve; 05/12/40, Second Army; 05/14/40, XXI Army Corps; 05/26/40, Second Army Reserves; 06/08/40, Colonial Army Corps; 06/10/40, VIII Army Corps; 06/18/40, dissolved): /36 BG Marcel-Charles-Joseph Lamson (Commanding General, II Army Corps) 08/26/39 MG Paul-Jean-Léon Bertin-Boussus (German prisoner-of-war) 06/18/40 dissolved.
- A. **Chief of Staff, 3rd Motorized Infantry Division** (08/25/39): LCol. Foglierini 06/18/40 dissolved.
- B. *Components - 3rd Motorized Infantry Division* (08/25/39)
    1. **51st Motorized Infantry Regiment**
    2. **67th Motorized Infantry Regiment**
    3. **91st Motorized Infantry Regiment**
    4. **42nd Divisional Artillery Regiment**
    5. **242nd Divisional Heavy Artillery Regiment**
- C. **Artillery, 3rd Infantry Division**: /38 Col. Paul-Jean-Léon Bertin-Boussus (08/26/39, Commanding General, 3rd Motorized Infantry Division) /38?

5th Motorized Infantry Division (pre-war; 08/23/39, organized in Military District III; 08/27/39, General Headquarters Reserve (First Army Zone); 09/11/39, General Headquarters Reserve (Third Army Zone); 10/02/39, General Headquarters Reserve; 01/08/40, First Army; 01/08/40, Ninth Army Reserve; 05/10/40, II Army Corps; 05/17/40,

First Army; 05/19/40, XI Army Corps; 05/20/40, First Army; 05/25/40, disbanded): /36 Col. Pierre-Louis-Célestin-Michel Champon (Commanding General, VII Army Corps) 08/23/39 MG Jean-Baptiste Limasset (killed in a car accident) 03/12/40 BG Eugène-Charles Dunoyer de Ségonzac (Infantry Commander, 5th Motorized Infantry Division) 03/22/40 MG Georges-Edgar Boucher (acting Commanding General, II Army Corps) 05/25/40 disbanded.

A. **Chief of Staff, 5th Motorized Infantry Division** (08/23/39): LCol. Tachet des Combes 03/40 LCol. Labarbe 05/25/40 dissolved.
B. *Components* - **5th Motorized Infantry Division** (08/23/39)
   1. **8th Motorized Infantry Regiment**
   2. **39th Motorized Infantry Regiment**
   3. **129th Motorized Infantry Regiment**: /39? Col. Marie-Cyrille-Victor Debeney (Infantry Commander, 30th Infantry Division) 10/28/39
   4. **11th Divisional Artillery Regiment**
   5. **211th Divisional Heavy Artillery Regiment**
C. **Infantry, 5th Motorized Infantry Division** (08/23/39): /36 Col. Louis-Germain Girol (Commanding General, Belfort Defense Sector & Belfort Subdivision Group) 08/23/39 Col. Eugène-Charles Dunoyer de Ségonzac (acting Commanding General, 5th Motorized Infantry Division 03/12/40 vacant 03/22/40 BG Eugène-Charles Dunoyer de Ségonzac (Commanding General, 239th Light Infantry Division) 06/01/40
D. **Artillery, 5th Motorized Infantry Division** (08/23/39): Col. Louis-Léon Dechaux (Artillery Commander, XII Army Corps) /40

9th Motorized Infantry Division (08/26/39, Military District V; 09/01/39, Fourth Army Covering Force; 09/06/39, Fourth Army Reserve; 09/07/39, V Army Corps; 09/25/39, VIII Army Corps; 10/01/39, III Army Corps; 10/03/39, XVI Army Corps; 03/06/40, Seventh Army Reserve; 03/28/40, I Army Corps; 05/10/40, XVI Army Corps; 05/16/40, Ninth Army; 05/19/40, dispersed): /38 MG Henri-Joseph-Martin Richter (retired) 11/13/39 MG Henri-Antoine Didelet (to /45, German prisoner-of-war) 05/19/40 dispersed.

A. **Chief of Staff, 9th Motorized Infantry Division** (08/26/39): Maj. Laureux 05/19/40 dissolved.
B. *Components* - **9th Motorized Infantry Division** (08/26/39)
   1. **13th Motorized Infantry Regiment**
   2. **95th Motorized Infantry Regiment**
   3. **131st Motorized Infantry Regiment**
   4. **30th Divisional Artillery Regiment**
   5. **230th Divisional Heavy Artillery Regiment**
C. **Infantry, 9th Motorized Infantry Division** (08/26/39): Col. Robert-Jules-Eugène Barthélémy (Commanding General, Flanders Defense Sector) 11/07/39

12th Motorized Infantry Division (08/23/39, Military District VI; 08/26/39, General Headquarters Reserve (Ardennes Army Detachment Zone); 09/04/39, General Headquarters Reserve (Third Army Zone); 09/10/39, Third Army; 09/14/39, Colonial Army Corps; 11/20/39, V Army Corps; 01/19/40, First Army; 05/10/40, V Army Corps; 05/29/40,

XVI Army Corps; 06/04/40, captured): /36 Col. Lucien Loizeau Commanding General, Military District VI) 08/23/39 BG Louis-Guillaume-Gaston Janssen (killed in action) 06/02/40 Col. Blanchon 06/04/40 captured.
- A. **Chief of Staff, 12th Motorized Infantry Division** (08/23/39): Maj. Michel 02/01/40 Maj. Palmieri 06/04/40 dissolved.
- B. *Components* - **12th Motorized Infantry Division** (08/23/39)
    1. **106th Motorized Infantry Regiment**
    2. **150th Motorized Infantry Regiment**
    3. **8th Motorized Zouave Regiment**
    4. **25th Divisional Artillery Regiment**
    5. **225th Divisional Heavy Artillery Regiment**
- C. **Infantry, 12th Motorized Infantry Division**: /39 BG André-Marie-François Dody (Commanding General, 8th Infantry Division) 04/01/40

15th Motorized Infantry Division (08/23/39; Military District VIII; 08/26/39 Covering Force Reserve (Eighth Army Zone); 09/05/39, Fifth Army; 09/08/39, VIII Army Corps; 10/05/39, Fifth Army Reserve; 10/10/39, 2nd Army Group Reserve; 10/23/39, General Headquarters Reserve; 05/10/40, IV Army Corps; 05/28/40, dispersed): /38 MG Henri Parisot (Military Attaché Italy) 02/01/40 MG Alphonse-Pierre Juin (to /41, German prisoner-of-war; /41, Deputy Commander-in-Chief, Morocco) 05/28/40 dispersed.
- A. **Chief of Staff, 15th Motorized Infantry Division** (08/23/39): LCol. Berlon 05/28/40 dissolved.
- B. *Components* - **15th Motorized Infantry Division** (08/23/39)
    1. **4th Motorized Infantry Regiment**
    2. **27th Motorized Infantry Regiment**
    3. **134th Motorized Infantry Regiment**
    4. **1st Divisional Artillery Regiment**
    5. **201st Divisional Heavy Artillery Regiment**
- C. **15th Motorized Infantry Division**: /37 Col. Eugène-Raphaël Échard (Commanding Officer, Escaut Fortified Sector) /39

25th Motorized Infantry Division (08/27/39, General Headquarters Reserve; 09/08/39, 2nd Army Group Reserve (Fourth Army Zone); 09/25/39, Fifth Army; 09/27/39, VIII Army Corps; 10/28/39, 2nd Army Group Reserve; 11/04/39, General Headquarters Reserve; 11/13/39, I Army Corps; 05/16/40, Belgian V Army Corps; 05/17/40, I Army Corps; 05/18/40, First Army Reserve; 05/19/40 XI Army Corps; 05/21/40 V Army Corps; 05/28/40, Group Molinié; 05/31/40, captured): /36 BG Alfred-Marie-Joseph-Louis Montagne (Commanding General, Military District XVIII) /38 unknown? 08/27/39 MG Jean-Baptiste-Emmanuel Molinié [+ 05/28/40, Commanding General, Group Molinié] (German prisoner-of-war) 05/31/40 captured.
- A. **Chief of Staff, 25th Motorized Infantry Division** (08/27/39): LCol. Donnat 03/25/40 LCol. de Bellegarde 05/31/40 dissolved.
- B. *Components* - **25th Motorized Infantry Division** (08/27/39)
    1. **38th Motorized Infantry Regiment**
    2. **92nd Motorized Infantry Regiment**

3. **121st Motorized Infantry Regiment**
   4. **16th Divisional Artillery Regiment**
   5. **216th Divisional Heavy Artillery Regiment**
C. **Infantry, 25th Motorized Infantry Division**: /38 Col. Pierre-Louis-Félix Lanquetot (Commanding General, 21st Infantry Division) 10/13/39 unknown? 05/31/40 dissolved.

Infantry Divisions
[Division d'Infanterie]

2nd Infantry Division (09/02/39, Military District I; 09/08/39, First Army; 10/05/39, III Army Corps; 12/04/39, VI Army Corps; 02/01/40, Third Army; 03/08/40, Colonial Army Corps; 05/22/40, VI Army Corps; 05/25/40, General Headquarters Reserve; 05/27/40, Sixth Army; 05/30/40, XXIII Army Corps; 06/11/40, Fourth Army; 06/15/40, XXIII Army Corps; 06/17/40, Second Army; 06/20/40, disbanded): MG Gaston-Ernest Renondeau (Commanding General, Bas-Rhin Defense Sector) 01/06/40 BG Albert-Frédéric Klopfenstein (?) 06/20/40 disbanded

A. **Chief of Staff, 2nd Infantry Division** (09/02/39): Maj. Villate 06/20/40 dissolved.
B. *Components* - **2nd Infantry Division** (09/02/39)
   1. **33rd Infantry Regiment**
   2. **73rd Infantry Regiment**
   3. **127th Infantry Regiment**
   4. **34th Divisional Artillery Regiment**
   5. **234th Divisional Heavy Artillery Regiment**

4th Infantry Division (08/26/39, II Army Corps; 09/12/39, V Army Corps; 09/20/39, XI Army Corps; 11/23/39, Third Army Reserve; 11/30/39, VI Army Corps; 01/13/40, General Headquarters Reserve (Seventh Army Zone); 05/12/40, Seventh Army Reserve; 05/15/40, First Army Zone; 05/20/40, IV Army Corps; 05/30/40, most of the division was evacuated at Dunkirk, the rest destroyed or captured): vacant 09/02/39 MG Jean-Frédéric Oehmichen 11/11/39 BG Félix-Joseph Musse (German prisoner-of-war) 05/30/40 most of the division was evacuated at Dunkirk, the rest destroyed or captured.

A. **Chief of Staff, 4th Infantry Division** (08/26/39): LCol. Jacques-Pierre-Louis de Grancey (Deputy Chief of Staff, Army of the Alps) 12/15/39 LCol. Chardon du Ranquet 05/30/40 dissolved.
B. *Components* - **4th Infantry Division** (08/26/39)
   1. **45th Infantry Regiment**
   2. **72ndInfantry Regiment**
   3. **124th Infantry Regiment**
   4. **29th Divisional Artillery Regiment**
   5. **229th Divisional Heavy Artillery Regiment**
C. **Infantry, 4th Infantry Division** (08/26/39): Col. Henri-Jean Lafontaine (Commanding General, 55th Infantry Division) 02/21/40 unknown? 05/30/40 dissolved.

6th Infantry Division (09/02/39, Military District III; 09/12/39, General Headquarters Reserve (Ardennes Army Detachment Zone); 10/24/39, General Headquarters Reserve (Ninth Army Zone); 11/23/39, XI Army Corps; 12/09/39, Ninth Army Reserve; 12/25/39, Third Army; 01/022/40, VI Army Corps; 03/21/40, Third Army Reserve; 03/28/40, 2nd Army Group Reserve; 04/15/40, Third Army Reserve; 05/12/40, Second Army; 05/14/40, XVIII Army Corps; 05/22/40, XVIII Army Corps Reserve; 05/23/40 XXI Army Corps; 06/21/40, Group Dubuisson): MG Auguste-Eugène Lucien (?) 06/23/40 disbanded.

A. **Chief of Staff, 6th Infantry Division** (09/02/39): Maj. Lalande 10/30/39 LCol. Gras 06/23/40 dissolved.
B. *Components* - **6th Infantry Division** (09/02/39)
    1. **36th Infantry Regiment**
    2. **74th Infantry Regiment**
    3. **119th Infantry Regiment**
    4. **43rd Divisional Artillery Regiment**
    5. **243rd Divisional Heavy Artillery Regiment**

7th Infantry Division (09/02/39, IV Army Corps; 01/11/40, XXIV Army Corps; 01/15/40, XLI Fortress Army Corps; 02/05/40, Ninth Army Reserve; 02/16/40, Colonial Army Corps; 05/05/40, Third Army Reserve; 05/11/40, Colonial Army Corps;05/16/40, Third Army; 05/19/40, General Headquarters Reserve; 05/28/40, XVII Army Corps; 06/15/40, Sixth Army (Group Hupel); 06/25/40, disbanded): BG François-Napoléon-Henri-Dieudonné Hupel (Commanding General, Constantine Territorial Division) 06/25/40 disbanded
A. **Chief of Staff, 7th Infantry Division** (09/02/39): LCol. Thouvenin de Villaret [+ 10/10/39, Chief of Staff, VI Army Corps] 10/21/39 Maj. Rihouey 03/24/40 Maj. Audry 06/25/40 dissolved.
B. *Components* - **7th Infantry Division** (09/02/39)
    1. **93rd Infantry Regiment**
    2. **102nd Infantry Regiment**
    3. **130th Infantry Regiment**
    4. **31st Divisional Artillery Regiment**
    5. **231st Divisional Heavy Artillery Regiment**
C. **Infantry, 7th Infantry Division** (09/02/39): Col. Marie-Marcel Bonnaissieux (Commanding General, 26th Infantry Division) 04/10/40

8th Infantry Division (04/01/40, Military District XVIII; 04/29/40, Third Army; 05/17/40, Military Governor of Paris; 05/20/40, Military Governor of Paris Reserve; 05/22/40, Sixth Army Reserve; 05/23/40, 3rd Army Group Reserve; 05/24/40, XVII Army Corps; 06/25/40, disbanded): MG André-Marie-François Dody (Commanding General, Meknès Territorial Division) 06/25/40 disbanded.
A. **Chief of Staff, 8th Infantry Division** (04/04/40): Maj. Gouyon /40 Capt. [Army] Bonnefay 06/25/40 dissolved.
B. *Components* - **8th Infantry Division** (04/01/40)
    1. **11th Foreign Legion Infantry Regiment** (removed 04/20/40)
    2. **12th Foreign Legion Infantry Regiment**
    3. **6th Infantry Regiment** removed 04/20/40)
    4. **82nd North African Artillery Regiment**
    5. **282nd North African Heavy Artillery Regiment**
    6. **137th Infantry Regiment** (added 04/27/40)
    7. **16th Infantry Half-Brigade** (added 04/27/40)

10th Infantry Division (08/23/39, Paris Military District; 08/27/39, General Headquarters Reserves (Second Army Zone); 09/11/39, Second Army; 09/21/39, XXI Army Corps;

01/16/40, Third Army; 01/22/40, VI Army Corps; 04/08/40, General Headquarters Reserve; 05/16/40, XXIII Army Corps; 06/11/40, Group Keller (41nd Infantry Division); 06/13/40, Group Klopfenstein (2nd Infantry Division); 06/16/40, Second Army; 06/25/40, disbanded): /36 Col. Henri-Louis Vary (09/05/39, Commanding General, Military District IX) /38 MG Eugène-Prosper-Joseph Sisteron (Director, Rear Areas, Sixth Army) 06/03/40 BG Georges-Albert Aymé (12/08/41?, Commanding General, Tonkin Division, Indochina) 06/25/40 disbanded.

A. **Chief of Staff, 10th Infantry Division** 08/23/39): LCol. Badel (Chief of Staff, X Army Corps) 02/12/40 Maj. René-Raphaël Valette 06/25/40 dissolved.
B. *Components* - **10th Infantry Division** (08/23/39)
   1. **5th Infantry Regiment**
   2. **24th Infantry Regiment**
   3. **46th Infantry Regiment**
   4. **32nd Divisional Artillery Regiment**
   5. **232nd Divisional Heavy Artillery Regiment**
C. **Infantry, 10th Infantry Division** /38 Col. François-Napoléon-Henri-Dieudonné Hupel (Commanding General, 7th Infantry Division) 09/02/39

11th Infantry Division (08/22/39, Military District XX; 08/25/39, XX Army Corps; 11/15/39, Fourth Army Reserve; 03/27/40, IX Army Corps; 05/18/40, General Headquarters Reserve; 05/22/40, Seventh Army; 06/06/40, XXIV Army Corps; 06/13/40, I Army Corps; 07/11/40, disbanded): MG Henri-Marie-Joseph Aymes (Commanding General, IV Army Corps) 01/15/40 MG Paul-Hippolyte Arlabosse (Commanding General, Bouches-du-Rhône) 07/11/40 disbanded.

[NOTE: one source lists /40 Col. Aimable-Adrien-Fernand Allemandet (/44, Commanding General, Military District XX); Col. Allemandet may have been acting commander.]

A. **Chief of Staff, 11th Infantry Division** (08/22/39): LCol. Cueff 01/27/40 Capt. [Army] Fabre 02/02/40 Maj. Cohendet 07/11/40 dissolved.
B. *Components* - **11th Infantry Division** (08/22/39)
   1. **1st Cavalry Half-Brigade**
   2. **26th Infantry Regiment**
   3. **170th Infantry Regiment**
   4. **8th Divisional Artillery Regiment**
   5. **208th Divisional Heavy Artillery Regiment**
C. **Infantry, 11th Infantry Division** (08/22/39): unknown? 01/15/40 Col. Fernand-Zacharie-Joseph Lenclud (Commanding General, 19th Infantry Division) 06/02/40
D. **Artillery, 11th Infantry Division** (08/22/39): Col. Aimable-Adrien-Fernand Allemandet (one source lists Commanding Officer, 11th Infantry Division) /40

13th Infantry Division (08/22/39, Military District VII; 09/01/39, General Headquarters Reserve (Eighth Army Zone); 10/16/39, XIII Army Corps, Eighth Army, General Headquarters Reserve; 03/01/40, VII Army Corps; 05/22/40, General Headquarters Reserve; 05/26/40, X Army Corps; 06/01/40, IX Army Corps; 06/09/40, X Army Corps; 06/12/40, XXV Army Corps; 06/23/40, 85th African Infantry Division (remnants); 06/26/40, disbanded): /36 BG Marie-Alphonse-Théodore-René-Adrian Desmazes (Commanding

General, VIII Army Corps) 05/19/40 MG [Retired] Jean-Roch-Charles-Numa Baudouin (retired) 06/26/40 disbanded.
A. **Chief of Staff, 13th Infantry Division** (08/23/39): Maj. Philippon 06/26/40 dissolved.
B. *Components - 13th Infantry Division* (08/23/39)
    1. **21st Infantry Regiment**
    2. **60th Infantry Regiment**
    3. **8th Moroccan Infantry Regiment**: Col. Marie-Eugène-Aimé Molle (Chief of Staff, 2nd Moroccan Infantry Division) /42
    4. **28th Divisional Artillery Regiment**
    5. **228th Divisional Heavy Artillery Regiment**
C. **Artillery, 13th Infantry Division** (08/23/39): Col. Georges-Marie Vermiel du Conchard (Artillery Commander, XV Army Corps) /39

14th Infantry Division (08/25/39, Eighth Army; 09/02/39, Eighth Army Reserve; 12/17/39, XX Army Corps; 04/25/40, General Headquarters Reserve (Fourth Army Zone); 05/13/40, Ninth Army Reserve; 05/14/40, Ninth Army; 05/15/40 XXIII Army Corps; 06/08/40, VIII Army Corps; 06/16/40, Fourth Army; 06/18/40, XXIII Army Corps; 06/25/40, disbanded): /36 Col. Jean-Gabriel Bouffet (Commanding General, II Army Corps) 01/04/40 BG Jean-Joseph-Marie-Gabriel de Lattre de Tassigny (Commanding General, Puy-de-Dôme Department, Military District XIII) 06/25/40 disbanded.
A. **Chief of Staff, 14th Infantry Division** (08/25/39): LCol. Auguste-Émile Barbier (05/40, Chief of Staff, II Motorized Army Corps) 03/26/40 Maj. Jean-Louis-Marie-Pouis Manhès 06/25/40 dissolved.
B. *Components - 14th Infantry Division* (08/26/39)
    1. **3rd Cavalry Half-Brigade**
    2. **35th Infantry Regiment**
    3. **152nd Infantry Regiment**: /39 Col. Auguste-Jean Gilliot (Chief of Staff, Fourth Army) /40
    4. **4th Divisional Artillery Regiment**
    5. **204th Divisional Heavy Artillery Regiment**
C. **Infantry, 14th Infantry Division**: /38 Col. Paul-Adrien Voinier (Commanding General, Mulhouse Fortified Sector) 01/07/40

16th Infantry Division (09/02/39, Military District VIII; 09/13/39, Fifth Army; 10/03/39, XII Army Corps; 12/01/39, Fifth Army; 02/11/40, XII Army Corps; 05/25/40, Fifth Army; 05/26/40, General Headquarters Reserve; 05/27/40, Seventh Army; 05/31/40, X Army Corps; 06/08/40, Seventh Army; 06/09/40, X Army Corps; 06/25/40, disbanded): MG Pierre-André-Antoine Marquis (retired) 11/15/40 BG Eugène Mordant (Commanding General, Groups of Colonial Camp, Southeast Asia; /40, Commander-in-Chief, Indochina) 06/25/40 disbanded.
A. **Chief of Staff, 16th Infantry Division** (09/02/39): LCol. Lucereau 01/13/40 Maj. Pochard 06/25/40 dissolved.
B. *Components - 16th Infantry Division* (09/02/39)
    1. **29th Infantry Regiment**
    2. **56th Infantry Regiment**

3. **89ᵗʰ Infantry Regiment**
4. **37ᵗʰ Divisional Artillery Regiment**
5. **237ᵗʰ Divisional Heavy Artillery Regiment**

17ᵗʰ Infantry Division (#1) (03/31/40; 05/26/40, disbanded): BG Georges-Eugène-Joseph Lascroux [+ Head, French Military Mission with the Dutch Army] (Commanding General, 17ᵗʰ Infantry Division (#2) 05/21/40 vacant 05/26/40 disbanded.
A. **Chief of Staff, 17ᵗʰ Infantry Division (#1)** (03/31/40):
B. *Components* - **17ᵗʰ Infantry Division (#1)** (03/31/40)
   1. **6ᵗʰ Infantry Regiment**
   2. **22ⁿᵈ Foreign Volunteer Infantry Regiment**
   3. **23ʳᵈ Foreign Volunteer Infantry Regiment**
   4. **97ᵗʰ Divisional Artillery Regiment**
   5. **297ᵗʰ Divisional Heavy Artillery Regiment**

17ᵗʰ Infantry Division (#2) (05/21/40, from remnants of the 55ᵗʰ Infantry Division and 71ˢᵗ Infantry Division; 05/26/40, redesignated **59ᵗʰ Light Infantry Division**): BG Georges-Eugène-Joseph Lascroux (Commanding General, 59ᵗʰ Light Infantry Division) 05/26/40 redesignated **59ᵗʰ Light Infantry Division** - see **59ᵗʰ Light Infantry Division**.
A. **Chief of Staff, 17ᵗʰ Infantry Division (#2)** (05/21/40): LCol. Jean-Charles-Louis Regnault (Chief of Staff, 59ᵗʰ Light Infantry Division) 05/26/40 dissolved.
B. *Components* - **17ᵗʰ Infantry Division (#2)** (05/21/40)
   1. **120ᵗʰ Infantry Regiment**
   2. **147ᵗʰ Infantry Regiment**
   3. **213ᵗʰ Infantry Regiment**
   4. **36ᵗʰ Divisional Artillery Regiment**
   5. **45ᵗʰ Divisional Heavy Artillery Regiment**

18ᵗʰ Infantry Division (08/23/39, Military District IX; 09/12/39, Fourth Army; 09/30/39, IX Army Corps; 12/06/39, Ninth Army; 12/10/39, General Headquarters Reserves; 01/11/40, XI Army Corps; 05/18/40, disbanded): BG Camille-Léon Duffet (?) 05/18/40 disbanded.
A. **Chief of Staff, 18ᵗʰ Infantry Division** (08/23/39): LCol. Hautcœur (Chief of Staff, XII Army Corps) 11/15/39 Maj. de Gouvello (Chief of Staff, 17ᵗʰ Light Infantry Division) 05/18/40 dissolved.
B. *Components* - **18ᵗʰ Infantry Division** (08/23/39)
   1. **66ᵗʰ Infantry Regiment**
   2. **77ᵗʰ Infantry Regiment**
   3. **125ᵗʰ Infantry Regiment**
   4. **19ᵗʰ Divisional Artillery Regiment**
   5. **219ᵗʰ Divisional Heavy Artillery Regiment**
C. **Deputy Chief of Staff, 18ᵗʰ Infantry Division** (08/23/39): unknown? /40 LCol. Marcel Rime-Bruneau (Chief of Staff, 4ᵗʰ Armored Division) 05/15/40
D. **Artillery, 18ᵗʰ Infantry Division** (08/23/39): BG Marie-Paul-Vincent Grollemund (Artillery Commander, XLV Fortress Army Corps) 02/09/40

19th Infantry Division (08/25/39, Military District IV; 09/10/39, Ardennes Army Detachment; 09/17/39, General Headquarters Reserves; 10/15/39, Ninth Army; 10/18/39, General Headquarters Reserves; 11/08/39, XX Army Corps; 11/10/39, General Headquarters Reserves; 11/18/39, XX Army Corps; 01/08/40, VII Army Corps; 01/15/40, General Headquarters Reserves; 03/01/40, XIII Army Corps; 05/17/40, Seventh Army; 05/19/40, I Army Corps; 07/11/40, disbanded): /36 BG Charles-Henri-Paul d'Arbonneau (Head, French Military Mission to Turkey) 12/28/39 BG Jean-Benigne-Auguste-Francis Toussaint (?) 06/02/40 BG Fernand-Zacharie-Joseph Lenclud (Commanding General, Lot Department, Military District XVII) 07/11/40 disbanded.

A. **Chief of Staff, 19th Infantry Division** (08/25/39): LCol. Durieux 06/07/40 Maj. Rocaut 07/11/40 dissolved.
B. *Components* - **19th Infantry Division** (08/26/39)
    1. **41st Infantry Regiment**
    2. **71st Infantry Regiment**
    3. **117th Infantry Regiment**
    4. **10th Divisional Artillery Regiment**
    5. **210th Divisional Heavy Artillery Regiment**
C. **Infantry, 19th Infantry Division** (08/26/39): /38 Col. Marie-Gustavé-Victor-René-Alfred Texier (01/01/40, Commanding General, 57th Infantry Division) 08/26/39 Col. Marie-Charles-Henri de Girval (Commanding General, Faulquemont Fortified Sector) 04/28/40

20th Infantry Division (09/02/39, Military District IV; 09/09/39, Second Army; 09/20/39, XXI Army Corps; 12/17/39, XVIII Army Corps; 01/08/40, Third Army; 01/22/40, Colonial Army Corps; 03/10/30, Third Army Reserve; 04/09/40, XLII Fortress Army Corps; 05/25/40, Third Army Reserve; 05/29/40, 2nd Army Group Reserve; 06/10/40, VII Army Corps; 06/15/40, captured and disbanded): BG René-Jean-Divy Corbé (/41, Commanding General, Vichy 9th Military Division) 06/15/40 captured and disbanded.

A. **Chief of Staff, 20th Infantry Division** (09/02/39): Maj. Callico /40? Col. Moyen 06/15/40 dissolved.
B. *Components* - **20th Infantry Division** (09/02/39)
    1. **2nd Infantry Regiment**
    2. **47th Infantry Regiment**
    3. **115th Infantry Regiment**
    4. **7th Divisional Artillery Regiment**
    5. **207th Divisional Heavy Artillery Regiment**
C. **Infantry, 20th Infantry Division** (09/02/39): unknown? /40 Col. Jean-Louis-Paul-Marie Petibon (German prisoner-of-war; /42, escaped; /42, served with the Resistance; /44, retired) 06/15/40 dissolved.

21st Infantry Division (08/25/39, Military District XI; 09/01/39 General Headquarters Reserve (Fourth Army Zone); 09/05/39, XX Army Corps; 09/09/39, V Army Corps; 09/21/39, XX Army Corps; 10/07/39, General Headquarters Reserve (Fourth Army Zone); 11/13/39, I Army Corps; 03/06/40, XVI Army Corps; 04/25/40, most of the division was

captured defending Boulogne; 05/10/40, Seventh Army; 05/15/40, I Army Corps; 05/17/40, General Headquarters Reserve; 05/22/40, Admiral North; 05/24/40, assigned to both XVI Army Corps and Flanders Fortified Sector; 06/25/40, disbanded): /38 BG Marie-Camille-Charles-Raymond Pigeaud (?) 10/13/39 BG Pierre-Louis-Félix Lanquetot (German prisoner-of-war) 06/25/40 disbanded.
- A. **Chief of Staff, 21st Infantry Division** (08/25/39): LCol. Barande 06/25/40 dissolved.
- B. *Components - 21st Infantry Division* (08/25/39)
    1. **48th Infantry Regiment**
    2. **65th Infantry Regiment**
    3. **137th Infantry Regiment**: /38 Col. Charles-Emmanuel Mast (Chief of Staff, X Army Corps) 02/15/40
    4. **35th Divisional Artillery Regiment**
    5. **235th Divisional Heavy Artillery Regiment**
- C. **Infantry, 21st Infantry Division** (08/25/39): Col. André-Lucien Caille (killed in action) /40 unknown? 06/25/40 dissolved.
- D. **Artillery, 21st Infantry Division**: /38 LCol. Paul-Gilbert-Eugène Frénal (Artillery Commander, Military District XI) /39

22nd Infantry Division (08/23/39, Military District XI; 09/08/39, Third Army; 09/30/39, Colonial Army Corps; 02/18/40, General Headquarters Reserve; 03/01/40, Ninth Army Reserve; 05/10/40, XI Army Corps; 05/18/40, disbanded after heavy losses defending the Meuse): MG Joseph-Louis-François Hassler 04/15/40 BG Pierre-Louis-Arthur-Marie Beziers-Lafosse (Infantry Commander, 22nd Infantry Division) 05/15/40 MG Joseph-Louis-François Hassler (Deputy Military-Governor, Paris) 05/18/40 disbanded.
- A. **Chief of Staff, 22nd Infantry Division** (08/23/39): LCol. Salaun 05/18/40 dissolved.
- B. *Components - 22nd Infantry Division* (08/23/39)
    1. **19th Infantry Regiment**
    2. **62nd Infantry Regiment**
    3. **116th Infantry Regiment**
    4. **18th Divisional Artillery Regiment**
    5. **218th Divisional Heavy Artillery Regiment**
- C. **Infantry, 22nd Infantry Division** (08/23/39): Col. Pierre-Louis-Arthur-Marie Beziers-Lafosse (Commanding General, 22nd Infantry Division) 04/15/40 unknown? 05/15/40 BG Pierre-Louis-Arthur-Marie Beziers-Lafosse (?) 05/18/40 dissolved.
- D. **Artillery, 22nd Infantry Division** (08/23/39): Col. [Retired '38] Joseph-Armand-Victor Gain (Artillery Commander, Military District II) 05/18/40 dissolved.

23rd Infantry Division (08/25/39, Military District IX; 09/06/39, 2nd Army Group; 09/07/39, V Army Corps; 09/25/39, VIII Army Corps; 10/04/39, Fifth Army Reserve; 11/13/39, XII Army Corps; 02/12/40, Fourth Army Reserve; 03/23/40, General Headquarters Reserve; 05/18/40, XXIV Army Corps; 06/25/40, disbanded): /36 BG Georges-Henri-Jean-Baptiste Misserey (Commanding General, Military District XIII) /39 MG Joseph-Charles-Robert Jeannel [+ 11/11/39 to 11/14/39, acting Commanding General, XII Army Corps] (Deputy Commander, Military District XII) 06/25/40 disbanded.
- A. **Chief of Staff, 23rd Infantry Division** ()8/25/39): LCol. Sale 06/25/40 dissolved.

B. **Components - 23rd Infantry Division** (08/25/39)
    1. **32nd Infantry Regiment**
    2. **107th Infantry Regiment**
    3. **126th Infantry Regiment**
    4. **41st Divisional Artillery Regiment**
    5. **241st Divisional Heavy Artillery Regiment**
C. **Infantry, 23rd Infantry Division** (08/25/39): /38 Col. Ainé-Gabriel-Hilaire-Jehan-Marie Sarrebourse de la Guillonnière (Commanding General, 62nd Infantry Division) 08/25/39 Col. Georges-Eugène-Joseph Lascroux (Commanding General, 17th Infantry Division (#1)) 03/31/40

24th Infantry Division (09/03/39, Military District IX; 09/14/39, Fourth Army; 09/26/39, General Headquarters Reserve; 11/22/39, Fourth Army; 11/24/39, XX Army Corps; 01/22/40, 2nd Army Group Reserve; 03/25/40, VIII Army Corps; 05/22/40, 2nd Army Group Reserve; 05/29/40, Seventh Army; 06/02/40, Tenth Army Reserve; 06/05/40, X Army Corps; 06/08/40, Tenth Army; 06/10/40, X Army Corps; 06/11/40, XX Army Corps; 06/12/40 XXV Army Corps and Bazelaire Group; 06/18/40, no contact; 06/25/40, XXV Army Corps; 06/26/40, disbanded): vacant 09/10/39 MG Étienne Bonnet (Commanding General, Rear Area Zones) 02/25/40 BG Paul-Albert Voirin (?) 06/26/40 disbanded.
A. **Chief of Staff, 24th Infantry Division** (09/03/39): Maj. Mousset 06/26/40 dissolved.
B. **Components - 24th Infantry Division** (09/03/39)
    1. **50th Infantry Regiment**
    2. **53rd Infantry Regiment**
    3. **78th Infantry Regiment**
    4. **21st Divisional Artillery Regiment**
    5. **221st Divisional Heavy Artillery Regiment**

26th Infantry Division (09/02/39, Military District XIII; 09/12/39, Third Army Reserve; 10/11/39, General Headquarters Reserve; 03/14/40, VI Army Corps; 05/21/40, VI Army Corps Reserve; 06/12/40, VI Army Corps; 06/21/40, Group Flavigny; 06/24/40, disbanded): BG René-Jules Troublé (?) 04/10/40 BG Marie-Marcel Bonnaissieux (?) 06/24/40 disbanded.
A. **Chief of Staff, 26th Infantry Division** (09/02/39): LCol. Chailly 06/24/40 dissolved.
B. **Components - 26th Infantry Division** (09/02/39)
    1. **86th Infantry Regiment**
    2. **98th Infantry Regiment**
    3. **1205h Infantry Regiment**
    4. **36th Divisional Artillery Regiment**
    5. **236th Divisional Heavy Artillery Regiment**
C. **Artillery, 26th Infantry Division** (09/02/39): BG [Retired] Marie-Félix-Henri Loiseau (retired) 06/24/40 dissolved.

27th Infantry Division (10/27/39, from **27th Alpine Infantry Division**, XIV Army Corps; 11/05/39, General Headquarters Reserve; 12/20/39, Fifth Army; 12/22/39, VIII Army Corps;

03/04/40, Fifth Army; 03/08/40, VII Army Corps; 06/02/40, Sixth Army Reserve; 06/06/40, XVII Army Corps; 06/14/40, VII Army Corps; 06/24/40, disbanded): MG Paul-André Doyen (Commanding General, XVIII Army Corps) 05/19/40 BG Henri-Charles-Marie de Bizemont (?) 06/14/40 Col. Lhuillier 06/15/40 Col. Marie 06/24/40 disbanded.

- A. **Chief of Staff, 27th Infantry Division** (10/27/39): Maj. Henri-Marie-Antoine-François Lorber 06/24/40
- B. *Components* - **27th Infantry Division** (10/27/39)
    1. **140th Infantry Regiment**
    2. **159th Infantry Regiment**
    3. **7th Alpine Infantry Half-Brigade**
    4. **58th Divisional Artillery Regiment**
    5. **258th Divisional Heavy Artillery Regiment**
- C. **Infantry, 27th Infantry Division** (10/27/39): Col. Paul-Wilhelm Boell (Commanding General, 51st Infantry Division) 01/07/40
- D. **Artillery, 27th Infantry Division** (10/27/39): Col. François Thierry

30th Infantry Division (pre-war; 10/28/39, from **30th Mountain Infantry Division**, VIII Army Corps; 12/09/39, 2nd Army Group Reserve; 12/26/39, General Headquarters Reserve; 03/10/40, Fifth Army; 03/13/40, Fifth Army Reserve; 03/18/40, XLIII Fortress Army Corps; 06/16/40, XII Army Corps; 06/25/40, disbanded): MG Amédée Duron (to /45, German prisoner-of-war; /45, retired) 06/25/40 disbanded.

- A. **Chief of Staff, 30th Infantry Division** (10/28/39): LCol. Pendaries 06/25/40 dissolved.
- B. *Components* - **30th Infantry Division** (10/28/39)
    1. **55th Alpine Infantry Regiment**
    2. **141st Alpine Infantry Regiment**
    3. **22nd Alpine Infantry Half-Brigade**
    4. **42nd Divisional Artillery Regiment**
    5. **242nd Divisional Heavy Artillery Regiment**
- C. **Infantry, 30th Infantry Division** (10/28/39): Col. Marie-Cyrille-Victor Debeney (Commanding General, 238th Light Infantry Division) 06/01/40

32nd Infantry Division (08/23/39, Military District XVI; 09/13/39, Third Army Reserve; 09/21/39, 2nd Army Group Reserve; 10/25/39, VI Army Corps; 12/19/39, First Army Reserve; 05/16/40 III Army Corps; 05/21/40, First Army Reserve; 05/23/40, III Army Corps; 05/29/40, XVI Army Corps; 06/01/40, XVI Army Corps Reserve; 06/07/40, regrouping Zone B; 06/14/40, XVI Army Corps; 06/12/40, redesignated **32nd Light Infantry Division**, 06/18/40, captured in the Falaise sector and disbanded): **32nd Infantry Division** 08/23/39 vacant 09/02/39 MG Marie-Martin-Jean-Alfred de Charry (Deputy Chief of Staff, Army of the Interior) 01/08/40 MG Maurice-Charles-Gabriel Lucas [+ to 03/05/40, Commanding General, Lauter Fortified Region] (Commanding General, 32nd Light Infantry Division) 06/12/40 redesignated **32nd Light Infantry Division** 06/12/40 MG Maurice-Charles-Gabriel Lucas 06/16/40 Col. François-Adolphe-Laurent Sevez (German prisoner-of-war; /41, released; /42, Chief of Staff, French North Africa) 06/18/40 captured and disbanded.

- A. **Chief of Staff, 32nd Infantry Division** (08/23/39): LCol. Jean-Paul Bergeron

(German prisoner-of-war; later escapes; Commanding Officer, Vichy Military Region XIX) 12/10/39 LCol. Dubois (Chief of Staff, 32nd Light Infantry Division) 06/12/40 redesignated **Chief of Staff, 32nd Light Infantry Division** 06/12/40 LCol. Dubois 06/14/40 LCol. Blanc 06/18/40 dissolved.
- B. *Components - 32nd Infantry Division* (08/23/39)
    1. **13th Zouave Infantry Regiment**
    2. **122nd Infantry Regiment**
    3. **143rd Infantry Regiment**
    4. **3rd Divisional Artillery Regiment**
    5. **203rd Divisional Heavy Artillery Regiment**
- C. *Components - 32nd Light Infantry Division* (06/12/40)
    1. **131st Infantry Regiment**
    2. **616th Infantry Regiment**
    3. **a battalion, 327th Divisional Artillery Regiment**
- D. **Infantry, 32nd Infantry Division** (08/23/39): Col. Auguste Alaurent (Commanding Officer, 153rd Fortress Infantry Regiment) /40

35th Infantry Division (09/02/39, Military District XVIII, 09/15/39, Fifth Army; 10/02/39, VIII Army Corps; 11/15/39, Fifth Army Reserve; 01/29/40, XII Army Corps; 05/21/40, General Headquarters Reserve (Second Army Zone); 05/23/40, XXI Army Corps; 05/26/40, Colonial Army Corps; 06/13/40, XXI Army Corps; 06/18/40, XXI Army Corps Reserve; 06/19/40, Group Dubuisson; 06/22/40, disbanded): MG Pierre-Nicolas-Louis Decharme (German prisoner-of-war; /41, released; /44, Commandant, Poly-technical School) 06/22/40 disbanded.
- A. **Chief of Staff, 35th Infantry Division** (09/02/39): LCol. de Caumia-Baillenx 03/20/40 Maj. Loustaunau Lacau 03/25/40 LCol. Jobin 06/22/40 dissolved.
- B. *Components - 35th Infantry Division* (09/02/39)
    1. **11th Infantry Regiment**
    2. **49th Infantry Regiment**
    3. **123rd Infantry Regiment**
    4. **14th Divisional Artillery Regiment**
    5. **214th Divisional Heavy Artillery Regiment**
- C. **Infantry, 35th Infantry Division** (09/02/39): Col. François-Claude-Philippe Delaissey (to /45, German prisoner-of-war) 06/22/40 dissolved.

36th Infantry Division (#1) (08/28/39, Military District XVIII; 09/08/39, General Headquarters Reserve (Second Army Zone); 09/22/39, Third Army; 09/30/39, Colonial Army Corps; 11/27/39, Second Army; 12/01/39, XXI Army Corps; 12/13/39, Third Army; 01/12/40, XXI Army Corps; 03/25/40, XLII Fortress Army Corps; 04/29/40, Third Army; 05/06/40, General Headquarters Reserve; 05/14/40, X Army Corps; 05/22/40, Colonial Army Corps; 06/21/40, captured while withdrawing between the Meuse and Moselle and disbanded): vacant 09/02/39 MG Marcel-Louis-Marie Aublet (?) 06/21/40 captured and disbanded.
- A. **Chief of Staff, 36th Infantry Division (#1)** (08/28/39): LCol. Soulet 06/21/40 dissolved.

B. *Components* - 36th Infantry Division (#1) (08/28/39)
    1. **14th Infantry Regiment**
    2. **18th Infantry Regiment**: /40 Col. André-Marie-Martial d'Anselme (Director, Personnel, General Staff) 42
    3. **57th Infantry Regiment**
    4. **24th Divisional Artillery Regiment**
    5. **224th Divisional Heavy Artillery Regiment**
C. **Infantry, 36th Infantry Division** (08/28/39): Col. Albert-Frédéric Klopfenstein (Commanding General, 2nd Infantry Division) 01/06/40

41st Infantry Division (09/02/39, Military District of Paris; 09/11/39, Fourth Army; 09/24/39, XVII Army Corps; 10/04/39, IX Army Corps; ; 12/25/39, General Headquarters Reserve (Third Army Zone); 01/15/40, XVIII Army Corps; 06/01/40, Second Army Reserve; 06/05/40, General Headquarters Reserve; 06/09/40 XVII Army Corps; 06/17/40, captured while withdrawing from the Aisne and disbanded): /38 BG Eugène-Marie-Louis Bridoux (German prisoner-of-war; /41, released; 04/18/42, Minister of National Defense and War) 06/17/40 captured and disbanded.
A. **Chief of Staff, 41st Infantry Division** (09/02/39): Maj. Eble 06/17/40 dissolved.
B. *Components* - 41st Infantry Division (09/02/39)
    1. **101st Infantry Regiment**
    2. **103rd Infantry Regiment**
    3. **104th Infantry Regiment**
    4. **13th Divisional Artillery Regiment**
    5. **213th Divisional Heavy Artillery Regiment**

42nd Infantry Division (08/20/39, Military District VI; 09/03/39, Third Army; 09/07/39, VI Army Corps; 10/02/39, Second Army; 11/12/39, Metz Fortified Region; 12/21/39, Colonial Army Corps; 01/05/40, General Headquarters Reserve; 03/31/40, Army Corps; Army Corps; *05/18/40, XXIII* Army Corps; 05/23/40, VI Army Corps; 06/09/40, XXIII Army Corps; 06/17/40, captured at Jarges and disbanded): vacant 09/02/39 MG Paul-Marie-Joseph de La Porte du Theil [+ 05/11/40, Commanding General, VII Army Corps] 06/17/40 captured and disbanded.
[NOTE: also listed by one source 04/30/40 MG François-Pierre-Louis Keller (?) /40]
A. **Chief of Staff, 42nd Infantry Division** (08/23/09 LCol. Marie-Joseph-Louis-Henri Noetinger (07/43, Artillery Commander, 1st Armored Division) 06/17/40 dissolved.
B. *Components* - 42nd Infantry Division (08/23/39)
    1. **80th Infantry Regiment**
    2. **94th Infantry Regiment**
    3. **151st Infantry Regiment**: /39? Col. Olivier-Charles-Marie Thierry d'Argenlieu (Chief of Staff, Ninth Army) 11/05/39
    4. **61st Divisional Artillery Regiment**
    5. **261st Divisional Heavy Artillery Regiment**
C. **Infantry, 42nd Infantry Division**: /36 Col. Maurice-Charles-Gabriel Lucas (01/07/40, Commanding General, Lauter Fortified Region & Commanding General, 32nd Infantry Division) /36

43rd Infantry Division (08/23/39, Military District XX; 08/26/39, Fifth Army; 09/10/39, Fortified Region de la Lauter; 10/06/39, XII Army Corps; 11/14/39, VIII Army Corps; 12/31/39, 2nd Army Group Reserve; 05/13/40, First Army; 05/16/40, V Army Corps; ; 05/23/40, First Army; 05/27/40, V Army Corps; 05/29/40, First Army; 06/08/40, Regrouping Zone B; redesignated **43rd Light Infantry Division**; 06/13/40, XVI Army Corps; 06/18/40, destroyed at Passais and disbanded): **43rd Infnatry Division** /37 MG Pierre-Paul-Jacques Grandsard (Commanding General, Military District VIII) 08/23/39 BG Henry-François Vernillat (Commanding General, 43rd Light Infantry Division) 06/13/40 redesignated **43rd Light Infantry Division** 06/13/40 BG Henry-François Vernillat (?) 06/18/40 destroyed and disbanded.

    A.   **Chief of Staff, 43rd Infantry Division**: Maj. Deruer (Chief of Staff, 32nd Light Infantry Division) 06/13/40 redesignated **Chief of Staff, 32nd Light Infantry Division** 06/13/40 Maj. Deruer 06/18/40 dissolved.

    B.   *Components* - **43rd Infantry Division** (08/23/39)
  1. **3rd Moroccan Infantry Regiment**
  2. **4th Light Infantry Half-Brigade**
  3. **158th Infantry Regiment**
  4. **12th Divisional Artillery Regiment**
  5. **212th Divisional Heavy Artillery Regiment**

    C.   *Components* - **43rd Light Infantry Division** (06/13/40)
  1. **54th Infantry Regiment**
  2. **158th Infantry Regiment**

    D.   **Artillery, 43rd Infantry Division**: /38 Col. Marie-Paul-Vincent Grollemund (Artillery Commander, 18th Infantry Division) 08/23/39

44th Infantry Division (03/01/40, General Headquarters Reserve; 04/11/40, Fifth Army; 05/16/40, XXIII Army Corps; 05/18/40, XVII Army Corps; 05/23/40, VII Army Corps; 06/14/40, dispersed and disbanded): MG Robert-Marie-Jules-Camille Boissau (Commanding General, Southeast Sahara) 06/14/40 dispersed and disbanded.

    A.   **Chief of Staff, 44th Infantry Division** (03/01/40): Maj. Moillard 06/14/40 dissolved.

    B.   *Components* - **44th Infantry Division** (03/01/40)
  1. **2nd Alpine Infantry Half-Brigade**
  2. **26th Alpine Infantry Half-Brigade**
  3. **173rd Alpine Infantry Half-Brigade**
  4. **91st Divisional Artillery Regiment**
  5. **291st Divisional Heavy Artillery Regiment**

45th Infantry Division (09/02/39, Military District V; 09/11/39, Fourth Army; 09/25/39, XX Army Corps; 11/30/39, 2nd Army Group Reserve; 01/17/40, XX Army Corps; 03/20/40, Fourth Army; 04/14/40, Fourth Army Reserve; 05/15/40, General Headquarters Reserve; 05/20/40, Sixth Army; 05/22/40, Sixth Army Reserve; 06/01/40, VII Army Corps; 06/14/40, dispersed and disbanded): Col.[Retired] Oscar-Auguste Roux (06/18/40, German prisoner-of-war; 01/03/44, Commanding Officer, 4th Tunisian Tirailleurs (Infantry) Regiment) 06/14/40 dispersed and disbanded.

    A.   **Chief of Staff, 45th Infantry Division** (09/02/39): Maj. Moulan 06/14/40 dissolved.

    B.   *Components* - **45th Infantry Division** (09/02/39)
  1. **31st Infantry Regiment**

2. **85th Infantry Regiment**
  3. **113th Infantry Regiment**
  4. **55th Divisional Artillery Regiment**
  5. **255th Divisional Heavy Artillery Regiment**

47th Infantry Division (09/02/39, General Headquarters Reserve; 09/07/39, Eighth Army Reserve; 10/15/39, VII Army Corps; 02/11/40, IX Army Corps; 05/26/40, General Headquarters Reserve; 06/01/40, I Army Corps; 06/25/40, disbanded): BG Marie-Joseph-Edmond Mendras [+ 04/14/40 to 04/26/40, Commanding General, Faulquemont Fortified Sector] (?) 06/25/40 disbanded.

A. **Chief of Staff, 47th Infantry Division** (09/02/39): LCol. Racadot 06/25/40 dissolved.
B. *Components - 47th Infantry Division* (09/02/39)
  1. **23rd Light Infantry Half-Brigade**
  2. **44th Infantry Regiment**
  3. **109th Infantry Regiment**
  4. **5th Divisional Artillery Regiment**
  5. **205th Divisional Heavy Artillery Regiment**

51st Infantry Division (09/02/39, Military District I; 09/10/39, III Army Corps; 10/04/39, I British Army Corps; 10/10/39, British Expeditionary Corps; 12/02/39, General Headquarters Reserve (Second Army Zone) 12/15/39 XXI Army Corps; 03/23/40, XLII Fortress Army Corps; 04/15/40, XXI Army Corps; 05/04/40, XXIV Army Corps; 05/18/40, XLII Fortress Army Corps; 06/23/40, disbanded): MG [Retired] Victor-Jean-Edmond Gillard [+ 09/09/39 to 12/02/39, Commanding General, Lille Defense Sector] (retired) 01/07/40 BG Paul-Wilhelm Boell (German prisoner-of-war; /40, released) 06/23/40 disbanded.

A. **Chief of Staff, 51st Infantry Division** (09/02/39): LCol. Marie-Paul-François Azaïs 01/07/40 Maj. Duperon /40 Capt. [Army] Aubertin 06/23/40 dissolved.
B. *Components - 51st Infantry Division* (09/02/39)
  1. **100th Infantry Regiment**
  2. **201st Infantry Regiment**
  3. **310th Infantry Regiment**
  4. **27th Divisional Artillery Regiment**
  5. **227th Divisional Heavy Artillery Regiment**

52nd Infantry Division (08/24/39, Ardennes Army Detachment; 09/22/39, IV Army Corps; 01/15/40, XLI Fortress Army Corps; 01/25/40, 2nd Army Group Reserve (Fourth Army Zone); 03/15/40, XX Army Corps; 05/30/40. XX Army Corps (Sarre Group); 06/22/40, disbanded): BG François-Arthur Portzert [+ 11/20/39 to 01/01/40, Commanding General, Ardennes Defense Sector; + 01/01/40, Commanding General, 102nd Fortress Infantry Division] 01/25/40 BG Eugène-Raphaël Échard [+ Commanding General, French Forces at the Sarre] (to /45, German prisoner-of-war) 06/22/40 disbanded.

A. **Chief of Staff, 52nd Infantry Division** (08/24/39): LCol. Jean-Adolphe-Léonce Curnier 01/25/40 LCol. Paul-Antoine Chassard 06/22/40 dissolved.
B. *Components - 52nd Infantry Division* (08/24/39)
  1. **291st Infantry Regiment**
  2. **348th Infantry Regiment**
  3. **148th Fortress Infantry Regiment**

    4.   **17th Divisional Artillery Regiment**
    5.   **217th Divisional Heavy Artillery Regiment**
C.   **Infantry, 52nd Infantry Division** (08/24/39): Col. François-Louis-Marie-Victor Haca 06/22/40 dissolved.

53rd Infantry Division (08/26/39; 09/02/39, Military District III; 09/12/39, Admiral North; 09/23/39, III Army Corps; 10/03/39 XVI Army Corps; 03/06/40, Seventh Army; 03/10/40, Military Governor of Paris; 04/30/40, General Headquarters Reserve (Ninth Army Zone); 05/10/40, Ninth Army; 05/12/40, XLI Fortress Army Corps; 05/15/40, Touchon Army Detachment and XXIII Army Corps; 05/17/40, General Headquarters Reserve; 05/31/40, redesignated **53rd Light Infantry Division**; 06/05/40, Fourth Army; 06/12/40, VIII Army Corps; 05/31/40, disbanded): **53rd Infantry Division** 08/26/39 BG [Retired '38] Louis-Émile-Charles-Henri Blin (retired) 05/31/40 redesignated **53rd Light Infantry Division** 06/01/40 BG Jean-Marie-Léon Etcheberrigaray (Commanding General, Cantal Department), Military District XIII 06/25/40 disbanded.
    A.   **Chief of Staff, 53rd Infantry Division** (08/26/39): Maj. Dufour (Chief of Staff, 53rd Light Infantry Division) 05/31/40 redesignated **Chief of Staff, 53rd Light Infantry Division** 05/31/40 Maj. Dufour 06/25/40 dissolved.
    B.   *Components* - **53rd Infantry Division** (09/02/39)
        1.   **208th Infantry Regiment**
        2.   **239th Infantry Regiment**
        3.   **329th Infantry Regiment**
        4.   **22th Divisional Artillery Regiment**
        5.   **222th Divisional Heavy Artillery Regiment**
    C.   *Components* - **32nd Light Infantry Division** (06/01/40)
        1.   **239th Infantry Regiment**
        2.   **329th Infantry Regiment**
    D.   **Infantry, 53rd Infantry Division** (08/26/39): Col. Elophe-Jean Larcher 06/25/40 dissolved.

54th Infantry Division (09/02/39, Military District IV; 09/14/39, General Headquarters Reserve; 12/25/39, Eighth Army Reserve; 12/29/39, VII Army Corps; 03/01/40, XIII Army Corps; 03/16/40, XIII Army Corps Reserve; 04/17/40, Eighth Army; 04/23/40, XIII Army Corps; 05/23/40, Eighth Army Reserve; 06/09/40, Army Corps; 06/22/40, disbanded): MG Fernand Vix (retired) 11/27/39 BG Louis-Gustavé-Adolphe Coradin (to /45, German prisoner-of-war) 06/22/40 disbanded.
    A.   **Chief of Staff, 54th Infantry Division** (09/02/39): LCol. Brasart 06/22/40 dissolved.
    B.   *Components* - **54th Infantry Division** (09/02/39)
        1.   **302nd Infantry Regiment**
        2.   **317th Infantry Regiment**
        3.   **330th Infantry Regiment**
        4.   **44th Divisional Mixed Artillery Regiment**

55th Infantry Division (03/09/39, Military District V and General Headquarters Reserve; 09/11/39, Second Army; 09/20/39, Governor-General of Verdun; 10/21/39, X Army Corps; 05/31/40, disbanded): BG [Retired '38] Paul-Émile Britsch (retired?) 02/21/40 BG Henri-Jean Lafontaine (?) 05/31/40 disbanded.

A. **Chief of Staff, 55th Infantry Division** (09/03/39): LCol. Lallemand de Liocourt (Chief of Staff, 235th Light Infantry Division) 05/31/40 dissolved.
B. *Components - 55th Infantry Division* (09/03/39)
   1. **213th Infantry Regiment**
   2. **295th Infantry Regiment**
   3. **331st Infantry Regiment**
   4. **45th Divisional Mixed Artillery Regiment**

56th Infantry Division (09/02/39, Military District VI; 09/08/39, Third Army Reserve; 11/24/39, Colonial Army Corps; 06/11/40, 2nd Army Group Reserve; 06/14/40, XVIII Army Corps; 06/16/40, captured after retreating over in Seine in the Aignay-le-duc region disbanded): MG Benjamin-François-Régis Michel (retired) 01/01/40 MG Jean Martin Gallevier de Mierry (?) (06/20/40, German prisoner-of-war) 06/16/40 captured and disbanded.
A. **Chief of Staff, 56th Infantry Division** (09/02/39): LCol. Klein 03/40 LCol. Bonne 06/16/40 dissolved.
B. *Components - 56th Infantry Division* (09/02/39)
   1. **294th Infantry Regiment**
   2. **306th Infantry Regiment**
   3. **332nd Infantry Regiment**
   4. **26th Divisional Artillery Regiment**
   5. **226th Divisional Heavy Artillery Regiment**

57th Infantry Division (08/22/39, Military District VII; 12/26/39, Army Corps du Jura; 01/12/40, XLV Fortress Army Corps; 06/07/40, General Headquarters Reserve; 06/09/40, XXIV Army Corps; 06/25/40, disbanded): MG [Retired] Marie-François-Armand-Roger Barbeyrac de Saint-Maurice [+ Commanding General, Military District II; + 09/02/39, Commanding General, 87th African Infantry Division] 01/01/40 MG Marie-Gustavé-Victor-René-Alfred Texier (?) 06/25/40 disbanded.
A. **Chief of Staff, 57th Infantry Division** (08/22/39): LCol. Belfils 02/10/40 Maj. Decageux 06/25/40 dissolved.
B. *Components - 57th Infantry Division* (08/22/39)
   1. **235th Infantry Regiment**
   2. **260th Infantry Regiment**
   3. **8th Light Infantry Half-Brigade**
   4. **47th Divisional Artillery Regiment**
   5. **247th Divisional Heavy Artillery Regiment**

58th Infantry Division (09/02/39, Military District VIII; 09/12/39, Third Army; 10/02/39, XVIII Army Corps; 10/06/39, Metz Fortified Region; 11/11/39, Third Army Reserve; 01/12/40, XXI Army Corps; 03/23/40, XLII Fortifies Army Corps; 04/14/40, XXI Army Corps; 05/01/40 XLII Fortress Army Corps; 05/20/40, XLII Fortress Army Corps Reserve; 05/24/40, XLII Fortress Army Corps; 06/22/40, disbanded): BG Georges-Eugène Paul (?) 12/11/39, MG Henri-Gilbert-Antoine Perraud (?) 06/22/40 disbanded.
A. **Chief of Staff, 58th Infantry Division** (09/02/39): Maj. Simon 06/22/40 dissolved.
B. *Components - 58th Infantry Division* (09/02/39)
   1. **204th Infantry Regiment**

2. **227th Infantry Regiment**
3. **334th Infantry Regiment**
4. **48th Divisional Artillery Regiment**
5. **248th Divisional Heavy Artillery Regiment**

60th Infantry Division (09/02/39, Military District IV; 09/17/39, Military District XI; 10/16/39, XVI Army Corps; 11/11/39, I Army Corps; 11/20/39, XVI Army Corps; 05/10/40, Seventh Army; 05/17/40, I Army Corps; 05/18/40, XVI Army Corps; 05/23/40, Belgian Cavalry Corps; 05/28/40, 1st Army Group; 05/29/40, XVI Army Corps; 06/04/40, captured on the fall of Dunkerque and disbanded): vacant 09/15/39 BG Jean-Georges-Henri Masson Bachasson de Montalivet (?) 01/01/40 BG Marcel-Émile Deslaurens (killed in action) 05/17/40 Col. de Chilly 05/27/40 BG Gustavé-Léon-Marius Teisseire (Greman prisoner-of-war) 06/04/40 captured and disbanded.

A. **Chief of Staff, 60th Infantry Division** (09/02/39): vacant 09/15/39 LCol. Schott /40? Maj. de Romemont 06/04/40 dissolved.
B. *Components - 60th Infantry Division* (09/15/39)
  1. **241st Infantry Regiment**
  2. **270th Infantry Regiment**
  3. **271st Infantry Regiment**
  4. **50th Divisional Mixed Artillery Regiment**

61st Infantry Division (09/02/39, Military District XI; 09/17/39, Military District of Paris; 12/1439, General Headquarters Reserve (Ninth Army Zone); 01/25/40, XLI Fortress Army Corps; 05/17/40, dislocated; 05/20/40, Military District III; 05/27/40, disbanded): MG Maurice-Jean-Joseph Abadié (retired) 12/07/39 MG Arsène-Marie-Paul Vauthier (Commanding General, 31st Alpine Infantry Division) 05/26/40 BG [Retired '38] Jacques-Jean-Louis Lhéritier (Commanding General, 241st Light Infantry Division) 05/27/40 disbanded.

A. **Chief of Staff, 61st Infantry Division** (09/02/39): LCol. Hallier (Chief of Staff, 241st Light Infantry Division) 05/27/40 dissolved.
B. *Components - 61st Infantry Division* (09/02/39)
  1. **248th Infantry Regiment**
  2. **265th Infantry Regiment**
  3. **337th Infantry Regiment**
  4. **51st Divisional Mixed Artillery Regiment**

62nd Infantry Division (09/02/39, Military District IX; 09/13/39, General Headquarters Reserve; 09/20/39, Fourth Army; 11/02/39, XX Army Corps; 11/23/39, Fourth Army; 12/27/39, Fifth Army Reserve; 01/31/40, XVII Army Corps; 05/16/40, 103rd Fortress Infantry Division; 06/14/40, Fifth Army; 06/15/40 103rd Fortress Infantry Division; 06/22/40, XLIII Fortress Army Corps; 06/23/40, disbanded): BG Ainé-Gabriel-Hilaire-Jehan-Marie Sarrebourse de la Guillonnière [+ 05/25/40 to 05/28/40, Commanding General, 103rd Fortress Infantry Division] (?) 06/12/40 BG René-Jacques Mortemart de Boisse (?) 06/23/40 disbanded.

A. **Chief of Staff, 62nd Infantry Division** (09/02/39): Col. de la Villeon 09/26/39 Maj. le Corguille 06/23/40 dissolved.
B. *Components - 62nd Infantry Division* (09/02/39)
  1. **250th Infantry Regiment**

2. **307th Infantry Regiment**
3. **326th Infantry Regiment**
4. **52nd Divisional Mixed Artillery Regiment**

63rd Infantry Division (09/03/39, Military District XIII; 10/18/39, XIV Army Corps; 11/18/39, Military District VII; 12/16/39, Army Corps du Jura; 01/12/40, XLV Fortress Army Corps; 05/23/40, Eighth Army; 05/25/40, Eighth Army Reserve; 06/09/40, Eighth Army; 06/13/40, XLIV Fortress Army Corps; 06/22/40, disbanded): MG [Retired '38] Gaspard-Henri-Marie-Gaston d'Humières (Commanding General, Military District XIII) 11/11/39 MG Maurice-René-Pierre Parvy (?) 06/22/40 disbanded.
  A. **Chief of Staff, 63rd Infantry Division** (09/03/39): LCol. Richefort 06/22/40 dissolved.
  B. *Components - 63rd Infantry Division* (09/03/39)
    1. **238th Infantry Regiment**
    2. **298th Infantry Regiment**
    3. **321st Infantry Regiment**
    4. **53rd Divisional Mixed Artillery Regiment**

66th Infantry Division (09/02/39, General Headquarters Reserve; 09/13/39, Military District III; 09/25/39, XV Army Corps; 10/07/39, Military District XV; 11/10/39, XIV Army Corps; 06/25/40, disbanded): MG Marie-Charles-Léon Spitz (retired) 11/16/39 BG Jean-Noël-Louis Boucher [+ 06/05/40 to 06/16/40, Commanding General, 240th Light Infantry Division] (?) 06/25/40 disbanded.
  A. **Chief of Staff, 66th Infantry Division** (09/02/39): Maj. Henri-Joseph-Charles-Marie de Cugnac (German prisoner-of-war; /44, died in concentration camp at Hartheim-Mathausen; /44, posthumously promoted to Brigadier General) 06/25/40 dissolved.
  B. *Components - 66th Infantry Division* (09/02/39)
    1. **215th Infantry Regiment**
    2. **281st Infantry Regiment**
    3. **343rd Infantry Regiment**
    4. **9th Divisional Artillery Regiment**
    5. **209th Divisional Heavy Artillery Regiment**

67th Infantry Division (08/26/39, Military District XVII; 10/15/39, Eighth Army; 10/28/39, XIII Army Corps; 11/20/39, Belfort Fortified Region; 03/16/40, XLIV Fortress Army Corps; 05/29/40, Eighth Army Reserve; 06/13/40, XLV Fortress Army Corps; 08/23/40, disbanded): 08/22/39 BG [Retired '37] Eugène-Henri-Étienne-Auguste Penavayre (Commanding General, Montauban Subdivision Group) 10/22/39 BG Henri-Aimé Boutignon [+ 10/29/39 to 11/20/39, Commanding General, Altkirch Fortified Sector; + 12/22/39 to 12/27/39, Commanding General, Belfort Fortified Region] (?) 08/23/40 disbanded.
  A. **Chief of Staff, 67th Infantry Division** (08/22/39): LCol. Lamasse 08/23/40 dissolved.
  B. *Components - 67th Infantry Division* (08/26/39)
    1. **211th Infantry Regiment**
    2. **214th Infantry Regiment**
    3. **220th Infantry Regiment**

    4.   **57th Divisional Mixed Artillery Regiment**

68th Infantry Division (01/16/40, from **North Coastal Group**, Admiral North; 05/18/40, XVI Army Corps; 06/04/40, captured at Dunkerque and disbanded): MG Maurice-Frédéric-Gaëtan Beaufrère (German prisoner-of-war) 06/04/40 captured and disbanded.
- A. **Chief of Staff, 68th Infantry Division** (01/16/40): LCol. Chabanier 06/04/40 dissolved.
- B. *Components - 68th Infantry Division* (01/16/40)
    1. **224th Infantry Regiment**
    2. **225th Infantry Regiment**
    3. **341st Infantry Regiment**
    4. **89th Divisional Artillery Regiment**
    5. **289th Divisional Heavy Artillery Regiment**
- C. **Infantry, 68th Infantry Division** (01/16/40): Col. Pierre-Servais Durand 06/25/40 dissolved.

70th Infantry Division (09/02/39, Military District XX; 09/12/39, Fifth Army Reserve; 10/06/39, XII Army Corps; 11/11/39, Fifth Army; 12/05/39, XII Army Corps; 02/07/40, Fifth Army Reserve; 04/25/40, XII Army Corps; 06/22/40, disbanded): BG Henri-Nicholas François [+ 06/05/40, Commanding General, 237th Light Infantry Division] 06/22/40 disbanded.
- A. **Chief of Staff, 70th Infantry Division** (09/02/39): Maj. Kocher 06/22/40 dissolved.
- B. *Components - 70th Infantry Division* (09/02/39)
    1. **223rd Infantry Regiment**
    2. **279th Infantry Regiment**
    3. **41st Light Infantry Half-Brigade**
    4. **44th Light Infantry Half-Brigade**
    5. **68th Divisional Artillery Regiment**
    6. **268th Divisional Heavy Artillery Regiment**

71st Infantry Division (09/03/39, Military District of Paris; 09/15/39, Fortress Army Corps; 10/12/39, X Army Corps; 04/05/40, Second Army Reserve; 05/11/40, X Army Corps; 05/21/40, disbanded): BG Joseph-Antoine-Jacques-Louis Baudet (?) 05/21/40 disbanded.
- A. **Chief of Staff, 71st Infantry Division** (09/03/39): LCol. Jean-Charles-Louis Regnault (Chief of Staff, 17th Infantry Division (#2)) 05/21/40 dissolved.
- B. *Components - 71st Infantry Division* (09/03/39)
    1. **120th Infantry Regiment**
    2. **205th Infantry Regiment**
    3. **246th Infantry Regiment**
    4. **38th Divisional Mixed Artillery Regiment**

Colonial Troops Morocco: /37 MG Pierre-Marius-Ernest Gibert (Commanding General, Oran Territorial Division) 09/39

Senselme March Division (06/13/40, from **XLIII Fortress Army Corps**; 06/24/40, surrendered):

A. **Chief of Staff, Senselme March Division**:
B. *Components* - **Senselme March Division**
   1. **154th Infantry Regiment**
   2. **165th Infantry Regiment**

March Division Besse (06/20/40, from remnants from **Bouley Fortified Sector**): Col. Jean-Joseph-René Besse 06/25/40 disbanded.

Mountain Divisions
[Division d'Infanterie type Montagne]

27th Alpine Infantry Division (08/22/39, regular unit, Military District XIV; 08/29/39, XIV Army Corps; 10/26/39, redesignated **27th Infantry Division**): /38 BG Georges-Eugène-Alphonse Cartier (Commanding General, 64th Alpine Infantry Division) 08/22/39 MG Paul-André Doyen (Commanding General, 27th Infantry Division) 10/26/39 redesignated **27th Infantry Division** - see **27th Infantry Division**.
- A. **Chief of Staff, 27th Alpine Infantry Division** (08/22/39) Maj. Henri-Marie-Antoine-François Lorber (Chief of Staff, 27th Infantry Division) 10/26/39 dissolved.
- B. *Components* - **27th Alpine Infantry Division** (08/22/39)
    1. **53rd Infantry Brigade**
    2. **54th Infantry Brigade**
    3. **93rd Mountain Artillery Regiment**
    4. **293rd Mountain Heavy Artillery Regiment (Motorized)**
- C. **Artillery, 27th Infantry Division** /36 LCol. Lucien-Julien-René André (09/01/39, Commanding Officer, Vosges Fortified Sector) /3?

28th Alpine Infantry Division (08/22/39, series "A" type, Military District XIV; 09/02/39, XIV Army Corps; 10/25/39, Fifth Army; 10/29/39, Fifth Army Reserve; 02/02/40, Lauter Fortified Region; 03/08/40, XLIII Fortress Army Corps; 03/27/40, Fifth Army Reserve; 05/16/40, XVII Army Corps; 06/08/40, VII Army Corps; 06/24/40, disbanded): MG Georges-Eugène Lestien (?) 06/24/40 disbanded.
- A. **Chief of Staff, 28th Alpine Infantry Division** (08/22/39): Maj. Maurice-Jules-Marie Collignon 06/24/40 dissolved.
- B. *Components* - **28th Alpine Infantry Division** (08/22/39)
    1. **55th Infantry Brigade**
    2. **56th Infantry Brigade**
    3. **2nd Mountain Artillery Regiment**
    4. **202nd Mountain Heavy Artillery Regiment (Motorized)**
- C. **Infantry, 28th Alpine Infantry Division** (08/22/39): BG Augustin-Marcelin Agliany (Commanding General, 5th North African Infantry Division) 04/19/40

29th Alpine Infantry Division (08/22/39, regular unit, Military District XV; 09/02/39, XV Army Corps; 11/12/39, General Headquarters Reserve; 01/23/40, IX Army Corps; 03/30/40, Fourth Army Reserve; 04/09/40, General Headquarters Reserve; 05/19/40, XXIV Army Corps; 05/26/40, Seventh Army Reserve; 05/31/40, I Army Corps; 06/21/40, Seventh Army; 06/25/40, disbanded): MG Paul-Henry Gérodias (Deputy Commander, Military District XV) 06/25/40 disbanded.
- A. **Chief of Staff, 29th Alpine Infantry Division** (08/22/39): Maj. Petetin 06/25/40 dissolved.
- B. *Components* - **29th Alpine Infantry Division** (08/22/39)
    1. **57th Infantry Brigade**
    2. **59th Infantry Brigade**
    3. **94th Mountain Artillery Regiment**
    4. **294th Mountain Heavy Artillery Regiment (Motorized)**

30th Alpine Infantry Division (08/22/39, series "A" type, Military District XV; 09/02/39, Sixth Army; 10/16/39, Fifth Army; 10/28/39, redesignated **30th Infantry Division**): MG Amédée Duron (Commanding General, 30th Infantry Division) 10/28/39 redesignated **30th Infantry Division** - see **30th Infantry Division**.
- A. **Chief of Staff, 30th Alpine Infantry Division** (08/22/39): LCol. Pendaries (Chief of Staff, 30th Infantry Division) 10/28/39 dissolved.
- B. *Components* - **30th Alpine Infantry Division** (08/22/39)
    1. **58th Infantry Brigade**
    2. **60th Infantry Brigade**
    3. **96th Mountain Artillery Regiment**
    4. **296th Mountain Heavy Artillery Regiment (Motorized)**
- C. **Infantry, 30th Alpine Infantry Division** (08/22/39): Col. Pierre-Désiré-Robert Didio (Commanding General, Mulhouse Fortified Sector) 01/12/40

31st Alpine Infantry Division (pre-war; 08/27/39, regular unit, Sixth Army Reserve; 09/01/39, Sixth Army; 09/16/39, Sixth Army Reserve; 09/20/39, XIV Army Corps; 09/30/39, Eighth Army; 10/15/39, XIII Army Corps; 02/20/40, Fifth Army; 02/24/40, VIII Army Corps; 05/22/40, 2nd Army Group Reserve; 05/29/40, Seventh Army; 05/31/40, Tenth Army; 06/01/40, IX Army Corps; 06/12/40, captured at St-Valéry-en-Caux and disbanded): /38 MG Marcel Ihler (Commanding General, IX Army Corps) 05/25/40 BG Arsène-Marie-Paul Vauthier (?) 06/12/40 captured and disbanded.
- A. **Chief of Staff, 31st Alpine Infantry Division** (08/27/39): LCol. Lacroisade 06/12/40 dissolved.
- B. *Components* - **31st Alpine Infantry Division** (08/27/39)
    1. **15th Alpine Infantry Regiment**
    2. **81st Alpine Infantry Regiment**
    3. **96th Alpine Infantry Regiment**
    4. **56th Mountain Artillery Regiment**
    5. **202th Divisional Heavy Artillery Regiment**
- C. **Infantry, 31st Infantry Division**: /35 Col. Marie-Martin-Jean-Alfred de Charry (Commanding General, 32nd Infantry Division) 09/02/39

64th Alpine Infantry Division (09/02/39, series "B" type, Military District XIV; 09/09/39, XIV Army Corps; 09/15/39, XVI Army Corps; 09/27/39, XIV Army Corps; 06/25/40, disbanded): MG Georges-Eugène-Alphonse Cartier (Commadning Officer, Lines of Communications [Rear Area], Sixth Army) 12/02/39 BG Louis-Albert-Pierre Robert de Saint-Vincent (Commanding General, Vaucluse Department, Military District XV) 06/25/40 disbanded.
- A. **Chief of Staff, 64th Alpine Infantry Division** (09/02/39): Maj. Lamothe 06/25/40 dissolved.
- B. *Components* - **64th Alpine Infantry Division** (09/02/39)
    1. **299th Alpine Infantry Regiment**
    2. **45th Alpine Infantry Half-Brigade**
    3. **47th Alpine Infantry Half-Brigade**
    4. **58th Divisional Artillery Regiment**
    5. **258th Divisional Heavy Artillery Regiment**
- C. **Infantry, 64th Alpine Infantry Division** (09/02/39): Col. René-André Gérin 06/25/40 dissolved.

65th Alpine Infantry Division (09/02/39, series "B" type, Military District XV; 09/09/39, Sixth Army; 10/23/39, XV Army Corps; 06/25/40, disbanded): BG [Retired '38] Charles Paquet 12/01/39 BG Marie-Joseph-André de Saint-Julien (?) 06/25/40 disbanded.

- A. **Chief of Staff, 65th Alpine Infantry Division** (09/02/39): LCol. Salmon [+ 02/09/40, Chief of Staff, Alps-Maritime Fortified Sector] 06/25/40 dissolved.
- B. *Components* - **65th Alpine Infantry Division** (09/02/39)
    1. **203rd Alpine Infantry Regiment**
    2. **42nd Alpine Infantry Half-Brigade**
    3. **46th Alpine Infantry Half-Brigade**
    4. **42nd Colonial Artillery Regiment**
    5. **242nd Colonial Heavy Artillery Regiment**
- C. **Artillery. 65th Alpine Infantry Division** (09/02/39): Col. Gauthier-Léon Niollet (?) 06/25/40 dissolved.

Light Mountain Divisions
[Division Légère de Chasseurs]

Light Mountain Division (02/08/40, formed as **High Mountain Brigade [Brigade de Haute Montagne]** French Scandinavian Expeditionary Force; 04/01/39, redesignated **1st Light Mountain Division**): Col. Marie-Emil-Antoine Béthouart (Commanding General, 1st Light Mountain Division) 04/01/40 redesignated **1st Light Mountain Division** - see **1st Light Mountain Division**.
- A. **Chief of Staff, Light Mountain Infantry Division** (02/08/40): Maj. Marcel-Étienne Paris (Chief of Staff, 1st Light Mountain Division) 05/01/40 dissolved.
- B. *Components* - Light Mountain Infantry Division (02/08/40)
    1. **5th Alpine Infantry Half-Brigade**
    2. **27th Alpine Infantry Half-Brigade**

1st Light Mountain Infantry Division (04/01/40, French Scandinavian Expeditionary Force; 04/28/40, British Expeditionary Force (Norway); 06/16/40, Brittany Command; 07/31/40, disbanded): BG Marie-Emil-Antoine Béthouart (Commanding General, Rabat Subdivision) 07/31/40 disbanded.
- A. **Chief of Staff, 1st Light Mountain Infantry Division** (04/01/40): Maj. Marcel-Étienne Paris 07/31/40 dissolved.
- B. *Components* - 1st Light Mountain Infantry Division (04/01/40)
    1. **5th Alpine Infantry Half-Brigade**
    2. **27th Alpine Infantry Half-Brigade**

2nd Light Mountain Infantry Division (04/18/40, formed as **Brigade "B"**. French Scandinavian Expeditionary Force; 05/31/40, disbanded): Col. Maurice-Georges-Constant Durand (Commanding General, 40th Alpine Infantry Division) 05/31/40 disbanded.
- A. **Chief of Staff, 2nd Light Mountain Infantry Division** (04/18/40): Maj. Piatte (/44? Commanding Officer, 5th Morocco Tirailleurs (Infantry) Regiment) 05/11/40 Maj. Valette d'Osia (Chief of Staff, 40th Alpine Infantry Division) 05/31/40 dissolved.
- B. *Components* - 2nd Light Mountain Infantry Division (04/18/40)
    1. **2nd Alpine Infantry Half-Brigade**
    2. **24th Alpine Infantry Half-Brigade**

3rd Light Infantry Division (has some mountain troops; 04/15/40, French Scandinavian Expeditionary Force; 05/16/4, Military Governor of Paris; 05/18/40 XXIV Army Corps; 06/25/40, disbanded): BG François-Jacques-André Duchemin 06/25/40 disbamded.
- A. **Chief of Staff, 3rd Light Infantry Division** (04/15/40): Maj. Lafaille 06/25/40 dissolved.
- B. *Components* - 2nd Light Infantry Division (04/15/40)
    1. **140th Alpine Infantry Regiment**
    2. **141st Alpine Infantry Regiment**

40th Alpine Infantry Division (05/30/40, General Headquarters Reserve; 06/03/40, Tenth Army; 06/06/40, IX Army Corps; 06/25/40, disbanded): BG Maurice-Georges-Constant Durand (?) 06/25/40 disbanded.

A. **Chief of Staff, 40th Alpine Infantry Division** (05/30/40): Maj. Valette d'Osia 06/25/40 dissolved.
B. *Components* - **40th Alpine Infantry Division** (05/31/40)
   1. **2nd Alpine Infantry Half-Brigade**
   2. **5th Alpine Infantry Half-Brigade**
   3. **24th Light Infantry Half-Brigade**
   4. **8th Colonial Artillery Regiment**
   5. **208th Colonial Heavy Artillery Regiment**

North African Infantry Divisions
[Division d'Infanterie Nord Africaine [DINA]]

1st North African Infantry Division (08/23/39, Military District XIV; 08/27/39, Sixth Army; 09/15/39, XVI Army Corps; 09/25/39, Second Army; 11/17/39, Colonial Army Corps; 12/21/39, General Headquarters Reserve; 05/15/40, XI Army Corps; 05/21/40, First Army; 05/22/40, Corps de Cavalerie; 05/24/40, Vernillat Group; 05/27/40, First Army; 06/09/40 redesignated **1st North African Light Infantry Division**; 06/13/40, XVI Army Corps; 06/17/40, virtually destroyed and disbanded): **1st North African Infantry Division** 08/23/39 BG Emmanuel-Urbain Libaud (Commanding General, XLI Fortress Army Corps) 01/15/40 BG Pierre-François-Joseph Tarrit (Commanding General, 1st North African Light Infantry Division) 06/09/40 redesignated **1st North African Light Infantry Division** 06/09/40 BG Pierre-François-Joseph Tarrit (?) 06/17/40 destroyed and disbanded.

A. **Chief of Staff, 1st North African Infantry Division** (08/23/39): LCol. Marmillot 06/09/40 redesignated **Chief of Staff, 1st North African Light Infantry Division** 06/09/40 Col. Serny 06/17/40 dissolved.
B. *Components* - **1st North African Infantry Division** (08/23/39)
   1. **27th Algerian Tirailleurs (Infantry) Regiment**
   2. **28th Algerian Tirailleurs (Infantry) Regiment**
   3. **5th Moroccan Tirailleurs (Infantry) Regiment**
   4. **58th North African Divisional Artillery Regiment**
   5. **258th North African Divisional Heavy Artillery Regiment**
C. *Components* - **1st North African Light Infantry Division** (06/09/40)
   1. **27th Algerian Tirailleurs (Infantry) Regiment**
   2. **1st Moroccan Tirailleurs (Infantry) Regiment**
D. **Artillery, 1st North African Infantry Division** (08/23/39): Col. Charles-René Donnio 06/17/40 dissolved.

2nd North African Infantry Division (08/22/39, Military District VI; 08/27/39, Third Army; 09/08/39, VI Army Corps; 11/10/39, 2nd Army Group Reserve; 12/18/39, III Army Corps; 05/24/40, V Army Corps; 05/29/40, XVI Army Corps; 06/01/40, surrendered and disbanded): /36 Col. Fernand-Joseph-Louis Lescanne (Commanding General, XLIII Fortress Army Corps) 01/01/40 BG Pierre Dame (German prisoner-of-war; /40, died in prison) 06/01/40 surrendered and disbanded.

A. **Chief of Staff, 2nd North African Infantry Division** (08/22/39): Maj. Dumoncel 09/39 LCol. Serny (Chief of Staff, 1st North African Light Infantry Division) 06/01/40 dissolved.
B. *Components* - **2nd North African Infantry Division** (08/22/39)
   1. **13th Algerian Tirailleurs (Infantry) Regiment**: /39 Col. François-Adolphe-Laurent Sevez (Commanding Officer, 32nd Light Infantry Division) 06/16/40
   2. **22nd Algerian Tirailleurs (Infantry) Regiment**
   3. **6th Moroccan Tirailleurs (Infantry) Regiment**: /36 LCol. Marcel-Georges François (Infantry Commander, 6th North African Infantry Division) 11/01/39
   4. **40th North African Divisional Artillery Regiment**
   5. **240th North African Divisional Heavy Artillery Regiment**
C. **Infantry, 2nd North African Infantry Division**: /36 Col. Henri-Nicholas François

(Commanding General, 70th Infantry Division) 09/02/39

3rd North African Infantry Division (08/23/39, Ministry of War; 08/26/39, XXI Army Corps; 09/11/39, Colonial Army Corps; 09/29/39, XVIII Army Corps; 10/06/39, Third Army; 10/11/39, General Headquarters Reserve; 10/17/39, X Army Corps; 12/02/39, General Headquarters Reserve; 12/39, Second Army; 04/04/40, X Army Corps; 05/14/40, XVIII Army Corps; 05/22/40, Second Army; 05/24/40, Colonial Army Corps Reserve; 05/29/40, XVIII Army Corps; 06/11/40, Second Army; 06/12/40, Colonial Army Corps; 06/25/40; disbanded): /36 BG Théodore-Marcel Sciard (Commanding General, Military District I) /39 vacant 08/26/39 MG Edouard-Charles-François Chapouilly (retired) 05/23/40 Col. Charles-Emmanuel Mast (/42, Chief of Staff, XIX Army Corps) 06/25/40 disbanded.
- A.   **Chief of Staff, 3rd North African Infantry Division** (08/23/39): LCol. Rivaud 06/25/40 dissolved.
- B.   *Components* - **3rd North African Infantry Division** (08/23/39)
    1. **14th Algerian Tirailleurs (Infantry) Regiment**
    2. **15th Algerian Tirailleurs (Infantry) Regiment**
    3. **24th Tunisian Tirailleurs (Infantry) Regiment**
    4. **20th North African Divisional Artillery Regiment**
    5. **220th North African Divisional Heavy Artillery Regiment**
- C.   **Infantry, 3rd North African Infantry Division** (08/23/39): Col. Pierre-François-Joseph Tarrit (Commanding General, 1st North African Infantry Division) 01/15/40

4th North African Infantry Division (08/22/39, Military District XX; 08/23/39, Fourth Army Reserve; 08/27/39, 20 Army Corps; 09/16/39, IX Army Corps; 11/09/39, Fourth Army Reserve; 11/29/39, XI Army Corps; 05/10/40, Ninth Army; 05/13/40, XI Army Corps; 05/20/40, captured and disbanded): /38 MG Jean-Frédéric Oehmichen (Commanding General, 4th Infantry Division) 09/02/39 MG Charles-Eugène Sancelme (to /45, German prisoner-of-war; /45, retired) 05/20/40 captured and disbanded.
- A.   **Chief of Staff, 4th North African Infantry Division** (08/22/39): LCol. Pots 05/20/40 dissolved.
- B.   *Components* - **4th North African Infantry Division** (08/22/39)
    1. **21st Algerian Tirailleurs (Infantry) Regiment**
    2. **22nd Algerian Tirailleurs (Infantry) Regiment**
    3. **25th Tunisian Tirailleurs (Infantry) Regiment**
    4. **33rd North African Divisional Artillery Regiment**
    5. **233rd North African Divisional Heavy Artillery Regiment**
- C.   **Infantry, 4th North African Infantry Division**: /36 Col. Camilee-Léon Duffet (Cammanding General, 18th Infantry Division) 08/23/39

5th North African Infantry Division (09/02/39, Military District XIV; 09/09/39, Third Army Reserve; 10/01/39, VI Army Corps; 12/03/39, First Army Reserve; 01/16/40, V Army Corps; 05/12/40, Belgian VII Army Corps and French V Army Corps; 05/29/40, XVI Army Corps; 06/01/40, destroyed defending Habourdin and disbanded): MG [Retired] Ferdinand-Prosper-Emmanuel-Léon Vieillard [+ Commanding General, 5th Colonial Division] (retired) 04/19/40 MG Augustin-Marcelin Agliany (German prisoner-of-war) 06/01/40 destroyed and disbanded.

[NOTE: listed in one source /40 MG Gustavé-Marie-Maurice Mesny (to /45, German

prisoner-of-war; /45, killed in Dresden) /40]
- A. **Chief of Staff, 5th North African Infantry Division** (09/02/39): LCol. Putinier /40? LCol. de Gournay 06/01/40 dissolved.
- B. *Components - 5th North African Infantry Division* (09/02/39)
    1. **11th Zouave Infantry Regiment**
    2. **12th Zouave Infantry Regiment**
    3. **14th Zouave Infantry Regiment**
    4. **22nd North African Divisional Artillery Regiment**
    5. **222nd North African Divisional Heavy Artillery Regiment**

6th North African Infantry Division (11/01/39, General Headquarters Reserve (Ninth Army Zone); 02/10/40, VI Army Corps; 04/26/40, Third Army; 05/13/40, Second Army; 05/18/40, XVIII Army Corps; 06/14/40 Group Dibuisson; 06/16/40, XXI Army Corps; 06/21/40, Group Dubuisson; 06/25/40, disbanded): BG Joseph-Antoine-Sylvain-Raoul de Verdillac (Chief of Staff, VI Army Corps) 06/25/40 disbanded.
- A. **Chief of Staff, 6th North African Infantry Division** (11/01/39): Maj. Voyron 05/30/40 Maj. Potier 06/25/40 dissolved.
- B. *Components - 6th North African Infantry Division* (11/01/39)
    1. **21st Algerian Tirailleurs (Infantry) Regiment**
    2. **9th Moroccan Tirailleurs (Infantry) Regiment**
    3. **24th Light Infantry Half-Brigade**
    4. **6th North African Divisional Artillery Regiment**
    5. **206th North African Divisional Heavy Artillery Regiment**
- C. **Infantry, 6th North African Infantry Division** (11/01/39): Col. Marcel-Georges François (Commanding Officer, 237th Light Infantry Division) 05/27/40

7th North African Infantry Division (03/16/40, General Headquarters Reserve; 05/18/40, I Army Corps; 06/25/40, disbanded): BG Georges-Edmond-Lucien Barré (Commanding General, Dordogne Department, Military District IX) 06/25/40 disbanded.
- A. **Chief of Staff, 7th North African Infantry Division** (03/16/40): Maj. Donin de Rosières 06/25/40 dissolved.
- B. *Components - 7th North African Infantry Division* (03/16/40)
    1. **31st Algerian Tirailleurs (Infantry) Regiment**
    2. **10th Moroccan Tirailleurs (Infantry) Regiment**
    3. **20th Tunisian Tirailleurs (Infantry) Regiment**
    4. **81st Divisional Artillery Regiment**
    5. **281st Divisional Heavy Artillery Regiment**
- C. **Artillery, 7th North African Infantry Division** (03/16/40): Col. Georges-Marie-Joseph Revers (09/12/40, Chief of Staff, II Group of Military Divisions) 06/25/40 dissolved.

Colonial Infantry Divisions
[Division d'Infanterie Coloniale [DIC]]

1st Colonial Infantry Division (08/23/39, Ministry of War (Military District XVIII); 08/29/39, First Army; 10/01/39, V Army Corps; 11/20/39, First Army; 12/11/39, Third Army; 12/19/39, VI Army Corps; 03/01/40, Third Army; 03/10/40, Second Army; 05/10/40, XVIII Army Corps; 05/13/40, Second Army Reserve; 05/14/40, XXI Army Corps; 06/12/40, Second Army Reserve; 06/13/40, Colonial Army Corps; 06/25/40, disbanded): /38 MG Maxime-Jean-Vincent Germain (Commanding General, XXIII Army Corps) 04/02/40 BG Guillaume-Charles Roucaud (to /41, German prisoner-of-war; /41, Chief of the General Staff of the Colonies) 06/25/40 disbanded.

- A. **Chief of Staff, 1st Colonial Infantry Division** (08/23/39): LCol. Rocafort 06/25/40 dissolved.
- B. **Components - 1st Colonial Infantry Division** (08/23/39)
    1. **3rd Colonial Infantry Regiment**
    2. **12th Sénégalais (African) Tirailleurs (Infantry) Regiment**
    3. **14th Sénégalais (African) Tirailleurs (Infantry) Regiment**
    4. **1st Colonial Divisional Artillery Regiment**
    5. **201st Colonial Divisional Heavy Artillery Regiment**
- C. **Artillery, 1st Colonial Infantry Division**: /38 Col. Jean-Jules-Ernest Picard (Artillery Commander, French West Africa) BG $_{[Retired]}$ Alphonse-Louis Cruciani (?) 06/25/40 dissolved.

2nd Colonial Infantry Division (08/22/39, Military District XV; 08/23/39, Toulon Naval District; 08/23/39, General Headquarters Reserve; 09/15/39, Sixth Army; 09/16/39, Sixth Army Reserve; 12/09/39, Army of the Alps Reserve; 04/20/40 XV Army Corps; 06/08/40, redesignated **2nd Colonial Light Infantry Division**; 06/13/40, Seventh Army; 06/15/40, XXIV Army Corps; 06/25/40, disbanded): /38 MG René-Paul Dubuisson [+ Commander-in-Chief, French West Africa] 09/02/39 MG Maignan (Commanding General, 2nd Colonial Light Infantry Division) 06/08/40 redesignated **2nd Colonial Light Infantry Division** 06/08/40 MG Maignan 06/25/40 disbanded.

- A. **Chief of Staff, 2nd Colonial Infantry Division** (08/23/39): LCol. Quenardel 03/21/40 Maj. Gonnet 06/25/40 dissolved.
- B. **Components - 2nd Colonial Infantry Division** (08/23/39)
    1. **Moroccan Colonial Infantry Regiment**
    2. **4th Sénégalais (African) Tirailleurs (Infantry) Regiment**
    3. **8th Sénégalais (African) Tirailleurs (Infantry) Regiment**
    4. **2nd Colonial Divisional Artillery Regiment**
    5. **202nd Colonial Divisional Heavy Artillery Regiment**
- C. **Components - 2nd Colonial Light Infantry Division** (06/08/40)
    1. **4th Pyrenean Infantry Half-Brigade**
    2. **8th Sénégalais (African) Tirailleurs (Infantry) Regiment**
- D. **Infantry, 2nd Colonial Infantry Division**: /38 Col. Frédéric Vallée (Commanding General, 103rd Fortress Infantry Division) 05/28/40
- E. **Artillery, 2nd Colonial Infantry Division** (08/23/39): unknown? 06/08/40 **Artillery,**

2nd Colonial Light Infantry Division: /39 Col. Georges-Eugène Paul (Commanding General, 58th Infantry Division) 09/02/39 unknown? 03/21/40 Col. Antoine-Dominique-Frédéric Aliotti 06/25/40 dissolved.

3rd Colonial Infantry Division (08/25/39, General Headquarters Reserve (Military District of Paris); 08/30/39, General Headquarters Reserve (Fifth Army Zone); 09/02/39, Military District of Paris; 09/10/39, General Headquarters Reserve; 09/13/39, Fifth Army; 09/16/39, VIII Army Corps; 11/05/39, Fifth Army; 11/29/39, XVIII Army Corps; 06/08/40, Second Army Reserve; 06/10/40, XXI Army Corps; 06/15/40, Group Dubuisson; 06/20/40, XXI Army Corps; 06/21/40, Group Dubuisson; 06/25/40, disbanded): MG Jean-Joseph-Guillaume Barrau (Member, The Army Council) 04/09/40 BG Maurice-Émile Falvy (German prisoner-of-war; /40, released; 12/08/40, Commander-in-Chief, Niger) 06/25/40 disbanded.
A. **Chief of Staff, 3rd Colonial Infantry Division** (08/25/39): Col. Cazeilles 02/03/40 Col. Renucci 06/25/40 dissolved.
B. *Components* - **3rd Colonial Infantry Division** (08/25/39)
   1. **1st Colonial Infantry Regiment**
   2. **21st Colonial Infantry Regiment**
   3. **23rd Colonial Infantry Regiment**
   4. **3rd Colonial Divisional Artillery Regiment**
   5. **203rd Colonial Divisional Heavy Artillery Regiment**
C. **Infantry, 3rd Colonial Infantry Division** (08/25/39): BG Henri-Gilbert-Antoine Perraud (Commanding General, 58th Infantry Division) 12/11/39 Col. Georges-Albert Aymé (Commanding General, 10th Infantry Division) 06/03/40 unknown? 06/25/40 dissolved.
D. **Artillery, 3rd Colonial Infantry Division**: /36 Col. Maurice Viant [+ to /39, Member, Consultative Committee for Colonial Defense; + /37 to /39, Member, Engineering Technical Committee] (Artillery Commander, Second Army) /40

4th Colonial Infantry Division (08/39, Military District XVIII; 08/27/39, Fifth Army; 09/07/39, VIII Army Corps; 09/20/39, General Headquarters Reserve; 10/03/39, Fifth Army; 10/13/39, XVII Army Corps; 01/31/40, VIII Army Corps; 04/01/40, 2nd Army Group Reserve; 05/18/40, Seventh Army; 05/20/40, I Army Corps; 06/01/40, Tenth Army and X Army Corps; 06/12/40, Army of Paris and XXV Army Corps; 06/18/40, XXV Army Corps; 06/25/40, disbanded): MG Marie-Joseph-Maurice de Bazelaire de Ruppiere (?) 06/25/40 disbanded.
A. **Chief of Staff, 4th Colonial Infantry Division** (08/39): Maj. Thomas 06/25/40 dissolved.
B. *Components* - **4th Colonial Infantry Division** (08/27/39)
   1. **2nd Colonial Infantry Regiment**
   2. **16th Sénégalais (African) Tirailleurs (Infantry) Regiment**
   3. **24th Sénégalais (African) Tirailleurs (Infantry) Regiment**
   4. **12th Colonial Divisional Artillery Regiment**
   5. **212th Colonial Divisional Heavy Artillery Regiment**
C. **Infantry, 4th Colonial Infantry Division** (08/27/39): Col. Jean-Dominique Quilichini (12/08/41?, Commanding General, Cochinchine-Cambodge Division) /40 Col. André-Georges-Louis Tranchant 06/25/40 dissolved.
D. **Artillery, 4th Colonial Infantry Division** (08/27/39): Col. Michel-Alexandre-

Maximilien Hanck (Artillery Commander, XXV Army Corps) /40 unknown? 06/25/40 dissolved.

5th Colonial Infantry Division (09/02/39, Military District XVI; 09/11/39, Third Army; 10/04/39, General Headquarters Reserve; 12/11/39, IX Army Corps; 02/17/40, Eighth Army; 05/19/40, X Army Corps; 05/20/40, Seventh Army Reserve; 05/21/40, X Army Corps; 05/24/40, Seventh Army Reserve; 05/20/40, Group "A"; 06/05/40, IX Army Corps; 06/07/40, dispersed; 06/21/40, Military District XII; 06/25/40, disbanded): MG [Retired] Ferdinand-Prosper-Emmanuel-Léon Vieillard [+ Commanding General, 5th North African Infantry Division] (retired) 12/39 BG Félix-Pierre-Marie Séchet (?) 06/25/40 disbanded.

A. **Chief of Staff, 5th Colonial Infantry Division** (09/02/40): LCol. Henri-Gustavé-André Borgnis-Desbordes (Commanding Officer, 4th Senegalese Regiment; /44, Infantry Commander, 19th Infantry Division) /40
B. *Components* - **5th Colonial Infantry Division** (09/02/39)
    1. **22nd Colonial Infantry Regiment**
    2. **44th Colonial Infantry Regiment**
    3. **53rd Colonial Infantry Regiment**
    4. **21st Colonial Divisional Artillery Regiment**
    5. **221st Colonial Divisional Heavy Artillery Regiment**
C. **Infantry, 5th Colonial Infantry Division** (09/02/39): Col. Germain-Stanislas-Victor Mennerat (Commanding General, 2nd Infantry Brigade, Tomkin Division) /40 MG Marie-Jules-Victor-Léon François (Commanding General, Tlemcen Subdivision) 06/25/40 dissolved.

6th Colonial Infantry Division (09/02/39, Military District IX; 09/12/39, Fourth Army; 09/16/39, IX Army Corps; 10/14/39, General Headquarters Reserve; 11/24/39, Fifth Army; 12/05/39, VIII Army Corps; 02/06/40, 2nd Army Group Reserve; 02/16/40, Third Army; 05/14/40, Second Army; 05/15/40, XXI Army Corps; 05/25/40, Second Army; 06/08/40, Colonial Army Corps; 06/17/40, Group Dubuisson; 06/22/40, captured and disbanded): MG Amédée-Alexandre-Gabriel-Henri Thierry (retired) 12/03/39 MG Émile-Jean-Gabriel Carlès (Commanding General, Colonial Corps) 06/06/40 BG [Retired '38] Lucien-Jean-Baptiste-Isidore Chaulard (retired) 06/11/40 BG Pierre-Marius-Ernest Gibert (to /45, German prisoner-of-war) 06/22/40 captured and disbanded.

A. **Chief of Staff, 6th Colonial Infantry Division** (09/02/39): Maj. de Saizieu 04/12/40 Maj. Meyer 04/23/40 Maj. de Saizieu 05/01/40 Maj. Glain 06/22/40 dissolved.
B. *Components* - **6th Colonial Infantry Division** (09/02/39)
    1. **5th Colonial Infantry Regiment**
    2. **6th Colonial Infantry Regiment**
    3. **43rd Colonial Infantry Regiment**
    4. **23rd Colonial Divisional Artillery Regiment**
    5. **223rd Colonial Divisional Heavy Artillery Regiment**
C. **Artillery, 6th Colonial Infantry Division** (09/02/39): BG [Retired '38] Lucien-Jean-Baptiste-Isidore Chaulard (Commanding General, 6th Colonial Infantry Division) 06/06/40

7th Colonial Infantry Division (09/01/39, Military District XVII; 09/11/39, Second Army; 09/12/39, Fortress Army Corps; 10/12/39, X Army Corps; 10/15/39, XVIII Army Corps;

11/26/39, Second Army; 12/04/39, General Headquarters Reserve; 12/27/39, XX Army Corps; 03/10/40, General Headquarters Reserve; 05/20/40, X Army Corps; 06/01/40, Seventh Army Reserve; 06/05/40, XXIV Army Corps; 06/14/40, I Army Corps; 06/25/40, disbanded): MG Louis-Émile Noiret (/44, arrested by the Germans; /44, killed in an Allied bombardment) 06/25/40 disbanded.
- A. **Chief of Staff, 7th Colonial Infantry Division** (09/01/39): LCol. Carton 06/25/40 dissolved.
- B. *Components - 7th Colonial Infantry Division* (08/01/39)
    1. **7th Colonial Infantry Regiment**
    2. **33rd Colonial Infantry Regiment**
    3. **57th Colonial Infantry Regiment**
    4. **32nd Colonial Divisional Artillery Regiment**
    5. **232nd Colonial Divisional Heavy Artillery Regiment**

8th Colonial Infantry Division (04/30/40, Military District XVIII; 05/16/40, General Headquarters Reserve (Army of the Alps Zone) 06/06/40 redesignated **8th Colonial Light Infantry Division**; 06/10/40, Army of Paris; 06/12/40, X Army Corps; 06/25/40, disbanded): BG Louis-Ernest Gillier (Commanding General, 8th Colonial Light Infantry Division) 06/06/40 redesignated **8th Colonial Light Infantry Division** 06/06/40 BG Louis-Ernest Gillier [+ acting Commanding General, X Army Corps] (?) 06/25/40 disbanded.
- A. **Chief of Staff, 8th Colonial Infantry Division** (04/30/40): Maj. Chrétien (Chief of Staff, 8th Colonial Light Infantry Division) 06/06/40 redesignated **Chief of Staff, 8th Colonial Light Infantry Division** 06/06/40 Maj. Chrétien (11/42?, Head, 2nd Bureau (Intelligence), North Africa) 06/25/40 dissolved.
- B. *Components - 8th Colonial Infantry Division* (04/30/40)
    1. **4th Colonial Infantry Regiment**
    2. **25th Sénégalais (African) Tirailleurs (Infantry) Regiment**
    3. **26th Sénégalais (African) Tirailleurs (Infantry) Regiment**
    4. **8th Colonial Divisional Artillery Regiment**
    5. **208th Colonial Divisional Heavy Artillery Regiment**
- C. *Components - 8th Colonial Light Infantry Division* (06/06/40)
    1. **4th Colonial Infantry Regiment**
    2. **26th Sénégalais (African) Tirailleurs (Infantry) Regiment**
    3. **9th Divisional Artillery Regiment**
- D. **Infantry, 8th Colonial Infantry Division** (04/30/40): Col. Hermann-Françis-Denis Delsuc (Infantry Commander, 8th Light Colonial Infantry Division) 06/06/40 redesignated **Infantry, 8th Light Infantry Division** 06/06/40 Col. Hermann-Françis-Denis Delsuc (Commanding General, 3rd Infantry Brigade, Tonkin Division) 12/08/41? unknown? 06/06/40 dissolved.

9th Colonial Infantry Division (06/15/40, but never formed): BG Pellet 06/15/40? never formed.
- A. **Chief of Staff, 9th Colonial Infantry Division** (06/16/40): unknown?
- B. *Components - 9th Colonial Infantry Division* (06/16/40)
    1. **27th Sénégalais (African) Tirailleurs (Infantry) Regiment**
    2. **28th Sénégalais (African) Tirailleurs (Infantry) Regiment**

3. **9th Colonial Divisional Artillery Regiment**
C. **Infantry, 9th Colonel Division** (06/16/40): Col. Georges-Ernest-Émile Duminy
D. **Artillery, 9th Colonial Division** (06/16/40): Col. Edouard Claerebout

Overseas Infantry Divisions
[Division d'Infanterie type Outre-Mer]

81st African Infantry Division (08/27/39, mobilized at Blida from **5th Algerian Infantry Brigade**, as a 1st Category Overseas Division; 09/39, North African Theater of Operations; 11/39, Tunisien Southern Front): vacant 09/02/39 BG Étienne-Paul-Émile-Marie Beynet (Commanding General, XIV Army Corps) 02/05/39 BG François-Antoine-Charles Chevallier (?) /40 BG Joseph-Jean de Goislard de Monsabert [+ /42, Commanding General, Vichy French African Corps] (Commanding General, Free French 3rd Algerian Division) 05/01/43

A.   **Chief of Staff, 81st African Infantry Division** (08/27/39): LCol. Pons
B.   *Components* - **81st African Infantry Division** (08/27/39)
    1.   **1st Algerian Tirailleurs (Infantry) Regiment**
    2.   **5th Algerian Tirailleurs (Infantry) Regiment**
    3.   **9th Algerian Tirailleurs (Infantry) Regiment**
    4.   **65th African Artillery Regiment**

82nd African Infantry Division (mobilized at Oran as a 1st Category Overseas Division; 09/02/39, Military District XIX; 09/25/39, sent to France; 10/05/39, War Ministry (Military District V); 10/22/39, V Army Corps; 04/04/40, Fourth Army; 04/12/40, XX Army Corps; 05/25/40, General Headquarters Reserve; 06/06/40, Fourth Army; 06/10/40, XXIII Army Corps; 06/15/40, destroyed in the retreat from the Marne to the Aube and disbanded): MG Gustavé-Marcellin Armengeat (German prisoner-of-war) 06/15/40 destroyed and disbanded.

A.   **Chief of Staff, 82nd African Infantry Division** (09/02/39): Maj. Tritschler 06/15/40 dissolved.
B.   *Components* - **82nd African Infantry Division** (09/02/39)
    1.   **1st Zouave Infantry Regiment**
    2.   **6th Algerian Tirailleurs (Infantry) Regiment**
    3.   **4th Moroccan Tirailleurs (Infantry) Regiment**
    4.   **66th African Artillery Regiment**

83rd African Infantry Division (mobilized at Constantine from **7th Algerian Infantry Brigade**, as a 1st Category Overseas Division; 09/01/39, Tunisien Southern Front; 11/39, Tunisien Front Reserve): BG Bernard-Marie-Alexis Vergès (Commanding General, Constantine Territory Division) 06/25/40 disbanded.

A.   **Chief of Staff, 83rd African Infantry Division** (09/01/39): Col. Lucien-Émile-Eugéne Monniot [+ to 10/15/39, Chief of Staff, V Motorized Army Corps]
B.   *Components* - **83rd African Infantry Division** (09/01/39)
    1.   **3rd Algerian Tirailleurs (Infantry) Regiment**
    2.   **7th Algerian Tirailleurs (Infantry) Regiment**
    3.   **11th Algerian Tirailleurs (Infantry) Regiment**
    4.   **67th African Artillery Regiment**

84th African Infantry Division (mobilized at Tunis as a 2nd Category Overseas Division; 08/26/39, Tunisien Southern Group; 11/21/39, North African Theater of Operations

Reserve; 05/40, sent to France; 05/26/40, General Headquarters Reserve; 06/08/40, Military District of Paris; 06/10/40, XXV Army Corps; 06/14/40, X Army Corps; 06/25/40, disbanded): MG Charles-Pierre-Martial Ardant du Picq (killed in action) 06/09/40 BG Paul-Amédée-Marie Goubaux (?) 06/25/40 disbanded.

- A. **Chief of Staff, 84th African Infantry Division** (08/26/39): LCol. Carcasses 06/25/40 dissolved.
- B. *Components* - 84th African Infantry Division (08/26/39)
    1. **4th Tunisian Tirailleurs (Infantry) Regiment**
    2. **8th Tunisian Tirailleurs (Infantry) Regiment**
    3. **18th Sénégalais (African) Tirailleurs (Infantry) Regiment**
    4. **88th African Artillery Regiment**

85th African Infantry Division (08/28/39, mobilized at Algiers as a 2nd Category Overseas Division; 09/07/39, Tunisien Southern Group; 04/24/40, North African Theater of Operations Reserve; 05/40, sent to France; 06/04/40, XXV Army Corps; 06/25/40, disbanded): MG Maurice-Arthur-Alphonse Wemaëre (?) 06/25/40 disbanded.

- A. **Chief of Staff, 85th African Infantry Division** (08/28/39): Maj. Pinson 06/25/40 dissolved.
- B. *Components* - 85th African Infantry Division (08/28/39)
    1. **3rd Zouave Infantry Regiment**
    2. **9th Zouave Infantry Regiment**
    3. **20th Tunisia Tirailleurs (Infantry) Regiment**
    4. **65th African Artillery Regiment**
- C. **Infantry, 85th African Infantry Division** (08/28/39): Col. Hector-Louis-Ferdinand Normand 06/25/40 dissolved.

86th African Infantry Division (mobilized at Oran as a 2nd Category Overseas Division; 09/39, Eastern Mediterranean Theater of Operations (Middle East); 10/01/39 Army Corps L; 10/23/39, Levant Expeditionary Force (Levant Mobile Force)): BG Jean Cazaban (?) /40

- A. **Chief of Staff, 86th African Infantry Division** (09/39): unknown?
- B. *Components* - 86th African Infantry Division (09/39)
    1. **2nd Zouave Infantry Regiment**
    2. **2nd Algerian Tirailleurs (Infantry) Regiment**
    3. **29th Algerian Tirailleurs (Infantry) Regiment**
    4. **86th African Artillery Regiment**
    5. **286th African Artillery Regiment**

87th African Infantry Division (mobilized at Constantine, as a 3rd Category Overseas Division; 08/29/39, Military District XIX, 09/05/39, Tunisien Front; 11/06/39, Military District XVI; 11/29/39, General Headquarters Reserve (Second Army Zone) 02/27/40 XX Army Corps; 05/02/40, 2nd Army Group Reserve; 05/17/40, XVII Army Corps; 05/31/40, XXIV Army Corps; 06/24/40, I Army Corps; 06/25/40, disbanded): 08/29/39 BG Victor-Paul-Auguste Duclos (/40, Commanding General, Sousse et de Gabés Subdivision) 09/02/39 MG [Retired] Marie-François-Armand-Roger Barbeyrac de Saint-Maurice [+ Commanding General, Military District II & to 01/01/40, Commanding General, 57th Infantry Division]

05/25/40, Col. Henri-Jules-Jean Martin (Commanding General, Marrakech Territorial Division) 06/25/40 disbanded.
- A. **Chief of Staff, 87th African Infantry Division** (08/29/39): LCol. Wisbecq 11/01/39 Maj. Roche 06/25/40 dissolved.
- B. *Components* - **87th African Infantry Division** (08/29/39)
  1. **17th Algerian Tirailleurs (Infantry) Regiment**
  2. **18th Algerian Tirailleurs (Infantry) Regiment**
  3. **19th Algerian Tirailleurs (Infantry) Regiment**
  4. **87th African Artillery Regiment**

88th African Infantry Division (mobilized at Constantine, as a 3rd Category Overseas Division; 09/39, Tunisien Northern Front): MG Jean-Pierre-Hector-Marie Bessières [+ 09/39, Commanding General, North Tunisian Front]
- A. **Chief of Staff, 88th African Infantry Division** (09/39): LCol. Léon-Alexis Guyot
- B. *Components* - **88th African Infantry Division** (09/39)
  1. **4th Zouave Infantry Regiment**
  2. **5th Sénégalais (African) Tirailleurs (Infantry) Regiment**
  3. **10th Sénégalais (African) Tirailleurs (Infantry) Regiment**
  4. **82nd African Artillery Regiment**

1st Moroccan Infantry Division (mobilized as a 1st Category Overseas Division; 09/02/39, Morocco Troops; 10/39, sent to France; 11/08/39, Ministry of War (Military District XVIII); 11/18/39, General Headquarters Reserve; 12/17/39, Colonial Army Corps; 02/01/40, General Headquarters Reserve; 04/01/40, V Army Corps; 05/10/40, IV Army Corps; 05/21/40, First Army Reserve; 05/24/40, Cavalry Corps; 05/26/40, V Army Corps; late-05/40, virtually destroyed defending Canteleu; 06/08/40, Regrouping Zone C; 06/11/40, XVI Army Corps; 06/25/40, disbanded): 09/02/39 MG Sylvestre-Gérard Audet [02/16/39, Commanding General, French Scandinavian Expeditionary Force] 02/27/40 BG Albert-Raymond Mellier (German prisoner-of-war) 06/25/40 disbanded.
- A. **Chief of Staff, 1st Moroccan Infantry Division** (09/02/39): Maj. Nardin 05/22/40 Capt. [Army] Castaing 06/25/40 dissolved.
- B. *Components* - **1st Moroccan Infantry Division** (09/02/39)
  1. **1st Moroccan Tirailleurs (Infantry) Regiment**
  2. **2nd Moroccan Tirailleurs (Infantry) Regiment**
  3. **7th Moroccan Tirailleurs (Infantry) Regiment**
  4. **64th African Artillery Regiment**

2nd Moroccan Infantry Division (09/02/39, mobilized at Rabat, as a 3rd Category Overseas Division; 09/02/39, Commander of the Troops in Morocco; 10/39, disbanded): BG Jean-Jules-Alexis Callies (/44, Commanding General, Pyrenees Front) 10/39 disbanded.
- A. **Chief of Staff, 1st Moroccan Infantry Division** (09/02/39): unknown? 10/39 dissolved.
- B. *Components* - **1st Moroccan Infantry Division** (09/02/39)
  1. **2nd Foreign Legion Infantry Regiment**
  2. **4th Foreign Legion Infantry Regiment**
  3. **3rd Sénégalais (African) Tirailleurs (Infantry) Regiment**

    4. **1st African Chasseurs (Armor) Regiment**
    5. **2nd Foreign Legion Cavalry Regiment**
    6. **Moroccan Colonial Artillery Regiment**

3rd Moroccan Infantry Division (pre-war; 09/02/39, mobilized at Rabat, as a 3rd Category Overseas Division; 09/02/39, Commander of the Troops in Morocco): BG Jean-Joseph-Lucien Mordacq [+ Commanding General, Méknes Territorial Diviison] (retired) 06/25/40
A. **Chief of Staff, 3rd Moroccan Infantry Division** (09/02/39): unknown?
B. *Components* - **3rd Moroccan Infantry Division** (09/02/39)
    1. **3rd Foreign Legion Infantry Regiment**
    2. **21st Zouave Infantry Regiment**
    3. **6th Sénégalais (African) Tirailleurs (Infantry) Regiment**
    4. **63rd African Artillery Regiment**
C. **Infantry, 3rd Moroccan Infantry Division**: /36 Col. Edouard-Charles-François Chapouilly (08/26/39, Commanding General, 3rd North African Infantry Division) /36

180th African Infantry Division (11/01/39, mobilized as a 3rd Category Overseas Division and titled **87th African Infantry Division (#2)**, to replace the **87th African Infantry Division** that was sent to Metropolitan France, but was redesignated **180th African Infantry Division**; 11/39, North Africa Theater of Operations): BG Jean-Baptiste-René-François Rochas
A. **Chief of Staff, 180th African Infantry Division** (11/01/39): Col. Louis Grélot (Commanding Officer, 38th Infantry Regiment; /39, Commanding Officer, 95th Infantry Regiment; /40 to /45, German prisoner-of-war) /39
B. *Components* - **180th African Infantry Division** (11/02/39)
    1. **22nd Zouave Infantry Regiment**
    2. **13th Sénégalais (African) Tirailleurs (Infantry) Regiment**
    3. **380th African Artillery Regiment**

181st African Infantry Division (09/39, mobilized at Algiers, as a 3rd Category Overseas Division; 09/39, Protection Forces (North Africa Theater of Operations)): BG Gendre /40? BG Despas
A. **Chief of Staff, 181st African Infantry Division** (09/39): Col. Perrossiet
B. *Components* - **181st African Infantry Division** (09/39)
    1. **29th Zouave Infantry Regiment**
    2. **13th Sénégalais (African) Tirailleurs (Infantry) Regiment**
    3. **385th African Artillery Regiment**

182nd African Infantry Division (09/39, mobilized at Oran, as a 3rd Category Overseas Division; 09/39, Protection Forces (North Africa Theater of Operations)): BG Jean-Gabriel-Edouard Thomas
A. **Chief of Staff, 182nd African Infantry Division** (09/39): Col. Camille-Hippolyte Caldairou
B. *Components* - **182nd African Infantry Division** (09/39)
    1. **1st Foreign Legion Infantry Regiment**
    2. **22nd Zouave Infantry Regiment**

3. **11ᵗʰ Sénégalais (African) Tirailleurs (Infantry) Regiment**
4. **386ᵗʰ African Artillery Regiment**

183ʳᵈ African Infantry Division (09/39, mobilized at Constantine, as a 3ʳᵈ Category Overseas Division; 09/39, Protection Forces (North Africa Theater of Operations)): BG Diclos
A. **Chief of Staff, 182ⁿᵈ African Infantry Division** (09/39): Col. Seminel
B. *Components* - **182ⁿᵈ African Infantry Division** (09/39)
   1. **344ᵗʰ Infantry Regiment**
   2. **23ʳᵈ Zouave Infantry Regiment**
   3. **15ᵗʰ Sénégalais (African) Tirailleurs (Infantry) Regiment**
   4. **387ᵗʰ African Artillery Regiment**

191ˢᵗ African Infantry Division (07/20/39, originally formed **1ˢᵗ Levant Mixed Brigade [1ˢᵗ Brigade Mixtes du Levant]**; 09/10/39, redesignated **1ˢᵗ Levant Infantry Division**; 10/01/39, Army Corps L; 10/23/39, Levant Expeditionary Force (Levant Mobile Force); 10/30/39, redesignated **191ˢᵗ African Infantry Division**): **1ˢᵗ Levant Mixed Brigade** 07/20/39 Col. Marie-Joseph-Gabriel Sarrade (Commanding Officer, 1ˢᵗ Levant Infantry Division) 09/10/39 redesignated **1ˢᵗ Levant Infantry Division** 09/10/39 Col. Marie-Joseph-Gabriel Sarrade (Commanding Officer, 191ˢᵗ African Infantry Division) 10/30/39 redesignated **191ˢᵗ African Infantry Division** 10/30/39 Col. Marie-Joseph-Gabriel Sarrade (?) /40
A. **Chief of Staff, 1ˢᵗ Levant Mixed Brigade** (07/20/39): LCol. Picot (Chief of Staff, 1ˢᵗ Levant Infantry Division) 09/10/39 **Chief of Staff, 1ˢᵗ Levant Infantry Division** 09/10/39 LCol. Picot (Chief of Staff, 191ˢᵗ African Infantry Division) 10/30/39 redesignated **Chief of Staff, 191ˢᵗ African Infantry Division** 10/30/39 LCol. Picot
B. *Components* - **191ˢᵗ African Infantry Division** (10/30/39)
   1. **12ᵗʰ Tunisia Tirailleurs (Infantry) Regiment**
   2. **16ᵗʰ Tunisia Tirailleurs (Infantry) Regiment**
   3. **24ᵗʰ Colonial Infantry) Regiment**
   4. **41ˢᵗ Colonial Artillery Regiment**

192ⁿᵈ African Infantry Division (07/20/39, originally formed **2ⁿᵈ Levant Mixed Brigade [2ⁿᵈ Brigade Mixtes du Levant]**; 09/10/39, redesignated **2ⁿᵈ Levant Infantry Division**; 10/01/39, Army Corps L; 10/23/39, Levant Expeditionary Force (Levant Mobile Force); 10/30/39, redesignated **192ⁿᵈ African Infantry Division**): **2ⁿᵈ Levant Mixed Brigade** 07/20/39 BG Georges-Julien Richard (Commanding General, 2ⁿᵈ Levant Infantry Division) 09/10/39 redesignated **2ⁿᵈ Levant Infantry Division** 09/10/39 BG Georges-Julien Richard (Commanding Officer, 192ⁿᵈ African Infantry Division) 10/30/39 redesignated **192ⁿᵈ African Infantry Division** 10/30/39 BG Georges-Julien Richard (?) /40
A. **Chief of Staff, 2ⁿᵈ Levant Mixed Brigade** (07/20/39): unknown? 09/10/39 **Chief of Staff, 2ⁿᵈ Levant Infantry Division** 09/10/39 unknown? 10/30/39 redesignated **Chief of Staff, 192ⁿᵈ African Infantry Division** 10/30/39 unknown?
B. *Components* - **192ⁿᵈ African Infantry Division** (10/30/39)
   1. **17ᵗʰ Sénégalais (African) Tirailleurs (Infantry) Regiment**
   2. **6ᵗʰ Foreign Legion Infantry Regiment**

3. **10th North African Infantry Half-Brigade**
4. **80th North African Artillery Regiment**

Light Infantry Divisions
[Division Légère d'Infanterie [DLI]]

1st Light Infantry Division (06/06/40, from **1st Motorized Infantry Division**; 06/06/40, Regrouping Zone D; 06/10/40, XVI Army Corps; 06/19/40 captured; 06/25/40, disbanded): 06/10/40 MG Paul-René Malivoire-Filhol de Camas (German prisoner-of-war) 06/25/40 disbanded.
- A. **Chief of Staff, 1st Light Infantry Division** (06/10/40): Col. Welschinger 06/25/40 dissolved.
- B. *Components* - **1st Light Infantry Division** (06/10/40)
    1. **43rd Infantry Regiment**
    2. **110th Infantry Regiment**
    3. **327th Divisional Artillery Regiment**

17th Light Infantry Division (05/31/40; 06/01/40, Military District IX; 06/05/40, General Headquarters Reserve; 06/07/40; IV Army Corps; 06/12/40, Group Dufour; 06/15/40, disbanded): BG René-Albert Darde (?) 06/15/40 disbanded.
- A. **Chief of Staff, 17th Light Infantry Division** (06/01/40): Maj. de Gouvello 06/15/40 dissolved.
- B. *Components* - **17th Light Infantry Division** (06/01/40)
    1. **90th Infantry Regiment**
    2. **114th Infantry Regiment**
    3. **97th Divisional Artillery Regiment**

32nd Light Infantry Division (06/12/40, from **32nd Infantry Division**): see **32nd Infantry Division**.

43rd Light Infantry Division (06/13/40, from **43rd Infantry Division**): see **43rd Infantry Division**.

53rd Light Infantry Division (05/31/40, from **53rd Infantry Division**):see **53rd Infantry Division**.

59th Light Infantry Division (05/26/40, from **17th Infantry Division (#2)**; 05/30/40, Second Army; 06/07/40, VIII Army Corps; 06/08/40, Second Army; 06/12/40, VII Army Corps; 06/13/40, destroyed south of Montmirail and disbanded): BG Georges-Eugène-Joseph Lascroux (Commanding General, Vienne Department, Military District IX) 06/13/40 destroyed and disbanded.
- A. **Chief of Staff, 59th Light Infantry Division** (05/26/40): LCol. Jean-Charles-Louis Regnault 06/13/40 dissolved.
- B. *Components* - **59th Light Infantry Division** (06/01/40)
    1. **83rd Infantry Regiment**
    2. **135th Infantry Regiment**
    3. **84th Divisional Artillery Regiment**

1st North African Light Infantry Division (06/09/40, from **1st North African Infantry Division**): see **1st North African Infantry Division**.

2nd Colonial Light Infantry Division (06/08/40, from **2nd Colonial Infantry Division**): see **2nd Colonial Infantry Division**.

8th Colonial Light Infantry Division (06/06/40, from **8th Colonial Infantry Division**): see **8th Colonial Infantry Division**.

235th Light Infantry Division (06/01/40, General Headquarters Reserve; 06/06/40, Sixth Army; 06/07/40, XXIII Army Corps; 06/12/40, destroyed on the retreat to the Marne and disbanded): BG François-Joseph-Marie-Amédée Trolley de Prévaux (?) 06/12/40 destroyed and disbanded.
- A. **Chief of Staff, 235th Light Infantry Division** (06/01/40): LCol. Lallemand de Liocourt 06/12/40 dissolved.
- B. *Components* - **235th Light Infantry Division** (06/01/40)
    1. **9th Infantry Regiment**
    2. **108th Infantry Regiment**
    3. **323rd Divisional Artillery Regiment**

236th Light Infantry Division (05/27/40, Military District XVIII; 06/04/40, General Headquarters Reserve; 06/08/40, Army Corps D (Tenth Army); 06/20/40; III Army Corps; 06/25/40, disbanded): vacant 06/01/40 BG Agathon-Jules-Joseph Deligne (Commanding General, Corsica) 06/25/40 disbanded.
- A. **Chief of Staff, 236th Light Infantry Division** (06/01/40) LCol. Ardellier
- B. *Components* - **236th Light Infantry Division** (06/01/40)
    1. **64th Infantry Regiment**
    2. **118th Infantry Regiment**
    3. **90th Divisional Artillery Regiment**

237th Light Infantry Division (05/27/40 at Rivesaltes; 06/05/40, General Headquarters Reserve; 06/09/40, 3rd Light Cavalry Division; 06/10/40, III Army Corps; 06/11/40, 3rd Light Mechanized Division; 06/12/40, Group Petiet; 06/13/40, III Army Corps; 06/25/40, disbanded): BG Marcel-Georges François (07/40, Commanding General, Landes Department, Military District XVIII) 06/05/40 BG Henri-Nicholas François (to /45, German prisoner-of-war) 06/25/40 disbanded.
- A. **Chief of Staff, 237th Light Infantry Division** (05/27/40): LCol. Labarre 06/25/40 dissolved.
- B. *Components* - **237th Light Infantry Division** (06/05/40)
    1. **236th Infantry Regiment**
    2. **274th Infantry Regiment**
    3. **95th Divisional Artillery Regiment**

238th Light Infantry Division (06/01/40, in the Arc-en-Barrois region; 06/07/40, Sixth Army Reserve; 06/08/40, XVII Army Corps; 06/25/40, disbanded): BG Marie-Cyrille-Victor Debeney 06/25/40 disbanded.

A. **Chief of Staff, 238th Light Infantry Division** (06/01/40): Maj. Caullet 06/25/40 dissolved.
B. *Components* - **238th Light Infantry Division**
   1. **25th Infantry Regiment**
   2. **144th Infantry Regiment**
   3. **324th Divisional Artillery Regiment**

239th Light Infantry Division (06/01/40, in the Arc-en-Barrois region; 06/01/40, General Headquarters Reserve; 06/09/40, Seventh Army; 06/11/40, XXIV Army Corps; 06/21/40, I Army Corps; 06/25/40, disbanded): BG Eugène-Charles Dunoyer de Ségonzac (?) 06/25/40 disbanded.
A. **Chief of Staff, 239th Light Infantry Division** (06/01/40): Maj. Fremiot 06/25/40 dissolved.
B. *Components* - **239th Light Infantry Division** (06/01/40)
   1. **59th Infantry Regiment**
   2. **138th Infantry Regiment**
   3. **325th Divisional Artillery Regiment**

240th Light Infantry Division (06/05/40, in the Bar-sur-Seine region; 06/14/40, XVIII Army Corps, Second Army, 2nd Army Group; 06/17/40, captured and disbanded): 06/05/40 BG Jean-Noël-Louis Boucher [+ Commanding General, 66th Infantry Division] 06/16/40 BG Louis-Léon-Marie-André Buisson [+ Commanding General, 3rd Armored Division] (German prisoner-of-war) 06/17/40 captured and disbanded.
A. **Chief of Staff, 240th Light Infantry Division** (06/05/40): Maj. Magny 06/17/40 dissolved.
B. *Components* - **240th Light Infantry Division** (06/14/40)
   1. **40th North African Infantry Half-Brigade**
   2. **42nd Colonial Infantry Regiment**
   3. **307th Divisional Artillery Regiment**

241st Light Infantry Division (05/27/40, in Louviers region; 05/27/40, Military District III; 06/05/40, XXV Army Corps; 06/26/40, disbanded): BG [Retired '38] Jacques-Jean-Louis Lhéritier (retired) 06/26/40 disbanded.
A. **Chief of Staff, 241st Light Infantry Division** (05/27/40): LCol. Hallier 06/26/40 dissolved.
B. *Components* - **241st Light Infantry Division** (05/27/40)
   1. **219th Infantry Regiment**
   2. **264th Infantry Regiment**
   3. **98th Divisional Artillery Regiment**

Light Division Burtaire (06/21/40): MG Maurice-Alphonse-Alfred Burtaire (?) 06/25/40 disbanded.

Foreign Infantry Divisions
[Division d'Infanterie de Volontaires Étrangers]

1st Polish (Polonaise) Infantry Division (10/39, in Coëtquidan region of Brittany; 10/39, General Headquarters Resewrve; 04/20/40, Fourth Army; 05/15/40, 2nd Army Group Reserve; 06/13/40, XX Army Corps; 06/21/40, disbanded): BG Duch (?) 06/21/40 disbanded.

- A. **Chief of Staff, 1st Polish Infantry Division** (10/39) LCol. Skrzydlewski [Polish] 06/21/40 dissolved.
- B. *Components - 1st Polish Infantry Division* (10/39)
    1. **1st Polish Infantry Regiment**
    2. **2nd Polish Infantry Regiment**
    3. **3rd Polish Infantry Regiment**
    4. **1st Polish Artillery Regiment**
    5. **1st Polish Heavy Artillery Regiment**

2nd Polish (Polonaise) Infantry Division (spring/40, at Saint-Loup sur Thouet; 03/40, General Headquarters Reserve; 05/24/40, 2nd Army Group and Third Army; 06/09/40, XLV Fortress Army Corps; 06/13/40, Belfort Defense; 06/14/40, XLV Fortress Army Corps; 06/20/40, crossed the Swiss border into internment): 03/40 BG Prugar Ketling (?) 06/20/40 crossed the Swiss border into internment.

- A. **Chief of Staff, 2nd Polish Infantry Division** (03/40): Col. Najymski [Polish] 06/20/40 dissolved.
- B. *Components - 2nd Polish Infantry Division* (03/40)
    1. **4th Polish Infantry Regiment**
    2. **5th Polish Infantry Regiment**
    3. **6th Polish Infantry Regiment**
    4. **2nd Polish Artillery Regiment**
    5. **202nd Polish Heavy Artillery Regiment**

1st Czechoslovakian (Tchécoslovaque) Infantry Division
- A. **Chief of Staff, 1st Czechoslovakian Infantry Division**
- B. *Components - 1st Czechoslovakian Infantry Division*
    1. **1st Czechoslovakian Infantry Regiment**
    2. **2nd Czechoslovakian Infantry Regiment**
    3. **3rd Czechoslovakian Infantry Regiment**
    4. **1st Czechoslovakian Artillery Regiment**

Cavalry Divisions
[Division de Cavalerie [DC]]

1st Cavalry Division (08/23/39, Ministry of War; 08/27/39, Ardennes Army Detachment; 10/15/39, Ninth Army; 02/10/40, redesignated **1st Light Division**): /35 BG Léon-Benoit de Fornel de La Laurencie (Commanding General, Military District III) 08/23/39 MG Jacques-Marie-Toussaint d'Arras (Commanding General, 1st Light Division) 02/10/40 redesignated **1st Light Division** - see **1st Light Cavalry Division**.
- A. **Chief of Staff, 1st Cavalry Division** (08/39): Maj. de Brecey 09/02/39 Maj. de Truchis de Varenne (Chief of Staff, 1st Light Division) 02/10/40 dissolved.
- B. *Components* - **1st Cavalry Division**
    1. **1st Cavalry Brigade**
    2. **2nd Cavalry Brigade**
    3. **1st Armored Car (Automitrailleuses) Regiment**
    4. **75th Artillery Regiment**

2nd Cavalry Division (08/22/39, Military District XX; 08/23/39, Military District VII; 09/06/39, XIII Army Corps; 10/09/39, Second Army; 02/10/40, redesignated **2nd Light Division**): **2nd Cavalry Division** /36 MG André Berniquet (Commanding General, 2nd Light Division) 02/10/40 redesignated **2nd Light Division** - see **2nd Light Cavalry Division**.
[NOTE: acting Commanding General /40 BG [Retired '39] Charles-Georges-Antoine Delestraint (06/02/40, Commanding General, 1st Armored Group) /40]
- A. **Chief of Staff, 2nd Cavalry Division** (08/22/39): LCol. Lejax (Chief of Staff, 2nd Light Division) 02/10/40 dissolved.
- B. *Components* - **2nd Cavalry Division** (08/22/39)
    1. **3rd Cavalry Brigade**
    2. **4th Cavalry Brigade**
    3. **2nd Armored Car (Automitrailleuses) Regiment**
    4. **73rd Artillery Regiment**

3rd Cavalry Division (08/27/39, Second Army; 08/28/39, XXI Army Corps; 09/04/39, Third Army; 09/14/39, Colonial Army Corps; 09/16/39, Third Army; 10/02/39 XXI Army Corps; 01/21/40, Third Army; 02/10/40, redesignated **3rd Light Division**): /38 MG Robert-Marie-Eduardo Petiet (Commanding General, 3rd Light Division) 02/10/40 redesignated **3rd Light Division** - see **3rd Light Cavalry Division**.
- A. **Chief of Staff, 3rd Cavalry Division** (08/27/39): LCol. de Villavielle (Chief of Staff, 3rd Light Division) 02/10/40 dissolved.
- B. *Components* - **3rd Cavalry Division** (08/27/39)
    1. **5th Cavalry Brigade**
    2. **6th Cavalry Brigade**
    3. **3rd Armored Car (Automitrailleuses) Regiment**
    4. **72nd Artillery Regiment**

Light Cavalry Divisions
[Division Légère de Cavalerie [DLC]]

1st Light Cavalry Division (02/10/40, as **1st Light Division**; 02/10/40, Ninth Army; 03/03/40, redesignated **1st Light Cavalry Division**; 05/13/40, 18th Infantry Division; 06/10/40, cease to exist and disbanded): **1st Light Division** 02/10/40 MG Jacques-Marie-Toussaint d'Arras (Commanding General, 1st Light Cavalry Division) 03/03/40 redesignated **1st Light Cavalry Division** 03/03/40 MG Jacques-Marie-Toussaint d'Arras (/49, arrested and charged with collaboration but was acquitted later that year) 06/10/40 ceased to exist and disbanded.
- A. **Chief of Staff, 1st Light Division** (02/10/40): Maj. de Truchis de Varenne (Chief of Staff, 1st Light Cvalry Division) 03/03/40 redesignated **Chief of Staff, 1st Light Cavalry Division** 03/03/40 Maj. de Truchis de Varenne 06/10/40 dissolved.
- B. *Components* - **1st Light Cavalry Division** (03/03/40)
  1. **11th Light Mechanized Infantry Brigade**
  2. **2nd Cavalry Brigade**
  3. **75th Artillery Regiment**

2nd Light Cavalry Division (02/10/40, as **2nd Light Division**; 02/10/40, Second Army; 03/05/40, redesignated **2nd Light Cavalry Division**; 05/15/40, XXI Army Corps; 05/23/40, Second Army; 05/24/40, Group A (Seventh Army); 05/27/40, Tenth Army; 05/31/40, IX Army Corps; 06/25/40, disbanded): **2nd Light Division** 02/10/40 MG André Berniquet (Commanding General, 2nd Light Cavalry Division) 03/05/40 redesignated **2nd Light Cavalry Division** 03/05/40 MG André Berniquet (killed in action) 06/11/40 BG Paul-Constant-Amédée Gastey (?   ) 06/25/40 disbanded.
- A. **Chief of Staff, 2nd Light Division** (02/10/40): LCol. Lejax (Chief of Staff, 2nd Light Cavalry Division) 03/05/40 redesignated **Chief of Staff, 2nd Light Cavalry Division** 03/05/39 LCol. Lejax 06/25/40 dissolved.
- B. *Components* - **2nd Light Cavalry Division** (03/05/40)
  1. **12th Light Mechanized Infantry Brigade**
  2. **3rd Cavalry Brigade**
  3. **73rd Artillery Regiment**

3rd Light Cavalry Division (02/01/40, as **3rd Light Division**; 02/10/40, Third Army; 03/05/40, redesignated **3rd Light Cavalry Division**; 05/15/40, Sixth Army; 05/21/40, Seventh Army; 05/23/40, Group A; 05/29/40, Tenth Army; 06/01/40, IX Army Corps; 06/0-9/40, III Army Corps; 06/13/40, Tenth Army Reserve; 06/14/40, Tenth Army; 06/19/40, III Army Corps; 06/25/40, disbanded): **3rd Light Division** 02/10/40 MG Robert-Marie-Eduardo Petiet (Commanding General, 3rd Light Cavalry Division) 03/05/40 redesignated **3rd Light Cavalry Division** 03/05/40 MG Robert-Marie-Eduardo Petiet [+ 06/12/40, Commanding General, Petiet Group] (Head, Reorganization of the Cavalry Controller; /40, President, Commission Reviewing Citations) 06/25/40 disbanded.
- A. **Chief of Staff, 3rd Light Division** (02/10/40): LCol. de Villavielle (Chief of Staff, 3rd Light Cavalry Division) 03/05/40 redesignated **Chief of Staff, 3rd Light Cavalry Division** 03/05/39 LCol. de Villavielle 05/30/40 Maj. de Virel 06/25/40 dissolved.

B. ***Components*** - **3rd Light Cavalry Division** (03/05/40)
   1. **13th Light Mechanized Infantry Brigade**
   2. **5th Cavalry Brigade**
   3. **72nd Artillery Regiment**

4th Light Cavalry Division (02/16/40, General Headquarters Reserve; 03/16/40, Ninth Army; 03/18/40, XI Army Corps; 05/10/40, Ninth Army; 05/13/40, II Army Corps; 05/21/40, General Headquarters Reserve; 06/05/40, disbanded): MG Paul-Louis-Arthur Barbe (killed in action) 05/15/40 Col. André Marteau (Commanding General, 7th Light Mechanized Division) 06/05/40 disbanded.
A. **Chief of Staff, 4th Light Cavalry Division** (02/16/40): Maj. Friess (Chief of Staff, 7th Light Mechanized Division) 06/05/40 dissolved.
B. ***Components*** - **4th Light Cavalry Division** (02/16/40)
   1. **14th Light Mechanized Infantry Brigade**
   2. **4th Cavalry Brigade**
   3. **77th Artillery Regiment**

5th Light Cavalry Division (02/15/40, from **5th Light Division**; 02/25/40, Second Army; 03/05/40, redesignated **5th Light Cavalry Division**; 05/13/40, X Army Corps; 05/14/40, XXI Army Corps; 05/14/40, Group Touchon; 05/15/40, X Army Corps; 05/17/40, Second Army; 05/23/40, Group A; 05/27/40, Tenth Army; 06/08/40, IX Army Corps; 06/12/40, captured at St-Valéry-en-Caux and disbanded): **5th Light Division** 02/15/40 vacant 02/25/40 MG Marie-Jacques-Henri Chanoine (Commanding General, 5th Light Cavalry Division) 03/05/40 redesignated **5th Light Cavalry Division** 03/05/40 MG Marie-Jacques-Henri Chanoine (German prisoner-of-war; /41, released; /41, retired) 06/12/40 captured and disbanded.
A. **Chief of Staff, 5th Light Cavalry Division** (02/15/40): Maj. de Virieu 06/12/40 dissolved.
B. ***Components*** - **5th Light Cavalry Division** (02/25/40)
   1. **15th Light Mechanized Infantry Brigade**
   2. **6th Cavalry Brigade**
   3. **77th Artillery Regiment**

6th Light Cavalry Division (mobilized in Oran area; 03/40, North African Theater of Operations): BG Denis-Marie-Joseph-Félix Clouet des Perruches (?) /40
A. **Chief of Staff, 6th Light Cavalry Division** (03/40): unknown?
B. ***Components*** - **6th Light Cavalry Division** (03/40)
   1. **16th Light Mechanized Infantry Brigade**
   2. **7th Cavalry Brigade**
   3. **1st Colonial Motorized Artillery Regiment**

Cavalry, Levant (Middle East): /41 BG Amédée-Paul-Georges-Joseph Keime (Commanding General, Troops, South Syria) /41

Light Mechanized Divisions
[Division Légère Mécanique [DLM]]

1st Light Mechanized Division (08/22/39, Ministry of War; 08/26/39, General Headquarters Reserve (Ardennes Army Department Zone and Second Army Zone); 09/10/39, General Headquarters Reserve (Second Army Zone); 11/10/39, Cavalry Corps; 11/22/39, General Headquarters Reserve (First Army Zone); 12/26/39, Cavalry Corps; 03/26/40, Seventh Army; 05/16/40, First Army; 05/17/40, Ninth Army; 05/19/40, Cavalry Corps; 06/20/40, Army of Paris; 06/21/40, Cavalry Corps; 06/25/40, disbanded): vacant 08/27/39 BG François Picard (?) 05/23/40 Col. de Beauchesne 06/25/40 disbanded.

A. **Chief of Staff, 1st Light Mechanized Division** (08/22/39): Maj. Bonvalot 01/25/40 Maj. Clay 06/25/40 dissolved.
B. *Components - 1st Light Mechanized Division* (09/02/40)
   1. **1st Light Mechanized (Armored) Brigade**
   2. **2nd Light Mechanized (Infantry) Brigade**
   3. **74th Mechanized Artillery Regiment**

2nd Light Mechanized Division (08/22/39, Ministry of War; 08/26/39, General Headquarters Reserve (First Army Zone); 11/10/39, Cavalry Corps; 11/22/39, General Headquarters Reserve; 12/26/39, Cavalry Corps; 05/15/40, V Army Corps; 05/17/40, Cavalry Corps; 05/26/40, British II Army Corps; 05/29/40, First Army; 05/30/40, Cavalry Corps; 06/13/40, X Army Corps; 06/24/40 Group Bougrain; 06/25/40, disbanded): MG Félix-René Altmayer (Commanding General, V Motorized Army Corps) 01/13/40 BG Gabriel-Marie-Joseph Bougrain (?) 06/25/40 disbanded.

A. **Chief of Staff, 2nd Light Mechanized Division** (08/22/39): LCol. de Blois 06/25/40 dissolved.
B. *Components - 2nd Light Mechanized Division* (09/02/39)
   1. **3rd Light Mechanized (Armored) Brigade**
   2. **4th Light Mechanized (Infantry) Brigade**
   3. **71st Mechanized Artillery Regiment**

3rd Light Mechanized Division (02/01/40, General Headquarters Reserve; 02/24/40, Cavalry Corps; 03/19/40, First Army; 03/26/40, Cavalry Corps; 05/26/40, First Army Reserve; 05/27/40, Cavalry Corps; 06/11/40, III Army Corps; 06/12/40, Group Petiet; 06/14/40, Cavalry Corps; 06/23/40, disbanded): MG Jean-Léon-Albert Langlois (Commanding General, Cavalry Corps) 05/26/40 BG Pierre-Jules-André-Marie de La Font Chabert (Commanding General, 4th Armored Division) 06/06/40 BG Marie-Joseph-Eugène Testard (?) 06/23/40 disbanded.

A. **Chief of Staff, 3rd Light Mechanized (Armored) Division** (02/01/40): Maj. Demange 06/21/40 Capt. [Army] de Brantes 06/23/40 dissolved.
B. *Components - 3rd Light Mechanized Division* (02/01/40)
   1. **5th Light Mechanized (Armored) Brigade**
   2. **6th Light Mechanized (Infantry) Brigade**
   3. **76th Mechanized Artillery Regiment**

4th Light Mechanized Division (06/10/40, at Rambouillet; 06/11/40, Seventh Army; 06/14/40, Welvert Mechanized Group; 06/19/40, XVII Army Corps; 06/20/40, Welvert Mechanized Group; 06/25/40, disbanded): Col. Roger-Alexander-Louis Leyer (/43, Chief of the Army General Staff) 06/25/40 disbanded.
- A. **Chief of Staff, 4th Light Mechanized Division** (06/10/40): Capt. [Army] de Villeneuve-Escalon 06/13/40 Capt. [Army] Daumont 06/25/40 dissolved.
- B. *Components - 4th Light Mechanized Division* (06/10/40)
  1. **1st Armored Car (Automitrailleuses) Regiment**
  2. **7th Mechanized Dragoon Infantry Regiment**
  3. **1st Mechanized Chasseurs Cavalry Regiment**
  4. **75th Mechanized Artillery Regiment**

7th Light Mechanized Division (06/05/40, in the Limours region; 06/05/40, General Headquarters Reserve; 06/08/40, Armored Group 2; 06/11/40, Fourth Army; 06/12/40, 82nd African Infantry Division; 06/13/40, XXIII Army Corps; 06/17/40, Second Army; 06/18/40, VIII Army Corps; 06/19/40, 14th Infantry Division; 06/21/40, Fourth Army; 06/25/40, disbanded): BG André Marteau (?) 06/25/40 disbanded.
- A. **Chief of Staff, 7th Light Mechanized Division** (06/05/40): Maj. Friess 06/25/40 dissolved.
- B. *Components - 7th Light Mechanized Division* (06/05/40)
  1. **14th Light Mechanized (Armored) Brigade**
  2. **4th Light Mechanized Cavalry Brigade**
  3. **77th Mechanized Artillery Regiment**

Armored Division
[Division Cuirassée de Reserve [DCR]]

1st Armored (Cuirassier) Division (01/01/40; 01/16/40, General Headquarters Reserve; 05/10/40, First Army Reserve; 05/14/40, XI Army Corps; 05/17/40, dispersed; 05/31/40, disbanded; 06/01/40, reformed and assigned, to General Headquarters Reserve; 06/05/40, Seventh Army and I Army Corps; 06/07/40, 3rd Army Group Reserve; 06/08/40, Seventh Army and I Army Corps; 06/10/40, Seventh Army; 06/13/40, Welvert Mechanized Group; 06/17/40, Sixth Army; 06/19/40, XVII Army Corps; 06/25/40, disbanded): **1st Armored (Cuirassier) Division (#1)** 010/140 vacant 01/15/40 BG Marie-Germain-Christian Bruneau (to /45, German prisoner-of-war; /45, retired) 05/19/40 Col. Pierre Sandrier 05/31/40 disbanded; reformed **1st Armored (Cuirassier) Division (#2)** 06/01/40 BG Marie-Joseph-Edmond Welvert [+ 05/17/40 to 06/02/40, Commanding General, I Armored Group or Welvert Mechanized Group; + Armor Commander, Sixth Army] (11/08/42, Commanding General, Constantine Territory Division) 06/25/40 disbanded.

- A. **Chief of Staff, 1st Armored Division** (01/01/40): Maj. Jousseaume de la Bretesche 06/25/40 dissolved.
- B. *Components - 1st Armored Division* (01/16/40)
    1. **1st Heavy Armored Half-Brigade**
    2. **3rd Light Armored Half-Brigade**
    3. **305th Mechanized Artillery Regiment**

2nd Armored (Cuirassier) Division (01/16/40; 05/13/40, General Headquarters Reserve; 05/14/40, Ninth Army; 05/16/40, Sixth Army and Ninth Army; 05/20/40, 3rd Army Group; 05/23/40, I Army Corps; 05/29/40, X Army Corps and Seventh Army Reserve; 06/01/40, Tenth Army; 06/03/40, British 51st Infantry Division; 06/05/40, Tenth Army; 06/06/40, X Army Corps; 06/07/40, IX Army Corps; 06/10/40, Armored Group; 06/18/40 Welvert Group; 06/19/40, VII Army Corps; 06/22/40, Sixth Army; 06/23/40, VII Army Corps; 06/25/40, disbanded): BG Albert-Charles-Émile Bruché (?) 05/20/40 Col. Perre 06/25/40 disbanded.

- A. **Chief of Staff, 2nd Armored Division** (01/16/40): Maj. Favier 06/25/40 dissolved.
- B. *Components - 2nd Armored Division* (01/16/40)
    1. **2nd Heavy Armored Half-Brigade**
    2. **4th Light Armored Half-Brigade**
    4. **300th Mechanized Artillery Regiment**

3rd Armored (Cuirassier) Division (03/01/40; 03/20/40, Armored Group; 05/12/40, Second Army; 05/14/40, XXI Army Corps; 05/19/40, Second Army Reserve; 05/23/40, XXI Army Corps; 05/25/40, First Army Reserve; 05/30/40, Second Army Reserve; 06/07/40, Armored Group 2; 06/09/40, Fourth Army; 06/10/40, Fourth Army and VIII Army Corps; 06/14/40, XVIII Army Corps; 06/18/40, disbanded): vacant 03/20/40 BG Georges-Louis-Marie Brocard (in reserve; /43, retired) 05/16/40 Col. Louis-Léon-Marie-André Buisson (Commanding General, II Armored Group) 06/07/40 Col. Le Brigant 06/11/40 BG Louis-Léon-Marie-André Buisson [+ 06/16/40, Commanding General, 240th Light Infantry Division] (German prisoner-of-war) 06/18/40 disbanded.

A. **Chief of Staff, 3rd Armored Division** (03/01/40): LCol. Alain-Robert-Étienne Devaux 06/18/40 dissolved.
B. *Components - 3rd Armored Division* (03/20/40)
   1. **5th Heavy Armored Half-Brigade**
   2. **7th Light Armored Half-Brigade**
   4. **319th Mechanized Artillery Regiment**

4th Armored (Cuirassier) Division (05/15/40, General Headquarters Reserve; 05/16/40, Sixth Army; 05/21/40, Seventh Army; 05/23/40, Group A; 05/30/40, Tenth Army; 06/01/40 Delestraint Armored Group; 06/06/40, XXV Army Corps; 06/09/40, Armored Group; 06/12/40, X Army Corps and Armored Group; 06/20/40, XXV Army Group; 06/23/40, Bougrain Mechanized Group (2nd Light Mechanized Division); 06/25/40, disbanded): Col. Charles-André-Joseph-Marie de Gaulle (Undersecretary of National Defense) 06/06/40 Col. Paul-Arthur-Marie Chaudessolle 06/07/40 BG Pierre-Jules-André-Marie de La Font Chabert (Commanding General, 8th Cavalry Brigade) 06/25/40 disbanded.
A. **Deputy Commander, 4th Armored Division** (05/15/40): Col. Paul-Arthur-Marie Chaudessolle [+ 06/06/40 to 06/07/40, acting Commanding Officer, 4th Armored Division] 06/25/40 dissolved.
B. **Chief of Staff, 4th Armored Division** (05/15/40): LCol. Marcel Rime-Bruneau (Chief of Staff, Military District XII) 05/23/40 Maj. Raymond-Emmanuel-Marie-Siméon Chomel 06/06/40 Maj. Faivre 06/25/40 dissolved.
C. *Components - 4th Armored Division* (05/15/40)
   1. **6th Heavy Armored Half-Brigade**
   2. **8th Light Armored Half-Brigade**

Fortress Infantry Divisions

101st Fortress Infantry Division (03/16/40, from **Maubeuge Fortified Sector**, in V Army Corps; 05/01/40, First Army; 05/24/40, III Army Corps; 06/25/40, disbanded): MG Louis-Ernest Béjard [+ 05/26/40, Commanding General l'Escaut Fortified Sector] 06/25/40 disbanded.
- A. **Chief of Staff, 101st Fortress Infantry Division** (03/16/40): Maj. Leroy 06/25/40 dissolved.
- B. *Components - 101st Fortress Infantry Division* (03/16/40)
    1. **84th Fortress Infantry Regiment**
    2. **87th Fortress Infantry Regiment**
    3. **13th Regional Protection Infantry Regiment**
    4. **18th Regional Construction Engineers (Travailleurs) Regiment**
    5. **19th Regional Construction Engineers (Travailleurs) Regiment**

102nd Fortress Infantry Division (01/01/40, from **Ardennes Defense Sector**, IV Army Corps; 01/11/40, XXIV Army Corps; 01/20/40, XLI Fortress Army Corps; 06/25/40, disbanded): MG François-Arthur Portzert [+ to 01/25/40, Commanding General, 52nd Infantry Division] (German prisoner-of-war) 06/25/40 disbanded.
- A. **Chief of Staff, 102nd Fortress Infantry Division** (01/01/40): Maj. Lafranc de Pompignan 06/25/40 dissolved.
- B. *Components - 102nd Fortress Infantry Division* (01/20/40)
    1. **148th Fortress Infantry Regiment**
    2. **42nd Colonial Infantry Demi-Brigade**
    3. **52nd Colonial Infantry Demi-Brigade**
    4. **160th Static Artillery Regiment**

103rd Fortress Infantry Division (03/05/40, from **Ras-Rhin Fortified Sector**, XVII Army Corps; 06/09/40, Fifth Army; 06/21/40, XLI Fortress Army Corps; 06/23/40, surrendered and disbanded): MG Gaston-Ernest Renondeau (Commanding General, XLII Fortress Army Corps) 05/25/40 BG Ainé-Gabriel-Hilaire-Jehan-Marie Sarrebourse de la Guillonnière [+ Commanding General, 62nd Infantry Division] 05/28/40 MG Frédéric Vallée (?) 06/23/40 surrendered and disbanded.
- A. **Chief of Staff, 103rd Fortress Infantry Division** (03/05/40): LCol. Remords 06/23/40 dissolved.
- B. *Components - 103rd Fortress Infantry Division* (03/05/40)
    1. **34th Fortress Infantry Regiment**
    2. **172nd Fortress Infantry Regiment**
    3. **226th Infantry Regiment**
    4. **237th Infantry Regiment**
    5. **155th Static Artillery Regiment**

104th Fortress Infantry Division (03/16/40, from **Colmar Fortified Sector**, XVII Army Corps; 05/07/40, XIII Army Corps; 05/27/40, XII Army Corps; 06/17/40, XIII Army Corps; 06/22/40, captured and disbanded): BG Edouard-Sylvain Cousse (German prisoner-of-war) 06/22/40 disbanded.

A. **Chief of Staff, 104th Fortress Infantry Division** (03/16/40): Maj. Gouget de Landres 06/22/40 dissolved.
B. *Components* - **104th Fortress Infantry Division** (03/16/40)
   1. **28th Fortress Infantry Regiment**
   2. **42nd Fortress Infantry Regiment**
   3. **242nd Infantry Regiment**

105th Fortress Infantry Division (03/16/40, from **Mulhouse Fortified Sector**, XIII Army Corps; 06/18/40, XLIV Fortress Army Corps; 06/20/40?, captured and disbanded): BG Pierre-Désiré-Robert Didio (?) 06/20/40? disbanded.
A. **Chief of Staff, 105th Fortress Infantry Division** (03/16/40): Maj. Leyraud 06/20/40? dissolved.
B. *Components* - **105th Fortress Infantry Division** (03/16/40)
   1. **10th Fortress Infantry Regiment**

Commands Equivalant to Divisions

Military-Governor, Metz: /40 MG Edouard-Octave-Jules Brussaux

Military-Governor, Toulouse: /44 MG Philibert Collet [+ Commanding General, Division Meknès].

French Somalia: /39 BG Paul-Louis-Victor-Marie Legentilhomme (replaced; /41, Commanding General, Free French Forces in Sudan & Eritrea) 06/27/40

Madagascar: /37 Col. Guillaume-Charles Roucaud (Commanding General, 1st Colonial Infantry Division) 04/02/40 unknown? 05/05/42 becomes **Madagascar Occupied Territories Administrators [Great Britain Command]** 05/05/42 MG Robert Grice Sturges [British] [+ Commander of Brirtish Forces] 11/05/42; 09/25/42 ANTHONY SILLERY [British] 01/07/43 occupied territories turned over to Free French; **Madagascar** 01/07/43 LG Paul-Louis-Victor-Marie Legentilhomme [+ Free French War Commissioner] (Deputy Commissioner of National Defense)05/03/43
    A.   **Director, Intendent [Quartermaster] Service Madagascar**: /38 BG Marie-Nicolas-Paul Poirel
    B.   **Director, Medical Services Madagascar**: /38 BG Maurice-Marie Blancdard (?) /4? BG François-Louis Toullec

Commanding General, Cambodia: /40 BG Yves-Marie-Jacques-Guillaume de Boisboissel (Deputy Commander, Military District XIX) /41

East Saharian Front [Front Est Saharien] (North Africa; forward defensive zone consisting of the Territory of the Oasis, the El-Oued annex of the Territory of Touggourt, and the area around Fort Saint in Tunisia; 09/19/39, the whole Territory of Touggourt was added along with the Biskra area from Batna Subdivision of Constantine; 04/15/40, the front was altered again with the area of southern Tunisia south of the Mechiguig-Hamajiet El Guelta line): Col. Azman
    A.   **Forward Troops, East Saharian Front**: Col. Carbillet

Commanding General, Southeast Sahara: 06/14/40 MG Robert-Marie-Jules-Camille Boissau (Commanding General, Oran Territorial Division) 11/08/42?

North Tunisian Front [Commandant de Front Tunisien du Nord] (/39, North Africa; commanded by Commanding Officer, 88th African Infantry Division): MG Jean-Pierre-Hector-Marie Bessières [+ Commanding General, 88th African Infantry Division]
    A.   *Components* - **North Tunisian Front**
        1.   **88th African Infantry Division**

Commander of Troops, North Syria [Général Commandant Troupes de Territorie Nord-Syrie et Euphrates] (Middle East): /38 BG Henri Monet (?) /40

Commander of Troops, South Syria [Général Commandant Troupes de Territorie

Sud-Syrie] (Middle East): /38 BG François-Pierre-Louis Keller (Commanding General, Army Corps L, Levant) /39 unknown? /39 BG François-Pierre-Louis Keller (Commanding General, 42nd Infantry Division) 04/30/40 BG Edmond-Gustavé-Armand Foiret (?) /41 BG Joseph-Antoine-Sylvain-Raoul de Verdillac (Deputy Commander-in-Chief, Levant) /41 BG Amédée-Paul-Georges-Joseph Keime (?) /41 BG Étienne-Charles-Ferdinand Delhomme

Commander of Troops, Lebanon [Général Commandant Troupes de Territorie Liban] (Middle East): /39 Col. Georges-Jacques-Frédéric Beucler 12/40 MG Paul-Hippolyte Arlabosse (Commanding General, Oran Territorial Division) /41 BG Georges-Jacques-Frédéric Beucler (/43, French Liaison Officer to United States Fifth Army) /42 MG Alfred-Maurice Cazaud [+ Commanding General, Division Côtière] (36th Infantry Division (#2)) 02/45.
A.   **Deputy Commander of Troops, Lebanon**: /41 Col. Paul-Henri-Maurice Garnier

Commanding General, French Forces in China: /38 Col. Henri-Frédéric-Paul Casseville (Director, Ministry of Colonies) /40 unknown? /45 MG Marcel-Jean-Marie Alessandri (High Commissioner, Northern Zone, Indochina) /45.

Western Sahara Detachment [Detachément Shara L'Ouest] (/43): MG Achille-Paul-Théophile Delay

Group Cartier (06/22/40; 06/25/40, disbanded): MG Georges-Eugène-Alphonse Cartier (?) 06/25/40 disbanded.

Group Conne (/43, temporary unit): MG Pierre-Félix Conne (Commanding General, Division Algiers) /43 disbanded.

Commands of the Maginot Line (Division Commands)

[Three types: Type A - Main Fortified Part of Maginot Line; Type B - Rest of Maginot Line; Type C - Along border with Spain]

Flanders Defense Sector (Secteur Défensif des Flandres)/Flanders Fortified Sector (Secteur Fortifié des Flandres) (Type B; 08/21/39, First Army; 09/08/39, III Army Corps; 10/03/39, XVI Army Corps; 11/15/39, Seventh Army; 01/20/40 upgraded to Fortified Sector, Seventh Army; 05/24/40, XVI Army Corps; 06/-4/40, captured): **Flanders Defense Sector** /38 BG Julian-Maurice Tencé [+ Military-Governor, Dunkerque, Military District I] (Commanding General, Northern Group; 12/27/39, Commanding General, Belfort Fortified Region) 08/21/39 BG Léon-Alexandre Rapenne 11/07/39 BG Robert-Jules-Eugène Barthélémy (?) 11/21/39 BG Léon-Alexandre Rapenne (Commanding General, Flanders Fortified Sector) 01/20/40 upgraded to **Flanders Fortified Sector** 01/20/40 BG Léon-Alexandre Rapenne (retired) 06/04/40 captured.
- A. **Chief of Staff, Flanders Defense Sector/Flanders Fortified Sector** (08/21/39): Maj. Chamboredon 06/04/40 dissolved.

Maubeuge Fortified Sector (Secteur Fortifié de Maubeuge) (Type B; 08/23/39, Military District I; 09/05/39, Esc-Maub Fortified Section Group; 10/01/39, V Army Corps; 03/16/40, disbanded and used to form the **101st Fortress Infantry Division**): BG Henri-Stanislas-Auguste Hanaut (Commanding General, Escaut Fortified Sector) 01/01/40 MG Louis-Ernest Béjard (Commanding General, 101st Fortress Infantry Division) 03/16/40 disbanded and used to form the **101st Fortress Infantry Division** - see **101st Fortress Infantry Division**.
- A. **Chief of Staff, Maubeuge Fortified Sector** (08/23/39): Maj. Leroy (Chief of Staff, 101st Fortress Infantry Division) 03/16/40 dissolved.
- B. *Components* - Maubeuge Fortified Sector (09/02/39)
    1. **84th Fortress Infantry Regiment**
    2. **87th Fortress Infantry Regiment**
    3. **13th Regional Protection Infantry Regiment**
    4. **18th Regional Construction Engineers (Travailleurs) Regiment**
    5. **19th Regional Construction Engineers (Travailleurs) Regiment**

Montmédy Fortified Sector (Secteur Fortifié de Montmédy) (Type A; 08/22/39, Military District I; 08/26/39, XXI Army Corps; 09/14/39, "F" Army Corps; 10/12/39 X Army Corps; 03/16/40, Second Army; 05/24/40, XVIII Army Corps; 06/13/40, Verdun Fortified Region; 06/14/40, Dubuisson Group; 06/21/40, surrendered): MG Maurice-Alphonse-Alfred Burtaire (Commanding General, Light Division Burtaire) 06/21/40, surrendered.
- A. **Chief of Staff, Montmédy Fortified Sector** (08/22/39): Maj. Georgin 06/21/40 dissolved.
- B. *Components* - Montmédy Fortified Sector (09/02/39)
    1. **136th Fortress Infantry Regiment**
    2. **147th Fortress Infantry Regiment**
    3. **156th Fortress Infantry Regiment**

    4.   **99th Fortress Artillery Regiment**

Crusnes Fortified Sector (Secteur Fortifié de Crusnes) (Type A; 08/21/39, Metz Fortified Region; 09/15/39, XXI Army Corps; 03/16/40, disbanded and with **Metz Fortified Region** used to form the **XLII Fortress Army Corps**): /38 Col. Pierre-François-Joseph Tarrit (Infantry Commander, 3rd North African Infantry Division) 08/21/39 Col. Maurice-Georges-Constant Durand (04/18/40, Commanding Officer, 2nd Light Mountain Infantry Division) 09/15/39 Col. Miserey 03/16/40 disbanded and with **Metz Fortified Region** used to form the **XLII Fortress Army Corps** - see **XLII Fortress Army Corps**.
A.   **Chief of Staff, Crusnes Fortified Sector** (08/21/39): Maj. Colin 03/16/40 dissolved.
B.   *Components* - **Crusnes Fortified Sector** (09/02/39)
    1.   **128th Fortress Infantry Regiment**
    2.   **132nd Fortress Infantry Regiment**
    3.   **139th Fortress Infantry Regiment**
    4.   **149th Fortress Infantry Regiment**

Thionville Fortified Sector (Secteur Fortifié de Thionville) (Type A; 08/22/39, Metz Fortified Region; 09/26/39, Colonial Army Corps; 05/22/40, VI Army Corps; 06/12/40, redesignated **Poisot March Division**; 06/21/40, captured): **Thionville Fortified Sector** 08/22/39 vacant 09/02/39 BG Edouard-Sylvain Cousse (Commanding General, Colmar Fortified Sector) 01/01/40 MG Louis-Gustavé-Abel Poisot (Commanding General, Poisot March Division) 06/12/40 redesignated **Poisot March Division** 06/12/40 MG Louis-Gustavé-Abel Poisot (?) 06/21/40 captured.
A.   **Chief of Staff, Thionville Fortified Sector** (09/02/39): Maj. Vuillaume 06/21/40 dissolved.
B.   *Components* - **Thionville Fortified Sector** (09/02/39)
    1.   **167th Fortress Infantry Regiment**
    2.   **168th Fortress Infantry Regiment**
    3.   **169th Fortress Infantry Regiment**
    4.   **70th Fortress Mixed Artillery Regiment**
    5.   **151st Static Artillery Regiment**

Boulay Fortified Sector (Secteur Fortifié de Boulay) (Type A; 08/22/39, Metz Fortified Region; 09/25/39, VI Army Corps; 06/20/40, captured): Col. Jean-Joseph-René Besse (Commanding Officer, March Division Besse) 06/20/40 captured.
A.   **Chief of Staff, Boulay Fortified Sector** (08/22/39): Maj. Claudel /40? Maj. Eberle 05/40 Maj. Francon 06/20/40 dissolved.
B.   *Components* - **Boulay Fortified Sector** (09/02/39)
    1.   **167th Fortress Infantry Regiment**
    2.   **168th Fortress Infantry Regiment**
    3.   **169th Fortress Infantry Regiment**
    4.   **70th Fortress Mixed Artillery Regiment**
    5.   **151st Static Artillery Regiment**

Faulquemort Fortified Sector (Secteur Fortifié de Faulquemort) (Type A; 08/21/39, Metz Fortified Region; 09/24/39, XVII Army Corps; 10/04/39, IX Army Corps; 05/27/40, XX

Army Corps; 07/02/40, captured): vacant 09/02/39 BG Jules-Georges-Jacques Baudolin (retired) 04/14/40 BG Marie-Joseph-Edmond Mendras [+ Commanding General, 47th Infantry Division] 04/28/40 BG Marie-Charles-Henri de Girval (?) 07/02/40 captured.
- A. **Chief of Staff, Faulquemort Fortified Sector** (08/21/39): Maj. Vergoz 07/02/40 dissolved.
- B. *Components* - **Faulquemort Fortified Sector** (09/02/39)
    1. **146th Fortress Infantry Regiment**
    2. **156th Fortress Infantry Regiment**
    3. **160th Fortress Infantry Regiment**
    4. **39th Fortress Mixed Artillery Regiment**
    5. **163rd Static Artillery Regiment**

Sarre Defense Sector (Secteur Défensif de la Sarre)/ Sarre Fortified Sector (Secteur Fortifié de la Sarre) (Type A; 08/21/39, Lauter Fortified Region; 08/22/39, Military District XX; 08/25/39, XX Army Corps; 09/16/39, IX Army Corps; 10/04/39, XX Army Corps; 03/15/40, redesignated **Sarre Fortified Sector**; 05/31/40, Sarre Group; 06/14/40 XX Army Corps; 06/14/40, becomes **Group Dagnan**): **Sarre Defense Sector** /38 BG Georges-Edgar Boucher (Commanding General, 5th Motorized Infantry Division) 01/02/40 Col. Dagnan (Commanding Officer, Sarre Fortified Sector) 03/01/40 redesignated **Sarre Fortified Sector** 03/01/40 Col. Marcel Dagnan 06/14/40 becomes **Group Dagnan** 06/14/40 Col. Marcel Dagnan
- A. **Chief of Staff, Sarre Defense Sector** (08/21/39): LCol. Didier (Chief of Staff, Sarre Fortified Sector) 03/01/40 redesignated **Chief of Staff, Sarre Fortified Sector** 03/01/40 LCol. Didier /40? Maj. Jacquet 06/14/40 becomes **Chief of Staff, Group Dagnan** 06/14/40 Maj. Jacquet
- B. *Components* - **Sarre Defense Sector** (09/02/39)
    1. **69th Fortress Infantry Regiment**
    2. **82nd Fortress Infantry Regiment**
    3. **174th Fortress Infantry Regiment**
    4. **49th Fortress Artillery Regiment**
    5. **166th Static Artillery Regiment**

Dagnan Provisional Defense Sector (Secteur Défensif Provisoire Dagnan) (09/16/39 by Fourth Army; 09/16/39, XX Army Corps; 10/04/39 Sarre Defense Sector; 10/05/39, dissolved): Col. Marcel Dagnan (01/02/40, Commanding Officer, Sarre Defense Sector) 10/04/39 dissolved.
- A. **Chief of Staff, Dagnan Provisional Defense Sector** (09/16/39): Col. Jean-Étienne Valluy (/43, Director, Colonial Forces) 09/25/39 Maj. Le Masle 10/04/39 dissolved.
- B. *Components* - **Dagnan Provisional Defense Sector** (09/16/39)
    1. **133rd Fortress Infantry Regiment**
    2. **41st Colonial Infantry Regiment**
    3. **51st Colonial Infantry Regiment**

Rohrbach Fortified Sector (Secteur Fortifié de Rohrbach) (Type A; 08/21/39, in Military District XX; 08/21/39, Lauter Fortified Region; 08/22/39, Military District XX; 08/25/39, XX Army Corps; 09/17/39, V Army Corps; 09/25/39, VIII Army Corps; 06/02/40, XLIII Fortress

Army Corps; 07/02/40, surrendered and disbanded): /38 Col. Henri-Aimé Boutignon [+ 09/01/39 to 09/25/39, Commanding General, Sarre Fortified Region; + 09/25/39 to 10/20/39, Commanding General, Fourth Army Fortified Region] (Commanding General, Altkirch Fortified Sector) 10/12/39 BG René-Jacques Mortemart de Boise (Commanding General, 62nd Infantry Division) 05/07/40 BG [Retired '32] Alfred Chastanet (Commanding General, Chastanet March Division de Marche Chastanet) 06/15/40, LCol. Bonlaron 07/02/40 surrendered and disbanded.

A. **Chief of Staff, Rohrbach Fortified Sector** (08/21/39): LCol. Thouvenin 07/02/40 dissolved.
B. *Components - Rohrbach Fortified Sector* (09/02/39)
   1. **133rd Fortress Infantry Regiment**: /39 Col. Victor-Paul-Auguste Duclos (Commanding General, 87th African Infantry Division) 08/29/39
   2. **153rd Fortress Infantry Regiment**: /40 Col. Auguste Alaurent (to /45, German prisoner-of-war) 06/40
   3. **166th Fortress Infantry Regiment**
   4. **59th Fortress Artillery Regiment**
   5. **150th Static Artillery Regiment**

Chastanet March Division (Division de Marche Chastanet) (06/15/40, from most of Rohrbach Fortified Sector; 06/23/40, surrendered and disbanded): BG [Retired '32] Alfred Chastanet (?) 06/23/40 surrendered and disbanded.

Vosges Fortified Sector (Secteur Fortifié des Vosages) (Type A; 08/21/39, in Military District XX; 08/21/39, Lauter Fortified Region; 09/02/39, Fifth Army; 09/07/39, VIII Army Corps; 10/19/39, Lauter Fortified Region; 03/05/40, XLIII Fortress Army Corps; 03/05/40, dissolved; with **Lauter Fortified Region** forms **XLIII Fortress Army Corps**): BG Aldophe-François Vieillard (?) 09/01/39 Col. Lucien-Julien-René André 01/19/40 Col. Lucien-Antoine Regard (Commanding Officer, Haguenau Fortified Sector) 03/05/40 dissolved with **Lauter Fortified Region** forms **XLIII Fortress Army Corps**)

A. **Chief of Staff, Vosges Fortified Sector** (08/21/39): Maj. Costard de Saint-Léger 03/05/40 dissolved.
B. *Components - Vosges Fortified Sector* (09/02/39)
   1. **37th Fortress Infantry Regiment**
   2. **154th Fortress Infantry Regiment**
   3. **165th Fortress Infantry Regiment**
   4. **60th Fortress Artillery Regiment**
   5. **168th Static Artillery Regiment**

Haguenau Fortified Sector (Secteur Fortifié de Haguenau) (Type A; 08/21/39 in Military District XX; 08/21/39, Lauter Fortified Region; 10/08/39, XII Army Corps; 06/18/40, XLIII Fortress Army Corps; 07/02/40, surrendered and disbanded): BG Louis-Ernest Gillier (Commanding General, 8th Colonial Infantry Division) 04/12/40 Col. Lucien-Antoine Regard 07/02/40 surrendered and isbanded.

A. **Chief of Staff, Haguenau Fortified Sector** (08/21/39): Maj. Laherre 05/14/40 LCol. Jacques-Fernand Schwartz (Infantry Commander, Constantine Territory Division) 07/02/40 dissolved.
B. *Components - Haguenau Fortified Sector* (09/02/39)

1. **22ⁿᵈ Fortress Infantry Regiment**
2. **23ʳᵈ Fortress Infantry Regiment**
3. **68ᵗʰ Fortress Infantry Regiment**
4. **79ᵗʰ Fortress Infantry Regiment**
5. **69ᵗʰ Fortress Artillery Regiment**
6. **156ᵗʰ Static Artillery Regiment**

Bas-Rhin Fortified Sector (Secteur Fortifié du Bas-Rhin) (Type A; 08/28/39 in Military District XX; 08/28/39, VIII Army Corps; 09/03/39, Fifth Army; 10/12/39, XVII Army Corps; 03/05/40, dissolved and use to form **103ʳᵈ Fortress Infantry Division**): /38 BG Jules Pichon (?) 01/05/40 MG Gaston-Ernest Renondeau (Commanding General, 103ʳᵈ Fortress Infantry Division) 03/05/40 dissolved and use to form **103ʳᵈ Fortress Infantry Division** - see **103ʳᵈ Fortress Infantry Division**.
  A. **Chief of Staff, Bas-Rhin Fortified Sector** (08/28/39): LCol. Remords (Chief of Staff, 103ʳᵈ Fortress Infantry Division) 03/05/40 dissolved.
  B. *Components* - **Bas-Rhin Fortified Sector** (09/02/39)
      1. **34ᵗʰ Fortress Infantry Regiment**
      2. **70ᵗʰ Fortress Infantry Regiment**
      3. **172ⁿᵈ Fortress Infantry Regiment**
      4. **226ᵗʰ Infantry Regiment**
      5. **155ᵗʰ Static Artillery Regiment**

Altkirch (Franken) Defense Sector (Secteur Défensif Altkirch (Franken)/Altkirch (Franken) Fortified Sector (Secteur Fortifié d'Altkirch (Franken)) (Type B; 08/21/39 in Military District VII; 08/21/39, Belfort Fortified Region 03/16/40, upgraded to **Altkirch (Franken) Fortified Sector**; 03/16/40, XLIV Fortress Army Corps; 06/21/40, 105ᵗʰ Fortress Infantry Division; 06/19/40, captured and disbanded): Col. Gard 10/29/39 BG Henri-Aimé Boutignon [+ Commanding General, 67ᵗʰ Infantry Division] 11/30/39 BG Louis-Germain Girol (03/15/40, Commanding General, Belfort Defense Sector & Belfort Subdivision Group) 12/15/39 BG Joseph-Étienne Salvan [+ to 01/07/40, Commanding General, Mulhouse Fortified Sector] (?) 06/19/40 captured and disbanded.
  A. **Chief of Staff, Altkirch (Franken) Defense Sector** (08/21/39) Capt. ₍ₐᵣₘᵧ₎ Lambelin 04/40 LCol. Perrin 06/19/40 dissolved.
  B. *Components* - **Altkirch (Franken) Defense Sector** (09/02/39)
      1. **12ᵗʰ Fortress Infantry Regiment**
      2. **171ˢᵗ Fortress Infantry Regiment**

Savoie Fortified Sector (Secteur Fortifié de Savoie) (Type B; 08/22/39, Military District XIV; 09/02/39, XIV Army Corps; 06/25/40, disbanded): /38 Col. Georges-Eugène Lestien (Commanding General, 28ᵗʰ Alpine Infantry Division) 08/22/39 unknown? 09/02/39 Col. André Marteau (05/15/40, Commanding Officer, 4ᵗʰ Light Cavalry Division) 01/01/40 Col. Michet de la Baume 06/25/40 disbanded.
  A. **Chief of Staff, Savoie Fortified Sector** (08/22/39): Maj. Chomel de Jarnieu 06/25/40 dissolved.
  B. *Components* - **Savoie Fortified Sector** (09/02/39)
      1. **16ᵗʰ Alpine Fortress Demi-Brigade**

2. **30th Alpine Fortress Demi-Brigade**
3. **164th Static Artillery Regiment**

Dauphiné Fortified Sector (Secteur Fortifié du Dauphiné) (Type B; 09/01/39, XIV Army Corps; 10/15/39, 27th Infantry Division; 11/03/39, XIV Army Corps; 06/25/40, disbanded): /38 BG Georges-Eugène-Alphonse Cartier (Commanding General, 27th Infantry Division) 01/39? Col. Henri-Louis-Léon Cyvogt (Commanding General, Department of Haut-Alps0 06/25/40 disbanded.
A. **Chief of Staff, Dauphiné Fortified Sector** (09/01/40): Maj. Daval 04/26/40 Maj. Languillaire 06/25/40 dissolved.
B. *Components* - **Dauphiné Fortified Sector** (09/02/39)
   1. **75th Alpine Fortress Demi-Brigade**
   2. **157th Alpine Fortress Demi-Brigade**
   3. **154th Static Artillery Regiment**

Alps-Maritimes Fortified Sector (Secteur Fortifié des Alps-Maritimes) (Type A; 08/24/39, Military District XV; 09/02/39, XV Army Corps; 06/25/40, disbanded): MG René-Alphonse-Joseph Magnien (?) 06/25/40 disbanded.
A. **Deputy Commander, Alps-Maritime Fortified Sector**: /38 BG René-Alphonse-Joseph Magnien (Commanding General, Alps-Maritime Fortified Sector) 08/24/39
B. **Chief of Staff, Alps-Maritimes Fortified Sector** (08/24/39): Maj. Lacoste 02/09/40 LCol. Salmon [+ Chief of Staff, 65th Alpine Infantry Division] 06/25/40 dissolved.
C. *Components* - **Alps-Maritimes Fortified Sector** (09/02/39)
   1. **40th Alpine Fortress Demi-Brigade**
   2. **58th Alpine Fortress Demi-Brigade**
   3. **61st Alpine Fortress Demi-Brigade**
   4. **157th Static Artillery Regiment**
   5. **158th Static Artillery Regiment**
   6. **167th Static Artillery Regiment**
D. **Artillery, Alps-Maritimes Fortified Sector**: /38 Col. Gaston-Auguste-Paul Lemière (Artillery Commander, XV Army Corps) 09/02/39

Southern Tunisian Fortified Region (Région Fortifiée du Sud Tunisien) (03/01/40, Southern Tunisian Front): BG Edouard-Georges Berthomé
A. **Chief of Staff, Southern Tunisian Fortified Region** (03/01/40): Maj. Roy
B. *Components* - **Southern Tunisian Fortified Region** (09/02/39)
   1. **5th Sénégalais Tirailleurs (Infantry) Regiment**
   2. **32nd Tunisian Tirailleurs (Infantry) Regiment**
   3. **35th Algerian Tirailleurs (Infantry) Regiment**
   4. **388th African Artillery Regiment**

Divisions in Overseas Colonies and Protectorates
[Under Minister of Colonies]

North Africa
Algeria

Algiers Territorial Division [Division d'Alger] (North Africa; HQ: Algiers, Algeria; 11/14/42, disbanded and used to form **Algerian March Division**; /44, reformed): /35 Col. Auguste-Marie-Émile Laure (Commanding General, Military District IX) /38 Col. Étienne-Paul-Émile-Marie Beynet (Commanding General, 81st African Infantry Division) 09/02/39 unknown? 11/08/42? MG Charles-Emmanuel Mast (Commanding General, Algerian March Division) 11/14/42 disbanded and used to form **Algerian March Division** [see **Algerian March Division**].
- A. *Components* - Algiers Territory Division
    1. **Algiers Subdivision**:
    2. **Miliana Subdivision**:
    3. **Médéa Subdivision**:
- B. *Components* - Algiers Territorial Division (07/40, Vichy France)
    1. **1st Zouaves Infantry Regiment**
    2. **1st Algerian Tirailleurs (Infantry) Regiment**
    3. **5th Algerian Tirailleurs (Infantry) Regiment**
    4. **9th Algerian Tirailleurs (Infantry) Regiment**
    5. **13th Algerian Tirailleurs (Infantry) Regiment**
    6. **29th Algerian Tirailleurs (Infantry) Regiment**
    7. **65th African Artillery Regiment**
    8. **1st Algerian Spahis (Cavalry) Regiment**
    9. **1st African Chasseurs (Armor) Regiment**
- C. **Intendant [Quartermaster] Services, Algiers Territorial Division**: /38 Col. Paul-Georges Willigens

Constantine Territorial Division [Division de Constantine] (North Africa: HQ: Constantine, Algeria; 11/08/42, disbanded): /34 Col. Eugène-Jules Rochard (Commanding General, Military District XVIII) /39 BG Bernard-Marie-Alexis Vergès (Commanding General, 83rd African Infantry Division) 09/01/39 unknown? 06/25/40 MG Bernard-Marie-Alexis Vergès (Commanding General, Morocco) /40 BG François-Napoléon-Henri-Dieudonné Hupel (?) /41 BG Jacques-Fernand Schwartz (/44, acting Commanding General, Military District X) 11/08/42 disbanded and used to form **Constantine March Division** - see **Constantine March Division**.
- A. *Components* - Constantine Territory Division
    1. **Constantine Subdivision**: /36 Col. Victor-Paul-Auguste Duclos [+ Commanding Officer, 3rd Algerian Infantry Brigade] (Commanding General, 133rd Fortress Infantry Regiment) /39

2. **Sétif Subdivision**:
3. **Bône Subdivision**:
4. **Batna Subdivision**:

B. *Components* - **Constantine Territorial Division** (07/40, Vichy France)
   1. **3rd Zouave Regiment**
   2. **3rd Algerian Tirailleurs (Infantry) Regiment**
   3. **7th Algerian Tirailleurs (Infantry) Regiment**
   4. **15th Algerian Tirailleurs (Infantry) Regiment**
   5. **7th African Artillery Regiment**
   6. **3rd Algerian Spahis (Cavalry) Regiment**
   7. **3rd African Chasseurs (Armor) Regiment**

C. **Infantry, Constantine Territorial Division**: 07/02/40 Col. Jacques-Fernand Schwartz (Commanding General, Constantine Territory Division) /41

Oran Territory Division [Division d'Oran] (North Africa; HQ: Oran, Algeria; 05/01/43, redesignated **Oran March Division**): /36 BG Raymond-Jules-Émile Poupinel (Commanding General, XIX Army Corps) 09/39 MG Pierre-Marius-Ernest Gibert (Commanding General, 6th Colonial Infantry Division) 06/11/40 MG Jean-Eugène-Marie Charbonneau (Commanding General, Colonial Forces in France) 12/41 MG Paul-Hippolyte Arlabosse (Commanding General, Vichy 12th Military Division) 11/08/42? MG Robert-Marie-Jules-Camille Boissau (Commanding General, Oran March Division) 05/01/43 redesignated **Oran March Division** - see **Oran March Division**.

A. *Components* - **Oran Territory Division**
   1. **Oran Subdivision**: /38 Col. Jean-Gabriel-Edouard Thomas (Commanding General, 182nd African Infantry Division) 09/39
   2. **Tlemcen Subdivision**: /40 MG Marie-Jules-Victor-Léon François (retired; /46, condemned to five years in prison; /48, pardoned) /42 BG Marcel-Georges François (Deputy Commander, Fèz Territorial Division) /42
   3. **Mascara Subdivision**: /38 Col. Denis-Marie-Joseph-Félix Clouet des Perruches (Commanding General, 3rd Spahis Brigade) 11/03/39 unknown? /42 BG Jean-Louis-Alai Touzet du Vigier [+ Commanding General, 1st Light Mechanized Brigade] (Commanding General, 1st Free French Light Mechanized Brigade) /43
   4. **Mostaganem Subdivision**:

B. *Components* - **Oran Territorial Division** (07/40, Vichy France)
   1. **2nd Zouaves Regiment**
   2. **2nd Algerian Tirailleurs (Infantry) Regiment**
   3. **6th Algerian Tirailleurs (Infantry) Regiment**
   4. **9th Algerian Tirailleurs (Infantry) Regiment**
   5. **66th African Artillery Regiment**
   6. **2nd Algerian Spahis (Cavalry) Regiment**
   7. **2nd African Chasseurs (Armor) Regiment**

Division Algiers (Algeria): /42 MG Agathon-Jules-Joseph Deligne (/48, Inspector-General of Infantry) /43 MG Pierre-Félix Conne (?) /44 BG Jean Breuillac.

Division Constantine (Algeria): /44 MG Raymond-Francis Duval.

Morocco

Casablanca (Independent) Territory Division (Moroccan Army Corps; HQ: Casablanca, Morocco): /39 BG Jean-Baptiste-René-François Rochas (Commanding General, 180th African Infantry Division) 11/01/39 BG Lebrun (?) /42 BG Jean-Sylvain-Louis Roubertie (Commanding General, Military District XIX) 11/08/42 BG Raymond-Charles-Émile Desre (acting; /43, Commanding General, Morocco Army Corps) 11/08/42? MG Marie-Emil-Antoine Béthouart (Head, French Military Mission to Washington, D. C.) /42

A. **Chief of Staff, Casablanca Territorial Division**: /40 Col. Jean Breuillac (Chief of Staff, Tunisia) /40
B. *Components* - **Casablanca Territory Division**
   1. **Casablanca Subdivision**: /38 Col. Jean-Baptiste-René-François Rochas (Commanding General, Casablanca Territory Division) /39
   2. **Rabat Subdivision** (07/31/40, Vichy France): BG Marie-Emil-Antoine Béthouart (Commanding General, Casablanca Territory Division) 11/08/42?
C. *Components* - **Casablanca Territorial Division** (09/12/40, Vichy France)
   1. **1st Morocco Tirailleurs (Infantry) Regiment**
   2. **6th Morocco Tirailleurs (Infantry) Regiment**
   3. **Morocco Colonial Infantry Regiment**
   4. **Morocco Colonial Artillery Regiment**
   5. **5th African Chasseurs Regiment**

Fèz Territory Division (Moroccan Army Corps): /37 MG Amédée-Ferdinand-Auguste Blanc (Commander-in-Chief, Tunisia) /38 unknown? 09/39 BG André-Joseph-Marie Lauzanne (?) /40 MG Georges-Eugène-Joseph Lascroux [+ /41, General Officer Commanding, Morocco] 11/08/42? MG Maurice-Marie Salbert (?) /43 BG Marcel-Georges François (Deputy Commander-in-Chief, Levant) /43

A. **Deputy Commander, Fèz Territory Division**: /42 BG Marcel-Georges François (Commanding General, Fèz Territory Division) /43
B. *Components* - **Fèz Territory Division**
   1. **Fèz Subdivision**: BG Maurice-Marie Salbert (Commanding General, Fèz Territory Division) 11/08/42?
   2. **Taza Subdivision**: /38 Col. André-Joseph-Marie Lauzanne (General Officer Commanding, Fèz Division) /39
C. *Components* - **Fez Territorial Division** (07/40, Vichy France)
   1. **4th Morocco Tirailleurs (Infantry) Regiment**
   2. **5th Morocco Tirailleurs (Infantry) Regiment**
   3. **11th Morocco Tirailleurs (Infantry) Regiment**
   4. **63rd African Artillery Regiment**
   5. **1st Foreign Legion Cavalry Regiment**

Marrakech Territory Division (Moroccan Army Corps; HQ: Marrakech, Morocco; 03/01/43, redesignated **3rd Marrakech Infantry Division**; 06/01/43, renamed **4th Moroccan Mountain Division**): /38 BG François-Marie-Jacques Fougère (Commanding General, XXIV Army Corps) 02/25/40 BG Panescoise 06/25/40 BG Henri-Jules-Jean Martin (Commanding General, 3rd Marrakech Infantry Division) 03/01/43 redesignated **3rd Marrakech Infantry Division** 03/01/43 MG Henri-Jules-Jean Martin (Commanding General, 4th Moroccan Mountain Division) 06/01/43 reformed as **4th Moroccan Mountain Division** - see rebuilt French Army (1943-1944) **4th Moroccan Mountain Division**.
A. *Components - Marrakech Territory Division*
 1. **Marrakech Subdivision**
 2. **Agadir Subdivision**
 3. **Ouarzazate Subdivision**
B. *Components - Marrakech Territorial Division* (07/40, Vichy France)
 1. **2nd Morocco Tirailleurs (Infantry) Regiment**
 2. **2nd Foreign Legion Infantry Regiment**
 3. **4th Morocco Spahis (Cavalry) Regiment**

Meknès Territory Division (Moroccan Army Corps; HQ: Meknès, Morocco): /36 BG Henri-Léon Caillault (Commander-in-Chief, Levant) /38 MG Pierre-Philippe-Marie-Adrien Compain (acting) /38 MG Sylvestre-Gérard Audet (Commanding General, 1st Moroccan Infantry Division) 09/02/39 BG Jean-Joseph-Lucien Mordacq [+ Commanding General, 3rd Moroccan Infantry Division] (retired) 06/25/40 MG André-Marie-François Dody (Commanding General, 2nd Moroccan Infantry Division) 05/01/43 redesignated **2nd Moroccan Infantry Division** - see French Army (1943) **2nd Moroccan Infantry Division**.
A. **Chief of Staff, Meknès Territory Division**: /40 Col. Paul-Arsène-Gérard Devinck (Vice Chief of Staff, Morocco) /40
B. *Components - Meknès Territory Division*
 1. **Meknès Subdivision**: /38 BG Gustavé-Antoine Petit
 2. **Atlas Central Subdivision**
 3. **Tafilalet Subdivision**
C. *Components - Meknès Territorial Division* (07/40, Vichy France)
 1. **7th Morocco Tirailleurs (Infantry) Regiment**
 2. **8th Morocco Tirailleurs (Infantry) Regiment**
 3. **64th African Artillery Regiment**
 4. **3rd Morocco Spahis (Cavalry) Regiment**: 11/42? Maj. Albert Le Bel

Division Meknès (/43, Morocco): MG Philibert Collet [+ /44, Military Governor, Toulouse].

Tunisia

Tunis Territory Division (Tunisian Army Corps): /38 BG Jean-Pierre-Hector-Marie Bessières (Commanding General, 88th African Infantry Division) /39
A. *Components - Tunis Territory Division*
 1. **Bizerte Subdivision**

2. **Tunis Subdivision**: /38 BG Jean-Pierre-Hector-Marie Bessières (acting Commanding General, Tunis Territory Division) /38 unknown? /42 BG Jean-Paul Bergeron (Commanding General, Tunisia) /43
B. **Infantry, Tunis Territory Division**: /38 Col. Paul-Amédée-Marie Goubaux (Commanding General, 84th African Infantry Division) 06/09/40

Sousse Territory Division (Tunisia Army Corps): /38 BG Maurice-Jean-Joseph Abadié (Commanding General, 61st Infantry Division) 09/02/39
A. *Components* - **Sousse Territory Division**
    1. **Sousse-Gabès Subdivision**: /40 BG Victor-Paul-Auguste Duclos (retired) /41
        a. **Sousse Subdivision**: /40? Col. Pierre-Marie-Edouard-Charles Trémeau (Commanding General, Sahel Group) /42? BG Louis-Henri Morel (arrested by the Germans; /44, died in Neuengamme Concentration Camp) /44
        b. **Gabès Subdivision**
B. **Infantry, Sousse Territory Division**: /38 Col. Edouard-Georges Berthomé (Commanding General, Southern Tunisian Fortified Region) 03/01/40

Sahel Group (Tunisia): /42 BG Pierre-Marie-Edouard-Charles Trémeau

French Indochina

Tonkin Division (Indochina Army Corps; HQ: Hanoi): /38 MG Henri-Joseph Cazin (?) 12/08/41? MG Georges-Albert Aymé (?) /4? unknown? /45 BG Raoul-Albert-Louis Salan.
A. **Chief of Staff, Tonkin Division**: /39 LCol. Lapierre
B. *Components* - **Tonkin Division**
    1. **1st Infantry Brigade, Tonkin Division**
    2. **2nd Infantry Brigade, Tonkin Division**
    3. **3rd Infantry Brigade, Tonkin Division**
    4. **4th Colonial Artillery Regiment**: 12/08/41? Col. Massimi

Cochinchine-Cambodge Division (Indochina Army Corps; HQ Saigon): /37 MG Maurice-Paul-Auguste Martin (Commander-in-Chief, Indochina) /38 MG Jean-Robert Derendinger (retired) 12/08/41? MG Jean-Dominique Quilichini (?) /42 MG Camille-Ange-Gabriel Sabattier (Commander-in-Chief, Indochina) /44
A. **Chief of Staff, Cochinchine-Cambodge Division**: /39 LCol. Joseph-Abraham-Auguste-Pierre-Edouard Magnan (/44, Commanding General, 9th Colonial Infantry Division) /40?
B. *Components* - **Cochinchine-Cambodge Division**
    1. **Cap Saint-Jacques [Sud Annam] Brigade**
    2. **Cambodge Brigade**
    3. **Cochinchine Brigade**

4. **5th Colonial Artillery Regiment**: 12/08/41? LCol. Ragot

C. **Infantry, Cochinchine-Cambodge Division**: /38 Col. Yves-Marie-Jacques-Guillaume de Boisboissel (Commanding General, Cambodia) /40

Air Divisions

1st Air Division [1re Division Aérienne] (05/10/40, assigned to Northern Zone of Air Operations):
A. **6th Bomber Group [Groupement de Bombardement 6]**: 05/10/40? Col. Lefort [FAF]
B. **9th Bomber Group [Groupement de Bombardement 9]**: 05/10/40? Col. François [FAF]
C. **18th Assault Bomber Group [Groupement de Bombardement d'Assaut 18]**: 05/10/40? Col. Girier [FAF]

3rd Air Division [3e Division Aérienne] (05/10/40, assigned to Eastern Zone of Air Operations):
A. **10th Bomber Group [Groupement de Bombardement 10]**: 05/10/40? LCol. Aribaut [FAF]
B. **15th Bomber Group [Groupement de Bombardement 15]**: 05/10/40? Col. Moraglia [FAF]

6th Air Division [6e Division Aérienne] (05/10/40, assigned to outhernern Zone of Air Operations):

South Eastern Bomber Training Command [Groupement d'Instruction de l'Aviation de Bombardement du Sud-Est (G. I. A. B. S. E.)]:
A. **1st Bomber Group [Groupement de Bombardement 1]**: 05/10/40? unknown?
B. **6th Bomber Group [Groupement de Bombardement 6]**: 05/10/40? Col. Lefort [FAF]
C. **7th Bomber Group [Groupement de Bombardement 7]**: 05/10/40? unknown?
D. **9th Bomber Group [Groupement de Bombardement 9]**: 05/10/40? Col. François [FAF]
E. **11th Bomber Group [Groupement de Bombardement 11]**: 05/10/40? LCol. Chopin [FAF]
F. **19th Assault Bomber Group [Groupement de Bombardement d'Assaut 19]**: 05/10/40? LCol. de Castets La Boulbène [FAF] (12/41?, Commanding Officer, Central Indochina Air Command [Group]) /40

North African Air Army (06/245/40, from **North African Zone of Air Operations**; downgraded to division status):
A. *Components* - **North African Zone of Air Operations** (11/08/42)
   1. **3rd Bomber Group [Groupement de Bombardement 3]**: 11/09/42? Col. de Turenne [FAF]
   2. **8th Bomber Group [Groupement de Bombardement 8]**: 11/09/42? LCol. Gérardot [FAF]
   3. **11th Bomber Group [Groupement de Bombardement 11]**: 11/09/42? Col. Auguste-Joseph-Marie de Lahoulle [FAF]
   4. **24th Fighter Group [Groupement de Chasse 24]**: 11/09/42? LCol. Derobert [FAF]
   5. **25th Fighter Group [Groupement de Chasse 25]**: 11/09/42? Maj. de Saint-Albin [FAF]

6. **26ᵗʰ Fighter Group [Groupement de Chasse 26]**: 11/09/42? Col. Cathal [FAF]
7. **15ᵗʰ Transport Group**: 11/09/42? Col. Georges Pelletier d'Oisy [FAF]

Naval Commands (Division equivalent)

1st Battle Division (HQ: Brest, France; 09/01/39, assigned to 1st Flotilla): 09/01/39? VA Marcel-Bruno Gensoul [FN] [Flag: battleship *Dunkerque*] [+ Commander-in-Chief, Raiding Force & Commander-in-Chief, 1st Flotilla] (Commanding Officer, High Seas Force) 12/20/39
A. *Components* - **1st Battle Division** (09/01/39)
    1. **BC *Dunkerque***
    2. **BC *Strasbourg***

2nd Battle Division (HQ: Oran, Algeria; 09/01/39, assigned to 2nd Flotilla): 09/01/39? RA P. J. E. Vallée [FN] [Flag: battleship *Lorraine*]
A. *Components* - **2nd Battle Division** (09/01/39)
    1. **BB Lorraine**
    2. **BB Bretagne**

3rd Battle Division (HQ: Brest, France; 09/01/39, assigned to II Naval Region): RA J. H. C. F. Moreau [FN] [Flag: BB *Paris*] (Commander-in-Chief, West Africa Naval Station; Commanding Officer, 5th Light Squadron; & Commanding Officer, 6th Cruiser Division) 09/01/39 Capt. P. L. Guillerm [FN] [Leader: BB *Paris*]
A. *Components* - **3rd Battle Division** (09/01/39)
    1. **BB *Paris***
    2. **BB *Courbet***

West Africa Naval Station (HQ: Dakar, Senegal): 09/01/39? RA J. H. C. E. Moreau [FN] [Flag: CL *Duguay-Trouin*] [+ Commanding Officer, 5th Light Squadron & Commanding Officer, 6th Cruiser Division] (Commanding Officer, Algiers Naval Force) 09/40 RA Landriau [FN] (Head, French Delegation to the Franco-German Armistice Commission) 08/42
A. *Components* - **West Africa Naval Station** (09/01/39)
    1. **5th Light Squadron**
        a. **6th Cruiser Division**
            I. **CL *Duguay-Trouin***
            ii. **CL *Primauguet***
        b. **7th Cruiser Division**
            I. **CL *Jeanne de Arc***
            ii. **CL *La Tour d'Auvergne [Pluton]***
B. *Components* - **West Africa Naval Station** (07/40)
    1. **BB *Richelieu***
    2. **CL *Primauguet***
    3. **CL *Montcalm***

Far East Naval Forces (HQ: Saigon, French Indochina): 09/01/39? VA Jean d'Decoux [FN] [+ Admiral Far East [Indochina}] (Governor-General, French Indochina) 06/25/40 VA Jules E. M. A. Terraux [FN] [+ Admiral Far East [Indochina}] (?) /45 VA Philippe Auboyneau [FN] [+ Admiral Far East [Indochina}].
A. *Components* - **Far East Naval Station** (09/01/39)

1. **5th Cruiser Division**
   a. **CL** *Lamotte Picquett*
   b. **CA** *Suffren*
2. **Yanztse Gunboats** (HQ: Shanghai, China; gunboats *Balny, Doudart de la Gree, Francis Garnier*): 09/01/39? Cdr. A. M. A. Rolin [FN] [Flag: PR [river gunboat] *Francis Garnier*]
3. **West River [Si Kiang] Gunboat** (HQ: Hong Kong, China, gunboat *Argus*): 09/01/39? LCdr. M. G. H. de Saint-George [FN] [Flag: PR [river gunboat] *Argus*]
4. **Indochina Gunboats** (HQ: Saigon, Indochina; gunboats *Avalanche, Commandant Bourdais*): 09/01/39? LCdr. M. J. L. Leparmentier [FN] [Flag: PG [gunboat] *Vigilante*]
   [stationed at Haiphong; gunboats *Mytho, Tourane, Vigilante*]
5. **Sloops** (HQ: Saigon, French Indochina; sloops *La Pérouse, Marne, Amiral Charner, Savorgnan de Brazza*):
   [stationed at Shanghai, China; sloop *Rigault de Genouilly*
   [stationed at Amoy, China, sloop *Tahure*]
6. **SS [submarine]** *l'Espoir*: 09/01/39? Lt. H. S. A. Tezenas du Montecel [FN]

Light Attack Forces [4th Cruiser Squadron] (HQ: Bizerte, Tunisia): 09/01/39? RA André A. A. Marquis [FN] [Flag: CL *Marseillaise*] [+ Commanding Officer, 3rd Cruiser Division] (Maritime Perfect and Governor of Toulon) 09/40 disbanded.
A. *Components - Light Attack Forces* (09/01/39)
   1. **3rd Cruiser Division**
      a. **CL** *Marseillaise*
      b. **CL** *Jean de Vienne*
      c. **CL** *La Galisonniere*
   2. **Bizerte Destroyers [4th Light Squadron]**
      a. **1st Destroyer Division**
      b. **3rd Destroyer Division**
      c. **11th Destroyer Division**
      d. **CM [minelayer]** *Émile Bertin* (part of 3rd Cruiser Division)

1st Cruiser Squadron (HQ: Toulon France; 09/01/39, assigned to 3rd Flotilla): 09/01/39? VA E. A. H. Duplat [FN] [Flag: heavy cruiser *Algérie*] [+ Commander-in-Chief, 3rd Flotilla & Commander, 1st Cruiser Division] (Head, French Delegation to the Franco-Italian Armistice Commission) 09/12/40 disbanded.
A. *Components - 1st Cruiser Squadron* (09/01/39)
   1. **1st Cruiser Division**
   2. **2nd Cruiser Division**

5th Light Squadron (HQ: Dakar, Senegal; 09/01/39, assigned to West Africa Naval Station): 09/01/39? RA J. H. C. E. Moreau [FN] [Flag: CL *Duguay-Trouin*] [+ Commander-in-Chief, West Africa Naval Station & Commanding Officer, 6th Cruiser Division] (Commanding Officer, Algiers Naval Force) 09/40 disbanded.
A. *Components - 5th Light Squadron* (09/01/39)

1. **6th Cruiser Division**
   a. **CL** *Duguay-Trouin*
   b. **CL** *Primauguet*
2. **7th Cruiser Division**
   a. **CL** *Jeanne de Arc*
   b. **CL** *La Tour d'Auvergne [Pluton]*

1st Submarine Flotilla (HQ: Toulon, France; 09/01/39, assigned to III Naval Region): 09/01/39? RA G. Walser [FN]
A. *Components - 1st Submarine Flotilla* (09/01/39)
   1. **3rd Submarine Squadron**
      a. **1st Submarine Division**
      b. **3rd Submarine Division**
      c. **5th Submarine Division**
   2. **5th Submarine Squadron**
      a. **13th Submarine Division**
      b. **15th Submarine Division**

Bizerta Naval Base (HQ: Bizerta, Tunisia; assigned to Tunis Force; 12/07/42, surrendered to the Germans): 11/08/42? VA E. H. H. N. Derrien [FN] [+ Commanding Officer, Tunis Naval Force] (German prisoner-of-war; 10/44, arrested; condemned to death and executed) 12/07/42 surrendered.
A. *Components - Bizerta Naval Base* (09/01/39)
   1. **Bizerte Submarine Base**
      a. **6th Submarine Squadron**
         i. **9th Submarine Division**
         ii. **10th Submarine Division**
         iii. **17th Submarine Division**
         iv. **20th Submarine Division**
      b. **AS [submarine tender]** *Castor*

Brigades

Commands of the Maginot Line (Brigade Commands)

[Three types: Type A - Main Fortified Part of Maginot Line; Type B - Rest of Maginot Line; Type C - Along border with Spain]

Lille Defense Sector (Secteur Défensif de Lille)/Lille Fortified Sector (Secteur Fortifié de Lille) (Secteur Fortifié de Lille) (Type B; 08/21/39. First Army; 09/08/39, III Army Corps; 10/03/39, XVI Army Corps; 11/15/39, Seventh Army; 03/16/40, upgraded to Fortified Sector, Seventh Army; 05/24/40, XVI Army Corps; 06/17/40, dissolved): **Lille Defense Sector** 08/21/39 vacant 08/23/39 Col. Charles-Joseph-Georges Bertschi 09/09/39 MG [Retired] Victor-Jean-Edmond Gillard [+ Commanding General, 51st Infantry Division] 12/02/39 Col. Charles-Joseph-Georges Bertschi (Commanding General, Lille Fortified Sector) 03/16/40 upgraded to **Lille Fortified Sector** 03/16/40 BG Charles-Joseph-Georges Bertschi (?) 06/17/40 dissolved.
- A. **Chief of Staff, Lille Defense Sector/Lille Fortified Sector** (08/23/39): Capt. [Army] Masson 06/17/40 dissolved.
- B. *Components* - Lille Defense Sector/Lille Fortified Sector (09/02/39)
    1. **16th Regional Construction Engineers (Travailleurs) Regiment**

l'Escaut Fortified Sector (Secteur Fortifié L'Escaut) (Type B; 08/20/39, Military District I; 09/05/39, Esc-Maub Fortified Section Group; 10/04/39, III Army Corps; 05/10/40, First Army; 05/19/40, III Army Corps): vacant 08/23/39 BG Eugène-Raphaël Échard (Commanding General, 52nd Infantry Division) 01/01/40 BG Henri-Stanislas-Auguste Hanaut (?) 05/22/40 MG Louis-Ernest Béjard [+ Commanding General, 101st Fortress Infantry Division] 06/25/40 disbanded.
- A. **Chief of Staff, l'Escaut Fortified Sector** (08/23/39): Maj. Fontaine
- B. *Components* - l'Escaut Fortified Sector (09/02/39)
    1. **54th Fortress Infantry Regiment**
    2. **17th Regional Construction Engineers (Travailleurs) Regiment**

Ardennes Defense Sector (Secteur Défensif des Ardennes) (Type B; 11/20/39, IV Army Corps; 01/01/40, disbanded and used to form the **102nd Fortress Infantry Division**): MG François-Arthur Portzert [+ Commanding General, 52nd Infantry Diviison] (Commanding General, 102nd Fortress Infantry Division) 01/01/40 disbanded and used to form the **102nd Fortress Infantry Division** - see **102nd Fortress Infantry Division**.
- A. **Chief of Staff, Ardennes Defense Sector** (11/20/39): unknown?
- B. *Components* - Ardennes Defense Sector (11/20/39)
    1. **148th Fortress Infantry Regiment**

Colmar Fortified Sector (Secteur Fortifié de Colmar) (pre-war; Type B; 08/21/39, in VII Military District; 09/02/39, Eighth Army; 10/06/39, VII Army Corps; 03/01/40, XIII Army Corps; 03/16/40, dissolved and used to form the **104th Fortress Infantry Division**): /38 BG

473

Louis-Gustavé-Adolphe Coradin [+ Commanding General, Colmar Independent Sub-Division] (Commanding General, 54th Infantry Division) 11/26/39 BG Louis-Gustavé-Abel Poisot (Commanding General, Thionville Fortified Sector) 01/01/40 BG Edouard-Sylvain Cousse (Commanding General, 104th Fortress Infantry Division) 03/16/40 dissolved and used to form the **104th Fortress Infantry Division** - see **104th Fortress Infantry Division**.
- A. **Chief of Staff, Colmar Fortified Sector** (08/21/39): Maj. Schindler (04/05/40, Chief of Staff, Jura Fortified Sector) 09/28/39 Maj. Gouget de Landres (Chief of Staff, 104th Fortress Infantry Division) 03/16/40 dissolved.
- B. *Components* - **Colmar Fortified Sector** (09/02/39)
  1. **28th Fortress Infantry Regiment**
  2. **42nd Fortress Infantry Regiment**

Mulhouse Fortified Sector (Secteur Fortifié de Mulhouse) (Type B; 08/21/39, Belfort Fortified Region; 10/05/39, VII Army Corps; 03/01/40, XIII Army Corps; 03/16/40, dissolved and used to form the **105th Fortress Infantry Division**): Col. Chaligne 09/16/39 BG André-Hubert-Léon Challe (retired) 11/30/39 Col. Joseph-Étienne Salvan [+ 12/15/39, Commanding General, Altkirch (Franken Defense Sector] 01/07/40 BG Paul-Adrien Voinier (?) 01/12/40 BG Pierre-Désiré-Robert Didio (Commanding General, 105th Fortress Infantry Division) 03/16/40 dissolved and used to form the **105th Fortress Infantry Division** - see and used to form the **105th Fortress Infantry Division**.
- A. **Chief of Staff, Mulhouse Fortified Sector** (08/21/39): Capt. [Army] de Saint-Germain /39? Capt. [Army] Delmau 01/10/40 LCol. Marty 03/16/40 dissolved.
- B. *Components* - **Mulhouse Fortified Sector** (09/02/39)
  1. **10th Fortress Infantry Regiment**

Belfort Defense (Defensé de Belfort) (08/21/39 in Military District VII; 08/21/39, Belfort Fortified Region; 01/25/40, Eighth Army; 03/16/40, XLIV Fortress Army Corps; 06/09/40, XLV Fortress Army Corps; 06/16/40, Eighth Army; 06/20/40, captured and dsibanded): vacant 08/30/39 BG Louis-Germain Girol [+ Commanding General, Belfort Subdivision Group] (Commanding General, Altkirch Fortified Sector) 10/29/39 Col. de Fleuriau 03/15/40 BG Louis-Germain Girol [+ Commanding General, Belfort Defense Sector] (?) 06/20/40 captured and disbanded.
- A. **Chief of Staff, Belfort Defense** (08/21/39): Capt. [Army] Laplante 01/06/40 Capt. [Army] Boudot 06/20/40 dissolved.
- B. *Components* - **Belfort Defense** (09/02/39)
  1. **371st Infantry Regiment**

Montbéliard Defense Sector (Secteur Défensif de Montbéliard)/Montbéliard Fortified Sector (Secteur Fortifié de Montbéliard) (Type B; 08/22/39 in Military District VII; 08/22/39, Belfort Fortified Region; 03/16/40, XLIV Fortress Army Corps; 05/29/40, XLV Fortress Army Corps; 06/16/40, Eighth Army; 06/18/40, destroyed and disbanded): Col. Henri-Charles-Marie de Bizemont (Commanding General, 27th Infantry Division) 05/19/40 Col. Gard 06/18/40 destroyed and disbanded.
- A. **Chief of Staff, Montbéliard Defense Sector** (08/22/39): Capt. [Army] Ronsin 06/18/40 dissolved.

Jura Fortified Sector (Secteur Fortifié du Jura) (Type B; 08/22/39, Military District VII;

12/16/39, Jura Army Corps; 01/12/40, XLV Fortress Army Corps; 05/23/40, Eighth Army; 06/13/40, XLV Fortress Army Corps; 06/25/40, disbanded): BG René-Pierre-Victor-Auguste Huet (?) 06/25/40 disbanded.

A. **Chief of Staff, Jura Fortified Sector** (08/22/39): Maj. Henri-Roger-Marie Méric de Bellefon 04/05/40 Maj. Schindler 06/25/40 dissolved.

Rhône Defense Sector (Secteur Défensif du Rhône) (Type B; 08/24/39; 08/28/39, XIV Army Corps; 09/15/39, XVI Army Corps; 09/28/39, XIV Army Corps; 06/03/40, Army of the Alps; 06/17/40, 2nd Army Group; 06/19/40, Army of the Alps; 06/22/40, XIV Army Corps; 06/25/40, disbanded): BG Louis-Michel-Marie-Joseph Michel (09/12/40, Commanding General, 17th Military Division) 06/25/40 disbanded.

A. **Chief of Staff, Rhône Defense Sector** (08/24/39): LCol. Juillard 05/19/40 Maj. Granger 06/25/40 dissolved.
B. *Components* - **Rhône Defense Sector** (09/02/39)
    1. **230th Alpine Fortress Demi-Brigade**

Infantry Brigades

53rd Infantry Brigade (08/22/39, 27th Alpine Infantry Division): /38 Col. Paul-Wilhelm Boell (Infantry Commander, 27th Infantry Division) 10/27/39 Col. Albert-Raymond Mellier (Commanding General, 1st Moroccan Infantry Division) 02/27/40 Col. Millier
A. **Components - 53rd Infantry Brigade** (08/22/39)
    1. 140th Alpine Infantry Regiment
    2. 7th Alpine Infantry Half-Brigade

54th Infantry Brigade (08/22/39, 27th Alpine Infantry Division): /37 Col. Paul-Wilhelm Boell (Commanding Officer, 53rd Infantry Brigade) /38
A. **Components - 54th Infantry Brigade** (08/22/39)
    1. 159th Alpine Infantry Regiment
    2. 27th Alpine Infantry Half-Brigade

55th Infantry Brigade (08/22/39, 28th Alpine Infantry Division): /39 BG Augustin-Marcelin Agliany (Infantry Officer, 28th Infantry Division) 08/22/39
A. **Components - 55th Infantry Brigade** (08/22/39)
    1. 99th Alpine Infantry Regiment
    2. 5th Alpine Infantry Half-Brigade (removed 02/06/40; added by 03/15/40)
    3. 2nd Alpine Infantry Half-Brigade (added 02/06/40; removed by 03/15/40)

56th Infantry Brigade (08/22/39, 28th Alpine Infantry Division):
A. **Components - 56th Infantry Brigade** (08/22/39)
    1. 97th Alpine Infantry Regiment
    2. 25th Alpine Infantry Half-Brigade

57th Infantry Brigade (08/22/39, 29th Alpine Infantry Division): /34 LCol. Bernard-Marie-Alexis Vergès (Commanding General, Constantine Territory Division) /39
A. **Components - 57th Infantry Brigade** (08/22/39)
    1. 112th Alpine Infantry Regiment
    2. 6th Alpine Infantry Half-Brigade

58th Infantry Brigade (08/22/39, 30th Alpine Infantry Division): Col. René-André Gérin (Infantry Commander, 64th Alpine Infantry Division) 09/02/39
A. **Components - 58th Infantry Brigade** (08/22/39)
    1. 55th Alpine Infantry Regiment
    2. 2nd Alpine Infantry Half-Brigade

59th Infantry Brigade (08/22/39, 29th Alpine Infantry Division):
A. **Components - 59th Infantry Brigade** (08/22/39)
    1. 3rd Alpine Infantry Regiment
    2. 26th Alpine Infantry Half-Brigade

60th Infantry Brigade (08/22/39, 30th Alpine Infantry Division):
A. **Components - 60th Infantry Brigade** (08/22/39)

1. **141st Alpine Infantry Regiment**
2. **22nd Alpine Infantry Half-Brigade**

1st Colonial Infantry Brigade: /39 Col. François-Claude-Philippe Delaissey (Infantry Commander, 35th Infantry Division) 09/02/39

2nd Colonial Infantry Brigade: /38 Col. Marie-Côme-Gaston Schmitt (Commanding General, 3rd Brigade, French West Africa) /40 unknown? /43 BG Diégo-Charles-Joseph Brosset (Commanding General, 1st Free French Division) 07/43

5th Colonial Infantry Brigade: /37 BG Jean-Robert Derendinger (Commanding General, Cochinchine-Cambodge Division) /38

6th Colonial Infantry Brigade: /36 Col. Charles-Pierre-Martial Ardant du Picq (Commanding General, 84th African Infantry Division) 08/26/39

1st Spahis (Cavalry) Brigade (08/22/39; disbanded 06/25/40):
A. *Components - 1st Spahis (Cavalry) Brigade*
 1. **4th Moroccan Spahis (Cavalry) Regiment**
 2. **5th Moroccan Spahis (Cavalry) Regiment**

1st Algerian Brigade (Algeria): /38 BG Paul-Émile Britsch (retired; /39, recalled; 03/09/39, Commanding General, 55th Infantry Division) /38

2nd Algerian Brigade (Algeria): /38 Col. Jean-Gabriel-Edouard Thomas (Commanding Officer, Oran Subdivision) /38

3rd Algerian Brigade (Algeria): /36 Col. Victor-Paul-Auguste Duclos [+ Commanding Officer, Constantine Subdivision] (Commanding General, 133rd Fortress Infantry Regiment) /39

4th Algerian Brigade (Algeria): 11/42 BG Marcel-Georges François (Commanding General Tlemcen Subdivision) /42

1st Infantry Brigade, Tonkin Division (Indochina; HQ: Hanoi): /38 Col. Marie-Jean-Georges Goudouneix (Deputy Commander, 1st Maritime Region) /39 Col. Benard
A. *Components - 1st Infantry Brigade*
 1. **4th Tonkinese Tirailleurs (Infantry) Regiment**: 12/08/41? LCol. Robert
 2. **19th Mixed Infantry Regiment**: 12/08/41? LCol. Digne

2nd Infantry Brigade, Tonkin Division (Indochina; HQ: Hanoi): unknown? /40 BG Germain-Stanislas-Victor Mennerat (?) 12/08/41? Col. Émile-René Lemonnier (killed by the Japanese) /45
A. *Components - 2nd Infantry Brigade*
 1. **1st Tonkinese Tirailleurs (Infantry) Regiment**
 2. **5th Foreign Legion Infantry Regiment**: 12/08/41? Col. Marcel-Jean-Marie Alessandri (Commanding General, Column Alessandri) /43

3rd Infantry Brigade, Tonkin Division (Indochina; HQ: Phu Lang Tuang): /38 BG Jean-Eugène-Marie Charbonneau (Commanding General, Sub-Division Hauts-Fleuves; /40, Commandant, Brest) /39 BG Rabut 12/08/41? BG Hermann-Françis-Denis Delsuc
- A. **Components - 3rd Infantry Brigade**
    1. **9th Colonial Infantry Regiment**: 12/08/41? LCol. Roger-Charles-André-Henri Blaizot (French Liaison Officer to Supreme Allied Commander Southeast Asia) /43?
    2. **3rd Tonkinese Tirailleurs (Infantry) Regiment**: 12/08/41? Col. Baleyrat-Rodannet

1st Brigade, French West Africa (French West Africa): /38 BG Jean-Louis-Laurent Méségué

2nd Brigade, French West Africa (French West Africa): /38 BG Henri-Gilbert-Antoine Perraud (Infantry Commander, 3rd Colonial Infantry Division) 08/25/39 BG Desgruelles

3rd Brigade, French West Africa (French West Africa): /39 BG Arnould /40 BG Marie-Côme-Gaston Schmitt

Annam Brigade (Indochina Army Corps; HQ: Hué): /38 Col. Marcel-Émile Deslaurens (Commanding Officer, Lines of Communication, Ninth Army) 11/05/39 BG Bourdeau 12/08/41? BG Auguste-Joseph-Charles-Antoine Turquin
- A. **Chief of Staff, Annam Brigade**: /39 Maj. de Kermer
- B. **Components - Annam Brigade**
    1. **10th Mixed Infantry Regiment**: 12/08/41? LCol. Charnier

Cap Saint-Jacques [Sud Annam] Brigade (Indochina; HQ: Cap Saint-Jacques): 09/39 unknown? 12/08/41? Col. James
- A. **Components - Cap Saint-Jacques [Sud Annam] Brigade**
    1. **16th Colonial Infantry Regiment**: 12/08/41? LCol. Bachetta

Cochinchine Brigade (Indochina; HQ: Saigon): 09/39 unknown? 12/08/41? BG Camille-Ange-Gabriel Sabattier (Commanding General, Cochinchine-Cambodge Division) /42
- A. **Components - Cochinchine Brigade**
    1. **11th Colonial Infantry Regiment**: 12/08/41? Col. Bouteil
    2. **Annamese Tirailleurs (Infantry) Regiment**: 12/08/41? Col. Genet

Cambodge Brigade (Indochina Army Corps; HQ: Pnom Penh): 09/39 unknown? 12/08/41? Col. Noël
- A. **Components - Cambodge Brigade**
    1. **Cambodian Tirailleurs (Infantry) Regiment**: 12/08/41? LCol. Denis

1st Brigade, Indochine (Indochina): /42 BG Gustavé-Amédée Bernard

Monclar Brigade (Eritrea; Free French unit): /41 Col. Monclar

Column Alessandri (/43, Indochina): BG Marcel-Jean-Marie Alessandri (Commanding General, French Forces in China) /45

Armored and Mechanized Brigades

2nd Armored Brigade: /36 BG Louis-Marie-Joseph-Ferdinand Keller (Inspector-General of Armored Troops) /39

3rd Armored Brigade: /36 Col. Charles-Georges-Antoine Delestraint (retired; 09/02/39, Commander Armored Forces, Seventh Army) /39 Col. Marie-Germain-Christian Bruneau (Commanding Officer, Armored, Third Army) 08/27/39

8th Armored Brigade: /43 BG Michel Malaguti (at disposal of the Commanding General, Southern Front) /44

1st Light Mechanized (Armored) Brigade: /39 BG Marie-Joseph-Eugène Testard (Commanding General, 3rd Light Mechanized (Armored) Brigade) 08/27/39 unknown? /42 BG Jean-Louis-Alai Touzet du Vigier [+ Commanding General, Mascara Subdivision] (Commanding General, 1st Free French Light Mechanized Brigade) /43
- A. *Components* - **1st Light Mechanized (Armored) Brigade**
  1. **4th Armored Cuirassier Regiment**
  2. **18th Armored Dragoon Regiment**

2nd Light Mechanized (Infantry) Brigade: /42 BG Henri-Jacques-Jean-François de Vernejoul (Commanding General, 2nd Free French Armored Division (#1)) 05/01/43
- A. *Components* - **2nd Light Mechanized (Infantry) Brigade**
  1. **4th Mechanized Dragoon Infantry Regiment**
  2. **6th Cuirassier (Reconnaissance) Cavalry Regiment**

3rd Light Mechanized (Armored) Brigade: /38 BG François Picard (Commanding General, 1st Light Mechanized Division) 08/27/39 BG Marie-Joseph-Eugène Testard (Commanding General, 3rd Light Mechanized Division) 06/06/40
- A. *Components* - **3rd Light Mechanized (Armored) Brigade**
  1. **13th Armored Dragoon Regiment**
  2. **29th Armored Dragoon Regiment**

4th Light Mechanized (Infantry) Brigade: /38 BG Gabriel-Marie-Joseph Bougrain (Commanding General, 2nd Light Mechanized Division) 01/13/40
- A. *Components* - **4th Light Mechanized (Infantry) Brigade**
  1. **4th Mechanized Dragoon Infantry Regiment**
  2. **8th Cuirassier (Reconnaissance) Cavalry Regiment**

5th Light Mechanized (Armored) Brigade (02/01/40, 3rd Light Mechanized Division): /38 Col. Louis-Ferdinand Bourguignon (Commanding General, Armored, Second Army) 08/27/39 unknown? /40 BG Pierre-Jules-André-Marie de La Font Chabert (Commanding General, 3rd Light Mechanized Division) 05/26/40
- A. *Components* - **5th Light Mechanized (Armored) Brigade** (02/01/40)
  1. **1st Armored Cuirassier Regiment**: /40 Col. Henri-Jacques-Jean-François de Vernejoul (Commanding Officer, 1st African Chasseurs (Armored)

Regiment) /41
2. **2ⁿᵈ Armored Cuirassier Regiment**: 02/01/40 unknown? /41? Col. Jean-Louis-Alai Touzet du Vigier (Commanding General, Mascara Subdivision) /42

6ᵗʰ Light Mechanized (Armored) Brigade (02/01/40, 3ʳᵈ Light Mechanized Division): /39 BG Emile-Henri Gailliard (Commanding General, 10ᵗʰ Cavalry Brigade) /40
A. *Components - 6ᵗʰ Light Mechanized (Armored) Brigade (02/01/40)*
   1. **11ᵗʰ Mechanized Dragoon Infantry Regiment**
   2. **12ᵗʰ Cuirassier (Reconnaissance) Cavalry Regiment**

11ᵗʰ Light Mechanized Infantry Brigade (03/03/40, 1ˢᵗ Light Cavalry Division): BG Georges-Saint-Ange Moulin
A. *Components - 11ᵗʰ Light Mechanized Infantry Brigade (03/03/40)*
   1. **1ˢᵗ Armored Car (Automitrailleuses) Regiment**
   2. **5ᵗʰ Mechanized Dragoon Infantry Regiment**

12ᵗʰ Light Mechanized Infantry Brigade (03/05/40, 2ⁿᵈ Light Cavalry Division): 12/03/39 Col. Paul-Constant-Amédée Gastey (Commanding General, 2ⁿᵈ Light Cavalry Division) 06/11/40
A. *Components - 12ᵗʰ Light Mechanized Infantry Brigade (03/05/40)*
   1. **2ⁿᵈ Armored Car (Automitrailleuses) Regiment**
   2. **3ʳᵈ Mechanized Dragoon Infantry Regiment**

13ᵗʰ Light Mechanized Infantry Brigade (03/05/40, 3ʳᵈ Light Cavalry Division): unknown?
A. *Components - 13ᵗʰ Light Mechanized Infantry Brigade (03/05/40)*
   1. **3ʳᵈ Armored Car (Automitrailleuses) Regiment**
   2. **2ⁿᵈ Mechanized Dragoon Infantry Regiment**

14ᵗʰ Light Mechanized Infantry Brigade (02/16/40, 4ᵗʰ Light Cavalry Division): unknown?
A. *Components - 14ᵗʰ Light Mechanized Infantry Brigade (02/16/40)*
   1. **4ᵗʰ Armored Car (Automitrailleuses) Regiment**
   2. **14ᵗʰ Mechanized Dragoon Infantry Regiment**

14ᵗʰ Light Mechanized (Armored) Brigade (06/05/40, 7ᵗʰ Light Mechanized Division): unknown?
A. *Components - 14ᵗʰ Light Mechanized (Armored) Brigade (06/05/40)*
   1. **4ᵗʰ Armored Car (Automitrailleuses) Regiment**
   2. **4ᵗʰ Armored Dragoon Regiment**

15ᵗʰ Light Mechanized Infantry Brigade (02/25/40, 5ᵗʰ Light Cavalry Division): unknown?
A. *Components - 15ᵗʰ Light Mechanized Infantry Brigade (02/25/40)*
   1. **5ᵗʰ Armored Car (Automitrailleuses) Regiment**
   2. **15ᵗʰ Mechanized Dragoon Infantry Regiment**

16ᵗʰ Light Mechanized Infantry Brigade (03/40, 6ᵗʰ Light Cavalry Division): unknown?
A. *Components - 16ᵗʰ Light Mechanized Infantry Brigade (03/40)*

1. **1st African Mechanized Chasseurs Cavalry Regiment**
2. **2nd African Mechanized Chasseurs Infantry Regiment**

7th Army Reconnaissance Group (11/13/39; disbanded 10/15/40): unknown?

Armored Group Langlade (/44): Col. Paul-Anne-Joseph-Alexandre Baron Girot de Langlade (Commanding General, 3rd Armored Division) /45

Cavalry Brigades

1st Cavalry Brigade (08/23/39, 1st Cavalry Division; 09/12/40, assigned to French Vichy Military District XIV and XV; 11/42, demobilized): /36 Col. Maurice-Arthur-Alphonse Wemaëre (Commanding General, 5th Cavalry Brigade) /38 unknown? 08/23/39 BG Emile-Henri Gailliard (Commanding General, 6th Light Mechanized (Armored) Brigade) /39 unknown? 11/42 demobilized.
- A. *Components - 1st Cavalry Brigade* (08/23/39)
    1. **1st Hussar Cavalry Regiment**
    2. **8th Cavalry (Chasseur à Cheval) Regiment**
- B. *Components - 1st Cavalry Brigade* (09/12/40)
    1. **1st Cavalry (Chasseur à Cheval) Regiment** (Vichy Military District XIV)
    2. **7th Cavalry (Chasseur à Cheval) Regiment** (Vichy Military District XV)

2nd Cavalry Brigade (08/23/39, 1st Cavalry Division; 02/10/40, 1st Light Division; 03/03/40, 1st Light Cavalry Division; 06/25/40, disbanded; 09/12/40, assigned to French Vichy Military District XVII; 12/42, demobilized): BG Alain-Bertrand-Marie-Gaston d'Humières (killed in action) 06/25/40 disbanded; reformed 09/12/40 unknown? 11/42 demobilized.
- A. *Components - 2nd Cavalry Brigade* (08/23/39, 02/10/40)
    1. **1st Cavalry (Chasseur à Cheval) Regiment**
    2. **19th Dragoon (Cavalry) Regiment**
- B. *Components - 2nd Cavalry Brigade* (09/12/40)
    1. **2nd Hussar Cavalry Regiment**
    2. **3rd Hussar Cavalry Regiment**

3rd Cavalry Brigade (08/22/39, 2nd Cavalry Division; 02/10/40, 2nd Light Division; 03/05/40, 2nd LightCavalry Division; 06/25/40, disbanded): BG Stanislas-Louis-Amédé de Bessey de Contenson (?) 06/25/40 disbanded.
- A. *Components - 3rd Cavalry Brigade* (08/22/39, 02/10/40, & 09/12/40)
    1. **18th Cavalry (Chasseur à Cheval) Regiment**: /41? Col. Guy Schlesser (Commanding Officer, 12th Dragoon Regiment) /42?
    2. **5th Cavalry (Cuirassiers) Regiment**

4th Cavalry Brigade (08/22/39, 2nd Cavalry Division; 02/16/40, 4th Light Cavalry Division; 06/25/40, disbanded): /38 BG Jean Martin Gallevier de Mierry (Commanding General, 56th Infantry Division) 01/01/40 unknown? 06/25/40 disbanded.
- A. *Components - 4th Cavalry Brigade* (08/22/39)
    1. **8th Dragoon (Cavalry) Regiment**
    2. **31st Dragoon (Cavalry) Regiment**: /40 LCol. Guy Schlesser (Commanding Officer, 18th Chasseurs Regiment) /41?

5th Cavalry Brigade (08/22/39, 3rd Cavalry Division; 02/01/40, 3rd Light Division; 03/05/40, 3rd Light Cavalry Division; 06/25/40, disbanded): /38 BG Maurice-Arthur-Alphonse Wemaëre (Commanding General, 85th African Infantry Division) 08/28/39 unknown? 06/25/40 disbanded.
- A. *Components - 5th Cavalry Brigade* (08/22/39)

1. **4th Hussar Cavalry Regiment**
2. **6th Dragoon (Cavalry) Regiment**

6th Cavalry Brigade (08/27/39, assigned to 3rd Cavalry Division; 02/25/40, 5th Light Cavalry Division; 06/25/40, disbanded): BG Émile-Louis-Gabriel Brown de Colstoun (?) 06/25/40 disbanded.
A. *Components* - 6th Cavalry Brigade (08/22/39)
    1. **11th Cavalry (Cuirassiers) Regiment**
    2. **12th Cavalry (Chasseur à Cheval) Regiment**

7th Cavalry Brigade (03/40, 6th Light Cavalry Division; 06/25/40, disbanded): unknown? 06/25/40 disbanded.
A. *Components* - 7th Cavalry Brigade (03/40)
    1. **1st Algerian Spahis (Cavalry) Regiment**
    2. **3rd Algerian Spahis (Cavalry) Regiment**

8th Cavalry Brigade (after 06/25/40): BG Pierre-Jules-André-Marie de La Font Chabert (Deputy Chief of the Vichy France Army General Staff) /40

10th Cavalry Brigade (/40): BG Emile-Henri Gailliard (to /45, German prisoner-of-war) 06/40

4th Light Mechanized Cavalry Brigade (06/05/40, 7th Light Mechanized Division): unknown?
A. *Components* - 4th Light Mechanized Cavalry Brigade (06/05/40
    a. **14th Mechanized Dragoon Infantry Regiment**
    b. **31st Mechanized Dragoon Infantry Regiment**

1st Spahis (Cavalry) Brigade (pre-war; /39, disbanded): /38 BG Jean-Barnard-Marie-Bertrand du Cor de Duprat de Damrémont (?) /39 disbanded.

2nd Spahis (Cavalry) Brigade (08/22/39; disbanded 06/20/40):
A. *Components* - 2nd Spahis (Cavalry) Brigade
    1. **7th Algerian Spahis (Cavalry) Regiment**
    2. **9th Algerian Spahis (Cavalry) Regiment**

3rd Spahis (Cavalry) Brigade (11/03/39; disbanded 06/07/40): BG Denis-Marie-Joseph-Félix Clouet des Perruches (Commanding General, 6th Light Cavalry Division) 03/40 BG Olivier-Marie-Alphonse Marc
A. *Components* - 3rd Spahis (Cavalry) Brigade
    1. **2nd Algerian Spahis (Cavalry) Regiment**
    2. **2nd Moroccan Spahis (Cavalry) Regiment**

4th Algerian Cavalry Brigade (unknown?): /38 BG Jean Cazaban (Commanding General, 86th African Infantry Division) /39 BG Adrian-Jules-Gustavé Burnol

Miscellaneous Brigades

7th Artillery Brigade: /36 BG Paul Fédary

Air Force Wings

Indochina Independent Air Force (Wing) (Indochina; HQ: Hanoi): 12/08/41? Col. Tavera [FAF]
A. *Components* - **Indochina Independent Air Force (Wing)**
    1. **Northern Indochina Air Command (Group)**: 12/08/41? Col. Weiser [FAF]
    2. **Central Indochina Air Command (Group)**: 12/08/41? Col. de Castet la Boulbène [FAF]

Naval Commands (Brigade equivalent)

Levant Naval Station (HQ: Beiruit, Lebanon): 09/01/39? RA M. F. L. F. de Carpentier [FN] (?) /41 RA Gouton [FN]
A. **Components**
   1. **11th Submarine Division**
   2. **Sloop *D'Iberville*** 09/01/39? Cdr. L. M. E. Arden [FN]

Casablanca Naval Station [Morocco Naval Force] (HQ: Casablanca, Morocco; 09/01/39, assigned to IV Naval Region): 09/01/39? RA L. M. J. Sable [FN] /42 RA Pierre-Alexis-Jean Ronarc'h [FN]
A. **Components - Casablanca Naval Station** (09/01/39)
   1. **9th Light Destroyer Division**
   2. **4th Submarine Division**

1st Cruiser Division (HQ: Toulon, France; 09/01/39, assigned to 1st Cruiser Squadron): 09/01/39? VA E. A. H. Duplat [FN] [Flag: heavy cruiser *Algérie*] [+ Commander-in-Chief, 3rd Flotilla & Commander, 1st Cruiser Squadron] (Head, French Delegation to the Franco-Italian Armistice Commission) 09/12/40 disbanded.
A. **Components - 1st Cruiser Division** (09/01/39)
   1. **CA *Algérie***
   2. **CA *Dupleix***
   3. **CA *Foch***

2nd Cruiser Division (HQ: Toulon, France; 09/01/39, assigned to 1st Cruiser Squadron): RA E. J. R. M. Kerdudo [FN] [Flag: heavy cruiser *Duquesne*]
A. **Components - 2nd Cruiser Division** (09/01/39)
   1. **CA *Colbert***
   2. **CA *Duquesne***
   3. **CA *Tourville***

3rd Cruiser Division (HQ: Birerte, Tunisia; 09/01/39, assigned to Light Attack Force [4th Light Squadron]): RA André A. A. Marquis [FN] [Flag: CL *Marseillaise*] [+ Commanding Officer, Light Attack Forces] (Maritime Perfect and Governor of Toulon) 09/40 disbanded; reformed 08/44 RA Philippe Auboyneau [FN] (Admiral Far East) /45.
A. **Components - 3rd Cruiser Division** (09/01/39)
   1. **CL *Marseillaise***
   2. **CL *Jean de Vienne***
   3. **CL *La Galisonniere***
   4. **CM [minelayer] *Émile Bertin*** (assigned to Bizerte Destroyers))

4th Cruiser Division (HQ: Brest, France; 09/01/39, assigned to 1st Flotilla [Squadron], Raiding Force): 09/01/39? RA C. J. L. Bourrague [FN] [Flag: light cruiser *Georges Leygues*]
A. **Components - 4th Cruiser Division** (09/01/39)
   1. **CL *Georges Leygues***

2. **CL** *Glorie*
   3. **CL** *Montcalm*

5th Cruiser Division (HQ: Saigon, French Indochina; 09/01/39, assigned to Far East Naval Forces): 09/01/39? RA Jules E. M. A. Terraux [FN] [Flag: CL *Lamotte Picquett*] (Admiral Far East [Indochina]) 06/25/40
A. ***Components - 5th Cruiser Division*** (09/01/39)
   1. **CA** *Suffren*
   2. **CL** *Lamotte Picquett*

6th Cruiser Division (HQ: Dakar, Senegal; 09/01/39, assigned to 5th Light Squadron): 09/01/39? RA J. H. C. E. Moreau [FN] [Flag: CL *Duguay-Trouin*] [+ Commander-in-Chief, West Africa Naval Station & Commanding Officer, 5th Light Squadron] (Commanding Officer, Algiers Naval Force) 09/40 disbanded.
A. ***Components - 6th Cruiser Division*** (09/01/39)
   1. **CL** *Duguay-Trouin*
   2. **CL** *Primauguet*

7th Cruiser Division (HQ: Dakar, Senegal; 09/01/39, assigned to 5th Light Squadron): 09/01/39? unknown?
A. ***Components - 7th Cruiser Division*** (09/01/39)
   1. **CL** *Jeanne de Arc*
   2. **CL** *La Tour d'Auvergne [Pluton]*

2nd Light Squadron (HQ: Brest, France; 09/01/39, assigned to 1st Flotilla): 09/01/39? RA E. M. Lacroix [FN] [Flag: DD *Mogador*]
A. ***Components - 2nd Light Squadron*** (09/01/39)
   1. **6th Large Destroyer Division**
   2. **8th Large Destroyer Division**
   3. **10th Large Destroyer Division**

3rd Light Squadron (HQ: Toulon, France; 09/01/39, assigned to 3rd Flotilla): 09/01/39? RA E. H. N. Derrien [FN] [Flag: destroyer *Maille Breze*] (Commanding Admiral, Bizerta Base) 11/42?
A. ***Components - 3rd Light Squadron*** (09/01/39)
   1. **5th Destroyer Division**
   2. **7th Destroyer Division**
   3. **9th Destroyer Division**

4th Light Squadron [Bizerte Destroyers] (HQ: Bizerte, Tunisia): 09/01/39? unknown?
A. ***Components - 4th Light Squadron*** (09/01/39)
   1. **1st Destroyer Division**
   2. **3rd Destroyer Division**
   3. **11th Destroyer Division**
   4. **CM [minelayer]** *Émile Bertin*

6th Light Squadron [Oran Naval Force] (HQ: Oran, Algeria; 09/01/39, assigned to IV Naval Region): 09/01/39? RA Y. V. M. Donval [FN] [Flag: AS [submarine tender] *Jules Verne*] 12/08/39 RA M. L. H. Jarry [FN] 11/08/42? VA Rioult [FN]
A. *Components*
1. **8th Light Destroyer Division**
2. **2nd Submarine Squadron**
    a. **12th Submarine Division**
    b. **14th Submarine Division**
    c. **18th Submarine Division**
3. **CVS *Commandant Teste***
4. **AS [submarine tender] *Jules Verne***

1st Light Destroyer Squadron (HQ: Oran, Algeria; 09/01/39, assigned to 2nd Flotilla, High Seas Force): 09/01/39? Capt. L. H. C. Longaud [FN] [Flag: DE *La Palme*] [+ Commander, 1st Light Destroyer Division]
A. *Components*
1. **1st Light Destroyer Division**
2. **3rd Light Destroyer Division**
3. **7th Light Destroyer Division**

2nd Light Destroyer Squadron (HQ: Brest, France; 09/01/39, assigned to II Naval Region; assigned to Naval Commander, Morocco; 11/09/42, destroyed): Capt. Y. F. C. A. M. Urvoy de Portzamparc [FN] [Flag: DE *Cyclone*] /42 RA R. E. Gervais de Lafond [FN] [Flag: CL *Primauguet*] (wounded) 11/09/42 destroyed.
A. *Components - 2nd Light Destroyer Squadron* (09/01/39)
1. **2nd Light Destroyer Division**
2. **4th Light Destroyer Division**
3. **5th Light Destroyer Division**
4. **6th Light Destroyer Division**

2nd Submarine Squadron (HQ: Oran, Algeria; 09/01/39, assigned to Oran Force [6th Light Squadron): 09/01/39? Cdr. P. J. M. Cadoret [FN]
A. *Components*
1. **12th Submarine Division**
2. **14th Submarine Division**
3. **18th Submarine Division**

3rd Submarine Squadron (HQ: Toulon, France; 09/01/39, assigned to 1st Submarine Flotilla): 09/01/39? Cdr. L. C. Vidil [FN]
A. *Components - 3rd Submarine Squadron* (09/01/39)
1. **1st Submarine Division**
2. **3rd Submarine Division**
3. **5th Submarine Division**

4th Submarine Squadron (HQ: Brest, France; 09/01/39, assigned to II Naval Region): Cdr. M. A. H. Leportier [FN] [Leader: SS *Surcouf*]

A. ***Components* - 4th Submarine Squadron** (09/01/39)
   1. **2nd Submarine Division**
   2. **4th Submarine Division**
   3. **6th Submarine Division**
   4. **8th Submarine Division**

5th Submarine Squadron (HQ: Toulon, France; 09/01/39, assigned to 1st Submarine Squadron): 09/01/39? Cdr. R. E. G. Fitte [FN]
A. ***Components* - 5th Submarine Squadron** (09/01/39)
   1. **13th Submarine Division**
   2. **15th Submarine Division**

6th Submarine Squadron (HQ: Bizerte, Tunisia; 09/01/39, assigned to Bizerte Submarine Base and subordinate to Bizerte Submarine Base): 09/01/39? Cdr. J. E. M. de Richoufftz de Manin [FN] [Flag: DD *Aigle*] [+ Commanding Officer, Bizerte Submarine Base]
A. ***Components* - 6th Submarine Squadron** (09/01/39)
   1. **9th Submarine Division**
   2. **10th Submarine Division**
   3. **11th Submarine Division** (detached to Levant Naval Division)
   4. **17th Submarine Division**
   5. **20th Submarine Division**

Toulon Submarine Base [Submarine Center at Toulon] (HQ: Toulon, France; 09/01/39, assigned to III Naval Region): 09/01/39? Cdr. R. M. de Bretteville [FN]
A. ***Components* - Toulon Submarine Base [Submarine Center at Toulon]** (09/01/39)
   1. **7th Submarine Division**
   2. **19th Submarine Division**
   3. **21st Submarine Division**

Bizerte Submarine Base (HQ: Bizerte, Tunisia; 09/01/39, assigned to IV Naval Region): 09/01/39? Cdr. J. E. M. de Richoufftz de Manin [FN] [Flag: DD *Aigle*] [+ Commanding Officer, 6th Submarine Squadron]
A. ***Components* - Bizerte Submarine Base** (09/01/39)
   1. **6th Submarine Squadron**
      a. **9th Submarine Division**
      b. **10th Submarine Division**
      c. **17th Submarine Division**
      d. **20th Submarine Division**
   2. **AS [submarine tender]** *Castor*

Indian Ocean Naval Station (HQ: Djibouti, French Territory of the Afars and the Issas): 09/01/39? Cdr. L. M. J. H. Fabre [FN] [Flag: Sloop *Bougainville*]

Pacific Ocean Naval Station (HQ: Papeete, Tahiti): 09/01/39? Cdr A. C. M. Arzur [FN] [Flag: Sloop *Dumont d'Urville*] 11/18/39 Cdr. P. G. Toussaint de Quievrecourt [FN]

Vichy French Army

Army of North Africa: see **Commander-in-Chief, North Africa Theater**.

Corps

I Group of Military Divisions (09/12/40; 11/42, demobilized): Gen. René-Henri Olry (retired) /42 LG Jean-Léon-Albert Langlois (retired) /42 LG Odilon-Léonard-Théophile Picquendar (Head, Preservation of War Material Service) 11/42 demobilized.
- A. **Chief of Staff, I Group of Military Divisions** (09/12/40): Col. Jacques-Pierre-Louis de Grancey (Commanding Officer, 26th Infantry Regiment) /41
- B. *Components - Group of Military Divisions* (08/12/40)
    1. **7th Military Division**
    2. **14th Military Division**
    3. **15th Military Division**
    4. **16th Military Division**

II Group of Military Divisions (09/12/40; 11/42, demobilized): Gen. Edouard-Jean Réquin (retired) /41 LG Aubert-Achille-Jules Frère [+ Member, The Army Council] (retired; /42, President, Investigating Commission of War Events) 11/42 demobilized.
- A. **Chief of Staff, Group of Military Divisions** (09/12/40): Col. Georges-Marie-Joseph Revers (Chief of Staff, Commander-in-Chief) 12/40 Col. Paul-Henri Dumas (Commanding Officer, 65th African Artillery Regiment) 12/41? unknown? 11/42 dissolved.
- B. *Components - Group of Military Divisions* (08/12/40)
    1. **9th Military Division**
    2. **12th Military Division**
    3. **13th Military Division**
    4. **17th Military Division**

19th Military Division: see **XIX Army Corps**
- A. *Components - Vichy France 19th Military Division [Algerian Army Corps]*
    1. **Algiers Division [Division d'Alger]**: see **Divisions in Overseas Colonies and Protectorates** Section.
    2. **Constantine Division [Division de Constantine]**: see **Divisions in Overseas Colonies and Protectorates** Section.
    3. **Oran Division [Division d'Oran]**: see **Divisions in Overseas Colonies and Protectorates** Section.

French African Corps: /42 MG Joseph-Jean de Goislard de Monsabert [+ Commanding General, 81st African Infantry Division] (Commanding General, Free French 3rd Algerian Infantry Division) 05/01/43 disbanded.

Tunisian Command: see **Tunisian Army Corps**.
- A. *Components - Tunisia Army Corps*

1. **Tunisian Division**: see **Vichy France Infantry Divisions**.

Moroccan Command: see **Moroccan Army Corps**.
A. *Components* - **Vichy France Morocco Army Corps**
1. **Casablanca (Independent) Territorial Division**: see **Divisions in Overseas Colonies and Protectorates** Section.
2. **Fèz Territorial Division**: see **Divisions in Overseas Colonies and Protectorates** Section.
3. **Marrakech Territorial Division**: see **Divisions in Overseas Colonies and Protectorates** Section.
4. **Meknès Territorial Division**: see **Divisions in Overseas Colonies and Protectorates** Section.

Indochina Army Corps: see **Indochina Army Corps** in **Army Corps** Section.
A. *Components* - **Vichy France Indochina Army Corps**
1. **Annam Division**: see **Divisions in Overseas Colonies and Protectorates** Section.
2. **Cochinshine-Cambodge Division**: see **Divisions in Overseas Colonies and Protectorates** Section.
3. **Tonkin Division**: see **Divisions in Overseas Colonies and Protectorates** Section.

Vichy France Divisions

France

2ⁿᵈ Military Division(/40; 09/12/40, redesignated **12ᵗʰ Military Division**): MG Jean-Marie-Léon Etcheberrigaray (Commanding General, 12ᵗʰ Military Division) 09/12/40 redesignated **12ᵗʰ Military Division** - see **12ᵗʰ Military Division**.
   A.   **Infantry, 2ⁿᵈ Military Division** (/40): BG Marcel-Georges François (Infantry Commander, 12ᵗʰ Military District) 09/12/40 dissolved.

7ᵗʰ Military Division (09/12/40; 11/42, demobilized): MG Louis-Albert-Pierre Robert de Saint-Vincent (Deputy Commander, 14ᵗʰ Military Division) /40 MG Maxime-Jean-Vincent Germain (Commanding General, 15ᵗʰ Military Division) /40 MG Marie-Alphonse-Théodore-René-Adrian Desmazes (42 to /45, German prisoner-of-war) /40 MG Louis-Marie-Joseph-Ferdinand Keller (/44, arrested by the Germans; /44, died in Buchenwald Concentration Camp) /41 MG Pierre-Louis-Charles-Constance Hanoteau (?) or MG Jean-Marie-Léon Etcheberrigaray (to /45, German prisoner-of-war; /45, retired) /42 MG Pierre-Jules-André-Marie de La Font Chabert (retired) 11/42 demobilized.
   A.   **Deputy Commander, 7ᵗʰ Military District** (09/12/40): unknown? /41 MG Fernand-Zacharie-Joseph Lenclud (Commanding General, 13ᵗʰ Military Division) /42
   B.   *Components - 7ᵗʰ Military Division*
       1.   **4ᵗᵗʰ Infantry Half-Brigade**
       2.   **65ᵗʰ Infantry Regiment**
       3.   **151ˢᵗ Infantry Regiment**
       4.   **61ˢᵗ Divisional Artillery Regiment**
       5.   **5ᵗʰ Dragoon (Cavalry) Regiment**
   C.   **Infantry, 7ᵗʰ Military Division** (09/12/40): BG Marie-Cyrille-Victor Debeney (Infantry Commander, 14ᵗʰ Military Division) /40

8ᵗʰ Military Division (09/12/40; 09/40, disbanded): MG Jules-Philippe-Octave Decamp (Deputy Commander, 15ᵗʰ Military Division) 09/40 disbanded.

9ᵗʰ Military Division (09/12/40; 11/42, demobilized): LG Alfred-Marie-Joseph-Louis Montagne (retired) /41 MG René-Jean-Divy Corbé (retired) /42 LG Jean-Léon-Albert Langlois (Commanding General, I Vichy Army Corps) /42 BG Marie-Henri-Pierre Préaud (?) 11/42 demobilized.
   A.   *Components - 9ᵗʰ Military Division*
       1.   **1ˢᵗ Infantry Regiment**
       2.   **27ᵗʰ Infantry Regiment**
       3.   **32ⁿᵈ Infantry Regiment**
       4.   **61ˢᵗ Divisional Artillery Regiment**
       5.   **8ᵗʰ Cuirassier (Cavalry) Regiment**

12ᵗʰ Military Division (09/12/40, from **2ⁿᵈ Division**; 11/42, demobilized): MG Jean-Marie-Léon Etcheberrigaray (Commanding General, 7ᵗʰ Military Division) /40 MG Joseph-Charles-

Robert Jeannel (retired; /44 to /45, in German prison) 11/18/42? MG Paul-Hippolyte Arlabosse (/43, Member, Commission in Charge of granting rewards of the war) 11/42 demobilized.
- A. **Deputy Commander, 12th Military Division** (09/12/40): unknown? /41 BG Henri-Louis-Léon Cyvogt (retired) 11/42 dissolved.
- B. *Components - 12th Military Division*
    1. **1st Infantry Half-Brigade**
    2. **26th Infantry Regiment**: /41 Col. Jacques-Pierre-Louis de Grancey (Commanding Officer, 5th Region, l'"Organisation Résistance de l'Armée) 11/18/40
    3. **41st Infantry Regiment**
    4. **35th Divisional Artillery Regiment**
    5. **6th Cuirassier (Cavalry) Regiment**
- C. **Infantry, 12th Military Division** (09/12/40): BG Marcel-Georges François (Commanding General, 4th Algerian Infantry Brigade) 11/42 dissolved.

13th Military Division (09/12/40; 11/42, demobilized): LG Pierre-Paul-Jacques Grandsard (retired; /43, arrested and deport by the Germans) /41 unknown? /42 LG Fernand-Zacharie-Joseph Lenclud (retired) 11/42 demobilized.
- A. **Deputy Commander, 13th Military Division** (09/12/40): unknown? /41 MG Jean-Joseph-Marie-Gabriel de Lattre de Tassigny (Commander-in-Chief, Tunisia) /41 MG Gaston-René-Eugène Roton (?) 11/42 dissolved.
- B. *Components - 9th Military Division*
    1. **5th Infantry Regiment**
    2. **92nd Infantry Regiment**
    3. **152nd Infantry Regiment**
    4. **4th Divisional Artillery Regiment**
    5. **8th Dragoon (Cavalry) Regiment**

14th Military Division (09/12/40; 11/42, demobilized): LG Aubert-Achille-Jules Frère [+ Military-Governor of Lyon] (Commanding General, II Group of Military Divisions & Member, The Vichy French Army Council) /41 MG Jean Mer (?) /41 LG Louis-Albert-Pierre Robert de Saint-Vincent [+ Military-Governor, Lyon] (retired) 11/42 demobilized.
- A. **Deputy Commander, 14th Military Division** (09/12/40): unknown? /40 MG Louis-Albert-Pierre Robert de Saint-Vincent (Commanding General, 14th Military Division & Military-Governor of Lyon) /41
- B. *Components - 14th Military Division*
    1. **3rd Mountain Infantry Half-Brigade**
    2. **153rd Mountain Infantry Regiment**
    3. **159th Mountain Infantry Regiment**
    4. **61st Divisional Artillery Regiment**
    5. **11th Cuirassier (Cavalry) Regiment**
    6. **1st Cavalry Brigade**
- C. **Infantry, 14th Military Division** (09/12/40): unknown? /40 BG Marie-Cyrille-Victor Debeney (Director of Infantry, Vichy Ministry of War) /41

15th Military Division (09/12/40; 11/42, demobilized): LG Henri-Fernand Dentz (Commander-in-Chief, Levant) 11/27/40 MG Maxime-Jean-Vincent Germain (Inspector of Colonial Forces & Member, the Army Council) /41 MG Jean-Louis-Auguste Humbert (/43 to /45, arrested by the Germans and deported to Buchenwald Concentration Camp) or MG Jules-Philippe-Octave Decamp (/44 to /45, German prisoner-of-war; /45, retired) 11/42 demobilized.
- A. **Deputy Commander, 15th Military Division** (09/12/40): unknown? 09/40 MG Jules-Philippe-Octave Decamp (Commanding General, 15th Military Division) /41
- B. *Components - 15th Military Division*
    1. **2nd Mountain Infantry Half-Brigade**
    2. **43rd Infantry Regiment**
    3. **21st Colonial Infantry Regiment**
    4. **10th Colonial Mountain Artillery Regiment**
    5. **12th Cuirassier (Cavalry) Regiment**
    6. **1st Cavalry Brigade**

16th Military Division (09/12/40; 11/42, demobilized): MG Félix-René Altmayer (retired) /42 MG René-Edouard-Joseph Bonnet de la Tour (?) 11/42 demobilized.
- A. **Deputy Commander, 16th Military Division** (09/12/40): BG René-Edouard-Joseph Bonnet de la Tour (Commanding General, Military District XVI) /42
- B. *Components - 16th Military Division*
    1. **8th Infantry Half-Brigade**
    2. **51st Infantry Regiment**
    3. **2nd Colonial Infantry Regiment**
    4. **61st Divisional Artillery Regiment**
    5. **3rd Dragoon (Cavalry) Regiment**

17th Military Division (09/12/40; 11/42 demobilized): LG Théodore-Marcel Sciard (retired; /44, at disposal of Military District XVIII for regroupment formation of North African and Colonial units) /40 MG Louis-Michel-Marie-Joseph Michel (?) /41 LG Sylvestre-Gérard Audet (in reserve; /42, retired) /42 MG Louis-Gustavé Bérard (/43, Head, French Delegation to the German Armistice Commission) 11/42 demobilized.
- A. **Deputy Commander, 17th Military Division**: 08/11/41 BG Henri Lacaille /41 BG Louis-Gustavé Bérard (Commanding General, 17th Military Division) /42
- B. *Components - 17th Military Division*
    1. **18th Infantry Regiment**
    2. **23rd Infantry Regiment**
    3. **150th Infantry Regiment**
    4. **24th Divisional Artillery Regiment**
    5. **2nd Dragoon (Cavalry) Regiment**
    6. **2nd Cavalry Brigade**

North Africa

Algeria

Algiers Territorial Division [Division d'Alger] (North Africa; HQ: Algiers, Algeria): see **Divisions in Overseas Colonies and Protectorates** Section.

Constantine Territorial Division [Division de Constantine] (North Africa: HQ: Constantine, Algeria): see **Divisions in Overseas Colonies and Protectorates** Section.

Oran Territorial Division [Division d'Oran] (North Africa; HQ: Oran, Algeria): see **Divisions in Overseas Colonies and Protectorates** Section.

Constantine March Division (11/08/42, North Africa: HQ: Constantine, Algeria; also known as **Welvert Division**; 04/30/43, disbanded and used to form on 05/01/43, the **3rd Algerian Infantry Division**): MG Marie-Joseph-Edmond Welvert (killed in action) 04/10/43 unknown? 04/30/43 disbanded and used to form the **3rd Algerian Infantry Division** - see rebuilt French Army (1943) **3rd Algerian Infantry Division**.

A. *Components* - **Constantine March Division** (11/08/42)
1. **Infantry**
    a. **1st Algerian Tirailleurs (Infantry) Regiment**
    b. **2nd Algerian Tirailleurs (Infantry) Regiment**
    c. **3rd Algerian Tirailleurs (Infantry) Regiment**
    d. **7th Algerian Tirailleurs (Infantry) Regiment**
    e. **9th Algerian Tirailleurs (Infantry) Regiment**: /39 Col. Joseph-Jean de Goislard de Monsabert (Commanding Officer, 81st Infantry Brigade) /39
    f. **4th Moroccan Tirailleurs (Infantry) Regiment**
    g. **7th Moroccan Tirailleurs (Infantry) Regiment**
    h. **15th Sénégalese Tirailleurs (Infantry) Regiment**
    i. **Constantine Goums**
    j. **2nd Moroccan Tabors**
2. **Cavalry and Armor**
    a. **7th Guard Cavalry Regiment**
    b. **8th Guard Cavalry Regiment**
    c. **3rd African Chasseurs (Armor) Regiment**
    d. **5th African Chasseurs (Armor) Regiment**
    e. **3rd Algerian Spahis (Cavalry) Regiment**
    f. **4th Tunisian Spahis (Cavalry) Regiment**
3. **Artillery**
    a. **62nd African Artillery Regiment**
    b. **64th African Artillery Regiment**
    c. **65th African Artillery Regiment**: 01/42? Col. Paul-Henri Dumas (Artillery Commander, I Free French Army Corps) /44

                d. **66ᵗʰ African Artillery Regiment**
                e. **Moroccan Colonial Artillery Regiment**
                f. **Levant Colonial Artillery Regiment**
                g. **410ᵗʰ Anti-Aircraft Regiment** (split with Algerian March Division)
                h. **411ᵗʰ Anti-Aircraft Regiment**
        4. **Engineer**
                a. **19ᵗʰ Engineer Regiment** (split with Algerian March Division)

Algerian March Division (11/14/42, North Africa; HQ: Algiers, Algeria; 06/09/43, disbanded): MG Charles-Emmanuel Mast (Head, French Military Mission to Syria & Egypt) 06/09/43 disbanded
A. *Components* - **Algerian March Division** (11/14/42)
    1. **Infantry**
            a. **1ˢᵗ Algerian Tirailleurs (Infantry) Regiment**
            b. **9ᵗʰ Algerian Tirailleurs (Infantry) Regiment**
            c. **1ˢᵗ Zouaves Infantry Regiment**: 11/14/42 Col. Jean-Charles-Marie-Joseph Gross (Commanding General, Base Command, Free French Expeditionary Corps, Italy) 09/43
    2. **Cavalry**
            a. **1ˢᵗ Algerian Spahis (Cavalry) Regiment**
            b. **1ˢᵗ African Chasseurs (Armor) Regiment**: /41 Col. Henri-Jacques-Jean-François de Vernejoul (Commanding General, 2ⁿᵈ Light Mechanized (Armored) Brigade) /42
    3. **Artillery**
            a. **65ᵗʰ African Artillery Regiment**
            b. **410ᵗʰ Anti-Aircraft Regiment** (split with Constantine March Division)
    4. **Engineer**
            a. **19ᵗʰ Engineer Regiment** (split with Constantine March Division)

Oran March Division (05/01/43, North Africa; HQ: Oran, Algeria; 06/30/43, disbanded): MG Robert-Marie-Jules-Camille Boissau (?) 06/30/43 disbanded.
A. *Components* - **Oran March Division** (05/01/40)
    1. **Infantry**
            a. **2ⁿᵈ Algerian Tirailleurs (Infantry) Regiment**
            b. **6ᵗʰ Algerian Tirailleurs (Infantry) Regiment**
            c. **15ᵗʰ Senegalese (African) Tirailleurs (Infantry) Regiment**: /42 Col. Louis-Constant Morlière (Infantry Commander, 9ᵗʰ Colonial Division) /44
            d. **1ˢᵗ Foreign Legion March Regiment**
    2. **Artillery**
            a. **66ᵗʰ African Artillery Regiment**
            b. **411ᵗʰ Anti-Aircraft Regiment**
            c. **412ᵗʰ Anti-Aircraft Regiment**

Algerian Light Mechanized Brigade (11/18/42, North Africa; 03/01/43, disbanded): unknown? 03/01/43 disbanded.

A. ***Components*** - **Algerian Light Mechanized Brigade**
   1. **Cavalry**
      a. **2nd African Chasseurs (Armor) Regiment**
      b. **5th African Chasseurs (Armor) Regiment**
      c. **9th African Chasseurs (Armor) Regiment**
   2. **Artillery**
      a. **1st Anti-Tank Regiment**
      b. **1st Zouave Infantry Regiment**

1st Armored Division (01/28/43, from elements of the **Algerian Light Mechanized Brigade**, although officially created 05/01/43; 08/43, becomes French Army (1943) **1st Free French Armored Division**): BG Jean-Louis-Alai Touzet du Vigier (Commanding General, 1st Free French Armored Division) 08/43 becomes French Army (1943) **1st Free French Armored Division** - see French Army (1943) **1st Free French Armored Division**.

A. **Deputy Commander, 1st Armored Division** (07/43): Col. Granier 08/43 see French Army (1943) **1st Free French Armored Division**.
B. ***Components*** - **1st Free French Armored Division** (07/43)
   1. **Light Mechanized Brigade**: /43 BG Jean-Louis-Alai Touzet du Vigier (Commanding General, Vichy French 1st Armored Division) 01/28/43
      a. **2nd Zouave Armored Regiment**
      b. **2nd African Armored Regiment**
      c. **8th African Armored Regiment**
      d. **12th African Armored Regiment**: /43? Col. Paul-Anne-Joseph-Alexandre Baron Girot de Langlade (Commanding Officer, Armored Group Langlade) /44
   2. **Cavalry Brigade**
   3. **68th Divisional Artillery Regiment**
C. **Artillery, 1st Armored Division** (07/43): Col. Marie-Joseph-Louis-Henri Noetinger 08/43 see French Army (1943) **1st Free French Armored Division**.

Morocco

Casablanca Territorial Division (North Africa; HQ: Casablanca, Morocco): see **Divisions in Overseas Colonies and Protectorates** Section.

Fèz Territorial Division (North Africa; HQ: Fèz, Morocco): see **Divisions in Overseas Colonies and Protectorates** Section.

Marrakech Territorial Division (North Africa; HQ: Marrakech, Morocco): see **Divisions in Overseas Colonies and Protectorates** Section.

Meknès Territorial Division (North Africa; HQ: Meknès, Morocco): see **Divisions in Overseas Colonies and Protectorates** Section.

Moroccan March Division (11/18/42, as **"A" Division**, North Africa; 11/29/42, redesignated **Moroccan March Division**; 12/05/42, redesignated **1st Moroccan March Division**; 06/15/43, disbanded): **"A" Division** 11/18/42 unknown? 11/29/42 redesignated **Moroccan March Division** 11/29/42 MG Maurice-Noël-Eugène Mathenet (Commanding General, 1st Moroccan March Division) 12/05/42 redesignated **1st Moroccan March Division** 12/05/42 MG Maurice-Noël-Eugène Mathenet

A. *Components* - **Moroccan March Division** (11/18/42)
  1. **Infantry**
      a. **7th Moroccan Tirailleurs (Infantry) Regiment**
      b. **3rd Foreign Legion Regiment**
      c. **1st Supplementary Moroccan Group**
  2. **Cavalry**
  3. **Artillery**
      a. **1st Moroccan March Artillery Regiment**

Tunisia

Tunis Territorial Division (Tunisia): see **Divisions in Overseas Colonies and Protectorates** Section.

Sousse Territorial Division (Tunisia): see **Divisions in Overseas Colonies and Protectorates** Section.

Tunisian Division (Tunisia):
A. *Components* - **Tunisian Division** (07/40)
  1. **4th Zouave Infantry Regiment** (07/40): Col. Marcel Rime-Bruneau (armistice leave; 12/26/42, Official Representative for the French at Allied Headquarters in Algiers) /41
  2. **4th Tunisian Tirailleurs (Infantry) Regiment**
  3. **10th Senegalese (African) Tirailleurs (Infantry) Regiment**
  4. **62nd African Artillery Regiment**

French Indochina

Cochinshine-Cambodge Division (Indochina Army Corps; HQ Saigon): see **Divisions in Overseas Colonies and Protectorates** Section.

Tonkin Division (Indochina Army Corps; HQ: Hanoi): see **Divisions in Overseas Colonies and Protectorates** Section.

Annam Brigade (Indochina Army Corps; HQ: Hué): see **Infantry Brigades** in **Brigades** Section.

Cambodge Brigade (Indochina Army Corps; HQ: Pnom Penh): see **Brigades** under French Army (pre-July 1940).

Free French Forces (1941 to 1943)

Corps

Free French, Africa (/41): MG Paul-Louis-Victor-Marie Legentilhomme (War Commissoner) 09/24/41

Divisions

Free French Forces, Great Britain: /41? MG René-Jean-Charles Chouteau (?) 01/43 LG François d'Astier de la Vigerie [FAF] [+ Member, Council & Assistant to BG Charles de Gaulle] /43 MG Charles-Jean-Roger Noiret (Commanding General, 10th Infantry Division (#2)) /45?

Free French Forces in Sudan & Eritrea: /41 Paul-Louis-Victor-Marie Legentilhomme (Commanding General, 1st Free French Infantry Division (#1), Syria) /41

Free French Forces in the Western Desert (/42, North Africa): MG René-Marie-Edgar de Larminat (Commanding General, 1st Free French Division) /43

Free French Forces, Libya: /42 Col. Achille-Fernand-Hector Dassonville (/45, Commanding General, French Southern Zone of Occupation, Germany) /43

1st Free French Infantry Division (#1) (/40, Syria; 05/10/41 in Quastina, Palestine; after Syria absorbed those French units who rallied to the Free French cause; becomes **Free French Group of Divisions**): MG Paul-Louis-Victor-Marie Legentilhomme (Commander-in-Chief, Free French, Africa) /41

A. **Chief of Staff, 1st Free French Infantry Division (#1)** (/40): Col. Marie-Joseph-Pierre-François Kœnig (Commanding General, 1st Independent French Brigade) /41

2nd Light Free French Division (from **Leclerc's Column [Colonne Leclerc]**; 08/24/43, becomes the **2nd Free French Armored Division (#2)**): <u>Leclerc's Column</u> /41 BG Philippe-François-Marie-Jacques Leclerc de Hauteclocque, Count of Hauteclocque [+ Commander-in-Chief, French Equatorial Africa] /41 redesignated <u>**2nd Light Free French Division**</u> /41 BG Alfred-Maurice Cazaud [+ Commanding General, 13th Foreign Legion Half-Brigade] (acting) /41

Division Côtière: /42 MG Alfred-Maurice Cazaud [+ Commanding General, Lebanon] (Commanding General, 36th Infantry Division (#2)) 02/45.

Brigades

4th Light Free French Infantry Brigade: /41 LCol. Pierre-François-Marie Joseph Garbay (Infantry Commander, 2nd Independent French Brigade) /41

Free French Oriental Brigade (11/12/40): BG René-Marie-Edgar de Larminat (Commanding General, 1st Free French Brigade) /41 Col. Charles-Raoul Magrin-Vernerey dit Monclar (Deputy Commander-in-Chief, Levant) /44

1st Independent French Brigade (/41, from **Free French Group of Divisions**): BG René-Marie-Edgar de Larminat (Commanding General, Free French Forces in the Western Desert) /42 BG Pierre-Paul Lelong (?) /42 BG Marie-Joseph-Pierre-François Kœnig (Commanding General, 1st Free French Infantry Division (#2)) 02/01/43 redesignated **1st Free French Infantry Division (#2)** - see French Army (1943) **1st Free French Infantry Division(#2)**.
  A. **Infantry, 2nd Independent French Brigade**: /41 LCol. Pierre-François-Marie Joseph Garbay (Deputy Commander, 2nd Independent French Brigade) /42 dissolved.

2nd Independent French Brigade (from **Free French Group of Divisions**) (/42): BG Alfred-Maurice Cazaud (Commanding General, Lebanon & Commanding General, Division Côtière) /42 unknown? /43 Col. Pierre-François-Marie Joseph Garbay (Infantry Commander, 1st Free French Infantry Division (#2)) /44
  A. **Deputy Commander, 2nd Independent French Brigade**: /42 Col. Pierre-François-Marie Joseph Garbay (Commanding Officer, 2nd Independent French Brigade) /44

1st Free French Armored Brigade: /42? BG Aimé Sudre (Deputy Commander, 1st Free French Armored Division) /43?

Free French Naval Forces

Free French Pacific Naval Forces (/40): Capt. Philippe Auboyneau [FN] [Naval [Leader: destroyer *Le Triomphant*] (Head, Navy and Merchant Navy Commission & Commander-in-Chief, Free French Navy) 04/42

Rebuilt French Army of 1943 - 1945

Armies

Commander-in-Chief, French Land Forces, North Africa (01/43): see **Commander-in-Chief, North African Theater** 05/43 disbanded.

French Forces of the Interior (FFI) [Forces Françaises l'Intérieur] (06/23/44, placed the resistance fighter under one command; 10/44, disbanded and were amalgamated into the French regular forces): MG Marie-Joseph-Pierre-François Kœnig [+ Military-Governor of Paris] 10/44 disbanded.
A. **Chief of Staff, French Forces of the Interior** (06/23/44): BG Pierre-Marie-Philippe Dejussieu-Pontcarrel (arrested and deported to Germany; /45, Inspectorate-General of the Army) /44

Commander-in-Chief, Army B (12/43): LG Jean-Joseph-Marie-Gabriel de Lattre de Tassigny (Commander-in-Chief, First Free French Army) 08/44 redesignated **First French Army** - see **First French Army**.
A. **Artillery, Army B** (12/43): BG René de Hesdin (Military-Governor, Rome, Italy) /44

Commander-in-Chief, First Free French Army (08/44): LG Jean-Joseph-Marie-Gabriel de Lattre de Tassigny.

    A. **Chief of Staff, First Free French Army** (08/44): BG Jean-Étienne Valluy (Commanding General, 9th Colonial Infantry Division) /45 BG François-Jean-Antonin-Marie-Amédée Gonzalès de Linarès.

    B. *Components* - First Free French Army
        1. **I Free French Army Corps**
        2. **II Free French Army Corps**
   3. **Reserves**
        a. **2nd Free French Armored Division**
        b. **1st Motor Infantry Division (later 1st March Infantry Division)**
        c. **10th Infantry Division**
        d. **14th Infantry Division**
        e. **27th Alpine Division**
C. **Vice Chief of Staff, First free French Army** (08/44): BG François-Jean-Antonin-Marie-Amédée Gonzalès de Linarès (Chief of Staff, First Free French Army) /45
D. **Armor, First Free French Army** (08/44): unknown? /45 MG Henri-Jacques-Jean-François de Vernejoul.
E. **Engineers, First Free French Army** (08/44): BG Robert-Henri-Eugène Dromard.
F. **Medical Services, First Free French Army** (08/44): BG Arthur Guirriec.
G. **Base Command, First Free French Army** (08/44): BG Jean-Charles-Marie-Joseph Gross

Corps

Commander-in-Chief, French Expeditionary Corps [FEC] in Italy [Corps Expéditionnaire Français en Italie (CEFI)] (09/43): LG Alphonse-Pierre Juin (Chief of the Free French General Staff) 07/44 disbanded.
- A. **Chief of Staff, French Expeditionary Corps** (09/43): BG Marcel-Maurice Carpentier (Commanding General, 2nd Moroccan Infantry Division) /44
- B. *Components* - French Expeditionary Corps in Italy
    1. **2nd Moroccan Motor Infantry Division**
    2. **3rd Algerian Infantry Division**
    3. **4th Moroccan Motor Infantry Division**
    4. **1st Free French Infantry Division (#2)**
    5. **Moroccan Goum**
- C. **Deputy Chief of Staff, French Expeditionary Corps** (09/43): Col. André-Marie Zeller (Head, French Transportation Mission to Belgian) /44
- D. **Artillery, French Expeditionary Corps in Italy** (09/43): Col. Claude-Philippe-Armand Chaillet
- E. **Engineers, French Expeditionary Corps in Italy** (09/43): Col. Robert-Henri-Eugène Dromard (Engineers, First Free French Army) 08/44
- F. **Indentend [Quartermaster] Service, French Expeditionary Corps in Italy** (09/43): BG Félicien-Alfred-Marie Monginoux
- G. **Medical Services, French Expeditionary Corps in Italy** (09/43): Col. Georges-André Hugonot (Director, Medical Services, Military District VIII) /44
- H. **Base Command, French Expeditionary Corps in Italy** (09/43): BG Jean-Charles-Marie-Joseph Gross (Commanding General, Base Command, First Free French Army) 08/44

I Free French Army Corps (08/16/43; Corsica): LG Henri-Jules-Jean Martin (Commanding General, XIX Army Corps) /44 LG Marie-Emil-Antoine Béthouart (French High Commissioner for Austria) /45.
- A. **Chief of Staff, I Free French Army Corps** (08/16/43): unknown? /44 BG André-Claude Chevillon.
- B. *Components* - I Free French Army Corps
    1. **1st Free French Armored Division**
    2. **4th Moroccan Motor Infantry Division**
    3. **9th Colonial Infantry Division**
- C. **Artillery, I Free French Army Corps** (08/16/43): unknown? /44 BG Paul-Henri Dumas.

II Free French Army Corps: 08/31/44 LG René-Marie-Edgar de Larminat (Commanding General, Atlantic Detachment) /44 LG Joseph-Jean de Goislard de Monsabert.
- A. **Chief of Staff, II Free French Army Corps** (08/31/44): BG Jean-Claude-Louis-Victor Bouley (Military-Governor, Rhine-Palatinate) /45.
- B. *Components* - II Free French Army Corps
    1. **5th Free French Armored Division**
    2. **2nd Moroccan Motor Infantry Division**

      3.   **3rd Algerian Infantry Division**

C.   **Artillery, II Free French Army Corps**: /44 Col. Henri-Marie-Jean Noël du Payrat /44 BG Fernand-Philippe-Alphonse Besançon (?) /45 BG André-Eugène Navereau.

III Free French Army Corps (/44, never fully formed; /44, disbanded): vacant /44 disbanded.

A.   **Chief of Staff, III Free French Army Corps** (/44): BG Raymond-Francis Duval (Infantry Commander, 3rd Algerian Division) /44 dissolved.

I Free French Armored Corps: /44? MG Oierre-Emannuel-André Dario.

Far East Expeditionary Corps (06/45): LG Philippe-François-Marie-Jacques Leclerc de Hauteclocque, Count of Hauteclocque.

French Forces in Great Britain (01/44): MG Marie-Joseph-Pierre-François Kœnig [+ French Liaison Officer to Supreme Headquarters Allied Expeditionary Force [see Volume III] (Commander-in-Chief, French Forces of the Interior & Military-Governor of Paris) 06/23/44

French Forces in Italy (/44): MG Charles-Paul-Augustin Louchet.

Atlantic Detachment [Detachément Altantique] (/44): LG René-Marie-Edgar de Larminat.

Infantry Divisions

1st Free French Infantry Division (#2) [Division Française Libre] (02/01/43, as North Africa; also known as **Kœnig Division**; 05/13/43, disbanded and used to form on 07/43, the **1st Light Infantry Division**; 04/44, French Expeditionary Corps in Italy): **1st Free French Infantry Division (#2)** 02/01/43 MG René-Marie-Edgar de Larminat (Chief of the Free French Army General Staff) /43 MG Marie-Joseph-Pierre-François Kœnig (Deputy Chief of National Defense Staff) 05/13/43 disbanded, reformed as **1st Light Infantry Division** 07/43 BG Diégo-Charles-Jospeh Brosset (killed in action) 08/24/43 redesignated **1st Motorized Infantry Division** - see **1st Motorized Infantry Division**.

A. **Chief of Staff, 1st Free French Infantry Division (#2)** (02/01/43): Col. Jean-Émile-Alexis Vautrin
B. *Components* - **1st Free French Infantry Division [Division Française Libre]** (02/01/43)
    1. **1st Independent French Brigade**: 04/44? Col. Delange
    2. **2nd Independent French Brigade**: - see **Free French Forces (after July 1941)**.
    3. **4th Independent French Brigade**: 04/44? Col. Raynal
    4. **1st Colonial Artillery Regiment**: 04/44? LCol. Maubert

1st Motorized Infantry Division (08/24/43, from **1st Light Division**; 08/43, French Expeditionary Corps in Italy; 05/01/44, renamed **1st March Division**; 08/44, French First Army, France): **1st Motorized Infantry Division** 08/24/43 unknown? 05/01/44 renamed **1st March Division** 05/01/44 BG Pierre-François-Marie Joseph Garbay.

A. *Components* - **1st Motorized Infantry Division** (08/24/43) & **1st Motorized Infantry Division** (08/15/44)
    1. **1st Brigade**
    2. **2nd Brigade**
    3. **4th Brigade**
    4. **1st Artillery Regiment**: /39? Col. Paul-Gabriel Arnaud (Inspector-General, Education & Experimental Techniques) /40?
B. **Infantry, 1st Motorized Infantry Division** (08/24/43): unknown? /44 Col. Pierre-François-Marie Joseph Garbay (Commanding General, 1st March Division) 05/01/44 redesignated **Infantry, 1st March Division** 05/01/44 unknown?

2nd Moroccan Infantry Division (05/01/43, from former Vichy French **Meknès Territorial Division**; 11/43, French Expeditionary Corps in Italy; 08/44, II Army Corps, French First Army, France): MG André-Marie-François Dody (Military-Governor, Metz & Commanding General, Military District XXI) /44 MG Marcel-Maurice Carpentier (Commanding General, Military District XV) /45.

A. **Chief of Staff, 2nd Moroccan Infantry Division**: /42 Col. Marie-Eugène-Aimé Molle.
B. *Components* - **2nd Moroccan Infantry Division** (11/43)
    1. **4th Morocco Tirailleurs (Infantry) Regiment**: 11/43? Col. Lappara /44? Col. Bridot
    2. **5th Morocco Tirailleurs (Infantry) Regiment**: 11/43? Col. Joppé /44? LCol.

Piatte
3. **8th Morocco Tirailleurs (Infantry) Regiment**: 11/43? Col. de Berchoux
4. **64th African Artillery Regiment**: 04/44? Col. Latarse
5. **3rd Morocco Spahis (Cavalry) Regiment**: 11/43? Col. Pique-Aubrun

C. **Artillery, 2nd Moroccan Infantry Division** (05/01/43): unknown? /44 BG Marie-Antoine-Arthur-Olivier Poydenot.

3rd Algerian Infantry Division: (05/01/43, from **Constantine March Division**; 12/43, French Expeditionary Corps in Italy; 08/44, II Army Corps, French First Army, France): MG Joseph-Jean de Goislard de Monsabert (Commanding General, II Free French Army Corps) 08/31/44 MG Augustin-Léon Guillaume (?) /45 MG Jean-Louis-Alai Touzet du Vigier.

A. *Components* - **3rd Algerian Infantry Division** (01/03/44)
1. **3rd Algerian Tirailleurs (Infantry) Regiment**: /43 Col. François-Jean-Antonin-Marie-Amédée Gonzalès de Linarès (Vice Chief of Staff, First Free French Army) /44
2. **7th Algerian Tirailleurs (Infantry) Regiment**: 01/03/44? Col. Chapuis
3. **4th Tunisian Tirailleurs (Infantry) Regiment**: 01/03/44? Col. [Retired] Oscar-Auguste Roux (killed in action) 01/27/44 LCol. Guillebraud
4. **3rd Algerian Spahis (Cavalry) Reconnaissance Regiment**: 01/03/44? LCol. Bonjour
5. **67th Algerian Artillery Regiment**:

B. **Infantry, 3rd Algerian Infantry Division** (05/01/43): Col. André-Claude Chevillon (Chief of Staff, I Free French Army Corps) /44 BG Raymond-Francis Duval (Commanding General, Division Constantine) /44? BG Jean-Maurice Richard

C. **Artillery, 3rd Algerian Infantry Division** (05/01/43): BG René de Hesdin (Chief of Staff, Army B) 12/43 Col. Fernand-Philippe-Alphonse Besançon (Artillery Commander, II French Army Corps) /44

4th Moroccan Mountain Infantry Division (06/01/43, from **3rd Marrakesh Infantry Division**; 02/44, French Expeditionary Corps in Italy; 08/44, I Army Corps, French First Army, France): MG Henri-Jules-Jean Martin (Commanding General, I Free French Army Corps) 08/16/43 MG François-Adolphe-Laurent Sevez (Deputy Chief of Staff, National Defense) /44 MG Charles-Paul-Augustin Louchet (acting Commanding General, French Forces in Italy) /44 MG René de Hesdin (/46, Military-Governor, Lyon) /45

A. *Components* - **4th Moroccan Mountain Infantry Division** (10/01/43)
1. **1st Morocco Tirailleurs (Infantry) Regiment**: 10/01/43? Col. Brissaud-Desmaillet
2. **2nd Morocco Tirailleurs (Infantry) Regiment**: 10/01/43? Col. Buot de l'Epine /44? Col. Deleuze
3. **6th Morocco Tirailleurs (Infantry) Regiment**: 10/01/43? Col. Cherrière
4. **4th Morocco Spahis (Cavalry) Reconnaissance Regiment**: 10/01/43? Col. Lambilly (killed in action) 05/18/44 LCol. Dodelier
5. **69th Mountain Artillery Regiment**: 10/01/43? LCol. Cerisier

B. **Infantry, 4th Moroccan Mountain Infantry Division** (10/01/43): BG Charles-Paul-Augustin Louchet (Commanding General, 4th Moroccan Mountain Infantry Division)

/44 Col. Paul-Louis Bondis.
- C. **Artillery, 4th Moroccan Mountain Infantry Division** (10/01/43): Col. André-Eugène Navereau (Artillery Commander, II Free French Corps) /45

9th Colonial Division (07/16/43; 08/44, I Army Corps, French First Army, France): /44 MG Joseph-Abraham-Auguste-Pierre-Edouard Magnan (Commander-in-Chief, French West Africa) /45 MG Jean-Étienne Valluy.
- A. *Components - 9th Colonial Division* (07/16/43)
    1. **4th Senegalese Tirailleurs (Infantry) Regiment**: /37 Col. Paul-Louis-Victor-Marie Legentilhomme (Commanding General, French Somalia) /39
    2. **6th Senegalese Tirailleurs (Infantry) Regiment**: /44 Col. Raoul-Albert-Louis Salan (Infantry Commander, 9th Colonial Division) /44
    3. **Moroccan Colonial Infantry Regiment**:
    4. **9th African Chasseurs (Armor) Regiment**: /43 Col. Guy Schlesser (Commanding General, Group 4, 5th Free French Armored Division) /44
    5. **Moroccan Colonial Artillery Regiment**:
- B. **Infantry, 9th Colonial Division** (07/16/43): unknown? /44 Col. Louis-Constant Morlière /44 Col. Raoul-Albert-Louis Salan (Commanding General, 14th Infantry Division) 03/20/45

1st Alpine Division FFI (11/44; 11/16/44, redesignated **27th Alpine Division (#1)**): **1st Alpine Division FFI** 11/44 unknown? 11/16/44 redesignated **27th Alpine Division (#1)** 11/16/44 unknown?
- A. *Components - 1st Alpine Division FFI or 27th Alpine Division (#1)* (11/16/44)
    1. **1st Demi-Brigade**:
    2. **2nd Demi-Brigade**:
    3. **3rd Demi-Brigade**:
    4. **4th Demi-Brigade**:
    5. **5th Demi-Brigade**:

1st Infantry Division (02/01/45; 04/45, assigned French First Army, France): unknown?

10th Infantry Division (#2) (09/30/44, assigned French First Army, France): MG Pierre-Armand-Gaston Billotte (Deputy Chief of the General Staff) /45 MG Charles-Jean-Roger Noiret.

14th Infantry Division (03/20/45; 04/45, assigned French First Army, France): BG Raoul-Albert-Louis Salan
- A. *Components - 14th Infantry Division* (03/20/45)
    1. **35th Infantry Regiment**:
    2. **152nd Infantry Regiment**:
    3. **12th Dragoon Regiment**: /42? Col. Guy Schlesser (Commanding Officer, 9th African Chasseurs Regiment) /43
    4. **4th Artillery Regiment**:

27th Alpine Division (#2) (02/45, assigned French First Army, France): unknown?

A. ***Components* - 27th Alpine Division (#2) (02/45)**
1. **5ᵗʰ Chasseur (Armor) Demi-Brigade**:
2. **7ᵗʰ Chasseur (Armor) Demi-Brigade**:
3. **159ᵗʰ Infantry Regiment**:
3. **5ᵗʰ Dragoon Regiment**:
4. **93ʳᵈ Mountain Artillery Regiment**:

36ᵗʰ Infantry Division (#2) (02/45): MG Alfred-Maurice Cazaud.

Moroccan Tabors (11/43, Moroccan Goum, French Expeditionary Corps in Italy): /40 BG Augustin-Léon Guillaume (Commanding General, 3ʳᵈ Algeria Infantry Division) 08/31/44
A. ***Components* - Moroccan Tabors (11/43)**
1. **1ˢᵗ Moroccan Tabor Group**: 04/44? Col. Leblanc
2. **3ʳᵈ Moroccan Tabor Group**: 04/44? Col. Massiet du Biest
3. **4ᵗʰ Moroccan Tabor Group**: 04/44? Col. Gautier

Military-Governor, Rome, Italy: /44 MG René de Hesdin (French Liaison Officer to United States Seventh Army) /44

Indochina

Cochinshine-Cambodge Division (Indochina Army Corps; HQ Saigon): see **Divisions in Overseas Colonies and Protectorates** Section.

Tonkin Division (Indochina Army Corps; HQ: Hanoi): see **Divisions in Overseas Colonies and Protectorates** Section.

Annam Brigade (Indochina Army Corps; HQ: Hué): see **Infantry Brigades** in **Brigades** Section.

Cambodge Brigade (Indochina Army Corps; HQ: Pnom Penh): see **Brigades** under French Army (pre-July 1940).

Armored Divisions

1st Free French Armored Division (08/43, from Vichy French **1st Armored Division**; 08/44, I Army Corps, French First Army, France): BG Jean-Louis-Alai Touzet du Vigier (Commanding General, 3rd Algerian Infantry Division) /45 MG Aimé Sudre.
- A. **Deputy Commander, 1st Free French Armored Division** (08/43): Col. Granier /43 BG Aimé Sudre (Commanding General, 1st Free French Armored Division) /45? BG Jean-Charles-Louis Caldairou
- B. *Components* - **1st Free French Armored Division** (08/43)
  1. **3rd Chasseurs d'Afrique [African Armored] Reconnaissance Regiment**
  2. **2nd Armored [Chasseurs] Regiment**
  3. **2nd Chasseurs d'Afrique [African Armored] Regiment**
  4. **5th Chasseurs d'Afrique [African Armored] Regiment**
  5. **9th African [d'Afrique] Anti-Tank Regiment**
  6. **68th Artillery Regiment**: /41 Col. René de Hesdin (Artillery Commander, XIX Army Corps) /42
- C. **Artillery, 1st Free French Armored Division** (08/43): Col. Marie-Joseph-Louis-Henri Noetinger

2nd Free French Armored Division (#1) (05/01/43, Rabat; 07/16/43, redesignated **5th Free French Armored Division**): MG Henri-Jacques-Jean-François de Vernejoul (Commanding General, 5th Free French Armored Division) 07/16/43 redesignated **5th Free French Armored Division** - see **5th Free French Armored Division**.
- A. *Components* - **2nd Free French Armored Division (#1)** (05/01/43)
  1. **Foreign Legion March (Motorized) Regiment**
  2. **1st Chasseurs d'Afrique [African Armored] Regiment**
  3. **6th Chasseurs d'Afrique [African Armored] Regiment**
  4. **1st Chasseurs [Armored] Regiment**
  5. **1st Foreign Legion Cavalry Regiment**
  6. **62nd African Artillery Regiment**

2nd Free French Armored Division (#2) (08/24/43, Rabat, from **2nd Light Free French Division**): MG Philippe-François-Marie-Jacques Leclerc de Hauteclocque, Count of Hauteclocque (Commanding General, French Far East Expeditionary Corps) 06/45.
- A. **Deputy Commander, 2nd Free French Armored Division (#2)**: /44 BG Pierre-Armand-Gaston Billotte (Commanding General, 5th Tactical Group, Paris; /44, Commanding General, 10th Infantry Division (#2)) 09/30/44
- B. *Components* - **2nd Free French Armored Division (#2)** (08/24/43)
  1. **Chad March Regiment**
  2. **1st Moroccan Spahis March (Reconnaissance) Regiment**
  3. **501st Battle Tank Regiment**
  4. **12th Chasseurs [Armored] Regiment**
  5. **12th Chasseurs d'Afrique [African Armored] Regiment**

3rd Free French Armored Division (09/01/43, to serve as a cadre unit to train troops for other armored divisions; 02/16/44, assigned to Territorial Command; 08/31/44, disbanded): MG Auguste-Marie Brossin de Saint-Didier (Head, French Military Mission, Washington, D. C.) 01/23/44 unknown? 08/31/44 disbanded.
  A.   *Components* - **3rd Free French Armored Division** (09/01/43)
        1.   **4th Chasseurs [Armored] Regiment**
        1.   **6th Chasseurs [Armored] Regiment**

5th Free French Armored Division (07/16/43, from **2nd Free French Armored Division (#1)**; 08/44, II Army Corps, French First Army, France): MG Henri-Jacques-Jean-François de Vernejoul (Armored Commander, First Free French Army) /45 MG Guy Schlesser.
  A.   **Deputy Commander, 5th Free French Armored Division** (07/16/43): unknown? /44 BG Paul-Arsène-Gérard Devinck.
  B.   *Components* - **5th Free French Armored Division** (10/02/43)
        1.   **Foreign Legion March (Motorized) Regiment**
        2.   **1st Chasseurs d'Afrique [African Armored] Regiment**
        3.   **6th Chasseurs d'Afrique [African Armored] Regiment**
        4.   **1st Chasseurs [Armored] Regiment**
        5.   **1st Foreign Legion Cavalry Regiment**
        6.   **62nd African Artillery Regiment**
  C.   *Components* - **5th Free French Armored Division** (/44)
        1.   **Group 4**: /44 BG Guy Schlesser (Commanding General, 5th Free French Armored Division) /45

Free French Mechanized Brigade: /42? BG Auguste-Marie Brossin de Saint-Didier (Commanding General, 3rd Free French Armored Division) 09/01/43

Part 3

MONACO

Monaco
(Area: 2 sq. km.)

While Prince Louis II's sympathies were strongly pro-French, he tried to keep Monaco neutral during World War II, and he supported the Vichy France government of his old army colleague Marshal Henri-Philippe-Benoni-Omar-Joseph Pétain. In 1943, the Italian army invaded and occupied Monaco, setting up a fascist government administration. Shortly thereafter, following Mussolini's collapse in Italy, the German army occupied Monaco and began the deportation of the Jewish population. Among them was RENÉ BLUM, founder of the Ballet de l'Opera, who died in a Nazi extermination camp.

Government of Monaco

Head of State: 06/26/22 Prince LOUIS II (LOUIS HONORÉ CHARLES ANTOINE GRIMALDI).
A. **Crown Council of Monaco** (advisers to the Prince):

Executive Branch

Minister of State (appointed by the monarch, from a list of three French or Monegasque national candidates presented by the French Government): 09/15/37 ÉMILE ROBLOT 09/29/44 PIERRE BLANCHY (acting) 10/13/44 PIERRE de WITASSE.
A. **Department of Interior**:

Legislative Branch

National Council (Conseil National) (unicameral legislative branch with 24 seats; elected by popular vote to serve a five-year term):
A. **President, National Council**: /33 HENRI SETTIMO /44 CHARLES BELLANDO de CASTRO

Judicial Branch

Two courts, both staffed by French judges, which are appointed among judges of French courts, members of the Conseil d'État and university professors.

Judicial Revision Court (Cour de révision judiciaire) (civil and criminal cases):

Supreme Tribunal (Tribunal suprême) (judicial review):

Monaco Government under Italian Control

Italian Consuls: 06/40? ANTONIO SAN FELLOW [Italian] /41 STANISLAO LEPRI (LEPRE) [Italian] /42?

Commander of the Italian Fourth Army: 11/16/42 Gen. Mario Vercellino [Italian] (?) 09/08/43 disbanded.

Monaco Government under German Control

Commander of the German Avignon Army (Hauptverbindungsstab): 09/08/43 MG Botho Elster [German] [+ Commandant, Marseille (France)] [see Volume I] 09/03/44 disbanded.

Mlitary Forces of Monaco

Monaco has a very limited military capacity. **Therefore, its military defense is depended upon by France.** The Department of the Interior is responsible for both policing and military activity within Monaco.

Prince's Company of Carabiniers (Compagnie des Carabiniers du Prince) (1817; ceremonial bodyguard unit; a small force, approximately 115, responsible for the defense of the Prince, the Prince's Palace, and members of the judiciary; it's officers are usually trained and served with the French military; commanded by a Commandant (Colonel)):

Corps des Sapeurs-Pompiers (09/18/1811; fire department; a small force, approximately 130, responsible for safety (fire and rescue), civil defense; it's officers have generally served in the French military or fire service; commanded by a Commandant (Colonel)):

Civil Police (has some quasi-military roles assigned to them, such as border patrol and border defense):

Part 4

ANDORRA

Andorra
(Area: 181 sq. mi.)

Andorra remained officially neutral for the duration of World War II. At the beginning of the war, a small detachment of French troops was stationed in the country which was left over from the Spanish Civil War, but these forces were withdrawn in 1940. When France fell, Marshal Henri-Philippe-Benoni-Omar-Joseph Pétain of the Vichy regime was declared the new French Co-prince. After the German invasion of Vichy France in 1942, a German military force moved to the Andorran border near Pas de la Casa but did not cross. In response, a Spanish force was established at La Seu d'Urgell, but it too remained outside Andorran territory. In 1944, BG Charles-André-Joseph-Marie de Gaulle established a new provisional government, and assumed the position of French Co-Prince. He ordered French forces to occupy Andorra as a "preventative measure" to secure order. Throughout the war, Andorra was used as a smuggling route between Spain and Vichy France, and an escape route for people fleeing German-occupied areas.

Government of Valleys of Andorra

Head of State (co-principality, with the President of France and the Bishop of Urgell (Catalonia), Spain as co-princes)
Co Prince - President of France: 05/10/32 ALBERT FRANÇOIS LEBRUN [French] [+ President of France] (fled France after surrender to Germany and replaced as President) 07/11/40 Marshal Henri-Philippe-Benoni-Omar-Joseph Pétain [French] [Vichy France] 06/03/44 BG Charles-André-Joseph-Marie de Gaulle [French] [Provisional Government of Free France].
A. **French Veguers** (representative of the President of France): 11/30/37 JEAN BAPTISTE LAUMOND [French] 12/02/40 EMILIEN LASMARTES [French] 09/14/44 ROBERT BARAN [French] 05/05/45 GEORGES DEGRAND [French].

Co Prince - Bishop of Urgell: 06/01/20 Bishop JUSTI GUITART I VILARDEBÒ [Spanish] 06/31/40 vacant 02/02/40 Bishop RICHARD FORNESA I PUIGDEMASA [Spanish] 04/15/43 Bishop RAMON IGLÉSIAS I NAVARRI [Spanish].
A. **Episcopal Veguers** (representative of the Bishop of Urgell): /37 Father JAUME SANSA [Spanish].

Legislative Branch

General Council (composed of twenty-eighth members, elected every four years. At least one representative from each parish must be present for the General Council to meet):
A. **First Syndics** (chosen by the General Council to implement its decisions. They serve a three-year term and may be reappointed once. Syndics have virtually no discretionary powers, and all policy decisions must be approved by the Council as a whole): /37 FRANCESC CAIRAT FREIXES.
B. **Subsyndic** (chosen by the General Council to implement its decisions. They serve

a three-year term and may be reappointed once. Syndics have virtually no discretionary powers, and all policy decisions must be approved by the Council as a whole):

Judicial Branch

High Court of Justice (five judges, one appointed by the Head of Government, one each by the Coprinces, one from the Syndic, and one by the judges and magistrates; presided over by the member appointed by the Syndic and the judges hold office for a six-year term; the High Court appoints judges, magistrates, President of the Criminal Law Court, and members of the Office of Attorney General):

Constitutional Court (Appeals) (responsible for interpreting the Constitution and reviewing all appeals; composed of four judges, one appointed by each of the coprinces and two by the General Council; they serve eight-year terms):

Criminal Law Court (this court and Magistrates Court applies the customary laws of Andorra, supplemented with Roman law and customary Catalan law)

Magistrates Court:

Military Forces

All able bodied men who own firearms must serve in its small army. The army has not fought in over 700 years. It's main responsibility is to present the Andorran flag at official ceremonies. Andorra has a small internal police force, around 140 police officers. **Defense of Andorra is dependent of France and Spain.**

Commander of French Gendarmes in Andorra: 07/36 RENÉ BAULARD [French] 06/40 disbanded.

:

APPENDIX

FOR

SECTION B

FRANCE

Appendix A

Table of Equivalent Ranks

French Army	United States & British Army
Marshal of France (Maréchal de France)	General of the Army (U. S.) Field Marshal (Brit.)
General (Général d'Armée)	General
Lieutenant General (Général de Corps d'Armée)	Lieutenant General
General Major (Général de Division)	Major General
Brigade General (Général de Brigade)	Brigadier General (U. S.) Brigadier (Brit.)
Colonel	Colonel
Lieutenant-Colonel	Lieutenant Colonel
Chef de Bataillon/Commandant	Major
Capitaine	Captain
Lieutenant	First Lieutenant (U. S.) Lieutenant (Brit.)
Second-Lieutenant (Sous-Lieutenant)	Second Lieutenant

Table of Equivalent Ranks

French Navy	United States & British Navy
Admiral of the Fleet (Amiral de la Flotte)	Fleet Admiral [U. S.] Admiral of the Fleet [Brit.]
Amiral (Admiral)	Admiral
Squadron Vice Admiral (Vice-amiral d'escadre)	Vice Admiral
Vice Admiral (Vice-amiral)	Rear Admiral
Counter Admiral (Contre-amiral)	Commodore
Ship-of-the-Line Captain (Capitaine de vaisseau)	Captain
Frigate Captain (Capitaine de frégate)	Commander
Corvette Captain (Capitaine de corvette)	Lieutenant Commander
Ship-of-the-Line Lieutenant (Lieutenant de vaisseau)	Lieutenant [U.S.] Lieutenant (Senior) [Brit.]
	Lieutenant (Junior Grade) [U.S.] Lieutenant (Junnior) [Brit]
Ship-of-the-Line Ensign First Class (Enseigne de vaisseau de première classe)	Ensign [U.S.] Sub-Lieutenant [Brit.]
Ship-of-the-Line Ensign Second Class (Enseigne de vaisseau deuxième classe)	Acting Sub-Lieutenant [Brit.] NO U. S. EQUIVALENT

Appendix B

Military Units in Selected Campaigns

The organizations of the following pages can be supplemented by reference to the previous sections in Part 2, which list the commanders for each unit.

French Army, May 10, 1940

1st Army Group
    First Army
        III Army Corps
            1st Motorized Infantry Division
            2nd North African Infantry Division
        IV Army Corps
            32nd Infantry Division
        V Army Corps
            5th North African Infantry Division
            101st Infantry Division
            VII Belgian Army Corps
                Belgian 8th Infantry Division
                Belgian 2nd "Ardennes" Infantry Division
        Cavalry Corps
            2nd Light Motorized Division
            3rd Light Motorized Division
    Second Army
        X Army Corps
            3rd North African Infantry Division
            55th Infantry Division
            71st Infantry Division
            5th Light Cavalry Division
        XVIII Army Corps
            1st Colonial Infantry Division
            41st Infantry Division
        Reserve Units
            2nd Light Cavalry Division
            1st Cavalry Brigade
    Seventh Army
        I Army Corps
            1st Light Motorized Division
            25th Motorized Infantry Division
        XVI Army Corps
            9th Motorized Infantry Division
        Reserve Units
            21st Infantry Division

                60th Infantry Division
                68th Infantry Division
Ninth Army
    II Army Corps
        5th Motorized Infantry Division
        4th Light Cavalry Division
    XI Army Corps
        1st Light Cavalry Division
        18th Infantry Division
        22nd Infantry Division
    XLI Army Corps
        102nd Fortress Division
        61st Infantry Division
        3rd Spahi Brigade
    Reserve Units
        4th North African Infantry Division
        53rd Infantry Division
British Expeditionary Forces
    British I Army Corps
        British 1st Infantry Division
        British 2nd Infantry Division
        British 48th Infantry Division
    British II Army Corps
        British 3rd Infantry Division
        British 4th Infantry Division
        British 50th Infantry Division
    British III Army Corps
        British 42nd Infantry Division
        British 44th Infantry Division
    British Reserve Units
        British 5th Infantry Division
        British 1st Armour Division (after May 10, 1940)
        British 52nd Infantry Division (after May 10, 1940)
        1st Canadian Infantry Division (after May 10, 1940)
        British 12th Territorial Infantry Division (after May 17, 1940)
        British 23rd Territorial Infantry Division (after May 17, 1940)
        British 46th Territorial Infantry Division (after May 17, 1940)
Belgian Army
    Belgian I Army Corps
        Belgian 1st Infantry Division
        Belgian 4th Infantry Division
        Belgian 7th Infantry Division
    Belgian II Army Corps
        Belgian 6th Infantry Division
        Belgian 11th Infantry Division
        Belgian 14th Infantry Division
    Belgian III Army Corps

                Belgian 1ˢᵗ "Ardennes" Infantry Division
                Belgian 2ⁿᵈ Infantry Division
                Belgian 3ʳᵈ Infantry Division
        Belgian IV Army Corps
                Belgian 9ᵗʰ Infantry Division
                Belgian 15ᵗʰ Infantry Division
                Belgian 18ᵗʰ Infantry Division
        Belgian V Army Corps
                Belgian 12ᵗʰ Infantry Division
                Belgian 13ᵗʰ Infantry Division
                Belgian 17ᵗʰ Infantry Division
        Belgian VI Army Corps
                Belgian 5ᵗʰ Infantry Division
                Belgian 10ᵗʰ Infantry Division
                Belgian 16ᵗʰ Infantry Division
        Belgian Cavalry Corps
                Belgian 1ˢᵗ Cavalry Division
                Belgian 2ⁿᵈ Cavalry Division

General Headquarters Reserve, behind 1ˢᵗ Army Group
        XXI Army Corps
                1ˢᵗ Armor Division
                1ˢᵗ Motorized Infantry Division
                12ᵗʰ Motorized Infantry Division
                15ᵗʰ Motorized Infantry Division
        Independent Units
                2ⁿᵈ Armor Division
                3ʳᵈ Armor Division
                4ᵗʰ Infantry Division
                43ʳᵈ Infantry Division
                1ˢᵗ North African Infantry Division

2ⁿᵈ Army Group
    Third Army
            VI Army Corps
                    26ᵗʰ Infantry Division
                    42ⁿᵈ Infantry Division
                    British 51ˢᵗ Highlander Infantry Division
            XXIV Army Corps
                    51ˢᵗ Infantry Division
                    58ᵗʰ Infantry Division
            XLII Army Corps
                    2ⁿᵈ Infantry Division
                    20ᵗʰ Infantry Division
                    56ᵗʰ Infantry Division
    Fourth Army
        IX Army Corps

    11th Infantry Division
    47th Infantry Division
  XX Army Corps
    82nd North African Infantry Division
    52nd Infantry Division
  Reserve Units
    45th Infantry Division
    87th North African Infantry Division

Fifth Army
  VIII Army Corps
    24th Infantry Division
    31st Infantry Division
  XII Army Corps
    35th Infantry Division
    44th Infantry Division
  XVII Army Corps
    62nd Infantry Division
    103rd Infantry Division
  XLIII Army Corps
    16th Infantry Division
    30th Infantry Division
    70th Infantry Division
  Reserve Unit
    4th Colonial Infantry Division

General Headquarters Reserve, behind 2nd Army Group
    3rd Motorized Infantry Division
    7th Infantry Division
    10th Infantry Division
    14th Infantry Division
    36th Infantry Division
    6th Colonial Infantry Division
    7th Colonial Infantry Division
    8th Infantry Division (still forming)
    1st Polish Infantry Division (still forming)

3rd Army Group
 Eighth Army
  XIII Army Corps
    54th Infantry Division
    104th Infantry Division
    105th Infantry Division
  XLIV Army Corps
    19th Infantry Division
    67th Infantry Division
  Reserve Units
    57th Infantry Division

63rd Infantry Division

General Headquarters Reserve, behind 3rd Army Group
    VII Army Corps
        13th Infantry Division
        27th Infantry Division
        2 Spahi Brigade
    XXIII Army Corps
        23rd Infantry Division
        28th Infantry Division
        29th Infantry Division
    Independent Units
        7th North African Infantry Division (still forming)
        5th Colonial Infantry Division (still forming)

Army of the Alps (defending the frontier with Italy)
        2nd Colonial Infantry Division
        + 7 fortress brigades.
    XIV Army Corps
        64th Infantry Division
        66th Alpine Infantry Division
        F. S. Savoy
        F. S. Dauphiné
    XV Army Corps
        65th Infantry Division
        Alpes Maritimes Fortified Section

During the campaign, between May 10, 1940 to June 22, 1940 another 18 divisions arrived at the front. These were:
        4th Armor Division
        17th Infantry Division
        40th Infantry Division
        3rd Light Infantry Division
        53rd Light Infantry Division
        59th Light Infantry Division
        235th Light Infantry Division
        236th Light Infantry Division
        237th Light Infantry Division
        238th Light Infantry Division
        239th Light Infantry Division
        240th Light Infantry Division
        241st Light Infantry Division
        2nd Polish Infantry Division
        7th North African Infantry Division
        8th Colonial Infantry Division
        84th African Infantry Division
        85th African Infantry Division

Appendix C

The Fleet of the French Navy

Light Aircraft Carriers [CVL]

Arromanches (ex-**Colossus**; Builder: Vickers-Armstrongs, Ltd.; Laid down: 01/06/42; Launched: 09/30/43; Completed: 12/16/42; for British Royal Navy; Lent to French Navy for five years; Colossus Class):

Béarn (Builder: La Seyne; Laid Down: 01/10/14; Launched: 04/20; Completed: 05/27; Béarn Class; 09/39, to slow for fleet service and was delegated to aircraft transportation duty; 09/01/39, assigned to 1st Flotilla): 09/01/39? Capt. M. M. A. Lafargue [FN] 10/07/39 Capt. Y. E. Aubert [FN]

Joffre (Builder: At & Ch de St. Nazaire-Penhoet; Laid Down: 11/26/39): NOT BUILT.

Escort Aircraft Carrier [CVE]

Dixmude (ex-**H. M. S. Biter**, ex-**Rio Parana**; Builder: Sun Shipbuilding; Laid down: 03/14/40; acquired by United States Navy, 05/20/41; converted by Atlantic Basin Iron Works; transferred to Royal Navy as Lend-Lease, 05/01/42; Charger Class/HMS Archer Class; taken over by French Navy, 04/09/45):

Seaplane Carrier [CVS]

Commandant Teste (Builder: F. et C. de la Gurande, Bordeaux; Laid Down: 05/27; Launched: 04/12/29; Completed: 1931; Class; 09/01/39, assigned to Oran Force [6th Light Squadron]): 09/01/39? Capt. M. Petyst de Morcourt [FN]

Battle Cruisers

Dunkerque (Builder: Brest Navy Yard; Laid down: 12/26/32; Launched: 10/02/35; Completed: 04/37; Dunkerque Class; 09/01/39, assigned to 1st Battle Division): 09/01/39? Capt. J. L. Negadelle [FN] 10/16/39 Capt. M. J. M. Seguin [FN] 11/27/42 damaged in dry dock in Toulon.

Strasbourg (Builder: Penhoëf; Laid down: 11/25/34; Launched: 12/12/36; Completed: 12/38; Dunkerque Class; 09/01/39, assigned to 1st Battle Division): 09/01/39? Capt. J. F. E. Bouxin [FN] (Commanding Admiral, 2nd Squadron, High Seas Force) 12/22/39 Capt. D. A. J. Collinett [FN] 11/27/42 scuttled in shallow water in Toulon.

Battleships

Bretagne (Builder: Lorient Navy Yard; Laid down: 07/01/12; Launched: 04/21/13; Completed: 09/15; Bretagne Class; 09/01/39, assigned to 2nd Battle Division): 09/01/39? Capt. M. J. M. Sequin [FN] (Commanding Officer, battleship *Dunkerque*) 10/16/39 Capt. L. R. E. Le Pivian [FN] 07/03/40 sunk by the British at Mers-el-Kebir.

Clemenceau (Builder: Brest Navy Yard; Laid down: 01/17/39; Uncompleted; Richelieu Class): NOT IN WORLD WAR II; UNCOMPLETED; 08/27/44 SUNK BY ALLIED HEAVY BOMBERS DURING THE SEIGE OF BREST.

Courbet (Builder: Lorient Navy Yard; Laid down: 09/01/10; Launched: 09/23/11; Completed: 09/13; Courbet Class; 09/01/39, assigned to II Naval Region): 09/01/39? Capt. A. M. J. Croiset [FN] 06/44 scuttled during Operation Neptune.

Gascogne (Projected; Richelieu Class): PROJECTED, BUT NEVER STARTED.

Jean Bart (Builder: Penhoëf, At & Ch de Loire; Laid down: 01/01/37; Launched: 03/06/40; Completed: 05/01/55; Richelieu Class): 01/15/40 Capt. Pierre-Alexis-Jean Ronarc'h [FN] (Commanding Admiral, Casablanca Naval Station) /42

Lorraine (Builder: Lorient Navy Yard; Laid down: 06/12; Launched: 09/30/13; Completed: 06/15; Bretagne Class; 09/01/39, assigned to 2nd Battle Division): 09/01/39? Capt. G. O. L. Aubin [FN] 10/16/39 Capt. M. L. M. Rey [FN]

Paris (Builder: F & Ch La Seyne; Laid down: 11/10/11; Launched: 09/28/12; Completed: 08/01/14; Courbet Class; 09/01/39, assigned to II Naval Region): 09/01/39? Capt. P. L. Guillerm [FN] [+ Commanding Officer, 3rd Battle Division]

Provence (Builder: Penhoëf; Laid down: 11/12; Launched: 04/20/13; Completed: 07/16; Bretagne Class): 09/01/39? Capt. G. T. E. Barois [FN] 07/03/40 severely damage at Mers-el-Kebir; taken to Toulon for refitting 11/27/42 damaged by her own crew at Toulon.

Richelieu (Builder: Brest Navy Yard; Laid down: 10/22/35; Launched: 01/17/39; Completed: 07/40; Richelieu Class; 07/08/40, slightly damage at Mers-el-Kebir): 09/01/39? unknown? 10/15/39 Capt. P. J. Marzin [FN]

Heavy Cruisers

Algérie (Builder: Brest Navy Yard; Laid Down: 03/19/31; Launched: 05/21/32; Completed: 09/15/34; Algérie Class; 09/01/39, assigned to 1st Cruiser Division): 09/01/39? Capt. L. H. M. Nouvel de la Fleche [FN] 11/27/42 scuttled at Toulon.

Colbert (Builder: Brest Navy Yard; Laid Down: 06/12/27; Launched: 04/20/28; Completed: 03/04/31; Suffren Class; 09/01/39, assigned to 2nd Cruiser Division): 09/01/39? Capt. E. H. M. A. A. du Tour [FN] 11/27/42 scuttled at Toulon.

Dupleix (Builder: Brest Navy Yard; Laid Down: 11/14/29; Launched: 10/09/30; Completed: 07/20/32; Suffren Class; 09/01/39, assigned to 1st Cruiser Division): 09/01/39? Capt. L. L. M. Harneury [FN] 11/27/42 scuttled at Toulon.

Duquesne (Builder: Brest Navy Yard; Laid Down: 10/30/24; Launched: 12/17/25; Completed: 12/06/28; Duquesne Class; 09/01/39, assigned to 2nd Cruiser Division): 09/01/39? Capt. P. S. R. Husson [FN] 11/20/39 Capt. G. E. Besineau [FN] 06/23/40 immobilized in the port of Alexandria, Egypt 05/43

Foch (Builder: Brest Navy Yard; Laid Down: 06/21/28; Launched: 04/24/29; Completed: 09/15/31; Suffren Class; 09/01/39, assigned to 1st Cruiser Division): 09/01/39? Capt. J. Mathieu [FN] 11/27/42 scuttled at Toulon.

Suffren (Builder: Brest Navy Yard; Laid Down: 04/17/26; Launched: 05/03/27; Completed: 01/01/30; Suffren Class; 09/01/39, assigned to 5th Cruiser Division): 09/01/39? Capt. R. J. M. Dillard [FN] 06/23/40 immobilized in the port of Alexandria, Egypt 05/43

Tourville (Builder: Lorient Navy Yard; Laid Down: 03/04/25; Launched: 08/24/26; Completed: 12/01/28; Duquesne Class; 09/01/39, assigned to 2nd Cruiser Division): 09/01/39? Capt. A. J. A. Marloy [FN] 06/23/40 immobilized in the port of Alexandria, Egypt 05/43

Light Cruisers

Duquay-Trouin (Builder: Brest Navy Yard; Laid Down: 08/04/22; Launched:08/14/23 ;  Completed: 11/02/26; Duguay-Trouin Class; 09/01/39, assigned to 6th Cruiser Division): 09/01/39? Capt. J. M. C. de Prevaux [FN] 06/23/40 immobilized in the port of Beiruit, Lebanon 07/43

Émile Bertin (minelaying cruiser; Builder: Penhoët, At & Ch St. Nazaire; Laid Down:  08/18/31; Launched: 05/09/33; Completed: 01/28/35; Émile Bertin Class; 09/01/39, assigned to Bizerte Destroyers [4th Light Squadron]): 09/01/39? Capt. R. M. J. Battet [FN] 06/23/40 immobilized in the port of Fort de France, French Antilles 05/43

Georges Leygues (Builder: At & Ch St. Nazaire; Laid Down: 09/21/33; Launched:  03/24/36; Completed: 11/15/37; La Galissonniere Class; also known as Gloire Class; 09/01/39, assigned to 4th Cruiser Division): 09/01/39? Capt. R. L. Perot [FN] 11/10/39 Capt. Bernaud [FN]

Gloire (Builder: F & Ch Gironde; Laid Down: 11/12/33; Launched: 09/28/35; Completed:  11/15/37; La Galissonniere Class; also known as Gloire Class; 09/01/39, assigned to 4th Cruiser Division): 09/01/39? Capt. F. H. R. de Belot [FN]

de Grasse (Builder: Lorient Navy Yard; Laid Down: 11/38; construction suspended during German occupation of Lorient; de Grasse Class): COMPLETED AFTER WORLD WAR II; LAUNCHED 09/11/46

Jean de Vienne (Builder: Lorient Navy Yard; Laid Down: 12/20/31; Launched: 07/31/35;  Completed: 02/10/37; La Galissonniere Class, assigned to 3rd Cruiser Division): 09/01/39? Capt. J. M. Missoffe [FN] 11/27/42 scuttled at Toulon.

Jeanne d'Arc (training cruiser; Builder: At & Ch de St. Nazaire; Laid Down: 08/31/28;  Launched: 02/14/30; Completed: 09/14/31; Jeanne d'Arc Class; 09/01/39, assigned to 7th Cruiser Division): 09/01/39? Capt. P. M. A. Rouyer [FN] 06/23/40 immobilized in the port of Pointe-a-Pitre, French Antilles 05/43

La Galissonniere (Builder: Brest Navy Yard; Laid Down: 12/15/31; Launched: 11/18/33; Completed: 04/01/36; La Galissonniere Class, assigned to 3rd Cruiser Division): 09/01/39? Capt. L.

M. L. Dupre [FN] 11/27/42 scuttled at Toulon.

La Tour d'Auvergne (ex-***Pluton***; Builder: Lorient Navy Yard; Laid Down: 04/16/28; Launched: 04/10/29; Completed: 10/01/31; Pluton Class; 09/01/39, assigned to 7th Cruiser Division; exploded before the change of name could occurred **[NOTE:** in some sources listed as ***La Tour d'Auvergne***, so listed under both names ***La Tour d'Auvergne*** and ***Pluton*]**): 09/01/39? Capt. H. J. E. Dubois [FN] 09/13/39 exploded while unloading armed mines in Casablanca, Morocco.

Lamotte-Picquet (Builder: Lorient Navy Yard; Laid Down: 01/17/23; Launched: 03/21/24; Completed: 03/05/27; Duguay-Trouin Class; 09/01/39, assigned to 5th Cruiser Division): 09/01/39? Capt. M. D. R. Bérenger [FN] 01/12/45 bombed and sunk.

Marseillaise (Builder: At & Ch de Loire; Laid Down: 10/23/33; Launched: 07/17/35; Completed: 10/10/37; La Galissonniere Class; 09/01/39, assigned to 3rd Cruiser Division): 09/01/39? Capt. Y. J. E. Hamon [FN] 11/27/42 scuttled at Toulon.

Montcalm (Builder: F & Ch La Seyne; Laid Down: 11/15/33; Launched: 10/26/35; Completed: 11/15/37; La Galissonniere Class; also known as Gloire Class; 09/01/39, assigned to 4th Cruiser Division): 09/01/39? Capt. Pierre-Jean Ronarc'h [FN] (Commanding Officer, battleship *Jean Bart*) 01/05/40 Capt. J. L. de Corbiere [FN]

Pluton (minelaying cruiser; Builder: Lorient Navy Yard; Laid Down: 04/16/28; Launched: 04/10/29; Completed: 10/01/31; Pluton Class; was to be renamed ***La Tour d'Auvergne*** but exploded before the change of name could occurred **[NOTE:** in some sources listed as ***La Tour d'Auvergne***, so listed under both names ***La Tour d'Auvergne*** and ***Pluton*]**): 09/01/39? Capt. H. J. E. Dubois [FN] 09/13/39 exploded while unloading armed mines in Casablanca, Morocco.

Primauguet (Builder: Brest Navy Yard; Laid Down: 08/16/23; Launched: 05/21/24; Completed: 04/01/27; Duguay-Trouin Class; 09/01/39, assigned to 6th Cruiser Division): 09/01/39? Capt. J. Constantin [FN] /40? Capt. Mercier [FN] 11/08/42 sunk by U. S. Task Force 38 at Casablanca, Morocco.

Minelayers [CM]

Pollux (HQ: Cherbourg, France): 09/01/39? Cdr. C. Blayo

Submarine Tender [AS]

Castor 09/01/39, assigned to 6th Submarine Squadron): 09/01/39? Lt. J. M. A. Duthu [FN]

Jules Verne (Builder: Lorient Navy Yard; Laid Down: unknown?; Launched: 02/03/31; Completed: unknown?; 09/01/39, assigned to Oran Force [6th Light Squadron]): 09/01/39? Capt. J. Tonnele [FN]

Destroyer Divisions

1st Destroyer Division (09/01/39, assigned to Bizerte Destroyers [4th Light Squadron]; destroyers *Épervier, Lion, Vauban*): 09/01/39? Capt. Chardenot [FN] [Leader: DD *Vauban*]

2nd Destroyer Division (09/01/39, assigned to II Naval Region; destroyers *Chacal, Jaguar, Léopard, Panthere*): 09/01/39? Capt. d'Res. Defforges [FN] [Leader: DD *Jaguar*]

3rd Destroyer Division (09/01/39, assigned to Bizerte Destroyers [4th Light Squadron]; destroyers *Guépard, Valmy, Verdun*): 09/01/39? Capt. R. le Chuitton [FN] [Leader: DD *Guepard*] 12/18/39 Cdr. R. E. Gervais de Lafond [FN] [Leader: DD *Guepard*] (Commanding Officer, 9th Light Destroyer Division) /40?

4th Destroyer Division (HQ: Toulon, France; 09/01/39, assigned to III Naval Region; destroyers *Lynx, Panthére, Tigre*): 09/01/39? Capt. C. G. de Vedrines [FN] [Leader: DD *Tigre*] 12/02/39 Capt. M. de La Forest Divonne [FN] [Leader: DD *Tigre*]

5th Destroyer Division (HQ: Toulon, France; 09/01/39, assigned to 3rd Light Squadron; destroyers *Chevalier Paul, Tartu, Vauquelin*): 09/01/39? Capt. J. M. Chomel [FN] [Leader: DD *Tartu*]

6th Destroyer Division (HQ: Brest; 09/01/39, assigned to 2nd Light Squadron; destroyers *Mogador, Volta*): 09/01/39? Capt. P. Maerten [FN] [Leader: DD *Mogador*] (Commanding Officer, Madagascar) 09/40

7th Destroyer Division (HQ: Toulon, France; 09/01/39, assigned to 3rd Light Squadron; destroyers *Albatros, Gerfaut, Vautour*): 09/01/39? Capt. G. F. J. M. Reboul Hector-Berlioz [FN] [Leader: DD *Vautour*]

8th Destroyer Division (HQ: Brest; 09/01/39, assigned to 2nd Light Squadron; destroyers *Le Malin, Le Triomphant, L'Indomptable*): 09/01/39? Capt. P. T. J. Barnard [FN] [Leader: DD *L'Indomptable*] 11/09/39 Capt. E. G.M. Barthes [FN] [Leader: DD *L'Indomptable*]

9th Destroyer Division (HQ: Toulon, France; 09/01/39, assigned to 3rd Light Squadron; destroyers *Cassard, Kersaint, Maillé Brézé*): 09/01/39? Cdr. H. M. E. A. Glotin [FN] [Leader: DD *Maille Breze*]

10th Destroyer Division (HQ: Brest; 09/01/39, assigned to 2nd Light Squadron; destroyers *L'Audacieux, Le Fantasque, Le Terrible*): 09/01/39? Capt. P. A. B. Still [FN] [Leader: DD *L'Fantasque*]

11th Destroyer Division (HQ: Bizerte, Tunisia; 09/01/39, assigned to Bizerte Destroyers [4th Light Squadron]; destroyers *Bison, Milan*): 09/01/39? unknown?

Light Destroyer Divisions

1st Light Destroyer Division (HQ: Oran, Algeria; 09/01/39, assigned to 1st Light Destroyer Squadron; destroyers *La Palme, Le Mars, Tempête*): 09/01/39? Capt. L. H. C. Longaud [FN] [Leader: DE *La Palme*] [+ Commander, 1st Light Destroyer Squadron]

2nd Light Destroyer Division (09/01/39, assigned to 2nd Light Destroyer Squadron; destroyers *Fougueux, Frondeur, l'Adroit*): 09/01/39? Cdr. C. A. Loisel [FN] [Leader: DE *Fougueux*] 10/09/39 Cdr. C. A. Poher [FN] [Leader: DE *Fougueux*]

3rd Light Destroyer Division (HQ: Oran, Algeria; 09/01/39, assigned to 1st Light Destroyer Squadron; destroyers *La Railleuse, Le Fortuné, Simoun*): 09/01/39? Cdr. C. M. L. d'Hespel [FN] [Leader: DE *Le Fortune*]

4th Light Destroyer Division (09/01/39, assigned to 2nd Light Destroyer Squadron; destroyers *Bourrasque, Orage, Ouragan*): 09/01/39? R. G. A. Fougue [FN] [Leader: DE *Boussasque*]

5th Light Destroyer Division (09/01/39, assigned to 2nd Light Destroyer Squadron; destroyers *Boulonnais, Brestois, Foudroyant*): 09/01/39? Cdr. J. G. Quebec [FN] [Leader: DE *Brestons*]

6th Light Destroyer Division (09/01/39, assigned to 2nd Light Destroyer Squadron; destroyers *Cyclone, Mistral, Sirocc*): 09/01/39? Capt. Y. F. C. A. M. Urvoy de Portzamparc [FN] [Leader: DE *Cyclone*] [+ Commander-in-Chief, 2nd Light Destroyer Squadron]

7th Light Destroyer Division (HQ: Oran, Algeria; 09/01/39, assigned to 1st Light Destroyer Squadron; destroyers *Tornade, Tramontane, Typhon*): 09/01/39? Cdr. R. M. J. A. Renault [FN] [Leader: DE *Tramontane*]

8th Light Destroyer Division (09/01/39, assigned to Oran Naval Force [6th Light Squadron]; destroyers *Bordelais, l'Alcyon, Trombe*): 09/01/39? Cdr. D. F. M. V. de Bourgoing [FN] [Leader: DE *Bordelais*]

9th Light Destroyer Division (09/01/39, assigned to Morocco Naval Force; destroyers *Basque, Forbin*): 09/01/39? unknown? /40? Capt. R. E. Gervais de Lafond [FN] (Commanding Officer, 2nd Light Destroyer Squadron) /42

11th Light Destroyer Division (HQ: Dunkirque, France; 09/01/39, assigned to I Naval Region; destroyer escorts *Branlebas, La Cordelière, L'Incomprise*): 09/01/39? Cdr. H. A. J. Robinet de Plas [FN] [Leader: DE *La Cordelière*]

12th Light Destroyer Division (HQ: Toulon, France; 09/01/39, assigned to IV Naval Region; destroyer escorts *La Bombarde, La Pomone' l'Iphigénie*): 09/01/39? Cdr. H. A. M. L. Pecqueur [FN] [Leader: DE *La Pomone*]

13ᵗʰ Light Destroyer Division (HQ: Toulon, France; 09/01/39, assigned to III Naval Region; destroyer escorts *Baliste*, *La Bayonnaise*, *Poursivante*): 09/01/39? Cdr. J. F. Rue [FN] [Leader: DE *Baliste*]

14ᵗʰ Light Destroyer Division (09/01/39, assigned to V Naval Region; destroyer escorts *Bouclier*, *La Flore*, *Melpoméne*): 09/01/39? LCdr P. Parion [FN] [Leader: DE *bouclier*]

Submarine Divisions

1st Submarine Division (09/01/39, assigned to 3rd Submarine Squadron; submarines *Le Conquérant, Le Glorieux, Le Héros, Le Tonnant*): 09/01/39? LCdr. R. E. Courson [FN] [Leader: SS *Le Heros*]

2nd Submarine Division (09/01/39, assigned to 4th Submarine Squadron; submarines *Achille, Casablanca, Pasteur*): 09/01/39? LCdr. F. M. Carre [FN] [Leader: SS *Casablanca*] 11/04/39 LCdr. R. L. B. Sacaze [FN] [Leader: SS *Casablanca*]

3rd Submarine Division (09/01/39, assigned to 3rd Submarine Squadron; submarines *Achéron, Acteon, Fresnel, Protée*): 09/01/39? LCdr. E. J. J. Gras [FN] [Leader: SS *Protee*]

4th Submarine Division (09/01/39, assigned to 4th Submarine Squadron but detached to Admiral South who assigned it to Morocco Naval Force; submarines *Argo, Henri Poincaré, Le Centaure, Pascal*): 09/01/39? unknown?

5th Submarine Division (09/01/39, assigned to 3rd Submarine Squadron; submarines *l'Espoir, Monge, Pégase*): 09/01/39? unknown?

6th Submarine Division (09/01/39, assigned to 4th Submarine Squadron; submarines *Ajax, Archimède, Persée, Poncelet*): 09/01/39? LCdr. M. J. B. Lapierre [FN] [Leader: SS *Persee*]

7th Submarine Division (09/01/39, assigned to Toulon Submarine Base; submarines *Redoubtable, Vengeur*): 09/01/39? unknown?

8th Submarine Division (09/01/39, assigned to 4th Submarine Squadron; submarines *Agosta, Bévéziers, Ouessant, Sidi Ferruch*): 09/01/39? LCdr. A. F. Beaussant [FN] [Leader: SS *Agosta*]

9th Submarine Division (09/01/39, assigned to 6th Submarine Squadron; submarines *Caiman, Morse, Souffleur*): 09/01/39? LCdr. J. B. A. Golse [FN] [Leader: SS *Caiman*]

10th Submarine Division (09/01/39, assigned to 6th Submarine Squadron; submarines *Dauphin, Espadon, Phoque*): 09/01/39? LCdr. J. F. M. P. Lagarrigue [FN] [Leader: SS *Phoque*]

11th Submarine Division (HQ: Beiruit, Lebanon; 09/01/39, assigned to 6th Submarine Squadron but detached to Levant Naval Station; submarines *Marsouin, Requin, Narval*): 09/01/39? Lt. J. E. L. A. Lorthioir [FN] [Leader: SS *Marsouin*]

12th Submarine Division (09/01/39, assigned to 2nd Submarine Squadron; submarines *Junon, Minerve, Ondine, Orion*): 09/01/39? LCdr. R. J. Cherdel [FN] [Leader: SS *Minerve*] 12/07/39 LCdr. L. V. H. M. P. Bazin [FN]

13th Submarine Division (09/01/39, assigned to 5th Submarine Squadron; submarines

Calypso, Circé, Doris, Thétis): 09/01/39? Lt. J. E. M. Favreul [FN] [Leader: SS *Doris*]

14th Submarine Division (09/01/39, assigned to 2nd Submarine Squadron; submarines *Ariane, Diane, Danaé, Eurydice*): 09/01/39? LCdr. R. H. J. L. Boyer-Besses [FN] [Leader: SS *Diane*]

15th Submarine Division (09/01/39, assigned to 5th Submarine Squadron; submarines *Cérès, Iris, Pallas, Vénus*): 09/01/39? LCdr. R. A. H. J. Mourral [FN] [Leader: SS *Iris*]

16th Submarine Division (HQ: Cherbourg, France; 09/01/39, assigned to I Naval Region; submarines *Amazone, Antiope, La Sybille, Orphée*): 09/01/39? LCdr. L. E. Y. M. Courson [FN] [Leader: submarine *Orphée*]

17th Submarine Division (09/01/39, assigned to 6th Submarine Squadron; submarines *Aréthuse, Atalante, La Sultane, La Vestale*): 09/01/39? Lt. G. F. A. Vidal [FN] [Leader: SS *La Vestale*]

18th Submarine Division (09/01/39, assigned to 2nd Submarine Squadron; submarines *Amphitrite, La Psyché, Méduse, Oréade*): 09/01/39? Lt. J. C. Leroy [FN] [Leader: SS *La Psyche*]

19th Submarine Division (09/01/39, assigned to Toulon Submarine Base; submarines *Argonaute, Galatée, Naiade, Sirène*): 09/01/39? LCdr. R. Bertrand [FN] [Leader: SS *Galatée*]

20th Submarine Division (09/01/39, assigned to 6th Submarine Squadron; submarines *Nautilus, Rubis, Saphir, Tourquoise*): 09/01/39? Lt. R. P. Wacogne [FN] [Leader: SS *Torquoise*]

21st Submarine Division (09/01/39, assigned to Toulon Submarine Base; submarines *La Perle, Le Diamant*): 09/01/39? unknown?

BIBLIOGRAPHY
BOOKS USED IN THIS SERIES

Abbott, Peter, et. al., *Germany's Eastern Front Allies 1941-45*. Men-at-Arms Series, #131. London: Osprey Publishing Ltd, 1982.

Adair, Paul. *Hitler's Greatest Defeat*. London: Arms and Armour, 1994.

Adam, Henry et al. *Italy at War.* Times-Life Books, World War II Series, Vol. 33. Chicago: Times-Life Books, 1982.

Alexander, Bevin. *How Hitler Could Have Won World War II*. New York: Crown Publishers, 2000.

Allen, Peter. *One More River: The Rhine Crossings of 1945.* New York: Charles Scribner's Sons, 1980.

Ambrose, Stephen E. *The Supreme Commander: The War Years of General Dwight D, Eisenhower.* Garden City, New York: Doubleday & Comp. Inc., 1969.

------. *D-Day June 6, 1944: The Climactic Battle of World War II*. New York. A Touchtone Book, Published by Simon & Schuster, 1994.

Anders, Wladyslaw. *Hitler's Defeat in Russia.* Chicago, Regnery, 1953.

------. *Russian Volunteers in Hitler's Army.* Bayside, New York: Axis Europa, 1998.

Argyle, Christopher. *Chronology of World War II: The Day by Day Illustrated Record 1939-45.* London: Marshall Cavendish, 1980.

Auerbach, William. *Last of the Panzers: German Tanks 1944-45.* Tank Illustrated #9. London: Arms & Armour Press, 1984.

The Australian Army at War: 1939-1944. London: His Majesty's Stationary Office, 1944.

Axworthy, Mark et. al., *The Romanian Army of World War 2.* Men-at-Arms Series, #246. London: Osprey Publishing Ltd, 1991.

------, et. al. *Third Axis Fourth Ally: Rumanian Armed Forces in the European War, 1941-1945.* London: Arms and Armour, 1995.

Bailey, Ronald H. et. al. *The Home Front: U.S.A.* Times-Life Books, World War II Series, Vol. 8. Chicago: Times-Life Books, 1978.

------. et al.*Partisans and Guerrillas.* Time-Life Books, World War II Series, Vol. 12. Chicago: Times-Life Books, 1978.

------ et. al. *The Air War in Europe.* Times-Life Books, World War II Series, Vol. 16. Chicago: Times-Life Books, 1979

------ et. al. *Prisoners of War.* Times-Life Books, World War II Series, Vol. 30. Chicago: Times-Life Books, 1981.

Bailey, Thomas A. And Paul B. Ryan. *Hitler vs. Roosevelt: The Undeclared Naval War.* New York: The Free Press, 1979.

Balin, George. *Afrika Corps.* Tank Illustrated #17. London: Arms & Armour Press, 1985.

Banyard, Peter. *The Rise of the Dictators 1919-1939.* New York: Aladdin Books, 1986.

Barker, A. J. *Pearl Harbor.* Ballantine's Illustrated History of World War II, Battle Book No. 10. New York: Ballantine Books, 1969.

Barnett, Correlli. *The Desert Generals.* Bloomington, Indiana: Indiana University Press, 1960.

------ (Edited by). *Hitler's Generals.* New York: Grove Weidenfeld, 1989.

Bekker, Cajus. *Hitler's Naval War.* New York: Zebra Books, Kensington Publishing Corp., 1977.

Benford, Timothy B., *The World War II Quiz & Fact Book*. New York: Berkley Books, 1984.
Bethell, Nicholas et. al. *Russia Besieged*. Times-Life Books, World War II Series, Vol. 6. Chicago: Times-Life Books, 1977.
Beyevor, Antony. *Stalingrad: The Fateful Siege: 1942-1943*. New York: Viking, 1998.
Bekker, Cajus. *Hitler's Naval War*. New York: Kensington Publishing Corp., 1971.
Bethell, Nicholas et. al. *Russia Besieged*. Times-Life Books, World War II Series, Vol. 6. Chicago: Times-Life Books, 1977.
Bidwell, Shelford. *The Chindit War: Stilwell, Wingate and the Campaign in Burma: 1944*. New York: Macmillan Publishing Co., Inc., 1979.
Bishop, Chris. *Order of Battle: German Infantry in WWII*. London: Amber Books, 2009.
------. *Order of Battle: German Panzers in WWII*. London: Amber Books, 2009.
Bishop, Edward. *Their Finest Hour: The Story of the Battle of Britain 1940*. New York: Ballantine Books, 1968
Blumenson, Martin. *Sicily: Whose Victory?*. Ballantine's Illustrated History of World War II, Campaign Book No. 3. New York: Ballantine Books, 1968.
------. *Eisenhower*. Ballantine's Illustrated History of the Violent Century, War Leader Book No. 9. New York: Ballantine Books, 1972.
Blumenson, Martin et al. *Liberation*. Times-Life Books, World War II Series, Vol. 14. Chicago: Times-Life Books, 1978.
Boatner, III, Mark M. *The Biographical Dictionary of World War II*. Novato, CA: Presidio, 1996.
Botting, Douglas et. al. *The Second Front*. Times-Life Books, World War II Series, Vol. 13. Chicago: Times-Life Books, 1978.
------ et al. *The Aftermath: Europe*. Times-Life Books, World War II Series, Vol. 38. Chicago: Times-Life Books, 1983.
Bowman, Martin W. *USAAF Handbook 1939-1945*. Mechanicsburg, Pennsylvania: Stackpole Books, 1997.
Bradley, Omar N. *A Soldier's Story*. New York: Henry Holt, 1951.
Bradley, Omar N. and Clay Blair. *A General's Life: An Autobiography*. New York: Simon & Schuster 1983.
Breuer, William B. *Operation Dragoon: The Allied Invasion of the South of France*. Novato, California: Presidio, 1987.
Britt-Smith, Richard. *Hitler's Generals*. San Rafael: Presidio Press, 1976.
Carell, Paul. *The Foxes of the Desert*. New York: E. P. Dutton, 1960.
------ *Hitler Moves East, 1941-43*. Boston: Little, Brown and Company, 1965 (republished by Bantam Books, New York: 1971.)
------. *Invasion: They're Coming*. New York: E. P. Dutton, . (republished by Bantam Books, New York: 1973.)
------. *Stalingrad: Defeat of the German 6th Army*. Atglen, Pennsylvania: Schiffer, 1993.
Calvert, Michael. *Slim*. Ballantine's Illustrated History of the Violent Century, War Leader Book No. 12. New York: Ballantine Books, 1973.
Chant, Christopher, ed. *Hitler's Generals*. New York: Chartwell Books, Inc., 1979.
Chapman, Guy. *Why France Fell: The Defeat of the French Army in 1940*. New York: Rinehart and Winston, 1968.
Chuikov, Vasili. *Battle for Stalingrad*. New York: Holt, Rinehart and Winston, 1964.
Churchill, Winston (Forwarded by). *D-Day, Operation Overlord*. London: Salamander Books Limited, 1993.

Clark, Alan. *Barbarossa: The Russian-German Conflict, 1941-45.* New York: William Morrow and Company, 1965.

Clark, Mark W. *Calculated Risk.* New York: Harper & Brothers Publishing, 1950.

Cole, Hugh M. *The Ardennes: The Battle of the Bulge.* United States Army in World War II: European Theater of Operations, Office of the Chief of Military History, United States Department of Army. Washington D. C.: United States Government Printing Office, 1965.

Collier, Basil. *The War in the Far East 1941-1945. A Military History.* New York: William Morrow & Company, Inc., 1969.

Collier, Richard et al. *The War in the Desert.* Times-Life Books, World War II Series, Vol. 7. Chicago: Times-Life Books, 1977.

Cooper, Matthew. *The German Army: 1933-1945.* Briarcliff Manor, N.Y.: Stein and Day/Publishers, 1978.

------ & James Lucas. *Panzer: The Armoured Forces of the Third Reich.* New York: St. Martin's Press, 1978.

Cormack, Andrew, et. al., *Germany's Eastern Front Allies 1941-45.* Men-at-Arms Series, #225. London: Osprey Publishing Ltd, 1990.

Costello, John. *The Pacific War 1941-1945.* New York: Quill 1982.

Cowley, Robert (Edited by). *The Collected What If?* New York: G. P. Putnam's, 1999.

Craig, William. *The Fall of Japan.* New York: Dell Publishing Group, 1967.

Creswell, Capt. John, R.N. *Generals and Admirals. The Story of Amphibious Command.* London: Longmans, Green and Company, 1952.

Cross, Robin. *Citadel: The Battle of Kursk.* London: Michael O'Mara Books Ltd., 1993

Davis, Franklin M., Jr. et. al. *Across the Rhine.* Times-Life Books, World War II Series, Vol. 22. Chicago: Times-Life Books, 1980.

Deighton, Len. *Fighter.* New York: Ballantine Books, 1977.

D'Este, Carlo. *Bitter Victory: The Battle for Sicily, 1943.* New York: Harper Perennial, 1991.

Dollinger, Hans. *The Decline and Fall of Nazi Germany and Imperial Japan.* New York: Bonanza Books, 1967.

Downing, David. *The Devil's Virtuosos: German Generals at War 1940-5.* New York: St. Martin's Press, 1977.

Duffy, Christopher. *Red Storm on the Reich.* New York: Atheneum, 1991.

Dupuy, Trevor N. *A Genius for War: The German Army and General Staff, 1807-1945.*

Editors of Time-Life Books et al. *Japan at War.* Times-Life Books, World War II Series, Vol. 26. Chicago: Times-Life Books, 1980.

------ et al. *The Aftermath: Asia.* Times-Life Books, World War II Series, Vol. 39. Chicago: Times-Life Books, 1983.

----- et al. *Absolute Victory: America's Greatest Generation and Their World War II Triumph.* New York: Time Inc. Home Entertainment, 2005

Edwards, Roger. *German Airborne Troops, 1939-45.* New York: Doubleday and Company, 1974.

Eisenhower, David. *Eisenhower at War 1943-1945.* New York: Vintage Books, 1987.

Eisenhower, Dwight D. *Crusade in Europe.* New York: Avon, 1968.

Elliott, MG J. G. *Unfading Honour: The Story of the Indian Army 1939-1945.* New York: A. S. Barnes and Co., Inc., 1965.

Ellis, John. *The World War II Databook.* London: Aurum Press Ltd, 1993.

Ellis, L. E. *Victory in the West. Volume I, The Battle of Normandy.* London: Her Majesty's

Stationery Office, 1962.

------, *Victory in the West. Volume II, The Defeat of Germany.* London: Her Majesty's Stationery Office, 1968.

Elson, Robert et. al. *Prelude to War.* Times-Life Books, World War II Series, Vol. 1. Chicago: Times-Life Books, 1979.

Elting, John R. et. al. *Battles for Scandinavia.* Times-Life Books, World War II Series, Vol. 28. Chicago: Times-Life Books, 1981.

Erickson, John. *The Road to Stalingrad.* Harper and Row, 1975.

------. *The Road to Berlin.* New York: Harper and Row, 1983.

Essame, MG H. *Normandy Bridgehead.* Ballantine's Illustrated History of World War II, Campaign Book No. 10. New York: Ballantine Books, 1970.

Ethell, Jeffrey. *U. S. Army Air Forces, World War II.* Warbirds Illustrated #38. London: Arms & Armour Press, 1986.

Faber, Harold. *Luftwaffe: A History.* Chicago: Times Books, 1977.

Falk, Stanley. *Liberation of the Philippines.* Ballantine's Illustrated History of World War II, Campaign Book No. 10. New York: Ballantine Books, 1971.

Farago, Ladislas (Edited by). *The Last Days of Patton.* New York: Berkley Books, 1982.

Fisher, Ernest F., Jr. *Cassino to the Alps.* United States Army in World War II: Mediterranean Theater of Operations, Office of the Chief of Military History, United States Department of Army. Washington D. C.: United States Government Printing Office, 1977.

Fodor, Denis J. et al. *The Neutrals.* Times-Life Books, World War II Series, Vol. 35. Chicago: Times-Life Books, 1982.

Forty, George. *Patton's Third War at War.* London: Arms and Armour Press, 1976.

Frank, Benis M. *Okinawa: Touchstone to Victory.* Ballantine's Illustrated History of World War II, Battle Book No. 12. New York: Ballantine Books, 1969.

Frankland, Noble. *Bomber Offensive: The Devastation of Europe.* Ballantine's Illustrated History of World War II, Campaign Book No. 7. New York: Ballantine Books, 1970.

Fuller, Richard. *Shōkan, Hirohito's Samurai, Leaders of the Japanese Armed Forces, 1926-1945.* London: Arms and Armour Press, 1992.

Gailey, Harry A. *The War in the Pacific: From Pearl Harbor to Tokyo Bay.* Novato, California: Presidio, 1995.

Gavin, James M. *On to Berlin.* New York: Viking, 1978.

German Army Order of Battle, October 1942. Military Intelligence Service. Lancer Militaria. Mt. Ida, Arkansas. (First published by Military Intelligence Service, 1942.)

German Order of Battle 1944: The Directory, Prepared by Allied Intelligence, of Regiments, Formations and Units of the German Armed Forces. Greenhill Books, London and Stackpole Books, Pennsylvania, 1994. (First published by Her Majesty's Stationery Office, 1944.)

Gilbert, Alton Keith. *A Born Leader: The Life of Admiral John Sidney McCann, Pacific Carrier Commander.* Philadelphia: Casemate, 2006.

Gilbert, Martin. *The Second World War: A Complete History.* New York: Henry Holt and Company, 1989.

Goerlitz, Walter. *Paulus and Stalingrad.* New York: Citadel, 1963.

Goolrick, William K. and Ogden Tanner et al. *The Battle of the Bulge.* Times-Life Books, World War II Series, Vol. 18. Chicago: Times-Life Books, 1979.

Goralski, Robert. *World War II Almanac, 1931-1945.* New York: G. P. Putnam's Sons,

1981.

Gow, Ian. *Okinawa 1945: Gateway to Japan.* Garden City, New York: Doubleday & Company, Inc. 1985.

Granatstein, J. L. *The Generals: The Canadian Army's Senior Commanders in the Second World War.* Toronto: Stoddart Publishing, 1993.

Green, William & Gordon Swanborough. *Flying Colors.* Carrollton, Texas: Salamander Books Ltd. And Pilot Press Ltd., 1981.

Grigg, John. *1943: The Victory That Never Was.* New York: Zebra Books, 1980.

Guderian, Heinz. *Panzer Leader.* New York: Ballantine Books, 1957.

Hamilton, Nigel. *Master of the Battlefield: Monty's War Years 1942-1944.* New York: McGraw-Hill Book Company, 1983.

------. *Monty: Final Years of the Field-Marshal 1944-1976.* New York: McGarw-Hill Book Company, 1987.

Hart, B. H. Liddell. *History of the Second World War.* 2 Vols. New York: G. P. Putnam's Sons, 1972.

------. *The German Generals Talk.* New York: Quill, 1979.

Haskew, Michael E., *Encyclopedia of the Elite Forces in the Second World War.* London: Amber Books, 2007.

Hastings, Max. *Overlord: D-Day & the Battle for Normandy.* New York: Simon and Schuster, 1964.

Haupt, Werner. *Assault on Moscow, 1941: The Offensive, the Battle, the Retreat.* Atglen, Pennsylvania: Schiffer, 1996.

------. *Army Group Center: The Wehrmacht in Russia.* Atglen, Pennsylvania: Schiffer, 1997.

------. *Army Group North: The Wehrmacht in Russia.* Atglen, Pennsylvania: Schiffer, 1997.

------. *Army Group South: The Wehrmacht in Russia.* Atglen, Pennsylvania: Schiffer, 1998.

------. *Elite German Divisions in World War II.* Atglen, Pennsylvania: Schiffer Publishing Ltd., 2001.

Heckmann, Wolf. *Rommel's War in Africa.* Garden City, New York: Doubleday & Comp. Inc. 1981.

Herzstern, Robert Edwin et al. *The Nazis.* Times-Life Books, World War II Series, Vol. 21. Chicago: Times-Life Books, 1980.

Hibbert, Christopher. *Anzio: The Bid for Rome.* New York: Ballantine Books, 1970.

Higgins, Trumbull. *Hitler and Russia: 1941-1946.* New York: Columbia Univ. Press, 1973.

Hoyt, Edwin P. *199 Days: The Battle: The Battle for Stalingrad.* New York: Doherty, 1993.

------. *Yamamoto: The Man Who Planned the Attack on Pearl Harbor.* Guilford, Connecticut: The Lyons Press, 2001.

Humble, Richard. *United States Fleet Carriers of World War II.* Dorset, United Kingdom: Blandford Press, 1984.

Irving, David. *The Trail of the Fox: The Search for the True Field Marshal Rommel.* New York: E. P. Dutton, 1979.

Jackson, Robert. *Churchill's Moat: The Channel War 1939-1945.* Shrewsbury, United Kingdom: Airlife Publinhing Ltd., 1995.

------. *The Royal Navy in World War II.* Annapolis, Maryland: Naval Institute Press, 1997.

Jackson, W. G. F. *The Battle for North Africa.* New York: Mason/Charter, 1975.

Jones, James. *WWII.* New York: Ballantine Books, 1975.

Jordan, David. *Wolfpack.* New York: Barnes & Noble Books, 2002.

Jukes, Geoffrey. *Stalingrad: The Turning Point.* Ballantine's Illustrated History of World

War II, Battle Book No. 3. New York: Ballantine Books, 1968.

Keegan, John. *Waffen-SS: The Asphalt Soldiers.* Ballantine's Illustrated History of World War II. New York: Ballantine Books, 1970.

------ (General editor). *The Rand McNally Encyclopedia of World War II.* Chicago: Rand McNally and Company, 1977.

------, *Who Was Who in World War II.* New York: Thomas Y. Crowell Publishers, 1978.

------ (Edited by). *Churchill's Generals.* New York: Quill & William Morrow Publishing, 1991.

Kemp, Anthony. *The Maginot Line: Myth & Reality.* New York: Military Heritage Press, 1988.

Koburger, Charles W. Jr., *The Cyrano Fleet, Franch and Its Navy, 1940-1942.* New York: Praeger, 1989.

Kursietis, Andris J. *The Hungarian Army and Its Military Leadership in World War II.* Bayside, New York: Axis Europa Books & Magazines, 1996.

Lanning, Lt. Col. (Ret.) Michael Lee. *The Military 100.* Secaucus, New Jersey: A Citadel Press Book, 1996.

Lash, Joseph P. *Roosevelt and Churchill 1939-1945.* New York: W. W. Norton & Company, Inc.,1976.

Lewin, Ronald. *Rommel as a Military Commander.* New York: Ballantine Books, 1970.

-------, *Montgomery as a Military Commander.* New York: Stein and day Publishers, 1971.

Lodge, Brett. *Lavarack: Rival General.* St. Leonards, Australia: Allen & Unwin, 1998.

Lord, Walter. *Incredible Victory: The Battle of Midway.* Short Hill, New Jersey: Burford Books, 1967.

Lucas, James. *Panzer Army Africa.* San Rafael, California: Presidio Press, 1977.

------. *War on the Eastern Front, 1941-1945: The German Soldier in Russia.* New York: Stein and Day Publishers, 1980.

------. *Storming Eagles: German Airborne Forces in World War Two.* London: Arms & Armour Press, 1988.

------ (General Editor). *Command: A Historical Dictionary of Military Leaders.* New York: Military Press, 1988.

------. *Hitler's Mountain Troops.* London: Arms & Armour Press, 1992.

------. *Battle Group!: German Kampfgruppen Action of World War Two.* London, Arms & Armour, 1993.

------. *Hitler's Enforcers: Leaders of the German War Machine 1939-1945.* London: Arms & Armour Press, 1996

------, *German Army Handbook 1939-1945.* Bridgend, London: Sutton Publishing Limited, 1998.

------. *Hitler's Commanders: German Bravery in the Field, 1939-1945.* London: Cassell & Company, 2000.

Luck, Hans von. *Panzer Commander.* New York: A Dell Book, Bantan Doubleday Dell Publishing Group, 1989

Lyall, Gavin (Edited by). *The War in the Air: The Royal Air Force in World War II.* New York: William Morrow & Company, Inc., 1968.

MacDonald, Charles B. *A Time for Trumpets: The Untold Story of the Battle of the Bulge.* New York: Bantam Books, 1984.

MacIntyre, Donald. *The Naval War Against Hitler.* New York: Charles Scribner's Sons, 1971.

Macksey, Maj. K. J. *Panzer Division: The Mailed Fist.* Ballantine's Illustrated History of

World War II, Weapons Book No. 2. New York: Ballantine Books, 1968.

------. *Afrika Korps*. Ballantine's Illustrated History of the Violent Century, Campaign Book No. 1. New York: Ballantine Books, 1968.

Macksey, Kenneth. *Guderian: Creator of the Blitzkrieg*. New York: Stein and Day Publishers, 1975.

------, *Guderian Panzer General*. London: Lionel Leventhal Limited, 1975.

------. *Military Errors of World War Two*. London: Arms & Armour, 1987.

------ (Edited by). *Hitler's Options: Alternate Decisions of World War II*. London: Greenhill Books, 1995.

Madej, W. Victor. *German Army Order of Battle 1939-1945*. New Martinsville, West Virginia: Game Marketing Comp., 1978.

------. *German Army Order of Battle 1939-1945: Volume I*. Allentown, Pennsylvania: Game Marketing Company., 1981.

------. *German Army Oder of Battle 1939-1945 Supplement*. Allentown, Pennsylvania: Game Marketing Company, 1981.

------, *Southeastern Europe Axis Armed Forces Order of Battle*. Allentown, Pennsylvania: Game Publishing Company, 19832.

------, *Red Army Order of Battle 1941 - 1943*. Allentown, Pennsylvania: Game Publishing Company, 1983.

------. *German Army Order of Battle: The Replacement Army, 1939-1945*. Allentown, Pennsylvania: Game Publishing Company, 1984.

------. *German Army Order of Battle: Field Army and Officer Corps 1939-1945*. Allentown, Pennsylvania: Game Publishing Company, 1985.

------. *Italian Army Order of Battle: 1940-1944*. Allentown, Pennsylvania: Game Publishing Company, 1987.

Mallmann Showell, Jak P. *The German Navy in World War Two*. Naval Institute Press. Annapolis, Maryland, 1979.

Malony, C. J. C. *The Mediterranean and the Middle East. Vol. 5. The Campaign in Sicily (1943) and the Campaign in Italy (3 Sept 1943 - 31 March 1944)*. London. Her Majesty's Stationery Office, 1973.

------. *The Mediterranean and the Middle East. Vol. 6. Victory in the Mediterranean Part I (1 Apr - 4 Jun 1944)*. London: Her Majesty's Stationery Office, 1984.

Manstein, Erich von. *Lost Victories*. Chicago: Henry Regnery, 1958.

March, Cyril, ed. *The Rise and Fall of the German Air Force, 1933-1945*. New York: St. Martin's, 1983.

Marston, Daniel. *The Pacific War Companion: From Pearl Harbor to Hiroshima*. Oxford, United Kingdom. Osprey Publishing, 2005.

Martienssen, Anthony. *Hitler and his Admirals*. New York: E. P. Dutton & Co., Inc., 1949.

Masson, Phillipe. *De Gaulle*. Ballantine's Illustrated History of the Violent Century, War Leader Book No. 7. New York: Ballantine Books, 1972.

Matanle, Ivor. *World War II*. Godalming, Surrey, England: Colour Library Books, Ltd., 1989.

Maurer, Maurer. (Edited by). *Air Force Combat Units of World War II*. Edison, New Jersey: Chartwell Books, 1994.

Mayer, S. L. (Edited by). *The Rise and Fall of Imperial Japan 1894-1945*. New York: Military Press, 1976.

Mayer, Sydney L. *MacArthur*. Ballantine's Illustrated History of the Violent Century, War Leader Book No. 2. New York: Ballantine Books, 1971.

McCombs, Don and Worth, Fred L. *World War II: Super Facts.* New York: Warner Books, 1983.

McKee, Alexander. *The Race for the Rhine Bridges.* New York: Stein and Day Publishers, 1971.

McNab, Chris. *Order of Battle: German Kriegsmarine in WWII.* London: Amber Books, 2009.

------. *Order of Battle: German Luftwaffe in WWII.* London: Amber Books, 2009.

Mellenthin, MG F. W. von. *Panzer Battles.* Norman: University of Oklahoma Press, 1956. (Republished by Ballantine Books, New York: 1971.)

------. *German Generals of World War II.* Norman: University of Oklahoma Press, 1977.

Miller, Russell et. al. *The Resistance.* Times-Life Books, World War II Series, Vol. 17. Chicago: Times-Life Books, 1979.

------. *The Commandos.* Times-Life Books, World War II Series, Vol. 31. Chicago: Times-Life Books, 1981.

Mitcham, Samuel W., Jr. *Rommel's Last Battle: The Desert Fox and the Normandy Campaign.* Briarcliff Manor, New York: Stein and Day Publishers, 1983.

------. *Hitler's Legions: The German Army Order of Battle, World War II.* Briarcliff Manor, New York: Stein and Day Publishers, 1985.

------. *Men of the Luftwaffe.* Novato, California: Presidio Press, 1988.

------. *Triumphant Fix.* New York: Jove Books 1990.

Mitcham, Samuel W., Jr. and Gene Mueller. *Hitler's Commanders.* Scarborough House. Lanham, Maryland, 1992.

Mitcham, Samuel W., Jr. and Friedrich von Stauffenberg. *The Battle of Sicily.* New York: Orion Books, 1991.

Morison, Samuel Eliot. *The History of the United States Naval Operations in World War II. 14 vols.* Boston: Little, Brown, 1947-62.

------. *The Two-Ocean War.* New York: Ballantine Books, 1963.

Moser, Don et. al. *Blitzkrieg.* Times-Life Books, World War II Series, Vol. 9. Chicago: Times-Life Books, 1978.

Mosley, Leonard. *The Reich Marshal: A Biography of Hermann Goering.* New York: Dell Publishing Co., Inc., 1974.

------ et. al. *The Battle of Britain.* Times-Life Books, World War II Series, Vol. 3. Chicago: Times-Life Books, 1977.

Moulton, J. L. *Battle for Antwerp.* New York: Hippocrene Books, Inc., 1978.

Murphy, Audie. *To Hell and Back.* New York: Bantam, 1979.

Natkiel, Richard. *Atlas of World War II.* New York: The Military Press, 1985.

Nafziger, George F. *German Order of Battle, World War II, Volume 1, Panzer, Panzer Grenadier, Light and Cavalry Divisions.* Privately Published, 1994.

------. *German Order of Battle, World War II, Volume 2, The Waffen SS, Luftwaffe, Fallschirmjager, Naval and Mountain Divisions.* Privately Published, 1994.

------. *German Order of Battle, World War II, Volume 3, German Artillery: Independent Battalions, Railroad, Coastal Flak, and Sturmgeschutz.* Privately Published, 1994.

------. *German Order of Battle, World War II, Volume 4, German Infantry Divisions.* Privately Published, 1994.

------. *German Order of Battle, World War II, Volume 5, German Infantry Divisions Nos 300-999, Named Divisions, and Corps Detachments.* Privately Published, 1994.

------. *German Order of Battle, World War II, Volume 6, German Security, Static/Garrison,*

Jager, Light, Reserve and Replacement and Training Divisions. Privately Published, 1994.

------. *Bulgarian Order of Battle, World War II, An Organizational History of the Bulgarian Army in World War II.* Pisgah, Ohio: Privately Published, 1995.

------. *French Order of Battle, World War II, 1939-1945, á la Gloire, de Ínfanterie Française.* Pisgah, Ohio: Privately Published, 1995.

------. *German Order of Battle, World War II, Foreigners in Field Gra, The Cossack, Russian, Croatian, and Italian Soldiers in the Wehrmacht.* Pisgah, Ohio: Privately Published, 1995.

------. *Rumanian Order of Battle, World War II, An Organizational History of the Rumanian Army in World War II.* Pisgah, Ohio: Privately Published, 1995

------. *Italian Order of Battle, World War II, Volume 1, An Organizational History of the Itlian Army in World War II: Armored, Motorized, Alpini & Cavalry Divisions.* Pisgah, Ohio: Privately Published, 1996.

------. *Italian Order of Battle, World War II, Volume 2, An Organizational History of the Itlian Army in World War II: The Infantry Divisions.* Pisgah, Ohio: Privately Published, 1996.

------. *Italian Order of Battle, World War II, Volume 3, An Organizational History of the Itlian Army in World War II: Black Shirt, Mountain, Assault & Landing Divisions, Corps Troops and 1944 Liberation Army.* Pisgah, Ohio: Privately Published, 1996.

------. *The Afrika Korps, An Organizational History, 1941-1943.* Privately Published, 1997.

Niehorster, Leo W. G. *The Royal Hungarian Army, 1920-1945. Volume I Organization and History.* New York: Axis Europa Books, 1998.

Packard, Jerrold M., *Neither Friend Nor Foe, The European Neutrals in World War II.* New York: Charles Scribner's Sons, 1992.

Paine, Lauran. *German Military Intelligence in World War II: The Abwehr.* New York: Military Heritage Press, 1984.

Parrish, Thomas (Edited by). *Simon and Schuster Encyclopedia of World War II.* New York: Simon and Schuster, 1978.

Payne, Robert. *The Life and Death of Adolf Hitler.* New York: Praeger Publishers, 1973.

Patton, George S., Jr. *War As I Knew It.* Boston: Houghton Mifflin, 1947.

Perret, Geoffrey. *There's a War to be Won: The United States Army in World War II.* New York: Ballantine Books, 1981.

------. *Winged Victory: The Army Air Forces in World War II.* New York: Random House, 1993.

Perrett, Bryan. *A History of Blitzkrieg.* New York: Stein and Day Publishers, 1983. (Republished by Jove Books, New York: 1989.)

Persons, Benjamin S. *Relieved of Command.* Manhattan, Kansas: Sunflower University Press, 1997

Pfannes, Charles E. And Victor A. Salamone. *The Great Commanders of World War II. Volume I: The Germans.* New York: Zebra Books, Kensington Publishing Company, 1980.

------. *The Great Commanders of World War II. Volume I: The Germans.* New York: Zebra Books, Kensington Publishing Company, 1981.

------. *The Great Commanders of World War II. Volume III: The Americans.* New York: Zebra Books, Kensington Publishing Company, 1981.

------. *The Great Admirals of World War II. Volume I: The Americans.* New York: Zebra

Books, Kensington Publishing Company, 1983.

Piekalkiewicz, Janusz. *The Air War 1939-1945.* Dorset, United Kingdom: Blandford Press, 1985.

Pitt, Barrie et al. *The Battle of the Atlantic.* Times-Life Books, World War II Series, Vol. 5. Chicago: Times-Life Books, 1977.

Playfair, I. S. O. *The Mediterranean and the Middle East. Vol. 1. The Early Success Against Italy (to May 1941).* London: His Majesty's Stationery Office, 1954.

------. *The Mediterranean and the Middle East. Vol. 2. The Germans Come to the Help of their Ally (1941).* London: His Majesty's Stationery Office, 1956.

------. *The Mediterranean and the Middle East. Vol. 3. British Fortunes Reach Their Lowest Ebb (9/41-9/42).* London: His Majesty's Stationery Office, 1960.

------ and C. J. C. Malony. *The Mediterranean and the Middle East. Vol. 4. The Destruction of the Axis Forces in Africa.* London: His Majesty's Stationery Office, 1966.

Poirier, Robert G. & Albert Z. Connor. *The Red Army Order of Battle in the Great Patriotic War.* Novato, CA: Presidio Press, 1985.

Porten, Edward P. von der. *The German Navy in World War II.* New York: Ballantine Books, 1969.

Powell, Geoffrey. *The Devil's Birthday: The Bridges to Arnhem 1944.* New York Franklin Watts, 1984.

Prange, Gordon W. With Donald M. Goldstein and Katherine V. Dillon. *Pearl Harbor: The Verdict of History.* New York: McGrew-Hill Book Company, 1986.

Preston, Anthony (Foreword by). *Jane's Fighting Ships of World War II.* London: The Random House Group Ltd, 2001.

Preston, Paul. *The Spanish Civil War: An Illustrated Chronicle 1936-39.* New York: Groves Press, Inc., 1986.

Price, Dr. Alfred. *The Luftwaffe Data Book.* London: Greenhill Books, 1997.

Quarrie, Bruce. *Hitler's Samurai: The Waffen-SS in Action.* Wellingborough, England: Patrick Stephens, Third Printing, 1986.

Ready, J. Lee, *World War Two, Nation by Nation.* London: Arms and Armour Press, 1995.

Reynolds, Clark G. *Famous American Admirals.* New York: Van Nostrand Reinhold Company, 1978.

Rich, Norman. *Hitler's War Aims.* New York: W. W. Norman & Company, Inc., 1973.

Rigge, Simon et al. *War in the Outposts.* Times-Life Books, World War II Series, Vol. 24. Chicago: Times-Life Books, 1980.

Rikmenspoel, Marc J. *Waffen-SS: The Encyclopedia.* Garden City, New York: The Military Book Club, 2002.

Rommel, Erwin. *The Rommel Papers.* New York: Harcourt Brace Jovanovich, 1953. (Edited by B. H. Liddell Hart.)

------. *Rommel and his Art of War.* London: Greenhill Books, 2003

Rooney, D. D. *Stilwell.* Ballantine's Illustrated History of the Violent Century, War Leader Book No. 4. New York: Ballantine Books, 1971.

Roskill, B. W. *The War at Sea 1939-45. Vol. 1. The Defensive.* London: Her Majesty's Stationery Office, 1954.

------. *The War at Sea 1939-45. Vol. 2. The Period of Balance.* London: Her Majesty's Stationery Office, 1956.

------. *The War at Sea 1939-45. Vol. 3. The Offensive Part 1.* London: Her Majesty's

Stationery Office, 1960.

------. *The War at Sea 1939-45. Vol. 4. The Offensive Part 2.* London: Her Majesty's Stationery Office, 1963.

Rottman, Gordon L. *World War II Pacific Island Guide: A Geo-Military Study.* Westport, Connecticut: Greenwood Press, 2002.

Ruffner, Kevin Conley, et. al., *Luftwaffe Field Divisions 1941-45.* Men-at-Arms Series, #229. London: Osprey Publishing Ltd, 1990.

Ruge, Friedrich. *Der Geefrieg. The German Navy's Story 1939-1945.* United States Naval Institute. Annapolis, Maryland, 1957.

------, *Rommel in Normandy.* San Rafael, Calif.: Presidio Press, 1979.

Russell, Francis et al. *The Secret War.* Times-Life Books, World War II Series, Vol. 29. Chicago: Times-Life Books, 1981.

Rutherford, Ward. *Blitzkrieg 1940.* New York: G. P. Putnam's Sons, 1980.

Ryan, Cornelius. *The Longest Day.* New York: Simon and Schuster, 1959.

------. *The Last Battle.* New York: Simon and Schuster, 1966.

------. *A Bridge Too Far.* New York: Simon and Schuster, 1974.

Salisbury, Harrison E. *The 900 Days: The Siege of Leningrad.* New York: Avon, 1969.

Schmidt, H. W. *With Rommel in the Desert.* London: Harrap, 1951.

Seaton, Albert. *The Battle for Moscow.* New York: Stein and Day, 1971.

------. *Russo-German War, 1941-45.* New York: Praeger, 1976.

------. *The Fall of Fortress Europe, 1943-1945.* London: Batsford, 1981.

Sharp, Charles C. *Soviet Order of Battle, World War II, Volume 1, "The Deadly Beginning" - Soviet Tank, Mechanized, Motorized Division and Tank Brigades of 1940 - 1942.* Published by George F. Nafziger, 1995.

------. *Soviet Order of Battle, World War II, Volume 1I, "School of Battle" - Soviet Tank Corps and Tank Brigades January 1942 to 1945.* Published by George F. Nafziger, 1995.

------. *Soviet Order of Battle, World War II, Volume 1II, "Red Storm" - Soviet Mechanized Corps and Guards Armored Units 1942 to 1945.* Published by George F. Nafziger, 1995.

------. *Soviet Order of Battle, World War II, Volume 1V, "Red Guards" - Soviet Guards Rifle and Airborne Units 1941 to 1945.* Published by George F. Nafziger, 1995.

------. *Soviet Order of Battle, World War II, Volume V, "Red Sabers" - Soviet Cavalry Corps, Divisions, and Brigades 1941 to 1945.* Published by George F. Nafziger, 1995.

------. *Soviet Order of Battle, World War II, Volume V1, "Red Thunder" - Soviet Artillery Corps, Divisions, and Brigades 1941 to 1945.* Published by George F. Nafziger, 1995.

------. *Soviet Order of Battle, World War II, Volume VI1, "Red Death" - Soviet Mountain, Naval, NKVD, and Allied Divisions and Brigades 1941 to 1945.* Published by George F. Nafziger, 1995.

------. *Soviet Order of Battle, World War II, Volume VIII1, "Red Legions" - Soviet Rifle Divisions Formed Before June 1941.* Published by George F. Nafziger, 1995.

------, *Soviet Order of Battle, World War II, Volume V1X, "Red Tide" - Soviet Rifle Divisions Formed June to December 1941.* Published by George F. Nafziger, 1996.

------, *Soviet Order of Battle, World War II, Volume X, "Red Swarm" - Soviet Rifle Divisions Formed From 1942 to 1945.* Published by George F. Nafziger, 1996.

------, *Soviet Order of Battle, World War II, Volume X1, "Red Volunteers" - Soviet Militia

Units, Rifle and s 1941 - 1945. Published by George F. Nafziger, 1996.

Sharp, Lee. *The French Army 1939-1940, Organisation: Order of Battle : Operational History, Volume 1.* Milton Keyes, Great Britain: The Military Press, 2002.

------, *The French Army 1939-1940, Organisation: Order of Battle : Operational History, Volume 1I.* Milton Keyes, Great Britain: The Military Press, 2001.

------, *The French Army 1939-1940, Organisation: Order of Battle : Operational History, Volume 1II.* Milton Keyes, Great Britain: The Military Press, 2003.

Shaw, Jonn et. al. *Red Army Resurgent.* Times-Life Books, World War II Series, Vol. 20. Chicago: Times-Life Books, 1979.

Shirer, William L. *The Rise and Fall of the Third Reich.* New York: Simon and Schuster, 1960.

Showalter, Dennis, *Patton and Rommel. Men of War in the Twentieth Century.* New York: The Berkley Publishing Group, 2005.

Shtemenho, S. M., *The Soviet General Staff at War /1941-1945/.* Moscow: Progress Publishers, 1970, Second Printing, 1975.

Shukman, Harold (Edited by). *Stalin's Generals.* New York: Weidenfeld and Nicolson, 1993.

Simons, Gerald et. al. *Victory in Europe.* Times-Life Books, World War II Series, Vol. 36. Chicago: Times-Life Books, 1982

Slaughterhouse: The Encyclopedia of the Eastern Front. The Military Book Club. Garden City, New York, 2002.

Smurthwaite, David. *The Pacific War Atlas 1941-1945.* London: Mirabel Books Ltd., 1995.

Snyder, Dr. Louis L. *Encyclopedia of the Third Reich.* London: Robert Hale, McGraw-Hill, Inc., 1976.

Sokolov, Marshal Sergei (Foreword by). *Battles Hitler Lost.* New York: Jove Books, The Berkley Publishing Group, 1988.

Spector, Ronald H. *Eagle Against the Sun. The American War with Japan.* New York: The Free Press, 1985.

Stanton, Shelby L. *World War II Order of Battle.* New York: Galahad Books, 1991.

Stein, George. *The Waffen-SS.* New York: Cornell University Press, 1966.

Steinberg, Rafael et. al. *Island Fighting.* Times-Life Books, World War II Series, Vol. 10. Chicago: Times-Life Books, 1978.

----- et. al. *Return to the Philippines.* Times-Life Books, World War II Series, Vol. 15. Chicago: Times-Life Books, 1980.

Stolfi, R. H. S. *Hitler's Panzers East: World War II Reinterpreted.* Norman, Oklahoma: University of Oklahoma Press, 1992.

Strategy and Tactics of the Great Commanders of World War II and Their Battles. Greenwich, Conn.: Dorset Press, 1990.

Strawson, John. *The Itatian Campaign.* London: Secker & Warburg, 1987.

Sulzberger, C. L. *The American Heritage Picture History of World War II.* New York: Crown Publishers, 1966.

Taylor, James and Shaw, Warren. *The Third Reich Almanac.* New York: World Almanac, 1987.

Thompson, R. W. *D-Day: Spearhead of Invasion.* Ballantine's Illustrated History of the the Violent Century, Battle Book No. 1. New York: Ballantine Books, 1968.

Toland, John. *The Last 100 Days.* New York: Random House, 1965.

------. *The Rising Sun: The Decline and Fall of the Japanese Empire 1936-1945 (2*

Volumes). New York: Random House, 1970.

------. *Adolf Hitler*. New York: Ballantine Books, 1977. (Originally published by Random House, New York: 1976.)

Tsouras, Peter G. (Edited by). *Panzers on the Eastern Front: General Erhard Raus and his Panzer Divisions in Russia, 1941-1945*. London: Lionel Leventhal Limited, 2002.

------ (Edited by). *Hitler Triumphant: Alternate Decisions of World War II*. London: Greenhill Books, 2006.

U. S. War Department. *Handbook on Japanese Military Forces*. London: Greenhill Books, 1991. (New Introduction by David Isby & Afterword by Jeffrey Ethell).

Wallace, Robert et. al. *The Italian Campaign*. Times-Life Books, World War II Series, Vol. 11. Chicago: Times-Life Books, 1978.

Warlimont, Gen. Walter. *Inside Hitler's Headquarters 1939-45*. Novato, California: Presidio Press, 1962.

Wernick, Robert et. al. *Blitzkrieg*. Times-Life Books, World War II Series, Vol. 2. Chicago: Times-Life Books, 1977.

West Point Military History Series. *The Second World War: Military Campaign Atlas*. Wayne, New Jersey: Avery Publishing Group Inc., 1989 (series editor Thomas E. Griess.)

------. *The Second World War: Asia & the Pacific*. Wayne, New Jersey: Avery Publishing Group Inc., 1989 (series editor Thomas E. Griess.)

------. *The Second World War: Europe & the Mediterranean*. Wayne, New Jersey: Avery Publishing Group Inc., 1989 (series editor Thomas E. Griess.)

Wheeler, Keith et. al. *The Road to Tokyo*. Times-Life Books, World War II Series, Vol. 19. Chicago: Times-Life Books, 1979.

------ et al. *War Under the Pacific*. Times-Life Books, World War II Series, Vol. 23. Chicago: Times-Life Books, 1981.

------ et al. *Bombers Over Japan*. Times-Life Books, World War II Series, Vol. 34. Chicago: Times-Life Books, 1982.

------ et al. *The Fall of Japan*. Times-Life Books, World War II Series, Vol. 37. Chicago: Times-Life Books, 1983.

Whipple, A. B. C. et. al. *The Mediterranean*. Times-Life Books, World War II Series, Vol. 27. Chicago: Times-Life Books, 1981.

White, David Fairbank. *Bitter Ocean: The Battle of the Atlantic 1939-1`945*. New York: Simon & Schuster, 2006.

Whiting, Charles. *Patton*. Ballantine's Illustrated History of World War II, War Leader Book No. 1. New York: Ballantine Books, 1970.

------. *Bradley*. Ballantine's Illustrated History of the Violent Century, War Leader Book No. 5. New York: Ballantine Books, 1971.

------. *West Wall: The Battle for Hitler's Siegfried Line*. Staplehurst, England: Spellmount1999.

Whiting, Charles et al. *The Home Front: Germany*. Times-Life Books, World War II Series, Vol. 32. Chicago: Times-Life Books, 1982.

Williams, John. *France: Summer 1940*. Ballantine's Illustrated History of World War II, Campaign Book No. 6. New York: Ballantine Books, 1969.

Wistrich, Robert. *Who's Who in Nazi Germany*. New York: MacMillan Publishing Company, 1982.

World War II Surrender Documents. *Germany Surrenders 1945*. Washington, D. C.: The

National Archives, 1976.
World War II Surrender Documents. *Japan Surrenders 1945*. Washington, D. C.: The National Archives, 1976.
Wykes, Alan. *The Siege of Leningrad*. Ballantine's Illustrated History of World War II, Battle Book No. 5. New York: Ballantine Books, 1968.
Young, Desmond. *Rommel: The Desert Fox.* New York: Harper and Row, Publisher, 1965.
Zoology, Steven J. Et al. *Operation Barbatossa*, Tank Illustrated #16. London: Arms & Armour Press, 1985.
Zaloga, Steven & Victor Madej. *The Polish Campaign 1939*. New York: Hippocrene Books, Inc, 1991.
Zinh, Arthur et. al. *The Rising Sun.* Times-Life Books, World War II Series, Vol. 4. Chicago: Times-Life Books, 1977.
Ziemke, Earl F. et. al. *The Soviet Juggernaut.* Times-Life Books, World War II Series, Vol. 25. Chicago: Times-Life Books, 1980.

INTERNET SITES

Ammentorp, Steen, The Generals of WWII, - www.generals.dk.
Barrass, M. B., The Royal Air Force, - www.rafweb.org/menu.htm.
Battleships of World War II, - www.voodoo.cz/battleships/
Clancey, Patrick, The Official Chronology of the U.S. Navy in World War II; transcribed and formatted for HTML by, - www.ibiblio.org/hyperwar/USN/USN-Chron/USN-Chron-1939.html.
D'Adamo, Cristiano, Francesco Cestra, Marc De Angelis, Pierluigi Malvezzi, Robert Maulini, Vince O'Hara, Andrea Piccinotti, Ammiraglio Attilio Ranieri, Achille Rastelli, Comandante Salvatore Romano, Alberto Rosselli, Sebastiano Tringali, and Francesco Mattesini, Regia Marina Italiana, - www.regiamarina.net.
Kuznetsov, V., About Admiral of the Fleet of the Soviet Union N. G. Kuznetsov, - admiral.centro.ru/start_e.htm.
Liddell Hart Center, King's College London, - www.kd.ac.uk?lhcma/search/ocsearch.html.
Naval War In The Pacific 1941-1945, pacific.valka.cz/personel.
Niehorster, Dr. Leo, World War II Armed Forces, - niehorster.orbat.com.
Nishida, Hiroshi, Imperial Japanese Navy, - homepage2.nifty.com/nishidah/e/ .
Senior Officers, November 1, 1940, - www.geocities.com/scs028a/seniorofficers1940.html?200515.
Smith, Gordon (edited by), NAVAL-HISTORY.NET - www.naval-history.net/index.htm.
Swigart, Soren & Axel Schudak, The World at War: From Versailles to the Cold War. worldatwar.net.
Tully, Anthony P., Jon Parshall, Allyn D. Nevitt, Robert Hackett with Sander Kingsepp, Imperial Japanese Navy Page, - www.combinedfleet.com.
United States Air Force, - www.af.mil/bios.
United States Marine Corps, History and Museums Division, - hqinet001.hqmc.usmc.mil/HD/Historical/Whos_Who.
Wendel, Marcus, Axis History Factbook, - www.axishistory.com.
WW2-Cruisers - www.world-war.co.uk

Index

CCRR - Royal Carabinieri
CCNN - Blackshirt
FAF - French Air Force
FN - French Navy
GdA - General of Artillery
GdFl - General of Fighters
GdI - General of Infantry
GN - German Navy

GdGebTr - General of Mountain Troops
GdPzTr - General of Panzer Troops
GFM - General Field Marshal
Luft. - German Air Force
MVSN - National Security Volunteer Militia
RIAF - Royal Italian Air Force
RIN - Royal Italian Navy

Andorra

FREIXES, FRANCESC CAIRAT, 519

France

ABADIE, JULES, 346 (2)
Abadié, MG Maurice-Jean-Joseph, 418, 466
Abrial, Adm. Jean-Marie-Charles [FN], 318, 335, 375, 395
Agliany, BG Augustin-Marcelin, 422, 428, 476
AHNNE, ÉDOUARD, 325
Alaurent, MG Auguste, 412, 459
Alessandri, MG Marcel-Jean-Marie, 390 (2), 455, 477, 479
ALIBERT, RAPHAËL, 336
Aliotti, BG Antoine-Dominique-Frédéric, 431
Allemandet, BG Aimable-Adrien-Fernand, 317, 405 (2)
Alombert-Goget, MG Pierre-Paul-Étienne, 365
ALPHAND, HERVÉ, 345
Altmayer, LG Félix-René, 314, 316, 380, 494
Altmayer, LG Marie-Robert, 309, 369 (2), 448
André, BG Lucien-Julien-René, 422, 459
Andreï, BG Joseph-Charles-Gaëtan, 384
ANDRIEU, JULES, 350
ANGELINI, ANTOINE-MARIE, 325
Angénot, MG Paul-Émile, 297
ANNET, ARMAND-LÉON, 322, 324
ANTONINE, ARISTIDE, 344
Apffel, MG Jacques-Albert, 317, 364
Ardant du Picq, MG Charles-Pierre-Martial, 436, 477
Ardellier, LCol., 442
Arden, Cdr. L. M. E. [FN], 485
Ardouin-Dumazet, LCol., 295
Arguerolle, MG, 306
Aribaut, LCol. [FAF], 468
Arlabosse, LG Paul-Hippolyte, 314, 340, 341, 369, 405, 455, 463, 493
Arlabosse, LCol. Pierre-Georges, 392
Armengeat, MG Gustavé-Marcellin, 435
Arnaud, BG Edouard-Joseph, 384

Arnaud, MG Paul-Gabriel, 340, 357, 505
Arnould, BG 478
Arzur, Cdr A. C. M. [FN], 489
ASSIER de POMPIGNAN, CHARLES-ANDRÉ-MAURICE, 322, 323
AUBERT, PIERRE-ÉMILE, 324 (2)
Aubert, Capt. Y. E. [FN], 532
Aubertin, Capt. [Army], 415
Aubin, Capt. G. O. L. [FN], 534
Aublet, MG Marcel-Louis-Marie, 412
Auboyneau, RA Philippe [FN], 301, 345, 357, 377 (2), 470, 486, 501
AUBRAC, LUCIE, 350
AUBRAC, RAYMOND, 350
Audet, LG Sylvestre-Gérard, 384, 387 (3), 389, 437, 465, 494
Audrieu, Col. Georges [FAF], 357
Audry, Maj., 404
AUPELLE, CAMILLE, 326
Auphan, VA Gabriel-Paul [FN], 335 (2), 342 (2)
AURIOL, JULES-VINCENT, 279
AVEL:INE, CLAUDE, 350
Aymé, MG Georges-Albert, 405, 431, 466
Aymé, BG Marie-Fernand, 315
Aymes, LG Henri-Marie-Joseph, 380, 405
Azaïs, Col. Marie-Paul-François, 415
Azan, LG Paul-Jean-Louis, 296
Azman, Col., 454

BABIN, RENÉ, 321
Bachetta, LCol., 478
Badel, LCol., 381, 405
Bailly, BG Louis-Ernest-Henri-Robert, 363
Baleyrat-Rodannet, Col., 478
Balourdet, MG Eugène-Jules-Octave, 380
BAMBRIDGE, GEORGES, 325
BARAN, ROBERT, 519
Barande, LCol., 409
Barbe, MG Blaise-Henry-Donatien, 285
Barbe, MG Paul-Louis-Arthur, 447
Barbeyrac de Saint-Maurice, MG Marie-François-Armand-Roger, 304, 417, 436
Barbeyrac de Saint-Maurice, BG Maurice-Paul-

Raoul, 317
Barbier, Col. Auguste-Émile, 379, 406
BARÉTY, LÉON, 281
Baril, Col. Louis, 361
Barnard, Capt. P. T. J. [FN], 540
Barois, Capt. G. T. E. [FN], 534
Barrau, MG Jean-Joseph-Guillaume, 285, 321 (2), 338 (2), 391 (2), 431
Barré, LG Georges-Edmond-Lucien, 309, 317, 341, 383, 389, 393, 429
BARTHÉLÉMY, JOSEPH, 336
Barthélémy, BG Robert-Jules-Eugène, 400, 456
Barthes, Capt. E. G.M. [FN], 540
BARTHÈS, RENÉ-VICTOR-MARIE, 325
BASTID, PAUL, 281
Bastidon, BG, 385
Battet, Capt. R. M. J. [FN], 537
Baudet, BG Joseph-Antoine-Jacques-Louis, 303, 420
Baudolin, MG Jules-Georges-Jacques, 458
Baudouin, BG Jean-Roch-Charles-Numa, 406
BAUDOUIN, PAUL, 279, 288, 334, 336
Baufine-Ducrocq, Maj., 364
BAULARD, RENÉ, 521
Baurés, Col. Jean-Baptiste-Henri, 340, 367
Baussac, LCol., 295, 340
BAYARDELLE, ANGE-MARIE-CHARLES-ANDRÉ, 324
Bazoche, MG, 306
Bazelaire de Ruppierre, MG Marie-Joseph-Maurice de, 431
Bazin, LCdr. L. V. H. M. P. [FN], 543
Beau, Col., 293
Beauchesne, Col. de, 448
Beaufrère, MG Maurice-Frédéric-Gaëtan, 420
Beaumont, BG Georges-Henri-Auguste, 380
Beaussant, LCdr. A. F. [FN], 543
BECH, V., 324
Béjard, MG Louis-Ernest, 452, 456, 473
Belfils, LCol., 417
BELIN, RENÉ, 336 (2)
Bellegarde, LCol. de, 401
Belot, Capt. F. H. R. de [FN], 537
Benard, Col. 477
Bénouville, BG Pierre de, 354
Benson, Col., 384
Bérard, MG Louis-Gustavé, 311, 341, 363, 494 (2)
Berchoux, Col. de, 506
Bérenger, Capt. M. D. R. [FN], 538
Bergeret, Gen. Jean-Marie-Joseph [FAF], 335, 348 (2)
Bergeron, BG. Jean-Paul, 316, 390, 393, 411, 466
BERJOAN, ANDRÉ-JOSEPH, 327 (2)
Berlon, LCol., 401
Bernard, BG Gustavé-Amédée, 478
Bernard, MG Joseph-Frédéric-Ange-Désiré, 300
Bernaud, Capt. [FN], 537
Berniquet, MG André, 445, 446 (2)

Berquet, BG Laurent-Maurice, 382
BERTAUT, MAURICE-PIERRE-EUGÈNE, 325
BERTHLOT, JEAN, 336
Berthomé, BG Edouard-Georges, 461, 466
Bertière, MG Edouard, 294
Bertin-Boussu, MG Paul-Jean-Léon, 399 (2)
Bertrand, Col. René-Gabriel-Henri, 364
Bertrand, LCdr. R. [FN], 544
BERTRAND, WILLIAM, 280, 288, 300
Bertschi, BG Charles-Joseph-Georges, 473 (3)
Besançon, MG Fernand-Philippe-Alphonse, 504, 506
Besineau, Capt. G. E. [FN], 536
Besse, BG Jean-Joseph-René, 421, 457
Bessey de Contenson, BG Stanislas-Louis-Amédé de, 483
Bessière, MG Jean-Pierre-Hector-Marie, 437, 454, 465, 466
Besson, Gen. Antoine-Marie-Benoit, 286 (2), 303, 339, 340, 363, 367
Béthouart, MG Marie-Emil-Antoine, 353, 356, 425 (2), 464 (2), 503
Beucler, BG Georges-Jacques-Frédéric, 357, 455 (2)
Beyne, BG Pierre-Jules-Émile, 299
Beynet, Gen. Étienne-Paul-Émile-Marie, 316, 317, 320, 341, 353, 356, 382, 435, 462
BEYRIES, JEAN-LOUIS, 321
Béziers-Lafosse, BG Pierre-Louis-Arthur-Marie, 310, 409 (3)
BICHELOONE, JEAN, 336 (2)
BIDAULT, GEORGES, 352, 354
Billotte, Gen. Gaston-Henri-Gustavé, 286, 291, 303, 363, 365
Billotte, MG Pierre-Armand-Gaston, 353, 355, 356, 507, 509
BILLOUX, FRANÇOIS, 354
Bineau, MG Henri-Marie-Auguste, 293
Bizemont, BG Henri-Charles-Marie de, 4101 474
BLACHER, LOUIS-PLACIDE, 322
Blaizot, MG Roger-Charles-André-Henri, 391, 478
Blanc, LCol., 390, 412
Blanc, LG Amédée-Ferdinand-Auguste, 389 (2), 464
Blanc, BG Jean-Clément, 285, 355
Blanchard, BG André-Jean-Marie, 285
Blanchard, Gen. Georges-Maurice-Jean, 286, 295, 296, 307, 339, 363, 365
Blanchard, BG Maurice-Marie, 454
Blanchon, Col., 401
Blayo, Cdr. C. [FN], 539
BLÉHAUT, HENRI, 335
Blin, BG Louis-Émile-Charles-Henri, 416
Bloch-Dassault, LG Darius-Paul, 284, 306, 340 (2), 365, 380
Blois, LCol. de, 448
BLUM, LÉON-ANDRÉ, 279 (4)
Boell, BG Paul-Wilhelm, 411, 415, 476 (2)
Boichut, Gen. Edmund-Just-Victor, 290
Boisboissel, LG Yves-Marie-Jacques-Guillaume de,

317 (2), 321, 327, 391, 454, 467
Boissau, MG Robert-Marie-Jules-Camille, 414, 454, 463, 496
Boissel, MG Joseph-Jean-Louis, 280
BOISSON, PIERRE-FRANÇOIS, 321 (2), 322, 324, 349
BONCOUR, AUGUSTIN-ALFRED-JOSEPH-PAUL, 279, 288
Bondis, Col. Paul-Louis, 507
Bonjour, LCol., 506
Bonlaron, LCol., 459
BONNAFOUS, MAX, 336
Bonnaissieux, BG Marie-Marcel, 404, 410
BONNARD, ABEL, 336
Bonne, LCol., 417
Bonnefay, Capt. [Army], 404
Bonnet, MG Étienne, 291, 293, 296, 410
BONNET, GEORGES-ÉTIENNE, 279 (2), 281, 288
BONNET, HENRI, 346
Bonnet de la Tour, MG René-Edouard-Joseph, 494 (2)
Bonvalot, Maj., 448
BONVIN, LOUIS-ALEXIS-ÉTIENNE, 323, 326
Borgnis-Desbordes, LCol. Henri-Gustavé-André, 383, 432
Boris, LG Pierre-Louis-André, 294, 306, 379
Botreau-Roussel, MG Jules-Marie-Antoine-Joseph, 369
Bouche, Int-Mil 3rd Class, 296
Boucher, BG Georges-Edgar, 379, 400, 458
Boucher, BG Jean-Noël-Louis, 419, 443
Boudet, BG Félix-Marie-Étienne, 382
Boudot, Capt. [Army], 474
Boudier, Maj., 295
Bouffet, LG Jean-Gabriel, 379, 406
Bougrain, MG Gabriel-Marie-Joseph, 448, 480
Bouisson, Méd-Col., 296
Bouley, MG Jean-Claude-Louis-Victor, 503
Bourcart, LCol., 392
Bourdeau, BG, 478
Bourély, MG Joseph-Edouard-Henri-Marie-André, 390
Bourget, BG Paul-Alexandre-Pierre, 362
Bourgoing, Cdr. D. F. M. V. de [FN], 541
Bourguignon, BG Louis-Ferdinand, 366, 480
BOURNAT, GILBERT de, 325
Bourrague, RA C. J. L. [FN], 486
Bourret, Gen. Victor, 287, 303, 366
Bouscat, Gen. René [FAF], 358, 372, 373
Bouteil, Col., 478
BOUTHILIER, YVES, 279, 281, 334
Boutignon, BG Henri-Aimé, 385, 386 (2), 419, 459, 460
Bouxin, RA J. F. E. [FN], 394, 533
Boyer-Besses, LCdr. R. H. J. L. [FN], 544
Braconnier, LG Joseph-Eugène-Charles, 279
Braconnier, BG Pierre-Marie, 319 (2), 389, 390

Brantes, Capt. de [Army], 448
Brasart, LCol., 416
BRASEY, LOUIS-ANTOINE-MARIE, 327
Bravais, BG Pierre-Auguste, 310
Brécard, Gen. Charles-Théodore, 334
Brecey, Maj. de, 445
Brenet, BG Marie-Joseph-Charles-François, 384
BRESSOLES, LOUIS-HENRI-FRANÇOIS-DENIS, 322, 325
Bret, BG, 316
Bret, MG, 308
Bretteville, Cdr. R. M. de [FN], 489
Breuillac, MG Jean, 353, 389, 463, 464
BRÉVIÉ, JOSEPH-JULES, 326, 335
Bridot, Col. 505
Bridoux, LG Eugène-Marie-Louis, 335, 413
BRINON, FERNAND de, 354
Brisac, BG Pierre-Salomon-Isaac, 351
Brissaud-Desmaillet, Col., 506
Britsch, MG Paul-Émile, 416, 477
Brocard, MG Georges-Louis-Marie, 450
Brosset, BG Diégo-Charles-Joseph, 355, 356, 369, 477, 505
Brossin de Saint-Didier, MG Auguste-Marie, 357, 510 (2)
BROSSOLETTE, PIERRE, 350 (2)
Brown de Colstoun, MG Émile-Louis-Gabriel, 484
Bruché, BG Albert-Charles-Émile, 296, 450
Bruneau, BG Marie-Germain-Christian, 366, 450, 480
BRUNOT, RICHARD-EDMOND-MAURICE-ÉDOUARD, 324, 325
Brussaux, MG Edouard-Octave-Jules, 307, 387, 454
Bucheton, MG Louis-Eugène-Fernand, 292
Buot de l'Epine, Col., 506
Bührer, Gen. Jules-Antoine, 287, 291 (2), 292 (2), 298, 341
Buisson, MG Louis-Léon-Marie-André, 284, 392, 443, 450 (2)
BUSSIÈRE, AMÉDÉE-FÉLIX, 331
Burnol, BG Adrian-Jule-Gustavé, 484
Burtaire, MG Maurice-Alphonse-Alfred, 443, 456

Cabotte, MG Pierre-Paul-Jacques, 307
Cadoret, Cdr. P. J. M. [FN], 488
Cahuzac, Int-Gen 1st Class, 364
Caillault, LG Henri-Léon, 288, 292, 320, 369, 465
Caille, BG André-Lucien, 409
Caldairou, BG Camille-Hippolyte, 438
Caldairou, BG Jean-Charles-Louis, 509
Callico, Maj., 408
Callies, MG Jean-Jules-Alexis, 437
Callin, Maj., 390
CALVEL, AUGUSTE, 322
Calvel, BG Henri-Alexandre, 296, 381
Campet, BG Jacques-Marie-Joseph-François, 334, 368
CAMPINCHI, CÉSAR, 280 (2), 281, 288 (2), 300 (2)

CAPAGORRY, JEAN-CHARLES-ANDRÉ, 323, 324
CAPITANT, RENÉ, 354
Carbillet, Col., 454
Carcasses, LCol., 436
CARCOPINO, JÉRÔME, 336
Cardin, Maj., 392
Carence, LG Jean-Jacques, 294
Carles, LCol., 391
Carlès, LG Émile-Jean-Gabriel, 297, 298, 323, 341, 385, 391, 432
CARLES, FERNAND, 331 (2)
Carpentier, RA M. F. L. F. de [FN], 486
Carpentier, MG Marcel-Maurice, 364, 388, 502, 505
CARRAS, HUBERT-EUGÈNE-PAUL, 324
Carre, LCdr. F. M. [FN], 543
Cartier, MG Georges-Eugène-Alphonse, 367, 422, 423, 455, 461
Carton, LCol., 433
CASAMATTE, FRANÇOIS, 323
Casseville, MG Henri-Frédéric-Paul, 335, 352, 455
CASSIN, RENÉ, 346 (2), 347
CASSOU, JEAN, 350
Castaing, Capt. [Army], 437
Castelnau, BG Jean-François-Marie-Joseph-Béranger de Curières de, 315 (2), 383
Castet la Boulbène, Col. de [FAF], 468, 485
Castex, VA Raoul-Victor-Patrice [FN], 290, 375
Cathal, Col. [FAF], 469
CATHALA, PIERRE, 334, 336
Catroux, Gen. Georges-Albert-Julien, 318 (2), 320 (2), 326, 345, 346 (2), 347, 354, 356, 369, 383
Caullet, Maj., 433
Caumia-Baillenx, LCol. de, 412
Causeret, BG Pierre-Jean-Joseph, 316, 366
Cavailher, BG Gustave-Bruno-Henri, 305
CAYLA, LÉON-HENRI-CHARLES, 321, 324 (2)
Cazeilles, Col., 431
Cazaban, MG Jean, 436, 484
Cazanove, BG Franck-Jules-Léon, 324
Cazaud, MG Alfred-Maurice, 388, 455, 500 (2), 501, 508
Cazin, MG Henri-Joseph, 466
CAZIOT, PIERRE, 336
CÉDILE, JEAN-MARIE-ARSÈNE, 326
Cerisier, LCol., 506
Chaban-Dalmas, BG Jacques-Pierre-Michel, 355, 356
Chabanier, LCol., 420
Chadebec de Lavelade, MG Georges-Jean-Émile-René, 320, 369
Chaillet, MG Claude-Philippe-Armand, 365, 503
Chailly, LCol., 410
Challe, MG André-Hubert-Léon, 474
Chaligne, Col., 474
Châlon, LCol., 295

CHALVET, JEAN-VICTOR-LOUIS-JOSEPH, 321, 324
Chambon, Col., 295
Chamboredon, Maj., 456
Champon, LG Pierre-Louis-Célestin-Michel, 297, 380, 382, 400
Chanoine, BG Marie-Jacques-Henri, 447 (2)
Chapouilly, MG Edouard-Charles-François, 428, 438
CHAPPEDELAINE, LOUIS de, 280 (2), 288, 300
CHAPSAL, FERNAND, 381 (2)
Chapuis, Col., 506
Charbonneau, MG Jean-Eugène-Marie, 310, 388, 463, 478
Chardenot, Capt. [FN], 540
Chardon du Ranquet, LCol., 403
Charnier, LCol., 478
Charry, MG Marie-Martin-Jean-Alfred de, 283, 411, 423
Chassard, Col. Paul-Antoine, 415
Chastanet, BG Alfred, 459 (2)
CHASTENET de GÉRY, FRÉDÉRIC-MARIE-JEAN-BAPTISTE, 325
CHATAIGNEAU, YVES, 318, 320
Châtel, LG Yves-Charles, 318, 326, 349
Chaudessolle, BG Paul-Arthur-Marie, 451 (2)
Chaulard, BG Lucien-Jean-Baptiste-Isidore, 432 (2)
Chautant, Maj., 296
CHAUTEMPS, CAMILLE, 279 (2)
Chauvin, MG Ange-Marie-Léon, 316
CHAZELAS, JEAN-BAPTISTE-VICTOR, 322
Chedeville, LG Charles-Joseph, 311
Cherdel, LCdr. R. J. [FN], 543
Cherrière, Col., 362 (2), 506
CHEVALIER, JACQUES, 336 (2)
Chevallier, BG François-Antoine-Charles, 389, 435
Chevillon, BG André-Claude, 503, 506
Chevrier, LCol., 361
Chevrier, Capt. Eugène-Marcel [FN], 357
CHIAPPE, JEAN, 320
CHICHERY, ALBERT, 281 (2)
Chilly, Col. de, 418
Chomel, Capt. J. M. [FN], 540
Chomel, Col. Raymond-Emmanuel-Marie-Siméon, 451
Chomel de Jarnieu, Maj., 460
Chomereau, Comte de Saint-André, BG Gaston-Marie-Joseph de, 303, 309 (2)
Chopin, LCol. [FAF], 468
CHOT-PLASSOT, ROBERT-PAUL, 325
Chouteau, MG René-Jean-Charles, 500
Chrétien, Col., 364 (433 (2)
Claerebout, BG Edouard, 434
Claudel, Maj., 457
Clay, Maj., 448
Clére, MG, 313
Clouet des Pesruches, BG Denis-Marie-Joseph-Félix, 447, 463, 484
Codechevre, Col., 366

Cohendet, Maj., 405
Colin, Maj., 457
Collet, MG Philibert, 316, 454, 465
Collignon, LCol. Maurice-Jules-Marie, 422
Collinett, Capt. D. A. J. [FN], 533
Colson, Gen. Louis-Antoine, 280, 283, 285, 286, 334
Compain, MG Pierre-Philippe-Marie-Adrien, 465
Condé, Gen. Charles-Marie, 286, 294, 363, 366
Conne, BG Pierre-Félix, 382, 455, 463
Constantin, Capt. J. [FN], 538
COPPET, JULES-MARCEL de, 324
Coradin, MG Louis-Gustavé-Adolphe, 308, 416, 474
Corap, Gen. André-Georges, 304, 367, 368, 371
Corbé, MG René-Jean-Divy, 408, 492
Corbel, BG [Mèd.-Gen.] Paul-Louis-Malie-Félix, 362
Cor de Duprat de Damrémont, BG Jean-Barnard-Marie-Bertrand du, 484
Corbiere, Capt. J. L. de [FN], 538
Cordier, LCol., 364
Cornet, BG Edgard-Marie-Julien, 385
Costard de Saint-Léger, Maj., 459
Coste, BG Jean-Auguste-Velentin, 312
COT, PIERRE, 280, 281, 288
Coudanne, MG, 306
Coudrain, Col., 362
Coudray, BG Ferdinand-Émile-Casimir, 285
Coudret, BG Pierre-Henri-Marie, 380
Coulon, BG Albert, 282
COURNARIE, PIERRE-CHARLES-ALBERT, 321, 324
Courson, LCdr. L. E. Y. M. [FN], **544**
Courson, LCdr. R. E. [FN], 543
Cousse, MG Edouard-Sylvain, 452, 457, 474
Couvy, MG Louis-Eugène-Benoit-Léon, 391
Croiset, Capt. A. M. J. [FN], 534
COURT, JOSEPH-URBAIN, 324
Coustey, Col. Pierre [FAF], 357
COUVE de MURVILLE, MAURICE, 345
Cristau, MG Xavier-Marie, 309, 368
CROCICCHIA, HORACE-VALENTIN, 322 (2)
Cruciani, BG Alphonse-Louis, 430
Cueff, LCol., 405
Cugnac, BG Henri-Joseph-Charles-Marie de, 419
Cumin, BG Jean-Jacques-Alexandre, 312
Cuq, BG Félix-François-Maurice, 305
Curnier, Col. Jean-Adolphe-Léonce, 415
CURTON, ÉMILE de, 325
Cussenot, BG Léon-Charles-Victor, 385
Cyvogt, MG Henri-Louis-Léon-Gaspard, 312, 461, 493

Dagnan, BG Marcel, 458 (4)
Daille, LG Marius, 307, 387, 388
Daine, BG Albert-Joseph, 380
DALADIER, ÉDOUARD, 279 (6), 283, 286, 288 (3), 290
Dame, BG Pierre, 366, 427
d'Anselme, MG André-Marie-Martial, 293, 339, 351, 355, 413
d'Arbonneau, MG Charles-Henri-Paul, 297, 408
Darde, BG René-Albert, 441
Dario, MG Pierre-Emannuel-André, 364, 504
Darlan, Adm. of the Fl. Jean-Louis-Xavier-François [FN], 280 (2), 289 (3), 300 (2), 301, 333 (2), 334, 335 (2), 336, 338, 341, 342, 348 (3)
d'Arras, MG Jacques-Marie-Toussaint, 445, 446 (2)
DARROUY, HENRI-JOSEPH, 331
Dassonville, BG Achille-Fernand-Hector, 355, 500
d'ASTIER de la VIGERIE, EMMANUEL, 346, 350
d'Astier de la Vigerie, Gen. François [FAF], 344, 372, 389, 500
d'ASTIER de la VIGERIE, HENRI, 343, 348, 350
Daudin, MG Ernest-André, 303
DAUGY, JEAN-MAECEL, 331
Daumont, Capt. [Army], 449
DAUTRY, RAOUL, 281
Daval, Maj., 461
d'Decoux, VA Jean [FN], 326, 377, 470
d'EAT, MARCEL, 280, 288
Debailleul, MG, 310
Debeney, MG Marie-Cyrille-Victor, 312, 334, 335, 339, 399, 411, 442, 492, 493
Debeney, Gen. Marie-Eugène, 290
Decageux, Maj., 417
Decamp, LG Jules-Philippe-Octave, 283, 313, 339, 492, 494 (2)
Decharme, MG Pierre-Nicolas-Louis, 303, 356, 412
Dechaux, BG Louis-Léon, 382, 400
DECHARTRE, MAURICE-XAVIER-JOSEPH, 325
Defforges, Capt. d'Res. [FN], 540
DEGAIN, CHARLES-JEAN, 321
DEGRAND, GEORGES, 519
DEJEAN, MAURICE, 344, 345
Dejussieu-Pontcarrel, BG Pierre-Marie-Philippe, 351 (2), 502
Delaissey, BG François-Claude-Philippe, 412, 477
Delange, Col., 505
Delay, MG Achille-Paul-Théophile, 455
Deleuze. Col., 506
DELBOS, YVON, 279, 281 (2), 288
Delègue, MG Louis-Clitus-Honoré, 390
Delestraint, LG, Charles-Georges-Antoine, 294, 351, 367, 392, 445, 451, 480
Delhomme, BG Étienne-Charles-Ferdinand, 455
Deligne, MG Agathon-Jules-Joseph, 314, 442, 463
Delmau, Capt. [Army], 474
Delmotte, MG Joseph-Dominique-Victor-Robert, 335
DELPECH, LÉONCE-JOSEPH, 322
DELSALLE, EDOUARD-ANDRÉ, 326
Delsuc, MG Hermann-Françis-Denis, 382, 433 (2), 478
Demain, MG Louis-Pierre-Henri, 297
Demange, Maj., 448

DENIS, 325
DENIS, PIERRE, 344
Denis, LCol., 478
DENNERY, ÉTIENNE, 344
Dentz, Gen. Henri-Fernand, 292, 293, 303, 313, 320 (2), 340, 369, 382 (2), 494
Deramond, RA [FN], 358
DÉRAVIN, RUBEN, 325
Derendinger, MG Jean-Robert, 466, 477
Derobert, LCol. [FAF], 468
Derrien, VA E. H. H. N. [FN], 397, 472, 487
Deruer, Maj., 414 (2)
DESANTI, JEAN, 322
DESCHAMPS, HUBERT-JULES, 321, 322, 324
Desgruelles, BG, 478
Deslaurens, BG Marcel-Émile, 368, 418, 478
Desmazes, MG Marie-Alphonse-Théodore-René-Adrian, 307, 381, 405, 492
Despas, BG 438
Desprez, BG Octave-Georges-Alexandre, 313
Desre, LG Raymond-Charles-Émile, 389, 464
Devaux, Col. Alain-Robert-Étienne, 451
Devinck, BG Paul-Arsène-Gérard, 310, 364, 389, 465, 510
Dewavrin, Cdr. André, 355
d'Hespel, Cdr. C. M. L. [FN], 541
d'Humières, BG Alain-Bertrand-Marie-Gaston, 483
d'Humières, MG Gaspard-Henri-Marie-Gaston, 311, 419
Diclos, BG 439
Didelet, MG Henri-Antoine, 296, 303, 400
Didier, LCol., 458 (2)
Didio, BG Pierre-Désiré-Robert, 313, 423, 453, 474
DIETHELM, ANDRÉ, 345 (4), 346 (3), 354
Digne, LCol., 477
Dillard, Capt. R. J. M. [FN], 536
Dodelier, LCol., 506
Dody, LG André-Marie-François, 317 (2), 401, 404, 465, 505
Doizelet, MG Émile-Auguste-Marie, 364
Donin de Rosières, Maj., 429
Donnat, LCol., 401
Donnio, BG Charles-René, 427
Donval, RA Y. V. M. [FN], 488
Dordilly, LCol. [FAF], 372
DORMOY, MARX, 290 (2)
Dosse, Gen. Edmond-Lois, 286, 292
Doumenc, Gen. Joseph-Edouard-Aimé, 287, 292, 293, 297, 304, 338, 339, 340 (2)
Doyen, LG Paul-André, 312 (2), 340, 383, 411, 422
Dromard, BG Robert-Henri-Eugène, 293, 502, 503
Drôme, BG Paul-Eugène-Maurice, 303, 385
Dubois, LCol., 412 (2)
Dubois, Capt. H. J. E. [FN], 538 (2)
Dubuisson, LG René-Paul, 291, 307, 321, 391, 393, 430

Ducasse, LG Eugène-Georges, 311
Duch, BG, 444
Duche, Col., 383
Duchemin, MG François-Jacques-André, 382, 425
Duclos, MG Victor-Paul-Auguste, 436, 459, 462, 466, 477
Duffet, MG Camilie-Léon, 407, 428
Dufieux, Gen. Julien-Claude-Marie-Sosthène, 295
Dufour, Maj., 416 (2)
Dufour, LG Jean-Baptiste-François-Paul, 294, 305, 386, 393
Duhautois, BG Louis-Joseph, 381
Duhesme, BG, 308
Dulac, Capt. [Army], 388
DUMAS, CHARLES-ANDRÉ, 321
Dumas, BG Paul-Henri, 339, 366 (2), 490, 495, 503
Du Mazel, Col., 361
Dumèmes, Col. [FAF], 372
Duminy, BG Georges-Ernest-Émile, 434
Dumoncel, Maj., 427
Dumont-Fillon, MG Paul-Ernest, 294, 389
Dumontier, MG Maurice-Henri, 356, 367
Dunoyer de Ségonzac, BG Eugène-Charles, 400 (3), 443
Duperon, Maj., 415
Duplat, VA E. A. H. [FN], 341, 394, 471, 486
DUPONT, EDMOND-GUSTAVE, 324
Dupre, Capt. L. M. L. [FN], 538
Durand, BG Maurice-Georges-Constant, 425 (2), 457
Durand, MG Pierre-Servais, 381, 420
Durieux, LCol., 408
Duron, MG Amédée, 313, 411, 423
Duthu, Lt. J. M. A. [FN], 539
du Tour, Capt. E. H. M. A. A. [FN], 536
Duval, MG Raymond-Francis, 319, 340 (2), 366, 464, 504, 506

Eberle, Maj., 457
Eble, Maj., 413
ÉBOUÉ, ADOLPHE-FÉLIX-SYLVESTRE, 323 (2), 347
Échard, MG Eugène-Raphaël, 401, 415, 473
ELBEL, PAUL, 280
El Ghozi, BG Jacob-Raoul, 314, 387, 388, 390
Ely, BG Paul-Henri-Romuald, 357
Emblanc, Capt. [Army], 391
Estéva, VA Jean-Pierre [FN], 319, 376
Estremé, Col., 383
Etcheberrigaray, LG Jean-Marie-Lèon, 287, 310, 311, 363 (2), 380, 416, 492 (3)
Étienne, LG, 306
EUTROPE, EUGÈNE-HENRI-ROGER, 327
ÉVEN, AUGUSTE-LÉON-VALENTIN, 323
EYNAC, LAUENT, 280, 288

FABIEN, PIERRE, 351
Fabre, Capt. [Army], 405

Fabre, Cdr. L. M. J. H. [FN], 489
Fagalde, LG Marie-Bertrand-Alfred, 314, 367, 383
Fagot, BG Firmin-Philippe-Edouard, 379
Faivre, Maj., 451
Falvy, LG Maurice-Émile, 285, 322, 431
Faucher, LG Louis-Eugène, 297
Faury, MG Louis-Augustin-Jos, 297
Favier, Maj., 450
Favreul, Lt. J. E. M. [FN], 544
Fayet, BG Antoine-Jean, 303
Fédary, MG Paul, 485
FELDMAN, VALENTIN, 350
Féquant, Gen. Philippe [FAF], 289, 299
Fernet, RA [FN], 334
Févre, BG, 308
FÉVRIER, ANDRÉ, 281 (2)
Fichet, MG Émile-Ange-Marie, 295
Fitte, Cdr. R. E. G. [FN], 489
FLANDIN, PIERRE-ÉTIENNE, 279, 288, 333 (2), 334
Flavigny, LG Jean-Adolphe-Louis-Robert, 310, 384
FLEMING, LOUIS-CONSTANT, 325
Fleuriau, Col. de, 474
Foglierini, LCol., 399
Foiret, BG Edmond-Gustavé-Armand, 455
Foisy, BG, 307
Fonsagrive, BG Joseph-Vincent-Félix, 381
Fontaine, Maj., 473
Fontan, BG Justin-François-Bertrand-Marcel-Angéli-Gustavé, 284
Fontanges, MG Géraud-Maurice-Marie-Joseph de, 380
FORTUNE, GABRIEL-ÉMILE, 323
Fougère, LG François-Marie-Jacques, 320 (2), 384, 465
Fougue, Cdr. R. G. A. [FN], 541
FOURNEAU, JACQUES-GEORGES, 322
Fournier, LG Henri, 317 (2), 367
Frainot, LG, 384
Franchet d'Esperey, Mar. Louis-Félix-Marie-François, 290
François, Col. [FAF], 468 (2)
François, MG Henri-Nicholas, 420, 427, 442
François, BG Marcel-Georges, 316, 320, 427, 429, 442, 463, 464 (2), 477, 492, 493
François, LG Marie-Jules-Victor-Léon, 319, 389, 432, 463
Francon, Maj., 457
FRÉMICOURT, CHARLES, 281
Fremiot, Maj., 443
Frénal, BG Paul-Gilbert-Eugène, 310, 381, 409
FRENAY, HENRY, 350
Frère, Gen. Aubert-Achille-Jules, 305, 309, 310, 312, 313, 317, 338, 341, 351, 367, 381, 490, 493
Freydenberg, LG Henri, 365, 385
Friess, Maj., 447, 449

Froissard Broissia, Col. de, 385
Froment, BG Georges-Joseph, 294
Frossard, MG Charles, 294
FROSSARD, LUDOVIC-OSCAR, 281 (4)

GABOLDE, MAURICE, 336
Gaglio, BG Paul-Alphonse-Léon, 314
Gailliard, MG Émile-Henri, 481, 463, 484
Gain, BG Jospeh-Armand-Victor, 305, 310, 409
Gainsette, Maj., 295
Galmiche, MG Marie-Olivier, 308
Gamelin, Gen. Maurice-Gustavé, 285, 286, 288, 291, 292, 293, 361
Garbay, BG Pierre-François-Marie-Joseph, 501 (4), 505 (2)
Garchèry, Gen. Jeanny-Jules-Marcel, 287, 294, 368
Gard, Col., 460, 474
Garnier, BG Paul-Henri-Maurice, 455
GARROUSTE, PIERRE-MARIE-JACQUES-FRANÇOIS, 326
GASHIER-DUPARC, ALPHONSE, 280
Gastey, BG Paul-Constant-Amédée, 379, 446, 481
Gauché, BG Maurice-Henri, 293 (2)
Gaucher, MG Fernand-Georges, 390
Gaulle, BG Charles-André-Joseph-Marie de, 280, 344 (2), 353 (3), 354 (2), 355 (2), 356, 367, 451, 500, 519 (2)
GAUTHIER, GEORGES-ARMAND-LÉON, 327
Gauthier, BG Maurice-Marie-Joseph, 379
Gautier, Col., 508
Gay-Bonnet, MG Charles-Yriex-Jean-Bernard, 302
Gendre., BG, 438
Genet, Col., 478
GENLIN, FERNAND, 281 (3)
Gensoul, VA Marcel-Bruno [FN], 374 (2), 394, 470
Georges, Gen. Alphonse-Joseph, 286, 291, 292, 298, 353, 361
Georgin, Maj., 456
Gérardot, LCol. [FAF], 468
Gérault de Langalene, MG de, 311
Gérin, BG René-André, 423, 476
Germain, BG Gaëtan-Louis-Elie [Georges-Louis], 310, 324
Germain, Gen. Maxime-Jean-Vincent, 291, 315, 338, 339, 384, 430, 492, 494
Gérodias, LG Paul-Henry, 313, 335, 339, 422
Gervais de Lafond, RA R. E. [FN], 488, 540, 541
Gest, MG Théodre-Benoit-Honoré-Louis, 303
GIACOBBI, ANTOINE-FÉLIX, 322
GIACOBBI, PAUL, 354
Gibert, LG Pierre-Marius-Ernest, 420, 432, 463
Gillard, BG Victor-Jean-Edmond, 415, 473
Gillier, MG Louis-Ernest, 381, 433 (2), 459
Gilliot, BG Auguste-Jean, 366, 406
Gimpel, BG Gaston, 379, 380
Giraud, Gen. Henri-Honoré, 287, 307 (2), 348 (3), 349, 353 (2), 356, 367, 368
Girier, Col. [FAF], 468

Girodet, Ins-Gen., 296
Girol, MG Louis-Germain, 308 (2), 400, 460, 474 (2)
Girot de Langlade, MG Baron Paul-Anne-Joseph-Alexandre, 482, 497
Girval, BG Marie-Charles-Henri de, 408, 458
Glain, Maj., 432
Glotin, Capt. H. M. E. A. [FN], 540
Glück, MG Gabriel-Léopold, 305
Godfroy, VA René-Émile [FN], 395
Goetschy, MG Joseph-Charles-Eugène, 295, 340
Goislard de Monsabert, LG Joseph-Jean de, 435, 490, 495, 503, 506
Golse, LCdr. J. B. A. [FN], **543**
Gondy, BG, 305
Gonnet, Maj., 430
Gonzalès de Linarès, BG François-Jean-Antonin-Marie-Amédée, 502 (2), 506
Goubaux, BG Paul-Amédée-Marie, 436, 466
Goudot, LG Victor-Nicolas, 314, 316
Goudouneix, BG Marie-Jean-Georges, 477
Gouget de Landres, Maj., 453, 474
GOUIN, FÉLIX, 354
Gouraud, Gen. Henri-Joseph-Eugène, 290
Gournay, LCol. de, 429
Goursolas, BG Antoine-Marie-Gabriel, 316, 368
Gouton, RA [FN], 486
Gouvello, Maj. de, 407, 441
Gouyon, Maj., 404
Goybet, Maj., 388
GRAFFEUIL, MAURICE-FERNAND, 326
Granboulan, BG Pierre-Jean Raymond, 283
Grancey, BG Jacques-Pierre-Louis de, 351, 369, 403, 490, 493
GRANDJEAN, ÉMILE-LOUIS-FRANÇOIS, 326 (2)
Grandsard, LG Pierre-Paul-Jacques, 308, 311, 381, 414, 493
Granger, Maj., 475
Granier, Col., 382, 497, 509
Gras, LCol., 386, 403
Gras, LCdr. E. J. J. [FN], 543
GRASSET, EDMOND, 336
Gravellat, BG Marie-Camille-Henri, 390
Grélot, BG Louis, 438
Grenet, MG Maurice-Jules-Zacharie, 308 (2), 341, 368
GRENIER, FERNAND, 345
Greot, Col., 380
Griveaud, MG Charles, 295, 304
Grollemund, BG Marie-Paul-Vincent, 387, 407, 414
Gross, BG Jean-Charles-Marie-Joseph, 364 (2), 496, 502, 503
Guedeney, LCol., 380
Guérin, Col., 381
Guérithault, BG Roger-Charles-Marcel, 311
GUERNUT, HENRI, 281

Guichard, Capt. [Army], 388
Guilbaud, LCol., 388
Guillard, LCdr. [FN], 396
Guillaumat, Gen. Marie-Louis-Adolphe, 290
Guillaume, MG Augustin-Léon, 364, 506, 508
Guillebraud, LCol., 506
Guillemont, MG Jean, 308, 385, 387
Guillerm, Capt. P. L. [FN], 470, 534
GUILLON, ARMAND, 319
Guillot, BG Jean-Gaston, 366
GUINGOUIN, GEORGES, 351
Guirriec, MG Arthur, 502
Guitry, LG Jean-Marcel-Robert, 309
Guyot, Col. Léon-Alexis, 437

Haca, BG François-Louis-Marie-Victor, 416
HACKIN, JOSEPH, 345
HAELEWYN, JEAN-MAURICE-NORBERT, 326 (2)
Halbwachs, BG, 293
Hallier, LCol., 418, 443
Hamon, Capt. Y. J. E. [FN], 538
Hanaut, BG Henri-Stanislas-Auguste, 456, 473
Hanck, BG Michel-Alexandre-Maximilien, 385, 432
Hanly, BG Maurice-Eugène-Marcel-Joseph, 385, 387
Hanote, LG Charles-Gustavé, 314
Hanoteau, MG Pierre-Louis-Charles-Constance, 293, 492
Happich, MG Paul-George, 282
Hardoun de Grosville, BG, 304
Harneury, Capt. L. L. M. [FN], **536**
Hartung, MG, 312
Hassler, MG Joseph-Louis-François, 314, 365, 409 (2)
HAUMANT, JEAN-CAMILLE, 325
Hautcœur, Col., 382, 407
Heckenroth, MG Frédéric-François-Marie, 390
HELLEU, JEAN, 320
Hème de la Cotte, LCol., 385
HÉRAUD, MARCEL, 281
Herlant, BG, 309
Herbillon, MG Pierre-Joseph, 303 (3)
Héring, Gen. Pierre, 286, 291, 303, 317, 365, 369
Hermil, Maj., 295
Herscher, LG Henri-Jospeh-Léon, 310
Hesdin, MG René de, 357, 361, 365, 384, 502, 506 (2), 508, 509
Hillairet, MG André-Pierre, 284
Hirsch, Maj. Étienne, 344 (2)
HOEFFEL, ERNEST-THIMOTHÉE, 326
HOPPENOT, HENRI, 324
Hornus, BG Pierre-Philippe, 368
Houdemon, Gen. [FAF], 373
HUARD, SERGE, 336
Hubert, LG Louis-Eugène, 307, 317, 340, 384, 385
Huet, LCol., 295
Huet, BG René-Pierre-Victor-Auguste, 475
Hugonot, MG Georges-André, 309, 340, 390, 503
Hugot, BG Paul-Charles-Joseph, 316

Humbert, Col. Jacques-Émile-Louis-Léon, 314, 363
Humbert, BG Jean-Louis-Auguste, 341, 361, 494
Huntziger, Gen. Charles-Léon-Clément, 287 (2), 320, 335, 339, 341, 363, 365, 369
Hupel, MG François-Napoléon-Henri-Dieudonné, 404, 405, 462
Hurault, MG Louis-Aristide-Alexandre, 285, 356
Huré, Gen. Antoine-Jules-Joseph, 286, 294, 339
Husson, BG Edmond-Edouard, 388
Husson, Capt. P. S. R. [FN], 536
Husson, BG Paul-Louis, 322, 323, 391

Ihler, LG Marcel, 381, 423
IMFELD, HANS, 327
INGEN, JACQUES, 344
Ingold, MG François-Jospeh-Jean, 323, 324, 354
Issaly, MG, 305
ITHIER, GEORGE, 350

Jacomet, MG Marie-Joseph-Paul-Laurent, 280
Jacomet, Controller General of the Army Robert, 283
Jacques, MG Henri, 364
Jacquet, Maj., 458 (2)
Jacquinet, LCol., 296
JACQUINOT, M. LOUIS, 354
Jame, Col. Lucien-Eugène-Paul-Gabriel, 303
James, Col., 478
Jamet, LG Louis-Marie, 288, 311
Jannekeyn, MG Jean-François [FAF], 335, 343
Janssen, MG Louis-Guillaume-Gaston, 401
Jarry, RA M. L. H. [FN], 488
Jaugard, VA [FN], 357
Jeannel, LG Joseph-Charles-Robert, 310 (2), 382, 409, 493
Jeanpert, BG, 313
Jeanpierre, MG Hippolyte-Maurice-René, 294
Jeanrot, Int-Mil. 1st Class, 296
Jenoudet, BG Charles-Léon, 399
Jobin, LCol., 412
Joppé, Col., 505
JORE, LÉONCE-ALPHONSE-NOËL-HENRI, 325
Jourdan, LCol., 364
Jousse, BG Moïse-Germain-Louis, 318, 353, 355, 364
Jousseaume de la Bretesche, Maj., 450
Juillard, LCol., 475
Juin, Gen. Alphonse-Pierre, 286, 287, 319, 353, 355 (2), 363 (2), 389 (2), 401, 503
JULES-JULIEN, ALFRED, 281
Jullien, MG Léon, 283
Jurion, BG Maurice-Charles-Henri-Félicien, 389

Kahn, MG Louis-Lazare, 281, 300 (2)
Keime, BG Amédée-Paul-Georges-Joseph, 388, 447, 455
Keller, MG François-Pierre-Louis, 388, 413, 455 (2)
Keller, MG Louis-Marie-Joseph-Ferdinand, 294, 392, 480, 492
Kerdudo, RA E. J. R. M. [FN], 486
Kergoat, BG François-Jean, 293, 295, 384
Kermer, Maj. de, 478
Ketling, BG Prugar, 444
Klein, LCol., 417
Klopfenstein, BG Albert-Frédéric, 403, 413
Kocher, Maj., 420
Koëltz, LG Marie-Louis, 293, 294, 316, 335, 357 (2), 368, 383
Kœnig, Gen. Marie-Joseph-Pierre-François, 324, 353, 355, 357, 365, 500, 501, 502, 504, 505

Labarbe, LCol., 400
Labarre, LCol., 442
LABARTHE, ANDRÉ, 344
La Bigot, VA J. J. G. M., 375
LABONNE, EIRIK, 319
Laborde, Adm. Count Jean J. J. de [FN], 374, 375
Lacaille, BG Henri, 335, 363, 365, 494
LA CHAMBRE, GUY, 280, 288
Laclos, BG Henry-Joseph-Gaston Choderlos de, 296, 311
Lacoste, Maj., 461
Lacroisade, LCol., 423
Lacroix, RA E. M. [FN], 487
LADURIE, JACQUES LE ROY, 336
Lafaille, Maj., 425
Lafargue, Capt. M. M. A. [FN], 532
Laffargue, LG Charles-Victor-André, 313
Laffitte, LCol. David, 385
Laffon, BG Marie-François-Joseph, 282
Lafont, LG Michel-Laurent-Marie-Joseph, 316
Lafontaine, BG Henri-Jean, 403, 416
La Font Chabert, LG Pierre-Jules-André-Marie de, 339 (2), 448, 451, 480, 484, 492
La Forest Divonne, Capt. M. de [FN], 540
Lafranc de Pompignan, Maj., 452
LAGARDE, GEORGES, 325
Lagarde, LCol., 293
LAGARDELLE, HUBERT, 336
Lagarrigue, LCdr. J. F. M. P. [FN], **543**
Laherre, Maj., 459
Lahoulle, Col. Auguste-Joseph-Marie de [FAF], 468
LAIGRET, CHRISTIAN-ROBERT-ROGER, 321, 325
Lalande, Maj., 404
La Laurencie, LG Léon-Benoit de Fornel de, 305, 314, 341, 379, 445
Lallemand de Liocourt, LCol., 417, 442
Lallement, BG, 305
Lambilly, Col., 506
Lamasse, LCol., 419
Lambelin, Capt. [Army], 460
Lamon, LCol. [FAF], 373
Lamothe, Maj., 423
LAMOUREUX, LUCIEN, 279

Lamson, LG Marcel-Charles-Jospeh, 304, 379, 399
Landriau, VA [FN], 341, 395, 470
Langlois, LG Jean-Léon-Albert, 311, 339, 365, 392, 448, 490, 492
Languillaire, Maj., 461
Lannes-Dehore, BG Pierre-Anselme-Léon, 285
Lanoix, LG Octave-Charles, 303 (2), 365
Lanquetot, BG Pierre-Louis-Félix, 402, 409
LAPIE, PIERRE-OLIVIER, 323, 344
Lapierre, LCol., 466
Lapierre, LCdr. M. J. B. [FN], 543
Laplante, Capt. [Army], 474
La Porte du Theil, LG Paul-Henri-Joseph de, 337, 380, 413
Lappara, Col., 505
Lapy, LCol., 391
Larcher, BG Elophe-Jean, 305, 383, 416
Larminat, MG René-Marie-Edgar de, 323, 347, 353, 355, 356, 362, 369, 500, 501 (2), 503, 504, 505
Lascroux, LG Georges-Eugène-Joseph, 297, 309, 389, 407 (2), 410, 441, 464
LASMARTES, EMILIEN, 519
Lassaie, Méd-LCol., 296
Latarse, Col., 506
LATRILLE, ANDRÉ-JEAN-GASTON, 322, 323 (2)
Lattre de Tassigny, Gen. Jean-Joseph-Marie-Gabriel de, 312, 355, 366, 389, 406, 493, 502 (2)
LAUMOND, JEAN BAPTISTE, 519
Laure, Gen. Auguste-Marie-Émile, 309, 333, 368, 381, 462
Laurens, Gen. [FAF], 373
LAURENT, AUGUSTIN, 354
Laurent, BG Edmond-Camille-Jean-Baptiste, 296
Laureux, Maj., 400
Lauzanne, BG André-Joseph-Marie, 464 (2)
LAVAL, PIERRE, 279, 332 (4), 334 (4), 336 (2)
la Villeon, Col. de, 418
Lavilléon, LCol., 362
LEBAS, JEAN-BAPTISTE, 281 (2)
LE BEAU, GEORGES, 318
Le Bel, Maj. Albert, 465
Leblanc, Col., 508
Le Bleu, BG Paulin-André-Jean, 307, 310
Le Brigant, Col., 450
Lebrun, BG, 464
LEBRUN, ALBERT FRANÇOIS, 279, 519
Le Chuitton, Capt. R. [FN], **540**
Leclerc de Hauteclocque, LG Philippe-François-Marie-Jacques, Count of Hauteclocque, 323 (2), 324, 347, 500, 504, 509
Le Corguille, Maj., 418
LÉDÉE, CLÉMENT, 325 (2)
LÉDÉE JEAN, 325
Lefèvre, BG Antoine-Charles, 389
Lefort, Col. [FAF], 468 (2)

Lefort, LG Ferréol-François-Gabriel, 285, 297
Legendre, LG Joseph-Jules-Marie, 292, 321, 387
Legentilhomme, MG Paul-Louis-Victor-Marie, 305, 324, 345 (3), 356, 454 (2), 500 (3), 507
LEHIDEUX, FRANÇOIS, 336
Lejax, LCol., 445, 446 (2)
Lelaquet, Maj., 362
LELEU, SYLVETTE, 350
Le Loarer, BG Émile-Jules-Pierre, 304
Lelong, MG Albert, 297
Lelong, BG Pierre-Paul, 501
Le Luc, VA Maurice-Athanase [FN], 300, 342 (2)
LEMAIGRE-DUBREUIL, JACQUES, 343
Le Masle, Maj., 458
LÉMERY, HENRY, 335
Lemière, MG Gaston-Auguste-Paul, 382, 461
Lemoine, BG, 314
Lemonnier, VA André G. [FN], 357
Lemonnier, BG Émile-René, 477
Lenclud, LG Fernand-Zacharie-Joseph, 312, 313, 316, 381, 405, 408, 492, 493
Lenglet, LCol., 388
LENS, JEAN de, 327
Leparmentier, LCdr. M. J. L. [FN], 471
LEPERCQ, AIMÉ, 354
Lepetit, MG Louis-Gabriel, 320
Le Pivian, Capt. L. R. E. [FN], 534
Leportier, Cdr. M. A. H. [FN], 488
Le Quintrec, BG Auguste-Marie-Maurice, 306
Leridon, Capt. [Army], 388
Leroy, Maj., 452, 456
Leroy, Lt. J. C. [FN], 544
Lescales, MG de, 390, 393
Lescanne, LG Fernand-Joseph-Louis, 387, 427
Lestien, MG Georges-Eugène, 422, 460
Le TROQUET, ANDRÉ, 345 (2)
LEWITSKY, ANATOLE, 350
LÉVY, JEAN-PIERRE, 350
Lévy, MG Lucien-Meyer, 366
Lévy, MG René, 307
Leyer, LG Roger-Alexandre-Louis, 339, 449
Leyraud, Maj., 453
Lhéritier, BG Jacques-Jean-Louis, 410, 418, 443
Lhuillier, Col., 411
Libaud, LG Emmanuel-Urbain, 384, 386, 427
Liebert, Monsieur le Rabbin, 296
Liégeois, MG Marcel, 293
Limasset, MG Jean-Baptiste, 293, 400
Linder, Col., 381
Lipman, LCol., 295
Loiseau, BG Marie-Félix-Henri, 410
Loisel, Cdr. C. A. [FN], 541
Loizeau, LG Lucien, 307 (2), 380, 401
Longaud, Capt. L. H. C. [FN], 488, 541
Lorber, Col. Henri-Marie-Antoine-François, 411, 422
Lorme, BG Pierre-Marie-Charles de, 381, 384
Lorthioir, Lt. J. E. L. A. [FN], **543**
Lortholary, BG Henri-Ernest-Christophe, 304, 314

Louchet, MG Charles-Paul-Augustin, 504, 506 (2)
Loustaunau Lacau, Maj., 412
LOUVEAU, EDMOND, 322
Lucas, MG Maurice-Charles-Gabriel, 385, 411 (2), 413
Lucereau, LCol., 406
Lucien, MG Auguste-Eugène, 403
Luguet, Col. Charles [FAF], 357

Maertan, Capt. P. [FN], 377, 540
MAESTRACCI, PIERRE-LOUIS, 321
Magnan, MG Joseph-Abraham-Auguste-Pierre-Edouard, 321, 391, 466, 507
Magnien, BG René-Alphonse-Joseph, 314, 461 (2)
Magnillat, Maj., 388
Magny, Maj., 443
Magrin-Vernerey dit Monclar, MG Charles-Raoul, 320, 388, 501
Maignan, MG, 430 (2)
Mainié, BG Henri, 367
Maisonnet, MG Pierre-Joseph-Félix-Romuald, 334, 367
Maisons, BG Paul, 295
Malaguti, MG Michel, 480
MALGLAIVE, PIERRE de, 344
Malivoire-Filhol de Camas, MG Paul-René, 399, 441
MALRAUX, ANDRÉ, 354
Mancier, BG Robert-Eugène-Hippolyte-Alexandre, 285
MANDEL, GEORGES, 280 (2)
Manhès, Col. Jean-Louis-Marie-Pouis, 406
MANSARD, EDMOND, 325
Marc, BG Olivier-Marie-Alphonse, 484
MARCHANDEAU, PAUL, 279 (2), 281
Marie, Col., 411
Marion, Capt. [Army], 362
MARION, PAUL, 336
Marin de Montmarin, MG Marie-Robert-Guy, 310
MARJOLIN, ROBERT, 344
Marloy, Capt. A. J. A. [FN], 536
Marmillot, LCol., 427
MAROSELLI, ANDRÉ, 354
MARQUET, ADRIEN, 281, 335
Marquis, VA André A. A. [FN], 398, 471, 486
Marquis, MG Pierre-André-Antoine, 291, 406
Marteau, MG André, 447, 449, 460
MARTEL, DAMIEN de, Count de Martel, 320
Martin, MG Clément, 285
MARTIN, ÉMILE, 325
Martin, MG Henri-Jules-Jean, 381, 383, 437, 465 (2), 503, 506
Martin, LG Julien-François-René, 294 (2), 310, 334, 343, 381
Martin, LG Maurice-Paul-Auguste, 326, 390, 466
Martin, Cdr. P. M. H. [FN], 377
Martin Gallevier de Mierry, MG Jean, 417, 483

MARTINE, FÉLIX, 322
Marty, LCol., 474
Marzin, Capt. P. J. [FN], 535
Massiet, LG Charles-Gabriel-Renaud, 294, 307, 388
Massiet du Biest, Col., 508
Massimi, Col., 466
Massip, Col. Jean, 344
MASSIGLI, RENÉ, 345
Masson, Capt. [Army], 473
MASSON, GEORGES-PIERRE, 319
Masson Bachasson de Montalivet, MG Jean-Georges-Henri, 418
Mast, LG Charles Emmanuel, 319, 357, 381, 383, 409, 428, 462, 496
Mathenet, MG Maurice-Noël-Eugène, 379, 498 (2)
Mathieu, BG Adolphe-Charles, 315
Mathieu, Capt. J. [FN], 536
Matter, BG Philippe-Paul, 297, 357
Maubert, LCol., 505
MAUDUIT, HENRY-JEAN-MARIE de, 322
MAYER, DANIEL, 350
MAYER, RENÉ, 346, 354
Mazen, MG Charles-Marie-François-Joseph, 380
Meillier, LCol., 296
Mellier, BG Albert-Raymond, 437, 476
MENDÈS-FRANCE, PIERRE, 345
Mendras, MG Marie-Joseph-Edmond, 415, 458
Menguy, Maj., 344
Menjaud, MG Henri-Jules-Alexis-Marie, 385
Mennerat, MG Germain-Stanislas-Victor, 432, 477
MENTHON, FRANÇOIS de, 346, 354
Menu, BG Charles-Léon-Ferdinand, 386, 387
Mer, MG Jean, 369, 493
MERCADIER, ALBERT, 322
Mercier, Capt. [FN], 538
Méric de Bellefon, Col. Henri-Roger-Marie, 475
Mesmay, BG Jean-Joseph-Marie de, 312
Mesny, MG Gustavé-Marie-Maurice, 428
Mességué, BG Jean-Louis-Laurent, 478
MESSMER, PIERRE, 326
Métrot, MG Georges-Gabriel, 283
Meunier, MG René-Romain-Marie-Robert, 285
Meyer, Maj., 432
Michel, Maj., 401
Michel, MG Benjamin-François-Régis, 417
Michel, BG Delphin-Joseph-Théodore, 282
Michel, MG Louis-Michel-Marie-Joseph, 303, 475, 494
MICHELET, EDMOND, 354
MICHINET, EDMOND, 352
Michelier, VA François-Félix [FN], 300, 348, 397
Michelin, LG Pierre, 306
Michet de la Baume, Col., 309, 460
Mignon, BG, 303
Milliau, LCol., 295
Millier, BG, 476
Millour, Méd-Gen., 390
MIRAUD, ÉMILE, 336

Miserey, Col., 457
Misserey, LG Georges-Henri-Jean-Baptiste, 311, 382, 409
Missoffe, Capt. J. M. [FN], 537
Mittlehauser, Gen. Eugène-Désité-Antoine, 292, 297 (2), 362, 369
MOCH, JULES, 281, 354
Moillard, Maj., 414
Molinié, MG Jean-Baptiste-Emmanuel, 393, 401
Mollard, MG Amédée-Jean-Joseph-Jules-Stanislas, 314 (2)
Molle, MG Marie-Eugène-Aimé, 406, 505
Monclar, Col., 478
Monet, BG Henri, 454
Monginoux, BG Félicien-Alfred-Marie, 503
Monod, Monsieur le Pasteur, 296
MONNET, GEORGES, 281 (2)
Monniot, BG Lucien-Émile-Eugène, 380, 435
Montagne, LG Alfred-Marie-Joseph-Louis, 303, 309, 316, 382 (2), 401, 492
MONTAGNÉ, MICHEL-LUCIEN, 322
MONTCHAMP, MARIE-HENRI-FERDINAND-AUGUSTE, 325
Montegny, Maj. de, 391
MONZIE, ANATOLE de, 281
Moraglia, Col. [FAF], 468
Mordacq, MG Jean-Joseph-Lucien, 389, 438, 465
Mordant, LG Eugène, 326, 390, 406
Moreau, Int-Mil. 1st Class, 296
Moreau, RA J. H. C. E. [FN], 397, 470 (2), 471, 487
Moreau, BG Pierre-Émile-Henri, 390
Morel, BG Louis-Henri, 466
Morin, MG Charles-Eugène, 390
Morisson, MG Roger-Albert-Firmin, 367
Morlière, MG Louis-Constant, 496, 507
Mortemart de Boisse, BG René-Jacques, 418, 459
Mouchard, Gen. [FAF], 372
Mouflard, BG Henri-Zéphir-Clément, 296
Moulan, Maj., 414
Moulin, BG Georges-Saint-Ange, 481
MOULIN, JEAN, 351 (2)
Mourral, Cdr. R. A.H. J. [FN], 544
Moussac, LCol. de [FAF], 372
Mousset, Maj., 410
MOUTET, MARIUS, 280
Mouton, BG Georges-Léon-Gustavé, 383
Moyen, Col., 408
Moyrand, LG Auguste-Edouard-Maurice, 371
Mulot, Col., 383
Murat, BG, 314
Muselier, VA Émile-Henri [FN], 325, 345, 347, 357 (2), 358
Musse, MG Félix-Joseph, 297, 403
Mussel, LG Saint-Cyr-Étienne, 315

Nardin, Maj., 437
Navereau, BG André-Eugène, 319, 499, 504, 507
Negadelle, Capt. J. L. [FN], 533

NICOL, YVES-MAURICE, 325
NICOLAS, HENRI-PIERRE, 324
Nicolet, BG Pierre-Léon, 306
Nicolle, BG André-Pierre, 304
NICOLLE, LOUIS, 281
Niessel, LG Henri-Albert, 297
Niollet, BG Gauthier-Léon, 391, 424
Noël, Col., 478
Noël, LG Onésime-Paul, 307, 315, 383
Noël du Payrat, BG Henri-Marie-Jean, 504
Noetinger, BG Marie-Joseph-Louis-Henri, 413, 497, 509
Noguès, Gen. Charles-Auguste-Paul, 286 (2), 318, 319, 349, 363, 389
Noiret, MG Charles-Jean-Roger, 362, 500, 507
Noiret, MG Louis-Émile, 335, 433
NORDMANN, LÉON-MAURICE, 350
Normand, BG Hector-Louis-Ferdinand, 436
NOUAILHETAS, PIERRE-MARIE-ELIE-LOUIS, 324
NOUTARY, JEAN, 322
Nouvel de la Fleche, Capt. L. H. M. [FN], 536

ODDON, YVONNE, 350
Odend'hal, VA [FN], 301 (2)
Odic, LG Robert [FAF], 342, 372
Odry, Capt. [Army], 388
Oehmichen, MG Jean-Frédéric, 403, 428
Olivie dit Oliva-Rogel, BG François-Fernand-Michel, 320
Olleris, MG Pierre-Armand-Marie-Robert, 339, 351, 392
Ollive, VA Emmanuel L. H. [FN], 374, 377, 394, 396
Olry, Gen. René-Henri, 313, 338, 339, 367, 369, 382, 490
ORSELLI, GEORGES-LOUIS-JOSEPH, 325

Pagézy, LG Eugène-Henri-Jacques, 304, 308 (2)
PALEWSKI, GASTON, 344
PALICETI, PIERRE-JEAN-ANDRÉ, 322
Palmieri, Maj.,
Panescoise, BG, 465
Paquet, BG Charles, 424
Paquin, BG François-Louis, 293
Parent, Col., 381
Parion, LCdr P. [FN], 542
Paris, Col. Marcel-Étienne, 425 (2)
PARISOT, GEORGES-HUBERT, 323, 325
Parisot, LG Henri, 297, 313, 341, 401
PARISOT, JEAN-PAUL, 321
Parmentier, BG Maurice, 379
Parvy, MG Maurice-René-Pierre, 419
Paul, BG Georges-Eugène, 417, 431
PAULHAM, JEAN, 350
Pecqueur, Cdr. H. A. M. L. [FN], 541
Pégay, MG Pierre-Jean-Marie, 305, 393
PELICIER, MARIE-MARC-GEORGES, 325
Pellet, BG, 433
Pelletier d'Oisy, Col. Georges [FAF], 469

Pellion, BG Charles-Eugène-Ladislas-Louis, 296, 379
Penavayre, BG Eugène-Henri-Étienne-Auguste, 315, 419
Pendaries, LCol., 411, 423
Penel, BG Pierre-Charles-Joseph, 285
Penfentyo de Kervereguin [FN], VA H. L. M. de, 397
Pennès, Gen. [FAF], 372, 373
Périer, BG Germain-Charles-Henri, 284
PERNOT, GEORGES, 281
Perot, Capt. R. L. [FN], 537
Perraud, MG Henri-Gilbert-Antoine, 417, 431, 478
Perre, Col., 450
PERRIER, 325
Perrin, Conservateur, 295
Perrin, LCol., 386, 460
Perrossiet, Col., 438
Pétain, Mar. Henri-Philippe-Benoni-Omar-Joseph, 279, 333, 334, 513, 519 (2)
Petetin, Maj., 422
Petibon, BG Jean-Louis-Paul-Marie, 292, 408
Petiet, LG Robert-Marie-Eduardo, 340, 445, 446 (2)
Petin, LG Victor-Eugène-Lucien-Gabriel, 297
Petit, Col., 295
Petit, MG Ernest-Émile, 297, 355, 356 (2)
Petit, MG Gustavé-Antoine, 465
Petitville, Maj. de, 369
PEYROUTON, MARCEL, 318, 319, 335
Petyst de Morcourt, Capt. M. [FN], 533
Pfister, MG Georges-Jean-Eugène, 339, 340, 379
PHILIP, ANDRÉ, 346 (2)
Philippe, LG Louis-Auguste-Julien, 294, 295
Philippon, Maj., 406
Piatte, LCol., 425, 506
Picard, BG François, 448, 480
Picard, BG Jean-Jules-Ernest, 391, 430
Pichon, MG Jules, 460
Picot, LCol., 439 (3)
Picquendar, LG Odilon-Léonard-Théophile, 284, 309, 339, 357, 490
PIERRE-ALYPE, MARIE-FRANÇOIS-JULIEN, 325
PIÉTRI, FRANÇOIS, 336
Pigeaud, MG Marie-Camille-Charles-Raymond, 409
Pijaud, LCol. Charles-Félix [FAF], 357 (2)
Pilod, MG Maurice-Louis-Étienne, 305, 356, 368
Pinsard, BG Armand [FAF], 372
Pinson, Maj., 436
Pique-Aubrun, Col., 364, 506
Piquet, BG Pierre-Émile-Gabriel, 292
Piraud, BG Barthélémy-Joseph-Alexandre, 313
Planche, BG Ernest-Alidor, 308
Plagnol, LCol., 386, 387
Platon, RA Charles [FN], 335 (2), 393
PLEVEN, RENÈ, 344, 345 (4), 354 (2)
Plisson, MG Lucien-Georges-Émile-Félicien, 295

Pochard, Maj., 406
Pognon, BG Félix-Étienne, 282
Poher, Cdr. C. A. [FN] 541
Poirel, MG Marie-Nicolas-Paul, 454
Poisot, MG Louis-Gustavé-Abel, 457 (2), 474
POMARET, CHARLES, 281 (2)
Pons, LCol., 435
PONTON, LOUIS-GEORGES-ANDRÉ, 325
Portzert, MG François-Arthur, 415, 452, 473
Potet, MG [Med.-Gen. Insp.] Maurice-Alphonse-Joseph-Marie, 364
Potier, Maj., 429
Pots, LCol., 428
Poupinel, LG Raymond-Jules-Émile, 316, 383, 393, 463
Poydenot, BG Marie-Antoine-Arthur-Olivier, 356, 506
Préaud, MG Marie-Henri-Pierre, 362, 492
Prételat, Gen. André-Gaston, 286, 363
Prevaux, Capt. J. M. C. de [FN], 537
Prieur, Capt. [Army], 295
PRIGENT, ROBERT, 354
Prioux, Gen. René-Jacques-Adolphe, 284, 294, 307, 348, 365, 392
PROUVOST, JEAN, 281
PUAUX, GABRIEL, 319, 320
PUCHEAU, PIERRE, 336 (2)
PUJES, ANDRÉ-ALEXANDRE, 331
PUJO, BERTRAND, 280, 288, 335
Putinier, LCol., 429

Quebec, Cdr. J. G. [FN], 541
Quenardel, LCol., 430
QUEUILLE, HENRI, 281 (2)
Quilichini, BG Jean-Dominique, 431, 466

Rabut, BG, 478
Racadot, LCol. 415
Ract-Madoux, MG René-Théodre-Marie, 294, 295
Ragot, LCol., 466
RAMADIER, PAUL, 281
Raoux, BG Marie-Henri-Charles, 382
RAPENNE, JEAN-ALEXANDRE-LÉON, 322
Rapenne, MG Léon-Alexandre, 456 (3)
Rausch, MG Louis-Philippe-Henri, 282
RAYARDELLE, ANGE-MARIE-CHARLES-ANDRÉ, 323.
Raynal, Col., **505**
Raynaud, Pay-Gen., 296
RÉALLON, LÉON-MAURICE-VALENTIN, 324
Rebeu, MG Pierre-Jules-Joseph, 296
Reboul Hector-Berlioz, Capt. G. F. J. M. [FN], 540
Regard, BG Lucien-Antoine, 459 (2)
Regnault, BG Jean-Charles-Louis, 407, 420, 441
Regnault de Premesnil, BG Jean-Charles-Louis, 382
Remords, LCol., 452, 460
Renault, Cdr. R. M. J. A. [FN], 541
Renondeau, MG Gaston-Ernest, 303, 386, 403, 452, 460

Renucci, Col., 431
REPENNE, JEAN-ALEXANDRE-LÉON, 325
Réquin, Gen. Edouard-Jean, 287, 290, 339, 366, 490
RESTE, DIEUDONNÉ-FRANÇOIS-JOSEPH-MARIE, 322
Revers, MG Georges-Marie-Joseph, 303, 338 (2), 351, 429, 490
Rey, Pharmacien-Maj., 296
REY, GEORGES-PIERRE, 321, 322
Rey, Capt. M. L. M. [FN], 534
REYNAUD, PAUL, 279 (4), 280, 281, 283, 286, 288 (3), 290
Riand, MG [Int-Gén 2nd Class] Marcel-Auguste, 295
Ricard, BG Émile-Pierre-Edouard, 283
Richard, BG Georges-Julien, 439 (3)
Richard, BG Jean-Maurice, 506
Richefort, LCol., 419
Richter, MG Henri-Joseph-Martin, 400
Richoufftz de Manin, Cdr. J. E. M. de [FN], 489 (2)
Riedinger, BG, 315
RIGAULT, JEAN, 343, 348
Rihouey, Maj., 404
Rimaud, LCol., 387
Rime-Bruneau, MG Marcel, 311, 319, 348, 407, 451, 498
Rinck, MG Henrich-Camille-Constant-Arthur, 292, 385, 388
Rinderneck, MG Charles-Eugène, 293
RIO, ALPHONSE, 280
Rioult, VA [FN], 488
RIPERT, GEORGES, 336
Rivaud, LCol., 428
RIVAUD, ALBERT, 281
Rivet, VA E. L. [FN], 396
Rivet, BG Pierre-Louis, 284
RIVIÈRE, ALBERT, 335
RIVOAL, HENRI-GEORGES, 326
Robert, LCol., 477
Robert, Adm. Georges-Achille-Marie-Joseph [FN], 324, 377
Robert de Saint-Vincent, LG Louis-Albert-Pierre, 286, 313, 314, 363, 367, 423, 492, 493 (2)
Robinet de Plas, Cdr. H. A. J. [FN], 541
Robinet-Marcy MG Marie-Philippe, 306
Rocafort, LCol., 430
Rocaut, Maj., 408
Rocca, BG, 305
Rochard, LG Eugène-Jules, 316, 383, 462
ROCHARD, GABRIËL-AUGUSTA-LÉON, 331
Rochas, MG Jean-Baptiste-René-François, 438, 464 (2)
Roche, Maj., 437
Roederer, LCol., 386
ROGUÉ, JACQUES-CAMILLE-MARIE, 323
Rolin, Cdr. A. M. A. [FN], 471
ROLLIN, LOUIS, 280, 281

Romatet, MG Jean-Charles [FAF], 342, 372
Romemont, Maj. de, 418
Ronarc'h, RA Pierre-Alexis-Jean [FN], 486, 534, 538
Ronin, MG Emmanuel-Auguste-Abel, 339
Ronsin, Capt. [Army], 474
ROQUES, ADRIEN-ANTHONY-MAURICE, 327
ROSEY, RAYNAL, 325
Roton, MG Gaston-René-Eugène, 293, 361, 493
Roubertie, BG Jean-Sylvain-Louis, 317, 386, 464
Roucaud, LG Guillaume-Charles, 339, 341, 430, 454
Roucy, LCol. de, 384
Roussel, BG Calixte-Louis-François-Joseph, 305, 367
Roux, BG Oscar-Auguste, 414, 506
Rouyer, Capt. P. M. A. [FN], 537
Roy, Maj., 458
ROY, HENRI, 280
Royer, LCol., 364
Rozan, Col., 295
Ruby, BG Edmund-Auguste, 465
RUCAST, MARC, 281 (3)
Rue, Cdr. J. F. [FN], 542
Ruot, LCol., 295
Rupied, BG Paul-Jean, 284

Sabattier, MG Camille-Ange-Gabriel, 326, 327, 384, 390, 466, 478
Sable, RA L. M. J. [FN], 486
Sacaze LCdr. R. L. B. [FN], 543
SADON, ANDRÉ-PAUL, 331
SADOUL, NUMA-HENRI-FRANÇOIS, 323
Sainctavit, BG Jean-Ernest-Anne, 316, 383
SAINT-ALARY, JEAN-FRANÇOIS de, 322
Saint-Albin, Maj. de [FAF], 468
SAINTENY, JEAN-ROGER, 326
SAINT-FÉLIX, MAX de MASSON de, 323
Saint-George, LCdr. M. G. H. de [FN], 471
Saint-Germain, Capt. de [Army], 474
Saint-Julien, BG Marie-Joseph-André de, 314, 424
SAINT-MART, PIERRE de, 323, 324
Saint-Paul de Sinçay, BG Léon-Joseph-Louis, 384
Saizieu, Maj. de, 432 (2)
Sala, RA A. [FN], 301
Salan, MG Raoul-Albert-Louis, 364, 391, 466, 509 (3)
Salaun, LCol., 409
Salbert, MG Maurice-Marie, 464 (2)
SALCETI, PIERRE, 322
Sale, LCol., 409
SALENGRO, ROGER-HENRI-CHARLES, 280
Salland, BG Camille-Roger, 379
SALLER, MICHEL-RAPHAËL-ANTOINE, 324
Salmon, LCol., 424, 461
Salvan, BG Joseph-Étienne, 460, 474
Sancelme, LG Charles-Eugène, 428
Sandrier, BG Pierre, 450
Sarrade, BG Marie-Joseph-Gabriel, 439 (3)
SARRAUT, ALBERT-PIERRE, 280 (3), 281

Sarrebourse de La Guillonière, BG Aimé-Gabriel-Hilaire-Jehan-Marie, 410, 418, 452
SAUTOT, HENRI-CAMILLE, 323, 325, 347
SAVARY, ALAIN, 325
Schickele, MG Marie-Joseph-Antoine, 317
Schindler, Maj., 474, 475
Schlesser, BG Guy, 483 (2), 507 (2), 510 (2)
Schmidlin, BG Georges-Auguste, 303
Schmitt, MG Marie-Côme-Gaston, 477, 478
Schneider, BG Auguste, 309, 366
Schott, LCol., 418
Schwartz, MG Jacques-Fernand, 310, 459, 462, 463
Schweizguth, LG Victor-Henri, 308 (2), 340
Sciard, LG Théodore-Marcel, 304, 315, 379, 428, 494
Séchet, MG Félix-Pierre-Marie, 432
SELLIER, HENRI, 281
Seminel, Col., 439
Sequin, Capt. M. J. M. [FN], 533, 534
Serant, MG Léon-Eugène, 317
Serny, Col., 427 (2)
SÉROL, ALBERT, 281 (2)
Séron, BG Adolphe-Pierre-Henri, 385
Servet, MG, 317
Sevez, MG François-Adolphe-Laurent, 353, 364, 411, 427, 506
Sicé, BG [Méd.-Gen.] Marie-Eugène-Adolphe, 322, 323, 324, 347, 356 (2), 382
SIMMONET, ALICE, 350
Simon, Maj., 417
Sisteron, MG Eugène-Prosper-Joseph, 367, 405
Sivot, MG Désiré-Louis, 385, 386
SMITH, VICTOR-VALENTIN, 323
SOLOMIAC, LÉON, 322 (2)
SORIN, CONSTANT-LOUIS-SYLVAIN, 325
Soulet, LCol., 412
SOUSTELLE, JACQUES, 344, 345, 354
SPITZ, GEORGES-AIMÈ, 325
Spitz, MG Marie-Charles-Léon, 419
STEEG, THÉODORE, 280
Stehlé, MG Charles-Jean-Baptiste, 283
Still, Capt. P. A. B. [FN], 540
Stockel, Col., 295
Suchet, MG Anne-Baltbazar, 309
Sudour, Monseigneur, 296
Sudre, MG Aimé, 501, 509 (2)
SURLEMONT, JULES-EUCHER, 325

Tachet des Combes, LCol., 400
TALLEC, JACQUES-VICTOR-FRANÇOIS, 325
TANGUY-PRIGENT, FRANÇOIS, 354
TAP, PIERRE, 322
TARBÉ de SAINT-HARDOUIN, JACQUES, 343, 348
Tarrit, MG Pierre-François-Joseph, 427 (2), 428, 457
Tassel, BG, 317
Tassin, BG Charles-Marte-Jules, 384
Tavera, Col. [FAF], 485
Teisseire, BG Gustavé-Léon-Maurice, 418
TEITGEN, PIERRE-HENRI, 354 (2)
Tencé, LG Julian-Maurice, 304, 385, 387, 456
Terraux, RA Jules E. M. A. [FN], 377, 470, 487
Tessier, Col. Raymond-Jules-Paul-Henri, 366
Testard, BG Marie-Joseph-Eugène, 448, 480 (2)
Tétevuide, BG Constant-André, 382
Têtu, Gen. Marcel [FAF], 322, 372 (2)
Texier, MG Marie-Guastave-Victor-René-Alfred, 408, 417
Tezenas du Montecel, Lt. H. S. A. [FN], 471
THELLIER, PAUL, 281
Théry, Int-Gen. 1st Class, 294
THIBAUDEAU, LÉON-EMMANUEL, 327
Thiébeauid, BG Charles-Amédée, 381
Thierry, BG, 388
Thierry, MG Amédée-Alexandre-Gabriel-Henri, 432
Thierry, BG François, 411
Thierry d'Argenlieu, RA Georges [FN], 346, 347, 356
Thierry d'Argenlieu, BG Olivier-Charles-Marie, 368, 413
Thomas, Maj., 431
THOMAS, EUGÈNE, 354
Thomas, BG Jean-Gabriel-Edouard, 438, 463, 477
Thomassin, BG Henri-Charles, 303
Thouvenin, LCol., 459
Thouvenin de Villaret, LCol., 380, 404
TILLON, CHARLES, 351, 354
TILLON, GERMAINE, 350
Tissier, MG Raymond, 355
TIXIER, ADRIEN, 336, 354
TOBY, JEAN-FRANÇOIS, 322 (2)
Tonnele, Capt. J. [FN], 539
Touchon, LG Robert-Auguste, 312 (2), 313, 367, 382
Toullec, BG François-Louis, 454
Tourret, LCol., 381
Toussaint, BG Jean-Benigne-Auguste-Francis, 296, 408
Toussaint de Quievrecourt, Cdr. P. G. [FN], 489
TOUZET, ANDRÈ, 327
Touzet du Vigier, MG Jean-Louis-Alai, 392, 463, 480, 481, 497 (2), 506, 509
Trancart, BG Jacques-Marie-Joseph-Edmond-Ignace, 379
Tranchant, BG André-Georges-Louis, 310, 431
Traub, VA M. E. F. [FN], 395
Trémeau, BG Pierre-Marie-Edouard-Charles, 466 (2)
Tresoul, LCol., 295
Trinquand, BG Marcel-Louis-Lucien, 384
Tritschler, Maj., 435
Trolley de Prévaux, BG François-Joseph-Marie-Amédée, 442
Troublé, BG René-Jules, 311, 410

Truchis de Varenne, Maj. de, 445, 446 (2)
TRUFFERT, 324
TRUITARD, LÉON-HIPPOLYTE, 322
Turenne, Col. de [FAF], 468
Turquin, MG Auguste-Joseph-Charles-Antoine, 478

Urvoy de Portzamparc, Capt. Y. F. C. A. M. [FN], 488, 541

Valette, Col. René-Raphaël, 405
Valette d'Osia, Maj., 425, 426
Valin, Gen. Martial [FAF], 345, 357, 358 (2)
Vallée, BG Frédéric, 430, 452
Vallée, RA P. J. E. [FN], 470
Vallet, BG André-Paul, 368
Valluy, MG Jean-Étienne, 356, 458, 502, 507
Van Hecke, Col., 343
Vanlande, BG Maurice-Yves-Séraphin-Joseph, 364
Vanssay, Col. de, 380
Vary, LG Henri-Louis, 309, 405
Vauthier, MG Arsène-Marie-Paul, 418, 423
Vautrin, BG Jean-Émile-Alexis, 505
VEBER, RENÉ, 325, 326
Vedrines, Capt. C. G. de [FN], 540
Velluz, Pharmacien-Maj., 296
Verdier, BG Joseph-Guillaume, 385
Verdillac, LG Joseph-Antoine-Sylvain-Raoul de, 307, 369, 380 (2), 429, 455
Vergès, LG Bernard-Marie-Alexis, 389, 435, 462 (2), 476
Vergoz, Maj., 458
Vermiel du Conchard, BG Georges-Marie, 382, 406
Verneau, MG Jean-Edouard, 339 (2), 341, 351, 364
Vernejoul, MG Henri-Jacques-Jean-François de, 480 (2), 496, 502, 509, 510
Vernillat, MG Henry-François, 307, 414 (2)
Véron, BG Jean-Émile-Louis, 368
Verret, BG Jean-Marie-Louis, 282
VIANNAY [nee MORDKOVITCH], HELENE, 350
Viant, LG Maurice, 291, 311, 321 (3), 365, 383, 391 (2), 431
Vidal, BG Joseph-Louis-Justin, 385, 387
Vidal, Lt. G. F. A. [FN], 544
Vidil, Cdr. L. C. [FN], 488
Vieillard, BG Aldophe-François, 385, 459
Vieillard, MG Ferdinand-Prosper-Emmanuel-Léon, 428, 432
Villain, LG Paul-Louis-François, 291, 308
Villate, Maj., 403
Villavielle, LCol. de, 445, 446 (2)
Villeneuve-Escalon, Capt. de [Army], 449
Villers, MG Roger-Gaston-Marie-Joseph, 317
VILLON, PIERRE [ROGER GINSBURGER], 351
(2)
Virel, Maj. de, 447
Virieu, Maj. de, 447
Vix, MG Fernand, 416
Voinier, BG Paul-Adrien, 406, 474
Voirin, BG Paul-Albert, 297, 410
Voisin, BG Jean-Baptiste-François, 379
Voyron, Maj., 429
Vuillaume, Maj., 457
VUILLAUME, PAUL, 323
Vuillemin, Gen. Joseph [FAF], 289, 299 (2), 342

Wacogne, Lt. R. P. [FN], 544
Walch, Gen. Camille, 339
Walser, RA G. [FN], 472
WALTER, PIERRE, 350
Watrin, BG Jules-Henri, 303, 304
Wattel, MG Jean-Charles-Edmond, 294
Weischinger, Col., 399
Weiser, Col. [FAF], 485
Welschinger, Col., 441
Welvert, MG Marie-Jospeh-Edmond, 367, 392, 450, 495
Wemaëre, MG Maurice-Arthur-Alphonse, 436, 483 (2)
Weygand, Gen. Maxime, 280, 285, 291, 292, 318 (2), 334, 348, 362
WILDE, BORIS, 350
Willigens, BG Paul-Georges, 462
Wisbecq, LCol., 437
Worms, BG Gustavé, 296, 366

YBARNEGARAY, JEAN, 281, 336

ZAY, JEAN, 281
Zeller, Col. André-Marie, 356, 357, 503
Zeller, Col. Henri, 351, 355

Germany

Adolph, Col. Ernst 329
Arnim, MG Friedemund von, 329 (3)
Auleb, MG Helge Arthur, 2328 (2)
Auloch, Col. d. Res. Hubertus von, 328
Baarth, MG Juergen [Jürgen] 329
Bartenwerffer, MG Gustav von 330
Beckmann, Col. Alfred, 330
Behlendorff, GdA Hans 330
Bertram, MG George 331
Blaskowitz, Gdl Johannes 328
Bock, MG Franz Karl von, 329
Boehm-Tettelbach [Böhm-Tettelbach], LG Alfred 330
Boie, MG Claus Sigurd, 329
Boineburg-Langsfeld, LG Hans Wilhelm Freiherr [Baron] von, 328
Brauchitsch, CG (Heinrich Alfred Hermann) Walther

von, 328
Brunner, SS-MG Karl, 49
Buechs [Büchs], LG Fritz 330
Buerger [Bürger], SS-Col. Karl-Heinz, 49
Choltitz, LG Dietrich von 328
Daser, LG Wilhelm, 331
Debes, SS-Gen. Lothar, 50
Deichmann, LG Paul, 49
Dostler, GdI Anton], 50
Elfenau, SS-Col. Eugen von, 50
Elster, MG Botho, 330, 514
Faber du Faur, LG Moritz von 329
Felber, GdI Hans-Gustav 329, 331
Feldt, LG Kurt 328
Fellmer, Maj. I. G. Reinhold, 96
Fuechtbauer [Füchtbauer], LG Heinrich Ritter [Knight] von, 328 (2), 332
Geib, GdA Theodor 329, 332
Greiff, GdI Kurt von, 330
Gyldenfeldt, Maj. Hans-Wessel von, 96
Hamel, LCol. Gustan, 192
Hederich, LG Wilhelm Hans, 328
Hildebrandt, SS-BG Ernst, 49
Hoppe, MG Henry, 227
Hueffmeier [Hüffmeier], VA Friedrich, 329
Jacobi, MG Alfred 329
Kesselring, FM Albert, 49 (3)
Kitzinger, GdFl Karl, 328
Koch-Erpach, GdK Rudolf, 330
Kuebler [Kübler], GdGebTr Ludwig, 49
Kuntzen, GdPzTr Adolf, 330
Kurnatowski, MG von, 329
Lucht, MG Enno von, 49
Model, GFM (Otto Moritz) Walter 328
Mueller [Müller], Col., 329
Nagel, Col. Walter, 69
Neubronn von Eisenburg, LG Alexander Freiherr [Baron] von 329, 332
Newmann-Neurode, LG Karl-Ulrich 328
Niehoff, GdI Johannes 329, 331, 332
Oelsner-Woller, LCol., 328
Pogrell, GdK Guenther [Günther] von, 330
RAHN, RUDOLF, 49
Ramcke, MG (Hermann) Bernhard 330
Rintelen, GdFl Enno von, 49 (2)
Roettiger [Röttiger], LG Hans, 49
Rommel, FM Erwin Johannes Eugen, 26, 49, 60, 139
Rotberg, LG Freiherr [Baron] von 328
Runstedt, GFM Karl Rudolf Gerd von 328
Schaumburg, LG Ernst 328
Schmettow, MG Robert Graf [Count] von 329 (2)
Schulz, GdI Friedrich Wilhelm "Fritz", 49
Speidel, LG Dr. phil. Hans 69, 328
Streccius, LG Alfred, 328
Stuelpnagel [Stülpnagel], GdI Karl Heinrich von 328
Stuelpnagel [Stülpnagel], GdI Otto von 328

Tensfeld, SS-MG Willi, 49
Theissen [Theißen], GdA Edgar, 328, 332
Tippelskirch, GdI Kurt von, 69
Viebahn, GdI Max von, 330
Vierow, GdI Dipl. Ing. Erwin 328
Vietinghoff genannt Scheel, CG Heinrich Gottfried von, 49 (2)
Vilsow, MG, 328
Waechter [Wächter], LG Friedrich-Karl Otto Gustav von, 49
Witthoeft [Witthöft], GdI Joachim, 50
Wolff, SS-Gen. Karl, 49 (2)
Xylander, Col. Rudolf Ritter [Knight] und Elder [Noble] von 329

Italy

Abbondanza, BG Ugo, 25, 107
Accoretti, RA Enrico [RIN], 40, 161
ACERBO, GIACOMO, 9
Adami, BG Guiseppe, 125, 144
Adami, BG Ugo, 118
Adami-Rossi, LG Enrico, 30, 46, 47, 113
Ademollo, MG Amedeo, 9
Ago, Gen. Pietro, 15, 239
Agosti, MG Tito, 209
Agostini, MG Augusto [MVSN], 76, 93, 171, 209
Agostinucci, MG Crispino, 8, 74
Ajmone-Cat, MG Mario [RIAF], 7, 18, 42, 99, 100
Alagia, MG Gastano, 26, 65, 68
Albert, BG Alessandro, 61, 214
Albini, BG Unberto [MVSN], 8, 12 (2), 36, 38, 43
ALDISIO, SALVATORE, 8
Alfieri, BG Dino [MVSN], 6 (2), 10
Aliberti, MG Alberto, 35, 67, 111, 149
Allegretti, MG Lorenzo [MVSN], 76
Alleva, BG Armando, 36
Almici, Col. Ugo, 78
Altavilla, Col. Enrico, 68 (2)
Amato, BG Attilio, 93, 110 (2), 182, 184
Amato, BG Luigi, 183
Ambrosio, Gen. Vittorio, 7, 18 (2), 19, 22, 23, 24, 63, 64, 84, 213, 239
Amé, BG Cesare, 19, 182
Amico, MG Giuseppe, 65, 67, 115, 123
Amico di Meane, MG Count Giovanni, 5
Amoroso, MG Frederico, 27
Anderson, BG Giacomo, 39
Andreini, BG Enrico 119
Andreoli, BG Giuseppe, 147
Angelica, BG Domenico, 84
Angelini, BG Ignazio, 194
Angioj, MG Paolo, 111. 121, 122
Antonelli, MG Francesco, 166
Antoniazzi, MG, 131
Aosta [Savoy-Aosta], Gen. His Royal Highness Prince Amadeo Umberto Isabella Luigi

Filippo Maria Giuseppe Giovanni di Savoia, 3rd Duke of, 23, 58, 239
Aporti, BG Alessandro, 20
Appiotti, LG Giacomo, 16, 20, 167
Arena, BG Francesco Antonio, 139, 142
Argentino, MG Francesco, 167
Arisio, LG Mario, 67, 79, 84, 110, 113, 137 (2), 182
Armando, LG Enrico, 72, 86, 123, 147
Armellini, LG Quirino, 14, 19, 45, 76, 82, 86, 149, 179
Arnato, BG Luigi, 129
Arnera, BG Alfredo, 46
Artale, LG Vito, 24
Asinari di Bernezzo, MG Vittorio, 79, 156
Assanti, MG Rosario, 110, 157
Asteriti, BG Massimo, 157
Astuti, BG Giovanni, 24
Avarna di Gualtieri, Duke MG Carlo, 20
Aventi, BG Giuseppe [MVSN], 33, 35
Aymonino, LG Aldo, 9, 81, 92
Azzi, LG Arnaldo, 114, 116, 134, 214

Babini, LG Valentono, 113, 122, 217
Babbini, LG Ezio, 79, 135
Baccari, BG Alfredo, 153
Baccarini, BG Giovanni [MVSN], 77
Bacchiani, MG Augusto [RIAF], 164
Bacci, VA Guido [RIN], 40, 98
Bachelet, MG Giovanni Battista, 28
Badino-Rossi, MG Mario, 28, 93, 128, 131, 147
Badoglio, 1st Mar. of Italy Pietro, Duke of Addis Abeba, Marquess of el Sabotino, 5 (2), 10, 11, 12, 13 (2), 18, 58, 239
Baistrocchi, Gen. Count Federico, 15, 239
Balbo, Mar. Of Italy Italo [RIAF], 11, 42, 60, 239
Balbo-Bertone, BG Samuele, 34
Baldassare, LG Ettore, 87, 90, 121, 139
Ballabio, BG G. [MVSN], 75
Balocco, LG Riccardo, 23, 80, 107, 108
Balotta, MG Mario, 25, 68, 83, 139
Balsamo, RA [RIN], 162
Bancale, LG Emilio, 82, 85, 121, 182
Bancheri Lecce, LCol. A. [RIAF], 99
Baratelli, MG Carlo [MVSN], 31
Baratelli, BG Pietro Andrea, 82
Baratono, BG Michele, 199
Barbacini, BG Arturo, 28
Barbara, BG Luigi, 156
Barbasetti di Prun, LG Count Curio, 20, 60, 61, 72, 78, 84, 151
Barbato, MG Antonio, 10
Barberini, BG Ennio [MVSN], 76
Barberis, MG Francesco, 156
Barbieri, LG Alberto, 83, 85, 86, 92, 122, 139
Barbò di Caselmorano, BG Count Guglielmo, 25, 184, 185
Barni, BG Count Antonio, 189

Barone, RA [RIN], 161
Barrilis, BG Carlo, 157
Bartiromo, BG Salvatore, 74
Bartolotta, BG Cesare, 189
BASILE, CARLO EMANUELE, 43
Basso, LG Antonio, 25, 75, 82, 84, 214
Bastianon, BG August [MVSN], 209
Bastico, Mar. of Italy Ettore, 6 (2), 15, 60 (2), 63 (2), 78, 79, 91, 166, 239
Battisti, LG Emilio, 59, 118, 145 (2)
Baudino, BG Carlo, 116, 182
Bazzarello, BG Guglielmo, 19, 192 (2)
Beato, BG Giuseppe, 157
Becuzzi, BG Emilio, 109, 140, 192
Beggiato, BG Francesco, 38
Beghi, BG Aido, 26
Belletti, MG Pietro, 25, 64, 109, 137
Bellini, BG Francesco [MVSN], 32 (3), 38
Bellocchi, BG Giuseppe, 30
Bellomo, MG Nicola, 156
Bencivenga, MG Roberto, 34, 36
Benelli, MG Cesare, 112
Benigni, BG Arturo, 151, 182 (2)
Benvenutti, BG Ettore, 183
Berardi, LG Paolo, 7, 18, 22, 23, 67, 78, 87, 107, 108, 183
Berardi, BG Umberto, 25
Beraudo di Pralormo, LG Emanuelle, 25, 140, 155, 216 (3)
Bergamini, Adm. Carlo [RIN], 40, 41, 62, 97 (3), 160 (2), 161, 240
Bergamo [Savoy-Genoa], Gen. His Royal Highness Prince Adalberto di Savoia, Duke of, 67 (3), 79, 112, 239
Bergonzi, BG Angelo, 193
Bergonzoli, LG Annibale, 88, 92, 104
Bernasconi, LG M. [RIAF], 100
Bernotti, VA Romeo [RIN], 40 (2)
Bertelli, BG Enrico, 81
Berti, LG Mario, 70, 85, 91 (2)
Berti, BG Raffaele, 46
Bertini, LG Francesco, 78 (2), 113
Bertoni, BG Mario [MVSN], 47, 199, 200
Bettoni Cazzago, Col. Alessandro, 185
Bevilacqua, MG Cesare Federico [MVSN], 82
Bianchi, MG Armando, 26, 67
Bianchi, Col. Mario, 105
BIANCHI, MICHELE, 10
Bianchi, BG Tancredi, 5, 26, 81
Bianchieri, VA Luigi [RIN], 160, 161
Bianco di San Secondo, BG Enrico, 117
Biani, Col. V., 164
Biasioli, Col. Rocco, 135
BIGGINI, CARLO ALBERTO, 10, 11, 12, 44
Biglioni, LG Carlo, 25, 68, 96, 135, 216
Bignami, BG Mario, 25
Bignami, BG Riccardo, 149 (2)
Bignamini, LG Ferruccio, 19, 32, 103

Binacchi, MG Gastano, 30, 129
Binelli, BG Alfonso, 38
Biraghi, MG Sergio [MVSN], 12, 46, 76
Biscaccianti, MG Alessandro [MVSN], 93, 170
Bisson, BG Emilio, 121, 182
Bitossi, MG Gervasio, 78, 87 (2), 140, 147
Bivona, Col. Pietro, 195
Blanchi, BG Alessandro, 31
Bobbio, Gen. Valentino, 15, 27, 239
Bocassi, BG Guglielmo, 46
Bocchetti, Col. Prof. Federico, 69
Bocchetti, BG Giovanni, 184
Bocchi, BG Erminio, 174
BOCCHINI, ARTURO, 8
Bocchio, BG Giovanni [MVSN], 209
Boglione, BG Gabriele, 111
Bollati, LG Ambrogio, 16
Bollea, MG Ottavio, 106
Bologna, MG Guido, 133, 137, 216 (3)
Bonagura, BG Unberto, 106
Bonamici, BG Sandro [MVSN], 76
Bondi, BG Ferrucio, 156
Bonelli, BG Arnaldo, 117, 169
Bonelli, Col. Livio, 193
Bonini, MG Silvio, 110 (2)
Bonola, LG A. [RIAF], 99
BONOMI, IVANOE, 5 (2), 8, 11, 51
Bonomi, MG Ruggero, 43, 164
Borelli, BG Romolo, 88
Borghese, Cdr. Prince Junio Valerio [RIN], 212, 272
Borghi, MG Mario [MVSN], 169
Borghini, BG Davide, 135
Borgnini, MG Valetti, 58
Borri, BG Dino [MVSN], 29, 32, 35, 38
Boscardi, LG Enrico, 144, 167
Boschi, BG Mario [RIAF], 164, 165 (2)
Boselli, MG Guido, 75, 112, 116, 135, 138
BOTTAI, GIUSEPPE, 13
Bottari, Col. E., 69
BOTTO, ERNESTO, 43
Bozzoni, MG Aurelio [MVSN], 37
Bracci, BG Angelo Cesare [MVSN], 169
Bracco, MG Carlo, 105, 123
Brancati, BG [MVSN], 204
Brandimarte, MG Piero [MVSN], 169
Brenta, RA Emilio [RIN], 160
Briganti, MG Alberto [RIAF], 99, 100
Brisotto, BG Silvio, 93, 113, 216
Brivonesi, RA Bruno [RIN], 40, 159, 162
Brivonesi, VA Bruto [RIN], 98, 160
Broccoli, BG Umberto, 71
Broglia, LG Enrico, 47, 114, 126, 179, 180
Brovarone Carnaro, BG Lorenzo, 32, 124
Brunelli, BG Giulio, 148
Brunetti, MG Brunetto, 25, 75, 113, 136
Bruni, BG Nicola, 33
Bruno, BG Francesco, 120
Bruzzone, Col. A., 144

Bucci, LG Emilio, 24
Bucciante, MG Alfredo, 26
BUFFARINI-GUIDI, GUIDO, 8, 43
Bulbo, BG Bertone, 183
Buoncompagni, LG Ugo, 70
Butta, BG Ugo, 126, 130

Cadorna, LG Raffaele, 25, 139, 141, 184, 214
Calamani, BG Camillo, 22
Calcagno, LG Riccardo, 9, 16, 92
Caldone, BG Nunzlo, 71
Calendi, BG Attilio, 71
Caligian, MG Ercola, 119
Calini, MG Giovanni, 10
Callierno, MG Antonio, 114, 123, 129
Calvani, BG Michele,
Calvi di Bergolo, MG Count Fiorgio, 26, 139 (2), 140 (2)
Calzini, BG Raffaello, 11, 118
Calzolari, BG Bruno [MVSN], 209
Campioni, VA Inigo [RIN], 6, 11, 40 (2), 62, 91, 97
Canale, LG Antero, 30, 79, 83, 85, 105, 151
Candelori, BG Mario [MVSN], 209
Canegallo, BG Carlo, 32
Canevari, BG Emilio, 45, 48
Caniglia, Col. V., 69
Canistrà, BG Domenico, 125 (2), 220
Cantaluppi, MG Gaetano, 24, 137, 149
Cantù, MG Casare, 8
Capelli, BG Giuseppe, 66
Capizzi, MG Manilo, 105, 137
Cappa, LG Ernesto, 22, 32, 106
Cappa, BG Guilo, 22
Cappa, BG Umberto [RIAF], 100
Cappi, MG Americo, 47
Capra, BG Enrico, 20
Caracciolo, MG Italo, 71, 116, 120
Caracciolo di Feroleto, Gen. Mario, 28, 60, 65, 66 (2), 87, 147, 239, 332
Caratti, BG Lorenzo, 25
Carboni, LG Giacomo, 19 (2), 24, 81, 87, 151, 175
Caretta, BG, 107
Carette, Col. Aminto, 148
Carini, MG Luigi, 178
Carlino, BG Enrico, 145
Carlino, BG Pietro, 26
Carloni, MG Mario, 148, 209 (3)
Carnellutti, BG Giuseppe, 25 (2)
Carnimeo, LG Nicolangelo, 35, 153
Carossini, BG Ettore, 116
Carraba, BG Gennaro, 156
Carrara, BG Biagio, 45
Carrera, BG Mario, 24
Carta, LG Angelico, 84, 106, 119
Carusi, BG Antonio, 36
Caruso, Gen. Filippo, 9
Caruso, LG Giovanni, 36
Casardi, VA Ferdinando [RIN], 40 (2), 159, 160 (2)

Casassa, LCol. G. B., 135
Cascella, BG (Res.) Sebastiano, 46, 76
Casella, MG Dante, 23
Cassata, BG Ruggiero, 1243
Castagna, MG Giacomo, 89, 108, 112, 114
Castellani, BG Ludovico, 192
Castellano, BG Giuseppe, 20, 26, 113, 217
Castriotta, BG Raffaele, 47, 64
Casula, MG Giovanni, 217
Catalano, BG Vincenzo, 81
Catardi, BG Raffaele [MVSN], 61
Cattaneo, RA Carlo [RIN], 159 (2), 160
Cavagnari, VA Domenico [RIN], 8. 18, 40 (2)
Cavallero, Mar. of Italy Count Ugo, 18, 19, 59 (2), 74, 239
Cavallo, BG Antonio, 5
Caviglia, Mar. of Italy Enrico, 75, 239
Ceccarini, MG Giuseppe, 29
Ceriana-Mayneri, MG Count Carlo, 28, 140, 147
Cerica, LG Angelo, 8, 33
Cerio, MG Giovanni, 113, 177
Cerrato, MG Anturo,
Cerruti, BG Guido, 108
Cerrutti, BG Guiseppe, 71
CERULLI, ENRICO, 13, 14 (2)
Cesaretti, BG Antonio, 107, 125, 220
Cesari, MG Cesare, 12
Cessari, BG Ruggero, 192
Cetroni, MG Bernado, 30
Chatrian, BG Luigi, 119, 131
Chiappe, BG Aristide, 47
Chiappe, MG Umberto [MVSN], 170
Chiappi, MG Armellini, 113, 182
Chiaramonti, BG Epifanio, 26, 135
Chierici, MG Renzo [MVSN], 8
Chiesa, Col. Umberto [RIAF], 165
Chiminelli, MG Ernesto, 115, 125
Chinnici, BG Domenico, 37
Chiolini, MG Luigi, 26, 118, 151, 182
Chirieleison, MG Domenico, 151
Chirubini, BG Florenzo, 47
Chitti, BG Carlo, 91
Chitti, MG Enrico, 91
Ciampa, BG Nicola, 112
Ciancarini, MG Ovidio, 20 (2)
Cianci, BG Fernando [MVSN], 9
CIANETTI, TULLIO, 10
CIANO, GIAN GALEAZZO, 2nd Count of Cortellazzo and Buccari, 5 (2), 6, 11 (2), 12
Ciardi, BG Giuseppe, 77
Cigala-Fulgosi, MG Alfonso, 65, 109, 184
Cimino, BG Ettore, 37
Cimolino, Col. Armando, 145
Cinti, LG Agostino, 85, 120
Cinti, BG Carlo, 115, 118
Cinti, BG Giuseppe, 85
Cipriani, BG Guido, 68

Clerici, LG Count Ambrogio, 15, 82
Clerico, BG Luigi, 116, 118
Cloza, Col. Giuseppe, 193
Cobianchi, BG Antonio, 76, 172
Cocconi, MG Giovanni, 108, 177
Coiro, MG Guido, 22
Colizza, BG Ugo [MVSN], 170
Colonna, BG Raffaele, 183, 218
Colombo, Col. Cesare, 148
Comerci, MG Giuseppe, 20
Cona, LG Fernandino, 85, 86, 106
Concialini, BG Arturo, 34
Consoli, MG Giuseppe, 91, 119
Contestabile, MG Carlo, 8
Conti, MG Egisto, 107, 119, 132
Conti, MG Riccardo, 9
Conticelli, MG Giuseppe, 12, 46, 76
Contini, Col. Massino, 104
Converso, BG Lorenzo, 83
Coppi, MG Americo, 38, 183, 185
Cordero di Montezemolo, MG Alberto, 117
Coronati, MG Emilio, 89, 108, 111, 125
Corrado, BG Uberto, 209
Corte, MG Giovanni, 31
Cortese, MG Giuseppe, 117, 179
Corti, BG, 81
Corvino, BG Cesare, 46
Coselschi, MG Eugenio,
Costa, BG Giuseppe, 139
Costa, BG Savario [MVSN], 23
Cotronei, BG Ettore, 105, 151, 152
Coturri, LG Renato, 80, 89, 115, 120, 179
Cozzolino, BG Antonio, 122
Cremascuoli, BG Giuseppe, 136
Crepas, MG Ettore, 38
Crimi, LG Filippo, 9 (3), 209
Cristani, BG Giorgio, 179
Cristiani, BG Gino, 118
Crivaro, LG Oreste, 26, 27 (2), 29, 86
Croce, BG Alessandro, 38
Cubeddu, MG Luigi, 109

da Barberino, BG Raul [RIAF], 164
Dabbeni, BG Ottorino, Battista, 108, 137, 184
d'Admo, MG (Res.) Michele, 23
Dagnino, BG Torello, 77
D'Agostino, BG Salvatore, 74
d'Alfonso, BG Augusto, 24
Dall'Ora, LG Fidenzio, 15, 90
Dall'Ora, LG Giuseppe, 21
Dalmazzo, LG Lorenzo, 28, 69, 74 (2), 80, 83, 87, 107, 153
Danioni, MG Carlo, 145
D'Antoni, BG Giovanni, 31, 123, 133
D'Antonio, MG Raffaelo, 27
DAODICE, GIUSEPPE, 13, 14
Dapino, BG Vincenzo, 121 (2), 144, 215
D'Aponte, MG Alberto, 116

d'Arle, BG Federico, 71, 113, 116
d'Arminio Monforte, BG Salvatore, 107, 119
D'Aurelio, BG Venceslao [RIAF], 164
Da Zara, VA Alberto [RIN], 40, 159, 160 (3), 161, 222 (2)
De Agazio, BG Alberto, 74
De Angelis, RA Cardo [RIN], 40
De Benedetti, MG Giovanni Antonio, 114
De Benedettis, BG, 220
de Bernadis, BG Vittorio, 85
De Biase, LG Luigi, 82, 114
de Blasio, MG Ettore, 148
De Bonis, BG Giovanni, 108
De Bono, Mar. of Italy Emilio, 10, 12 (2), 15 (2), 16, 28 (2), 57, 58, 59, 239
De Carolis, BG Ugo, 25, 86, 93, 137
de Castiglione, LG Lazzaro Maurizio, 36, 145 (2)
De Castiglione, BG Massimo [MVSN], 46, 47
De Cia, MG Amedeo, 47, 121, 131, 145
De Corné, BG Guido, 24
De Courten, VA Raffaele [RIN], 7, 8, 18, 40, 160 (2)
De Ferrari, BG Aldo, 184
De Franchis, BG Corrado, 84
de GASPERI, ALCIDE, 5, 11
Degiani, MG Stefano, 25, 27 (2)
De Giorgis, LG Fedele, 120, 144
De Guidi, BG Alessandro, 122
de Laurentis, BG Augusto, 129
De Lauso, MG Pietro, 10
De Leone, BG Adolfo, 87
Del Giudice, BG Giovanni, 48, 112
Della Bona, LG Giulio, 89, 122
Della Mura, BG Vincenzo, 122
de Lorenzis, MG Ugo, 152, 216, 217, 220
Del Ponte, MG Cesare, 36
Del Totto, BG Ettore, 157
De Marinis, BG Gilberto, 174
de Michelis, BG Attilio, 113, 157
Denti Amari, VA Salvatore [RIN], 40
De Nobili, MG Nicholas [MVSN], 77
De Pasquale, BG Italo [MVSN], 47
de Pignier, LG Augusto, 25, 27, 84
de Porcellinis, BG Carlo,
de Rienzi, BG Alfredo, 111 (2)
de Rosa, MG Alfredo, 36
De Rose, BG Francesco, 112
de Simone, LG Carlo, 6, 14, 94, 139, 154
de Simone, LCol. Ugo, 148
Dessy, MG Francesco [MVSN], 77
de Stefanis, LG Giuseppe, 22, 87, 90, 112, 134, 139, 214
de Vecchi di Val Cismon, BG Count Cesare Maria, 6, 10, 11, 91, 127, 130
Degiani, LG Stefano,
Del Totto, BG Ettore,
D'Havet, BG Achille, 26, 117, 128, 145
Diamanti, MG Filippo [MVSN], 47 (2), 48, 199 (2)
di Caccuri, MG Carlo Petra, 75, 114, 117, 217

Di Gaetano, BG Michele, 92
di Giorgio, MG Umberto, 34, 92, 148
di Marino, Col. Giuseppe, 68
di Nisio, MG Ismaele, 35, 82, 117, 139, 141
Di Rodeano, BG Elchi [MVSN], 47
D'Oro, MG Giovanni [MVSN], 47, 169
Drago, Col. Carlo [RIAF], 96, 163, 164
Dromm, Col. Ernesto, 106
Du Pont, MG Francesco, 89, 95, 105, 137 (2)
Durante, Col. Enrico, 194
Dusmet, BG Davide, 37

Elti di Rodeano, MG Count Giandavide [MVSN], 77
Esposito, MG Giovanni, 28, 46, 120, 145, 182

Faccenda, MG Ettore [RIAF], 99
Falangola, VA Mario [RIN], 97
Falasca, BG Marrigo, 21
Faldella, LG Emilio, 23, 66, 144
Falugi, MG Giuseppe, 110, 133
Fantazzini, BG Paolo, 68
Fantoni, MG Attilio, 31
Farina, MG Amilcare, 48, 209
Farinacci, MG Roberto [MVSN], 77
Fassi, BG Carlo, 145
Fattarappa-Sandri, MG, 46
Fattori, BG Mario, 34
Fautilli, LG Ubaldo, 21
Fava, BG Giovanni, 72
Favagrossa, LG Carlo, 10 (2), 24, 109
Fazzini, BG Luigi, 182, 184
Felici, Col. Ercole, 148
Felici, BG Guido [MVSN], 47, 76, 171, 200
FELSANI, ARMANDO, 14
Fenoglietto, BG Carlo, 30
Fenulli, BG Dardano, 148
Ferone, BG Ernesto, 117, 119
Ferrannini, BG Mario, 71
Ferrari, BG Augusto, 220
Ferrari, BG Vito, 151
Ferrari Orsi, LG Federico, 28, 83, 87, 90, 147 (2)
Ferrero, LG Alberto, 20, 74, 88, 145 (2)
Ferrero, MG Carlo, 22, 110
FERRINI, FERRUCCIO, 43
Ferroni, MG Vito, 110, 134
Fettarappa Sandri, MG Carlo, 10
Ficalbi, BG Gino, 128
Fietta d'Asolo, BG Pietro, 38
Filippi, BG Carlo, 28, 91, 144
Fiocca, BG Ildebrando, 158
Fioravanti, LCol. Evaristo, 137
Fioravanzo, RA Giuseppe [RIN], 160 (2)
Fiore, MG Basilio, 37
Fiorentino, LG Oscar, 34
Fiorenza, BG Ignazio, 23
Fiorenzuoli, LG Benedetto, 80, 108 (2)
Fioretti Fiume, Col. P., 124
Flaminio, BG [MVSN], 145

Florio, BG Giacomo, 157
Focanti, Col. Ettore, 194
Fogliani, BG Luigi, 64, 80
Fongoli, MG Ugo, 111, 151, 194
Fontana, LG Giovanni, 71
Forgiero, LG Arnaido, 25, 27, 29, 78, 91, 107
Foriero, MG Arnaldo, 68
Formisano, MG Antonio, 106
FORNACIARI, BRUNO, 8
Fortunato, BG Auturo, 25 (2), 71
Fougier, LG Rino Corso [RIAF], 7, 18, 42, 99
Franceschini, BG Antonio, 112, 135, 142
Franchini Timavo, Col. O., 124
Francisci, MG Enrico [MVSN], 166, 199
FRANGIPANI, AGENORE, 13, 14
Franzini, BG Camillo, 78
Fraticelli, BG Giuseppe, 152, 156
Frattali, BG Gualtiero, 45 (2)
Frattini, LG Enrico, 26, 89, 149 (2)
Frichione, MG Gastano, 35
Froio, BG Guido, 183 (2), 220
Frongia, BG Cicito, 21
Frusci, LG Luigi, 13, 14, 27, 86, 91, 93, 104, 151, 153, 192
Fuselli, BG Tito, 66

Gabba, Gen. Melchiade, 12, 16 (2), 239
Gabutti, MG Gualtiero, 115, 119
Gaeta, BG G. [RIAF], 165
Gaggiotti, BG Cino, 47
Gagliotti, BG Gino, 30
GAI, SILVIO, 43
Galamini, MG Count Alberto [MVSN], 76, 166
Galbiati, LG Enzo Emilio [MVSN], 12, 46, 71 (2), 76
Galletti, Commo [RIN], 196
Gallina, LG Sebastiano, 154, 193
Gallo, BG Annibale, 84
Gamaleri, LG Mario, 79, 86, 180
Gambara, Gen. Gastone, 6, 46, 60, 82, 83, 85, 86 (2), 91 (2), 240
Gambelli, LG Remo, 8, 63, 82, 109 (2)
Gamerra, LG Emillio,
Gamondi, MG Paolo, 9 (2)
Gandin, MG Antonio, 23 (2), 115
Gandini, LG Cesare, 19, 71, 135 (2)
Gangi, BG Salvatore, 9
Ganini, MG Luigi, 71
Garasano, MG Pietro, 38
Garavano, BG Agostino, 80, 84
Garavelli, LG Emilio, 133 (2), 134
Garelli, BG Antonio, 114, 217, 220
Gariboldi, Gen. Italo, 6, 58, 60 (2), 66, 67, 70, 80, 114, 239
Garino, Col. Carlo, 195
Gatti, BG Eugenio, 96, 120
Gatti, Gen. Giuseppe, 10
Gay, Col. Pietro, 145
Gazzale, MG Enrico, 105, 128

Gazzera, Gen. Pietro, 13, 14, 16, 58 (2), 94, 153, 240
Gelich, LG Count Fernando, 115, 151 (2)
Geloso, Gen. Carlo, 14, 58, 65, 70 (3), 80, 82, 88, 239
GEMELLI, BRUNO, 43
Genova [Savoy-Genoa], VA His Royal Highness Prince Ferdinando Umberto Filippo Adalberto di Savoia, 3rd Duke of [RIN], 98
Gerboni, BG Michale, 30
Germino, BG Alfredo, 26
Ghe, BG Carlo, 92
Ghemi, BG Fausto, 6
Gherzi, BG Luigi, 38, 116, 121 (2), 125, 142
Ghiringhelli, Col. Giuseppe, 137
Giamberini, MG Curgio, 21
Giangreco, BG Francesco, 126
Giani, BG Nicolo, 174
Giani, BG Umberto, 61, 174
Giannantoni, MG Ottorino [MVSN], 60
Gianni, MG Giuseppe, 64, 121
Giannuzzi, MG Ettore, 108, 110
Giardina, MG Vincenzo, 125, 209
Gigliarelli Fiumi, LG Ugo, 109
Giglio, BG Italo, 79
Giglio, MG Umberto, 43 (2), 46, 64
Giglioli, MG Emilio, 59, 60, 111 (2), 117
Gignolini, BG Marcello, 45
Gilardi, BG Achille, 176
Gilioli, BG E., 123
Gioda, LG Benvenuto, 25, 83, 86, 151
Gioia, BG Flavio, 89
Giordano, MG Eduardo, 95
Giorgetti, BG Enrico, 156
Giovannelli, BG Renzo, 31
Giovannelli, MG Vittorio, 135
Girandinetti, Col. [RIAF], 164
Girlando, MG Emanuele, 113, 142, 177
Girola, BG Enrico Guido, 27
Girotti, LG Mario, 144, 146, 183
Giuliana, Col. Egidio, 185
Giusfredi, BG Gino [MVSN], 199
Gloria, LG Alessandro, 80, 87, 88, 89, 92, 104, 116, 136, 178
Goiran, VA Ildebrando [RIN], 40, 98
Gonnella, MG Felice, 19, 89, 108, 129
Gonzga del Vodice, BG Ferrante, 84, 88, 115, 131
GORINI, POMPEO, 14
Gorlier, MG Marlo, 146
Gotti, LG Carlo, 29, 35, 130, 134, 136
Gotti-Porcinari, BG Count Guilio Cesare, 92, 120
Gozzi, BG Celestino, 30
Granata, LG Gino, 32, 81, 216
Grande Brindisi, Col. E. [RIAF], 99
Granozio, BG Mario, 80
Grassi, LG Augusto, 79
Grassi, BG Giovanni. 75, 117
Grassi, MG Noe, 26

Grattarola, MG Attilio, 29 (2), 118, 183
Graziani, Col. F., 69
Graziani, Mar. of Italy Rodolfo, Marquis [Marchese] of Neghelli, 6, 7, 13 (2). 18, 22, 23, 43, 45 (2), 60, 83, 201, 239
Grazioli, Gen. Francesco, 6, 16 (3), 240
Grazioci, BG Antonia, 144
Graziosi, LG Eugenio, 15
Gregori, BG Claudio, 107
Griffin, BG [MVSN], 204
Grillo, BG Arrigo, 83
Grillo, BG Pietro [MVSN], 209
Grimaldi, Col. E., 79
Grimaldi, BG Paolo,109
Grimaldi, MG Roberto, 21
Gritti, BG Oscar, 184
Grossi, Gen. Camillo, 15, 19, 58, 63, 65, 239
Grosso, MG Luigi, 60
Grosso (I), BG Mario, 30
Grosso (II), BG Mario, 26
Grosso, BG Vittorio, 78
Guala, BG Francesco, 174
Gualano, LCol. A., 69
GUARIGLIA, RAFFAELE, 5, 11
Guasconi, Col. A., 105
Guassardo, MG Mario, 47, 116
Guiccione, MG Giovanni Battista, 67, 125, 214
Guidi, Gen. Francesco, 15, 70, 79, 239
Gusberti, Col., 104
Guzzoni, Gen. Alfredo 7, 14, 18, 19, 21, 58, 65, 66, 74, 83, 208, 239, 332

Hazon, LG Azzolino, 8 (2)

Iacoe, MG Vincenzo, 23
Ienco, BG Luigi, 83
Ilari, LG Eraldo [RIAF], 99 (2)
Imperiali de Franscavilla, BG Giavanni, 183
Infante, LG Adolfo, 5, 26, 63, 112, 139
Infante, MG Mario [RIAF], 99
Ingravalle, LG Alfredo, 24
Invrea, Col. Massimo, 192 (2)
Iorio, LG Ilio, 5
Isasca, BG Carlo, 110
Ivaldi, LG Giuseppe Cesare, 72

Jachino, Adm. Angelo [RIN], 40, 41, 62, 159 (2), 240
Jacomoni, BG Viceroy Francesco, 74
Jacopetti, BG Giuseppe, 137
Jalla, BG Luigi, 47, 79, 95, 145

Kellner, BG Arturo, 134 (2)
Kellner, BG Enrico, 147 (3)
Krall, MG Luigi, 126, 137

Laccetti, BG Luigi, 89
La Corte, MG Antonio [MVSN], 170
La Ferla, MG Francesco, 129, 134

Laina, MG Carlo, 130
Lama, BG Guido, 81, 82 (2)
Lanari, BG Pietro, 9
Lannuti, Col. Sebastiano, 195
Lapenna, LCol. Giacomo, 105
La Rocca, MG Vittorio Emanuele, 65
Lastrico, BG Luigi, 28
La Strucci, BG Romolo, 70
Lavinao, MG Francesco, 109 (2), 122
Lavizzari, Col. Fausto, 145
Lazzarini, BG Attilio, 79, 131
Legnani, VA Antonio [RIN], 43, 97 (2), 160
Lenti, BG Luigi, 9
Leonardi, MG Ugo [MVSN], 76, 173, 209
Leone, BG Domenico, 24
LEPRI (LEPRE), STANISLAO, 514
Lerici, LG Roberto, 82, 136, 137, 176
LETO, GUIDO, 8
Levis, MG Egidio, 39, 133, 178
Liberati, BG Amedeo, 123, 154
Liberati, BG Egido, 7
Licari, BG Giuseppe, 29
LIVERANI, AUGUSTO, 44
Loasses, MG Francesco Paolo, 23, 37
Lodolo, VA Pietro [RIN], 98
Lomaglio, MG Cesare, 93, 147, 185
Lombardi, BG Carlo, 148, 185
Lombardi, BG Francesco, 134
Lombardi, BG Giacomo, 25, 136, 144
Lombardi, BG Guiseppe, 147
Lombardi, RA Giuseppe [RIN], 160, 162
Longo, LG Ulisse [RIAF], 100
Lorenzelli, MG Dante, 89, 111, 151, 180
Lorenzini, BG Orlando, 193 (2)
Losurdo, BG Giovanni, 9
Lotti, BG Michele, 47
Lubrano, BG Armando, 83, 112, 144
Ludovico Valona, Col. D. [RIAF], 100
Lugli, BG Enrico, 118, 192
Luna, BG Nunzio [MVSN], 202
Luraschi, MG Benesperando [MVSN], 76
Luridiana, BG Antonio, 125, 148
Lussiana, MG Augusto, 27

Maccario, MG Alessandro, 108 (2), 149, 217
Maccario, MG Giovanni, 144, 145, 183
Maestrelli, BG Guiseppe, 184
Maffei, BG Achille, 140, 183
Magaldi, BG Gherardo, 46 (2)
Maggiani, MG Mario, 108, 120
Maggiani, MG Pietro, 79, 104, 106 (2), 120 (2), 136, 182
Maggio, Col. Paolino, 105
Maggiore-Perni, BG Luigi, 111
Magli, MG Giovanni, 19, 75, 78, 81, 116, 139, 181
Magliano, MG Emilio, 29, 144, 145, 215
Magneri, BG Carlo, 130
Magri, BG Federico, 46, 158

Magrini, LCol. Agostino, 193
Maj, Col. G., 91
Majnardi, MG Odoardo, 58, 92
Majnoni D'Intignano, MG Count Gerolamo, 147
Majoli, LG Giovanni, 23, 109, 182
Malaguti, BG Bruno, 68, 137
Malavasi, BG Carlo [MVSN], 200
Maletti, BG Pietro, 113, 153 (3)
Maltese, LG Enrico, 112
Mambretti, Gen. Ettore, 15, 239
Manardi, BG Guido, 136, 209
Manca di Mores, LG Marquis Ettore, 27, 118, 127
Mancinelli, LG Giuseppe, 19, 20, 63 (2), 106
Manera, MG Mario, 22
Manetti, Col. Manlio, 194
Manfredi, Col. Giacomo, 105
Manfredi, Col. Luigi, 145
Manildo, BG Giovanni, 128
Mannerini, LG Alberto, 92, 96
Manzi, MG Luigi, 25, 79, 113, 137, 181
Maraffa, BG Riccardo, 14
Maraghini, VA Giotto [RIN], 40, 98
Maranghini, BG Umberto, 39
Marangio, BG Vittorio, 81
Maraventano, Col. Saverio, 193
Maravigna, Gen. Pietro, 23, 78, 82, 239
Marazzani, LG Mario, 28 (2), 148 (2)
Marchesi, BG Umberto, 113, 129, 220
Marchesi, LG Vittorio [RIAF], 100
Marchi, BG Mario, 85
Marchini, BG Paolo, 185
Marciani, BG Giovanni, 7, 121
MARCONI, Marquis [Marchese] GUGLIELMO, 11
Marenco di Moriondo, VA Alberto [RIN], 159
Marescalco, BG Orazio, 85
Marfuggi, BG Ugo, 89
Marghinotti, LG Mario, 82 (2), 107, 116, 136, 182
Marinetti, LG Adriano, 15, 27, 63 (3), 81, 239
Marinetti, LG Giulio, 5
Marino, BG Ettore, 36
Marino, MG Mario [MVSN], 47, 48, 170
Mariotti, LG Adamo, 37, 66 (2), 115
Mariscalco, BG Orazio, 179, 184
Marotta, MG Pasquale, 37
Marrajeni, BG Francesco, 45
Marras, LG Efisio, 20, 26 (3), 66, 82
Martinat, BG Guilio, 80, 85, 90, 145 (2)
Martinesi, MG Luigi [MVSN], 166, 171
Martini, BG Giovanni, 169
Martorrelli, MG Mario, 79, 117
Marziani, MG Alfio, 22, 91
Masciocchi, MG Silvio [MVSN], 170
Masi, MG Raul, 61
Masina, BG Giorgio, 110, 117, 134
Masini, BG Luigi, 182
Masnoni D'Intiganano, MG Count Girolamo [MVSN], 31
Masserano, BG Guido, 80

Massone, BG Riccardo, 148
Matarelli, MG Leonida, 34
Matiotti, Col. Lorenzo, 96
Matteucci, BG Mario, 183
Matteucci, RA Pellegrino [RIN], 159, 161
Mattioli, BG E., 20
Mattioli, BG Riccardo di Belfiore, 114, 136
Matucci, BG Giuseppe, 36
Maugeri, RA Franco [RIN], 40, 267
Maugeri, Col. Dr. N., 69
Maugliam, BG Fedele [MVSN], 200
Mauro, BG Fortunato, 115
Mayer, BG Francesco, 74
Mazzari, MG Pier Domenico, 31, 106
Mazzerelli, BG Francesco, 71, 120, 174
Mazzetti, BG Armando, 21
Mazzetti, MG Loreto, 24, 26
Mazzini, MG Luigi, 26, 115
Mazzocchi, Col. Armandi, 135
Mazzolini, BG Quinto, 19
Mazzucco, MG Renato [RIAF], 101
MEDICI, FRANCESCO CAMERO, 13
Medoni, BG Francesco, 45
Medori, BG Ugo, 108, 130
Melchiori, MG Allessandro [MVSN], 12, 76
Melotti, MG Carlo, 106
Menghini, BG Aldo, 82
Mentasti, LG Luigi, 20, 84, 104
Meranghini, BG Umberto, 39
Mercadante, MG Ginesio, 32
Mercalli, LG Camillo, 74, 79, 89, 142
Merzari, MG Fablo, 167
Messe, Mar. Of Italy Giovanni, 7, 18, 19, 22, 23, 28, 63 (2), 74, 89, 90, 95 (2), 148, 239
Mezzacapo, BG Vincenzo, 5, 11
MEZZASOMA, FERNANDO, 44
Mezzetti, LG Ottorino, 13, 16
Micheletta, BG Carlo, 21
Micheletti, BG Paolo, 118, 144
Miele, BG Oliviero, 60
Milazzo, BG Gioacchino, 9
Milocco, BG Giuseppe, 188
Minaja, BG Eduardo, 130
Minola, Col. Bartolomeo, 194
Mirabelli, MG Arrigo, 20
Mischi, LG Archimede [MVSN], 45
Mischi, LCol. Cesiro, 68
Mittica, BG Domenico [MVSN], 47, 199
Moccagatta, Cdr. Vittorio [RIN], 272
Modestini, MG Paolo, 22
Moizo, LG Riccardo, 8, 15
MOLFESE, MANLIO, 43
Molinari, MG Michele, 119
Molinero, BG Giuseepe, 37, 92, 189
Monacci, BG Ettore, 84, 216
Mondadori, MG Umberto, 105
Mondino, LG Umberto, 81, 88, 89, 117, 143
Monetta, BG Antonio,

Montagna, BG Francesco [MVSN], 25, 44, 135
Montagna, MG Renzo [MVSN], 45, 46, 47 (3), 167
Montella, Col. D., 68
Monti, LG [RIAF], 101
Monti, LG Edoardo, 63, 84
Monti, MG Enrico, 21
Monticelli, MG Furio, 108, 118, 147
Montuorisanseverino, BG Carlo, 34
Mora, BG Manlio, 122, 123, 128
Moramarco, BG Giovanni, 32
MORANDI, RODOLFO, 51
Moreno, LG Mario, 189
Morera, MG Umberto, 48
Moretti, MG Giuseppe [MVSN], 200
Moretto, BG Augusto, 46, 72
Morgari, MG Guglielmo, 112, 142, 143
Mori, BG Antonio, 33
Morigi, BG Giorgi, 93, 216, 217
Moro, Col. Federico, 144
MORONI, EDOARDO, 44
Morra, Col. E., 123
Morsero, BG [MVSN], 166
Mosca, BG Amedeo [MVSN], 47
Mozzoni, MG Adolfo [MVSN], 170
Mugnai, BG Lorenzo, 122
Murari della Corte Brà, LG Count Sebastiano, 28, 84, 135
Musinu, BG G., 69
MUSSOLINI, 1st Mar. of the Empire Il Duce BENITO AMILCARE ANDREA, 5 (7), 7 (3), 8, 10, 11 (4), 18, 19 (3), 21, 43 (2), 51, 239
Muti, BG Ettore [MVSN], 100
Muttini, BG Enrico, 156
Muzzioli, BG Augusto, 20

Naldi, MG Rodolfo, 82, 113
Naldoni, Col. Giovanni, 105
Nam, BG Cesare, 193
Nannei, BG Mario, 114
Napoletano, MG Gaetano, 36
Nasci, LG Gabriele, 28, 78, 86, 88, 90 (2), 93, 144
Nasi, Gen. Guglielmo Ciro, 13 (3), 14 (3), 15, 16, 58, 94, 153, 239
Navarini, LG Enea, 48, 86, 87 (2), 120
Navarra-Viggiani, BG Marquis Francesco, 190
Nebbia, MG Edoardo, 78, 83, 105, 135, 137
Negri, MG Paride, 81, 116, 125
Negri Cesi, LG Luigi, 90, 145
Negro, MG Guglielmo, 59, 82, 133, 151
Negro, BG Livio, 126 (2)
Negro, MG Matteo, 25, 82, 117
Negroni, MG Giacomo, 31
Nicchiarelli, MG Niccolò [MVSN], 46, 95, 167, 169
Nicolini, BG Michelangelo, 83
Nicolosi, LG Mario, 81, 83
Nicotra, BG Giovanni, 71
Ninci, BG Luigi, 29

Ninchi, Col., 95
Nomis di Pallone, RA Amadeo [RIN], 161
Notari, BG Alberto, 84
NUDI, FRANCESCO, 8
Nurchis, BG Virgilio [MVSN], 203
Nuvoloni, MG Luigi, 83, 134 (2), 144

Obici, BG Alfredo, 29
Oddo, BG Umberto, 81
Odetti, BG Count Eduardo, 29
Odone, BG Angelo, 24
Ojetti, BG Ugo, 86
Oliva, RA Romeo [RIN], 160
Olivieri, MG Bernardo, 61
Ollearo, LG Alfonso, 45, 87, 104
Olmi, BG Roberto, 121, 135 (2)
Orengo, BG Guglielmo, 156
Orlandi, Col. Enrico, 145
Orlando, LG Taddeo, 7, 8, 19, 21, 87, 89, 110
Orrigo, Col. Flaminio, 193
Ottone, BG Paolo, 85
Oxilia, LG Giovanni Battista, 7, 18, 21, 23, 65, 68, 110, 136, 215

Pacini, LG Leonida, 23
Paderini, BG Luigi, 91
Padovani, Col. Ezio [RIAF], 100
Pafundi, LG Giuseppe, 81 (2), 85, 90, 113, 136
Paganuzzi, BG Feruccio, 75, 120
Pagliano, Col. Carlo, 185
Paglieri, BG Guiseppe, 174
Paladini, VA Riccardo [RIN], 40, 97, 98
Paladino, BG Francesco, 27
Paleologo, BG Giuseppe, 37
Pallieri, MG Vittorio, 21
Pallotta, BG Michele [MVSN], 81
Palma, BG Vittorio, 73
Paoletti, BG Alpinolo, 33, 185
Paoletti, BG Verecondo, 34
Paolini, MG Vincenso, 126, 145 (2)
Paolocci, BG Luigi, 157
Papaleo, MG Antonio, 9
Papini, BG Erberto, 116, 142
Papone, MG Agostino, 28
Pariani, Gen. Alberto, 6, 7 (2), 18 (2), 21, 22, 23, 74, 239
Parona, RA Angelo [RIN], 40, 159
Parri, BG Dino, 83, 92, 122, 133, 136
Pascolini, BG Etelvoldo, 126
Pasetti, VA Antonio [RIN], 40, 98
Pasini, BG Vittorio, 20
Pavolini, MG Alessandro, 10, 44, 210
Peano, BG Emilio, 75
Peano, BG Ottavio [MVSN], 46, 75
Pederzini, BG Amedeo, 115, 139
Pedrazzoli, LG Gino, 118, 179
Pedrotti, BG Bartolomeo, 25, 80, 131, 216 (2)
Peirolo, BG Eugenio, 106, 119, 135

Pellegrini, LG Aldo [RIAF], 99
Pellegrini, MG Carlo, 25, 104
PELLEGRINI, DOMENICO GIAMPIETRO, 43
Pellegrini, BG Felice, 184
Pellegrini, BG Francesco, 32
Pelligra, LG Raffaele, 64, 108
Pelligra, BG Salavtore, 65, 86
Peluso, BG Luigi, 33, 93
Pentimalli, MG Natale, 82, 178
Pentimalli, LG Riccardo, 86, 115, 125
Perdomo, Maj. A., 69
Perego, LG Luigi, 23
Permeti, BG Half Ismail, 39
Peroglio, BG Domenico, 183
Perotti, BG Giuseppe, 22
Perrelli, BG Mario, 89
Perrod, BG Adriano, 89
Perrod, BG Paolo, 88
Perugi, MG Giulio, 36, 109, 119, 142 (4)
Perugini, BG Ilo Giacomo, 47 (2)
Pescatore, BG Alberto, 27
Pescatori, MG Armando, 122, 153
Pesenti, LG Gustave, 6, 153, 157
Pession, MG Ugo, 84
Petillo, Col. V., 93
Petromilli, BG Luigi, 38
Pettinau, BG Ettore, 139, 220
Pezzi, MG Enrico [RIAF], 68, 96, 165, 207
Piacentini, MG Giuseppe, 70
Piacentini, MG Pietro [RIAF], 7, 18, 42
Piacenza, BG Guido, 87, 95, 142
Pialorsi, MG Guido, 111, 193, 217
Piatti del Pozzo, MG Umberto, 46, 48, 96
Piazzi, BG Rodolfo, 157
Piazzoni, MG Alessandro, 81, 86, 104 (2), 109, 118, 119, 134
Piccini, BG Gino, 114 (2), 114, 115, 117 (2)
Piccini, BG Mario [RIAF], 165
Piccinini, BG Carlo, 137
Piccolo, BG Felice, 92
Piccone, BG Marcello, 38, 120, 137
Pieche, MG Guiseppe, 8 (2)
Piemonte, Mar. Of Italy His Royal Highness Umberto di Savoia, Crown Prince of Italy (Piemonte) and Viceroy, 27, 57 (3), 59 (2), 64, 72, 239
PIERACCINI, GAETANO, 51
Pietracaprina, MG Pietro, 118, 127
Pignetti, LG Ugo, 9, 109
Pini, VA Vladimiro [RIN], 98 (2)
Pinna, LG Pietro [RIAF], 100
Pinto, BG Luigi, 189
Pintor, Gen. Ben Pietro, 19, 63, 83, 86, 239
Pipito, MG Giuseppe,
Pirro, Col. F., 69
Pirzio-Biroli, Gen. Alessandro, 6, 13, 69, 74, 75, 93, 239
Pistoia, Gen. His Royal Highness Prince Filiberto Lodovico Massimilano Emanuele Maria di Savoia [Savoy-Genoa], Duke of, 27, 67, 79, 240
PISENTI, PIETRO, 43
Pitassi-Manella, LG Enrico, 87, 110
Pittagula, BG Gerolamo, 135
Pittau, BG Beniamino, 120
Pivano, LG Giovanni Angelo, 20, 111
Pizzarello, BG Ugo, 122
Pizzolato, BG Gavino, 139, 147, 149
PIZZONI, ALFREDO "Longhi", 51
Poccetti, Col. Weiss, 185
Podio, BG Luigi, 27, 118, 137
Pognisi, MG Attilio, 46
Poli, MG Francesco, 9 (3)
Policardi, BG Angelo, 86, 89
Porro, LG Felice [RIAF], 99, 100
Porzio Giovanola, RA Guido [RIN], 159
Prenk, BG Perrizi, 39
Presti, BG Ubaldo [MVSN], 14
Preti, MG Educardo [MVSN], 170
Pricolo, MG Francesco [RIAF], 7, 18, 42
Primieri, LG Clemente, 59, 64, 80, 105, 215, 216 (2)
Prina, Col. Francesco, 193
Princivalle, MG Aldo, 107, 108, 135, 209
Priore, LG Mario, 81, 89, 133, 137
Properzj, BG Per Giulio,
Provanzano, BG, 184
Puntoni, BG Paolo, 5, 106

Quarra, BG Ferruccio [MVSN],
Quarra-Sito, MG Eduardo, 125 (2), 181
Quarto, MG Arturo, 23
Quasimodo, MG Santi [MVSN], 201

Racca, BG Carlo, 156
Radice, MG Emilio, 36
Raffaldi, MG Vittorio [MVSN], 76, 171, 209
RAGGHIANTI, CARLO, 51
Ranza, LG Ferruccio [RIAF], 99, 100
Rastrelli, BG Carlo [MVSN], 166, 167, 203, 205
Ravera, MG Francesco, 78
Re, MG Giovanni Carlo, 20, 26, 148, 216
REALE, VITO, 8
Rean, Col. Tiburzio, 193
Reginella, Col. Alfredo, 135
Reisoli-Matthieu, LG Gustavo, 84, 106, 182
Relligra, MG Raffaele, 67
Renzoni, BG Luigi, 157
Rerone, BG Ernesto, 119
REVAL, 9
Reverberi, LG Luigi, 63, 144
Ribella, Col. [RIAF], 99
Ricagno, LG Umberto, 74, 144, 145
Riccardi, Adm. Arturo [RIN], 8, 18, 40 (3), 240
Riccardi, LG Count Enrico, 142, 156
Ricci, MG Goffredo, 47, 48, 209
Ricci, MG Renato [MVSN], 10, 12, 46

Ricci, MG Tito, 21
Ricci, BG Umberto, 8, 33, 156
Ricciuti, MG Michele, 156
Richieri, BG Lorenzo, 68
Rima, BG Balilla, 25, 79
Riviera, BG Lauro, 106
Rivolta, MG Carlo, 80, 119, 123
Rizzo, BG Antonio, 108, 193, 220
Roatta, LG Mario, 7 (2), 18 (2), 22 (2), 23 (3), 26, 64 (2), 66, 75, 104
Robertielli, MG Vincenzo, 105, 106, 108
Robino, BG Silvio, 70, 74
Robotti, LG Mario, 64 (2), 83
Roda, LG Alberto, 87, 106, 151
Rogadeo, RA Franco [RIN], 40
Rolandi, LCol. Giorgio, 194
Roluti, MG Francesco, 108 (2)
Romano, MG Giuseppe, 24 (2), 35, 113, 126, 129
Romano, Maj. Luigi, 194
ROMANO, RUGGERO, 44
Rombola, BG Antonio, 36
Romegialli, MG Italo [MVSN], 46 (2), 169
Romei Longhena, LG Count Giovanni, 15
Romeres, Col. Gaetand, 126
Romero, LG Federico, 78, 82, 108
Roncaglia, LG Ercole, 84, 95, 133
Ronco, BG Ercole, 91, 114, 216, 217
Ronco, MG Francesco, 134, 149
Rosa, Maj. G., 69
Rosi, Gen. Ezio, 7, 18, 22, 23, 59, 66 (2), 80, 177, 239
Rosica, BG Achille, 27, 155
Rosmini, MG Achille, 20, 22
Rossi, LG Aldo, 24, 137
Rossi, LG Angelo, 79, 84, 122
Rossi, LG Camillo, 79, 82
Rossi, LG Carlo (I), 85 (2), 88 (2), 116, 144
Rossi, MG Carlo (II), 137
Rossi, BG Cesare, 38, 137 (2)
Rossi, MG Domenico, 135
Rossi, LG Edmondo, 81, 106
Rossi, LG Francesco, 19 (2), 78
Rossi, BG Giuseppe, 60
Rossi, BG Luigi [MVSN], 169
Rossi, LG Silvio, 19, 35
Rossillon, LG Duke Giuseppe Marion Asinari, 5, 15, 16
Rosso, BG Eligio, 66
Roux, LG Matteo, 22, 74, 83, 105 (2)
Rovebe, BG Enrico, 23
Roveda, BG Mario, 183
Rovida, BG Erminio, 138
Ruffo, BG Nicola, 104
Ruggeri, MG Umberto, 21, 27
Ruggero, BG Vittorio, 30, 59, 111, 121
Ruggiero, MG Giunio, 46, 110, 111, 142, 177
Russo, MG Biagio, 82, 151, 182
Russo, MG Luigi [MVSN], 12, 46, 76

Russo, BG Mario, 183
Russo, BG Ugo, 27

Sabatini, BG Luigi, 65
Sacchi, BG Emilio, 25
Sacco, MG Francesco [MVSN], 77
Salazar y Munatores, BG Count Diego [MVSN], 76
Salomon, BG Giovan Battista, 88
Saltini, BG Guido, 60
Salvatores, BG Pasquale, 36
Salvatores, Col. U., 185
Salvi, Col., 87
Salvi, BG Constantino, 128
Salvi, Col. Giulio Cesare, 126
Sandali, MG Renato [RIAF], 7 (2), 18, 42
Sandicchi, BG Fortunato, 36
SAN FELLOW, ANTONIO, 514
Sannia, BG Attilio, 85
Sansanelli, MG Nicola [MVSN], 77
Sansonetti, VA Luigi [RIN], 40, 159 (2), 160
Sant' Andrea, BG Creste, 130
Santin, BG Alessandro, 92
Santini, Col. Biagio, 137
Santini, BG Leone, 19, 33
Santini, Gen. Ruggero, 6, 15 (2), 16, 78, 79, 94, 239
Santovito, LG Ugo, 81, 86, 89, 144
Sapienza, BG Francesco, 112, 149
Saporetti, BG Vincenzo, 89, 114
Sardi, BG Adolfo, 25, 82
Sardu, Col. G. [MVSN], 199
Sarracino, MG Luigi, 21
Sartoris, MG Francesco, 106, 115
Scala, LG Alessandro, 45
Scala, MG Edoardo, 121
Scala, LG Ettore, 123
Scalabrino, BG Giovanni Maria, 27
Scalise, MG Guglielmo, 112
Scanagatta, MG Ubaldo, 114, 123, 180
Scaroina, MG Michele Giacomo, 108, 118, 176
Scaroni, BG Silvio [RIAF], 101
Scattaglia, MG Nazzarono, 130, 135
Scattini, LG Arturo, 93, 149, 216
Scavazzi, MG Giulio, 180
Schreiber, MG Ottorino, 129, 137, 142
Scipioni, BG Pietro, 120
SCOCCIMARRO, MAURO, 14
Scognamillo, Col. G., 93
Sclavo, BG Francesco, 85
Scopelliti, BG Giovanni, 74
Scordato, BG Salvatore, 75
Scorza, MG Carlo [MVSN], 11, 12
Scotti, MG Francesco, 134, 142
Scuero, LG Antonio, 7, 18, 21, 80, 121
SENISE, CARMINE, 8 (2)
Sequi, BG Roberto, 91
Serena, BG Adelschi [MVSN], 10, 11 (2), 12 (2)
Serimin, Col. Luigi, 145
Sesini, MG Ralmondo, 88

Sibilla, MG Ascanio, 128
Sibille, MG Luigi, 128, 153
Siciliani, LG Domenico, 92, 166
Signorelli, MG Enrico, 29
Signorini, Col. Paolo, 144
Silimbani, BG Giacomo [MVSN], 20
Siliprandi, Col. Gioegio, 194
Silvestri, MG Fernando [RIAF], 164
SINISCALCHI, ALFREDO, 13
Sisinni, BG Peitro, 36
Soati, MG Angelo, 33
Soddu, Gen. Ubaldo, 7, 18, 19, 21, 23, 59, 239
Sogno, LG Vittorio, 78, 81, 86, 89, 151
Soldarelli, MG Mario, 72, 86, 106, 122, 214
Solinas, MG Giaocchino, 47, 48, 111, 117, 148
Somma, LG Umberto, 16 (2), 87, 135, 167
Sommavilla, BG Angelo [MVSN], 47
Sorice, LG Antonio, 7 (2), 18, 19, 21 (3), 22
Sorrentino, MG Amedeo, 89, 156
Sorrentino, BG Rosario, 45
Sozzani, MG Gino [RIAF], 100
Sozzani, MG Nino, 46, 114, 117, 138, 141
SPARZANI, GIUSEPPE, 43
Spatocco, LG Carlo, 79 (2), 89, 92, 122
Spicacci, MG Guglielmo, 63, 69, 79, 81, 110
Spigo, LG Umberto, 82, 86, 110
SPINELLI, GIUSEPPE, 44
Spinelli, MG Nicola, 20, 111, 123
Spoleto [Savoy-Aosta], VA Aimone Roberto Margherita Marie Giuseppe Torino di Savoia, King Designate of Croatia, 4th Duke of Aosta and Duke of [RIN], 98
Sportiello, RA [RIN], 161
Sprega, BG Ugo, 82, 113
Stampioni, MG, 134
Starace, MG Achille [MVSN], 11, 12, 46, 76, 148
Stefanelli, MG Giuseppe, 105, 123, 185
Stefanini, BG Gino, 22
Stirati, BG Giovanni, 6
Stirpe, LG Angelo, 22, 109, 112 (2), 178
Stivala, BG Rodolfo, 29, 74

Tabellini, MG Ugo, 133, 193
Tade Grottaglie, Col. S. [RIAF], 100
Tagliavacche, BG Filippo, 86
Talinucci, BG Evandro [MVSN], 205
Tamassia, BG Cesare, 91
Tanese, MG Rodolfo [MVSN], 76, 173, 209
Tarabin, MG Alessandro [MVSN], 77, 146
Taranto, LG Arturo, 31, 86 (2), 89
TARCHI, ANGELO, 43
Tedeschini-Lalli, LG Gennaro [RIAF], 99 (2)
Tei, BG Gaetano, 30
Tellera, LG Guiseppe, 60, 70, 121
Teruzzi, MG Attillo [MVSN], 12 (2), 167
Terziani, LG Alberto, 33, 104
TESSARI, ARRIGO, 43
Tessiore, BG Carlo, 80

Tessitore, MG Vincenzo, 93
Tessore, MG Francesco, 90
Testa, LG Umberto, 23, 90, 145
Testi, LG Franco, 144 (2)
TIBALDI, ETTORE, 52
Ticchioni, MG Carlo, 75, 134, 140, 147, 216
TIENGO, 10
Tirelli, MG Mario, 89, 95
Tirindelli, Col. Achille, 104
Tissi, BG Antonio, 133 (2)
Toccolini, LG Tullio [RIAF], 99
Tonareli, BG Giacomo, 112
Toraido di Francia, MG Marquis [Marquise] Orazio, 23
Torelli, Col. Adriano, 194
Torresan, MG Rodolfo, 107, 113
Torriano, MG Arturo, 119, 123, 135
Tortella, BG Alfredo, 31
Tosatto, MG Silvio, 91
Toscano, RA Antonino [RIN], 40, 159
Tosi, BG Angiolo, 115, 130
Tosti, BG Carlo, 194
Trabucchi, LG Alessandro, 65
Tracchia, LG Ruggero, 121, 122, 134
Traditi, MG Alessandro, 167
Traina, BG Francesco, 34
Traniello, BG Ottaviomo, 108
Trevissio, BG Alberto, 118
Trezzani, LG Claudio, 58, 90
Tricoli, BG Conradino, 88
Tringali, MG Casanuova Antonio [MVSN], 9, 12, 43
Trionfi, BG Marquis Alberto, 24, 34, 111, 119, 120, 121
Trionfi, BG Marquis Luigi, 95, 107, 116
Troilo, LCol. Ettoro, 220
Tua, Gen. Angelo, 15, 63, 239
Tucci, MG Carlo, 74, 110
Tur, VA Vittorio [RIN], 161

Ulrich Bansa, BG Oscar, 29
Urbani, MG Aldo [RIAF], 101
Utili, LG Umberto, 19, 25, 89, 95, 214, 215, 216 (2)

Vacca-Maggiolini, Gen. Arturo, 15 (2), 19, 239
Vaccaneo, BG Alessandro, 71
Vaccari, BG Renzo, 79, 189
Vaccari, MG Umberto, 32, 147
Vaccarisi, LG Achille, 109
Vaccaro, MG Giorgio [MVSN], 77
Vaccaro, BG Michele, 104 (2)
Valle, MG Giuseppe [RIAF], 7, 18, 42
Vallerini, BG Giuseppe, 114, 136
Vallesi, BG Arturo, 84
Valletti Borgnini, BG Felice, 47, 58
Vanden Heuvel, MG Carlo, 66
Vanden Heuvet, BG Giulio, 217
Vanden Heuvel, MG Mario, 66
Vannetti, BG Federigo, 37

Varda, LG Giovanni, 116, 145
Varese, BG Mario, 86
Vargas, Col. Gaetano, 89
Vasarri, MG Alberto, 105, 169, 189
Vecchi, LG Giovanni, 84, 88, 110, 114 (2)
Vecchiarelli, LG Carlo, 19, 70, 72, 78, 80, 86, 111, 139
Vece, BG Mario, 142
Vegni, MG Ezio, 118
Vercellino, Gen. Mario, 5, 65 (2), 66, 69, 239, 332 (2), 514
Vespignani, MG Ottorino [RIAF], 101
Viale, BG Carlo, 124, 125, 126
Viale, Col. Mario, 104
Vianini, Col. I., 199
Vicini, MG,
VICTOR EMMANUEL III [Victor Emmanuel di Savoia, House of Savoy], 1st Mar. of Italy His Royal Highness King, 5 (3), 18, 239
Vietina, RA [RIN], 207
Villa Santa, LG Nino Salvatore, 20, 110
Visconti, BG Giuseppe [MVSN], 76, 172
Visconti di Oleggio, BG Vitaliano, 31
Visconti Prasca, LG Sebastiano, 26 (2), 59, 70, 74, 79, 88, 147
Vitelli, BG Giuseppe, 182
Vivaldi, BG Lorenzo, 144
Volante, BG Giuseppe [MVSN], 48, 75, 209
Voli, BG Emilio, 26
Volpi, BG Giuseppe, 33
Volpini, MG Giovan Battista, 14
Vox, MG Donato, 32

Zaccone, MG Ernesto, 117
Zaccone, MG Mario, 78, 182
Zaglio, MG Pietro, 38, 135, 142 (2)
Zambon, MG Bortolo, 27, 136
Zanella, BG Giovanni [MVSN], 201
Zanghieri, LG Giovanni, 78, 86
Zani, MG Francesco, 75, 108, 110, 112
Zannini, BG Erico, 10
Zannini, LG Licurgo, 88, 107, 111, 112 (2), 179
Zanotti, BG Bianco [MVSN], 91
Zanotti, BG Mario, 31, 134
Zanuccoli, MG Giambattista, 74
Zanussi, LG Giacomo, 23, 64, 66, 117, 216
Zarri, BG Camillo, 71, 155
Zatti, MG Vittorio, 120
Zauli, BG Adolfo, 31
Zauli, BG Dino [MVSN], 169
Zenati, MG Giovanni Battista, 84, 114
ZERBINO, PAOLO, 43
Zicavo, MG Ferruccio, 36
Zingales, LG Francesco, 67, 84, 85, 87, 89 (3), 90, 95 (2), 133
Zingales, BG Leone, 20
Zitnik, LCol. Egon, 147
Zo, BG Luigi, 35, 123

Zocchi, Maj. A., 69
Zoppi, Gen. Ottavio [MVSN], 12, 15, 239

Japan

FUJIO, MINODA, 326
Iida, LG Shojiro, 327
ISHIBASHI, 327
KUBO, 327
KUMAO, NISHIMURA, 326
Machijiri, LG Viscount Kazumoto, 327
MASAYUKI, YOKOYAMA, 326
Nishimura, LG Takuma, 327
SAKO, MASANORI, 327
Tsuchihashi, LG Yuitsu, 327

Monaco

BLANCHY, PIERRE, 513
BLUM, RENÉ, 513
CASTRO, CHARLES BELLANDO de, 513
Prince LOUIS II (LOUIS HONORÉ CHARLES ANTOINE GRIMALDI), 513
ROBLOT, ÉMILE, 513
SETTIMO, HENRI, 513
WITASSE, PIERRE de, 513

Poland

Najymski, Col., 444
Skrzydlewski, LCol., 444

San Marino

BALDA, MARINO DELLA, 225
BALSIMELLI, CARLO, 225 (2)
BALSIMELLI, FRANCESCO, 225
BELLUZZI, SETTIMIO, 225 (2)
BORGHESI, ANGELO MANZONI, 225
BORGHESI, BARTOLOMEO MANZONI, 225
CASALI, ALVARO, 225
FOSCHI, SALVATORE, 225
GOZI, CELIO, 225 (2)
GOZI, FEDERICO, 225
GOZI, GINO, 225
GOZI, GIULIANO, 225 (2)
GOZI, MANLIO, 225
LONFERNINI, GIOVANNI, 225 (2)
LONFERNINI, SANTE, 225
LONFERNINI, TEODORO, 225
MARTELLI, RENATO, 225
MENICUCCI, SECONDO, 225
MICHELOTTI, MARINO, 225 (2)
MORRI, MARINO, 225
MULARONI, FILIPPO, 225
MULARONI, LUIGI, 225
REFFI, ORLANDO, 225

RIGHI, POMPEO, 225
ROSSI, MARINO, 225
VALENTINI, SANZIO, 225
VALENTINI, VITTORIO, 225
VALLI, LEONIDA SUZZI, 225

Somaliland

Dinke, Olol, Sultan of Sciavelli, 192

Spain

NAVARRI, Bishop RAMON IGLÉSIAS I, 519
PUIGDEMASA, Bishop RICHARD FORNESA I, 519
SANSA, Father JAUME, 519
VILARDEBÒ, Bishop JUSTI GUITART I, 519

Switzerland

Altishofen, Cmdt. Heinrich Pfyffer von, 234
d'Aspremont, Cmdt. Georg von Sury, 234

United Kingdom

Alexander, FM Sir Harold Rupert Leofric Geogre, 53 (2)
Mason-MacFarlane, LG Sir (Frank) Noel, 53
McMILLAN, MAURICE HAROLD, 53
Partridge, Brig. Henry Cuthbert, 227
SILLERY, ANTHONY, 454
Sturges, MG Robert Grice, 454
Wilson, FM Sir Henry Maitland, 53

United States

Clark, Gen. Mark Wayne, 53
Eisenhower, Gen. Dwight David, 53
Joyce, MG Kenyon Ashe, 53
STONE, ELLERY W., 53 (2)

Vatican City

CANALI, Cardinal NICOLA, 232
MAGLIONE, Cardinal LUIGI, 233
POPE PIUS XI (Cardinal Achille Ambrogio Damiano Ratti), 231
POPE PIUS XII (Cardinal Eugenio Maria Giuseppe Giovanni Rascelli), 231
RASCELLI, Cardinal EUGENIO MARIA GIUSEPPE GIOVANNI, 231, 233
SERAFINI, Marquis [Marchese] CAMILLO, 231

Vietnam

NGUYEN VAN SAM, 326

www.ingramcontent.com/pod-product-compliance
Lightning Source LLC
Chambersburg PA
CBHW082018300426
44117CB00015B/2267